THE CHANGING AMERICAN
COUNTRYSIDE

RURAL AMERICA

Hal S. Barron
David L. Brown
Kathleen Neils Conzen
Carville Earle
Cornelia Butler Flora
Donald Worster

Series Editors

THE CHANGING AMERICAN COUNTRYSIDE
RURAL PEOPLE AND PLACES

EDITED BY EMERY N. CASTLE

FOREWORD BY CLIFTON WHARTON, JR.

University Press of Kansas

Published by the University Press of Kansas (Lawrence, Kansas 66049), which was
organized by the Kansas Board of Regents and is operated and funded by Emporia State
University, Fort Hays State University, Kansas State University, Pittsburg State University,
the University of Kansas, and Wichita State University

Library of Congress Cataloging-in-Publication Data

The changing American countryside : rural people and places / edited by Emery
   N. Castle ; foreword by Clifton Wharton, Jr.
      p.   cm. — (Rural America)
   Includes bibliographical references (p.) and index.
   ISBN 0-7006-0724-2 — ISBN 0-7006-0725-0 (pbk.)
   1. United States—Rural conditions.   2. Rural poor—United States.
   I. Castle, Emery N.   II. Series: Rural America (Lawrence, Kan.)
   HN59.2.A447   1995
   307.72'0973—dc20   95-8076

British Library Cataloguing in Publication Data is available.

Printed in the United States of America

10 9 8 7 6 5 4 3 2 1

The paper used in this publication meets the minimum requirements of the American
National Standard for Permanence of Paper for Printed Library Materials Z39.48–1984.

CONTENTS

v

ILLUSTRATIONS

Tables

Photographs

FOREWORD

Professor Frederick Merk, of Harvard, was a great historian. I can still recall sitting in his classes some fifty years ago and reacting to the clarity and excitement he conveyed as he expounded his theme of the American frontier. His understanding of the frontier, the forces that pushed it back, and how it came to influence so many facets of American culture and life made an indelible impression on me. One of the unintended lessons from Merk's lectures surfaced in my consciousness many years later when I, too, toiled in the scholarly vineyards. I learned that a successful scholar must do more than push back the frontiers of knowledge by providing new facts, new analysis, and new insights. The scholar also must communicate that knowledge so that it is accepted and so that it influences the thoughts and actions of both scholar and public.

That is a goal which Emery Castle and his colleagues have sought to achieve in this book. They have reached their mark splendidly. They have clarified the confused stereotyping of "rural" America by identifying its complicated and ever-changing diversity. They have highlighted the complex factors involved in any sound approach to better understanding rural affairs by emphasizing the dangers involved in conventional approaches and by stressing the interdependence of rural and urban issues. And most important, they have succeeded in giving new perspective and a new sense of urgency to this all-too-neglected dimension of our nation.

This daunting challenge has been met not only by the skill and scholarly perceptiveness of the authors but also by the multidisciplinary approach adopted in constructing the book and defining the issues. It is an important and necessary recognition that economics, agriculture, ethnicity, environment, education, and history, among other disciplines, are elements without which such a broad tapestry as rural America cannot be properly considered.

The Kellogg Foundation is to be commended for its support of the National Rural Studies Committee (NRSC), which included the diverse group of scholars whose experience and insights illumine this effort. This book of readings, though intended primarily for use in a college curriculum, will—and should—be of value to a far wider audience. The richness of the work and analysis, as well as the newer perspectives and sensitive insights, are a welcome treasure for anyone interested in rural life.

I was particularly impressed with the sections on "Distress and Poverty" and "Regional and Ethnic Diversity." The persistence of poverty in the United States has long been a source of fascination and concern to me, and it threatens to turn our country into what I have called a "two-tier" nation divided along lines of wealth and opportunity. It is an issue that continues to bedevil scholars and policymakers. How, in a rich, advanced nation, where real per capita income has reached levels no one would have dared predict four or five decades ago, can abject poverty continue to exist? Once we assumed that poverty predominated in rural regions like Appalachia, but we quickly learned only too well that it is also rampant in the centers of our greatest cities.

And once we assumed, too, that poverty was an aberrant thing, a weak counterpart to overall prosperity—and a condition that would respond to a proper mix of programs and dollars. So that was what we tried, to the tune of billions of dollars. The result: some amelioration but increasing political discord—and the perpetuation of poverty. Moreover, the ills usually identified with the big city—such as AIDS and narcotics—are being found more and more often in the small towns and rural areas. No longer are we so naive as to believe there is a simple fix, but still the answers, lost somewhere in a sea of economic general well-being, elude us.

The persistence of poverty abroad also affects us at home. Unlike the United States, poverty in the Third World countries after World War II appeared from the outside to be more fundamental, a by-product of population growth, scarce resources, preindustrial technologies, and ineffective or corrupt political systems. Our answers were to send in the agricultural economists (of which I was one), promote technology transfers, establish Peace Corps missions, and address social problems. Yes, there was progress in some areas, but too often what we seemed to have in mind was a wholesale reinvention of entire societies in the image of our own. Yet democratic principles will continue to resist implantation as long as the line between poverty and wealth remains so sharply drawn as it is in many countries.

The reality of our shrinking planet and of the growing global interdependence of nations will be keenly influenced by our ability to deal with regional and ethnic diversity. What happens in Tibet or Tadzhikistan is no longer a subject for oral storytellers like Marco Polo but the substance of the evening's television news on CNN. Cultural and value differences will be brought increasingly to bear upon our policies and decisions, both domestic and foreign, over the next century. The growth in trade, the globalization of financial markets, and new, all-enveloping communications linkages are but a few of the major forces at work. So, too, are such problems as environmental degradation and pollution, which have no respect for political or even geographic boundaries.

We must begin by knowing ourselves. We will never be able to fully comprehend what makes other countries tick—and formulate our foreign policies effectively—until we better understand our own nation and find the solutions to our own problems. Professor Castle and his colleagues have provided in *The Changing American Countryside: Rural People and Places* a major source of knowledge about one of the critical dimensions of our society.

There is much more that could be said about this outstanding work, but let me add only that this book should be required reading for all those who care deeply about the issues that affect our lives.

Clifton R. Wharton, Jr.

ACKNOWLEDGMENTS

This book of readings has been approximately nine years in the making, and many people have contributed. Some contributions were so important that it would be a travesty if the book were to appear without their being recognized.

Barbara Baldwin, editor at the Western Rural Development Center (WRDC), Oregon State University, has been a linchpin for the entire operation. She has been involved in the work of the National Rural Studies Committee (NRSC) since it first came into existence in 1987. She read and commented on many of the chapters when they were first drafted, and she and I have consulted on the book at every stage of its creation. It is clear to me the book would be a very different, but inferior, product in the absence of her skillful and diplomatic work. I am deeply in her debt.

Elizabeth Davis, Barbara Baldwin, and I served as an editorial review committee as the book was taking shape. Elizabeth prepared a written evaluation of every version of each chapter. In my experience it is unusual for authors to say kind things about reviewers, but in this case many did, crediting Elizabeth for major improvement in their revisions. Certainly the book is better integrated and has greater integrity than it would have had without her efforts. My long-time colleague, Donna Mull, assisted me greatly with administrative details and did the necessary clerical work. Her good humor and pleasant demeanor contributed greatly to harmonious working relations both internally and externally.

The book has benefited from the sage advice and experience of all members of the NRSC. Most have contributed chapters to this book, and the two who did not, Julian Wolpert and Edward Bergman, supported the effort in numerous tangible ways. Julian reviewed the entire manuscript at one point and provided valuable advice on balance and emphasis. Ed's advice on regional economic development was exceedingly useful.

Finally, I recognize the help and support of Russell Youmans, director of the WRDC. Since the NRSC came into existence in 1987, Russ has been exceedingly supportive, and his support has contributed greatly to the work of the NRSC and to making this book possible. The WRDC is a small organization and the NRSC work and activities associated with this book of readings were not always easy to assimilate. Russ, and the readers of this book, should know I recognize and appreciate this fact.

I record here my apologies to anyone whose contribution has not been recognized.

Emery N. Castle

PART ONE
AN INTRODUCTION

1
THE FORGOTTEN HINTERLANDS

EMERY N. CASTLE

Rural people and places in America are poorly understood and largely ne-glected by the people who write, speak, and thereby influence attitudes about social problems and public policy. Misunderstanding and neglect are preva-lent in much of academia as well, and it is academics who typically provide the literature and the base of knowledge on which public opinion ultimately de-pends. The result is a paucity of literature and an absence of informed people to advise public discussion and debate when rural issues arise.

The consequences of such under-attention are serious. Too often rural problems are either not identified or simply ignored. When problems are recognized, unrealistic solutions are often advanced. This situation is quite different from what prevails in many other arenas where concerns are recognized—urban studies, resource and environmental policy, monetary and fiscal policy, and international economics, for example.

This book attempts to improve on this state of affairs by presenting thoughtful and informed discussions of numerous facets of rural life and rural conditions. It is addressed to people who will influence public opinion and general understanding in the long term; specifically, it is hoped college and university professors and students will find it useful and will be stimulated to create an even richer literature. The book also is intended to be of value to those who make decisions, in either their private or public lives, about rural people and rural places. Perhaps it will kindle interest in the place we call rural America and suggest solutions for some of the problems identified.

It is trite to say that our nation has a rural heritage—most people accept the truth of such a statement without question—but the rapidity and the ex-tent to which we have become a predominately urban nation is not always fully appreciated. At the beginning of the nineteenth century approximately three-quarters of the population were rural residents; today three-quarters reside in urban areas. We often glorify our rural heritage and accept, uncritically, the notion that rural places still are very much the way they were when the nation was a rural one. Although we know better, habitually we tend to think of rural places as being inhabited mainly by farm people. This tendency leads to easy but inaccurate conclusions that farm policy constitutes rural policy and that agricultural conditions measure the health of rural America.

That "agricultural and rural are synonymous" is only one of the many stereotypes. The countryside is huge, complex, and diverse, as documented and illustrated throughout the succeeding chapters, and there is therefore an understandable need to simplify in order to communicate about it. We may think of rural America as being similar to the community where our grandparents' farm was located. Of course, your grandparents may have lived in Vermont while mine settled in Nebraska and our neighbors' came from Alabama. Alternatively, our view of rural America may be shaped, albeit unconsciously, by the literary word pictures of a John Steinbeck or a Garrison Keillor. Sometimes our images are favorable, and positive values are attributed to the countryside. Words such as "stable," "solid," "shrewd," "independent," and "self-reliant" are often used to reflect positive rural values. But "bumpkin," "rube," "backward," and "unprogressive" have also been used to describe rural conditions and rural life. When the surface is scratched, rural complexity reveals itself.

But why bother? What matter if most Americans know little about the people who live in the more sparsely populated places of our nation? Is it not true that most of the major changes that will affect us originate in urban places or from outside the United States? Such questions deserve serious answers. If one advocates the discovery and communication of more information about the countryside, one should identify demonstrable benefits.

The main reason for learning more about rural people and rural places is that we will all be better off if we do so. Rural and urban places are highly interdependent. Urban people should have an interest in rural education because rural young people migrate to urban places, and they will influence the nature of the urban places to which they go. Persistent rural poverty means that some people do not contribute as much to total productivity as they are capable of contributing. Moreover, much of the space of the nation is cared for and managed by rural people, so those people who are concerned about natural resource and environmental policy need to be aware of conditions in rural America, where most of the natural environment is to be found. Self interest aside, compassionate citizens should want to know about and, if possible, improve the welfare of the one-quarter of the population that lives outside the metropolitan areas.

THE SOCIAL HEALTH OF THE COUNTRYSIDE

All is not well in rural America. Stress and distress are much in evidence. Superficial observation in the plains of the Dakotas, Nebraska, Kansas, Oklahoma, or Texas provides evidence of the decline of communities and the flight of younger, better-educated residents, and if one visits the rural South, persistent rural poverty is noticeable. Stress can be observed in the management of the natural environment, as conflict often exists between the "users" of natural resources—farmers and foresters, for example—and the people who are mainly interested in the natural amenities. There are many other examples of problems and concerns that could be cited.

Some rural places and people are, in fact, doing well. Many places located near the metropolitan areas are thriving economically, and others flourish because of unique cultural, social, or natural features. The material presented in the following pages indicates the importance of rural studies and the urgent need for a solution to the numerous problems that are identified. At issue here is about one-fourth of the nation's population and approximately 97 percent of the land area. Diversity in conditions mitigates against simplistic approaches and stereotyped policies. Clearly the urban population has an interest in a healthy rural America, but it is much less clear how this interest can be translated into informed and consistent attitudes and policies. This book is therefore designed to contribute to informed attitudes and enlightened policies.

The National Rural Studies Committee

This book has been made possible by the work of the National Rural Studies Committee (NRSC), whose members and their institutional affiliation and discipline are as follows:

Name	Academic Discipline	Institutional Affiliation
Edward Bergman	Regional Science	University of North Carolina
David Brown	Sociology	Cornell University
Emery Castle	Economics	Oregon State University
Pierre Crosson	Economics	Resources For the Future
William Howarth	Literature	Princeton University
Edwin Mills	Economics	Northwestern University
Ronald Oakerson	Political Science	Houghton College

Sonya Salamon	Anthropology	University of Illinois
Gene Summers	Sociology	University of Wisconsin
Bruce Weber	Economics	Oregon State University
Julian Wolpert	Geography	Princeton University

Former members:

| Bonnie Dill | Sociology | University of Maryland |
| Carol Stack | Sociology | University of California at Berkeley |

The NRSC members were chosen to reflect the viewpoints of numerous academic disciplines in both public and private institutions of higher learning. Some members are scholars who have devoted most of their professional life to studying rural people and places; others were chosen, not because of their knowledge of rural people or places, but because they provided a unique vantage point on rural America. Even so, the NRSC has never felt self-sufficient in its knowledge and expertise, and as the need has arisen, it has drawn on other knowledgeable people both in academia and elsewhere.

The W. K. Kellogg Foundation has long had an interest in rural America, and in 1987 it made possible the formation of the National Rural Studies Committee (NRSC) by a grant to Oregon State University. As a member of the faculty at Oregon State University, I had written on the neglect of rural America by people concerned with public policy and in academia and had proposed establishing the NRSC to assist institutions of higher education better use their resources to improve conditions for rural people and places.

Much of the work of the committee has revolved around meetings in rural regions of the United States. Meetings were held in Hood River, Oregon; Stoneville, Mississippi; Cedar Falls, Iowa; Reading, Pennsylvania; Las Vegas, New Mexico, and local people and rural practitioners were involved in each. Proceedings were issued for each meeting, and they provide the raw material for much that is in this book. But the book is not simply a compilation of these proceedings. Material has been revised and rewritten, and additional chapters were commissioned as well. Nevertheless, the highly diverse conditions, problems, and circumstances that were observed in these regional meetings over a five-year period did much to influence the thinking of the NRSC as to what should be in the book and to whom it should be addressed.

Should Rural Studies Have a Place in the University Curriculum?

The place, if any, of rural studies in the teaching program of the university has commanded the attention of the National Rural Studies Committee (NRSC) throughout its life. Should there be any special effort to include rural issues in the curriculum beyond that which is currently taught? If the answer is "yes," where and how should such issues be included? Should new, multidisciplinary curricula be established or should existing courses be reorganized to give greater attention to rural affairs?

The NRSC has conducted its affairs during a period of financial stress for many academic institutions. Most have been searching for opportunities to reduce, rather than to assume more obligations. If recommendations for the inclusion of new material in the curriculum are to taken seriously they must be supported by compelling arguments.

The NRSC was assembled with the knowledge that higher education in the United States is complex and diverse, just as rural America is complex and diverse. It was assumed from the outset that private institutions, as well as public, have the potential of contributing to a better rural America. Thus, four-year colleges as well as prestigious graduate universities were involved in NRSC work. Among the publicly supported institutions, land-grant universities were accorded an important but by no means an exclusive role in rural studies education. This point of view is reflected in the institutional affiliation and the disciplinary mix of NRSC members.

Given this background it is perhaps not surprising that the NRSC quite early in its existence decided there was no simple "best" way to incorporate rural studies in the university curriculum. Some institutions may well decide, indeed some have decided, to offer special programs of study with rural affairs as a particular focus. Others may wish to introduce new courses into established curricula; still others will modify existing courses.

This book will assist those who are addressing such issues by illustrating that a wide range of social problems exists in rural America and by demonstrating how a number of academic disciplines provide valuable insights into such problems. In short, the book provides an example of the intellectual fare of rural studies. One can observe, by reading the chapters that follow, the response to this area of study of scholars in literature, geography, demography, economics, sociology, anthropology, regional science, and political science. When this material is viewed from the vantage point of a particular academic institution, the place of rural studies in the curriculum becomes more clear.

ORGANIZATION AND CONTENT

No single book can possibly do justice to the vastness, the complexity, and the diversity of rural America, and, certainly this book has no such ambitious objective. It is not an exhaustive treatment of the countryside: some important subjects, such as rural health, have necessarily been neglected or under-represented. Nevertheless, the contribution good scholarship can make to understanding rural phenomena is illustrated. Some chapters report on recent research, others synthesize existing factual information, even as some provide new treatments of rural phenomena. Certain chapters will be of the greatest value to policymakers, others may appeal more to the budding scholar who is considering specializing in rural studies. Still other chapters will interest mature scholars who are following research developments in a particular area.

An effort has been made to make the book understandable to any intelligent person with an interest in the subject. There are two major reasons for doing so. One is to reach as many people as possible to inform them of the principal characteristics of the countryside. The other is to stimulate communication across disciplines so that serious scholars can form opinions about where the frontiers of knowledge exist in subjects other than their own.

A professor of American literature at Princeton University, William Howarth, has prepared the chapter for Part 2 in which he explores the basis of our interest in the rural and the pastoral. Is it nostalgia for a lifestyle, perhaps even an imagined lifestyle, or is it concern about the natural environment that move us? Perhaps both forces are at work. Our interest in things rural may spring from motivations and aspirations that are fundamental to our natures.

Such motivations have been translated into more pragmatic concerns in the remainder of the book. Part 3 relates the rural America of today to the one we may have imagined was present yesterday. The next part describes and analyzes the economic wealth of rural America in the context of money, jobs, and space. Part 5 examines rural poverty—places where the economic health is not good. Regional and ethnic diversity provide the focus for Part 6, which illuminates the enormous complexity and diversity of the countryside. Part 7 is concerned with the social and institutional context within which group decisions are made. The conclusion provides an interpretation of the material covered in the book.

ON THE DEFINITION OF RURAL

The use of terms such as "rural," "nonmetropolitan," "countryside," and "hinterlands" in this volume have the potential for creating misunderstanding. A word of explanation at the outset may avoid subsequent difficulty.

Hart (Chapter 4), Fuguitt (Chapter 5), and other authors note that "rural" and "nonmetropolitan" are specific definitions when used in official publications to describe particular data. In essence, they are residuals which measure everything that is nonurban or nonmetropolitan as the case may be. Used in this way they are by no means synonymous.

In Chapter 2 Lewis raises question about the continued relevance of the term "rural." His point is that recent settlement patterns have played hob with the traditional use of such terms as "urban" and "rural."

The National Rural Studies Committee has struggled with the term "rural" from the beginning. We have been troubled both by the specific, technical meaning of the term as used in official government publications as well as by the connotations, both favorable and unfavorable, that the term often evokes, yet we have been unable to identify an alternative term that would serve the general purpose we wished to serve.

When all of these considerations were taken into account, the decision was made not to impose rigid requirements each time the terms are used. Properly warned, we believe the reader will be able to know how these terms are being used from the context. In some cases (Hart, Chapter 4, Fuguitt, Chapter 5, Mills, Chapter 6, and Summers, Chapter 11, for example) the authors state precisely how the terms are used and what they are intended to measure empirically. In other instances, (Chapters 1 and 26, for example) such terms describe generic conditions and are often used interchangeably.

PART TWO
READING THE LAND: LITERATURE AND THE COUNTRYSIDE

Some people know rural America because they have lived there. They have had the sensual experience of turning the soil and then harvesting the produce of the seed they have planted. They may have attended a small country school and graduated in a high school class of fewer than one hundred students. Many other people have lived their entire life in a small town, although they are a decreasing percentage of the total population. These people are often well-educated and well-traveled, and all of them know about the countryside from first-hand experience.

Americans who have not spent most of their life in rural America must depend on others for their impressions about the place. Information may come from the oral histories of people who have experienced rural life—perhaps a family member of an earlier generation—or from media fragments. The most lasting impressions, however, often come from the serious literature that we read or that is read by those whose business it is to inform or entertain us. What, then, is the impression one gets of the countryside from reading American literature?

William Howarth concerns himself with such matters in Chapter 2. He takes his readers on a journey from a time before Jesus Christ to the present. He tells us why we are dependent on city writers to tell us about rural places: the answer, in part, is because the rural cannot be understood independent of the urban. The city provides the perspective from which the rural is viewed and interpreted—and therein lies the danger. Unless one understands the perspective, one may not be able to evaluate the claims of the literature. The Howarth chapter is, then, particularly valuable and appropriate to open this book of readings, for he helps us appreciate and evaluate the perspective of city writers on rural subjects.

2
LAND AND WORD: AMERICAN PASTORAL

WILLIAM HOWARTH

PASSING LAND

Willa Cather's novel, *My Ántonia* (1918), begins with a reunion of two child-hood friends who meet again at midlife on a train crossing Iowa. The time is late summer, just before harvest. From seats in an observation car, they look with fond reminiscence upon the passing land:

> While the train flashed through never-ending miles of ripe wheat, by country towns and bright-flowered pastures and oak groves wilting in the sun, we sat in the observation car, where the woodwork was hot to the touch and red dust lay deep over everything. The dust and heat, the burning wind, reminded us of many things.
>
> We were talking about what it is like to spend one's childhood in little towns like these, buried in wheat and corn, under stimulating extremes of climate: burning summers when the world lies green and billowy be-neath a brilliant sky, when one is fairly stifled in vegetation, in the color and smell of strong weeds and heavy harvests; blustery winters with little snow, when the whole country is stripped bare and grey as sheet-iron. We agreed that no one who had not grown up in a little prairie town could know anything about it. It was a kind of freemasonry, we said.

The mood is nostalgic because neither friend has lived in this region for many years. Their train is rolling east to New York, where both long ago moved to take up urban lives: affluent, fast-paced, crowded with social rites, and not entirely happy.

Cather's scene sketches a complex view of American land, evoking its tangled history of wonder, loss, and alienation. Once the prairie was a vast treeless plain covered with lush grasses, taller than a man on horseback. Great herds of elk and buffalo grazed the region on seasonal treks, trailed by Indian hunters. Then a generation of settlers arrived, scoring the land into roads and fields that became "miles of never-ending wheat," dotted with pasture and wilting oaks. Plows broke the soil and hot, dry winds eroded it, spreading clouds of red dust "deep over everything." Progress brought profits, but also ominous changes. Towns now lie "buried" in crops and "stifled" by growth; harsh seasons mold the residents into insular pride, the "freemasonry" that narrows and ritualizes their lives.

The two friends see this country with the ambivalence of native exiles, bound by sentiment yet also departing. Their situation measures a dialectical process in civilized life, the rural-urban interaction. However opposite they appear, rural and urban places define each other. Willa Cather knew that well, for she left Nebraska to live in Manhattan, where she wrote of western lands. In the East she escaped small-town strictures, yet her city vantage made the country into Paradise lost, a place she left in order to know it as home. *My Antonia* relates how generations of Americans passed from their agrarian origins to urban modernity. The book verifies that social progress empties the countryside yet also raises its cultural status. The sources of this paradox are not recent, but rooted in four millennia of social evolution. In summary, these are its prime factors:

- Language. Ancient Greeks use one word, *polis,* to mean city-state, but Roman laws distinguish *rur* from *urb,* and both words are urban inventions. The antithesis of "urban" is "rural"—sparsely settled, agricultural, quiet, simple, artless—and those values are positive or negative, depending on a user's urbanity. One person's simple, rustic serenity is another's dull, rude, inelegance. These distinctions affect synonyms for rural, such as bucolic, rustic, and pastoral.
- Literature. Rural writing is also an urban product. The first pastoral poet is Theocritus; in the third century B.C. he was living in Alexandria and homesick for the countryside of Sicily. Throughout literary history, from Virgil to Cather, city writers produce the country books. Two reasons: writers need distance (exile) to find their themes, and they create literature in and for urban markets.
- History. The nostalgia that writers associate with pastoral scenes is a reaction to change, usually age or dislocation. The greater the change, the stronger the nostalgia. Pastoralism, a high esteem for rural life, accelerates in periods of rapid urban growth, caused by economic devel-

opment. Societies that invest heavily in progress also sentimentalize "primitive" rural ways. A countryside seen as "empty" or "open" counters the negative aspects of city life: crowding, disease, crime, violence.

* Sociology. Rural people may accept urban myths, but their folklore (oral, not written), often documents the actual conditions of country life, positive and negative. The most accurate accounts of rural society grant its residents uncensored speech. Otherwise, even scholars devoted to empirical research will perpetuate urban bias.

The rural-urban interaction is widely recognized, yet historians read it quite variously. Cultural critic Raymond Williams says urban values prevail because cities concentrate the force of economic capital. Landscape historian John Stilgoe emphasizes design, finding that layouts of rural farms and roads initially shape urban streets and houses, until those agrarian forms turn industrial, producing mills and factories that consume rather than sustain resources. Biologist Edward O. Wilson takes a longer view, suggesting that urban parks may be efforts to preserve humanity's first home, the savannah: a rolling, grassy plain with few trees and no cultivation—as on the early American plains.

PASTORAL TRADITION

A common element in these readings is land, which cultures possess through acts of language. People bring names to places, telling stories of this hill or that shore, and the earth makes their ideas tangible. The earliest recorded tales in Western tradition arise in the Mediterranean. From Babylon to Greece, that region's adverse climate and terrain promote a market economy at village or city places (*plateia, plaza*). Markets generate literacy and history, the use of notched sticks (*talea*) to tally sums, and tales to recount the deeds of gods or heroes. One common fable is of a Golden Age, a time when mortals dwelled in gardens known as Arcadia, the Hesperides, or Paradise.

In a harsh world, order and security reside in cultivated images of garden and pastor. The Hebrew scriptures depict God as a shepherd who tends the world through acts of firm partition: dark-light, water-land, man-woman. *Genesis* defines life as antithetical—and also verbal, for God creates with dicta: "Let there be . . . ." Mankind occupies the garden Eden until sin leads to exile, an outcast life of pain and labor. That legend confirms the Jews' long history as stateless nomads, ever seeking a Messiah who will return them to a homeland. During centuries of dispersal they sustain their heritage with sacred writings, translated into Greek in the third century B.C. by Jewish scholars at Alexandria.

As imperial city-states develop, rural life acquires its counterappeal. At Ptolemy's court in Alexandria, Theocritus writes his *Idylls,* nostalgic love songs that depict Sicily as a peaceful countryside. Sicily is, in fact, often racked by civil mutiny; but his view from afar is of a kindly realm. So begins a classical tradition known as bucolic, georgic, eclogue; pastoral verses that portray rural folk as gentle planters and herders. The simple tone of pastoral masks its ironic and often political allegory. In his *Eclogues* (43–37 B.C.) Virgil alludes to Roman wars and land grabs, mocking imperial dominion in a series of song contests between rustic swains.

The empire's nemesis is an itinerant pastor, Jesus of Nazareth. Born in a stable and trained as a carpenter, Jesus travels the countryside to preach to farmers and fishers. His parables use simple rural images to attack official corruption, while his miraculous deeds transform soil and food into spiritual emblems. In cities Jesus confronts greed, lust, and betrayal; eventually he is crucified by the Roman masters of Jerusalem. His ultimate triumph over death promises followers not earthly reward but a celestial home, the Kingdom of Heaven. This revolutionary gospel wins converts throughout the Mediterranean, ultimately founding a new Church in the declining imperial capitols of Constantinople and Rome.

Victory on earth dilutes the heavenly kingdom, until Church patriarchs raise a new vision of history. In 426 A.D. Augustine of Hippo completes *The City of God,* a treatise that attributes Christian success to a redemptive prophecy, in which the church (*Civitas Dei*) justly occupies Rome (*Civitas Terra*). In coming to urban power, Christianity divides the world into civil and wild domains, the latter held by unconverted pagans (*paganus,* country dwellers) and barbarians (*barbarus,* foreign). Land acquires piety, its godly cities built on open shores and plains, while demons occupy interior uplands, a realm of forest (*foris,* outside) and heathen (*heath,* untilled land). Such rhetoric converts pastoralism into an instrument of dominion, using the forces of clearing and cultivation to save an imperfect, fallen world.

Driven by fear of unsettled lands, the Church spreads its mission to northern Europe during the early Middle Ages. Through conversion and alliance, barbarian kingdoms give way to holy empire, directed by Rome and aided by monastic priests. They clear forests and plant crops at monasteries, small cities of God, around which settlements grow. Priests teach literacy, establishing schools and universities that promulgate study as cultivation of a field (*campus*). The Church also condones feudal aristocracy and its manorial system of land use. From Denmark to England, lords and vassals occupy manors, great houses seated amid villages and fields that peasants work in tenancy. This pastoral economy sustains a strict hierarchy of social classes, with unlanded peasants at the bottom.

As fortunes of church and state improve, urban growth intensifies. Regions acquire population centers at market towns (*seignory, ville, burg*), linked by roads to rural districts. In Germany, the solitary *landschaft*, a clearing ringed by marsh and forest, gives way to tenant farmsteads leased from manor owners. After 1100, Norman invaders spread manorial rule to England, seizing land and erecting elegant vaulted cathedrals, which form town centers. Normans introduce to English many Romance words, including *urban* and *rural*, the latter meaning rustic, rude, primitive; it attributes to country people a narrow outlook and crude manner. At university those students who fail and must depart are said to "rusticate," exiled into ignorance.

In the late Middle Ages, urban centers steadily deplete rural populations. A series of plagues and famines after 1300 shrink the pool of skilled labor, attracting agricultural peasants to towns and skilled trades. Common people (*vulgus*) enter craft or commodity guilds, acquire capital, and participate in expanding trade. A chain of political consolidation ensues: towns strengthen regions, regions press for national sovereignty; monarchs form alliances with or against other states. As Europe affiliates, its Christian mission of settlement aligns with market-driven policy. Rich trade in spices and metals opens with the far East, yet sea travel is costly and land routes are blocked by Muslim empires. In 1492 a newly united Spain expels the Moors, discarding eight centuries of Arabic culture for Christian enterprise. A voyager named Columbus seeks a western route to Asia, sailing beyond the fabled Hesperides.

NEW WORLD

When Columbus sets forth in 1492 he pursues a medieval version of the pastoral dream, to redeem pagan lands on behalf of a holy empire. The "new world" he finds is not as blank as imagined, for its "Indians" have built a strong civilization and use intertribal trade. Yet he prevails over these resourceful people, often using the advantage of literacy. With his pen he maps and renames land, for documents seal the legality of imperial mission. A classic instance of such revision occurs on November 12, 1492, when he lands at "Cuba" to trade gifts with the natives. Columbus distributes beads and caps, "things of small value." They give tobacco and corn, their most useful and sacred goods. To the natives these gifts say peace and life, but he reads them as groceries.

Between the native and the European lie radical differences of thought respecting language, land, and property. In the new world only Mayans had attained precontact literacy, but they had declined in the same era as Rome. The tribes Columbus meets use hand signs, which in time can evolve into writing, as they did for Neolithic Europeans. Thriving in an oral culture, the natives root their faith in earthly objects and see words as primary, having the mysterious power of dreams and prayers. In this view, language preexists and thus creates nature. Reflecting its roots in oral tradition, *Genesis* also attributes God's primacy to words, the power to command and name. But the ability to *write* gives words lasting authority, setting forth laws and bounds, recording events as history, converting ideas into plans and designs. Pastoral tradition long ago became scripture, the Bible that Columbus reads each day. Now its rhetoric of dominion advances with him, into an age of conquest.

Columbus strives to inscribe "the Indies," yet words alone will not possess this land, his first glimpse of the tropics. The "savage" harvests large tracts of land, builds extensive villages, and mines precious metals. He succeeds by adapting to his land, which at times also becomes his natural mentor. In less tactical hours he simply enjoys the exotic birds and forests, or the great waterfalls that course down mountainsides, expressing "the delight that he had received from seeing and looking at the beauty and freshness of those lands." Columbus had come in order to possess the Indies but they enchant him, remaining so elusive that "a thousand tongues would not suffice to tell it or his hand to write it" (Columbus 1989, 116). This clash between design and wonder eventually becomes a dominant rhythm in American pastoral.

After 1500 the wealth and knowledge amassed from global exploration spurs Europe into a cultural Renaissance, a period of vibrant urban growth. In the capitols of Florence, Paris, and London, a new secularism emerges, versed in science and classical humanism. Rediscovery of pre-Christian thought inspires greater tolerance of dissent, spurring the Protestant reformation. In the arts, classical revivals create villas and eclogues, and now these ancient forms absorb the tensions of modern change. The pastoral poems of Spenser or Sidney are set in countryside, but their characters dress and speak as courtiers. Shakespeare's dramatic pastoral, *As You Like It* (1600), depicts aristocrats playing at country life, regressing to an idyllic agrarian order. In fact, rural Britain is rapidly emptying, as emigrants depart to colonize America. Pastoral poets romanticize a lost past, yet also ironize changing prospects.

The Renaissance awakes to time, then to place. Science charts anatomy and cartography; artists adopt an empirical realism, exact line and portion bathed in light and color. Paintings give new emphasis to natural outdoor scenes, bringing exact locations to the fore instead of hiding them in vague background. Italians call the works *pastorale,* since they depict green hills dotted with flocks and shepherds, but north of the Alps this tradition is *paysage moralise,* the "moral country" that gleams with natural atmosphere, even though its realistic trees and flowers also express religious allegory. In the low-lying Netherlands, country reclaimed from the sea, the new painting is *landskap,* or "shaped land," measuring the solid, earthy realism of Holland, a tidy nation that runs a vast colonial trade. Soon the English also paint rural *landscape,* a term for general outdoor scenery, from country vistas to urban parks and gardens.

This heightened cultural appreciation of land comes as its economic value is changing. In the colonial era, wealth derives less from resources than products and services. Cities expand, rural tenants decline, and absentee landlords own most of the countryside. By 1600 *landscape* means grand estate grounds, both natural and cultivated; while farms are merely low, functional *rural* land. This social bias imparts to landscape a broad range of privileged meanings: wholesome and spacious (panorama), containing future prospects (horizon), and providing a general epitome (vista). These notions inform the British view of North America, which is seen not as rural land, fit for planting and harvesting, but as a great landscape, full of potential as a new pastoral civilization.

During its early phase of settlement, American land receives and reforms European ideas. At the outset no explorer knows the continent's true mass, only that it is vast and open, with greatly varied terrain. Europeans sail west and stake out claims according to latitudes: Spaniards to the south, French on the north, British along the eastern seacoast. In planting colonies, each culture brings the pastoral tradition into new places. Forested slopes become woodlot and clearings yield pasture, while meadows and floodplain suit as plowed fields. These forms shape livestock pens and fencing, lines that direct paths and roads. America is not a space of exile or dreamy innocence, but voluntary and constructed. The task is to fill an "empty" space, and if that attitude is ruthless, its necessity is also clear. As Robert Frost later wrote, "The land was ours before we were the land's" (Frost 1979, 348).

The early literature of America is not pastoral in the European sense, for no writer may depict unknown terrain as rural pasture, full of piping shepherds and fair maidens. Royal patrons seek profit from their colonial lands, not rustic entertainment. The first American books are reports or "relations" directed to distant investors. That means *Good News from Virginia* (1613), where the soil is warm and well-drained, but in Massachusetts the Puritans face a harsh climate and stony land. To survive there is a tribute to the faith that *Wonders of the Invisible World* (1693) must lie beyond New England. Like their Christian ancestors, the Puritans not only endure but prosper, challenging them to ask if their plantation is a "city upon a hill," God's model for the world to admire and follow.

PEOPLE OF CULTIVATORS

The sense of purpose in American settlement changes in the 1700s, driven by rising prosperity and resentment over absentee governance of colonial resources. Many conservative leaders of the American Revolution are wealthy planters who write political tracts styled as correspondence. In *Letters from a Farmer in Pennsylvania* (1768), John Dickinson offers a Tory critique of British imperialism, asserting that America is a land where work distinguishes citizens more than class origins and fashion. J. Hector St. Jean de Crevecoeur goes farther in his *Letters from an American Farmer* (1782), asserting that the fundamental American identity is agrarian:

> Some few towns excepted, we are all tillers of the earth, from Nova Scotia to West Florida. We are a people of cultivators, scattered over an immense territory, communicating with each other by means of good roads and navigable rivers, united by the silken bands of mild government, all respecting the laws, without dreading their power, because they are equitable. We are all animated with the spirit of an industry which is unfettered and unrestrained, because each person works for himself. (Crévecoeur 1963, 61)

This definition of a homogenous America, where the poor of Europe enjoy "a pleasing uniformity of decent competence," reflects general conditions after the Revolution. The new nation is predominantly rural, its people occupying farms and villages along the eastern seaboard. In that settled space Americans seem natural republicans, connected mainly to their land and local governance. Yet elements of national consolidation exist, in the survey grids and roads that form corridors to community spaces of churches, schools, or meeting houses. These rural forms identify Americans as free and self-governing, the sort of pastoral yeomen that Thomas Jefferson saw as natural aristocrats, ready to improve upon Old World errors. *The Farmer's Almanac*

(1793) popularizes this ideal by depicting the American as one man on a plot of ground, yet connected to the cosmic round of sun, moon, and stars.

In strong contrast, royal pastoralism sinks to frivolity at the court of Versailles in 1785, when Louis XVI builds for Marie Antoinette a rustic hamlet of thatched cottages. Some favorite cows wear gilded hooves, and titled "maids" carry golden milk pails. In the evenings, costumed swains revive the gavotte, a medieval peasant dance. By 1793 the monarchs and their patronage of the arts expire, swept away by revolutions. An industrial economy arises, drawing fresh waves of peasants to urban tenancy, imposed by low wages and slum housing. Yet cities also promote education and literacy, assisted by high-speed presses that publish for middle-class readers, who give writers income and independence. The new demography does not kill pastoral, for the tradition broadens its class appeal. In the *Lyrical Ballads* (1800) of Wordsworth and Coleridge, two urban poets celebrate English lake country but use the simple words of rural speech, "the real language of men in a state of vivid sensation" (Wordsworth 1802, 141). This idealizing of natural form and style spreads to painting and music, as in Beethoven's *Pastoral Symphony* (1816).

During the early 1800s American population rises steeply, as settlers cross the Appalachians into the Ohio valley and central prairie. Although this rolling, well-drained soil is suited to farming, Alexis de Tocqueville predicts in his *Democracy in America* (1838) that the expanding country will develop new enterprises. Agriculture is too slow and stable, not suited to a rising middle class: "Democracy not only swells the number of working-men, but leads men to prefer one kind of labor to another; and while it diverts them from agriculture, it encourages their tastes for commerce and manufactures" (Tocqueville 1965, 163–164). But national development is not uniform. The Northeast turns industrial while the South remains agrarian, and those opposed economies produce deep sectional rivalry. Northern industry replaces planting with manufacture; this new emphasis on artifice crowds the landscape with mines and mills, factories that create wealth faster than fields. Given its scant population and long growing season, the South chooses to plant its cash crops with African slaves. The result is a human and ecological tragedy, for cotton and tobacco monocultures exhaust Southern soil, and slavery defames the legal heritage of property rights, born in the demise of Europe's manorial-peasant system. Sectional tensions only increase as settlers emigrate to the western plains and mountain plateaus, for Manifest Destiny, the call to expel foreign holdings, also defines a Union that federates all regions.

The literary culture of American romantics straddles this schism, echoing long-held conflicts in the pastoral tradition. Conservatives celebrate the familiar rustic ways of their regions, as with the "schoolroom poets" of New England—Bryant, Whittier, Lowell, and Longfellow. James Fenimore Cooper writes his Leatherstocking novels about prerevolutionary New York to denounce western expansion, blaming it first for destroying the wilderness and native people, and then for discarding an agrarian republic. In such novels as *The Prairie* (1827), the frontier becomes an ominously leveling region, promoting class intermarriage and encouraging peasants to embrace the new spirit of Jacksonian democracy.

Liberals trust the masses but seek to reform their culture. "Prospects," the final chapter in Emerson's *Nature* (1836), asks readers to trust in change: "Build therefore your own world. As fast as you conform your life to the pure idea in your mind, that will unfold its great proportions" (Emerson 1957, 56). Yet Emerson declines to test his ideas, refusing an invitation to join Margaret Fuller and other reformers at Brook Farm, an agrarian commune. Nathaniel Hawthorne, a skeptical resident, later satirizes their utopian experiment in *The Blithedale Romance* (1852). In this era many Shaker, Amish, and Mennonite sects live in religious communes, but an important social experiment is Henry Thoreau's sojourn at Walden Pond in 1845–1847. Thoreau resolves the conflict between pastoral ideal and rural land that eluded fellow Transcendentalists. In *Walden* (1854) he integrates action and principle by attending fully to his physical life: building a house near a wooded pond, baking bread at an open fire. Thoreau seeks an economy that fuses word to land, like a plant to soil and light: "What though I value the seeds of these beans, and harvest them in the fall of the year? This broad field which I have looked at so long looks not to me as the principal cultivator, but away from me to influences more genial to it, which water and make it green. These beans have results which are not harvested by me. Do they not grow for woodchucks partly?" (Thoreau 1981, 150).

TERRITORY AHEAD

The Civil War nearly shatters this idealism, but not the American sense of its identity as Nature's nation. Walt Whitman, styling himself "a kosmos, of Manhattan the son," is an urban poet who persistently depicts America with pastoral images. Responding, like Thoreau, to dynamic advances in the new earth sciences of geology and biology, Whitman takes as his central metaphor for democracy the grass, a common plant. Each blade of grass is distinct—

grasses have a complex lineage, with many species—yet in a field the leaves blend together, one united into many. *Leaves of Grass,* a single book of many editions (1855–1892), spans a half-century of history and limns the democratic ties of self and society, states and union. The poetry celebrates a full spectrum of rural imagery, from a farmer's humble compost heap, decaying matter that feeds new life, to the fields of rising grain that salute President Lincoln's coffin, tokens of resurrection for a grieving nation.

Western settlement booms after 1865, as railroads and homesteaders advance into the Great Plains. This region becomes the American heartland, directing its meat and grain to the commodities market in Chicago, an urban center that defines the rural frontier. City writers also shape frontier culture. Edward Eggleston, *The Hoosier School-Master* (1883), writes of prairie hamlets, and Mark Twain recalls drowsy river villages on the Mississippi. Each author sees the West from an eastern perspective, for Eggleston is a minister in Brooklyn, while Twain writes about Missouri from his mansion in Hartford, Connecticut. The ending of *Adventures of Huckleberry Finn* (1885), where Huck says he will "light out for the Territory" before yielding to civilization, is doubly ironic, both for Twain and his nation.

By 1885 little open territory remains in America, a condition that thwarts the westering impulse in national culture. The last Indian lands in Oklahoma open to homesteading in the 1890s, and when Frederick Jackson Turner writes "The Significance of the Frontier in American History" (1893), he defines an enduring myth of rugged, questing, self-reliant discovery just as its terrain appears to vanish, four centuries after Columbus arrived. Turner signals that America is no longer an empty land to fill, but a space with finite limits. Over four millennia, pastoralism led civilization from the Mediterranean to Europe, and then to the Americas; what happens when surveyor's grids and fences close the open range; when the Territory becomes states and federal "public land," when most of the population lives in urban or metropolitan centers?

That trend has been apparent for a century, as census after census confirms that Americans are shifting to towns and cities. After 1890 the countryside empties rapidly, especially across the South as mechanized agriculture displaces black and white tenant farmers, forcing them to abandon subsistence lives and migrate to wage earning, often in factories. By the early 1900s most new writers come from cities, where they have trained as newspaper reporters—a breed with tough, urbanized values. In *Maggie* (1896) and *Sister Carrie* (1900), Stephen Crane and Theodore Dreiser depict young women as sexually defamed by city life, while such authors as Jacob Riis, *The Battle with the Slums* (1902), Lincoln Steffens, *Shame of the Cities* (1904), and Upton Sinclair, *The Jungle* (1906), bluntly describe urban-industrial squalor. These reporters, "muckrakers" to angry politicians, agree with Marxist and Darwinian theory that life is determined by competitive material struggle. Most books of this era find little pastoral innocence, even in rural settings. Fiction by Hamlin Garland, *Main-Travelled Roads* (1891), and Frank Norris, *The Octopus* (1901), portray farmers as tiny, pathetic figures pitted against harsh land and climate, snared in the coils of market or railroad monopolies. Americans are no longer a nation of free, republican farmers; now they are enslaved and lost amid a vast, indifferent landscape.

In the new century, combined shocks of international war and intense urbanization transform the American image of rural life. A modern pastoral literature, reminiscent yet etched with dark introspection on death and failure, emerges in the poems of Robert Frost, "North of Boston" (1914), Edgar Lee Masters, "Spoon River Anthology" (1915), and Carl Sandburg, "Corn-Huskers" (1918), and in the early prairie novels of Willa Cather, *O Pioneers!* (1913), *The Song of the Lark* (1915), and *My Antonía* (1918). Little of this work focuses on the realities of farming in 1915, but on memories of forty years earlier: homesteads, small towns, railroads. To writers of this era, rural life is less an economic resource than a cultural heritage, vanishing into national mythology. In 1920 the census confirms a long-apparent trend, that America is now a predominantly urban nation.

With that turn, pastoral literature becomes an experimental realm, where writers explore Freudian themes of sexual and psychological obsession. In *Winesburg, Ohio* (1919) Sherwood Anderson populates his fictional country village with dreamers and ravers, people compelled by sexual drives and thwarted by repressive neuroses. To Ernest Hemingway the woods and streams of northern Michigan become havens for a convalescing war veteran in search of childhood security. "Big Two-Hearted River," published in *In Our Time* (1924), enacts the state of repression by never alluding to war or a wound—yet every moment of camping or fishing threatens to awake the hero's violent memories. The countryside depicted is not safe but broken, its abandoned farms and shuttered mill towns a portent of oncoming national failure.

For indeed the Depression that strikes industrial cities in the 1930s is old news in the country. From 1910 on, American agriculture experiences widespread shocks, jolted by prolonged drought and the arrival of tractor mechanization. These changes end Southern land tenancy and force millions of farm workers to migrate to the far West. Popular literature focuses on rural rather than urban depression, and mainly on agricultural collapse in the South. Since the Civil War that region has suffered seventy years of economic stagnancy, and the image of its rural decay is now firmly etched in the novels of William Faulkner, Erskine Caldwell, and John Steinbeck.

Faulkner and Steinbeck create two controversial images of modern rural life, working from opposite visions of history. Faulkner's fourteen novels and many stories (1929–1962) about a mythical "Yoknapatawpha" present a conservative saga, reminiscent of Fenimore Cooper, in which the landed gentry of northern Mississippi decline through moral bankruptcy, the old wages of slavery, while poor whites rise as parvenu merchants, the new possessors of capital. In *The Grapes of Wrath* (1939) Steinbeck poses a Marxist analysis of the Depression, describing poor white sharecroppers who migrate from the Cotton Belt to the central valley of California, where they fall victims to the fascist practices of corporate agriculture. Although a gigantic bestseller, his book draws fire from critics on both the political left and right. Especially offended are California's "Okies," a subculture still united by dialect, food, music—and undying enmity for John Steinbeck. Yet the novel is historically significant because it is the last major popular book to treat the working lives of American farmers.

As urban and international problems intensify in the late twentieth century, many writers ignore rural land. Wars fought on international fronts, the horrors of genocidal and nuclear destruction, spread a pall across these decades, now glumly identified as postmodern. In literature of the era, long silent and ignored groups of Americans—women, blacks, ethnics, homosexuals—turn and attack the forces that deny them identity. The unnamed black hero of Ralph Ellison's *Invisible Man* (1952) recapitulates racial history, migrating from rural South to urban North, where he is still treated as a cipher. Rootless and transient, other nomads of a Nuclear Age reject politics, religion, or any ideology that presumes a common social contract. Angry and disillusioned descendants of Puritan stock, the characters of Lillian Hellman, Carson McCullers, Flannery O'Connor, John Updike, and Thomas Pynchon live in paranoiac worlds, fractured by ignorant bias. In the postmodern call for a multicultural America, people affirm difference, not similarity. They know who but not *where* they are, having lost the old core of American identity, a strong sense of regional or social place.

Although ignored in postmodern literature, the country itself is still there, forming a panoramic backdrop for the continental journeys of Jack Kerouac, Robert Pirsig, Joan Didion, Tom Wolfe, and Leslie Silko, whose counterculture heroes compulsively take to the road in frenzied replays of the old westering history—and of their pastoral ancestors, dressed in native and rancher costume. Few note that the West is now a toxic waste dump and nuclear arms range, studded with abandoned family farms. In *The Nine Na-*

tions of North America (1981), Joel Garreau dubs that region "The Empty Quarter," a barren interval lying between the two coasts, merely a background to the figure of society.

ENVIRONMENTAL ERA

Yet the pastoral lives on, reviving in the 1960s as an environmental movement that affects nonfiction essays, memoirs, and journalism—as in the writings of John McPhee, Annie Dillard, Barry Lopez, or Gretel Erlich. Many of their books describe the northern edges of Alaska and upper Canada, a fragile Arctic ecosystem sadly miscast as "the last frontier." Spurred by findings of ecologists, environmental writers report that human populations have outgrown the carrying capacity of natural systems. This news, resisted by advocates of traditional expansion, coincides with evidence of global decline: destruction of habitat and species, pollution of air, water, and soil; rapid viral mutation and infection; spreading social decay.

Media broadcast these alarms, yet America is dumbing down, one in three citizens illiterate. As the nation descends the knowledge ladder, from books to pictures to talk, Bill McKibben glimpses in *The Age of Missing Information* (1992) that just ahead may lie an old story reborn, of outcast and wandering exile:

> A day of television reminds you that except for whatever specialty you earn your living with, you live in a vastly simpler place. A place where your physical location hardly matters. We dwell at the intersection of *Oprah* and *Love Connection*, of *General Hospital* and *You Deserve a Break Today* and *Hawaii Five-O* and *She's the Sheriff*, all of which make as much sense in Seattle as they do in Miami, all of which can be dubbed or copied around the planet and enjoyed by nineteen-year-olds and ninety-year-olds; all of which can be understood in a matter of seconds by someone who switched them on halfway through. If my endless day of television reminded me of anything, it's that electronic media have become an environment of their own—that to the list of neighborhood and region and continent and planet we must now add television as a place where we live. And the problem is not that it exists—the problem is that it supplants. Its simplicity makes complexity hard to fathom. (McKibben 1993, 52–53)

Other media are more promising, such as digital mapping of the earth, which has created what Stephen Hall calls "new geographies." This technology confirms what pastoral has long indicated, that land is a text read and written, a mix of cognition and rational planning. Other disciplines see land as a set of signs; a cultural "construction" or social "production" shaped by policy, ideology, and technology. Philosophers and critics now analyze the shapes of everyday life, from suburbs to theme parks, while landscape historians reaffirm the cultural meaning of America as shaped places, synthetic in their mix of natural space and human custom. Such findings have led environmental historians to review the lore of continental discovery and settlement. They agree that Africa, North America, and Australia were conquered by language, lands possessed by the inscriptive names and maps of settlers.

In the new field of landscape ecology, pastoral has shaped the work of science, as observers read human-land interactions to see how regions are altered by design. Recognizing that disturbance is a normal condition in nature, they look for structures common to both rural and urban areas, then create a spatial language to analyze those forms by shape, function, and change. Although land often appears complex and varied, its elements are deeply intertwined as ecosystems. The systems show where distribution patterns lie; what they give and take through flow or exchange; and what changes they alter or influence in time. A formal analysis of landscape thus strongly resembles one of history and literature, a mosaic of elements that share common structures and relations of development, disturbance, flow, and change. This reading has strong implications for land management, since users must balance diversity and productivity, evaluating an area's quality before trying to change it.

In the twenty-first century environmentalism can only accelerate, whether America's population expands or declines. Citizens will live mainly in urban centers, working at service trades and rarely producing their own material goods. Groceries will reach the table, but their place of origin may remain unknown. Also forgotten will be the skills required to chop cotton or buck hay, or to hitch a team in driving rain. Those labors bear tangible rewards, and if they vanish so will the values they sustain. But the pastoral itself will not vanish, for it thrives on the losses that time always brings.

In "Fat Girls in Des Moines" (1988) Bill Bryson, an American long exiled in England, writes of his native Iowa, and not always kindly. He recalls a plain, dull country, where men wear feed caps and women resemble "elephants dressed in children's clothing," yet he also sees that land as his native theme:

On another continent, 4,000 miles away, I am quietly seized with that nostalgia that overcomes you when you have reached the middle of your life and your father has recently died and it dawns on you that when he went he took a part of you with him. I want to go back to the magic places of my youth—to Mackinac Island, Estes Park, Gettysburg—and see if they were as good as I remember them. I want to hear the long, low sound of a Rock Island locomotive calling across a still night, and the clack of it receding into the distance. I want to see lightning bugs, and hear cicadas shrilling, and be inescapably immersed in that hot, crazy-making August weather that makes your underwear scoot up every crack and fissure and cling to you like latex, and drives mild-mannered men to pull out handguns in bars and light up the night with gunfire. I want to look for Ne-Hi Pop and Burma Shave signs and go to a ball game and sit at a marble-topped soda fountain and drive through the kind of small towns that Deanna Durbin and Mickey Rooney used to live in in the movies. It's time to go home. (1988, 43)

Once more a traveler crosses the central plains, reading its land and heading east for a distant city. The world Bryson describes has long ago vanished, its marble-topped soda fountains gone to fast-food emporia and shopping malls. Yet his insistent recollection measures the vitality of pastoral, which thrives on the pace and affluence of urban life.

Today an enduring pastoralism shapes our culture: it appears in city parks and suburban gardens, second country homes and wilderness treks, Winnebagos on the road and Bambi in the VCR. As nations grow more technological, as economies turn from producing goods to services, those trends guarantee the tenacity of pastoral values. Hence a paradox is clear: faster, busier, more artificial and technological lives will cling ever more strongly to pastoral themes. The reason? Humans are irrational beings; they seek but also resist change. Wanting to be close to soil is a fable that secures the hopes and fears aroused by history.

Societies that invest in progress are deliberately courting change, and modernization inevitably brings the crowded, swifter pace of urban life. The pastoral monitors that social change: for all classes, it assuages fears of progress and posits a stable continuity in nature. To the critic William Empson, pastoral is a means of "putting the complex into the simple," expressing intricacy clearly, which explains why the impulse waxes with the quickened pace of history. The pastoral endures because it travels well, adjusting to changes of style and substance. In a world now driven by ideology and information, pastoral reminds us of unmediated labor, the pleasure of raking leaves or stacking firewood. The view from a moving train or car must be pastoral, to preserve our dream of unfallen Paradise.

Country books shall thus always come from city writers, telling a fable of time, out of their own exile and alienation, to make a story of a lost place. For Americans they will hold out that old illusion of wild and open land, "the clean, fresh breast of America" that Scott Fitzgerald thought the first explorers saw. But America always had finite limits; the myth of its discovery preserves the fiction of human property. The truth: on the land all people are tenants, paying rent for a while before they return to its dust. The pastoral mediates our fear of that change, hence its constant ambivalence in form and tone. It celebrates what has vanished and could not exist without the diminished here and now. It bonds all people into a secret and ritual society, "a kind of freemasonry," as Willa Cather wrote, that rides cross-country in an observation car, bound ahead but looking back, telling of early and happy days.

WORKS CONSULTED

Passing Land

Cather, Willa. *My Antonía*. New York: Knopf, 1918.

Levy, Helen Fiddyment. *Fiction of the Home Place: Jewett, Cather, Glasgow, Porter, Welty, and Naylor.* Jackson: University Press of Mississippi, 1992.

Stilgoe, John R. *Common Landscape of America, 1580 to 1845*. New Haven: Yale University Press, 1982.

Turner, Frederick. *Spirit of Place: The Making of an American Literary Landscape.* San Francisco: Sierra Club, 1989.

Williams, Raymond. *The Country and the City.* New York: Oxford University Press, 1973.

Wilson, Edward O. *Biophilia*. Cambridge: Harvard University Press, 1984.

Winters, Laura. *Willa Cather: Landscape and Exile.* Selinsgrove, Penn.: Susquehanna University Press, 1993.

Pastoral Tradition

Bechmann, Roland. *Trees and Man: The Forest in the Middle Age.* New York: Paragon, 1990.

Halperin, David M. *Before Pastoral: Theocritus and the Ancient Tradition of Bucolic Poetry.* New Haven: Yale University Press, 1983.

Harrison, Robert Pogue. *Forests: The Shadow of Civilization.* Chicago: University of Chicago Press, 1992.

Patterson, Annabel. *Pastoral and Ideology: Virgil to Valéry.* Berkeley: University of California Press, 1987.

Wells, Peter S. *Farms, Villages, and Cities: Commerce and Urban Origins in Late Pre-historic Europe.* Ithaca, N.Y.: Cornell University Press, 1984.

New World

Flint, Valerie I. J. *The Imaginative Landscape of Christopher Columbus.* Princeton: Princeton University Press, 1992.

Heimert, Alan, ed. *The Puritans in America: A Narrative Anthology.* Cambridge, Mass.: Harvard University Press, 1985.

Josephy, Jr., Alvin M., ed. *America in 1492: The World of the Indian Peoples Before the Arrival of Columbus.* New York: Knopf, 1992.

Kadir, Djelal. *Columbus and the Ends of the Earth: Europe's Prophetic Rhetoric as Conquering Ideology.* Berkeley: University of California Press, 1992.

Murray, David. *Forked Tongues: Speech, Writing and Representation in North American Indian Texts.* London: Pinter, 1991.

Nabakov, Peter, ed. *Native American Testimony: A Chronicle of Indian-White Relations from Prophecy to the Present, 1492–1992.* New York: Penguin, 1992.

Ong, Walter J. "Orality and Literacy: The Technologizing of the Word." In *New Accents,* ed. Terence Hawkes. New York: Methuen, 1982.

Sale, Kirkpatrick. *The Conquest of Paradise: Christopher Columbus and the Columbian Legacy.* New York: Knopf, 1991.

Tedlock, Dennis, ed. *Teachings from the American Earth: Indian Religion and Philosophy.* New York: Liveright, 1975.

Zerubavel, Eviatar. *Terra Incognita: The Mental Discovery of America.* New Brunswick, N.J.: Rutgers University Press, 1992.

People of Cultivators

Cowdrey, Albert E. *This Land, This South: An Environmental History.* University Press of Kentucky, 1983.

Cronon, William. *Changes in the Land: Indians, Colonists, and the Ecology of New England.* New York: Hill and Wang, 1983.

Evernden, Neil. *The Social Creation of Nature.* Baltimore: Johns Hopkins University Press, 1992.

Gray, Richard J. *Writing the South: Ideas of an American Region.* New York: Cambridge University Press, 1986.

Howarth, William. *The Book of Concord: Thoreau's Life as a Writer.* New York: Viking, 1982.

Kolodny, Annette. *The Lay of the Land: Metaphor as Experience and History in American Life and Letters.* Chapel Hill: University of North Carolina Press, 1979.

Lane, Belden C. *Landscapes of the Sacred: Geography and Narrative in American Spirituality.* In *Isaac Hecker Studies in Religion and American Culture,* ed. John A. Coleman. New York: Paulist, 1988.

Lawson-Peebles, Robert. *Landscape and Written Expression in Revolutionary*

America: The World Turned Upside Down. Cambridge and New York: Cambridge University Press, 1988.

Meinig, D. W. *Atlantic America, 1492–1800, The Shaping of America: A Geographical Perspective on 500 Years of History*. New Haven: Yale University Press, 1986.

Regis, Pamela. *Describing Early America: Bartram, Jefferson, Crevecoeur, and the Rhetoric of Natural History*. De Kalb: Northern Illinois University Press, 1991.

Riese, Teut Andreas. *Vistas of a Continent: Concepts of Nature in America*. Heidelberg: Carl Winter Universitatsverlag, 1979.

Tichi, Cecelia. *New World, New Earth: Environmental Reform in American Literature from the Puritans Through Whitman*. New Haven: Yale University Press, 1979.

Ziff, Larzer. *Writing in the New Nation: Prose, Print and Politics in the Early United States*. New Haven: Yale University Press, 1991.

Territory Ahead

Batteau, Allen W. *The Invention of Appalachia*. Tempe: University of Arizona Press, 1990.

Brand, Dana. *The Spectator and the City in Nineteenth-Century American Literature*. Cambridge: Cambridge University Press, 1991.

Cronon, William. *Nature's Metropolis: Chicago and the Great West*. New York: Norton, 1991.

Czitrom, Daniel J. *Media and the American Mind*. Chapel Hill: University of North Carolina Press, 1982.

Danly, Susan, ed. *The Railroad in American Art: Representations of Technological Change*. Cambridge, Mass.: MIT Press, 1988.

Dorman, Robert L. *Revolt of the Provinces: The Regionalist Movement in America, 1920–1945*. Chapel Hill: University of North Carolina Press, 1993.

Fisher, Philip. *Hard Facts: Setting and Form in the American Novel*. New York: Oxford University Press, 1985.

Goldsmith, Arnold L. *The Modern American Urban Novel: Nature as "Interior Structure."* Detroit: Wayne State University Press, 1991.

Harrison, Elizabeth Jane. *Female Pastoral: Women Writers Re-Visioning the American South*. Knoxville: University of Tennessee Press, 1991.

Heyne, Eric, ed. *Desert, Garden, Margin, Range: Literature on the American Frontier*. New York: Twayne, 1992.

Machor, James L. *Pastoral Cities: Urban Ideals and the Symbolic Landscape of America*. Madison: University of Wisconsin Press, 1987.

Madison, James H. *Heartland: Comparative Histories of the Midwestern States*. Bloomington: Indiana University Press, 1988.

Marx, Leo. *The Machine in the Garden: Technology and the Pastoral Ideal in America*. New York: Oxford University Press, 1964.

Meinig, D. W. *Continental America, 1800–1867, The Shaping of America: A Geographical Perspective on 500 Years of History*. New Haven: Yale University Press, 1993.

Noble, Allen G., ed. *To Build in a New Land: Ethnic Landscapes in North America*. Baltimore: Johns Hopkins University Press, 1992.

Novak, Barbara. *Nature and Culture: American Landscape and Painting, 1825–1875.* New York: Oxford University Press, 1980.

Relph, Edward C. *The Modern Urban Landscape: 1880 to the Present.* Baltimore: Johns Hopkins University Press, 1987.

Ruzicka, William T. *Faulkner's Fictive Architecture: The Meaning of Place in the Yoknapatawpha Novels.* Ann Arbor: UMI Research Press, 1987.

Schuyler, David. *The New Urban Landscape: The Redefinition of City Form in Nineteenth-Century America.* Baltimore: Johns Hopkins University Press, 1986.

Simonson, Harold P. *Beyond the Frontier: Writers, Western Regionalism, and a Sense of Place.* Fort Worth: Texas Christian University Press, 1989.

Wyatt, David. *The Fall into Eden: Landscape and Imagination in California.* New York: Cambridge University Press, 1986.

Environmental Era

Berry, Wendell. *The Gift of Good Land: Further Essays, Cultural and Agricultural.* San Francisco: North Point Press, 1981.

Calthorpe, Peter. *The Next American Metropolis: Ecology, Community, and the American Dream.* Princeton: Princeton University Press, 1993.

Devall, Bill, and George Sessions. *Deep Ecology: Living as if Nature Mattered.* Layton, Utah: Gibbs M. Smith, 1985.

Dowling, David. *Fictions of Nuclear Disaster.* London: Macmillan, 1987.

Eckersley, Robyn. *Environmentalism and Political Theory: Toward an Ecocentric Approach.* Albany: State University of New York Press, 1992.

Foreman, Richard T., and Michel Godron. *Landscape Ecology.* New York: Wiley, 1986.

Gore, Al. *Earth in the Balance: Ecology and the Human Spirit.* New York: Penguin, 1992.

Hall, Stephen S. *Mapping the Next Millennium: The Discovery of New Geographies.* New York: Random House, 1992.

Hiss, Tony. *The Experience of Place.* New York: Knopf, 1990.

Inge, Tonette Bond, ed. *Southern Women Writers: The New Generation.* Tuscaloosa: University of Alabama Press, 1990.

McCay, Bonnie J., ed. *The Question of the Commons: The Culture and Ecology of Communal Resources.* Tucson: University of Arizona Press, 1990.

Meyrowitz, Joshua. *No Sense of Place: The Impact of Electronic Media on Social Behavior.* New York: Oxford University Press, 1985.

Ryden, Kent C. *Mapping the Invisible Landscape: Folklore, Writing, and the Sense of Place.* Iowa City: Iowa University Press, 1993.

Sorkin, Michael. *Variations on a Theme Park: The New American City and the End of Public Space.* New York: Hill and Wang, 1992.

Strehle, Susan. *Fiction in the Quantum Universe.* Chapel Hill: University of North Carolina Press, 1992.

Tuan, Yi-Fu. *Space and Place: The Perspective of Experience.* Minneapolis: University of Minnesota Press, 1977.

Biographical Data

Howarth, William. *The Book of Concord: Thoreau's Life as a Writer.* New York: Viking Penguin, 1982.
Thoreau, Henry D. *Thoreau in the Mountains,* ed. William Howarth. New York: Farrar, Straus, and Giroux, 1982.

READINGS: AMERICAN PASTORAL

Colonial and Revolutionary

William Bradford, *History of Plimoth Plantation*
Richard Byrd, *Journey to the Land of Eden*
J. H. St. J. de Crèvecoeur, *Letters from an American Farmer*
John Dickinson, *Letters from a Farmer in Pennsylvania*
Thomas Jefferson, *Notes on Virginia*
Cotton Mather, *Wonders of the Invisible World*
Alexander Whitaker, *Good News from Virginia*

Romanticism and Transcendentalism

James Fenimore Cooper, *The Pioneers, The Prairie*
Ralph Waldo Emerson, *Nature*
Nathaniel Hawthorne, *The Blithedale Romance*
Washington Irving, *A Tour on the Prairies*
Sylvester Judd, *Margaret*
Henry Wadsworth Longfellow, *Evangeline*
James Russell Lowell, *The Biglow Papers*
Henry D. Thoreau, *Walden, The Maine Woods*
Alexis de Tocqueville, *Democracy in America*
Walt Whitman, *Leaves of Grass*
John Greenleaf Whittier, *Legends of New England*

Realism

Mary Austin, *The Land of Little Rain*
Kate Chopin, *Bayou Folk*
Edward Eggleston, *The Hoosier School-Master*
Joel Chandler Harris, *Uncle Remus*
E. W. Howe, *The Story of a Country Town*
Sarah Orne Jewett, *A Country Doctor, Country of the Pointed Firs*
Clarence King, *Mountaineering in the Sierra Nevada*

Mark Twain, *Roughing It, Adventures of Huckleberry Finn*
Owen Wister, *The Virginian*

Naturalism

Stephen Crane, *Maggie, A Girl of the Streets*
Theodore Dreiser, *Sister Carrie*
Hamlin Garland, *Main-Travelled Roads, Rose of Dutcher's Cooly*
Jack London, *The Call of the Wild*
Frank Norris, *McTeague, The Octopus, The Pit*
Jacob Riis, *The Battle with the Slums*
Charles Rosenfeld, *Songs from the Ghetto*
Upton Sinclair, *The Jungle*
Lincoln Steffens, *Shame of the Cities*
Thorstein Veblen, *Theory of the Leisure Class*

Modernism

Sherwood Anderson, *Winesburg, Ohio; Poor White*
Erskine Caldwell, *Tobacco Road, God's Little Acre*
Willa Cather, *O Pioneers!, The Song of the Lark, My Antonia*
William Faulkner, *As I Lay Dying; Light in August; Go Down, Moses*
Robert Frost, *North of Boston*
Ellen Glasgow, *Barren Ground*
Ernest Hemingway, *In Our Time*
Sinclair Lewis, *Main Street*
Edwin Arlington Robinson, *The Town Down the River*
Ole Rolvaag, *Giants in the Earth*
Carl Sandburg, *Corn-Huskers*
John Steinbeck, *Of Mice and Men, The Grapes of Wrath*
Robert Penn Warren, *All the King's Men*
Glenway Wescott, *The Grandmothers*

Postmodernism

Saul Bellow, *Dangling Man, Henderson the Rain King*
Joan Didion, *Play It As It Lays, The White Album*
Ralph Ellison, *Invisible Man*
Jack Kerouac, *On the Road, The Dharma Bums*
Robert Pirsig, *Zen and the Art of Motorcycle Maintenance*
Thomas Pynchon, *The Crying of Lot 49, Gravity's Rainbow*
Hunter Thompson, *Fear and Loathing in Las Vegas*
John Updike, *Rabbit, Run; Rabbit Redux; Rabbit Is Rich*
Tom Wolfe, *The Electric Kool-Aid Acid Test*

Environmental and Regional

Edward Abbey, *Desert Solitaire, Down the River*
Annie Dillard, *A Pilgrim at Tinker Creek*
Edward Hoagland, *Walking the Dead Diamond River*
Bill Holm, *Prairie Days*
Garrison Keillor, *Lake Woebegone Days*
Charles Kuralt, *On the Road*
Aldo Leopold, *A Sand County Almanac*
Barry Lopez, *Of Wolves and Men, Arctic Dreams*
John McPhee, *Coming into the Country, Basin and Range*
Rob Schultheis, *The Hidden West*

PART THREE
CHANGE IN THE COUNTRYSIDE

In the preceding chapter William Howarth identifies some of the constants in city-countryside relations and attitudes. In Part 3 attention shifts to changes in city-countryside relationships. In this century those changes have been enormous, especially since World War II.

Peirce Lewis leads off the section by describing the emergence of a new kind of "galactic city" that calls into question the usefulness of the traditional concepts of rural and urban. The kind of development Lewis discusses is not confined to any particular region of the country, although its obvious impact is greater in more populous places.

One of the more enduring myths of our time is that "rural" and "farm" are synonymous. In Chapter 4 John Fraser Hart attacks this notion head-on. He shows that however such a notion might have been based historically, that basis has been destroyed in this century. Nevertheless, as we learn later in the book, the myth continues to influence the institutions of the countryside, even though most of the people who live there are neither farmers nor dependent on agriculture for their livelihood.

In Chapter 5 Glenn Fuguitt documents and compares demographic trends in metropolitan and nonmetropolitan America. He compresses an enormous amount of detail into a few pages characterizing the people who live in nonmetropolitan places. Not only does Fuguitt's essay help put Chapters 3 and 4 in perspective, it also provides a foundation for the chapters that follow. There are, to be sure, distinctive demographic differences between metropolitan and nonmetropolitan places, but there is also enormous variation within nonmetropolitan America itself. The reader will encounter such diversity repeatedly as he moves through the book and considers new subjects.

All of the authors emphasize the fact that the United States has become an urban nation. Whether one prefers to use the term "rural" or "nonmetro-politan," it is clear that conditions in such places are influenced enormously by developments in more densely populated places such as cities and metro-politan areas. Thus rural or nonmetropolitan America should not be studied in isolation from its larger environment.

3

THE URBAN INVASION OF RURAL AMERICA: THE EMERGENCE OF THE GALACTIC CITY

PEIRCE LEWIS

For as long as history has recorded such matters, Americans have been saying how much they dislike cities and how much they admire the values of rural life. At precisely the same time, America has been busily and self-consciously converting itself from a rural to an urban country.

The conversion from rural to urban life has provoked mixed emotions. Nostalgia is one—a feeling of loss for a golden age of farms and small towns, preserved in Currier and Ives lithographs and resurrected in the Main Streets of Disneyland and DisneyWorld. A feeling of resignation is another, for in most parts of the United States, the battered remains of rural life is under siege from a relentless urban assault, and in many parts of the country, traditional forms of rural life have virtually disappeared. A sense of outrage, often accompanied by confusion, is also manifest, for the tattered remnants of rural territory are being invaded by a kind of city that nobody has ever seen before. And because this new American city is unprecedented, nobody has yet invented rules to govern or guide its growth—much less to check it. To many Americans, scholars and lay people alike, observing the urban invasion of rural America is like watching the Nazi blitzkrieg roll across the old-fashioned rural countryside of northern France in June 1940. Nobody had ever seen an invasion like it before and nobody knew what to do about it.

THE DECLINE OF THE OLD URBAN ORDER

Until the time of World War II, the battle between urban and rural territory had been fought along traditional and clearly marked lines. The order of

39

Downtown Detroit, circa 1925, archetypical of a prosperous nucleated city of the early twentieth century. Newly built skyscrapers dwarf the Victorian city hall and low-rise business buildings of the nineteenth-century city. The cluster of high buildings reflected high rents in the downtown area, but they were also visible symbols of commercial vitality and civic pride. Although autos are present, most travel was by streetcar or on foot.

battle was determined by the geographic form of cities that existed at the time—a time when cities had sharply defined boundaries.

One can read a description of such cities in any sixth-grade geography book written before the war.[1] That city had a well-defined commercial nucleus, usually called "downtown." Industry was lined up along the railroad tracks, and residential areas were arrayed around the edges and usually segregated internally along lines of income, ethnicity, and race. At the edge of the city, the countryside began, and the boundary between city and country was sharp.[2] To be sure, there were often suburbs beyond the city's edge, but the suburbs had sharp boundaries too. There was little debate about where the city was or where the country was (see Figure 3.1).

That form of nucleated city, which Americans founded in great numbers during the nineteenth century, was a creature of the railroad. The railroad station was the gateway to the city, and the land with highest value clustered nearby—occupied, quite naturally, by high-bidding commercial establishments. There the biggest cities built skyscrapers, visible monuments to the high value of center-city land. Industries located near the railroad track be-

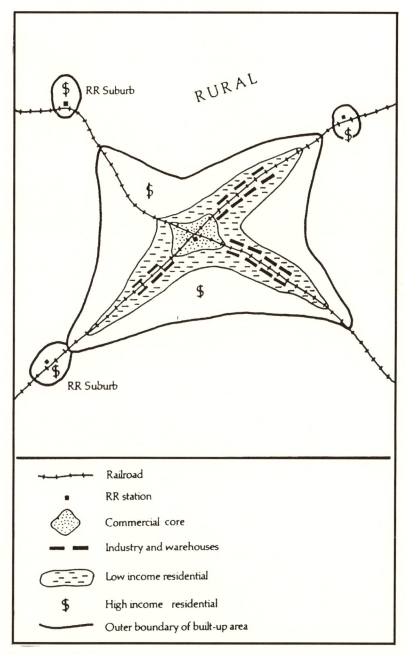

RURAL

RR Suburb

$

$

$

RR Suburb

┼─┼─┼	Railroad
▪	RR station
◇	Commercial core
▬ ▬	Industry and warehouses
⬭	Low income residential
$	High income residential
──	Outer boundary of built-up area

Figure 3.1. Idealized map of the compact nucleated city that grew up with railroads in the nineteenth century. City and country are divided by a sharp unambiguous line. Within the city, commercial, industrial, and residential areas are sharply segregated. The city was a creation of the railroad, and its core was the railroad station, the city's functional and ceremonial entryway. Before the automobile arrived, both city and suburbs were necessarily compact.

cause it was the most economical place to receive raw materials and ship out finished products. Poor people lived in disagreeable areas near the edge of the commercial district, or, more commonly, close by their place of industrial employment, often under squalid circumstances in the shadow of belching chimneys. With the help of trolley cars, affluent people moved to the outer edges of the city, or, if they could afford it, to a nearby suburb. But even suburbanites had to live near railroad stations, and even the most affluent suburbs were necessarily fairly compact. Like the city itself, farmland began along an unambiguous line at the edge of the suburb. The city limits were literally that: where the city ended and the country began. What we now call "sprawl" was confined to a few roadside locations near interurban electric lines. For the most part, country was country and city was city.

THE RISE OF THE GALACTIC CITY

That arrangement, of course, was blown apart by the Model-T Ford, that democratizer of geography, which allowed Americans of moderate means to live anywhere they wanted, provided only that they had access to an all-weather road and a job somewhere within commuting distance (Lewis 1987).

Several things began to happen all at once. First, as railroads lost their monopoly over personal transportation and access to railroad stations became less important, both nucleated cities and nucleated suburbs began to lose their magnetism. The sharp geographic boundaries between city and country grew fuzzy as real estate speculators began to buy up cheap farmland and sell it off as residential lots to middle-class people who had recently acquired automobiles. Shortly after World War II the enterprising Levitt family built Levittown on Long Island—an instant suburb, complete with mass-produced houses. Levittown and its imitators excited choruses of derision from architects and dismay from social critics, but they were so successful that two more Levittowns were built near Philadelphia, and imitations erupted across the face of the land.

As more and more people moved beyond the urban fringes into suburbs with increasingly diffuse geographic forms, commercial entrepreneurs followed in hot pursuit. By the early 1950s Victor Gruen and others were experimenting with the design of exurban shopping centers equipped with huge parking lots to accommodate shoppers who came no longer by streetcar but by privately owned automobile. The parking lots, of course, consumed

Aerial view of galactic urban development carved out of the rural countryside. The photograph was taken in the mid-1970s thirty miles or so northwest of Chicago, but it could well be located in almost any urbanizing region of the United States—and not necessarily close to a traditional nucleated city. It is tempting to call such residential developments "suburban," but unlike the suburbs in Figure 3.1, it is not really "sub" to any traditional "urb."

huge spaces, but the buildings were space-consumptive too. Unlike downtown properties, rural land was cheap, so that buildings were spread out horizontally, unlike the old multistoried downtown department stores. The new suburbanites gleefully discovered that they no longer needed to go downtown to do their shopping and presently ceased to do so. Meanwhile, industries began to move from cramped obsolete buildings on the railroad track to new quarters beyond the urban fringe, often at considerable distances from the old city, but increasingly nearby the newly mobile labor force. From a distance, the profile of these new factories resembled shopping centers—low-slung horizontal buildings surrounded by vast areas of pavement for employee parking and loading ramps for trucks. When, in 1956, Congress passed the Interstate Highway Act, with its ingenious formula for financing limited-access highways from a mandated gasoline tax, the effect was like pouring that gasoline on an already blazing fire that was consuming rural land at an unprecedented pace.

In retrospect, it is easy to see what happened. From the beginning of their national history, Americans had lusted for the economic benefits that came from living in a city but at the same time wanted the environmental amenities

Aerial view of a post–World War II shopping center in Blair County, Pennsylvania. Because the land was cheap, there was no encouragement to conserve it. Unlike the downtowns, which such centers replaced, low-profile buildings and parking lots are hugely space consumptive—lending a characteristically horizontal profile to the postwar commercial landscape.

Aerial view of post–World War II industrial installations in northwestern Oklahoma circa 1967. Typical of manufacturing plants in the galactic city, this one is surrounded by rural countryside, but its function is entirely urban. Cheap rural land permits and encourages prodigal use of land. As with the shopping center, buildings are low-slung and sprawling and there are huge parking lots and loading areas.

of country living. The solution was to live in the green countryside near the city but not in it.[3] Before the arrival of the automobile, only the affluent could afford that luxurious combination. What the automobile did was to democratize this heretofore impossible dream and put it within the reach of Everyman.

Considerable confusion reigned in the early stages of the process. Urban planners and social critics complained loudly about what they called "suburban sprawl," as if this new arrangement of people and roads and structure were some kind of unusual event that should be stopped—and that could be stopped, if only Americans could be persuaded to pause and reflect on their collective iniquity.[4] And, because the process was going on conspicuously in southern California, many planners in the east contemptuously dismissed it as some kind of West Coast aberration. A famous eastern sneer described Los Angeles as "fifty suburbs in search of a city."

But it was not an aberration, nor was it merely an expansion of traditional suburban growth. What Americans were doing, far beyond the old urban fringe, was building nothing less than an altogether new form of city—doing all the things that cities had traditionally done, but arranging them in a new geometric form (see Figure 3.2). I have called this new urban form "the galactic city," not because I enjoy coining trendy terminology, but because I know of no other term that accurately describes the new city that we have built. It is a city where all the traditional urban elements float in space like stars and planets in a galaxy, held together by mutual gravitational attraction but with large empty spaces in between.

Although the whole new structure was nourished by a new transportation system of democratized cars and democratized freeways, it is plain that transportation planners simply did not understand what was going on. Certainly they did not understand the seismic implications of their own plans, as we know from the now-famous experience of Boston, where planners after World War II decided to build a bypass around the old nucleated city and call it Massachusetts Route 128. What promptly happened is now history: At the interchanges between old roads and the new "bypass," some ten miles from downtown Boston, high-tech industry began to spring up, fed by the work force, money, and brains that had already moved out beyond the suburbs.[5] It was not long before Route 128 (later renamed I-95) became so clogged that it was necessary to build yet another bypass around the Boston conurbation. The new road, twenty miles farther out, was called I-495: a bypass to bypass the bypass, so to speak. In time, one suspects, I-495 will become another version of 128 and another bypass will be needed.

Neither of those roads really have much to do with Boston—not with the old downtown hub, at any rate. Those roads are no more or less than one of the several main streets of a galactic city which now spreads untidily from Maine to Virginia and beyond. Massachusetts Route 128 has its analogues in the Baltimore and Washington beltways, and it is hardly coincidental that transportation planners are now debating whether a new outer beltway should be built east of the city across the swamps of tidewater Maryland or through the hunt country of Loudoun and Fauquier Counties, Virginia, west of Washington. Meantime, the tone of the debate among the affluent residents of Fauquier County (not a few of whom wield considerable political influence) makes it clear that people know that bypasses aren't bypasses any more but powerful agents of urban growth. At this writing, the project is stalled, partly because of its prodigious cost, partly because of very effective local opposition who know well that a new "outer beltway" will inevitably bring the galactic city to their green bucolic idyll.

In some ways, this new urban form was foretold in the prescient book *Megalopolis* (1961), wherein the geographer Jean Gottman describes the

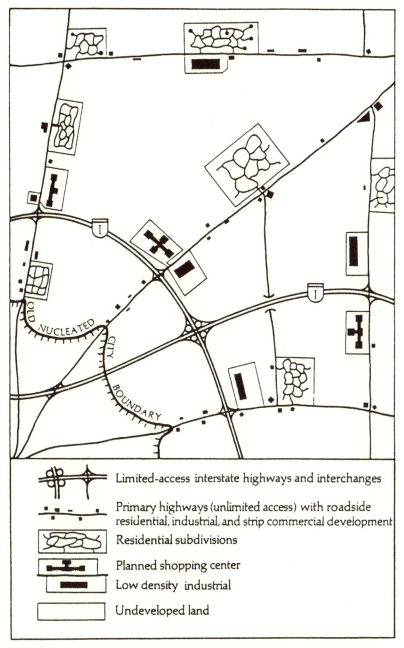

Figure 3.2. Idealized map of the galactic city in its early post–World War II form, here attached to the fringe of a nineteenth-century nucleated city (lower left). Later on, as the galactic city developed in many areas of the United States, it took on a variety of geographic forms, defying any attempt to capture its image on a single map.

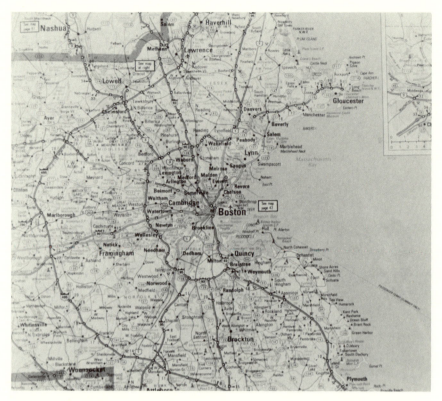

Interstate highways around Boston. Note the "inner" bypass, Massachusetts Route 128 (later I-95). Route 128 was one of America's first high-tech corridors, and it became so congested that a second "outer" bypass had to be constructed (I-495). These limited-access highways have become the main streets of the post–World War II galactic city, this one covering most of eastern Massachusetts and adjacent New England.

gradual growing together of the big old East Coast cities—Boston, New York, Philadelphia, Baltimore, and Washington—to form a supermetropolis that stretches along the Atlantic coast from southern Maine to northern Virginia. But today's galactic city has exploded far beyond the margins of Megalopolis—no matter how generously we define it. Adams County, Pennsylvania, for example, whose county seat is Gettysburg, used to be a quiet conservative rural area of fruit farms, cornfields, and a sprinkling of villages, the very image of nineteenth-century rural America. In Biglerville, a village not far from Gettysburg, the main action used to be direct sales of apple butter from Musser's Fruit Farm and midday chicken dinners for $4.95 at the Biglerville Hotel, replete with mashed potatoes, gravy, and chow-chow. Dur-

The I-270 technology corridor, Frederick County, Maryland, fifty-odd miles northwest of Washington, D.C. Ostensibly, I-270 links Frederick with the Capitol Beltway, but it functions like Massachusetts Route 128 as a main street of one of the nation's galactic cities.

ing the last ten years or so, however, the galactic city has arrived in Adams County. Rural land prices have skyrocketed and so have real-estate taxes. Boutiques have arrived in Biglerville and lesser places nearby. The roads, designed for country traffic, are clogged with commuters every weekday morning and evening, and weekends are no better, as fleamarkets and garage sales erupt along those not-so-countrylike roads.

Where do the commuters work? Very few go to nearby Gettysburg, whose main business continues to be selling motel rooms and caloric meals and Civil War souvenirs to tourists along the commercial strip of U.S. Highway 15. Most of the commuters head in the direction of Washington, although very few really go that far. Washington, after all, is seventy-five miles away, and the traffic is fierce. Their destination, most commonly, is some part of the new galactic city which sprawls untidily along the axis of Interstate Highway 270, the self-styled "Technology Corridor" which connects the Washington Beltway with Frederick, Maryland, and the Great Valley.

Not so long ago, I-270 was an unsurprising four-lane interstate highway, with a wide grassy median, traversing some of the handsomest agricultural country in the United States. The state of Maryland, admirably conscious of roadside amenities, had planted flowering trees along the margins; it was a nice road for a Sunday drive. Today, after fifteen years of continual "upgrading," I-270 has begun to look like the New Jersey Turnpike through Perth Amboy, with six express lanes, four local lanes and a skein of on-ramps, off-ramps, overpasses, concrete traffic dividers, and large signs warning motorists not to drive on the shoulders. Fluorescent orange signs tell motorists to beware of construction zones ahead and to "expect delays." Significantly, I-270 is now being lined with sound barriers to protect the tranquillity of new residents who think they live in Frederick County, but in fact are living in a galactic city which has no name aside from a collection of zip codes.

Meantime, Frederick itself, only recently a depressed and somewhat gritty railroad town, now sports new paint and new prosperity. North Market Street is bedecked with flowers and lined with chic new restaurants and fern-bars, catering to young childless couples who drive BMWs and Mercedes convertibles. Much the same sort of thing is happening on a smaller scale to the once-sleepy town of Shepherdstown, West Virginia. Shepherdstown is sixty miles from Washington, much of it over twisting mountain roads, and therefore Washington, as an urban place, is socially, politically, and economically irrelevant to the people who are living in the town's freshly-built "suburbs" or, increasingly, in houses on one-acre plots along the once-rural roads between Shepherdstown and Sharpsburg and Charlestown and a host of smaller places in the West Virginia panhandle. The residents of these houses are city dwellers, but the center of that city is not Washington; indeed, there is no single center to that new galactic city they inhabit. The residents make their home in one place, but they work in a second place some miles away, they shop in yet a third or fourth or fifth, and they travel between these places by high-speed roads across country that is mainly farm or forest.

In short, this new galactic city is an urban creation different from any sort Americans have ever seen before. And because it does not spread across the rural landscape along a solid front the way cities used to, many people—scholars included—fail to recognize it for what it is, a genuine city. It performs all the functions that American cities have always performed: commercial, industrial, residential, and social. What makes it different is its geographic arrangement, which to many casual observers (and even some of its inhabitants) seems disorderly and even unsettling.

Most unsettling, perhaps, is the ubiquity of the galactic city in contemporary America. When it first came into being some fifty years ago, it flourished most luxuriantly on the outer fringes of established nineteenth-century cities: along the Atlantic coast from Boston to Washington; in the Midwest in the

Galactic residential tissue recently carved out of rural land in Mifflin County, central Pennsylvania. Apartments in the middle-distance are incongruously modeled after eighteenth-century row houses more commonly found in densely packed nucleated cities.

old industrial belt between Cleveland, St. Louis, and Minneapolis; and along the West Coast, most conspicuously around Los Angeles, the San Francisco Bay Area, and the urban corridor from Portland, Oregon, to Vancouver, B.C. For that reason, it has been tempting to think of the galactic city as merely a continuation of existing suburban tendencies, enlarged and inflamed by bigger highways, more cars, and general affluence. It has been equally tempting to think of such urban tissue as confined to the fringes of conventional urbanized areas. That would be a serious misunderstanding of what is happening in America today. With very few exceptions, wherever Americans are creating new urban tissue today, that tissue takes galactic form. Any attentive traveler can see the galactic city from the window of a car or a high-flying airplane in almost any quarter of the inhabited United States. It erupts in rural Iowa as well as in urbanized Massachusetts, it appears in the potato fields of southern Idaho just as fifty years ago it appeared in the prune orchards at the southern end of San Francisco Bay. Even in the two regions that Americans have traditionally thought most immune to urbanization, the mountains and deserts of the cowboy West and the supposedly traditional rural country of the Old South, the galactic city is flourishing. In the Piedmont of the Carolinas and north Georgia, elements of the galactic city are rarely out of sight along the old rural roads that once saw mules and cotton gins. In the arid West, considerable territory remains virtually empty for want of water, but in the presence of water, wherever people are building cities and towns in

New Mexico and Arizona, the bulk of that building takes galactic urban form. It can be seen the length and breadth of the upper Rio Grande valley in New Mexico, the Salt River valley of Arizona, and along the lower Colorado all the way from Las Vegas, Nevada, to the Mexican border south of Yuma. It is the standard form of new human settlement over huge expanses of the mid-continent that Americans have traditionally imagined as rural. Indeed, because of the large empty spaces that separate its constituent parts, it usually looks disorderly, and to most Americans it does not look like a city. But it is. It contains all of the elements that the old nucleated city contained, and it performs all of the old urban functions, albeit often in somewhat different ways. It does indeed differ powerfully from the old city in two fundamental aspects: appearance and geographic arrangement.

Like the nucleated city before it, however, this galactic city contains a good deal of order and a good deal of internal variety, its often untidy appearance and huge empty areas notwithstanding. Scholars and critics would do well to recognize that internal order, rather than denouncing the whole thing as a kind of sprawling excrescence or, more commonly, ignoring it.

FOUR ELEMENTS WITHIN THE GALACTIC CITY

The first and most basic element of the galactic city is its internal transportation system. We should stop thinking about interstate and limited-access highways as merely big country roads that allow cars and trucks to move rapidly and uneventfully from one city to another across a greensward of rural landscape. Such roads are, at least potentially, urban arteries, some better developed than others. Interstate highway I-270 in Montgomery County, Maryland, and Route 128 in Massachusetts are, among other things, the main streets of high-tech industrial districts. A continent away, the same situation prevails along I-680, the outer bypass for the San Francisco Bay metropolitan area.

A second feature of the new galactic city is a considerable degree of internal commercial clustering. Despite the vast geographic extent of the galactic city, despite its generally low density of people and buildings, and despite its extremely horizontal form, there is plain evidence that the tendency toward urban nucleation has not disappeared but is simply being resurrected under new geographical circumstances. Unsurprisingly, these new commercial clusters tend to be located at the intersection of main arterial highways. People have been clustering at the intersection of important roads since the founding of

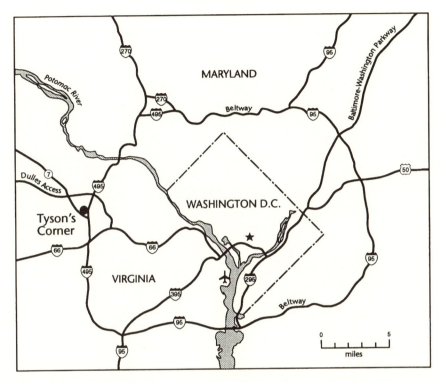

Figure 3.3. Tyson's Corner in the context of the Washington-area limited-access highway system. The location of Tyson's is typical of successful "edge cities" all across the country—near the intersection of an urban bypass (here the Washington Beltway) and a clustering of limited-access highways: I-66, the Dulles Airport Access Road, and Virginia Route 7, in the process of conversion from a two-lane country road into a multilane arterial highway.

Babylon. In contemporary America, the main crossroads occur where interstate and primary highways intersect.

There are many such intersections and many such clusters within America's enormous galactic city. Two examples will suffice. One is Valley Forge, where the Pennsylvania Turnpike has an interchange with two limited-access U.S. highways (U.S. 30 and U.S. 202), and a major interstate link, the Schuylkill Expressway (I-76), which leads to center city Philadelphia. The other (and more egregious) example is Tyson's Corner, where the Washington Beltway intersects I-66 to Charlottesville, two limited-access highways to Dulles Airport, and Virginia Route 7, which is the main highway between the Washington Beltway and the affluent hunt country of northern Virginia (Figure

Tyson's Corner, Virginia. Fifteen years before the photograph was taken in 1992, this was agricultural countryside. Tyson's now contains more commercial floor space than the entire city of Miami.

3.3). Tyson's is, to put it mildly, very accessible—providing, of course, one has an automobile.

Tyson's deserves special mention, for it is one of the most arresting bits of urban geography to emerge in the United States within memory. As recently as 1975, Tyson's Corner was just what its name implied: a country crossroad on the fringe of Washington's Virginia suburbs. By 1990 Tyson's had sprouted a sizable crop of eye-catching postmodern skyscrapers; two of the biggest shopping centers on the East Coast; a considerable number of large and small corporate offices; half a dozen major department stores; a bewildering array of shops, restaurants and warehouses; and a Byzantine complex of on-ramps, off-ramps, roads, and multidecked parking lots. With the exception of downtown Washington itself, Tyson's contains the largest assemblage of commercial space in the entire capital area and includes more commercial floor space than all of downtown Miami (Garreau 1991).

Joel Garreau of the *Washington Post,* one of the most perceptive observers of America's changing geography (see Garreau 1981), calls things like Tyson's and Valley Forge "edge cities," and, at latest count, identifies eighteen such clusters in and around the Washington metropolitan area. Edge cities, Garreau says, represent "the biggest change in 100 years in how Americans

Pacific Telesis's headquarters, Bishop Ranch, Pleasanton, California. The headquarters of a highly sophisticated communications system, the grounds are designed to resemble a country estate or college campus. Although the function is quintessentially urban, urban symbolism is rigorously excluded.

live and work" (Garreau 1988, 51). Whether that is true or not, they are springing up like patches of urban asparagus around the edges of Atlanta, Dallas, Los Angeles, and the fringes of San Francisco Bay, to mention only the biggest and most flamboyant examples.

Joel Garreau is a talented and perceptive observer, and his writings are among the most authoritative and lucid accounts of new American urban forms that I know. But I would take issue with his choice of language. The new clusters like Tyson's and Valley Forge are not cities in their own right, but merely parts of the much larger galactic city that extends over many thousand square miles, not just in the Northeast but in many other parts of the United States. Exactly how many square miles is impossible to say; nobody has yet discovered a way to map the whole thing.

A third kind of district within the galactic city is industrial, but these new industrial districts often look more like country clubs than dark Satanic mills. The reason for the difference is partly architectural, partly functional. The great smokestacks and Bessemer converters that are associated with nine-teenth-century industry are gone for the simple reason that a good part of

American industry has shifted from making steel to making computer chips. Moreover, since most of the galactic city's factories were built after World War II, most are designed vaguely in some variant of the International Style and tend to look like consolidated high schools (which were often built at the same time and according to the same stylistic rules). Furthermore, while industrial enterprises become less immediately noxious, management has increasingly sought to ingratiate itself with local government and its residential neighbors by planting large expanses of flower beds and green lawns, identifying themselves with modest groundsigns in Helvetica lettering, and referring to their lushly planted grounds as a "campus." Some large industrial operations, especially those combined with company offices, have become corporate symbols and are landscaped with such opulence that they have come to resemble golf clubs or vacation resorts. But the bucolic appearance is deceptive. These elegant new factories and corporate headquarters, set in the midst of rolling green countryside, are integral to the new galactic city just as the old smokestack industries were integral to the nineteenth-century nucleated city.

The fourth element of the galactic city is residential. In area, it is by far the largest part of the galactic city and the part that causes lovers of rural America the most acute gastric pain. The galactic city's residential areas come in a wide variety of forms, but they all tend to be extremely consumptive of space. The most familiar version takes its original form from Levittown, created by the brothers Levitt outside of New York City on Long Island after World War II to meet the housing needs of returning veterans and their burgeoning families. The Levitts' formula for success was devastatingly simple. First, they catered to the long-standing American appetite for a privately owned single-family house, separated from all others on a privately owned piece of land, set back from the street and separated from its neighbors by at least a modicum of lawn and landscaping. Second, the Levitts succeeded because they kept the cost of housing low: they invented ways to build mass-produced houses on the site, and the cost of land in then-rural Long Island was much cheaper than conventional residential building lots inside the five boroughs of New York.

The Levitts became famous because they built houses on a scale unprecedented in America (several more Levittowns were built, in New Jersey and Pennsylvania), and hosts of imitators across the land followed their lead. Most of them built on a much smaller scale than the Levitts, but followed the same general formula: buying rural land and converting it to low-density residential housing developments. The formula paid off for the same reason that Levittown paid off. A real-estate speculator could afford to buy farm land at prices that were much higher than agricultural uses would command and quite dizzying to hard-working farmers who were dumbfounded to learn that even the most marginal land could fetch such inflated prices. For the developer-buyer, on the other hand, the price of farmland was much lower than residential land within the city. Building was often cheaper, too, because zoning and building codes were lax or absent. Thus, a real-estate speculator could pay a farmer prices for eighty acres of cornfield that were well above the going rate for farmland and turn the land into a residential subdivision of houses of vaguely colonial design and streets named "Canterbury Lane" or "Devon Boulevard." Such developments often tended to be homogeneous in demography and appearance, and they were the target of ferocious attacks from social and architectural critics from coast to coast. Commerce and industry were routinely excluded from most of these housing developments, and, since population density was too low to justify public transportation, residents necessarily depended on automobiles for driving to work or even for doing the most modest shopping.

This arrangement, the basic residential building block of the galactic city, can be found nearly everywhere in America in one form or another. Upscale versions are commonly surrounded by walls, and entrance from the outside world is restricted at a gatehouse, equipped with uniformed guards, formidable (but dignified) iron gates, manicured landscaping, and a vaguely British name. ("Inverness Hills" or "Canterbury Crossing" are typical.) At the lower end of the economic scale are "mobile-home parks" (sometimes still called trailer parks), but they share a family resemblance with the galactic city's other residential developments. Almost universally, they have been carved out of rural land and continue to be surrounded by it.

Another conspicuous residential form within the galactic city is rarely mentioned in the standard literature of urban geography. It is the kind of residential settlement that occurs when farmers sell off two or three or five-acre plots of roadside frontage to expatriate urbanites, who then build ranch houses, raise families, and plant large lawns which they mow with John Deere garden tractors and tend with loving care. Nearly every paved road from southern New Hampshire to central Virginia has at least a few such plots along it, and along some roads in southeastern Pennsylvania, houses are arrayed so closely along the rural roadside they constitute a modern American equivalent of a German *strassendorf*—the traditional medieval form of European rural villages. Seen from a low-flying airplane, those houses on five-acre plots are one of the most conspicuous features of the human landscape. There are uncounted thousands of them, and from the commuter plane that I frequently fly from the University Park Airport at Penn State to Philadelphia or Balti-

Aerial photograph of a galactic residential development between Lebanon and
Harrisburg, Pennsylvania, circa 1990. The overwhelming majority of buildings in
the photograph are residential and have been built during the last thirty years.
Although this is some of the richest farmland in the eastern United States, only a
tiny fraction of the population makes its living from agriculture.

more or Washington-Dulles, those roadside houses are almost never out of
sight. One does not need to live in Pennsylvania to see such things, of course.
They can be found here and there in all but the most sparsely populated parts
of the United States.

Except in anecdotal terms, we know very little about the residents of those
houses, even as a statistic. We know—because we can see them from the airplane window—that they are very numerous. But we don't even know just
how many there are, because the Census hasn't found a way of counting
them yet. That is not for want of trying. The Census cannot count them unless they first define them and so far that has proved impossible, at least for
statistical purposes. They remind us of Justice Potter Stewart's celebrated re-
mark about pornography, that it was hard to define, but he knew it when he
saw it.

These houses along the rural roadsides are collectively treated as residential
pariahs. Environmentalists denounce them as space-consumptive obscenities;
planners deplore them as ecological disasters; officials in local government
wring their hands when they try to find money to provide them with munici-

pal services at reasonable cost. Students of rural culture simply don't discuss them because they are too urban, and urbanists usually ignore them because they don't look urban enough—a view echoed by the residents, who proudly claim rural status and are indignant when it is suggested that they are really residents of a city.

THINKING ABOUT THE GALACTIC CITY

Nobody has discussed this phenomenon better than Robert Riley, whose writings about rural America are among the most sympathetic and perceptive I know (e.g., Riley 1985). Riley, who has described several forms of such residential settlement in rural areas of east-central Illinois (1990), calls this assemblage of roadside houses "the new rural landscape," but immediately hedges. "The new rural landscape," Riley says, "is a residence, and occasional workplace, for people whose livelihood depends not at all upon the land per se." (Confronted with a Massey-Ferguson harvester or combine, for example, most residents of these scattered houses would know nothing about it—except perhaps how to turn on the stereo and air-conditioning in the machine's glass-enclosed cab.) In Riley's view, this new form of settlement is a radical and fundamental departure from age-old forms of rural life. In Riley's words again: "The humanized nonurban landscape, throughout human history, has been almost completely shaped by people who worked and lived on that land. The new nonurban landscape, in the United States at least, is being shaped largely by *people to whom the rural landscape is nothing more or nothing less than an alternative residential location*. Whether they be commuters, retirees, or desktop publishers earning a living from their den, to them, *the rural landscape is not a productive system or a way of life, but a locational amenity*" (1990, 3; emphasis added).

How do we go about classifying or even describing the people who inhabit these thousands and thousands of houses? The Census, of course, has tried repeatedly and for a time took evasive refuge in the portmanteau term "rural non-farm," a category that was so large and loosely defined that it was eventually abandoned as meaningless. I would suggest cutting the verbal Gordian knot, and calling these people what they really are: genuinely urban people who cannot afford five acres of well-groomed lawn in Bryn Mawr or Chevy Chase, but can afford it in "rural" Pennsylvania or Maryland or upstate New York. But to call these people "rural" is to stretch the term beyond the limits of any reasonable lexicon. They are urban in social outlook, urban in their personal relations, urban in the way they make their living. Only in their political opinions do they differ significantly from residents of the old nucleated city. Almost universally, residents of these dispersed houses resist the imposition of urban authority, and the idea of being administered by any form of urban government is anathema. Consistently such people resist annexation, political consolidation, and most kinds of land-use controls, except under the most extreme duress. They are, I submit, despite these opinions, nothing more nor nothing less than residents of the galactic city.

If I am right on that score, we must (along with Robert Riley) face up to the fact that much of the land in what we call "rural America," at least in the Northeast, is less important for its farm produce than as a residential stage set. That may be a distasteful idea to many admirers of rural America, but that is the way it is, at least in the view of many of the new inhabitants. If present trends continue, that is the way more and more of "rural America" is going to be. The reason is simple: we are not looking at just another bit of "exurban sprawl"; we are looking at a large and predictable part of the galactic city. That city and its urban inhabitants are not going to go away, even if we wanted them to. The obvious course for academics, it seems to me, is to do what academics always do when they confront a new and unfamiliar circumstance: to describe it as accurately and dispassionately as they can and then try to understand how it works. Only then can we make sensible policy for planning and government.

The task will not be easy, although the process of analysis is now under way. Academics have been very slow to get their minds around this business of the galactic city. Much of the best writing about it has come from journalists like Joel Garreau and John Herbers (1986), from landscape architects like Robert Riley, and from two brilliant historians of suburbs, Robert Fishman and Kenneth Jackson. Thomas Baerwald, in a seminal paper on the Minneapolis beltway, concluded that the new agglomeration of people and buildings presaged the design of a wholly new kind of city. Erickson and Gentry described similar events along the Baltimore beltway (1985). More recently, John Fraser Hart, among the most knowledgeable and sympathetic observers of America's rural geography, has written about what he calls "the perimetropolitan bow wave"—the precursors to urbanization that are found on the outer fringes of big cities like New York (1991b). Janet Fitchen, in a splendid work on rural poverty, provides one of the few accurate descriptions I know of the way "rural" trailer parks operate, and how their inhabitants tend to behave as a part of a larger geographic nexus (1988). And, as always, J. B. Jackson provides us with the most thoughtful reflections on the meaning of these changes in our ordinary landscapes (1970, 1980, 1984, 1990). Only very recently has a standard textbook in urban geography confronted the issue of the galactic city and tried to include it within a larger context of urban studies (Knox 1994).

Such studies are badly overdue. The galactic city has been under construction in the United States since the mass adoption of the automobile in the 1920s, and it was pushing aggressively into rural territory all over the Northeast by the end of World War II (Lewis 1987). Now, almost half a century later, traditional forms of rural life have totally disappeared in much (if not most) of the Northeast and in nearly all of California and the Southwest outside of Indian reservations. In much of the remaining territory it is an endangered species. An overwhelming majority of America's population already lives in the city—a large number in the old nucleated cities and suburbs, of course, but an increasing number (perhaps a majority) in some part of a spreading galactic city that bids fair to dominate a large part of the United States.

Language is important. We cannot talk about phenomena unless we possess the vocabulary to describe them, and many observers still cannot agree on what to call this new amorphous form of urban geography. As we try to come to grips with the question of urban pressures on rural America, it is crucial, I think, that we stop using worn-out terms like "suburban sprawl," terms that carry all sorts of obsolete intellectual freight along with them and get in the way of our understanding what is really happening along the frayed boundaries between urban and rural America today. Those ranch houses along those winding macadam roads in southeastern Pennsylvania and along those section-line roads in Iowa are not just scattered bits of exurbia. Those freeways are not just big fast roads. They are inherent parts of the galactic city. The sooner we realize that fact, the sooner we can come to terms with it.

NOTES

1. An excellent example of the genre, and a very good book, is J. Russell Smith's *Home Folks* (Philadelphia: Winston, 1930). Smith was professor of economic geography at Columbia and took elementary education seriously. My father gave the book to me for Christmas when I was six years old, and I cherish it, not merely for sentiment, but for its clinical portraits of the rural and urban landscapes of America before the automobile had arrived on the scene.

2. Vernacular speech reveals that the geographic division was accompanied by considerable hostility. For country people, city-dwellers were "city slickers." For residents of the city, country folk were "rubes," "hicks," or "hayseeds."

3. Two excellent histories of suburbanization are Fishman 1987 and K. Jackson 1985. Fishman's account traces the process of suburbanization back to seventeenth-century England. Jackson focuses mainly on the evolution of American suburbs within a national context of urbanization.

4. Polemics of this kind are still common. See, e.g., Kunstler, 1993.

5. Baerwald, 1978, describes the process in detail along I-494, the Minneapolis bypass.

4

"RURAL" AND "FARM" NO LONGER MEAN THE SAME

JOHN FRASER HART

The classification of rural people can be based on what they do or on where they live. The distinction was unimportant in horse-and-buggy days, when people lived where they worked. The traditional concept of rural America conjoined people and place and was based on the fact that people in certain occupations (such as farming, forestry, and mining) lived in the sparsely populated open countryside, because their livelihood required relatively extensive areas of land. The association between occupation and the open countryside is no longer as compelling as it once was, however, for increasing numbers of people with other occupations have been moving to sparsely populated places, and one can no longer assume that the people who live in the open countryside have traditional rural occupations.

The most generally accepted identification of rural people and places in the United States is based on the backhanded definition used by the Bureau of the Census: "rural" includes everything that is not urban. "The urban population consists of all persons living in urbanized areas and in places of 2,500 or more inhabitants; all other population is classified as rural" (1985a). Surprisingly, no one knows how or why the threshold population of 2,500 persons was originally chosen (Truesdell 1949). It was first used in a supplementary census report in 1906 with no explanation or justification, but it has been accepted so generally that the Census Bureau has used it ever since. Of course other federal agencies are not required to use the census definition, and some economic development programs use more liberal definitions to enable them to bestow their largesse on greater numbers of people.

In 1910 the census classified slightly more than half of the population of the United States as rural (Table 1). The rural population has increased steadily since 1910, but at a rate slower than the national rate, and by 1990 it

Table 4.1. Number of persons by place of residence, United States, 1910–1990

Year	United States Total	Rural Total	Farm	Incorporated Places	Other
1910	91,972,268	49,348,883	32,077,313	8,118,825	9,152,745
1920	105,710,620	51,406,017	31,358,640	8,963,125	11,084,252
1930	122,775,046	53,820,223	30,157,513	9,183,453	14,479,257
1940	131,669,275	57,245,573	30,216,188	9,342,677	17,686,708
1950					
old	150,697,361	61,769,897	23,076,539	10,504,463	28,188,895
new[a]	150,697,361	54,229,675	23,076,539	10,504,463	20,648,673
1960	183,285,009	54,054,425	13,444,898	10,327,818	30,281,709
1970	207,976,452	53,886,996	10,588,534	10,507,880	32,790,582
1980	226,545,805	59,491,167	5,617,903	10,900,310	42,972,954
1990	248,709,873	61,656,386	3,871,583	10,851,908	46,932,894

Source: *U.S. Census of Population,* appropriate years.

[a] In 1950 the urban population was redefined to include people living on the densely settled fringes of 50,000 people or more.

had dropped to only a quarter of the national total. The Census Bureau identifies three principal components of the rural population: people who live on farms, people who live in incorporated small towns and villages of less than 2,500 persons, and all the rest.

CHANGES IN FARMING

The farm population of the United States hovered above 30 million people between 1910 and 1940, but thereafter it dropped precipitously, and by 1990 fewer than 4 million people lived on farms (see Figure 4.1 and Table 4.1). In 1910 farm people comprised 65.0 percent of the rural population and 34.9 percent of the total population, but by 1990 their share had shriveled to only 6.3 percent of the rural population and a paltry 1.6 percent of the total population.

The decline of the farm population is merely one facet of the dramatic changes that have revolutionized American agriculture during the twentieth century (Hart 1986). The number of farms in the United States dropped from a peak of nearly 7 million in 1934 to just over 2 million in 1987, but the farms that persist have become much larger and far more productive; the average size of farms tripled from 153 acres in 1934 to 462 acres in 1987. Farmland has become so expensive that many farmers have enlarged their op-

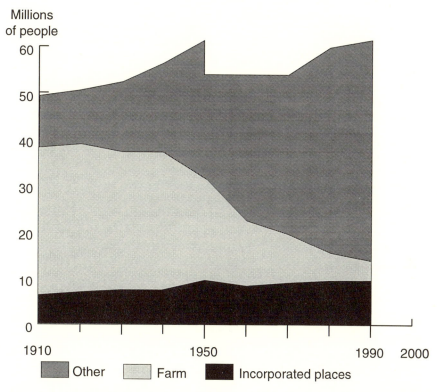

Figure 4.1. Components of the rural population of the United States, 1910–1990. Until 1950 the rural population included people who lived in places of 2,500 or fewer persons, and in that year the rural population dropped sharply because people living on the densely settled fringes of cities of 50,000 people or more were reclassified as urban. The "other" rural population includes all rural people who do not live on farms or in incorporated places of fewer than 2,500 people. The rural farm population includes all people who live on places that produce a modest minimal amount of agricultural products; the actual dollar value has varied from census to census.

erations by renting land from neighbors who had stopped farming rather than by buying it outright, and part-ownership has been the preferred strategy for farm enlargement in most areas (Hart 1991a).

Farming, like the grocery business, has changed from low volumes with high markups to huge volumes with minuscule profits per unit. Just as the supermarket has replaced the traditional corner grocery store, so the high-volume family farm business has replaced the traditional family farm that produced a little bit of everything but none of it very well. Farmers have increased their volume of production by using bigger and better machines to

Table 4.2. Measures of nonfarm farms

Farm Operators	United States		Iowa	
	1987	1982	1987	1982
Total number	2,087,759	2,240,976	105,180	115,413
Number who worked off farm 200 days or more	737,206	774,844	25,240	25,928
Number with nonfarm principal occupation	949,580	1,006,189	29,901	29,372
Number with farm sales less than $25,000	1,356,352	1,436,591	39,985	39,388

Source: *1987 Census of Agriculture.*

farm more acres and by using improved varieties of crops and better fertilizers and pesticides to extract greater yields from each acre. They have learned to specialize in doing what they can do best, and they have eliminated their less profitable activities. They have had to learn to manage money just as skillfully as they manage machines and crops and livestock, and ulcers have replaced blisters as one of their principal occupational hazards. A successful modern family farm is a business with a larger capital investment and greater gross income than most of the businesses on Main Street, and many modern farmers are more widely traveled and more cosmopolitan than many city dwellers, from whom they differ primarily in income and place of work.

Many of the 2 million farms in the United States are farms only by definition. In 1987 the Census of Agriculture defined a farm as any place that produced $1,000 or more of agricultural products. This definition includes large numbers of what I have dubbed "nonfarm farms": undersized, part-time, low-income, weekend, retirement, and hobby farms (Hart 1992). In 1987 one-third of all "farm" operators in the United States worked off their farms 200 days or more, almost half said that farming was not their principal occupation, and two-thirds sold less than $25,000 worth of farm products (Table 4.2). At least one-third, and probably more than half, of the farms reported in the Census of Agriculture cannot be considered farms by the wildest stretch of anyone's imagination.

In 1987 the United States had 300,000 farms that sold more than $100,000 worth of agricultural products. These farms produced more than three-quarters of the national total, suggesting that 300,000 to 500,000 farms can easily satisfy the food and fiber requirements of one-quarter of a

Table 4.3. Farm workers

	United States	Iowa	
	1980	1980	1990
Total population	226,545,805	2,913,808	2,776,755
All employed persons	97,639,355	1,375,504	1,340,242
Farm occupation	2,623,793	125,336	92,107
Operators and managers	1,298,670	92,346	69,031
Farm workers	1,334,123	32,990	24,076
Agriculture industry	2,760,213	130,520	103,520
Rural farm population	3,871,583	391,070	256,562

Source: *U.S. Census of Population,* 1980 and 1990.

billion American people in addition to producing an embarrassing surplus for which export markets must be found.

To an increasing degree the truly competitive farms of the United States are becoming concentrated in the most productive agricultural areas. The agricultural heartland of the nation is the plains of the midcontinent, flaring from central Ohio northwestward to the Dakotas and southwestward to the Texas Panhandle. Smaller but still important agricultural areas are the Central Valley of California and the alluvial plain of the lower Mississippi River (the Delta). In these areas much of the countryside remains predominantly agricultural. The rest of rural America has some good and prosperous farms, to be sure, but agriculture has lost its dominance, and the countryside is being transformed by people whose occupations, outlooks, and values are decidedly nonagricultural.

The censuses of agriculture and population publish a plethora of data about farms and farm workers that can easily confuse and mislead a naive or careless person who fails to understand how the various categories are defined. For example, the Census of Agriculture publishes data on numbers of farms and characteristics of farm operators (Table 4.2), and the Census of Population publishes data on the total labor force, the numbers of people employed in farm occupations and in the agriculture industry, and the number of people who live on farms (Table 4.3). Aggregate labor force data for the nation had not been published at the time of writing, but data for Iowa reveal that in 1987 the quintessential agricultural state had 105,180 farm operators and in 1990 it had 93,107 workers whose occupation was farming, 103,520 workers employed in the agriculture industry, and 256,562 persons who lived on farms. So how many "farm workers" has the state of Iowa?

SMALL TOWNS AND VILLAGES

The number of people who live in incorporated places of less than 2,500 persons slowly crept up from 8 million in 1910 to almost 11 million in 1990 (Table 4.1). Throughout the twentieth century these places have had an impressively steady 16 to 19 percent of the total population of rural America. Most of them originated as central places to serve the surrounding countryside. They were collecting and shipping points for the products of the land, and some of these products were processed to reduce their bulk before they were shipped. The central place was a retail center where local people could buy the goods they needed, and it offered a variety of public and private services. Its focus was Main Street, which became the symbol of small-town rural America.

Small towns and villages were spaced at horse-and-buggy distances, and many became redundant when automobiles enabled local people to travel greater distances in search of the goods and services they needed. Their retail and service functions gradually shifted up the urban hierarchy to larger places, and the long, slow, lingering death of Main Street was already under way well before World War II.

Almost imperceptibly, however, many small towns and villages were developing a new function. Employment in manufacturing was trickling down the urban hierarchy from larger to smaller places while retail trade was moving up, and many small towns and villages became minor cogs in the national system of manufacturing centers (Hart 1988). Some of the new manufacturing establishments were branch plants of large corporations, attracted by easy access to the cream of the surplus farm labor force, but an impressive number were homegrown, the brainchildren of local entrepreneurs. Some of these establishments process local commodities, but many rely on the local area only for cheap labor and cheap floor space, and they produce an astonishing variety of goods. Visitors often underestimate the importance of manufacturing in a small town: although the planned industrial park at the edge of town may be occupied only by lush stands of weeds, many of the new "factories" are in fact well-nigh invisible in recycled older buildings. Former schoolhouses are particularly popular for this purpose, for they had to be sturdy enough to withstand the kids.

Their new function as minor manufacturing centers enabled small towns and villages to continue growing fitfully in the postwar era, but the 1980s were tough for them. Industrial investment slowed down, and places that struggled to attract new industry discovered that they no longer had the necessary labor force. The number of farms had dwindled, and the remaining farm population was aging because young people had departed for the big city. The only small towns and villages that gained population in the 1980s were those within commuting distance of a metropolis, and they now function as bedroom communities for the metropolis. The long-awaited demise of small towns and villages beyond the metropolitan periphery, which has been predicted for half a century or so, finally seems at hand.

OTHER PEOPLE OF RURAL AMERICA

In 1910 two-thirds of the people of rural America lived on farms, one-sixth lived in small towns and villages, and one-sixth lived in other rural areas (Table 4.1). By 1990 only one of every sixteen rural people lived on a farm, the percentage of citizens living in small towns and villages had hardly changed, and more than three-quarters of rural Americans lived in other kinds of rural areas.

In 1910 probably one-quarter to one-half of the "other" rural Americans were engaged in such traditional activities as forestry, fishing, and mining, which are still important employers in some areas (Morrison 1990, 84–86). Comparisons over time are not easy, because concepts and definitions have changed so greatly, but it appears that employment in the forest industry remained stable at close to a million workers for much of the twentieth century. The principal areas of employment in this industry are the Pacific Northwest and the Southeast, with lesser areas in the Upper Great Lakes states and New England. The Northwest leans toward lumber production, and the Southeast toward pulp and paper. Forestry blossomed in the Southeast in the two decades after World War II, when new pulp and paper mills were built to capitalize on the bonanza pine forest that had colonized abandoned cotton fields, but few new mills have been built since 1975.

Mining resists generalization even more than forestry, because mining is by definition a boom-and-bust activity; minerals are nonrenewable resources, and all mining areas are temporary; every mineral deposit will ultimately be exhausted, and every mining area is destined to be worked out and abandoned. During the twentieth century employment in mining has fluctuated more than employment in forestry, but it has also stayed slightly under a million workers. Important mining areas today include the coal fields of Appalachia and southern Illinois, the "oil patch" of Texas and adjacent states, the iron ranges of the Upper Great Lakes states, and the deposits of oil, gas, and metallic ores scattered through the West. Still, the only certainty of any mining area is uncertainty.

In 1910 the agricultural labor force was six to ten times the size of the labor force in forestry, fisheries, and mining combined, but by 1990 it had dropped to nearly their level, and altogether the traditional rural activities of farming, forestry, fisheries, and mining employed little more than one-tenth of the total rural labor force.

It is apparent that the greatest change in rural America during the twentieth century, even greater than the decimation of the farm population, has been the massive influx of city people. Before World War I suburban development consisted largely of the homes of well-to-do people clustered near stops on rapid transit lines, but thereafter the automobile enabled city people to penetrate virtually every nook and cranny of the adjacent countryside. At first they came just to visit, but then they talked farmers into selling them plots of land on which they could build houses, and soon clever developers were buying up entire farms and subdividing them.

By 1950 built-up areas had sprawled beyond the official corporate limits of most American cities, but the densely settled areas outside the city limits were still officially classified as rural. The Census Bureau rectified this situation by expanding its definition of "urban" to include the urban fringe. The urban fringe is the densely settled (1,000 or more persons per square mile) area contiguous to a city of 50,000 persons or more. The entire built-up area, including both the city and its urban fringe, is designated the urbanized area. It keeps expanding as the city grows, so it must be defined anew for each census. It is an excellent indicator of the actual geographical extent of the city at the time when it is defined, but it is a poor unit for statistical comparisons over time because it grows larger at every census.

The new urban definition reclassified 7.5 million people, one-quarter of the "other" rural population, from rural to urban (Table 4.1), and a high percentage of the "other" people of rural America still live just beyond the urban fringe (Hart 1984a). In 1990 at least two of every five of these "others" lived within fifty miles of a city of 50,000 or more people, and a large but unknown number lived within commuting distance of smaller places. The perimetropolitan fringes, where urban people are moving to rural areas, are the fastest growing areas in the nation. They accounted for a major share of its total population growth in the 1980s, and they seem destined to continue to do so.

People who live on farms and in small towns and villages may work close to home, but most other rural Americans must live reasonably close to cities because they commute to work. The much vaunted telecommuting economy seems to exist mainly in the perfervid imaginations of futurologists and journalists. Any reporter worth his or her salt certainly can find someone who has moved to and works from a distant home, maintaining contact with the rest of the world by cable, wire, fax, Internet, and other marvels of the electronic age, but there is little evidence that such folk are numerous. One must assume that their numbers will increase, especially on the outer fringes of major metropolitan areas, but personal interaction with other human beings apparently remains more important than the amenity of isolated life in the country.

Commuting from distances that might seem extreme is not the chore it appears to be, because many commuters travel only to the nearest edge of the city, not to its center. Many of the best new jobs are in the office buildings, malls, stores, and factories interspersed among the motels, eating places, and filling stations that line the bypass and the major routes at the edge of the city, and they are just as accessible from distant rural areas as from the older built-up areas of the city. Long-distance commuting from rural areas also is facilitated by carpooling. The first rural carpools developed informally when several people drove to a convenient crossroads, parked their cars there for the day, and made the long trip to work in a single vehicle. Highways departments in many states have institutionalized this system by creating special carpool parking lots at major intersections, especially at interchanges on interstate highways in rural areas.

City people have feathered out so far and wide through rural areas that the traditional rural-urban dichotomy has become a continuum. The ends of this continuum are not debatable. No one, for example, would argue that midtown Manhattan is rural, or that a field of wheat in North Dakota is urban, but the rural-urban continuum has no unambiguous "natural" break that is generally recognized and accepted. Furthermore, one's inherent sense of what is "rural" varies from region to region. In North Dakota, for instance, a place of 1,500 people can seem like a veritable metropolis, whereas a place of the same size in New Jersey may seem little more than a crossroads hamlet. To a Manhattanite much of New Jersey seems pretty rural, but a North Dakotan is oppressed by how built-up and crowded and urban it is.

The form of urban occupancy of rural areas seems to vary regionally. In the Northeast virtually the entire countryside seems to have been taken over by city people, and traditional forms of rural life have largely disappeared. In the South many landowners have been only too happy to sell off small roadside building plots, and the urban occupancy of the countryside has taken the form of interminable strips of residences along major highways, with expensive homes in unembarrassed proximity to mobile and manufactured homes. The agricultural heartland, where farmland remains in strong hands, has fewer signs of urban occupancy in rural areas, but as in all other parts of the United States, such signs become noticeably thicker and more prominent as one approaches a metropolis, because the great majority of rural Americans are perimetropolitan.

City people have come to the countryside in search of residence and recreation. Their residences have had to be within commuting distances of the places where they work, but the development of high-speed automobiles and high-speed highways since World War II has enabled them to travel much farther afield in search of outdoor recreation in areas that are blessed with bodies of water, scenic uplands, or pleasant climates. Greater disposable income and longer vacations have stimulated the growth of tourism, which has expanded from a summer-only to a year-round activity. Resort areas have developed such necessities as hotels, motels, eating places, and gift shops, and supplemented them with such additional attractions as amusement parks, commercial entertainments, golf courses, ski resorts, and gambling casinos (Hart 1984b).

Resort areas have become popular places for affluent people to build second homes, which can be status symbols in a society that equates worth with income. People are no longer tied to their place of work after they retire, and many convert their second homes into primary residences; some even routinely migrate between summer homes in the North and winter homes in the Sunbelt. The influx of retired people and the maturation of the resort and retirement economy create more and better jobs in construction, maintenance, and the provision of services, especially health services. Local young people no longer have to migrate to the city in search of work, so rural recreation, resort, and retirement areas, like the perimetropolitan peripheries, enjoyed above-average rates of population increase during the 1980s, and presumably rural second-home areas in the Upper Great Lakes states, the Ozarks, the Texas hill country, the Sierra Nevada foothills, the Blue Ridge Mountains, and southern Arizona, Texas, and Florida will remain areas of population growth.

Much has been made of the potential clash of values, attitudes, perceptions, and lifestyles when urban people move into rural areas, but my own observations and conversations suggest that the first generation of city people who move to the open countryside may be better attuned to the rural people among whom they live than to the people living in the city from which they have fled. An unknown but probably sizable number of these "city" people are "elbowroomers," who grew up on the sparsely settled fringe of the metropolis and felt compelled to leapfrog farther out when they sensed that the built-up area of the city was starting to crowd in on them too closely.

Table 4.4. Population of the United States, 1990 (millions of people)

	Total	Urban	Rural
Total	248.7	187.1	61.6
Metropolitan	192.7	166.2	26.5
Nonmetropolitan	56.0	20.9	35.1

Source: *1990 Census of Population.*

Newcomers unquestionably have had confrontations with oldtimers, although the battle lines rarely are so neatly drawn, and these clashes may have been excessively publicized, because amicable relationships between neighbors rarely make the headlines. The most serious clashes seem to stem not from the initial invasion but from development of such scale and density that it gives the people who live in the countryside, oldtimers and newcomers alike, the threatening sense that they are becoming overwhelmed by suburbanization. The "gangplank mentality" seems to be most highly developed in resort areas that are feeling heavy pressure for development.

RURAL AND NONMETROPOLITAN

Anyone who studies an area larger than a single state must usually rely heavily on federal data, principally the Bureau of the Census, which distinguishes between urban and rural, or between metropolitan and nonmetropolitan. It has become increasingly common for casual users to assume that nonmetropolitan is synonymous with rural, but it is not; in 1990, 43.0 percent of the rural people of the United States lived in metropolitan areas, and 37.3 percent of the nonmetropolitan people lived in urban places (Table 4.4).

Both "nonmetropolitan" and "rural" are defined negatively; they include whatever happens to be left over after "metropolitan" and "urban" have been defined. A metropolitan area consists of one or more entire counties (except in New England) that have a city or population cluster of 50,000 people or more, at least in theory; in practice the advantages of metropolitan status are so great that this threshold has been stretched and relaxed periodically. Between 1950 and 1990 the number of metropolitan areas in the United States nearly doubled as new areas were added to the list, and their total area almost tripled, because new counties were added to existing areas (Table 4.5). The increasing number and size of metropolitan areas is steadily reducing and changing the nation's nonmetropolitan area. In 1990 metro-

Table 4.5. Metropolitan areas, United States, 1950–1990

Year	Number	Land area (square miles)	Population
1950	168	207,573	84,509,680
1960	212	310,233	112,885,178
1970	243	387,616	139,418,811
1980	318	566,148	169,430,623
1990	284	580,137	192,725,741

Source: *U.S. Census of Population,* appropriate years.

politan areas encompassed one-fifth of the total land area of the contermi-
nous United States, or the equivalent of two-thirds of the total land area east
of the Mississippi River.

The origin of and the rationale for the 50,000-person threshold for metropolitan status are just as mysterious as the origin of and rationale for the
2,500-person threshold for urban status. It is quite remarkable that both of
these critical threshold values seem to have been pulled out of the hat, so to
speak, with no apparent justification, but both have now been around for so
long that they are widely and generally accepted, and many people would be
uncomfortable if anyone were to propose changing them.

Metropolitan areas provide a stable geographical base for data collection
and for statistical comparisons over time, because their boundaries follow
county lines (except in New England), and it is easy to reconstitute data for
metropolitan areas that have been redefined simply by adding or subtracting
data for individual counties. Because they include entire counties, however,
it is inevitable that metropolitan areas will include extensive tracts of land
that are not heavily built-up and groups of people who are so close to the
rural end of the rural/urban continuum that they would not be classified
as urban no matter what definition was used. In other words, large parts of
metropolitan areas are patently rural; in the United States as a whole one of
every seven residents of metropolitan areas in 1990 was classified as rural, and
more than two of every five rural Americans lived in a metropolitan area
(Table 4.4).

The metropolitan area of St. Cloud, Minnesota, shows how the concepts
of metropolitan relate to and overlap with the concept of rural (Figure 4.2).
In 1990 the city of St. Cloud had a population of 48,812 people. The St.
Cloud urbanized area had a population of 74,037 people, which included
25,225 in the urban fringe, and the St. Cloud metropolitan area, which included three entire counties, had a population of 190,921 people. A total of

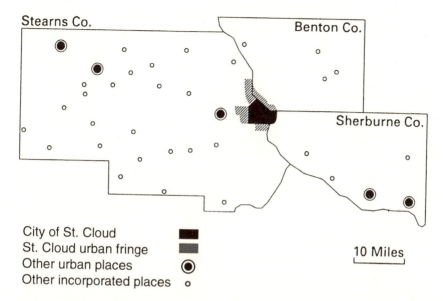

City of St. Cloud
St. Cloud urban fringe
Other urban places
Other incorporated places

10 Miles

Figure 4.2. The St. Cloud, Minnesota, metropolitan area. Including three entire counties, the area focuses on the city of St. Cloud, with 48,812 people in the incorporated city and 25,225 more in the densely settled urban fringe. A total of 23,692 people live in five other incorporated places of 2,500 people or more, but 93,192 people, or 48.8 percent of the total metropolitan area population of 190,921 people, are officially classified as rural. Many other metropolitan areas also have large rural populations.

116,884 people lived in the metropolitan area outside the urbanized area, but 23,692 of these people lived in five other places of 2,500 or more persons, leaving a residual rural population of 93,192 people. In short, almost half of the people who lived in the St. Cloud metropolitan area in 1990 were officially classified as rural, and it would be quite erroneous to think of the entire St. Cloud metropolitan area as urban.

Conversely, the people who live in nonmetropolitan areas are not all rural. In 1990, 37 percent of the nonmetropolitan people of the United States lived in urban places, and 10 million of the nation's 56 million nonmetropolitan people lived in cities of 10,000 to 49,999 persons (Table 4.6), too small to be metropolises, but hardly rural. The urban population of nonmetropolitan areas would be even larger if the census identified urbanized areas for cities of submetropolitan size, but the densely settled overspill areas just outside these cities are still classified as rural, despite their urban character, and they exaggerate the rural population of nonmetropolitan areas.

Table 4.6. Nonmetropolitan population, by size of place, United States, 1960–1990

Year	Total	Places of 10,000–49,999	Places of 2,500–9,999	Other
1960	66,437,997	16,172,839	13,247,424	37,017,734
1970	63,793,115	14,381,123	11,239,097	38,172,895
1980	57,115,182	11,432,348	9,890,416	35,792,418
1990	55,984,132	9,873,345	9,458,347	36,652,440

Source: *U.S. Census of Population,* appropriate years.

The preceding data confirm the observations beginning this chapter: the traditional dichotomy between rural and urban no longer exists. Yet the need to understand and define the concept of rural becomes all the more urgent as that concept becomes ever less clear.

NOTES

I am grateful to Alan Willis and Mui Le for having drafted the figures, and to Wendy Treadwell, Joel Sobel, and Don Dahmann for their help in tracking down elusive data.

5
POPULATION CHANGE IN NONMETROPOLITAN AMERICA

GLENN V. FUGUITT

The United States today is predominantly urban and metropolitan. This phenomenon was not always true; indeed, as recently as 1910 more than one-half of the population lived in rural areas. This proportion has decreased considerably over the succeeding seventy years so that now it is less than 25 percent. The rural and nonmetropolitan territory has undergone corresponding fundamental economic and social change. Fewer and fewer residents depend on farming, and today the number and proportion of farmers is very low. Urban influence has extended outward from large and small cities, with deconcentration of the population and of traditionally urban economic activities. Although important differences in socioeconomic levels remain, the lifestyles and outlook of people in rural and urban America appear to be more and more similar, with the modernization of rural communities, easier access to and increased interchange with large urban centers, and common exposure to the mass media (Fuguitt, Brown, and Beale 1989). These trends have led some to question the need for special attention to rural and nonmetropolitan areas today. But differences do remain. And precisely because of this continuing transition and the need to better understand its consequences, low density areas continue to deserve our attention.

Rural demographers are concerned about rural or nonmetropolitan as a location or type of residence within the larger settlement structure. They seek to explain the distribution and change in population numbers and composition and the demographic components of these changes. This inquiry must proceed with a recognition of the ever more extensive ties between rural and urban or metropolitan areas through migration and social and economic integration. With these needs in mind, we will first review the concepts of rural and nonmetropolitan, then consider metropolitan-nonmetropolitan population distribution and change since 1950 and the accompanying trends in age structure, sex composition, and the population by race and Hispanic status.

Three important themes emerge in this review. First is the increasing complexity of the interrelations between urban and rural that leads to conceptual difficulties in interpreting the results. Second is the significant recent change in population and related economic trends that do not display a unitary direction. Third is the great variability that exists in rural America across regions, subregions, and local areas, which is reflected in population growth experience, age composition, and race and ethnic diversity.

RURAL AND NONMETROPOLITAN

The rural-urban concept is commonly employed to distinguish demographic, economic, and sociocultural differences by residence. Much of the controversy regarding the definition of rural rests on confusion or implicit disagreement about the importance of these three different components. The approach of most demographers is to restrict the definition to more precise and less ambiguous demographic conditions relating to low size and density. Whether or not occupational and sociocultural differences are associated with these demographic conditions is thus an empirical question. According to current census practice, "rural" includes only residents of places (villages) of a population less than 2,500 or those living in other territory (open country) outside thickly settled nodes having at least 50,000 people.[1]

Concern about properly identifying the increasing interpenetration of rural and urban settlement, particularly around large cities, led in 1950 to the establishment of a census definition of metropolitan based on county. Although the precise definition has been modified several times since then, metropolitan areas may be considered to constitute counties or groups of counties that include large cities and their suburbs.[2] Other counties are classed as nonmetropolitan. Counties adjacent to those having large cities may be included in a metro area if they show sufficient integration, primarily through commuting. Since counties rarely change boundaries, such an approach is advantageous for considering changes over time.[3] (For ease of discourse the terms "metro" and "nonmetro" will be used here.)

Many scholars concerned about rural America have restricted their attention to nonmetro areas, and some have even used the terms rural and nonmetropolitan interchangeably. There are good reasons to focus on nonmetropolitan areas, but the two terms are not synonymous, as Table 5.1

Table 5.1. Population, rural and urban, by metro-nonmetro status, 1990[a]

	Metro	Nonmetro	Total
Urban	166,337	20,715	187,052
Percent	88.9	11.1	100.0
Rural	26,791	34,867	61,658
Percent	43.5	56.5	100.0
Total	193,128	55,582	248,710
Percent	77.7	22.3	100.0
Percent Population			
Urban	86.1	37.3	75.2

Source: U.S. Bureau of the Census.

[a] In thousands. Metro-nonmetro designation of 1990, using OMB-designated metro county equivalents (NECMAS) in New England, where official metro areas follow township rather than county lines. Yuma County, Arizona, split after 1980, and a new county, LaPaz, was established. For comparability across decades, we combined these two counties for 1990, making them both metro, although LaPaz was designated as nonmetro at the time. The use of New England NECMAS added 388,824 and the Yuma-LaPaz combination added 13,843 to our metro total above that in the 1990 Census reports (192,725,741). The latter number, rounded to millions, is shown in Table 5.4.

demonstrates for the year 1990. Almost one-half of the rural population is metropolitan, whereas 11 percent of the urban population is nonmetropolitan. Even if one were to argue that the metro population classed as rural is not "really" rural in terms of other aspects of the definition, it is important to recognize that 37 percent of the nonmetro population is actually urban. In any event, the greater interest in the territory some distance from large cities, the advantages of measuring change with county units, and the limited data available with cross-classifications of rural-urban by metro-nonmetro status have led me to concentrate on nonmetro areas and metro-nonmetro comparisons in this chapter.[4]

NONMETROPOLITAN POPULATION CHANGE AND COUNTY SHIFTS

Nonmetro population trends parallel those of the rural population, for there has been a continuation of the metropolitanization process since the metro concept was established in 1950. That is, there has been a steady decline in the nonmetro population, from 66 million to 56 million, which also dropped proportionally from 44 to 22 percent of the total population (Table 5.2).

Table 5.2. Metro and nonmetro trends, 1950–1990[a]

	Population		Percent Distribution		Number of Counties	
Year	Metro	Nonmetro	Metro	Nonmetro	Metro	Nonmetro
1990	193,128	55,582	77.7	22.3	726	2,362
1980	170,493	56,053	75.3	24.7	704	2,384
1970	140,759	62,542	69.2	30.8	461	2,627
1960	114,180	65,146	63.7	36.3	347	2,741
1950	85,421	65,904	56.4	43.6	273	2,815

Source: U.S. Bureau of the Census.
[a] In thousands. Metro-nonmetro designation as of the year indicated.

This population shift owes primarily to the spread of metro growth, as the number of metro counties has grown from 273 to 726. Both the increased spread around large cities and the establishment of new metro areas are represented in this shift. The number of different metro areas increased from 168 to more than 300 over the forty-year period, as formerly rural small towns grew up to become metropolitan centers.

The absolute decline in the nonmetro population over each of the four decades since 1950 (shown in the second column of Table 5.2) is due entirely to county reclassification. Groups of counties that were classed as nonmetro at the beginning of the period grew over each decade, and the same is true for counties classed as nonmetro at the end of each decade. Only in 1970–1980, however, are these nonmetro growth rates without county shifts greater than the corresponding metro growth rates. From the nonmetro perspective, it is perhaps a paradox that the most "successful" (i.e., most rapidly growing) counties in any decade end up being classified as metro, leaving the others behind.

Growth by reclassification should be distinguished from growth in constant areas. Here, in making comparisons, I usually follow the conventional practice of using a metro-nonmetro classification at the beginning of a period, in order to follow the same counties over time. To compare growth over several decades, a single metro-nonmetro designation may be used, or, alternatively, change may be compared using the designation at the beginning of each time interval considered (see Fuguitt, Heaton, and Lichter 1988). The latter approach is usually preferable, since it reflects the situation as it existed during each time interval under consideration.

This dynamic process means that we need to avoid as much as possible thinking of nonmetropolitan America as a separate, static category. Nonmetro-metro integration does not begin when a county is reclassified metropolitan but characterizes all nonmetropolitan and metropolitan areas today. It is a truism to note that improvements in transportation and communication have deepened these ties, and the simple process of spread and multiplication of metropolitan areas means that geographic accessibility has been greatly expanded. The limitations of a metro-nonmetro dichotomy are also revealed in this dynamic process, since smaller new metro areas may have more in common with similar nonmetro areas than with major metropolitan centers. For the "first cut" of available data in a general overview such as this chapter, it may be necessary to focus on the metro-nonmetro dichotomy starting from a particular point in time, but we must not lose sight of the dynamic, integral relations between what has been called metropolitan and nonmetropolitan America.

RECENT NONMETROPOLITAN POPULATION TRENDS

The last thirty years have seen two dramatic shifts in the pattern of rural and nonmetropolitan population change. In contrast to previous decades, the 1970s was a period of renewed and widespread nonmetropolitan growth, which overall was at a higher level than metropolitan growth. Much of this differential was due to migration, with the number of metro-to-nonmetro migrants exceeding the number going in the opposite direction. This unanticipated trend generated a great deal of interest and research, but most observers were unprepared for yet another change in the 1980s, during which nonmetropolitan growth slowed considerably and was again outpaced by growth in metropolitan areas. In a further development, which may or may not foreshadow a new trend for the 1990s, the late 1980s and the 1991 county population estimates show a rebound in nonmetro growth across the country (Beale and Fuguitt 1990; Johnson and Beale 1993).

Trends since 1950 in nonmetro and metro population change for the United States as a whole are given in Figure 5.1. (In calculating change, county shifts are not included and the metro-nonmetro designation at the beginning of each decade is used.) The unique population change pattern of the decade from 1970 to 1980 clearly stands out here. Nonmetro growth was one and one-half times that of metro growth in that period, with a strong decrease in metro growth and increase in nonmetro growth in comparison with the preceding decade. In the 1980s, however, there was a return to the differential favoring metro growth. When the percentage changes were partitioned into two components for natural increase and net migration, there was a nonmetropolitan net migration loss for all decades except 1970–1980.

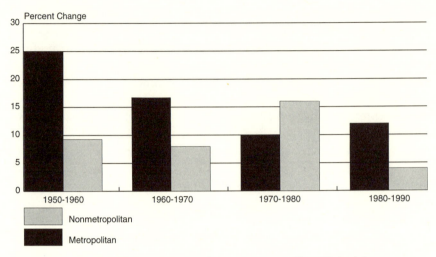

Figure 5.1. Population change metropolitan-nonmetropolitan United States, 1950–1990.

With the aging of the baby boomers, natural increase has become smaller for both metro and nonmetro areas across these time periods. Further deterioration of nonmetro natural increase has occurred relative to metro, however, primarily due to the continued migration of young people. Nonmetro net migration rates for young people aged 15 to 30 were strongly negative during the 1960s and 1980s, and even somewhat negative during the rapid growth phase of the 1970s.

County Type

A number of generalizations have been made regarding the kinds of non-metro counties that are associated with growth. Given the metro basis for the structure of most economic opportunities, location with respect to metro centers has generally shown a positive association with commuting counties, counties in the intermetropolitan corridors and other urban counties growing faster than most other counties. This pattern held true in the 1950s, the 1960s, and again in the 1980s, but less so in the 1970s when growth was widespread and extended into remote rural areas. During the 1970s also recreation-retirement counties emerged as growth magnets, and this tendency continued into the 1980s, with these counties as a whole growing even faster than metropolitan commuting counties. Throughout this entire period, counties dependent upon agriculture grew slowly or declined, reflecting a steady decline in farm numbers and employment opportunities in farm-related activities. The small number of counties specializing in mining grew in the 1970s but tended to decline in other periods. Rural manufacturing was an important component of the resurgence of economic activity in the 1960s and 1970s, but the growth of manufacturing counties did not match commuting or retirement counties in any decade.[5]

The wide extent of revived growth in the 1970s is illustrated by the fact that *all* types of counties had their highest growth in the 1970–1980 period. Conversely, during the 1980s, all groups showed considerably reduced levels of growth, and only retirement counties grew faster than all U.S. counties, indicating continued population concentration relative to the remainder of the country.

Place-Nonplace Comparisons

Within nonmetropolitan areas, another part of the new trend in the 1970s was a pattern of local deconcentration, with the population outside incorporated cities and villages generally growing faster than the population in such places, including even those communities located quite far from metro areas. In other words, the familiar pattern of deconcentration of residences and activities around large cities appeared to have a counterpart even in the hinterlands of smaller remote nonmetro centers, so that the decade from 1970 to 1980 could be termed a time of regional, metro-nonmetro, and local-level deconcentration across the nation (Long 1981; Lichter and Fuguitt 1982). Despite the strong downturn in overall growth in the 1980s, the population outside cities and villages increased while, overall, cities and villages declined slightly in population. The dispersed settlement pattern at the local level is a continuation of the trend of the 1970s, but in this slow growth era, many small villages and cities have faced difficult economic and political problems related to population decline.

Individual County Trends

In the 1960s and later in the 1980s, 50 percent of the nonmetropolitan counties lost population and less than one in five gained more than the United States as a whole. In the 1970s the pattern was reversed, with one-half of the counties gaining more than the United States as a whole and 19 percent declining. Nonmetro areas as a whole gained population in all three decades because counties with smaller populations were more likely to show decline. Shifting the focus to the individual, more than four-tenths nonmetropolitan residents in 1980 lived in counties that declined over the succeeding decade, whereas only one-tenth of the nonmetro residents in 1970 and one-third of the nonmetro residents in 1960 lived in counties that declined. There is a core of declining counties, located primarily in the corn belt and the Great Plains, characterized by a high dependence on commercial agriculture and related activities. Some of these counties have declined over the past three or four decades (Albrecht 1993). The "farm crisis" of the 1980s hit particularly hard in this area, affecting farmers and community businesses alike. Other notable areas of decline include southern Appalachia, which despite a history of decline had grown in the 1970s in part due to the energy boom. The Mississippi Delta and other parts of the Old South also showed declining counties. By contrast, nonmetro counties around large cities as well as those in rapidly growing parts of the South and Southwest tended to grow faster than the United States as a whole throughout the forty-year period. The extent of high-growth counties was greatest, however, in the 1970s, particularly in the Pacific Northwest and the Rocky Mountain states, where the turndown in energy and timber extraction had a negative effect on growth in the 1980s.

Yet Another Turnaround?

The "turnaround" to widespread nonmetro growth in the 1970s took most observers by surprise, but by the late 1970s many were predicting an extended continuation of the new trend. Then the 1980s presented another surprise, as the growth pattern reverted, by and large, to the pre-1970 model. Now there is limited evidence of a new upturn in nonmetro growth. Figure 5.2 shows the annual rates of net migration for the years 1970–1991. The estimates are centered on July 1 of each year.[6] Although metro rates have fluctuated over a narrow range, nonmetro rates have varied widely, peaking in 1974–1975, and declining steadily to 1985–1986. After that year, however, rates have increased, with the one estimate following the 1990 census showing the nonmetro rate above the metro again, using the metro-nonmetro designation of 1983. It is too early to say this is a definitive trend, and the methodology of the 1991 estimates differ from those in earlier years (Johnson and Beale 1993; see also Beale and Fuguitt 1990). But the five-year series since 1985 does indicate some recovery in nonmetro areas.

Discussion

This review of recent nonmetro population trends underscores how remarkable and unique the experience of the 1970–1980 decade was for nonmetro

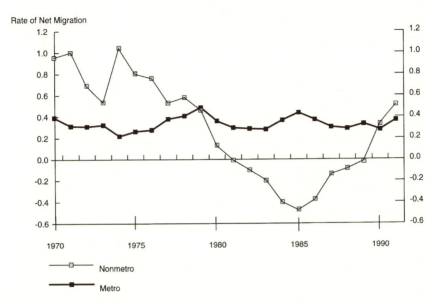

Figure 5.2. Annual rate of net migration/100, metropolitan-nonmetropolitan United States, 1970–1992.

America. Several specific reasons for this growth are reflected in the patterns shown here, including relatively more prosperous agriculture during the period, increased employment related to mineral extraction brought on by the energy crisis, a continuing deconcentration of manufacturing, an increased migration to attractive locations for recreation and retirement, and a continuing build-up of population and economic activities in nonmetro areas around larger metropolitan centers.

In a return to the pattern of the 1960s or 1950s, growth in the 1980s once more favored metro areas. Due in part to the decline in fertility, however, aggregate levels of nonmetro growth were often lower in the 1980s than ever before. With the farm crisis of the early 1980s, areas dependent on agriculture were particularly hard-hit economically, as shown in the county map. The energy boom of the 1970s was followed by sharp declines in demand during the 1980s, and manufacturing went into a national decline that was felt particularly in nonmetro areas. Recreation and retirement counties continued to grow more rapidly than the metropolitan population as a whole but at a markedly slower pace than previously, and counties with a high degree of commuting to metro areas showed slower but moderate growth in the 1980s. Finally, by the late 1980s there was evidence of another nonmetro growth upturn, which may have been a response to improved economic conditions.

This brief summary suggests a set of explanations for both the turnaround in growth and its reversal over the forty-year period, particularly as they relate to the ups and downs of extractive industries. Previously, those seeking to explain the turnaround often emphasized noneconomic issues related to "quality of life," and many researchers were attracted to speculations that we were entering a new era of "information society" in which work location was less important and people's preferences for desirable places to live were more compelling. Preferences may indeed be important, particularly for areas that offer many amenities, but the subsequent decade has made it clear that locational constraints have not been repealed and that economic considerations are fundamental: nonmetro America suffered an economic slump throughout most of the period that corresponded to the downturn in population, but is now experiencing a slight recovery.[7]

AGE AND SEX COMPOSITION

A major demographic trend shaping the social and economic structure of local communities and the nation has been the marked change in the age composition since 1950. Age and sex composition changes through variations in levels of fertility, mortality, and migration. Over the past forty years the most important of these elements for the age structure has been fertility. We are perhaps too familiar with accounts of the baby boomers as they collectively restructure the age distribution of our population. Meanwhile, declines in mortality, particularly among women, have led to greater than expected numbers in the higher age groups in recent years. Migration is always age-related, and differential migration has been particularly important in influencing the age and sex composition of local populations.

There have been characteristic differences in age structure and sex composition between rural and urban and metro and nonmetro areas. Consistent with earlier findings, the nonmetropolitan population has, in 1990, a somewhat lower proportion of people aged 15 to 64 and a higher proportion who are younger than 15 and older than 64 (Table 5.3). The metro-nonmetro differences in the proportion aged less than 15 are only one percentage point, and indeed other studies show that metro-nonmetro fertility differences are today quite small and by some measures nonexistent (Fuguitt, Beale, and Reibel 1991).

Table 5.3. Age-sex composition by metro-nonmetro residence, 1990

	Metropolitan	Nonmetropolitan	Total
Percent aged:			
Less than 15	21.3	22.3	21.5
15–64	66.7	63.0	65.9
65+	12.0	14.7	12.6
Total	100.0	100.0	100.0
Dependency ratios:[a]			
Youth	31.9	35.4	32.6
Elderly	18.0	23.3	19.1
Total	49.9	58.7	51.7
Sex ratio[b]	94.9	96.0	95.1

Source: U.S. Bureau of the Census.
[a] Youth: (number less than 15/number 15–64) × 100; elderly: (number 65 up/number 15–64) × 100
[b] Males per 100 females × 100

The metro-nonmetro difference in the proportion of the population aged 65 and over is more pronounced. In both metro and nonmetro areas, however, there is a higher proportion of elderly in urban areas than in rural areas (data for rural and urban not shown). The fact that nonmetropolitan urban places and villages have attracted retired rural people has long been acknowledged (Nelson 1961), though more recent metro-origin retirees moving to nonmetro areas have tended to seek rural settings with scenic amenities.

The sex ratio, conventionally expressed as number of males per one hundred females, indicates a predominance of women in metropolitan areas and a higher proportion of men in nonmetro areas. In this case, however, it appears that the small metro-nonmetro difference shown in Table 5.3 owes to the higher proportion of the nonmetro population living in rural areas, since the ratio for the urban nonmetro component is only 90.1, lower than the 93.9 for the urban metro component. Furthermore, both metro and nonmetro rural areas have sex ratios of about 100. The lower nonmetro urban ratio may well be due at least partly to the fact that the nonmetro segment has a higher proportion of elderly, and the elderly population, given sex differences in survival rates, has a higher proportion of women. Although selective migration of women to urban areas, including short-distance moves to urban nonmetro areas, may well continue to be important as a reason for the higher rural sex ratios, I found no overall metro-nonmetro differences in 1980–1990 net migration rates by sex.

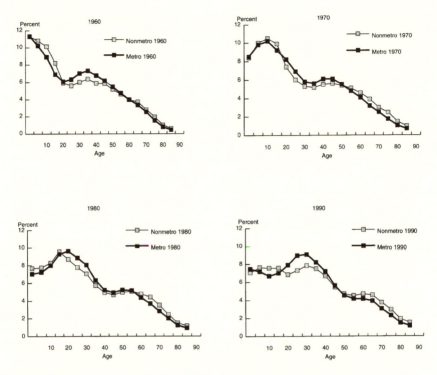

Figure 5.3. Percent distribution by age, metropolitan-nonmetropolitan United States, 1960–1990.

Another way to look at residential differences is in terms of the dependency ratio. This ratio shows the number of youth or elderly relative to the adult population age 15 to 64. As the name suggests, it may approximate a measure of those not economically active relative to those who are, although of course some people younger than 15 and older than 64 are economically active and many 15 to 64 are not. These ratios magnify the differences in age distribution by residence. The nonmetro youth dependency ratio is higher than the metro ratio, and this difference is even more pronounced for the elderly dependency ratios. Consequently, the total dependency ratio for nonmetro is close to ten points higher than the metro total ratio.

Trends Since 1960

More details on the differences between metropolitan and nonmetropolitan age distributions are given in Figure 5.3. This figure shows the percentage distribution by age for five-year age groups in the last four censuses using the metro-nonmetro county designations as of each census year indicated. Each graph clearly reveals the relative deficiency of adults in the age group from 20 through 44 in the nonmetro sector, though this is most pronounced for 1990. There is a smaller surplus for youth five years and over after 1960, and a corresponding larger surplus of the elderly population 65 and over. Perhaps the most notable thing about this figure, however, is the shift in the bulge of the baby boom population as it passes through and out of the younger age groups in both metro and nonmetro areas. For both metro and nonmetro categories, the largest percentage in the 1960 figure is 0 to 4, and this shifts forward ten years at each census to 10 to 14 in 1970, 20 to 24 in 1980 (here nonmetro is an exception with a peak at 15 to 19), and 30 to 34 in 1990. Note that in 1960 the nonmetro age groups range from more than 11 percent for 0 to 4, to 6 percent for 40 to 44, yet in 1990 all age groups under 44 range from 6 to 8 percent. This large decline in the relative importance of young people has important implications for services and institutions in rural areas and may presage further declines in population as these young people reach adulthood.

These age groups are summarized into dependency ratios in Figure 5.4. In every case, for each census beginning in 1960, nonmetro areas had larger dependency ratios both for young people and for the elderly population. Consistent with the graphs in Figure 5.3, a rather remarkable overriding trend across both residence categories is the decline in the youth dependency ratio with the passing of the baby boom out of the young age groups and the corresponding smaller increase in the elderly dependency ratio. Because of this shift, the overall total dependency ratio declined over time by about fifteen points in metropolitan and nonmetropolitan areas alike between 1960 and 1990.

The long-term trend in the United States has been a decline in the sex ratio, but the ratio has changed little since 1970 for the total or for the metro or nonmetro components. One would perhaps expect a continuing decline in the ratio, given the aging of the population, but this decline may be compensated in part by the international migration of young adults, since undocumented workers, in particular, are likely to be male.

The Elderly Population

The growing importance of the elderly population is a major demographic trend in the United States and throughout the Western world. This fastest growing age group continues to increase in relative importance. Today 12.3

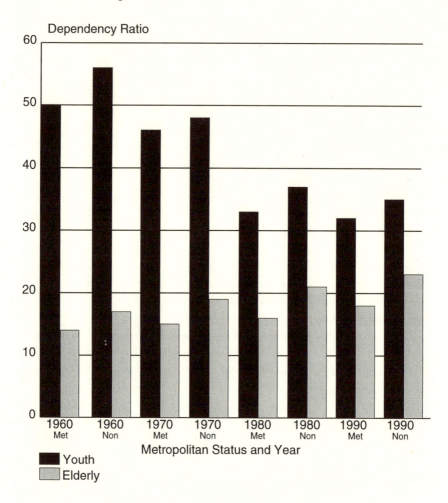

Figure 5.4. Dependency ratios metropolitan-nonmetropolitan United States, 1960–1990.

percent of the U.S. population is over 65, but a recent series of population projections predicts an increase to 20 percent by the year 2030 (U.S. Bureau of the Census 1992b).

Although metro and nonmetro areas share in this trend, there are notable differences by residence. Although the number of persons over 65 has grown rapidly in nonmetro areas, growth was slower than in metro areas during 1980–1990 and 1960–1970, and both residence groups grew at the same rate during 1970–1980. This showing for nonmetro areas is due to a lower level of elderly "natural increase," partially compensated by a small net migration gain that was larger during the 1970s than in other decades. A detailed examination of the data shows that higher rates of elderly natural increase for metro areas were due to a larger proportion reaching 65 over each decade, there being little relative difference by residence in the proportion dying (Fuguitt and Beale 1993). This phenomenon no doubt reflects the history of prior migration of persons reaching age 65, with the losses of younger adults in nonmetro areas and gains in metro areas through population movement. Nevertheless, from 1980 to 1990 the number of persons 65 and over increased by more than 20 percent in nonmetro areas, in contrast to a total nonmetro growth of about 4 percent.

Differential growth by age has led to an increase in the nonmetro proportion 65 and over, from 10.6 to 14.5 percent between 1960 and 1990. At the nonmetro county level there is wide variation in the proportion 65 and over. Over 1,300 nonmetro counties out of approximately 2,400 had more than 15 percent of their populations aged 65 and over, the national nonmetro proportion, and 368 had proportions of 20 percent or more. These high percentage counties—particularly those in the highest group—are concentrated in the Great Plains subregion extending from North Dakota to central Texas.

Like the absolute increase discussed above, the growth in the proportion of elderly is due to natural increase and net migration, but in this case, change in the population under 65 may affect the proportion as part of the denominator. In particular, outmigration of younger people may be more important than inmigration of the elderly for many nonmetro counties. Great Plains counties that are growing in the proportion of elderly do so largely through natural increase and the outmigration of young people. The circumstances facing the elderly in these areas, where long-time residents age in a setting with limited economic opportunities, must be quite different from that in growing counties experiencing the inmigration of elderly. As noted previously, "retirement" counties were the fastest growing nonmetro counties, with sustained, albeit slower, growth in the 1980s as compared with the 1970s. A number of these widely scattered counties are visible on the map in Florida, northern Arkansas, southern Missouri, northern Wisconsin and Michigan, and the Pacific Coast. Elderly migrants are younger, more likely to be married, and have higher educational and economic status than other older people; thus the characteristics of the elderly in retirement counties are generally rather different from those in declining aging-in-place counties. Indeed, the proportion 65 and over may not even be growing in some retirement counties, for young people are inmigrating along with older people. In part, this tendency must reflect the increased opportunities in providing goods and services for the expanding elderly populations there. These important differences between areas, associated with the demographic processes of aging, may have significant social and economic implications. Moreover, the possible consequences for nonmetro elderly of small community size, greater geographic distances, and limited community growth potentials may impinge on our capacity and ability to meet the health and other service needs of this growing population group.

RACE AND HISPANIC COMPOSITION[8]

Certainly one of the most significant demographic trends in the United States today is the increased racial and ethnic diversity of the population. By 1990 one-fourth of the population could be considered minority, that is, of nonwhite race or Hispanic ethnic status. Because of differential growth rates, projections have the non-Hispanic white population, by far the predominant group from the nation's inception up to now, dropping from 75 percent to 53 percent of the total by 2050 (U.S. Bureau of the Census 1992b; Pollard 1993).

The fact of increased racial and cultural diversity affects virtually every policy issue facing the nation. As a major factor in minority growth, immigration, both legal and illegal, is a matter of great concern. A general question underlying this trend toward greater diversity is whether the old "melting pot" metaphor, thought to describe the experience of European immigrants in the past, is viable to describe contemporary processes. Are we not, in fact, becoming a different sort of multicultural society, with continued and perhaps increasing social and economic diversity and protracted problems in achieving consensus? (O'Hare 1992; Lieberson 1993).

As with other major demographic trends, the population of rural and nonmetro America follows the nation in having experienced increased race and ethnic diversity in recent decades. Yet there are differences that reflect both the nature of these residence groupings and local geographic variation. The population distribution by race and Hispanic status is given for metro and nonmetro residence groupings in Table 5.4. Overall, nonmetro areas were less diverse than metro areas in 1990. They had lower proportions than metropolitan areas in all groups except whites and American Indians. Indians were almost 50 percent nonmetro in 1990, and most of these people lived on or near reservations. Rural-urban differences (not shown) parallel metro-nonmetro differences. Within both metro and nonmetro areas, the urban component reveals higher proportions of each group except non-Hispanic

Table 5.4. Race and Spanish origin of population, 1990 (in thousands)

Race or Spanish Origin	Metropolitan[a]	Nonmetropolitan	Total
Total	192,726	55,984	248,710
White	150,863	48,823	199,686
Black	25,122	4,864	29,986
Indian, Eskimo, Aleut	1,003	956	1,959
Asian and Pacific			
Islander	6,824	450	7,274
Other[b]	8,914	891	9,805
Hispanic[c]	20,205	2,149	22,354
White, non-Hispanic	141,005	47,420	188,425
Percentage of Total			
White	78.3	87.2	80.3
Black	13.0	8.7	12.1
Indian, Eskimo, Aleut	0.5	1.7	0.8
Asian and Pacific			
Islander	3.6	0.8	2.9
Other[b]	4.6	1.6	3.9
Hispanic[c]	10.5	3.8	9.0
White, non-Hispanic	73.2	84.7	75.8

Source: U.S. Bureau of the Census.
[a] Metropolitan-nonmetropolitan designation of 1990.
[b] Predominantly persons who wrote "Hispanic" for race.
[c] Hispanics may be of any race.

whites. This distribution is not the sole reason for the metro-nonmetro differences, however, since both the urban and rural nonmetro components are less diverse than corresponding urban and rural metro components.

Within nonmetro areas the concentrations of minority groups are quite distinct, considerably more so than in metro areas. The regional location of nonmetro black concentration is still essentially what it was just after the Civil War. In 1880, 94 percent of rural blacks lived in the South; in 1990 this number had dropped only to 91 percent. Similarly, of the nonmetro black population, 91 percent lived in the South in 1990, and almost all of the counties with more than 10 percent black were in the Southern areas of long-time rural black settlement, including those traditionally specializing in cotton, peanut, and tobacco farm production.

Hispanics are concentrated in the Southwest and West, with three-fourths found in the western census region and the state of Texas. This concentration is also true for almost all of the counties with more than a 10 percent His-

Table 5.5. Percentage change by race and Hispanic origin by residence, 1980–1990

Groups	Metropolitan[a]	Nonmetropolitan	Total
Total	11.6	3.9	9.8
White	7.1	2.9	6.0
Black	15.4	3.1	13.2
Indian, Eskimo, Aleut	44.3	31.7	37.9
Asian and Pacific Islander	112.2	56.6	107.7
Other[b]	47.2	26.7	45.1
Hispanic[c]	56.2	28.5	53.0
White, non-Hispanic	5.0	2.4	4.3

Source: U.S. Bureau of the Census.
[a] Metro-nonmetro designation of 1990.
[b] Predominantly persons who wrote "Hispanic" for race.
[c] Hispanics may be of any race.

panic population. Similarly, two-thirds of the nonmetro Indians are found in the western states, along with Oklahoma.

The lack of overlap in the concentration of blacks, Indians, and Hispanics is remarkable. Of the 831 nonmetro counties with more than 10 percent minority population, only 36 had more than 10 percent in two groups. Only four nonmetro counties have more than 10 percent Asian and Pacific Islander, including Kodiak Island, Alaska, and Kauai and Maui counties in Hawaii. Again, none of these overlap with concentrations of the other three minority groups.

As in metro areas, there was an increasing concentration of minorities in nonmetro America between 1980 and 1990 (see Table 5.5). Asians, with a very small population base, were by far the fastest growing minority, followed by Indians and Hispanics. The number of nonmetro blacks grew quite slowly, faster than non-Hispanic whites but slower than the nonmetro category as a whole, so that the proportion of blacks dropped from 8.8 to 8.7 percent. Hispanics increased their share of the nonmetro population from 3.1 to 3.9, Indians increased their share from 1.4 to 1.7 percent, and Asians from 0.5 to 0.8. Through this differential growth the non-Hispanic white segment declined from 86.3 to 85.1 percent of the total.

We see that the rather substantial growth rates for Hispanics, Indians, and Asians in Table 5.5 have resulted in only small increases in their proportional importance over the decade. Yet even though these minorities remain only about 15 percent of the nonmetro population, they contributed 46 percent of the absolute growth of this residential grouping between 1980 and 1990.

About one-half of this absolute growth of minorities came from the Hispanic population.

All minority and white population groups grew more rapidly in metro than nonmetro areas, and each of these groups also became more metropolitan over the decade, using a constant 1990 metro-nonmetro county designation. The increased metro proportions for the minority groups are even greater if they include the effect of county shifts in metro status over the decade, but in no case is the increase more than three percentage points.[9]

There are several sources of this rapid growth for the Hispanic, Asian, and Indian populations. The U.S. census uses a self-identification approach in measuring race and ethnicity, and therefore some of the differences between censuses may be due to an increased or decreased tendency to identify with a particular group. Many more persons reported themselves to be Indians, for example, in both 1980 and 1990, than could be attributed to natural increase for the preceding decade. Changes in wording for the race question also may have had an effect. In terms of demographic factors, higher fertility for minorities than for non-Hispanic whites is certainly important. For Hispanics and Asians, international migration also is significant. Although we do not have information on such migration according to residence for specific minority groups, we can identify the 1990 total of foreign-born population that came to this country since 1980. For metro areas, this population constitutes 40 percent of the absolute population change since 1980 but only 19 percent of the change for nonmetro areas. Thus much of the differential metro-nonmetro growth in the 1980s was due to the greater importance of international migration in and around large cities. Without this component metro areas would have grown only 6.8 percent overall instead of 11.6, and nonmetro areas only 3.1 percent instead of 3.9.

A small change has occurred since 1980 in the minority and white population distribution within nonmetro areas. There are slightly fewer counties with concentrations of black residents and a corresponding increase in counties that report more than 10 percent Indian and Hispanic populations.

In 1990, 513 counties had populations that were more than 10 percent black whereas in 1980 there were 529 counties with that minority concentration. There were 88 counties having more than 10 percent Indian in 1990 instead of only 70 as there were in 1980, and 228 with more than 10 percent Hispanic compared to a total of 183 in 1980. Although the number of Asians continues to be small, they also have become somewhat more widely scattered. In 1980, 30 percent of nonmetro counties recorded fifty or more Asians, but by 1990 this proportion had risen to 38 percent.

Another way to look at internal distribution focuses on differences between pairs of race/minority groups. The most common approach here is the index of dissimilarity, based upon comparisons of the percentage distributions of groups among geographic units. The index ranges from 0 for identical distributions to 100 for the situation of no overlap (Shryock and Siegel 1971). This measure is often used to show the degree of residential segregation among blacks and whites or other groups with small units, like blocks within metropolitan areas. Here the units are counties across the United States. With these larger units, the interpretation must be somewhat different. Counties may describe approximate areas within which people live and work, but a low index here does not mean that people of different races are necessarily living next door to each other. The index of dissimilarity may be interpreted as the proportion of people who would have to move to make the percentage distributions of each group the same.

The indexes for each pair of race/minority groups are given in Table 5.6 by residence and year. Consistent with the map that shows little overlap among the minority groups, nonmetro indexes are all quite large, and all are greater than corresponding metro indices. Comparing 1980 with 1990 in both metro and nonmetro areas, in most cases the indexes show that the increased numbers and proportions of minorities during the 1980s has been accompanied by a small decline in residential differentiation across counties. Exceptions are between whites and Hispanics and blacks and Hispanics in nonmetro areas, where the index increased by less than one point, and between Indians and Hispanics in metro areas, where the index increased less than two points.

CONCLUSION

Demographic factors form the basis of many distinguishing aspects of low-density areas in the United States. Population growth and decline, more diffuse settlement, and more interdependence have helped to make the conceptualization of settlement types difficult. Rural and urban are not synonymous with metropolitan and nonmetro, simple dichotomy may disguise important detail, and most important, the spread of metro areas means that rural and nonmetro America is not a firm location "out there," but a shrinking target.

Trends in population growth and decline have been quite variable during the last three decades. The turnaround decade from 1970 to 1980 stands out as a time of widespread renewed growth. What remains unanswered is whether this period is an anomaly along the continuing road of slow growth

Table 5.6. Indexes of dissimilarity between race/Hispanic groups by residence, 1980 and 1990[a]

Comparisons[b]	Metropolitan[c]	Nonmetropolitan
White vs. all other		
1990	44	54
1980	44	57
White vs. Indian		
1990	40	71
1980	44	74
White vs. black		
1990	43	65
1980	44	67
White vs. Hispanic		
1990	56	65
1980	57	64
Black vs. Hispanic		
1990	54	81
1980	55	80
Indian vs. Hispanic		
1990	50	72
1980	49	74
Indian vs. black		
1990	56	86
1980	60	89

Source: U.S. Bureau of the Census.
[a] The index of dissimilarity ranges from 0 to 100, with 0 indicating identical percentage distributions for the two groups across counties and 100 indicating no overlap in the distribution (see text).
[b] The white category in this table is non-Hispanic white.
[c] Metro-nonmetro designation of 1990.

and decline for most low-density areas or a harbinger of further fluctuations in the metro-nonmetro growth balance fueled by the special social and economic circumstances of the time.

The age structure of both metro and nonmetro areas has been affected most by changes in fertility, particularly the aging of the baby boom generation. But across recent decades there continues to be an effect caused by the migration of young adults from nonmetro to metro areas. This extended loss of able young people seeking better opportunities must have an important impact on many nonmetro communities, notably in the most recent decade of widespread population decline (Lichter, McLaughlin, and Cornwell 1992). The growing importance of the elderly population is an issue that transcends residence, but nonmetro areas stand out as having a higher proportion of the elderly. Local areas increasing in numbers of elderly through aging in place, with the proportion increasing also through the out-migration of young people, differ markedly from those places attracting retirement migrants by virtue of natural amenities. The former areas may face somewhat different challenges in meeting the special needs of their elderly populations.

Cities in both metro and nonmetro counties have lower ratios of men to women than do rural areas. This long-standing situation has changed little in recent decades, and the overall ratio has been stable since 1970. Despite the recent increase in research concerned with gender, the demographic aspects as they relate to residence still require detailed scrutiny. For example, the sex selectivity of metro-nonmetro or rural-urban migration streams has received relatively little attention, and its relation to employment and family structure needs to be further addressed. Unfortunately, space did not permit a consideration of family and household composition in this chapter, but the higher ratio of men to women in rural areas is associated with a greater proportion of husband-wife families there (Fuguitt, Brown, and Beale 1989).

Nonmetro America is less diverse ethnically than metro America, and there is much less overlap in the location of various minority groups. Although minority groups other than blacks are growing rapidly, nonmetro America continues to be the bastion of the white non-Hispanic population.

Finally, this overview has underscored the high degree of variability across nonmetropolitan regions and subregions. Despite advances in transportation and communication and greatly increased interdependence and social interpenetration across residence groups, nonmetro America is far from homogeneous geographically. In Figure 5.2, for example, the heartland of the nation stands out as a rather contiguous area of recent and often long-term population decline, elderly population concentration, and ethnic homogeneity. Such subregional and local variability has important implications beyond demography, for as areas of population grow or decline, different types of ethnic concentration or elderly concentration correspond to differences in settlement history, socioeconomic status, or political processes.

NOTES

Support for this research was provided by the College of Agricultural and Life Sciences, University of Wisconsin, Madison; the Agriculture and Rural Economy Division, Economic Research Service, U.S. Department of Agriculture through a cooperative agreement; and the Center for Demography and Ecology, University of Wisconsin-Madison, through a grant for the Center for Population Research of the National Institute of Child Health and Human Development. The contributions of John Fulton and Richard Gibson, who assisted in the analysis and graphics, and Diane Venden, who prepared the manuscript, are gratefully acknowledged.

1. The current official definitions of urban and metropolitan are found in Appendix A of most any volume of the 1990 Census of Population.

2. Townships are used instead of counties in New England in defining metropolitan areas. For consistency in this chapter, I use instead the official delineation of New England county equivalents.

3. Serious efforts are now under way to design a substantial revision of the metropolitan definition. So far considerable interest is being shown in the option of employing subcounty geographic areas and including all counties in the nation in a metro-nonmetro delineation (Fitzsimmons and Forstall 1993).

4. The occupational activity of farming is no longer closely identified with the conventional rural farm residence distinction, and so the census-defined rural farm population is not considered separately here (see Fuguitt, Brown, and Beale 1989; Butler 1993). Since 1960 this population has declined from 13 million to less than 4 million in 1990. The lack of fit between nonmetro and rural is further illustrated by the fact that one-third of this small population was found in 1990 metro areas, and it is true that smaller metro areas in particular may include important commercial farming operations as well as other traditionally rural people.

5. The USDA classification of counties based on economic activity is employed here (Bender et al. 1985). For a more detailed presentation of the results in this section, see Fuguitt 1992.

6. Net migration is estimated by the residual method, based on annual county population estimates (Federal-State Cooperative Program through the U.S. Bureau of the Census) and recorded births and deaths.

7. Frey (1993) offers a good evaluation of the perspectives on recent metro-nonmetro trends, which he organizes into period, deconcentration, and regional restructuring explanations. Regional restructuring refers to the reorganization of production as the United States has become much more closely integrated with the global economy. This restructuring led to the prediction that the decline of large metropolitan areas in the 1970s, associated with the shift of our economy away from manufacturing production, would moderate and turn around, particularly in areas associated with high technology and producer services. This expectation was largely confirmed in the 1980s with the end of the nonmetro turnaround. The greater integration of nonmetro America in the global economy must be associated with the increase in low-wage manufacturing in nonmetro America and its subsequent decline, as well as period effects such as the energy boom and agricultural prosperity in the

1970s. On the nonmetro side, it is not yet easy to fathom what is a "period effect" and what is more long-term "restructuring." Wardwell (1989), the theorist most closely identified with the deconcentration perspective, has reviewed implications of the recent trends, including a consideration of motivations and residential preferences, as well as the equilibrium-convergence approach emerging from the human ecology tradition.

8. A parallel paper that includes detailed maps for many different ethnic groups is Roseman (1993).

9. The effect of county shifts is determined by comparing the 1980 minority and white composition using the metro and nonmetro county designation of 1980 with the 1990 composition using the county designation of 1990.

PART FOUR
MONEY, JOBS, AND SPACE

The economic welfare of those who inhabit the countryside has been a matter of concern ever since the United States became a nation. Developments during the 1980s brought the matter to the forefront again. A combination of high interest rates and tight money, unfavorable exchange rates, and the flight of much rural manufacturing caused significant distress in many rural places. But development in the 1990s make it clear that fundamental forces work to the disadvantage of many such places even as others prosper.

Edwin Mills compares the economic activity of metropolitan and nonmetropolitan areas, both nationally and regionally, in the lead chapter of this section. Though revealing the remarkable aggregate similarity between the two areas, he notes that economic activity varies greatly within nonmetropolitan areas. Those nonmetropolitan areas adjacent to other metropolitan areas have very different economies from isolated nonmetropolitan areas. Mills also draws attention to the enduring importance of nonfarm economic activity in nonmetropolitan places. He concludes that about 25 percent of U.S. workers have been rural nonfarm throughout most of our history.

In Chapter 7, Pierre Crosson discusses the use and management of rural land. Because of the enormous substitution of capital and human knowledge for land and labor in agricultural production, it has been possible to produce much more on fewer acres with fewer farmers than ever before. The urban "invasion" of rural America referred to earlier by Lewis has not threatened American agriculture by diverting agricultural land to urban uses. As Crosson notes, 97 percent of the total land of the United States is still rural land, and policymakers with environmental concerns must necessarily consider rural land use. Most of the nonhuman life is found there, most of the waters arise there, and most of the atmosphere is above such land.

The economies of the extractive industries and the economic interdependence of rural and urban areas are treated by Bruce Weber in Chapter 8. As the efficiency of extractive industries increases, labor is released for other productive purposes. Unless the areas where the extractive industries are located can develop other economic enterprises, they will lose population, suffer economic decline, or both. Weber also discusses the economic conditions that determine the extent to which urban and rural places will positively or negatively affect the other.

Chapter 9, by Mark Drabenstott and Tim Smith, geographically identifies the nonmetropolitan counties that have prospered or declined economically. Their findings are consistent with those of Weber and Mills: those places that have done the best are either close to metropolitan areas or have something unique to offer, such as outstanding scenic amenities. Counties that have been able to attract retirees or outdoor recreation activities have done relatively well, although the supply of such places clearly far exceeds the demand for them.

The section concludes with a study of rural labor markets by Gene Summers, Francine Horton, and Christina Gringeri, who report that the earnings of rural workers fall below those of urban workers and that the situation is getting worse. They conclude that since rural labor markets differ in important ways from urban ones, prevailing theories of labor markets should be applied to rural areas only if particular attention is given to these differences.

6

THE LOCATION OF ECONOMIC ACTIVITY IN RURAL AND NONMETROPOLITAN UNITED STATES

EDWIN S. MILLS

There are two extraordinary characteristics of the farm and rural sectors in the United States. First is the small size and high productivity of the U.S. farm sector. Only about 2.4 percent of U.S. workers are employed in farming. No other country in the world that comes close to feeding itself with domestic farm production does so with such a small percentage of its work force in agriculture. Not only does the farm sector feed the U.S. population very well, it also accounts for 10 percent of U.S. exports.

Second is the tiny fraction of workers resident in rural areas who work in farming. About one-quarter of the U.S. population lives in rural areas, and about 27 percent of U.S. workers reside in rural areas, but only about 2.4 percent of U.S. workers work on farms. Given that about 2.5 million workers resident in urban areas also have farm jobs, the clear implication is that more than 90 percent of U.S. workers resident in rural areas have nonfarm jobs.[1] In no other country in the world is the percentage of workers who live in rural areas and have nonfarm jobs as great as in the United States. Only Canada and a few northern European countries even approach the U.S. figure.

This peculiar phenomenon forms the main subject of this chapter. In what nonfarm sectors of the economy do these large numbers of workers who live in rural areas work? Does the distribution by employment sector vary among regions? Do most rural workers serve the farm community? If not, why do they live in rural areas? The indications are strong that the number of farm workers will not increase significantly during coming years. Thus, rural growth will depend almost exclusively on growth in nonfarm rural employment. What are the prospects for such growth?

The crucial fact here is that the employment pattern in nonmetro counties is strikingly similar to that in metro areas. Only about 7.6 percent of non-metro employment is in farming. The remaining nonmetro workers are distributed among sectors in patterns remarkably similar to those of metro workers. Meanwhile, metro suburbanization is gradually providing much the same variety of employment and life-style opportunities within metro areas as is found in nonmetro counties.

Two technical issues arise. First, some of the data in this paper refer to the rural/urban distinction and some to the nonmetro/metro distinction. The two are by no means the same, as noted earlier in Chapters 4 and 5. A metro area contains one or more cities with at least 50,000 residents and any surrounding counties that are metropolitan in character and relate to the city or cities. A county is either entirely inside or entirely outside the metro area. Thus, some metro areas are larger than their urban parts, since counties may be quite large, especially in the western regions of the country. A place is urban if it is a community of at least 2,500 residents. Metro areas contain both urban and rural areas; in addition, many urban areas are outside metro areas. In 1990, 77.7 percent of U.S. residents lived in metro areas, and 75.2 percent of the population lived in urban areas. Thus, the numbers of metro and urban residents are nearly the same, and most people who fall in one category are also in the other. However, considerable numbers of rural people live in metro areas and considerable numbers of urban people live outside metro areas. It just happens that the number of rural metro residents and the number of urban nonmetro residents are about the same.

Second, most of the population and employment data here refer to places of residence. A worker is classified as being in an urban or metro area if the worker lives in an urban or metro area. Most workers both live and work either in a metro or nonmetro area. In 1980, 3 percent of workers commuted between metro and nonmetro areas, most from nonmetro residences to metro jobs. Distinguishing between place of residence and place of work is thus not very important in making the metro/nonmetro distinction. It is, however, important in making the urban/rural distinction. We know how many workers reside in rural areas, but we don't know whether they work in rural areas. Many urban areas outside metro areas are small, creating little doubt that many workers resident in rural areas commute to urban jobs, and at least some workers resident in nonmetro urban areas undoubtedly commute to jobs in rural areas. The exception is farm workers. Most farm workers work in rural areas, because there are almost no farms in urban areas. Some farm workers work in the rural parts of metro areas, but farming is the only sector in which rural/urban place of work is indicated by the sector's name.

Table 6.1. Population that is rural and nonmetro and workers in agriculture
(in percent)

Year	Workers in Agriculture	Population that Is Rural	Population that Is Nonmetro
1820	71.8	92.7	
1830	70.5	91.5	
1840	68.6	89.5	
1850	63.7	84.9	
1860	58.9	80.3	
1870	53.0	74.4	
1880	49.4	71.9	
1890	42.6	64.9	
1900	37.5	60.4	
1910	30.9	54.3	
1920	27.0	48.8	
1930	21.2	43.8	
1940	17.4	43.5	44.9
1950	11.6	40.4	41.0
1960	6.1	36.9	37.0
1970	3.6	26.5[a]	32.4
1980	2.7	26.2[a]	25.2
1990	2.4	24.8[a]	22.5

Source: Woods and Poole Economics, *The Complete Economic and Demographic Source 1992,* 3 vols. (Washington, D.C., 1992).

[a] Based on the new definition of urban. The effect of the redefinition was to increase the measured percent urban by several percentage points.

URBAN/RURAL AND METRO/NONMETRO GROWTH AND LOCATION

Table 6.1 reveals a remarkably close correlation between the percentage of the population that is rural and the percentage of workers that are in agriculture. In fact, the difference between the two columns has been between 20 and 22 percentage points in almost every year covered by the table. These data have two important implications: that urbanization certainly has been closely related to the decline in agricultural employment, and that the difference between the two percentages is almost constant over this long period of history. In other words, about 25 percent of the work force has lived in rural areas but has held nonfarm jobs for most of our history.[2] The 25 percentage-point difference has of course been a much larger percentage of rural workers in recent decades than in earlier decades. Nevertheless, about 25 percent of U.S. workers have been rural nonfarm workers throughout most of our history. Even when nonfarm sectors were much smaller parts of total employment, large numbers of rural workers were employed in those sectors.

Table 6.1 also shows the percentage of the population living outside metro areas for the census years since metro or comparable data have been collected. Until the 1970s, the metro population was somewhat smaller than the urban population, but for 1980 and 1990 the metro population exceeded the urban population, implying a substantial decline since the 1970s in the percent of workers that live outside metro areas and work off-farm.

In the postwar period, during which most workers have had cars and rural roads have been paved, it is likely that many nonfarm workers resident in rural areas have worked in nearby towns. Commuting from a metro to a nonmetro area is known to be uncommon, and it is therefore worthwhile to check the conclusions suggested by Table 6.1 with metro data. From 1950, only about 3 percent more jobs than resident workers have been located in metro areas. At least 20 percent of U.S. workers, then, both live and work in nonmetro areas but work in nonfarm sectors. Thus the decline in the percentage of the population residing in nonmetro areas, shown in Table 6.1, undoubtedly represents at least some decline in the proportion of workers who live in nonmetro areas and work in nonmetro and nonfarm jobs.

The data suggest that number of workers who both live and work in nonfarm, nonmetro jobs is both large and persistent. Although we know how many workers live and work in nonmetro areas and how many people live in rural areas, we do not know how many workers who live in rural areas also work in rural areas; many of them probably commute to nonmetro urban areas.[3]

REASONS FOR METRO/URBAN GROWTH

Sectoral shift is a crucial prerequisite to urban/metro growth. In all poor societies, the vast majority of workers are employed in agriculture because food productivity is so low that nearly all workers are needed to grow enough food to feed the population. As the economy grows, productivity increases in both agricultural and other sectors, whereas food consumption increases only slowly as incomes rise. The income elasticity (percent change in quantity demanded divided by percent change in price) of food demand declines as income increases and is only about .10 in the United States. The result is a shift of workers from agriculture to sectors for whose products and services the income elasticities of demand exceed one. In early stages of economic growth the major shift is to manufacturing. In later stages of growth the major shift is to various service sectors. In the United States the share of employment in manufacturing peaked at about 27 percent in 1960 and is now down to about 14 percent. The vast majority of U.S. workers has been in service sectors for about a half century. As we have seen, urbanization has been almost perfectly correlated with these sectoral shifts throughout U.S. history.

Why do nonfarm sectors concentrate in metro and urban areas? Despite much scholarly and popular writing on the subject, the answer is surprisingly simple. (For more detail, see Mills 1992.) Metro areas and, to a lesser extent. small nonmetro urban areas provide proximity to a large variety of producer and consumer groups, which permits inexpensive exchanges of goods, services, workers, and information. Many such exchanges are within the metro or urban area, but some occur between groups in the urban or metro area and groups elsewhere. Most metro areas are located on navigable bodies of water, which provided the original means of exchange with the outside world. More recently, roads, rail, and airports have become more important. And most recently, electronic exchanges of messages have become significant, and large metro areas have more sophisticated infrastructures for such exchanges than do other places. Large metro areas allow production at sufficient scale and diversification to exhaust scale economies and permit inexpensive exchanges of inputs and outputs. They also facilitate the exchanges of information necessary for technological innovation.

The preceding story is prosaic but the forces indicated are powerful. They account for the largest metro areas and for the smallest communities at the intersections of rural roads. Land prices are the best measure of the economic value of metro locations to businesses and consumers. The concentration of people and production in metro areas has driven land values there to ten to a hundred times their magnitudes outside metro areas. If metro locations were not extremely advantageous, firms would not pay metro prices for land and the higher wages and other input prices implied by high land values; instead, they would scatter throughout the country in relatively uniform density patterns.

If the benefits of proximity are so great, why are approximately 20 percent of workers employed outside metro areas in nonfarm sectors? The popular claim that many people just don't like big cities is irrelevant. A metro area need have only 50,000 people and an urban area need have only 2,500 people. Even if one dislikes living in a large town or small city, it is possible to live in a small town or rural area and commute to a larger town or city. Indeed, many metro suburbs have the small-town character that popular writers claim Americans like. There are hundreds of places where rural or small-town residence is easily consistent with metro or urban employment, and some workers take advantage of them. Nonetheless, only about 3 percent of the work force lives outside a metro area and commutes to a job in a metro area. What circumstances, then, make it profitable to produce nonfarm products outside metro areas, paying workers wages that induce them to work there?

The easy answer to the question is that some nonmetro businesses buy inputs from or sell outputs to the farm sector, in which case nonmetro locations economize on transportation costs. Food and fiber processors, for example, buy farm products as inputs; other businesses buy, sell, finance, and insure farm property; still others sell and service farm equipment, sell seeds and fertilizer to farms, or provide information and advice to farmers. We can estimate the size of this group of rural workers by examining detailed data on rural business sectors, as we shall do in the next section. At a rough glance, however, it seems inconceivable that 20 percent of workers are employed to serve the 2.4 percent of workers that are employed on farms, that is, eight nonfarm, nonmetro workers serve each farm worker, a ratio much greater than in other countries. It seems certain that the vast majority of nonfarm, nonmetro workers are located outside metro areas because nonmetro locations have advantages unrelated to farming that outweigh those of metro locations.

The advantages are in fact quite easy to identify. Wage rates are lower in rural areas than in metro areas, mainly because land values are much lower. Cheap land means cheap housing, and thus lower living costs. In addition, cheap land is directly important to some businesses, especially to manufacturing businesses that must produce on just one level and therefore require large amounts of land relative to output. Moreover, unions are weaker in rural areas; the result is not only lower wages, but also avoidance of the rigidities in production imposed by strong unions. Local taxes and crime rates are lower in rural areas. Regulations on land use are fewer and less stringent in rural areas, a factor that has been important only during the last forty or fifty years, but has become increasingly so. Furthermore, as transportation and communication become cheaper over long distances, metro locations actually provide fewer advantages. Thus the interstate highway system apparently induced some manufacturing firms to locate outside metro areas altogether (Dahmann and Dacquel 1990, 1992). Finally, the computer revolution has permitted inexpensive transmission of data and messages over long distances. Recently, some organizations that do business by phone and fax have located in very small towns. An 800 number for reservations for a hotel or car rental chain may be connected to an operator in North Dakota. It should, however, be noted that computers have been commercially important for less than forty years. Inexpensive long distance transmission of computer inputs and outputs has been possible only since the early 1980s. Whereas the computer revolution may be important for future growth of nonmetro employment, then, it cannot explain the long term magnitude and stability of nonmetro employment that is off-farm.

SECTORAL AND REGIONAL TRENDS IN METRO AND NONMETRO EMPLOYMENT AND EARNINGS[4]

All the tables presented in this section and in the Appendix concern a classification that divides all workers into one-digit sectors defined by the national government.[5] There are 13 one-digit sectors, shown on lines 1 to 13 and repeated on lines 14 to 26 of each table. Lines 1 and 14 refer to farm employment; lines 2 and 15 refer to employment in private businesses that provide services to the farm sector. Most other sectoral titles are self-explanatory. Lines 6 and 19 refer to transportation, communication, and public utilities; lines 9 and 22 refer to finance, insurance, and real estate (FIRE); and lines 10 and 23 refer to business and household services such as accounting, law, medicine, advertising, consulting, and domestic work. The data discussed in this section pertain to 1970, 1980, and 1990, since census data are available in comparable and machine-readable form only for those years.

Tables 6.2, 6.3, and 6.4 present national data and data for all metro and nonmetro counties for 1970, 1980, and 1990. In these and all subsequent tables, employment and earnings are for full-time equivalent workers. Earnings are annual in thousands of dollars at 1987 prices. Also shown on lines 27 to 31 are overall income, earnings, and demographic data (income and earnings are also in thousands of 1987 dollars per capita or per full-time equivalent worker).

Line 1 in Table 6.2 confirms the trend shown in Table 6.1 of a declining share of employment on farms.[6] Line 2 shows a steady increase in employment in farm services, though it accounts for only 1 percent of total employment. Undoubtedly, growth in agricultural services employment has facilitated decline in farm employment, just as growth in service firms that serve manufacturing has facilitated decline in manufacturing employment. The major employment trends shown on lines 3 to 13 are the decline in manufacturing's employment share and large increases in FIRE and in services. Declines are shown on lines 11 and 12 in both federal government employment sectors.

Lines 14 to 26 show that farm services and farming consistently have the lowest earnings per worker of any sector. Line 30 of Table 6.2 shows that real

Table 6.2. Nationwide earning and employment data, 1970–1990

Variable	1970	1980	1990
1. % Employment in farming	4.4	3.4	2.2
2. % Employment in agricultural services	0.6	0.8	1.0
3. % Employment in mining	0.8	1.1	0.7
4. % Employment in construction	4.9	5.0	5.2
5. % Employment in manufacturing	21.9	18.5	14.2
6. % Employment in transport, communication, and public utilities	5.4	5.0	4.8
7. % Employment in wholesale trade	4.6	5.1	4.8
8. % Employment in retail trade	15.2	15.9	16.5
9. % Employment in finance, insurance, real estate	5.5	6.7	7.5
10. % Employment in services	18.5	21.7	27.7
11. % Employment in federal civilian government	3.2	2.7	2.4
12. % Employment in federal military	3.6	2.2	1.9
13. % Employment in state/local government	11.4	11.9	11.0
14. Earning/worker in farming	13.10	10.63	15.12
15. Earning/worker in agricultural services	16.00	14.00	12.37
16. Earning/worker in mining	27.93	39.30	32.98
17. Earning/worker in construction	27.35	28.01	25.39
18. Earning/worker in manufacturing	25.02	27.97	28.45
19. Earning/worker in transport, communication, and public utilities	27.55	31.72	29.85
20. Earning/worker in wholesale trade	26.75	27.98	28.44
21. Earning/worker in retail trade	14.78	13.13	12.04
22. Earning/worker in finance, insurance, real estate	20.48	18.10	19.64
23. Earning/worker in services	17.61	18.04	20.39
24. Earning/worker in federal civilian government	27.85	28.53	28.07
25. Earning/worker in federal military	13.13	13.63	15.11
26. Earning/worker in state/local government	18.89	18.85	21.78
27. Income per capita	11.37	13.89	16.31
28. % population 20–64 years	52.3	56.8	58.7
29. % white in population	87.6	85.9	83.9
30. Mean earning per worker	20.59	21.02	21.32

earnings per worker grew only 3.5 percent during the twenty-year period. The metro growth rate was 3.3 percent and the nonmetro growth rate was 2.2 percent. (The national average is greater than either of its components because the more rapidly rising component received a larger weight in 1990 than in 1970.) Real earnings have risen from 1970 to 1990 in each sector except farm services, construction, retail, and FIRE. Lines 27 and 30 show that real income per capita has risen much faster than real earnings per worker. The reason is that a much larger fraction of the population was of

Table 6.3. MSA earning and employment data, 1970–1990

Variable	1970	1980	1990
1. % Employment in farming	1.8	1.4	1.0
2. % Employment in agricultural services	0.5	0.7	0.9
3. % Employment in mining	0.5	0.7	0.5
4. % Employment in construction	5.0	5.0	5.2
5. % Employment in manufacturing	22.4	18.4	13.5
6. % Employment in transport, communication, and public utilities	5.7	5.2	4.9
7. % Employment in wholesale trade	5.2	5.5	5.2
8. % Employment in retail trade	15.3	16.1	16.5
9. % Employment in finance, insurance, real estate	6.1	7.4	8.1
10. % Employment in services	19.4	23.0	29.2
11. % Employment in federal civilian government	3.5	2.9	2.6
12. % Employment in federal military	3.6	2.2	1.9
13. % Employment in state/local government	11.0	11.5	10.5
14. Earning/worker in farming	13.35	13.13	16.49
15. Earning/worker in agricultural services	16.41	14.25	12.83
16. Earning/worker in mining	30.02	43.66	35.52
17. Earning/worker in construction	28.51	29.05	26.68
18. Earning/worker in manufacturing	26.34	29.51	30.52
19. Earning/worker in transport, communication, and public utilities	28.17	32.53	30.46
20. Earning/worker in wholesale trade	27.40	28.92	29.67
21. Earning/worker in retail trade	15.18	13.44	12.50
22. Earning/worker in finance, insurance, real estate	21.18	18.93	20.93
23. Earning/worker in services	18.59	18.80	21.38
24. Earning/worker in federal civilian government	28.42	29.09	28.64
25. Earning/worker in federal military	13.64	14.21	15.75
26. Earning/worker in state/local government	20.08	19.72	22.95
27. Income per capita	12.15	14.75	17.35
28. % population 20–64 years	53.1	57.8	59.6
29. % white in population	87.2	84.9	82.6
30. Mean earning per worker	21.74	22.07	22.45

working age, as shown on line 28, in 1990 than in 1970. Thus, the fraction of the population that is working has increased.

Comparison between Tables 6.3 and 6.4 reveals the remarkable similarity in the sectoral shares of employment between metro and nonmetro counties. Agriculture, farm services, and mining are, of course, much larger shares of nonmetro than of metro employment. Construction shares are about the same. Manufacturing's share was greater in metro areas in 1970 but, incredibly, has become greater outside metro areas in 1980 and 1990. Manufactur-

Table 6.4. Non-MSA earning and employment data, 1970–1990

Variable	1970	1980	1990
1. % Employment in farming	14.4	10.9	7.6
2. % Employment in agricultural services	1.0	1.2	1.5
3. % Employment in mining	1.9	2.6	1.6
4. % Employment in construction	4.6	5.2	5.2
5. % Employment in manufacturing	20.2	18.9	17.1
6. % Employment in transport, communication, and public utilities	4.2	4.3	4.2
7. % Employment in wholesale trade	2.5	3.5	3.2
8. % Employment in retail trade	14.6	15.1	16.3
9. % Employment in finance, insurance, real estate	3.1	4.3	4.9
10. % Employment in services	15.2	16.9	21.6
11. % Employment in federal civilian government	2.1	1.9	1.7
12. % Employment in federal military	3.4	2.1	2.0
13. % Employment in state/local government	12.8	13.3	13.2
14. Earning/worker in farming	12.99	9.36	14.39
15. Earning/worker in agricultural services	15.27	13.43	11.14
16. Earning/worker in mining	26.02	34.86	29.88
17. Earning/worker in construction	22.57	24.21	19.99
18. Earning/worker in manufacturing	19.50	22.20	21.54
19. Earning/worker in transport, communication, and public utilities	24.37	27.93	26.80
20. Earning/worker in wholesale trade	21.65	22.28	20.05
21. Earning/worker in retail trade	13.19	11.85	10.09
22. Earning/worker in finance, insurance, real estate	15.28	12.58	10.51
23. Earning/worker in services	12.93	14.02	14.73
24. Earning/worker in federal civilian government	24.30	25.23	24.50
25. Earning/worker in federal military	11.07	11.26	12.47
26. Earning/worker in state/local government	15.05	15.99	17.87
27. Income per capita	8.77	11.11	12.72
28. % population 20–64 years	49.8	53.7	55.4
29. % white in population	89.1	89.2	88.7
30. Mean earning per worker	16.23	17.02	16.58

ing was the first sector to suburbanize on a substantial scale and the phenomena identified in the previous section have caused a large part of the sector to move out of metro areas during recent decades. Other evidence indicates that most of the manufacturing that has moved out of metro areas during the last thirty years does not purchase inputs from the farm sector. Wholesale's share is greater in metro areas, and retailing's is about the same. Services and FIRE are more concentrated in metro areas, and government employment shares add up to about the same percentages in metro and nonmetro counties. Nonmetro earnings were lower than metro earnings in each sector in each year covered by the tables. The nonmetro population is older and has a smaller minority share than the metro population.

Tables 6.5 to 6.20 in the Appendix show the same metro and nonmetro data for the same years for eight regions that comprise the country.[7] Only the highlights of this set of remarkable data can be pointed out here.

The shares of nonmetro employment that are in farming vary enormously among regions, from a low of 1.9 percent in New England to a high of 13.1 percent in the Plains. The shares of nonmetro employment in farm services also vary enormously among regions. Surprisingly, they barely correlate with farm employment shares. New England has one farm service worker for each farm worker and the Far West has two-thirds as many farm service as farm workers. The national nonmetro average shown in Table 6.4 was about 20 percent as many farm service workers as farm workers. By contrast, the Plains region has only one nonmetro farm service worker for twelve farm workers. These data make clear that most nonmetro, nonfarm workers do not serve the farm sector.

Manufacturing's share of nonmetro workers varies by only about a factor of two among regions. Not only are the nonmetro manufacturing shares similar among regions, but regions tend to have similar metro and nonmetro manufacturing shares. Likewise, there is remarkably little regional variation among nonmetro employment shares in most of the sectors in the Appendix tables.

Metro and nonmetro earnings per worker vary rather little among regions in most sectors. In all regions, farm service workers are among the lowest paid nonmetro sectors, along with retailing and FIRE. Nonmetro farm workers in the Far West are substantially better paid than farm workers of all other regions.

Time trends of regional nonmetro employment trends also accord with national averages. Manufacturing's share falls and the service sector's share rises during the twenty-year period in virtually all regions. The share for FIRE also rises in all regions. Retailing's share rises slightly in most regions.

The data lead to the following conclusions: farm and farm service workers are small shares of nonmetro workers in all eight regions of the country, although their nonmetro employment shares vary greatly among regions. In sectors not related to agriculture, the nonmetro employment pattern is remarkably similar to the metro pattern: nonmetro employment shares differ rather little among regions and are remarkably similar to metro shares; and nonmetro sectoral shares show time trends during the twenty-year period that are remarkably similar to metro trends. The important difference between metro and nonmetro shares is that the nonmetro shares of the three sectors related to extractive activities (agriculture, agricultural services, and mining) are much larger than the metro shares. However, their total employment share is so small that it causes only modest differences between metro and nonmetro shares in other sectors. (The sum of shares in any column must be 100, except for rounding errors.)

Earnings are higher in metro than in nonmetro areas in almost every sector and region. Earnings data are deflated by the national consumer price index, so they do not take account of lower prices in nonmetro than in metro areas. The recorded metro-nonmetro differences therefore exceed real earnings differences. Evidence and the fact that nonmetro to metro area migration continues indicate that real metro earnings are somewhat greater than real nonmetro earnings. However, differences shrink over time and are undoubtedly smaller than those in countries with lower incomes.

SUBURBANIZATION

Everyone knows that metropolitan suburbanization has been massive since World War II. Suburbanization is at least a century old and has been happening worldwide since about 1950, but it has proceeded farther and faster in the United States in the postwar period than in any other time or place. As recently as 1950, about 57 percent of metro residents lived in central cities and about 70 percent of metro jobs were located there. By 1990 the two percentages were about 35 and 45 (see Mieszkowski and Mills 1993, and Mills and Hamilton 1993). The result is that U.S. metro areas have lower population and employment densities than metropolitan areas of similar size in any other country.

Suburbanization is important to the future of metropolitan areas. Many people believe that most Americans have a strong preference to live in relatively small towns and cities compared with metro areas. Opinion surveys indicate a preference of many people to reside in towns or cities of 50,000 to 75,000 people. Such opinion surveys are defective in that they focus on "quality of life" issues and do not take account of the fact that earnings and employment opportunities and the variety of goods and services available are greater in larger metro areas.

Metropolitan suburbanization has made it increasingly easy to combine metropolitan and small-town life styles. About 85 percent of workers who live in suburbs also work there. In a large metro area such as Chicago, some metro residents live forty or fifty miles from downtown Chicago and work twenty or thirty miles from downtown. By the year 2000, it will not be uncommon to live sixty miles from downtown and work forty miles from down-town, with both locations being within the metro area. Such arrangements permit people who so desire to combine many of the advantages of small-town lifestyles and metro workplaces.

It should not be inferred from this discussion that the distinction between metro and nonmetro is meaningless. In a previous article I have shown that central cities and suburbs do tend to grow and shrink together, although the tendency is not very strong and appears to become weaker each decade (Mills 1990). Growing up in Challis, Idaho (population 1,073 in 1990), is an ut-terly different experience from growing up in Queens, New York, and people are forever stamped by either experience. Growing up in Harvard, Illinois (population 5,900 in 1990, sixty miles from downtown Chicago, but still in the greater Chicago metropolitan area), is a still different experience. My point is that as each decade passes, lifestyle is dictated less and less by metro or nonmetro residence. Metro areas are not so much draining nonmetro places as they are reaching out to engulf large numbers of small towns and large amounts of what was formerly countryside. The percentage of U.S. land area that was in metro areas nearly doubled during the thirty years from 1960 to 1990, whereas the metro population increased only 70 percent. But counties are not arbitrarily reclassified from nonmetro to metro status; instead, reclas-sification reflects workers' shifts in occupation and sector. The sectoral shifts are from the extractive sectors represented on lines 1 to 3 in the tables to the other ten sectors.

THE FUTURE OF NONMETRO POPULATION AND EMPLOYMENT

Table 6.1 shows that the vast majority of workers who live outside metro ar-eas have been employed off-farm ever since metro-related data were first col-lected in 1940. Nevertheless, the percentage of all workers who live outside metro areas and work off-farm has declined during the thirty-year period from 1960 to 1990. Metro population and employment are increasing faster than farm employment is decreasing. Although the data have not been pre-sented in this paper, the increasing national metro share of population and employment has been reflected in each region of the country.

It is almost certain that the percentage of people who live and work outside metro areas will continue to decline in coming decades. The percentage of people who live and work in metro areas has risen inexorably each decade in the last fifty years. The growth in the percentage has slowed in recent decades and will probably rise only slowly in coming decades. A good guess is that the percentage of the population that lives in metro areas will rise from its 1990 value of 77.5 to about 79 by the year 2000 and will increase by about 1 percentage point per decade for several decades after that. Since only 2.2 percent of workers were employed on farms in 1990, the percentage cannot fall much farther in future decades. As a matter of arithmetic, the foregoing implies that the percentage of workers who work off-farm outside metro areas will continue to decline somewhat during future decades.

Tables 6.3 and 6.4 demonstrate that, except for about 10 percent of nonmetro workers in jobs related to extractive sectors, the sectoral distribution of nonmetro workers is remarkably similar to the sectoral distribution of metro workers. Appendix tables reveal that the pattern holds for most sectors in most regions of the country. Earnings per worker are lower in nonmetro than in metro areas, and the pattern is repeated in nearly every sector in nearly every region. Earnings differences are almost certainly somewhat greater than can be accounted for by higher metro living costs relative to nonmetro costs.

As metro areas continue to grow and decentralize during coming decades, the differences between employment, earnings, and lifestyle opportunities in metro and nonmetro areas will continue to become less important. Metro-area suburbs, where most Americans live and most workers work, offer a rich variety of employment and lifestyle opportunities, ranging from rural and small town to cities that are larger than almost any located outside metro areas.

NOTES

I thank Luan' Sende Lubuele for valuable research assistance in the preparation of this chapter and Elizabeth Davis for comments on an earlier draft. Emery Castle and other committee members have provided my entire education on rural matters during my years of service on the National Rural Studies Committee. I am deeply indebted.

1. Even among workers who live on farms, about half have nonfarm jobs. Statistics in this paragraph are from Dahmann and Dacquel 1992.

2. If urban and rural labor force participation rates were the same, the difference between the two columns would equal the percentage of the labor force that is rural but nonfarm. In recent decades, the rural labor force participation rate has been somewhat greater than the urban rate, implying that the percentage of workers who are urban is somewhat less than the percentage of the population that is urban. Thus, the 20 to 24 percent difference between the two columns in Table 6.1 understates the difference in employment rates. Hence the 25 percent figure in the text. It is not

known if rural labor force participation rates exceeded the urban rates before about 1940.

3. There is an almost definitional limit to the amount of nonfarm employment that can cluster in one rural area. Suppose a factory locates in what was formerly a farm area and employs 500 people. Suppose twice that number of workers are attracted to provide retailing, banking, etc. for the factory workers and for each other. Then total employment in the community is 1,500 and total population is likely to be about 2,500, since about 60 percent of the U.S. population is employed. The resulting community of 2,500 people qualifies as an urban area.

4. All the data presented in this section are from U.S. censuses of population. The diskettes from which data in the tables were calculated were prepared by Woods and Poole Economics, Washington, D.C. The hard copy is in Woods and Poole, 1992. Some of the 1980 earnings in the mining sector are suspiciously high. However, the entries have been checked carefully and are in accord with data on the diskettes. Extreme entries may result from the small numbers of workers represented or from the erratic nature of resource sectors in the late 1970s and early 1980s.

5. Federal government data classify production sectors of the economy by increasingly detailed one-to-seven-digit designations. "Motor vehicles" is a two-digit sector of the manufacturing sector, "automobiles" is a three-digit sector, and so on.

6. Data in Table 6.1 are from different sources from those presented in this section. Discrepancies in farm workers result from the fact that many farm workers also have other jobs, frequently on a seasonal basis. Different sources use different criteria as to which sector such workers are assigned to.

7. A few metro areas, such as St. Louis, fall in two regions. In such cases, the metro area was included in the region that contains the state listed first in the metro title. Regions are those used in census data, except that my Plains region combines census West North Central and West South Central Regions.

APPENDIX: REGIONAL TABLES ON METRO AND
NONMETRO EMPLOYMENT AND EARNINGS

Table 6.5. New England MSA earning and employment data

Variable	1970	1980	1990
1. % Employment in farming	0.6	0.6	0.3
2. % Employment in agricultural services	0.5	0.6	0.8
3. % Employment in mining	0.1	0.1	0.1
4. % Employment in construction	4.9	3.8	5.2
5. % Employment in manufacturing	27.6	24.3	16.2
6. % Employment in transport, communication, and public utilities	4.5	4.1	3.9
7. % Employment in wholesale trade	4.7	5.1	5.2
8. % Employment in retail trade	15.9	15.9	16.3
9. % Employment in finance, insurance, real estate	6.0	7.0	8.6
10. % Employment in services	20.4	24.7	31.3
11. % Employment in federal civilian government	2.2	1.7	1.6
12. % Employment in federal military	2.9	1.5	1.1
13. % Employment in state/local government	9.7	10.7	9.3
14. Earning/worker in farming	15.33	9.92	18.52
15. Earning/worker in agricultural services	16.09	15.39	15.77
16. Earning/worker in mining	43.09	121.85	58.57
17. Earning/worker in construction	28.67	26.64	29.28
18. Earning/worker in manufacturing	24.51	26.68	31.27
19. Earning/worker in transport, communication, and public utilities	26.68	29.80	29.81
20. Earning/worker in wholesale trade	26.17	26.81	31.92
21. Earning/worker in retail trade	14.36	12.24	13.81
22. Earning/worker in finance, insurance, real estate	22.33	19.98	23.09
23. Earning/worker in services	18.90	17.51	22.51
24. Earning/worker in federal civilian government	27.40	28.18	27.97
25. Earning/worker in federal military	10.17	10.59	12.75
26. Earning/worker in state/local government	20.66	19.45	24.54
27. Income per capita	12.83	15.20	20.09
28. % population 20–64 years	52.7	57.6	60.6
29. % white in population	95.8	94.3	91.8
30. Mean earning per worker	21.19	20.72	23.81

Table 6.6. New England non-MSA earning and employment data

Variable	1970	1980	1990
1. % Employment in farming	4.5	3.6	1.9
2. % Employment in agricultural services	1.3	1.8	1.9
3. % Employment in mining	0.2	0.1	0.1
4. % Employment in construction	6.2	5.7	8.1
5. % Employment in manufacturing	23.6	21.6	15.3
6. % Employment in transport, communication, and public utilities	3.7	3.6	3.6
7. % Employment in wholesale trade	2.0	3.1	3.0
8. % Employment in retail trade	14.8	16.3	17.8
9. % Employment in finance, insurance, real estate	3.6	4.8	6.1
10. % Employment in services	18.9	22.9	27.9
11. % Employment in federal civilian government	3.3	2.6	2.2
12. % Employment in federal military	6.2	2.4	1.7
13. % Employment in state/local government	11.5	11.4	10.4
14. Earning/worker in farming	13.73	8.15	11.78
15. Earning/worker in agricultural services	13.50	12.17	12.50
16. Earning/worker in mining	25.99	85.72	49.63
17. Earning/worker in construction	23.28	22.16	22.74
18. Earning/worker in manufacturing	19.78	21.87	23.79
19. Earning/worker in transport, communication, and public utilities	23.03	24.70	23.09
20. Earning/worker in wholesale trade	21.67	20.63	22.81
21. Earning/worker in retail trade	13.89	11.69	11.96
22. Earning/worker in finance, insurance, real estate	18.33	12.22	10.36
23. Earning/worker in services	14.29	13.83	16.52
24. Earning/worker in federal civilian government	26.36	27.02	27.32
25. Earning/worker in federal military	13.88	12.81	15.44
26. Earning/worker in state/local government	15.62	16.06	19.42
27. Income per capita	10.46	12.59	16.70
28. % population 20–64 years	50.8	55.3	58.1
29. % white in population	99.0	98.8	98.4
30. Mean earning per worker	17.22	16.67	17.75

Table 6.7. Mideast MSA earning and employment data

Variable	1970	1980	1990
1. % Employment in farming	0.7	0.7	0.5
2. % Employment in agricultural services	0.3	0.5	0.6
3. % Employment in mining	0.2	0.2	0.1
4. % Employment in construction	4.4	3.8	4.8
5. % Employment in manufacturing	24.2	19.5	13.1
6. % Employment in transport, communication, and public utilities	6.2	5.6	5.1
7. % Employment in wholesale trade	5.3	5.8	5.5
8. % Employment in retail trade	14.5	14.7	15.0
9. % Employment in finance, insurance, real estate	6.9	7.7	8.6
10. % Employment in services	20.2	24.9	31.6
11. % Employment in federal civilian government	3.7	3.6	3.1
12. % Employment in federal military	2.0	1.2	1.0
13. % Employment in state/local government	11.1	11.7	10.9
14. Earning/worker in farming	16.26	10.21	14.22
15. Earning/worker in agricultural services	18.64	15.75	15.93
16. Earning/worker in mining	36.87	70.90	48.15
17. Earning/worker in construction	30.25	29.14	29.56
18. Earning/worker in manufacturing	26.37	29.48	31.33
19. Earning/worker in transport, communication, and public utilities	29.40	33.84	32.13
20. Earning/worker in wholesale trade	29.01	29.22	31.66
21. Earning/worker in retail trade	15.50	13.27	13.33
22. Earning/worker in finance, insurance, real estate	24.40	23.24	30.16
23. Earning/worker in services	20.87	19.97	23.84
24. Earning/worker in federal civilian government	29.92	30.35	30.24
25. Earning/worker in federal military	10.36	10.13	11.92
26. Earning/worker in state/local government	21.31	21.02	26.06
27. Income per capita	13.16	15.27	19.43
28. % population 20–64 years	54.1	57.9	59.9
29. % white in population	85.9	83.4	80.0
30. Mean earning per worker	23.21	23.16	25.17

Table 6.8. Mideast non-MSA earning and employment data

Variable	1970	1980	1990
1. % Employment in farming	5.3	4.5	2.8
2. % Employment in agricultural services	0.7	0.8	1.0
3. % Employment in mining	1.2	1.3	0.8
4. % Employment in construction	5.4	5.1	6.6
5. % Employment in manufacturing	20.9	17.2	12.7
6. % Employment in transport, communication, and public utilities	4.5	4.0	4.2
7. % Employment in wholesale trade	2.6	3.4	3.2
8. % Employment in retail trade	16.0	16.7	17.8
9. % Employment in finance, insurance, real estate	4.0	4.9	5.8
10. % Employment in services	17.7	21.7	27.3
11. % Employment in federal civilian government	5.0	4.8	4.0
12. % Employment in federal military	3.3	2.0	2.1
13. % Employment in state/local government	13.6	13.6	11.7
14. Earning/worker in farming	12.56	7.26	11.95
15. Earning/worker in agricultural services	13.95	12.07	12.50
16. Earning/worker in mining	27.24	37.91	31.63
17. Earning/worker in construction	24.32	23.66	23.58
18. Earning/worker in manufacturing	21.69	24.41	24.58
19. Earning/worker in transport, communication, and public utilities	25.24	27.70	26.57
20. Earning/worker in wholesale trade	22.40	23.51	25.45
21. Earning/worker in retail trade	14.75	12.83	12.41
22. Earning/worker in finance, insurance, real estate	16.31	13.50	13.68
23. Earning/worker in services	17.03	16.49	18.99
24. Earning/worker in federal civilian government	30.25	29.26	30.19
25. Earning/worker in federal military	12.78	13.02	16.73
26. Earning/worker in state/local government	17.68	17.74	21.80
27. Income per capita	10.91	12.79	15.81
28. % population 20–64 years	51.9	56.5	59.1
29. % white in population	93.7	89.8	86.1
30. Mean earning per worker	18.98	18.69	19.62

Table 6.9. Great Lakes MSA earning and employment data

Variable	1970	1980	1990
1. % Employment in farming	1.5	1.3	0.8
2. % Employment in agricultural services	0.3	0.4	0.6
3. % Employment in mining	0.2	0.2	0.2
4. % Employment in construction	4.5	4.2	4.5
5. % Employment in manufacturing	30.5	24.5	18.3
6. % Employment in transport, communication, and public utilities	5.4	4.8	4.7
7. % Employment in wholesale trade	5.3	5.4	5.4
8. % Employment in retail trade	15.7	16.6	17.3
9. % Employment in finance, insurance, real estate	5.5	6.8	7.3
10. % Employment in services	17.3	21.8	28.1
11. % Employment in federal civilian government	2.0	1.7	1.6
12. % Employment in federal military	1.4	0.9	0.8
13. % Employment in state/local government	10.4	11.5	10.4
14. Earning/worker in farming	12.22	11.35	11.79
15. Earning/worker in agricultural services	18.42	16.43	13.97
16. Earning/worker in mining	33.62	60.51	36.72
17. Earning/worker in construction	32.07	31.91	28.06
18. Earning/worker in manufacturing	28.81	34.04	33.63
19. Earning/worker in transport, communication, and public utilities	28.96	33.84	30.32
20. Earning/worker in wholesale trade	29.08	30.60	30.43
21. Earning/worker in retail trade	15.26	13.17	11.54
22. Earning/worker in finance, insurance, real estate	20.98	18.85	20.32
23. Earning/worker in services	18.86	18.89	20.60
24. Earning/worker in federal civilian government	28.29	29.49	28.19
25. Earning/worker in federal military	10.31	10.01	11.34
26. Earning/worker in state/local government	20.18	20.09	22.17
27. Income per capita	12.30	14.88	16.92
28. % population 20–64 years	52.3	57.3	58.9
29. % white in population	87.4	84.8	83.3
30. Mean earning per worker	23.26	23.75	22.83

Table 6.10. Great Lakes non-MSA earning and employment data

Variable	1970	1980	1990
1. % Employment in farming	11.5	10.0	6.9
2. % Employment in agricultural services	0.6	0.7	0.9
3. % Employment in mining	1.3	1.7	1.1
4. % Employment in construction	4.4	4.5	4.5
5. % Employment in manufacturing	24.9	21.8	19.8
6. % Employment in transport, communication, and public utilities	4.8	4.5	4.4
7. % Employment in wholesale trade	2.4	3.4	3.3
8. % Employment in retail trade	15.9	16.2	17.2
9. % Employment in finance, insurance, real estate	3.4	4.7	5.0
10. % Employment in services	14.2	17.2	21.9
11. % Employment in federal civilian government	1.8	1.5	1.4
12. % Employment in federal military	1.6	1.1	1.2
13. % Employment in state/local government	13.0	12.7	12.4
14. Earning/worker in farming	11.86	10.16	11.59
15. Earning/worker in agricultural services	19.12	14.80	11.99
16. Earning/worker in mining	28.12	36.99	29.72
17. Earning/worker in construction	25.45	26.33	21.80
18. Earning/worker in manufacturing	23.10	26.45	24.93
19. Earning/worker in transport, communication, and public utilities	25.87	29.25	26.85
20. Earning/worker in wholesale trade	23.25	24.13	21.13
21. Earning/worker in retail trade	13.37	11.60	9.57
22. Earning/worker in finance, insurance, real estate	15.24	12.27	10.30
23. Earning/worker in services	14.22	14.16	14.57
24. Earning/worker in federal civilian government	24.70	24.49	25.11
25. Earning/worker in federal military	10.05	10.35	11.50
26. Earning/worker in state/local government	15.26	16.20	18.23
27. Income per capita	9.69	11.97	13.26
28. % population 20–64 years	49.8	54.1	55.6
29. % white in population	97.5	97.1	96.5
30. Mean earning per worker	17.80	18.25	17.15

Table 6.11. Plains MSA earning and employment data

Variable	1970	1980	1990
1. % Employment in farming	2.3	1.9	1.3
2. % Employment in agricultural services	0.3	0.4	0.6
3. % Employment in mining	0.5	0.5	0.3
4. % Employment in construction	4.9	4.7	4.6
5. % Employment in manufacturing	20.9	17.9	14.0
6. % Employment in transport, communication, and public utilities	6.7	6.1	5.7
7. % Employment in wholesale trade	6.1	6.2	5.6
8. % Employment in retail trade	16.2	16.8	17.1
9. % Employment in finance, insurance, real estate	6.5	7.6	8.2
10. % Employment in services	19.4	23.1	29.0
11. % Employment in federal civilian government	3.1	2.4	2.2
12. % Employment in federal military	2.5	1.5	1.5
13. % Employment in state/local government	10.7	10.8	9.9
14. Earning/worker in farming	14.10	6.34	10.74
15. Earning/worker in agricultural services	20.53	16.76	13.63
16. Earning/worker in mining	27.10	42.96	28.27
17. Earning/worker in construction	28.92	29.76	25.63
18. Earning/worker in manufacturing	26.67	29.75	30.50
19. Earning/worker in transport, communication, and public utilities	27.83	32.58	30.05
20. Earning/worker in wholesale trade	27.73	30.19	29.17
21. Earning/worker in retail trade	14.62	12.62	11.21
22. Earning/worker in finance, insurance, real estate	19.47	17.71	18.35
23. Earning/worker in services	16.63	16.97	18.57
24. Earning/worker in federal civilian government	27.37	27.60	27.70
25. Earning/worker in federal military	11.31	12.25	13.06
26. Earning/worker in state/local government	18.80	18.81	21.11
27. Income per capita	11.76	14.80	16.94
28. % population 20–64 years	51.5	57.3	59.3
29. % white in population	92.4	91.2	89.8
30. Mean earning per worker	21.05	21.28	20.81

Table 6.12. Plains non-MSA earning and employment data

Variable	1970	1980	1990
1. % Employment in farming	21.4	17.1	13.1
2. % Employment in agricultural services	1.0	0.9	1.1
3. % Employment in mining	1.0	1.2	0.8
4. % Employment in construction	4.6	5.1	4.3
5. % Employment in manufacturing	11.7	12.4	12.5
6. % Employment in transport, communication, and public utilities	4.4	4.5	4.3
7. % Employment in wholesale trade	2.7	4.8	4.3
8. % Employment in retail trade	16.3	15.8	15.8
9. % Employment in finance, insurance, real estate	3.4	4.5	5.0
10. % Employment in services	14.7	17.2	21.9
11. % Employment in federal civilian government	1.9	1.6	1.5
12. % Employment in federal military	3.5	2.0	2.0
13. % Employment in state/local government	13.5	13.0	13.4
14. Earning/worker in farming	16.45	8.66	16.27
15. Earning/worker in agricultural services	18.21	16.74	13.31
16. Earning/worker in mining	20.90	28.23	20.68
17. Earning/worker in construction	22.17	23.69	18.42
18. Earning/worker in manufacturing	20.01	22.39	20.27
19. Earning/worker in transport, communication, and public utilities	24.27	28.11	27.04
20. Earning/worker in wholesale trade	23.79	23.51	19.65
21. Earning/worker in retail trade	12.95	11.05	9.02
22. Earning/worker in finance, insurance, real estate	14.83	13.12	10.78
23. Earning/worker in services	12.70	13.16	13.12
24. Earning/worker in federal civilian government	22.56	23.89	22.71
25. Earning/worker in federal military	9.87	10.38	10.68
26. Earning/worker in state/local government	14.37	15.37	16.56
27. Income per capita	9.33	11.65	13.51
28. % population 20–64 years	48.5	52.4	53.1
29. % white in population	97.9	97.3	96.6
30. Mean earning per worker	16.16	15.52	15.39

Table 6.13. Southeast MSA earning and employment data

Variable	1970	1980	1990
1. % Employment in farming	2.6	1.9	1.2
2. % Employment in agricultural services	0.5	0.7	1.0
3. % Employment in mining	0.6	0.7	0.4
4. % Employment in construction	6.1	6.3	6.0
5. % Employment in manufacturing	19.2	16.1	12.3
6. % Employment in transport, communication, and public utilities	5.8	5.6	5.2
7. % Employment in wholesale trade	5.2	5.6	5.3
8. % Employment in retail trade	14.8	16.2	17.5
9. % Employment in finance, insurance, real estate	5.4	7.0	7.7
10. % Employment in services	19.2	21.0	26.8
11. % Employment in federal civilian government	3.7	3.1	2.6
12. % Employment in federal military	5.8	3.6	3.1
13. % Employment in state/local government	10.9	12.1	10.9
14. Earning/worker in farming	10.46	10.39	16.02
15. Earning/worker in agricultural services	14.13	12.29	10.90
16. Earning/worker in mining	28.68	41.25	33.10
17. Earning/worker in construction	22.34	23.72	21.32
18. Earning/worker in manufacturing	21.54	24.77	25.78
19. Earning/worker in transport, communication, and public utilities	24.79	29.78	28.04
20. Earning/worker in wholesale trade	24.05	25.83	26.42
21. Earning/worker in retail trade	14.00	12.85	11.55
22. Earning/worker in finance, insurance, real estate	19.07	16.28	16.27
23. Earning/worker in services	14.93	16.86	19.13
24. Earning/worker in federal civilian government	26.54	27.95	27.34
25. Earning/worker in federal military	14.13	15.07	16.45
26. Earning/worker in state/local government	16.59	17.19	20.16
27. Income per capita	10.15	12.84	15.48
28. % population 20–64 years	52.6	57.0	59.0
29. % white in population	79.5	78.7	77.9
30. Mean earning per worker	18.31	19.43	19.57

Table 6.14. Southeast non-MSA earning and employment data

Variable	1970	1980	1990
1. % Employment in farming	13.3	9.2	5.8
2. % Employment in agricultural services	0.8	1.0	1.2
3. % Employment in mining	1.9	2.3	1.3
4. % Employment in construction	4.5	5.4	5.6
5. % Employment in manufacturing	23.9	23.0	20.4
6. % Employment in transport, communication, and public utilities	3.6	3.9	4.2
7. % Employment in wholesale trade	2.4	3.3	3.2
8. % Employment in retail trade	12.7	13.9	15.8
9. % Employment in finance, insurance, real estate	2.7	3.9	4.7
10. % Employment in services	15.4	15.8	20.5
11. % Employment in federal civilian government	2.7	2.6	2.3
12. % Employment in federal military	4.7	2.8	2.6
13. % Employment in state/local government	11.3	12.9	12.3
14. Earning/worker in farming	9.55	6.41	12.02
15. Earning/worker in agricultural services	13.40	11.93	10.42
16. Earning/worker in mining	28.03	37.20	33.52
17. Earning/worker in construction	19.62	21.43	19.27
18. Earning/worker in manufacturing	16.87	19.56	19.84
19. Earning/worker in transport, communication, and public utilities	22.99	26.53	27.86
20. Earning/worker in wholesale trade	20.52	21.96	21.87
21. Earning/worker in retail trade	12.88	12.04	10.55
22. Earning/worker in finance, insurance, real estate	15.53	13.22	12.08
23. Earning/worker in services	11.70	14.64	16.85
24. Earning/worker in federal civilian government	28.01	28.87	28.02
25. Earning/worker in federal military	13.12	13.43	14.94
26. Earning/worker in state/local government	14.36	15.15	17.40
27. Income per capita	7.88	10.36	12.60
28. % population 20–64 years	50.3	54.3	56.9
29. % white in population	78.2	79.4	79.6
30. Mean earning per worker	15.01	16.56	17.13

Table 6.15. Southwest MSA earning and employment data

Variable	1970	1980	1990
1. % Employment in farming	2.1	1.3	0.8
2. % Employment in agricultural services	0.6	0.6	0.8
3. % Employment in mining	2.1	3.3	2.2
4. % Employment in construction	6.2	7.1	5.2
5. % Employment in manufacturing	15.4	14.4	10.9
6. % Employment in transport, communication, and public utilities	5.7	5.4	5.2
7. % Employment in wholesale trade	5.8	6.1	5.1
8. % Employment in retail trade	16.1	16.7	16.9
9. % Employment in finance, insurance, real estate	6.1	7.3	8.5
10. % Employment in services	19.5	21.1	28.1
11. % Employment in federal civilian government	4.1	2.7	2.6
12. % Employment in federal military	5.4	2.9	2.3
13. % Employment in state/local government	10.9	11.1	11.3
14. Earning/worker in farming	11.38	8.74	14.55
15. Earning/worker in agricultural services	15.38	14.25	11.28
16. Earning/worker in mining	27.73	35.61	32.49
17. Earning/worker in construction	25.05	29.00	24.45
18. Earning/worker in manufacturing	25.03	28.72	29.49
19. Earning/worker in transport, communication, and public utilities	26.87	32.45	29.29
20. Earning/worker in wholesale trade	25.23	30.02	28.82
21. Earning/worker in retail trade	14.12	13.89	12.03
22. Earning/worker in finance, insurance, real estate	19.03	18.24	17.07
23. Earning/worker in services	16.39	18.68	19.85
24. Earning/worker in federal civilian government	27.19	28.52	28.43
25. Earning/worker in federal military	15.31	15.22	15.96
26. Earning/worker in state/local government	17.36	18.09	20.52
27. Income per capita	10.71	14.25	14.97
28. % population 20–64 years	52.4	57.4	59.0
29. % white in population	88.2	87.3	85.8
30. Mean earning per worker	19.79	21.95	20.90

Table 6.16. Southwest non-MSA earning and employment data

Variable	1970	1980	1990
1. % Employment in farming	17.5	12.5	9.2
2. % Employment in agricultural services	1.3	1.4	1.6
3. % Employment in mining	5.3	6.9	4.5
4. % Employment in construction	5.0	6.2	5.5
5. % Employment in manufacturing	10.1	10.9	9.3
6. % Employment in transport, communication, and public utilities	4.4	4.7	4.4
7. % Employment in wholesale trade	2.8	3.3	3.0
8. % Employment in retail trade	15.5	15.2	15.9
9. % Employment in finance, insurance, real estate	3.1	4.2	5.0
10. % Employment in services	16.1	16.4	21.7
11. % Employment in federal civilian government	3.1	2.6	2.5
12. % Employment in federal military	3.3	2.0	2.0
13. % Employment in state/local government	12.8	13.6	15.4
14. Earning/worker in farming	12.63	8.18	15.83
15. Earning/worker in agricultural services	14.06	13.98	10.86
16. Earning/worker in mining	23.04	29.87	23.84
17. Earning/worker in construction	23.41	27.18	20.97
18. Earning/worker in manufacturing	19.70	23.82	22.49
19. Earning/worker in transport, communication, and public utilities	24.18	28.72	28.66
20. Earning/worker in wholesale trade	20.52	22.84	19.63
21. Earning/worker in retail trade	12.90	12.54	10.23
22. Earning/worker in finance, insurance, real estate	15.43	12.97	10.72
23. Earning/worker in services	12.84	14.26	14.10
24. Earning/worker in federal civilian government	23.55	24.77	23.89
25. Earning/worker in federal military	12.39	12.62	13.27
26. Earning/worker in state/local government	14.72	15.81	17.48
27. Income per capita	8.39	11.01	11.76
28. % population 20–64 years	49.2	52.0	53.3
29. % white in population	87.6	87.5	86.4
30. Mean earning per worker	15.93	17.51	16.57

Table 6.17. Rocky Mountain MSA earning and employment data

Variable	1970	1980	1990
1. % Employment in farming	2.0	1.3	0.9
2. % Employment in agricultural services	0.3	0.5	0.8
3. % Employment in mining	1.5	1.8	1.0
4. % Employment in construction	5.4	6.2	4.6
5. % Employment in manufacturing	12.6	12.3	10.6
6. % Employment in transport, communication, and public utilities	6.0	5.6	5.5
7. % Employment in wholesale trade	5.6	5.8	4.8
8. % Employment in retail trade	16.1	16.7	16.6
9. % Employment in finance, insurance, real estate	6.5	8.3	8.9
10. % Employment in services	19.0	22.3	29.1
11. % Employment in federal civilian government	6.1	4.0	3.5
12. % Employment in federal military	6.1	3.3	2.9
13. % Employment in state/local government	12.8	11.8	10.9
14. Earning/worker in farming	18.59	9.20	11.69
15. Earning/worker in agricultural services	14.71	13.54	10.85
16. Earning/worker in mining	28.70	41.99	36.17
17. Earning/worker in construction	26.75	28.96	23.98
18. Earning/worker in manufacturing	25.44	28.13	28.68
19. Earning/worker in transport, communication, and public utilities	27.55	33.07	30.98
20. Earning/worker in wholesale trade	26.13	28.80	27.36
21. Earning/worker in retail trade	14.30	13.20	11.11
22. Earning/worker in finance, insurance, real estate	17.25	15.58	14.58
23. Earning/worker in services	16.31	17.42	18.20
24. Earning/worker in federal civilian government	27.09	27.80	27.01
25. Earning/worker in federal military	13.95	14.20	15.78
26. Earning/worker in state/local government	17.60	19.16	20.47
27. Income per capita	11.12	14.14	15.76
28. % population 20–64 years	51.9	57.7	58.4
29. % white in population	96.3	95.1	93.7
30. Mean earning per worker	19.89	20.96	19.77

Table 6.18. Rocky Mountain non-MSA earning and employment data

Variable	1970	1980	1990
1. % Employment in farming	15.9	10.3	8.0
2. % Employment in agricultural services	1.2	1.3	1.9
3. % Employment in mining	3.8	5.8	2.9
4. % Employment in construction	4.9	6.7	5.3
5. % Employment in manufacturing	9.4	8.3	8.0
6. % Employment in transport, communication, and public utilities	5.3	5.3	4.9
7. % Employment in wholesale trade	2.5	3.5	3.0
8. % Employment in retail trade	16.3	16.6	17.1
9. % Employment in finance, insurance, real estate	3.6	5.3	5.8
10. % Employment in services	16.0	18.6	24.3
11. % Employment in federal civilian government	3.7	3.0	2.7
12. % Employment in federal military	2.7	1.7	1.5
13. % Employment in state/local government	14.6	13.5	14.6
14. Earning/worker in farming	17.58	14.22	15.15
15. Earning/worker in agricultural services	13.08	11.36	9.44
16. Earning/worker in mining	26.80	38.30	36.47
17. Earning/worker in construction	26.04	27.68	20.69
18. Earning/worker in manufacturing	20.34	24.37	22.30
19. Earning/worker in transport, communication, and public utilities	25.68	29.91	27.97
20. Earning/worker in wholesale trade	21.95	22.13	19.78
21. Earning/worker in retail trade	13.41	12.11	9.78
22. Earning/worker in finance, insurance, real estate	14.26	11.85	9.76
23. Earning/worker in services	14.10	15.37	14.52
24. Earning/worker in federal civilian government	25.00	24.59	24.62
25. Earning/worker in federal military	7.84	8.31	10.16
26. Earning/worker in state/local government	14.52	16.27	16.87
27. Income per capita	9.34	12.30	12.69
28. % population 20–64 years	49.4	54.3	54.2
29. % white in population	97.1	96.7	95.9
30. Mean earning per worker	17.30	18.66	16.34

Table 6.19. Far West MSA earning and employment data

Variable	1970	1980	1990
1. % Employment in farming	2.6	2.0	1.4
2. % Employment in agricultural services	0.9	1.4	1.7
3. % Employment in mining	0.3	0.4	0.3
4. % Employment in construction	4.4	4.7	5.2
5. % Employment in manufacturing	17.3	15.8	12.9
6. % Employment in transport, communication, and public utilities	5.6	4.9	4.4
7. % Employment in wholesale trade	4.9	5.1	5.0
8. % Employment in retail trade	15.4	16.1	15.7
9. % Employment in finance, insurance, real estate	6.5	8.0	8.4
10. % Employment in services	20.5	24.4	29.9
11. % Employment in federal civilian government	4.0	2.9	2.4
12. % Employment in federal military	5.8	3.1	2.6
13. % Employment in state/local government	11.9	11.2	10.1
14. Earning/worker in farming	16.51	23.81	23.69
15. Earning/worker in agricultural services	15.79	13.80	12.23
16. Earning/worker in mining	32.64	52.64	43.80
17. Earning/worker in construction	33.52	34.81	30.25
18. Earning/worker in manufacturing	28.59	29.59	31.02
19. Earning/worker in transport, communication, and public utilities	30.51	33.82	32.24
20. Earning/worker in wholesale trade	28.27	29.88	30.19
21. Earning/worker in retail trade	17.10	14.99	14.03
22. Earning/worker in finance, insurance, real estate	20.22	18.03	19.70
23. Earning/worker in services	20.41	20.33	22.83
24. Earning/worker in federal civilian government	28.23	28.50	27.87
25. Earning/worker in federal military	15.30	15.67	17.30
26. Earning/worker in state/local government	23.66	22.13	25.17
27. Income per capita	13.19	16.14	17.94
28. % population 20–64 years	54.2	59.3	60.4
29. % white in population	89.1	85.5	81.6
30. Mean earning per worker	23.12	22.97	23.52

Table 6.20. Far West non-MSA earning and employment data

Variable	1970	1980	1990
1. % Employment in farming	11.8	8.8	6.4
2. % Employment in agricultural services	2.3	3.3	4.1
3. % Employment in mining	1.0	1.1	1.3
4. % Employment in construction	4.2	5.4	5.3
5. % Employment in manufacturing	15.4	12.9	10.7
6. % Employment in transport, communication, and public utilities	4.8	4.5	4.3
7. % Employment in wholesale trade	2.4	2.8	2.6
8. % Employment in retail trade	14.9	15.9	16.6
9. % Employment in finance, insurance, real estate	3.6	5.4	5.6
10. % Employment in services	15.7	19.3	24.1
11. % Employment in federal civilian government	3.4	2.9	2.4
12. % Employment in federal military	5.2	2.7	2.5
13. % Employment in state/local government	15.4	15.0	14.1
14. Earning/worker in farming	18.54	26.01	22.38
15. Earning/worker in agricultural services	15.99	14.54	11.67
16. Earning/worker in mining	31.07	45.08	40.29
17. Earning/worker in construction	32.55	32.93	25.54
18. Earning/worker in manufacturing	24.98	29.21	25.19
19. Earning/worker in transport, communication, and public utilities	27.59	32.47	30.11
20. Earning/worker in wholesale trade	22.30	22.90	20.62
21. Earning/worker in retail trade	15.16	13.42	11.42
22. Earning/worker in finance, insurance, real estate	13.77	10.79	9.18
23. Earning/worker in services	16.52	15.87	16.43
24. Earning/worker in federal civilian government	26.62	25.67	24.82
25. Earning/worker in federal military	13.95	13.76	15.20
26. Earning/worker in state/local government	19.66	20.83	21.97
27. Income per capita	10.66	13.54	14.00
28. % population 20–64 years	51.9	56.5	56.6
29. % white in population	90.9	90.4	89.0
30. Mean earning per worker	19.93	20.93	18.75

7

THE USE AND MANAGEMENT OF
RURAL SPACE

PIERRE CROSSON

Rural space is here defined as the land and water area of the forty-eight contiguous states that lies outside of towns and cities with populations of 2,500 or more. The latter are defined by the Census Bureau as urban places. In this chapter, therefore, rural space is nonurban space.[1]

Although this definition of rural space is generally accepted, most students of rural and urban land use are dissatisfied with it (see, e.g., Freshwater 1989 and other papers in the symposium of which Freshwater's paper is a part). The complaint is that "nonurban" does not adequately describe all the dimensions in which uses of rural space differ from the uses of urban space. Freshwater argues that the generally held view of the term rural is that it incorporates notions of distance between points, low population density, specialized resource-dependent economies, and diverse climatic, topographic, and socioeconomic characteristics of the population. These notions are not fully captured by "nonurban." Deavers (1992) also criticizes the nonurban definition, for essentially the same reasons as Freshwater. I share these reservations. However, much of the data, especially the land-use data relevant to an account of the use of rural space, are based on the "rural-is-not-urban" definition. Accordingly, I have adopted that working definition here.

Different rural spaces are characterized by distinctive physical features of terrain, soils, climate, and proximity to rivers, streams, and lakes, all of which influence in varying degree the uses to which the spaces are put. It is useful to assume that at any time the use of rural space reflects the cumulative responses of people to these physical characteristics and that the responses draw on accumulated stocks of knowledge about how the characteristics can best be managed to serve the vast range of human purposes. Whereas these physical characteristics change relatively slowly, knowledge accumulates and human purposes alter at a much faster rate.

Why should we be interested in uses of rural space? Given that the uses indicate the human purposes served by rural space, understanding the uses can help us to better understand the purposes, how they evolve, and how rural space both accommodates and contributes to those changes. Whatever support rural space may give to other than human interests is outside the scope of this discussion, and the exclusion of nonhuman interests in the uses of rural space may trouble some readers. There are people—I would include David Thoreau, Wes Jackson, and Wendell Berry among them—who seem to regard the land, a principal component of rural space, as having intrinsic value, that is, value quite apart from whatever human purposes the land may serve.[2] I do not accept the notion that something can have value independent of human purposes. Nor, however, do I believe my position to be inconsistent with the particular notion of intrinsic value apparently held by people such as Thoreau, Jackson, and Berry. They would have humans use the land in ways consistent with its presumed intrinsic value, thus essentially urging people to use the land in a way to serve a particular human purpose—that of Thoreau, Jackson, Berry and others who share their belief. To the extent that people adopt this belief, they will change the uses of the land from what otherwise would be the case.

CHANGES IN RURAL LAND AREA SINCE 1950

Table 7.1 shows the area in urban and rural uses in the forty-eight states in 1950, 1969, and 1987. (The years chosen are agricultural census years for which detailed rural land-use data are available.) Several features of the table are noteworthy. The urban area more than tripled from 1950 to 1987 but at the end of the period still was only 3 percent of the total land area of 1,896 million acres. The area in rural uses declined 46 million acres (2.4 percent), somewhat more than the increase in urban area because the total land area of the country declined slightly, reflecting, in part, the submersion of some land under irrigation reservoirs. All of the decline in rural land area was accounted for by a reduction of land in farms. Farmland declined 99 million acres from 1950 to 1969 and by an additional 99 million acres from 1969 to 1987 (Table 7.1). The amount of rural land in nonfarm uses actually increased 152 million acres—21 percent—from 1950 to 1987.

In broad outline the reasons for the decline are not mysterious. Beginning in the 1930s, and with a rush after World War II, American agriculture un-

Table 7.1. Amounts of rural and urban land, forty-eight states, 1950, 1969, and 1987 (in millions of acres)

	1950	1969	1987	Change 1950–1987
Total land	1,903.8	1,897.0	1,895.7	−8.1
Urban	18.3[a]	31.0	55.9	+37.6
Rural	1,885.5	1,866.0	1,839.0	−45.7
Farm	1,159.0	1,060.0	961.0	−198.0
Nonfarm	726.5	806.0	878.8	+152.3

Sources: Total and farmland 1950 and 1969 from USDA (1974), and 1987 from USDA (1992a). Urban land from USDA (1990). Rural land is the difference between total land and urban land, and rural nonfarm land is the difference between total rural land and farmland. Total land declined because of the increase in the area of water bodies greater than 40 acres.

[a] Refers to 1949

derwent a revolution involving a vast substitution of knowledge embodied in technology, people, and institutions for land and manual labor. So powerful was the substitution effect that despite a 17 percent reduction in the amount of farmland from 1950 to the late 1980s, total farm output increased almost 90 percent (U.S. Department of Agriculture [USDA] 1992).[3] After 1950 the knowledge revolution in farming thus released almost 200 million acres of rural land that could then be turned to urban and nonfarm rural uses. And despite its diminished aggregate size, farmland in 1987 still accounted for over half of all rural land.

The land, whether in urban, farm, or nonfarm rural uses, provides two fundamental services to humans: residence space and space in which to conduct all the many production and other activities that engage people.

RURAL SPACE AS RESIDENCE FOR PEOPLE: THE FORTY-EIGHT STATES

The conversion of an additional 38 million acres of rural land to urban uses from 1950 to 1987 (Table 7.1) reflected the expansion of the national economy in this period, especially in land-intensive activities such as manufacturing, financial services, and others in which so-called "agglomeration economies" resulting from proximity of buyers and sellers, providers and clients, are significant (Fischel 1991; Mills, Chapter 6). By providing space to accommodate the increase in these activities, the conversion of rural land contributed markedly to the country's economic growth and in the process provided residential space for the rapidly increasing urban population.

Table 7.2 shows the urban-rural distribution of the population of the forty-eight states in 1950 and 1990 and the intensity of occupation of rural and urban space measured by population per square mile. The increasing share of urban areas in the distribution of the total population and the corresponding decline in the rural area share are widely known. The only "surprise" here to the lay reader may be the fact that the current 75 percent share of urban areas was almost all accomplished by 1970.

Not so well known, and therefore of greater interest, may be the fact that the entire decline of the rural area share of the national population was attributable to the decline in the farm population. Notice in Table 7.2 that the farm population decline was not just relative to total population. The number of people resident on farms declined from 15.2 million in 1950 to 4.6 million in 1990.[4] The magnitude of the revolution that transformed American agriculture after 1950 is suggested by the fact that from 1949–1951 to 1988–1990 the number of labor hours devoted to farm work declined 72 percent (USDA 1992).

The forces leading to the massive emigration of people from agriculture after 1950 are complex, and a detailed examination is inappropriate here. Briefly put, however, most economists probably would agree that although the knowledge revolution was the proximate "cause" of the emigration, a more fundamental factor was the rising opportunity cost of labor in agriculture in post–World War II America. There is a consensus among agricultural economists that in the United States these opportunity costs are set in nonagricultural employments (see, e.g., Johnson n.d.). In the postwar period the nonagricultural economy was expanding rapidly and associated wages were rising, forcing up thereby the opportunity costs of farm labor and encouraging the development of the farm technologies and management practices that produced the labor-substituting characteristics of the knowledge revolution.[5]

The emigration of people from agriculture thus reflected both "push" factors—the labor-substituting effects of the knowledge revolution—and "pull" factors—the attractiveness of high and rising wages in the nonfarm sector. The power of these twin factors is evident in the farm population figures in Table 7.2.

Where did the more than 10 million people who left farming after 1950 go? As far as I know there are no studies that address this question in any detail. Clearly, however, many of the farm people must have gone to urban areas. Table 7.2 suggests, however, that some, perhaps many, of them stayed with their families in nonfarm rural areas. The table indicates that the non-

Table 7.2. Population and population density, 1950, 1970, 1990

	1950		1970		1990	
Population	Number (in millions) and percentage					
Total	151.3	100.0	203.2	100.0	248.7	100.0
Urban	96.8	64.0	149.6	73.6	187.0	75.2
Rural	54.5	36.0	53.6	26.4	61.7	24.8
Farm	23.0	15.2	9.7	4.8	4.6	1.8
Nonfarm	31.5	20.8	43.9	21.6	57.1	23.0
Density	Population per square mile					
Total	50.9		68.6		84.0	
Urban	3,385.8		3,088.5		2,140.7	
Rural	18.5		18.4		21.5	
Farm	12.7		5.9		3.1	
Nonfarm	27.8		34.9		41.6	

Sources: 1950 and 1970 population from U.S. Department of Agriculture and U.S. Department of Commerce (1992, 2–3). Data include Alaska and Hawaii, the total of which were 600,000 in 1950 and 1,078,000 in 1970. 1990 population data from U.S. Bureau of the Census (1992a).

Total land area and farm area are from the sources indicated in Table 7.1. Urban area is from U.S. Department of Agriculture (1990) and is for the years 1949, 1969, and 1987. In this source are urban area data comparable over time. To calculate density, the population figures in each category were divided by the corresponding land figures in Table 7.1, converted to square miles. 640 acres = 1 mile, creating a certain distortion in the density figures because the population figures are not for exactly the same years as the land figures. However, the land figures change slowly enough from year to year to make the distortion slight.

farm rural population increased almost 26 million—81 percent—from 1950 to 1990 and that the share of this segment of the population in total population increased slightly. Students of urban and rural population trends have dwelt heavily on the "rural turnaround" of the 1970s, that is, the faster percentage growth of rural than of urban populations in that decade. On a net basis, however, the "turnaround" involved not farm people but nonfarm rural people. Note in Table 7.2 that from 1970 to 1990 the increase in the nonfarm rural population—30 percent—exceeded the urban population increase—25 percent.

Changes in the percentage distribution of the population among urban, farm, and nonfarm areas is one way of expressing changes in the use of rural space as residence for people. Another way of expressing these changes is in terms of the density of population, that is, the number of people per unit of land in urban, farm, and rural nonfarm uses. The bottom part of Table 7.2 shows these changes in population density. Density across the country as a whole of course increased from 1950 to 1990 because population grew while the land area of the country remained virtually unchanged. The more interesting aspects of density are the marked decline of 37 percent in urban density and the 50 percent increase in rural nonfarm density.

The decline in urban density must reflect the suburbanization of urban living that occurred after World War II. Affluence, low interest rates (until the 1970s), the automobile, an improving system of urban streets and roads, and government policies favoring individual home ownership all promoted the movement of people to the suburbs. Beginning in the 1960s deteriorating social conditions in central cities seem to have had a similar effect. Whatever the causes, the urban population of the country was substantially more dispersed in 1990 than in 1950, with the greater part of the dispersion occurring after 1970.

As noted, the population density of the rural nonfarm area increased 50 percent from 1950 to 1990. This increase in density is particularly notable because it occurred even though the amount of rural nonfarm land rose 21 percent in that period (Table 7.1). The "rural turnaround" of the 1970s no doubt in part explains the rising density of rural nonfarm settlement. More generally, the increase in density may reflect some "spillover" effect of the same forces that led to the diminishing density of urban areas. That is, the increasing density of rural nonfarm areas may be, at least in part, an extension into those areas of the same processes that led to the greater suburbanization of urban areas. In this connection Dahmann and Dacquel (1992, 3) assert that "it appears certain that rural area population growth during the 1980s was linked to metropolitan settlements rather than the more dispersed nonmetropolitan forms of settlement."

RURAL SPACE AS RESIDENCE FOR PEOPLE: USDA REGIONS

This discussion of the use of rural space as residence has dealt thus far with changes in residential uses of land between rural and urban areas and between farm and nonfarm rural areas for the forty-eight states as a whole. These aggregate data conceal substantial differences among regions with respect to the residential uses of the land. Table 7.3 presents data showing the 1950 and 1990 distributions of urban and rural land and population among the ten producing regions designated by the USDA. Several features of the table stand out:

Table 7.3. Regional distribution of rural and urban land and population, forty-eight states, 1950–1990

		1950 Urban		1950 Rural			1990 Urban		1990 Rural	
	Total	No.	%	No.	%	Total	No.	%	No.	%
Land: (in thousands of miles)										
Northeast	175.6	6.4	3.6	169.2	96.4	175.6	15.5	8.8	160.1	91.2
Lake States	191.7	2.8	1.5	188.9	98.5	191.7	6.4	3.3	185.3	96.7
Corn Belt	258.4	4.6	1.7	253.7	98.2	258.4	11.5	4.5	246.9	95.5
Northern Plains	305.4	0.8	0.3	304.6	99.7	305.4	1.8	0.6	303.6	99.4
Appalachian	194.7	2.1	1.1	192.6	98.9	194.7	8.5	4.4	186.2	95.6
Southeast	194.1	2.9	1.5	191.2	98.5	194.1	13.1	6.7	181.0	93.3
Delta	145.1	1.3	0.9	143.8	99.1	145.1	3.8	2.6	141.3	97.4
Southern Plains	332.5	2.0	0.6	330.5	99.4	338.5	10.4	3.1	322.1	96.9
Mountain	857.3	1.4	0.2	855.9	99.8	857.3	5.8	0.7	851.5	99.3
Pacific	319.8	4.2	1.3	315.6	98.7	319.8	10.6	3.3	309.2	96.7
Total	2,970.6	28.6	1.0	2,946.1	99.0	2,976.6	87.4	2.9	2,887.2	97.1
Population: (in millions)										
Northeast	42.9	34.0	79.3	8.9	20.7	56.9	45.1	79.3	11.8	20.7
Lake States	12.8	8.1	63.3	4.7	36.7	18.6	12.8	68.8	5.8	31.2
Corn Belt	27.2	18.4	67.6	8.8	32.4	35.7	26.5	74.2	9.2	25.8
Northern Plains	4.5	2.0	44.4	2.5	55.6	5.4	3.4	63.0	2.0	37.0
Appalachian	15.6	6.1	39.1	9.5	60.9	23.2	13.2	56.9	10.0	43.1
Southeast	11.4	5.5	48.2	5.9	51.8	26.9	19.4	72.1	7.5	27.9
Delta	6.8	2.7	39.7	4.1	60.3	9.1	5.3	58.2	3.8	41.8
Southern Plains	9.9	6.0	60.1	3.9	39.9	20.1	15.8	78.6	4.3	21.4
Mountain	5.1	2.8	54.9	2.3	45.1	13.7	10.9	79.6	2.8	20.4
Pacific	14.5	10.9	75.2	3.6	24.8	39.1	34.6	88.5	4.5	11.5
Total	150.7	96.5	64.0	54.2	36.0	248.7	187.0	75.2	61.7	24.8

Sources: Total land area from Bureau of the Census (1953) and for convenience of calculation assumed to be the same in 1990 as in 1950. In fact the total area declined slightly in some regions but not enough to make a difference in these calculations. Urban land is from USDA (1990) and is for 1949 and 1987 (see note to Table 7.2 indicating the slight distortion this introduces in the calculation of the population density figures). Population data for 1950 and 1990 are from Bureau of the Census (1953 and 1992, respectively), and exclude Hawaii and Alaska.
Note: Northeast is New England plus NY, PA, NJ, DE, and MD; Lake States is MI, WI, MN; Corn Belt is OH, IN, IL, IA, MO; Northern Plains is KS, NE, SD, ND; Appalachian is VA, WV, NC, KY, TN; Southeast is SC, GA, FL, AL; Delta is AR, MS, LS; Southern Plains is TX and OK; Mountain is all the states between the Northern and Southern Plains on the east and Pacific on the west; Pacific is CA, OR, and WA.

First, the urban area of the forty-eight states increased about 3 times, but the increases among the ten regions varied widely and systematically from this. In the Northeast (see the note to Table 7.3 for the states included in each of the ten regions) and across the northern tier of states through the Northern Plains, the urban area increased less than 3 times. In all the rest of the country except the Mississippi Delta and the Pacific coast, the urban area increased more than 3 times—4 times in Appalachia, 4.5 times in the Southeast, 6.2 times in the Southern Plains, and 3.5 times in the Mountain region. The urbanization process after 1950 tended to make the distribution of urban land more even among the ten regions because the increase in urban share was greatest in regions that previously had been less urban than the national average.

The second notable feature is that the Northeast was easily the most urbanized region in the country in both 1950 and 1990, the percentage of regional land in urban uses in the latter year being 8.8. Still, the land base of the region was overwhelmingly rural, as it was even more so in the other nine regions.[6]

Third, with respect to population, only in the Northeast did the percentage of the population living in urban areas fail to rise. (The percentage was already 79.3 in 1950.) Interestingly, in 1990 the urban percentage was as high in the "wide open spaces" of the Mountain States as it was in the Northeast. In the Pacific region, the urban percentage in 1990 was well above that in the Northeast.

Fourth, and finally, from 1950 to 1990 the percentages of rural population growth among the regions varied from −20 in the Northern Plains to 32.6 in the Northeast. The rural population increase for the country as a whole was 64.4 percent, most of which must have reflected natural increase. Clearly there was substantial net migration from rural areas in all ten regions. Only in the Northern Plains and the Delta, however, was there an actual decline in rural population.

Table 7.4 shows the total, urban, and rural densities of population in 1950 and 1990. By far the largest increases in total density were in the Southeast (which includes Georgia and Florida as well as South Carolina and Alabama), in the Southern Plains, Mountain States, and Pacific States. In the other six regions the density increases lagged far behind. Since total land area of the regions changed insignificantly from 1950 to 1990, the regional differences in density increases are implicit in the population numbers in Table 7.3. The numbers show that whereas in the forty-eight states total population increased 65 percent over the period, population more than doubled in the four regions with relatively high percentage increases in density.

Table 7.4. Population density by rural and urban uses, forty-eight states, 1950 and 1990

	1950			1990			% Change		
	Total	Urban	Rural	Total	Urban	Rural	Total	Urban	Rural
Northeast	244.6	5,272.4	52.9	323.7	2,900.7	73.7	32	-45	39
Lake States	66.7	2,911.5	24.7	96.8	2,011.1	31.0	45	-31	25
Corn Belt	105.1	3,987.2	34.6	138.2	2,303.2	37.3	31	-42	8
N. Plains	14.7	2,486.1	8.2	17.7	1,929.0	6.4	20	-22	-22
Appalachian	80.2	2,955.0	49.1	119.0	1,538.2	53.8	48	-4	89
Southeast	58.7	1,873.7	30.9	138.8	1,483.5	41.6	136	-21	35
Delta	46.7	2,061.9	28.3	63.0	1,414.8	26.9	35	-31	-5
S. Plains	29.9	3,014.7	12.0	60.5	1,521.4	13.6	102	-50	13
Mountain	5.4	2,056.5	2.7	15.9	1,870.5	3.3	169	-9	22
Pacific	45.3	2,553.9	11.5	122.3	3,282.9	14.5	170	29	26
Total	50.7	3,376.9	18.4	83.6	2,141.3	21.4	65	-37	16

Source: Calculated from Table 7.3.

The regional differences in increases in density caused some reduction in interregional differences in total density, because four of the six regions that lagged in density growth (Northeast, Lake States, Corn Belt, and Appalachia) had higher than average densities in 1950. The nationwide decline in urban population density noted in Table 7.2 was spread, in varying degree, across all of the ten regions except the Pacific, where urban density rose 29 percent (Table 7.4). The 16 percent increase in rural density (Table 7.4) was spread quite unevenly across eight of the ten regions, from a 22 percent decline in density in the Northern Plains to a 39 percent increase in the Northeast.

Recall from Table 7.2 that the rise in rural density was the net result of a sharp decline in density of the farm population that was more than offset by a 51 percent increase in the density of the rural nonfarm population. Table 7.5 shows these relationships for the ten USDA production regions in 1950 and 1990. Note that the slight nationwide rise in rural population density from 1950 to 1990 was the net outcome of a very sharp drop (80 percent) in on-farm density combined with a 54 percent increase in density in rural non-farm areas. The nationwide 80 percent decline in on-farm density was fairly evenly distributed across the ten regions, from 90 percent in the Mississippi Delta to 67 percent in the Lake States. In contrast, the 54 percent increase in nonfarm rural density was the net outcome of highly variable experience among the ten regions, from small declines in density in the Corn Belt and Northern Plains to an 83 percent increase in the Mountain States.

RURAL SPACE FOR PRODUCTION AND OTHER ACTIVITIES

Aside from providing area to accommodate expanding urban and rural populations, rural space is used also in an enormous range of activities to provide production and other services. The services include all those that pass through markets, such as crop and animal products and timber, as well as tourist services provided in rural areas. Nonmarketed services are included as well, such as those that wildlife provide to hunters and bird watchers and that scenic wonders such as those in Monument Valley provide to all who come to that area in the Southwest to view them. Rural space also is "used" in the sense of having value for, by all those people who attribute intrinsic value to it, who value it for its mere existence, and who worry that its existence, or some significant part of it, may be irreversibly altered by conversion from its natural state to some tangible human use.

Table 7.5. Land use in the forty-eight United States, 1950–1987

	1950		1969		1987	
	Acres (in millions)	%	Acres (in millions)	%	Acres (in millions)	%
Total	1,904	100.0	1,897	100.0	1,896	100.0
Urban	18	0.9	31	1.6	56	3.0
Rural	1,886	99.1	1,866	98.4	1,840	97.0
Farm	1,159	60.9	1,060	55.9	961	50.7
Cropland	409	35.3	384	36.2	399	41.5
Pasture[a]	620	53.5	599	56.5	492	51.2
Forestland not grazed	85	7.3	50	4.7	39	4.1
Farmsteads, lanes, ponds, etc.	45	3.9	27	2.5	31	3.2
Nonfarm rural	727	39.1	806	44.1	879	46.3
Pasture and range	399	54.9	287	35.6	296	33.7
Forestland not grazed	201	27.6	355	44.0	365	41.5
Rural transportation	23	3.2	26	3.2	25	2.8
Rural parks and wildlife areas	28	3.9	53	6.6	84	9.6
Defense and industrial	21	2.9	23	2.9	19	2.2
Other land[b]	55	7.6	62	7.7	90	10.2

Sources: Farmland in 1950 and 1969 from USDA (1960 and 1974); 1987 farmland from U.S. Bureau of the Census (1989); nonfarm rural land from USDA (1990).

Note: Numbers in parentheses are area in a specific use as a percentage of the area in one of the two major categories of use. For example, the 478 million acres of cropland in 1950 were 41.2 percent of the total farmland area that year. Cropland includes cropland used only for pasture.

[a] Includes cropland used only for pasture and grazed forestland.
[b] Includes miscellaneous special uses such as industrial and commercial sites in rural areas, cemeteries, golf courses, mining and quarry sites, marshes, swamps, sand dunes, bare rocks, deserts, tundra, and other unclassified land.

These various uses of rural space can be described by a number of aspects: the kinds of production and other activities occupying rural space and the amount of space occupied by each kind of activity; the amounts of production and other activities per unit space (to the extent that quantitative measures are available); the kinds and quantities of other resources used in combination with the space to provide the production and other services; and the characteristics of the space that condition the various uses of it.

Given space limitations, two approaches must suffice here to characterize the uses of rural space. The first approach presents data showing amounts of land in agricultural and forestry production and in rural parks and wildlife areas in 1949 or 1950 and 1987. The main focus is changes over time in these uses of the land, both at the national level and among ten USDA production regions. The second approach deals, albeit partially, with the income yielded from agricultural and nonagricultural uses of rural land.

Table 7.5 shows the amounts of farmland and rural nonfarmland in a variety of uses in 1950, 1969, and 1987. With respect to rural land use as a whole there definitely seems to have been a shift from 1950 to 1987 toward less intensive use, measuring intensity by marketed output per unit area. The only reason why the shift cannot be unequivocally affirmed is the increase in nonfarm rural land in "other" uses. As the note to Table 7.5 indicates, this category includes among other things "industrial and commercial sites in rural areas." If most of the increase in this "other" land category were in these uses, the statement about a trend toward less intensive use of rural land might need modification, for industrial and commercial activities are much more intensive uses of the land than, say farm or ungrazed forest uses.

With this caveat, the evidence for a trend toward less intensive use of rural land runs along the following lines: in four categories of rural land-use—cropping, grazing, forestry, and parks and wildlife—cropping is the most intensive use (highest value of output per acre) and parks and wildlife the least intensive. Grazing and forest uses are intermediate and generalization about their relative intensity is difficult. Land devoted to grazing dairy cows or to cow-calf operations in the Great Plains must be more intensively used than the large amount of forestland, particularly that in private, nonindustrial uses that yields little marketable output. But much forestland is intensively managed for wood product markets, and much rangeland in the Mountain States supports only a few animals per acre. In any case, it can be calculated from Table 7.5 that cropland was 21.7 percent of total rural land in both 1950 and 1987, that grazed land decreased from 54 percent to 42.8 percent, that forestland not grazed increased from 15.2 percent to 22 percent, and that rural parks and wildlife areas increased from 3.9 percent to 9.6 percent. If in general grazing is a more intensive use of the land than forestry, then these changes unequivocally were toward less intensive use of rural land. Even if forestry generally is a more intensive use than grazing, the trend toward less intensive use is evident in the numbers since the forest share of rural land did not increase as much as the grazing share declined. In this latter case, however, the trend would be much less marked.

Among the uses of farmland there was a shift toward more intensive use. This trend is indicated by the 8 percentage point increase in the share of cropland in total farmland and the declining shares of pasture and forestland not grazed.

Table 7.6 shows the distribution among the ten USDA producing regions of the various uses of rural land. The westward shift of cropland from the East Coast, which must have been under way at least since Independence, continued from 1950 to 1987. The Northeast, Southeast, and Appalachian regions, which by 1950 had only 17.2 percent of the nation's cropland, saw the share drop to 12.2 percent in 1987. Among the other seven regions the share of the nation's cropland declined only in the Southern Plains. Most of the increase in share was in the Corn Belt, Northern Plains, and Mountain States.

In 1950 over 40 percent of the nation's grazed land was in the Mountain States, with another 22.5 percent in the Northern and Southern Plains. By 1987 these three regions had 74.9 percent of the nation's grazed land, the Mountain States alone having 46.5 percent. The losses in share of grazed land were spread more or less evenly across the other 7 regions.

In 1950 the Corn Belt, Northern Plains, and Southern Plains were essentially bare of ungrazed forest land. The Northeast, Lake States, and Pacific States between them had 48.8 percent of the nation's stock of land in this use. The Southeast, Appalachia, and Delta regions jointly had 32.8 percent of this land. By 1987 the latter three regions had increased their share to 39.7 percent and the share of the Northeast, Lake States, and Pacific States had declined to 40.4 percent. These changes reflect the well-known fact that over the last forty years the forest industry in the United States has tended to shift from the northern tier of states to the southern tier.

Between 1950 and 1987 every region increased the amount of land in rural parks and wildlife areas, in percentages varying from 69 in the Northeast to 345 in the Mountain States. However, the distribution of this land across the ten regions became decidedly less even over the period. Only three regions—the Corn Belt, Southeast, and Mountain States—increased their shares of this land, and the increases in the Corn Belt and Southeast were trivial. The Mountain States, which in 1950 already had the largest share—27.4 percent—of any region in rural parks and wildlife areas substantially increased its share to 40.2 percent.

Table 7.7 provides another way of looking at changes in the regional distribution of the four kinds of rural land use. The measure here is an index of regional specialization in the four kinds of use, the index for each use being

Table 7.6. Uses of rural land by region, forty-eight states, 1949 and 1987

	1949		1987	
	Acres (in millions)	%	Acres (in millions)	%
Northeast				
Cropland	20.3	5.0	13.4	3.4
Grazed land	18.2	1.8	6.7	0.8
Forestland not grazed	55.7	19.5	67.4	16.7
Rural parks and wildlife areas	4.2	15.2	7.1	8.5
All other uses	9.9	6.9	7.2	5.0
Total	108.3	5.7	101.8	5.5
Lake States				
Cropland	40.7	10.0	40.0	10.0
Grazed land	28.0	2.7	11.3	1.4
Forestland not grazed	38.4	13.4	43.2	10.7
Rural parks and wildlife areas	2.8	10.1	8.4	10.0
All other uses	11.0	7.7	15.2	10.5
Total	120.9	6.4	118.1	6.4
Corn Belt				
Cropland	81.0	19.8	89.2	22.4
Grazed land	49.8	4.9	29.8	3.7
Forestland not grazed	11.1	3.9	22.6	5.6
Rural parks and wildlife areas	0.5	1.8	1.9	2.3
All other uses	20.0	13.9	13.9	9.6
Total	162.4	8.6	157.4	8.6
Northern Plains				
Cropland	96.0	23.5	99.6	25.0
Grazed land	84.8	8.3	78.9	9.8
Forestland not grazed	1.7	0.6	2.1	0.5
Rural parks and wildlife areas	0.7	2.5	1.8	2.1
All other uses	11.7	8.2	10.8	7.5
Total	194.9	10.3	193.2	10.5
Appalachian				
Cropland	26.2	6.4	20.7	5.2
Grazed land	39.6	3.9	20.3	2.5
Forestland not grazed	45.2	15.8	65.5	16.2
Rural parks and wildlife areas	1.5	5.4	3.8	4.5
All other uses	10.8	7.5	8.1	5.6
Total	123.3	6.5	118.4	6.4
Southeast				
Cropland	23.6	5.8	14.2	3.6
Grazed land	53.3	5.2	23.8	2.9
Forestland not grazed	32.7	11.4	63.8	15.8

(continued)

Table 7.6. *(continued)*

	1949		1987	
	Acres (in millions)	%	Acres (in millions)	%
Rural parks and wildlife areas	1.4	5.1	4.6	5.5
All other uses	11.4	7.9	8.9	6.1
Total	122.4	6.5	115.3	6.3
Delta States				
Cropland	18.4	4.5	19.9	5.0
Grazed land	48.5	4.8	27.8	3.4
Forestland not grazed	16.1	5.6	30.9	7.7
Rural parks and wildlife areas	0.8	2.9	1.7	2.0
All other uses	8.2	5.7	9.3	6.4
Total	92.0	4.9	89.6	4.9
Southern Plains				
Cropland	45.0	11.0	37.7	9.4
Grazed land	145.3	14.2	150.5	18.6
Forestland not grazed	4.9	1.7	7.1	1.8
Rural parks and wildlife areas	1.2	4.3	2.2	2.6
All other uses	15.2	10.6	7.5	5.2
Total	211.6	11.2	205.0	11.1
Mountain States				
Cropland	35.5	8.7	41.8	10.5
Grazed land	434.9	42.6	376.2	46.5
Forestland not grazed	34.8	12.2	48.8	12.1
Rural parks and wildlife areas	7.6	27.4	33.8	40.2
All other uses	35.0	24.4	43.0	29.7
Total	547.8	29.1	543.6	29.5
Pacific States				
Cropland	21.8	5.3	22.5	5.6
Grazed land	117.3	11.5	82.9	10.3
Forestland not grazed	45.6	15.9	52.4	13.0
Rural parks and wildlife areas	7.0	25.3	18.7	22.3
All other uses	10.3	7.2	20.9	14.4
Total	202.0	10.7	197.4	10.7
48 States				
Cropland	408.5	21.7	399.0	21.7
Grazed land	1,019.7	54.1	808.2	43.9
Forestland not grazed	286.2	15.2	403.8	21.9
Rural parks and wildlife areas	27.7	1.5	84.0	4.6
All other uses	143.5	7.6	144.8	7.9
Total	1,885.6	100.0	1,839.8	100.0

Source: USDA (1990)

Note: Among the regions percentages are shares of national totals, e.g., in 1949 the Pacific region had 5.3 percent of the nation's cropland

Table 7.7. Indexes of regional specialization in rural land uses, forty-eight states, 1949 and 1987

	1949	1987
Cropland		
Lake States	1.56	1.56
Cornbelt	2.30	2.60
Delta		1.02
Northern Plains	2.28	2.38
% cropland	53.30	57.40
Grazed land		
Southern Plains	1.27	1.68
Mountain	1.46	1.58
Pacific	1.07	
% grazed land	56.80	65.10
Forestland not grazed		
Northeast	3.42	3.04
Lake States	2.09	1.67
Appalachian	2.43	2.53
Southeast	1.75	2.51
Delta	1.14	1.57
Pacific	1.49	1.21
% forestland not grazed	81.60	80.10
Rural parks and wildlife areas		
Northeast	2.67	1.55
Lake States	1.58	1.56
Mountain		1.36
Pacific	2.36	2.08
% rural parks, etc.	50.60[a]	89.20

Source: Derived from Table 7.6.

Note: The indexes of rural specialization are found by dividing the region's share of each land use by its share of total rural land.
[a] 78.0 including mountain.

the ratio of the region's percentage share of the use to its percentage share of all rural land. A ratio greater than 1 for a use indicates that the region is specialized in that use. The greater the ratio in excess of 1 for a use, the greater the degree of specialization in that use. Thus in 1987 the Lake States region was specialized in cropland because its share of the nation's cropland was 56 percent more than its share of all rural land. However, the Lake States was less specialized in cropland than the Cornbelt because that region's share of all cropland was 2.6 times its share of all rural land.

Table 7.7 indicates substantial specialization among the four uses and substantial stability in specialization over time. In 1949 seven of the ten regions were specialized in only one use, and none were specialized in all four. The Lake States were specialized in three uses, as were the Pacific States, although for that region the degree of specialization in grazed land was slight (a ratio of 1.07). The Northeast was specialized in two uses in 1949. By 1987 the pattern of specialization was little changed. The Delta emerged, barely, as specialized in cropland, the Pacific region was no longer specialized in grazed land, and the Mountain States shifted from unspecialized to specialized in rural parks and wildlife areas. That region thus was specialized in two uses in 1987.

The regions that were specialized in cropland and grazing land in 1949 tended to be more so in 1987 (leaving aside the Delta in cropland and the Pacific in grazed land). Of the six regions specialized in ungrazed forestland, three became more specialized from 1949 to 1987 and three became less specialized. The emergence of the Mountain States as specialized in rural parks and wildlife areas meant a decline in the degree of specialization of the other three regions specialized in this use. (Although the Mountain region had 27.4 percent of the nation's land in rural parks and wildlife areas in 1949, more than any other region, it was not specialized in this use because its share of all rural land was more than 27.4 percent. The note to Table 7.7 indicates that the share of the three regions specialized in rural parks and wildlife areas in 1949, when added to the share of the Mountain States, would give the four regions 78 percent of the nation's land in this use.)

ASPECTS OF THE MANAGEMENT OF RURAL SPACE

The changes in uses of rural land presented in the several tables reflect decisions by those with rights to or responsibilities for the management of the land. A majority of farmland—61 percent of rural land in 1950 and 52 percent in 1987—is privately owned as is much nonfarmland in forests. Significant amounts of other nonfarm rural land also is privately owned. But much rural land also is owned by public agencies. Indeed, when Alaska is included, rural land in the country is divided roughly 50–50 between the public and private sectors (Oakerson, Chapter 21). The federal government is by far the largest single landowner in the country with holdings of about 690 million acres (again, including Alaska), most of it rural. Add 165 million acres, also mostly rural, held by state and local governments and on Indian reservations, and the total of publicly held rural land is only about 100 million acres less than the 960 million acres of land in farms (Table 7.1).

Private owners of land manage land with an eye to maximizing the income they receive from it. This income includes profit the land generates over time.

Long-term erosion-induced losses of soil productivity, for example, are low, suggesting that farmers are alert to the threat of erosion to future income and take steps to hold the threat within limits consistent with maximizing long-term profit (Crosson 1986 and 1991a). Private owners of nonfarm rural land probably take comparable steps to maximize the income they receive from the land over time.

Except for farming, the amount of income generated by marketable products and services of privately owned rural land is unknown. I have, however, noted that in the late 1980s income from farming contributed only about 9 percent of the total income received by rural people for marketed goods and services (Crosson 1991b). In 1987 farmland accounted for over half of all rural land, suggesting that as far as income generation is concerned, farming is a very low intensity use of rural land relative to nonfarm uses. This suggestion has to be treated with caution, however, because of the lack of data on how much income is generated by nonfarm uses of rural land. Although roughly 90 percent of the income of people living in rural areas comes from nonfarm sources, it does not necessarily follow that those sources involve nonfarm uses of rural land. In 1989, for example, 92 percent of employed people over the age of fifteen living in rural areas were working in such nonfarm jobs as mining, construction, manufacturing, public utilities, trade, and services (LeClere and Dahmann 1990). Many of these people may have been working in nonurban communities, but many, perhaps most, must also have been commuting from their rural residences to work in urban areas. Their income, therefore, did not reflect a use of rural land.

In contrast to the profit-maximizing incentive that drives managers of privately owned rural land, the incentives to which managers of publicly owned land respond are not, and for the most part cannot be, driven by market signals. Even where there is a marketable product, as on federally owned forestland and grazing land, the agencies responsible for these lands are enjoined by law to so manage them that they generate also some measure of unmarketed environmental services.

It has long been recognized that rural land generates both marketed goods and services as well as unmarketed environmental services. And it is increasingly recognized that the public sector has a special role to play in assuring that market-driven management of the land does not so dominate land use that the supply of environmental services is socially inadequate. The public role in management of rural land seems likely to grow for two reasons. First, the American people perceive environmental values to be of increasing social importance, and they are aware, if not always capable of articulating it well, that private markets cannot always be counted on to provide these values in socially desired amounts. Second, a people concerned about environmental values must necessarily be concerned also about the management of rural land and space. Most nonhuman life is found there, most of the waters arise there, and most of the atmosphere is found above such land. The immense importance of rural land as a source of environmental values powerfully affects the management of publicly held rural land.

Public recognition of the importance of rural land in the provision of environmental values is not however the reason for the present large holdings of the federal and other governments in rural land. The size of those holdings is an institutional artifact dating from the founding of the nation when most land was publicly held and almost all of it, as today, was rural. Through much of the country's history the government has sought to convert its holdings of rural land to private hands in ways that would promote national economic development and, occasionally, equity.

The prime current example of the role of environmental values conditioning management of publicly held rural land is the pressure from the environmental community on the U.S. Forest Service to manage its holdings of old-growth forest in the Pacific Northwest to protect the habitat of the Northern Spotted Owl. More generally, the threefold increase in land in rural parks and wildlife areas from 1950 to 1987 (Table 7.6) must have been the policy response of governments, principally the federal government, to the increasing appreciation of the American people for the environmental values (here including recreational values) of land in these uses. The government's ability to protect and enhance the environmental values of rural land where the land is owned by government is reasonably strong, although certainly not absolute. Nonetheless, the institutional conditions for expressing the public interest in the environmental values of rural land are more favorable on publicly owned than on private land.

The institutional problem of assuring that the management of rural land, public and private, finds a proper balance between the provision of market and environmental values is likely to get more difficult. The demand for environmental services rises at least in proportion to per capita income, and perhaps more. Certainly the experience of the United States and other affluent countries since the end of World War II is consistent with this assessment, although the underlying connection between rising per capita income and rising demand for environmental services is still not well understood. Indeed, for people like Thoreau, Berry, and Jackson, there likely is no connection between income and the reverence they feel for the nonpecuniary values of the land. For most people, however, it may be that as the more pressing needs for food, shelter, and other basic conditions of life are met, demands for the less material values of life begin to surface. The dictum that man does not live by bread alone may be a sufficient explanation for the observed relationship between per capita income and demand for environmental services.

In any event, should per capita income in the United States continue to rise over the next several decades—and most economists seem to think that it will—the demand for environmental services of rural land can be expected to rise also. It is questionable whether the country's institutions engaged in managing rural land can generate increases in the supply of environmental services on a sufficient scale. The fact that environmental services for the most part are not traded in markets suggests that managers of privately owned land will at best respond sluggishly to the rising demand for services. Finding ways to induce greater responsiveness from private landowners likely will increasingly challenge the imagination and political skills of the policy-makers responsible for enhancing the environmental values of rural land.

The challenge to those with responsibility for the public lands will be different but perhaps no less imposing. The absence of price signals reflecting increasing demand for the land's environmental services makes it difficult to judge the strength of the demand relative to the demand for the marketed services of the land. And the system of incentives that motivates managers in public agencies is more complex, or at least less well understood, than in private markets where the drive to maximize profit is dominant and the conditions for achieving it are reasonably clear.

A major, although not the only, institutional problem in enhancing the supply of environmental values of rural land is competition for the land to produce marketed products. These products are overwhelmingly agricultural. The stiffer this competition, the greater the pressure on land management institutions to satisfactorily supply both marketed and environmental services of the land. It follows that continued development of agricultural technologies that increase output per unit of land would ease the competition for land between agriculture and environmental values. Continued support for research to develop yield-increasing agricultural technologies may, therefore, contribute significantly to solving the institutional problem of meeting future demands for environmental services of rural land. The yield-increasing approach would apply almost entirely to privately owned land, but, as previously indicated, this land presents the most difficult institutional problem. Without ignoring the problems of environmental management on public lands, those policymakers most concerned with the overarching issue of enhancing the environmental values of rural land might best serve that end by pressing for sustained development of higher-yielding agricultural technologies.

NOTES

1. The chapter excludes Alaska and Hawaii because they are so far away from the other forty-eight states. Alaska is excluded also because it is so large relative to the rest of the country and its patterns of land use so atypical.

2. See, e.g., Thoreau (1960); Jackson (1991); Berry (1981).

3. For an account of the knowledge revolution in American agriculture and its impact on use of farmland, see Crosson (1991a).

4. The 4.6 million figure for 1990 somewhat overstates the decline in farm population from 1950 because in the interim the definition of a farm was changed and eliminated from the statistics some operations previously counted as farms. In 1980, the last year for which comparisons of the old and new definitions can be made, the farm population was 7.2 million under the old definition and 6.1 million under the new one (Dahmann and Dacquel 1992, p. 1).

5. For a detailed analysis of the forces shaping the demand for farm labor (and land) in American (and Japanese) history from the nineteenth century to the late twentieth century, see Hayami and Ruttan (1985).

6. For an account of changing patterns of rural and urban land-use in the Northeast, see Lewis (1991).

8
EXTRACTIVE INDUSTRIES AND RURAL-URBAN ECONOMIC INTERDEPENDENCE

BRUCE A. WEBER

Extractive industries (agriculture, forestry, energy extraction, and mining) are not, as is sometimes supposed, a homogeneous set of declining industries that are economically important only in rural America. In fact, these industries and the immediate processing activities that depend on them are diverse in terms of growth and economic stability and are geographically dispersed; they respond in different ways to international and domestic economic market forces and public policies, as well as to technical change; collectively, they are an important economic base of rural America, providing 20 percent of the income in nonmetropolitan counties; and, finally, they provide more jobs and income in metropolitan counties than in nonmetro counties, though representing a smaller share (5 percent) of metropolitan county incomes.

The economic performance of the counties that depend on extractive industries for their economic base naturally tends to reflect the conditions in those industries. Extractive-industry conditions also affect urban centers, however, particularly the service industries in such counties, because of the large presence of extractive industries in metro counties and because of economic linkages between rural extractive-industry counties and their metropolitan service centers.

Extractive industries have been the economic mainstay of rural economies, historically providing work and income for most rural people and using (even today) the vast majority of rural land. The historical and current economic importance of these industries suggests that an understanding of life and work in today's American countryside must be based in an appreciation for the economic dynamics of the extractive industries.

155

This chapter, therefore, provides an economic profile of the economic contribution of U.S. extractive industries in rural and urban America, reviews the major forces affecting these industries, and explains how these factors may have affected extractive-industry growth and stability during the past two decades.

EXTRACTIVE INDUSTRIES IN RURAL AND URBAN AMERICA[1]

The four industries generally regarded as extractive industries are agriculture, forestry and wood products, energy extraction, and nonenergy mining. Extractive industries are defined in this paper using the Standard Industrial Code (SIC) classifications:

- Energy includes anthracite coal mining (SIC 11), bituminous coal mining (SIC 12), and oil and gas extraction (SIC 13).
- Mining includes mining of ores of metals such as iron, copper, gold, silver, and molybdenum (SIC 10) and the production of nonmetallic minerals (excluding fuels), such as stone, sand and gravel, clays, phosphate rocks, and sulfur (SIC 14).
- Forestry and wood products include forestry (SIC 08), lumber and wood products (SIC24), furniture and fixtures (SIC 25), and pulp and paper (SIC 26).
- Agriculture includes farm proprietors and labor, food processing (SIC 20), and agricultural services (SIC 07).

The industry categories are defined to include extractive activity, direct services to primary producers, and processing done in the vicinity of primary production. Elo and Beale have pointed out, however, that these categories "include certain amounts of furniture production that are not closely linked to local timber production, or of food processing, such as bakery goods, that are more closely tied to location of people than raw material. On the other hand, the categories exclude mineral smelting and refining, some of which is done near production sites and is directly dependent on continued local mining activity" (1983).

Economic Contribution

Extractive industries contributed about 7 percent of U.S. real labor and proprietor income on average over the 1969–1991 period. Over one-half (55

Table 8.1. Real earnings in U.S. extractive industries, 1969–1991 annual average

Industry	United States		Metro		Nonmetro	
	Million dollars	Percent of total	Million dollars	Percent of total	Million dollars	Percent of total
Agriculture	96,653	4.09	58,718	2.92	37,936	10.73
Farm income	44,598	1.89	17,512	0.87	27,087	7.70
Services	10,049	0.43	7,649	0.38	2,400	0.68
Food and kindred products	42,006	1.78	33,557	1.67	8,449	2.39
Forestry and wood products	47,384	2.01	30,587	1.52	16,797	4.75
Forestry	513	0.02	208	0.01	305	0.09
Paper and allied products	20,938	0.89	15,464	0.77	5,474	1.55
Lumber and wood	16,302	0.69	7,702	0.38	8,600	2.43
Furniture and fixtures	9,631	0.41	7,213	0.36	2,418	0.68
Energy	26,735	1.13	15,308	0.76	11,428	3.23
Coal mining	8,817	0.37	2,212	0.11	6,606	1.87
Oil and gas extraction	17,918	0.76	13,096	0.65	4,822	1.36
Mining	6,412	0.27	3,460	0.17	2,952	0.83
Metal	2,986	0.13	1,466	0.07	1,520	0.43
Nonmetallic, except fuels	3,426	0.15	1,994	0.10	1,432	0.40
Total extractive industries	177,184	7.49	108,073	5.37	69,113	19.54
Total all industries	2,361,414	100.00	2,007,760	100.00	353,654	100.00

Source: U.S. Department of Commerce, Bureau of Economic Analysis Response Economic Information System. "Personal Income by Major Source and Earnings by Industry," Table CA5, 1993; Implicit Price Deflators from *Economic Report of the President,* February 1992, Table B-3.

Note: Values expressed in 1987 dollars. Totals may not add up exactly because of rounding.

percent) of this labor and income was in agriculture (Table 8.1). Extractive industries provided 20 percent of earnings in nonmetro counties during this period, with the same proportion (54 percent) contributed by the agricultural industry.

Metropolitan counties actually derived more earnings from extractive industries than nonmetro counties, even though these industries accounted for only 5 percent of total earnings. Metropolitan counties contain most of the food processing, agricultural services, furniture and fixtures, paper and allied products, and oil and gas extraction activity. Those sectors requiring large amounts of relatively inexpensive land for production (agricultural production, forestry) are located primarily in nonmetro counties, as are activities that use these commodities as inputs and that lose weight in processing, such as lumber and plywood milling. Most of the lumber and wood processing (logging, lumber, and plywood mills) and farm income is earned in nonmetro areas. Energy extraction and metal mining, however, establish themselves at the resource sites. For metal mining and coal mining, these are primarily nonmetro areas. The metro orientation of oil and gas extraction may reflect in part the location of oil offshore of major metropolitan centers on the Gulf of Mexico and in southern California.

The location of other extractive industries in metro areas may reflect the need for proximity to markets or the importance of agglomeration economies. Nonmetallic minerals production (largely stone, sand, and gravel used in construction) is an example of the importance of proximity due to transport costs of a low value product. Agricultural services may be an example of an industry locating in metropolitan areas because of agglomeration or scale economy factors. The preference of food and kindred products, furniture and fixtures, and paper products industries for metro areas may reflect both factors.

Growth and Stability

Global market forces; domestic economic, resource, and environmental policy; and technical change interact variously in different natural resource industries to determine their growth and stability. This interaction can be illustrated by examining the economic performance of these industries during the 1970s and 1980s. These decades saw first a rapid growth and then a decline in mining and energy extraction, stagnation in agriculture, and slow growth in the forest industries. All of these extractive industries, except for food processing and paper and allied products components, which are closest to the final consumer, showed considerable instability in income relative to the national economy. Table 8.2 reports growth (compounded annual growth rate) and the stability (standard deviation of the mean annual growth rate) of each industry for the 1969–1991 period.

The energy industry as a whole is the most unstable of the four extractive industries. Energy extraction experienced tremendous growth during the 1970s. Oil prices increased in the 1970s in response to attempts by the Organization of Petroleum Exporting Countries (OPEC) to control oil supplies. The high oil prices stimulated U.S. oil and gas extraction in the 1970s and induced firms and households to conserve energy and invest in energy-

Table 8.2. Growth and stability in real earnings of U.S. extractive industries, 1969–1991

	Growth[a] Compounded growth rate (%)			Stability[b] Standard deviation of the growth rate		
	United States	Metro	Non-metro	United States	Metro	Non-metro
Agriculture	−1.041	−0.199	−2.313	10.49	4.58	21.93
Farm income	−2.970	−1.817	−3.727	26.89	15.04	40.92
Services	3.260	3.900	1.330	7.37	6.65	10.00
Food and kindred products	−0.005	−0.289	1.140	1.58	1.47	2.36
Forestry and wood products	1.113	0.921	1.472	5.29	4.90	6.32
Forestry	1.020	1.697	0.557	30.60	20.68	41.25
Paper and allied products	1.120	0.804	2.013	3.30	3.30	3.42
Lumber and wood	1.400	1.603	1.222	8.51	8.45	8.69
Furniture and fixtures	0.670	0.468	1.284	7.41	7.27	8.22
Energy	2.455	2.925	1.847	13.78	15.94	11.87
Coal mining	1.340	0.117	1.728	13.20	17.31	12.12
Oil and gas extraction	3.030	3.405	2.014	16.75	17.55	23.80
Mining	−0.084	0.109	−0.330	6.24	6.78	6.78
Metal	−0.880	−0.159	−1.590	10.57	13.16	10.14
Nonmetals, except fuels	0.520	0.243	0.927	4.31	4.83	4.57
Total extractive industries	0.005	0.491	−0.736	6.56	3.87	11.79
Total all industries	2.161	2.313	1.295	2.59	2.48	3.84

Source: U.S. Department of Commerce, Bureau of Economic Analysis Response Economic Information System. "Personal Income by Major Source and Earnings by Industry," Table CA5, May 1993; Implicit Price Deflators from *Economic Report of the President*, February 1992, Table B-3.

[a] The compounded annual growth rate is the regression coefficient from a simple regression of the log of real earnings against the year for the 1969–1991 period.
[b] Standard deviation of the mean annual growth rates of real earnings for the 1969–1991 period. A growth rate computed for each year is the basis of this calculation.

saving equipment. A slackening of aggregate demand in the early 1980s and the reduced demand for energy resulting from conservation measures combined with OPEC's inability to control supply and led to a precipitous decline in oil prices in the early 1980s. Energy projects conceived during the period of high prices were abandoned and oil and gas and coal production and income declined sharply. These declines stabilized in the late 1980s. Notwithstanding the declines, however, oil and gas extraction remains the extractive sector that shows the most income growth over the 1969–1991 period, an annual income growth of 3.03 percent per year. Coal mining, despite an almost uninterrupted decline in real income since 1980, shows a 1.34 percent annual increase in real income over the same period.

Overall, the mining sectors displayed little economic vitality during the 1969–1991 period, with a trended average income growth of –.08 percent. Increases in income in the 1970s and declines in the 1980s for metal mining (iron ore, copper, lead, gold, silver, uranium, molybdenum) were responses to international competition and commodity price fluctuations. The stability of metal mining was also affected by domestic policy decisions, such as environmental restrictions on mining, pollution-control regulation affecting the use of lead in gasoline and platinum in gasoline engines, embargoes on imports from certain countries, and targets for stockpiles of strategically important metals.

The forestry and wood products sector experienced modest growth in income over the 1969–1991 period, averaging around 1 percent per year. This average masks the impressive growth in the 1970s (fueled by low interest rates and strong demand for housing as the baby boomers entered adulthood) followed by a precipitous crash in the early 1980s caused, in part, by increases in interest rates. The late 1980s saw a sharp increase in production and income as interest rates eased and consumers adjusted expectations on housing costs. Technical advances and capital investment allowed the Oregon wood products industry, for example, to maintain output and decrease employment.

Instability in lumber and wood products is primarily a function of shifts in demand caused by changes in the interest rate and by fluctuations in the exchange rate. The instability of lumber and wood products is also, however, partly a function of domestic supply shifts generated by forest policy and environmental restrictions on production and harvesting practices. Laws designed to protect endangered species and recognize the value of nonmarket assets on public lands have removed much publicly owned timber from harvest. The desire to reserve some forests for wilderness recreation has further decreased the timber base. State regulation of forest practices has also increased with the objective of enhancing the value of nonmarket goods produced by the forest ecosystem. To the extent that pesticide spray restrictions cause an outbreak of insect or disease infestation, as happened several years ago with the southern pine beetle, the need to harvest infested timber quickly may cause large increases in timber supply. Perhaps more important, to the extent that such policy contributes to an atmosphere of uncertainty in the business climate, the scheduling of the timber harvest may be affected.

Agriculture saw a decline in real income during the 1969–1991 period, a combination of significantly reduced farm income and no growth in food and kindred products. The small agricultural service sector experienced a rapid growth in income, probably reflecting the increased subcontracting of work (fertilizing, harvesting, marketing, accounting) previously done on the farm. Reduced farm income reflects, in part, the nearly century-old decline in the number of commercial farms. Domestic policy has affected the supply of land in agriculture. The Conservation Reserve Program has taken 36.5 million acres of highly erodible or environmentally sensitive land (8 percent of U.S. cropland) out of production (Heimlich and Osborne 1993) and endangered species protection is also expected to affect the amount of land available for irrigation in the Pacific Northwest.

The instability of farm incomes is a function of the price-taking nature of agricultural production. Income depends on highly variable prices often determined in world markets. When demand declines, the more competitive industries, like farming, which are dominated by small proprietorships, tend to maintain output. The result is lower commodity prices and reduced income for the proprietors of these small businesses. By contrast, industries dominated by larger firms, like energy, mining, and much of forestry and wood products, respond to a decline in demand or a curtailment of supply by reducing output, which leads to unemployment or decreases in wages or both. Farmers who remain in farming are often able to withstand the highly variable annual income stress because their households depend also on off-farm income, which is much more stable. Indeed, farm households overall get only 13 percent of their household income from farming. About 80 percent of farm households received more income off the farm than on the farm. This figure includes a large number of farms in which the major occupation of the farm operator is not farming. However, even large farms (those farms with gross farm sales exceeding $250,000) depend significantly on off-farm income, which represents 21 percent of household income. For one-third of these larger operations, off-farm income exceeds farm income (Ahearn, Perry, and El-Osta 1993).

Table 8.3. Extractive-industry dependent counties, selected years

County Type	1969	1979	1984	1989
Energy	70	172	162	78
Mining	39	39	33	30
Forestry	167	165	167	128
Agriculture	504	1,003	759	803
All extractive industries	780	1,379	1,211[a]	1,039
Total U.S. counties	3,106	3,106	3,106	3,106

Source: U.S. Department of Agriculture, Economic Research Service. Special analysis conducted with unpublished Bureau of Economic Analysis data.

[a] There were actually 1,185 counties that were dependent on extractive industries, for the categories are not mutually exclusive. Twenty-six counties were dependent on both agriculture and one of the other extractive industries. Ten of 15 agriculture energy counties were in Texas, one-half of the 10 agriculture-forestry/wood products counties were in Georgia. One Nevada county was dependent on both agriculture and mining.

EXTRACTIVE INDUSTRIES AND THE LOCAL ECONOMY

Extractive industries are generally slow-growing or declining and economically unstable. In this chapter, a county is considered dependent on an extractive industry (agriculture, for example) if that industry contributed 20 percent or more of labor and proprietor income in 1984. The identity of counties included in this category changes dramatically over time, as might be anticipated given the volatility in the industries. Table 8.3 shows the number of counties that depended on each of the extractive industries for 1969, 1979, 1984, and 1989. Between 1969 and 1979 the number of dependent counties almost doubled because of increases in agriculture and energy counties. Between 1979 and 1984 the number of agriculture counties decreased 25 percent. And between 1984 and 1989 there were significant decreases in the number of energy and forestry counties. Agriculture counties are likely moving in and out of the agriculture-dependent category without a fundamental change in economic structure, whereas changes in energy and forestry counties are more likely to signal real changes in economic structure. I chose to analyze the 1984 set of extractive-industry counties because it best represents the counties that were structurally dependent on the various extractive industries during the early 1980s.

Extractive-Industry Dependent Counties

In 1984 over one-third (36 percent) of U.S. counties depended on extractive industries. The location of the counties that depend on these industries re-

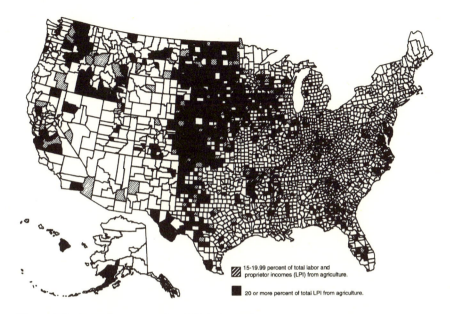

Figure 8.1. Agriculture counties, 1984. Agriculture includes farm labor and proprietor income, food processing, and agricultural services. (Prepared by Economic Research Service, USDA)

flects the geographic distribution of the resources (Figures 8.1–8.4). Forestry counties are concentrated in the Pacific Northwest, the extreme Northeast, the upper Midwest, and parts of the Southeast. Agricultural counties are found in the central part of the country, California's Central Valley, irrigated areas in the Snake and Columbia Basins of the Pacific Northwest, the Ozarks, and parts of the Atlantic coastal plains. Counties that depend on mining are found in the upper Midwest (iron ore), Rocky Mountains (copper, lead, silver, uranium, and molybdenum), Nevada (gold, tungsten), Missouri (lead), and the Southwest (copper, molybdenum). Most counties dependent on energy extraction are in the coal- and natural gas-producing areas of the Rocky Mountains, the oil-producing areas of Texas, Oklahoma, and the Gulf Coast, and the coal fields of southern Illinois, eastern Kentucky, and the Appalachian Mountains. Although many extractive industries are concentrated in regions where the particular resources are abundant, there is almost no state or region without counties dependent on agriculture or one of the other extractive industries. Southern New England, with its diverse economy, is the only exception to this generalization.

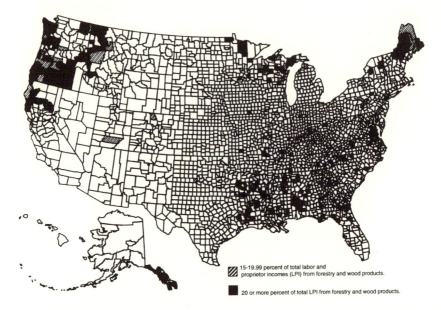

Figure 8.2. Forestry and wood products counties, 1984. Forestry includes lumber, wood, furniture, fixtures, pulp, and paper. (Prepared by Economic Research Service, USDA)

Performance of Extractive-Industry Dependent Counties in the 1980s

Regional economics suggests that the economic performance of a small regional economy is influenced by local supply factors (such as local availability and prices of lumber, capital, and natural resources) and demand for locally produced goods and services, as well as by the location of the region in relation to its major markets.

In a region specialized in extractive-industry production, market conditions (particularly external demand and prices) for the major commodity might be expected to explain much of the region's economic performance. Changes in population, median income, and poverty for the extractive-industry dependent counties during the 1980s may generally reveal the extent to which these changes tracked the changes in real income in the extractive industries.

Counties dependent on extractive industries have smaller populations, lower household incomes, and higher poverty rates than the average U.S. county (Table 8.4). During the 1980s, they also grew more slowly in both population and income than the U.S., reflecting slower overall real growth in

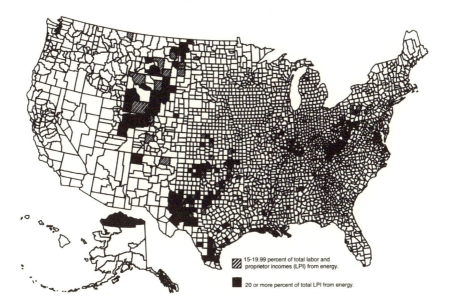

Figure 8.3. Energy counties, 1984. Energy includes coal mining and oil and gas extraction. (Prepared by Economic Research Service, USDA)

the extractive industries. Energy counties fared the worst during the decade, reflecting conditions in an industry in which real earnings declined by 38 percent between 1979 and 1989. Average population declined in these counties, particularly in the Midwest; median household income declined, particularly in the West and Northeast, and poverty rates increased. In the other types of extractive-industry dependent counties, however, populations and incomes grew, albeit more slowly than in the United States as a whole. Although real earnings in mining declined by 22 percent in the 1979–1989 period, population increased 6 percent and median household income increased 0.5 percent in mining-dependent counties. This increase suggests that these counties, many of which are small, isolated, and situated in the mountainous western states, were able to diversify their economic activities.

Real earnings in agriculture, although facing a long-term decline over many decades, grew 0.6 percent in the decade from 1979 to 1989. Population and median household incomes grew slightly in counties dependent on agriculture. These averages mask significant regional variations however. Population declined 7.6 percent and median income grew by only 2.7 percent in the midwestern agriculture-dependent counties, suggesting that farm consolidation allowed surviving farms to earn somewhat larger incomes.

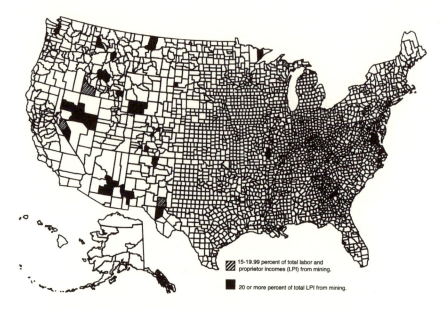

Figure 8.4. Mining counties, 1984. Mining includes metal and nonmetal mining, except fuels. (Prepared by Economic Research Service, USDA)

Western agriculture-dependent counties grew 17.8 percent in population and 3.8 percent in real median household income. Much of the agricultural growth in the West is dependent on the use of low-wage labor, consistent with the large population growth and slower than average income growth.

Real earnings in the forestry industry grew 6.5 percent over the decade and both population and median household income grew in forestry-dependent counties. Again, there are significant regional variations in the growth of population and income. In the western forest-dependent counties, real median household income declined by 1.7 percent, poverty increased by 1.8 percentage points, and population grew 5.8 percent. These trends probably reflect the decline in wood products employment and real earnings in the industry and the immigration of retirees into many of these counties. Meanwhile, southern forest-dependent counties experienced real median household income growth of 8.3 percent, a decline in poverty of .3 percentage points, and population growth of only 2.0 percent. This pattern suggests a real increase in the well-being of county residents engaged in the forest industry.

Market conditions for the major commodity produced in a county depen-

Table 8.4. Population, income growth, and poverty change in extractive-industry dependent counties during the 1980s

County Type	Counties[a] 1984	Average County Population and % Change		Average Median Household Income and % Change		Poverty and % Point Change	
		1990	1980– 1990	1989	1979– 1989[b]	1989	1979– 1989
Energy	162	22,308	−2.5	$21,663	−8.3	20.7	+4.4
Mining	33	13,882	+6.0	23,728	+0.5	16.6	−1.4
Forestry	167	26,794	+4.0	22,521	+4.4	17.4	+0.5
Agriculture	759	14,909	+2.2	21,608	+4.5	17.5	−0.1
Total U.S. counties	3,106	80,074	+9.8	30,056	+12.5	13.1	+0.7

Source: U.S. Bureau of the Census, U.S. Department of Commerce, Census of Population and Housing, 1980 and 1990.

[a] Number of counties that derived 20 percent or more of income from the indicated industry in 1984.
[b] Adjusted for inflation.

dent on extractive industry should be an important factor in economic performance. In the 1980s, however, the growth of a particular county economy may have depended as much on its proximity to metropolitan areas and on its natural and cultural amenities as on the market situation of its primary commodity (see Drabenstott and Smith, Chapter 9).

ECONOMIC INTERDEPENDENCE OF EXTRACTIVE-INDUSTRY DEPENDENT RURAL HINTERLANDS AND URBAN CENTERS

Rural areas are part of an urban-rural system in which urban centers are both markets for rural products and sources of inputs that thrive mainly in large cities. It is often useful to think of rural areas as a hinterland of an urban center, as a periphery of an urban core. This perspective encourages a focus on the economic interdependence of rural and urban parts of the system. In this chapter, more specifically, it encourages a recognition of the role of urban centers not just as significant contributors to extractive-industry production and processing (recall Table 8.1), but also as suppliers of goods and services and of labor, capital, and technical knowledge to rural industry. Through

Table 8.5. Core-periphery trade flows in the Portland, Oregon, trade area, 1982 (billions of $)

	Portland Metro	Trade Area Periphery	Rest of the World	Total Industrial Output
Portland Metro	19.6	2.4	9.4	31.4
Trade Area Periphery	1.0	20.0	11.5	32.6
Rest of the World	11.3	13.4		
Gross Regional Demand	32.0	35.9		

Source: Waters, Edward C., David Holland, and Bruce A. Weber. "Interregional Effects of Reduced Timber Harvests: The Impact of the Northern Spotted Owl Listing in Rural and Urban Oregon." *Journal of Agricultural Resource Economics* 19 (July 1994): 141–160.

trade and movement of capital and labor among regions, urban economic development may be affected by the performance of extractive industry in its rural hinterland.

Little empirical work has been done on the economic relationships between urban centers and rural hinterlands. However, one recent study by Holland, Weber, and Waters (1992) estimated 1982 trade flows between the Portland, Oregon, metropolitan area and its trade area periphery of western Oregon and southwest Washington, a region that has long depended on agriculture and wood products. Estimates from this study suggest the extent of rural-urban trade in one urban system and the impact of extractive-industry changes on both urban core and rural periphery.

Urban-Rural Interdependence: Evidence from the Pacific Northwest

The economies of the Portland metropolitan area and its hinterland are of almost equal size, $31.4 billion and $32.6 billion, respectively (Table 8.5). Each region exports over one-third of its output (37 and 38 percent). The metropolitan area, however, is more dependent on the hinterland as a market for exports than vice versa: 20 percent ($2.4 billion) of the $11.8 billion in metro exports goes to the hinterland, whereas only 8 percent ($1.0 billion) of hinterland export of $12.5 billion goes to the Portland area (Figure 8.5). (Looked at another way, the hinterland is more dependent on Portland as a source of imports than vice versa. Our discussion will emphasize the export side of the trade flows.)

The Portland metro area and its periphery are more interdependent in the agriculture-related sectors than in total trade. Portland's agricultural sector produces and exports livestock, crops, landscaping, and agricultural services. The metro region ships 21 percent ($32 million) of its agricultural exports to

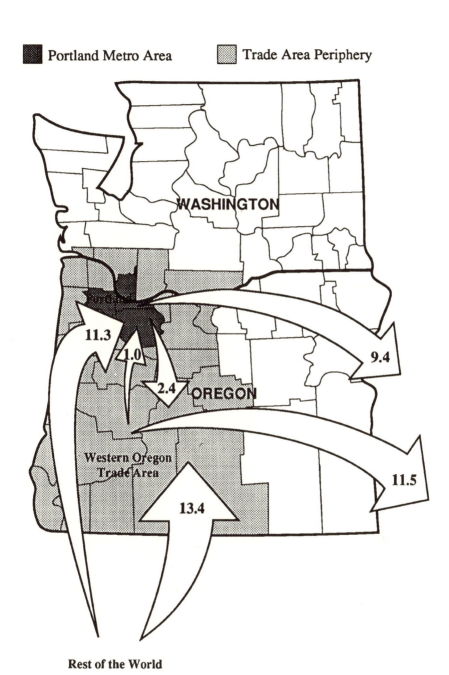

Rest of the World

Figure 8.5. Trade flows, Portland and its trade periphery, 1982 (in millions of dollars).

the rural periphery—all of this in landscaping and agricultural services (LAS) (Figure 8.6). The rural periphery ships 17 percent ($127 million) of its agricultural exports to the Portland metro economy. In food processing, Portland sends 28 percent ($170 million) of its food processing exports to the rural periphery. The rural periphery sends 9 percent ($50 million) of its food processing exports to Portland (Figure 8.7).

In forestry and wood products (FWP), including pulp and paper processing, rural and urban Oregon are much less interdependent. Portland sends 8 percent ($129 million) of its forestry and wood products exports to the periphery. The periphery sends 2 percent of its FWP sector exports to the metro area (Figure 8.8). National and world markets absorb most FWP exports from both regions.

There are indirect links between the urban core and the regional periphery, in addition to the direct trade links. The exports of extractive-industry products to national and world markets generate income that is respent in both the urban core and the rural hinterland. A measure of this interdependence is the multipliers derived from a rural-urban multiregional input/output (MRIO) model. These multipliers estimate the impact on output in both rural and urban Oregon of a $1 change in export sales in one region. Table 8.6 contains such multipliers for the extractive industries for Portland metro and rural periphery regions.

These multipliers have three components: the own-region impact, the cross-region impact, and the feedback effect. The metro food-processing sector, for example, has a total multiplier of 1.88. Each dollar of metro food-processing exports increases total output in the combined metro and periphery economy by $1.88 (column 4), the dollar of initial sales plus $.88 of sales and household income generated by the responding of the dollar in both regions. Most ($.67) of the $.88 is generated in the metro region because of responding in the metro region out of the initial dollar. Some of the responding, however, occurs in the periphery because food processing buys crops to process and other inputs from the surrounding region and because metro households that are paid by the food-processing industry to produce the dollar of export sales also make purchases in the periphery. This responding of the $1 of export sales generates $.19 in the periphery (the cross-regional impact).

Part of the $.19 of additional sales and income in the periphery may be respent in the Portland metro area. This feedback effect in the metro region of the initial dollar of metro exports occurs because metro industries and households affected by the initial dollar of export sales made purchases in the periphery and the affected periphery industries and households in turn made purchases in the metro area. The feedback effect in the metro area of $1 of

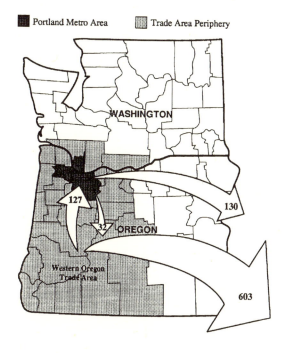

WASHINGTON

127

32 OREGON

Western Oregon
Trade Area

130

603

Figure 8.6. Trade flows in
agriculture, Portland and its
trade periphery, 1982
(in millions of dollars).
Agriculture includes
livestock, crops, landscaping,
and agricultural services.

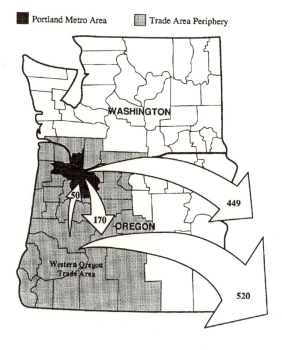

WASHINGTON

50

170 OREGON

Western Oregon
Trade Area

449

520

Figure 8.7. Trade flows in
food processing, Portland
and its trade area periphery,
1982 (in millions of
dollars).

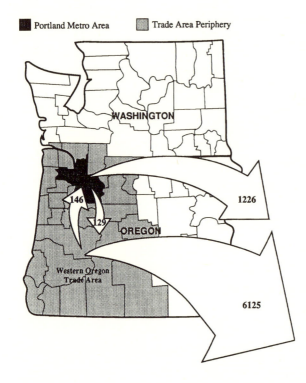

■ Portland Metro Area   ▨ Trade Area Periphery

Figure 8.8. Trade flows in forestry and wood products, Portland and its rural periphery, 1982 (in millions of dollars).

metro food-processing sales is $.02. The total impact in the metro area of $1 of metro food-processing exports is then $.69: $.67 of own-region impact and $.02 of feedback.

For the metro region, there are significant cross-regional linkages in the extractive-industry sectors. One dollar of total extractive-industry exports from the metro region generates $.15 of sales in the rural periphery. Wood products and food-processing exports from the metro region generate the most rural output per dollar ($.26 and $.19) of exports because of purchases of rural inputs by the metro firms in these sectors. Other metro sectors do not have the same rural linkages: $1 of exports in nonextractive industries generates only $.08 of rural output. (The only nonextractive metro sector with large rural linkages is utilities, which makes large purchases of rural electric power: $1 of metro utility exports generates $.21 of rural output.)

Exports from the periphery region have more impact on the metro region per $1 of exports than metro exports have on the periphery economy. This observation holds true for both extractive-industry and other sectors, because rural businesses purchase significant amounts of metro services. The

Table 8.6. Selected output multipliers for Portland, Oregon, and its rural trade area

Sector	Metro Own-region	Cross-region	Feed-back	Total	Periphery Own-region	Cross-region	Feed-back	Total
Livestock	1.63	0.13	0.02	1.78	1.76	0.18	0.01	1.95
Crops	1.80	0.13	0.02	1.95	1.62	0.18	0.01	1.81
Forestry Products and Logging	1.76	0.18	0.02	1.96	1.83	0.14	0.01	1.98
Landscaping and Agricultural Services	1.74	0.11	0.01	1.86	1.59	0.18	0.01	1.78
Mining	1.57	0.08	0.01	1.66	1.47	0.14	0.01	1.62
Food Processing	1.67	0.19	0.02	1.88	1.78	0.25	0.01	2.03
Wood Products	2.09	0.26	0.03	2.38	2.16	0.21	0.01	2.39
Pulp and Paper Products	1.68	0.13	0.01	1.81	1.65	0.19	0.01	1.85
Extractive Industries	1.75	0.15	[a]	1.90	1.74	0.18	[a]	1.93
Nonextractive Industries	1.64	0.08	[a]	1.72	1.50	0.16	[a]	1.66
All Industries	1.68	0.10	[a]	1.78	1.58	0.16	[a]	1.74

Source: Waters, Edward C., David Holland, and Bruce A. Weber. "Interregional Effects of Reduced Timber Harvests: The Impact of the Northern Spotted Owl Listing in Rural and Urban Oregon." *Journal of Agricultural and Resource Economics* 19 (July 1994): 141–160.
[a] Feedback effects are included in own region multipliers.

metro impact of $1 of rural extractive sector exports is $.18; the metro impact of $1 of rural exports by other sectors is $.16.

The rural extractive sectors whose exports have the most metro impact are food processing and wood products. One dollar of rural exports generates $.25 and $.21 of metro sales, respectively. The rural nonextractive sector with the most metro impact is "eating, drinking, and lodging": one dollar of rural exports generates $.22 of metro sales.

A recent study of the impact on the economies of rural and urban Oregon of listing the Northern Spotted Owl as an endangered species provides an example of the importance of cross-regional impacts. Waters et al. (1994), using the Portland urban-rural MRIO model, found that under the most likely scenario this government policy decision could reduce timber jobs in the rural periphery by 15,661 jobs (22.5 percent) and overall jobs in the periphery by 27,217 (5.0 percent). The impact on the metro area was estimated at 4,403 jobs. From an urban perspective, this impact represented less than 1 percent of metro jobs. From the perspective of the larger urban-rural region, a significant portion (14 percent) of the regional impact of an action that directly affected only the rural periphery occurred in the urban core.

More generally, it is possible to estimate the impact of each region's extractive-industry exports on the economy of the other region. Using cross-regional multipliers from Table 8.6 and estimates of regional exports from Holland, Weber, and Waters, it is estimated that the $2.1 billion of Portland extractive-industry exports generates $356 million in the rural periphery, about 1 percent of total periphery output. Periphery extractive-industry exports have an even larger impact on the Portland economy. The $7.6 billion in extractive-industry exports from the rural periphery generates $1.46 billion in the metro economy, almost 5 percent of the output of the metro economy.

One wonders if the level of interdependence estimated from the Portland trade area is typical for cities of its size; one suspects that smaller cities in natural-resource dependent areas might show greater interdependence at any given point in time. Proximity to metropolitan areas has been observed to affect the growth of rural counties (see, for example, Drabenstott and Smith, Chapter 9), suggesting that there may be something in the economic dynamics of rural-urban interdependence not captured in the static trade relationships estimated in an input-output model.

The Dynamics of Urban-Rural Development

An issue raised by Myrdal (1957), Hirschman (1958), Kaldor (1970), and others is whether the relationship between regions such as urban core and rural periphery is ultimately beneficial to both, or whether one region's growth and another's stagnation are mutually reinforcing. Does growth in urban centers, for example, generate important beneficial "spread" effects (to use Myrdal's term) in rural areas (increased demand for rural goods and services, new technical knowledge and investment in rural areas, increased productivity and wages in rural areas)? Or does urban growth generate harmful "backwash" effects (reductions in demand for rural goods because competitive urban goods underprice rural products, rural out-migration of the most productive workers, less reinvestment in rural enterprises) that more than counteract any spread effects? The position that backwash effects have dominated spread effects in the relationship between rural hinterlands and urban centers in recent decades is supported by the recent divergence of per capita incomes in rural and urban areas of the United States. During the 1980s, nonmetro per capita incomes declined from 77 percent of metro per capita incomes to 73 percent (Galston 1993).

As shown previously in Table 8.4, counties dependent on extractive industries appear to have lost ground relative to the rest of the United States during this period as well. Median household income grew much more slowly in these counties than elsewhere in the United States between 1979 and 1989. Whether this sluggishness is due solely to the economic forces affecting these industries (global market forces, domestic policy, technical change) or also to a disequilibrating dynamic in the relationship between rural areas dependent on extractive industry and their urban centers is a subject for future study.

Kaldor has argued that a principal mechanism for self-reinforcing growth in urban centers and for their faster growth relative to rural areas is the "existence of increasing returns to scale—using that term in its broadest sense—in processing activities. These are not just the economies of large-scale production, commonly considered, but the cumulative advantages arising from growth of industry itself—the development of skill and know-how; the opportunities for easy communication of ideas and experience; the opportunity of ever-increasing differentiation of processes and of specialization in human activities" (1970, 340). In Kaldor's model the increasing returns that come during the growth of industry increase labor productivity, reducing production costs per unit and allowing growing areas to underprice lagging areas. Lower prices in turn boost demand for the growing region's output, leading to further increases in labor productivity. Regions specializing in production of goods and services that are highly income elastic are at an advantage because increases in national or world income can give such regions the initial boost they need to start the self-reinforcing growth process. Conversely, regions that specialize in extractive industries, whose product is not generally very income elastic, are at a distinct disadvantage in this model.

EXTRACTIVE INDUSTRIES, PUBLIC POLICY, AND REGIONAL ECONOMIC CHANGE

Extractive industries—agriculture, forestry and wood products, energy extraction, and mining—are a highly diverse collection of slow-growing and economically unstable sectors. Most extractive industries compete in international markets and are thus much influenced by international economic forces and policies that affect resource supply and exchange rates. United States monetary and fiscal policies also bear considerably on these industries through their effect on interest rates (production in these industries often requires large investments, and demand for wood products and construction materials is affected by interest rates) and exchange rates (a strong dollar encourages imports and discourages exports).

Domestic resource and environmental policies play an increasingly important role in all extractive industries. Pressures for environmental protection and reduced extraction of resources come from those who value the amenities produced on resource lands; those harmed by the pollution associated with agricultural production or resource extraction or use; those who wish to preserve biological diversity and species that are threatened by resource extraction or development; and those who support extraction only within a context of sustainability. Some policies (such as those calling for reduced sulphur emissions) may affect demand for the resource (reducing demand for coal with high sulphur content and increasing demand for substitutes). Others (such as the Endangered Species Act affecting timber harvest) may reduce the supply of the resource available for harvest or extraction. Still others (such as those affecting irrigation withdrawals, soil erosion, or groundwater quality) may affect the production technology.

Technical change does not simply respond to policy shifts; it is induced by competitive forces as well. Technical change has generally involved the substitution of capital for labor, leading to displacement of labor in the extractive industries.

Rural areas are still highly dependent on extractive industries. In 1984 almost one-half (44 percent) of the nonmetro counties in the United States were dependent on one of the four extractive industries for 20 percent or more of earnings (Weber, Castle, and Shriver 1988). Today that proportion is probably around 40 percent of nonmetro counties. The future of rural areas that are dependent on natural resource extraction will be influenced, in part, by the conditions in the extractive industries. As the extractive industries continue to become more productive in the face of stagnant demand for output, labor in these industries will very likely continue to be displaced. The local opportunities for this labor will depend on the particular region's capacity for growth.

Drabenstott and Smith (see Chapter 9) identify the rural areas that have been most successful during the 1980s. Their analysis suggests that the following rural areas are best positioned to create new opportunities:

- those areas closest to growing metropolitan areas
- those areas with significant natural amenities (climate, proximity to water, mountains, forests, wildlife)
- those areas enjoying appropriate investments in communications and transportation infrastructure

- those areas able to specialize in production of goods and services that are not sensitive to economies of agglomeration
- those areas able to achieve necessary economies of size or agglomeration through new institutional arrangements

Policymakers who wish to influence the potential of rural areas to develop can focus on three factors: the capacity of a rural region to specialize in "increasing returns" industries, the region's predilection for institutional innovation, and the region's ability to capitalize on interregional linkages with urban centers.

Increasing Returns and the Dynamics of Development

Recent work in economics on the determinants of economic growth, mostly at the national level, identifies three themes that may be important for rural areas. First, growth in an economy may have positive feedbacks due to increasing returns, suggesting that growth may be self-reinforcing. Economies that can specialize in growing industries subject to increasing returns may thus put themselves on a self-reinforcing growth path (Arthur 1990). Although extractive industries generally do not manifest these characteristics, sectors within these broad industry classifications do face both growing demand and increasing returns. Second, technological progress, and hence growth, may be faster where the level of human knowledge is greater. An educated work force is therefore important for economic growth (Lucas 1988; Romer 1990; Grossman and Helpman 1991; as summarized in Gould and Ruffin 1993). Third, the future of an economy depends partly on its historical growth path, and random events can influence this path (Arthur 1990).

Institutions

Other work in economics focuses on the important role that institutions play in the extraction of resources and the development of economies. North defines institutions as rules, conventions, and codes of behavior: "the framework within which human interaction takes place" (1990, 4). Insights from this literature include the notion that the adjustment of an economy to outside forces is, in part, dependent on the institutional structure of the economy; this dependency implies that growth and stability can be influenced by altering institutions (Bromley 1985). Moreover, changing resource endowments, technologies, and factor prices lead to "institutional innova-

tions"; institutions thus evolve partly in response to how an economy develops and uses its resources (Ruttan 1979). Finally, the long-run performance
of an economy depends on its institutional structure; the path of institutional
change, like that of technological change, may be self-reinforcing due to
positive feedbacks (North 1990).

Rural-Urban Interdependence

The extractive industries of agriculture, forestry, energy extraction, and mining and their associated immediate processing generate significant amounts
of local output and income in both metro and nonmetro counties. Often
overlooked, however, is the extent of interdependence between the rural and
urban parts of an urban-centered trade area. Metropolitan extractive-industry
exports depend importantly on rural hinterlands for inputs, and changes in
demand for metro extractive industries exports significantly affect the surrounding rural economy. Changes in demand for rural extractive-industry exports (or supply restrictions), meanwhile, can have great impact on the metropolitan area because of the size of the extractive industries in rural areas and
because natural resource industries in the rural periphery depend on firms in
their metropolitan core for business and professional services.

The significant presence of extractive-industry activity in metropolitan areas and the interdependence of urban core and rural periphery in the natural
resource sectors suggest that national policies that affect extractive industries
may directly affect metro more than nonmetro economies in dollar terms (although they certainly will have a greater proportional impact on nonmetro
economies); and that the indirect effects of changes in extractive activity on
nonextractive sectors have important cross-regional dimensions: declines in
rural extractive activity, in particular, have large indirect and induced impacts
on the metro service sector.

More fundamentally, the interdependence of rural and urban areas can be
a source of dynamic "spread" and "backwash" effects. Metro economies that
specialize in industries facing growth in demand and subject to agglomeration economies are the major growth nodes in the United States. A critical
issue here is whether the positive "spread" effects of this growth will dominate the negative "backwash" effects (as Hirschman hopes) or whether the
ensuing urban-rural dynamics will follow the "cumulative causation" model
of Myrdal (1957) and Kaldor (1970) as formalized by Dixon and Thirwall
(1975). In Hirschman's analysis, the mutually beneficial relationship between core and periphery regions in the course of development depends on

political cooperation between them, a development that, in part, emerges as the regions grow at different rates (see Hirschman 1958, esp. 185–201).

Public policy that aims at strengthening the economic links between urban and rural areas and creating institutional incentives for political and economic cooperation could be the most effective rural policy. Such a strategy would also capitalize on the comparative advantage of rural areas in land-using extractive industries and natural amenity-based industries and of urban areas in services and manufacturing that benefits from agglomeration economies and urban densities.

NOTES

The writing of this paper was made lighter by the many hands that contributed to the work. Monica Fisher put together tables 8.1–8.3, using data made accessible to us by Craig Schaefer of the Federal Reserve Bank of Kansas City, and Table 8.4, using data retrieved from the 1980 and 1990 Census by Jennifer Burnet, Jared Schneider, and Steven Zahler. John Hession of the USDA's Economic Research Service produced the maps in figures 8.1–8.3. Edward Waters, drawing on previous work with David Holland, constructed Table 8.6 and the data for figures 8.5–8.8. The insightful comments of Emery Castle and Elizabeth Davis substantially improved the organization and clarity of the paper.

This section of the chapter draws on and updates "The Performance of Natural Resource Industries" by Bruce A. Weber, Emery N. Castle, and Ann L. Shriver in Rural Economic Development in the 1980s: Prospects for the Future, Economic Research Service, Washington, D.C., 1988.

FINDING RURAL SUCCESS: THE NEW RURAL ECONOMIC LANDSCAPE AND ITS IMPLICATIONS

MARK DRABENSTOTT
TIM R. SMITH

Powerful forces are reshaping the rural economic landscape, creating a new era for rural people, businesses, and institutions. For more than a decade, rural economic growth has been anemic, trailing well behind the national economy. And rural America no longer shares economic growth equally. Agriculture no longer proves a strong enough tide to lift all farming communities. Manufacturers are reinventing the way they do business, leaving fewer plants and jobs in rural places. Energy and timber production face new pressures from international competition and environmental regulations. And rural America generally has not benefited from a surging service sector elsewhere. Even as these forces of change hit the rural economy, a new pattern of economic growth is writ large across much of the nation's heartland. Growth is concentrating in pockets, in the towns and counties that seem to have everything going for them.

In short, fundamental economic forces have redrawn the rural economy. Winners on this new map are scarce and appear to depend on economic synergy and lifestyle amenities rather than on the natural resource endowments that used to guarantee rural success.[1] Meanwhile, the numerous ranks of rural economic losers remain tied to traditional industries that have undergone seismic structural changes and unrelenting competition from foreign producers.

What does the new economic landscape suggest about the future of the nation's rural communities? This chapter reviews the broad contours of the nation's new rural economic map, provides a profile of rural places that have been economically successful, and suggests policies rural communities might pursue in light of the economic trends at work. For communities with scenic amenities and growing service sectors, growth may come easily. For remote communities that lack economic synergies, economic development options will be fewer and the policy challenge more difficult.

THE NEW RURAL ECONOMIC LANDSCAPE

A useful way to examine the new economic landscape in rural America is to map out economic winners and losers during the past decade.[2] Though other definitions are possible, we defined economic winners as rural counties that had above average annual growth in both employment and income for the period 1980–1990. According to that definition, winners were rural counties with average annual growth in employment of 1.3 percent and growth in income of 1.7 percent. (The rural averages compared with 2.2 percent and 2.7 percent, respectively, for metropolitan counties.)

By using the average annual growth in both employment and income to identify winners and losers, some counties turned out to be neither. For example, a county that had above average employment growth but less than average income growth was considered to be neither a winner or a loser. Slightly less than a quarter of the nation's rural counties were winners in the 1980s. For the decade as a whole, 569 of the 2,357 nonmetro counties had above-average growth in employment and income. On average, in fact, the rural winners that met that test outperformed the nation's metro areas. Employment growth, for example, averaged 2.7 percent a year through the 1980s for rural winner counties, while real income growth managed 3.1 percent.

Who were the winners? In terms of economic base, 25 percent were retirement counties and another 35 percent were rural trade centers.[3] About 20 percent were manufacturing-dependent counties. Finally, only 3 percent were farm-dependent counties. In other words, if you lived in a farm-dependent county in the 1980s, you had a 1-in-35 chance of living in a rural county that had above-average growth.[4]

Geographically, the winners were clustered, but clusters appeared in many parts of the nation (Figure 9.1). Scenic amenities were important; there were clusters of winners in the Ozarks, the North Lake country, the Rockies, and the West Coast. The Eastern Seaboard also did well, as rural areas benefited from spillover from prosperous metropolitan areas. East Texas and Florida round out the list.

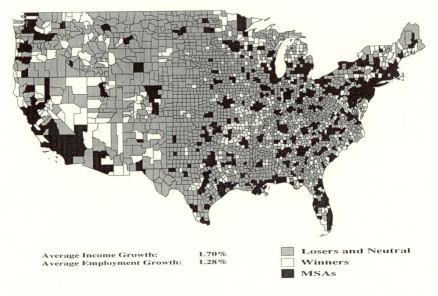

Average Income Growth: 1.70%
Average Employment Growth: 1.28%

Losers and Neutral
Winners
MSAs

Figure 9.1. Rural winning counties.

Forty-five percent of winning rural counties with above-average growth in the 1980s were located next to a metropolitan area. To be sure, some remote counties achieved above-average growth—one-sixth of the rural winners had no urban center. And roughly the same proportion of these completely rural counties were winners. Thus, the record of the past decade suggests that completely rural counties can prosper, although success appears to come mainly at the expense of other rural counties. Nearly two-thirds of the rural losing counties, meanwhile, were not adjacent to a metro area.

Nearly half of all rural counties were in the loser category. Of 1,146 counties with subpar employment and income growth, 37 percent were trade dependent. These are the counties that did not become trade centers, or put another way, did not benefit from the presence of a major retailer. Farm-dependent counties were 22 percent of the losers. Another 16 percent of the losers were manufacturing dependent, suggesting that some rural manufacturers did quite well in the 1980s, while others did quite poorly.

Geographically, the losers were clustered in the nation's midsection (Figure 9.2). Rural counties in the Great Plains, the Western Corn Belt, and the northern Rockies all did poorly. So did farm-dependent parts of the Delta. In short, one can think of a "heartland triangle" that takes in most of the losers, where in this case heartland might be defined as the region bounded triangularly by a line drawn from Chicago to Dallas, a line from Dallas to Seattle,

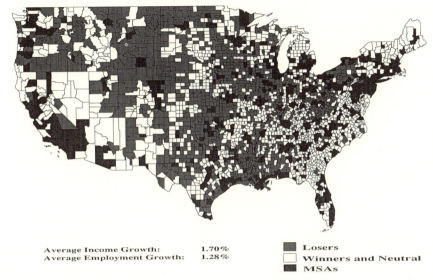

Average Income Growth:	1.70%		Losers
Average Employment Growth:	1.28%		Winners and Neutral
			MSAs

Figure 9.2. Rural losing counties.

and the Canadian border. This huge area is dominated by rural counties with subpar economic growth. Heavily dependent on traditional natural resource industries, this region appears to pose particularly difficult challenges to economic development.

CHARACTERISTICS OF RURAL WINNERS

Whereas the rural winners can easily be sorted by industrial base and geographical location, it is somewhat more difficult to identify the underlying characteristics that may have led to their relatively rapid growth amid the overall rural decline of the 1980s. The business location literature identifies several characteristics as potential determinants of business location and regional growth.[5] Location theory suggests that firms expand or locate in places where they expect their profits to be highest. Revenues usually vary according to the proximity of a location to final markets; variation in profitability across locations, then, can be explained by variations in costs—where transportation costs capture the locational effects on revenues.

Table 9.1 lists the characteristics most often associated with business location and rural economic growth. The first column of the table lists location factors often cited in the literature: labor and other business costs, transpor-

Table 9.1. Selected characteristics of rural U.S. counties

Characteristics	Winners	Losers
Labor and other business costs		
Relative wage rate		
(as a percent of the United States)	73.8	75.2
Housing costs		
(median value of owner-occupied housing units)	37,383	30,041
Right to work		
(percent of counties in right-to-work states)	46.0	46.0
Local taxes per capita	304.84	379.89
Transportation factors		
Interstate highway miles		
(per 1,000 square miles)	14.95	9.92
Adjacent to metro areas		
(percent of counties adjacent to metro areas)	44.8	35.2
Agglomeration		
Employees per square mile	25.6	13.8
Health care factors		
Hospital beds (per 100,000 population)	464.4	556.5
Doctors (per 100,000 population)	89.7	64.2
Nursing home beds (per 100,000 population)	863.5	1,174.5
Educational factors		
Local government education expenditures		
per capita	442.29	508.25
College (percent of counties with colleges)	39.4	26.3
Percent of population with 16 or more years		
education	11.6	9.8
Industry mix factors		
Retirement counties (percent)	24.1	4.6
Farm and Mining Income		
(as share of total income)	3.8	8.9

Sources: *Union Sourcebook;* Beale Code, Bureau of Economic Analysis, USDA; U.S. Department of Transportation, Federal Highway Administration; Bureau of Economic Analysis, Regional Economic Information System; U.S. Department of Commerce, *City and County Data Book* (1988); *Higher Education Directory* (1993); higher education publications; U.S. Department of Agriculture, Economic Research Service; and Bureau of Economic Analysis, Regional Economic Information System.

tation costs, agglomeration, health care, education, and industry mix. A measure of each factor is given for the 569 winning counties in the second column and for the 1,146 losing counties in the third column.[6]

Labor and Other Business Costs

Labor is a significant input to both manufacturing and service firms. At any time, the cost of this input can vary considerably across locations. All else being equal, lower labor costs at the beginning of the study period should be positively related to growth.

One measure of labor costs is relative wage rates. If a county's wage rates are high relative to other counties, then the increased labor costs are expected to discourage firms from moving to or expanding in that county. As expected, winner counties had lower average wage rates than loser counties, though the difference was small.

A second measure of labor costs is cost of living. Because no cost-of-living index is available at the county level, the median value of owner-occupied housing was used as a proxy. Counties with lower housing costs should, all else being equal, attract new and expanding firms, thus leading to higher income and employment growth. Contrary to expectations, the cost of living was generally higher for winning counties than for losing counties during the 1980s. One explanation for this unexpected result is the potential importance of retirement in winning counties. Cost of living may be less important in retirement counties where the value of amenities outweigh the added costs of housing. Moreover, retirees who have sold their homes and may be relocating to smaller homes may be less sensitive to high housing costs than younger migrants.

A third indicator of labor costs is the degree of unionization in a county. Although labor unions may affect work rules and other labor-force characteristics, their largest effect is on wages. Counties in states with right-to-work laws generally maintain lower wages because they are not highly unionized; thus they should be more conducive to business startups and expansions. This characteristic, however, does not appear to distinguish rural winners from losers. Forty-six percent of counties in both groups were located in states with right-to-work laws.

Taxes, too, may influence location choice. Bartik (1991) stresses the importance of taxes in studies of business location. High local taxes are thought to discourage business location and growth. Of course, this conclusion assumes the levels of government services provided are the same across counties. Per capita local taxes can thus be viewed as the price of government services in a county. If the level of government services is the same across counties, then higher taxes per capita are expected to be associated with lower growth. Although the comparisons in Table 9.1 do not control for the levels of public services, winning counties had significantly lower taxes per capita than losing counties.

Transportation Costs

Transportation costs are important to businesses because they affect both the cost of acquiring inputs and the cost of shipping products to their final markets. Lower transportation costs increase a firm's net profits by improving access to markets. Given a choice between two counties with the same non-transportation characteristics, a firm will choose to locate in a county that has lower transportation costs. Meanwhile, transportation costs are likely to be higher for a firm that locates in a county farther from final markets.

One proxy for county transportation costs is the number of miles of interstate highways. Counties with more interstate highway miles are expected to enjoy lower costs of transporting goods to markets and thus are expected to grow faster than comparable counties with fewer interstate highway miles. To control for the wide variance in land area across counties, Table 9.1 lists interstate highway miles per thousand square miles. As expected, winners had a much larger number of highway miles than losers.

Proximity to metropolitan areas is another proxy for transportation costs. Counties located near metropolitan areas are likely to have lower costs of shipping products to markets and lower costs of acquiring inputs. Other things being equal, these counties are expected to grow faster than counties that are not adjacent to metropolitan areas. As expected, nearly 45 percent of winning counties were adjacent to metropolitan areas compared with 35 percent of losing counties.

Agglomeration

Agglomeration—the concentration of economic activity—lowers business costs by increasing the availability of specialized supplier networks, such as those for materials of business services. Carlino (1985) argues that agglomeration economies in manufacturing contributed to the growth in rural counties in the 1970s. In addition to taking advantage of specialized supplier networks, businesses gain from agglomeration by being able to network with other companies in the same industry, exchanging technology and market intelligence. Examples of agglomeration include high-technology firms in Silicon Valley, insurance firms in Des Moines, and telemarketing firms in Omaha.

One proxy for this agglomeration effect is the number of employees per square mile. Using this measure, agglomeration does appear to be associated with higher county growth. Winning counties averaged 25.6 employees per square mile, whereas losing counties averaged only 13.8 employees per square mile.

Health-care Factors

Availability of quality health care at low cost is expected to attract both businesses and retirees, thus influencing an area's economic growth. Unfortunately, good measures of health-care costs and quality are difficult to obtain. In this chapter, the number of hospital beds, doctors, and nursing homes are used to approximate the county health care environment. Given the difficulty of measuring the quality of health care across all of its numerous dimensions, these measures should be considered only approximations of a county's health-care environment. Winning rural counties had more doctors but fewer hospital and nursing home beds than losers. Perhaps businesses view doctors as low-cost health care inputs and see hospitals and nursing homes as high-cost inputs.

Educational Factors

Businesses appear to be paying increased attention to education when they make location decisions, and this link has been receiving increasing attention in the regional growth literature.[7] Educational characteristics of an area generally reflect the quality of its work force. The county educational characteristics included in this chapter are local government expenditures on education, the presence of a college or university, and the proportion of the population with sixteen or more years of education. Like the measures used to characterize health care, these indicators should be considered rough proxies.

Education generally appears to influence rural growth. As expected, more winning counties (39.4 percent) had a college or university than losing counties (26.3 percent). The proportion of the population with a college education was significantly larger in winning counties than in losing counties. Local spending on education, however, was lower on average in winning counties than in losing counties. This apparent inconsistency may be explained partly by the fact that retirement was the engine of growth in many winning counties. Education spending is presumably less important in retirement-dependent counties than in counties where the economic base is more diversified.

Industry Mix Factors

The examination of rural winners and losers in the first section of this chapter suggested a broad relationship between rural success and industry mix. The two most important economic features of the rural economic landscape appear to be retirement and natural resource dependence. To capture these features, Table 9.1 shows the percent of winners and losers that fall under the USDA definition of retirement counties and the share of county income derived from farming and mining. A much larger share of winners were retirement counties; moreover, a significantly smaller share of winners' income was derived from farming and mining than losers' income.

The list of characteristics in Table 9.1 present a detailed profile of rural winners and losers. The composite picture of numerous location factors displays two prominent features: remoteness and scenic amenities.[8] Rural counties that were winners had low transportation costs and high agglomeration economies, often due to proximity to metropolitan areas. By contrast, counties that were far removed from product markets and metropolitan areas were overwhelmingly losers. Thus, remoteness appears to matter. Winners were often found in areas with mountains (the intermountain west, the Ozarks) or lakes (the northern lakes region). Moreover, the frequency of retirement counties among rural winners suggests that scenic amenities may play an important role in rural growth.

Remoteness, presumably the essence of being rural is in fact a liability in today's economy. The record of the 1980s is clear: indeed, one of the most striking pictures of economic activity in the 1980s derives from an analysis of how the economy performed in terms of proximity to metropolitan areas.[9] In brief, rural growth declined in direct proportion to the distance from a metro area (Figure 9.3). The conclusion holds whether "income" or "jobs" forms the economic yardstick. One of the profound features of the new rural economy, then, is that geography matters, despite the fanfare that the information age economy is no respecter of places. The fact is that metropolitan areas appear to be the real engines of our economy.

Remoteness will likely remain a liability in the 1990s. First, rural places are removed from markets. Consumer expectations are increasingly specific and volatile. Firms that change products to meet consumer expectations are re-

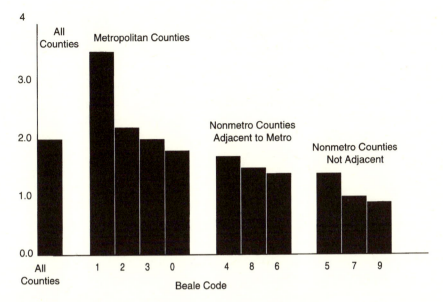

Figure 9.3. Employment growth by Beale Code, 1980–1990.

warded; firms that do not shift quickly are punished. Firms in metropolitan areas tend to be closer to their customers and may respond more nimbly to changing demand. Second, rural places are removed from centers of information, technology, and innovation. Silicon Valley sprang up where it did because it was close to several universities with world-class technological innovations. Few rural places can claim to be centers of technological innovation. Third, rural places are removed from the social and cultural opportunities now deemed essential by many citizens who do not believe amenities can be duplicated via satellite television.

Still, remoteness can operate as a growth virtue. Our nation increasingly recognizes the problems found in our major cities, such as crime, pollution, and congestion. These problems are encouraging a well-documented migration out of places like southern California. The pattern of the 1980s suggests, however, that the rural places that benefit will be mainly those with scenic amenities, particularly those in the intermountain West. Indeed, despite the general tide away from rural areas, some rural places were actually magnets for growth in the 1980s, and their magnetism seems likely to continue in the 1990s. Offering mountains, lakes, or other scenic assets, these places lure the nation's retirees and adaptable entrepreneurs.

Among rural economic bases, retirement-dependent counties were the

only rural counties that outperformed metro areas in income and employment growth over the past decade—and many retirement-dependent counties claim scenic amenities. The Ozark region (southwestern Missouri, northwestern Arkansas, and northeastern Oklahoma) is a good example. As it turns
out, in fact, a scenic amenity is one of the best assets upon which to build a
rural economy. Colorado's rural counties nestled along the Front Range or in
the mountains offer obvious recreational opportunities. Building on those
opportunities, those rural counties saw their employment grow 2.3 percent a
year in the 1980s, as compared to an average job growth of just .5 percent a
year in the state's eastern rural counties located in the plains.

IMPLICATIONS FOR RURAL DEVELOPMENT POLICY

The growth factors discussed above suggest a mixed rural economy in the
1990s. Overall, the rural economy will likely trail the rest of the nation as
economic growth continues to migrate toward metropolitan areas or to rural
areas adjacent to them. Across the nation's heartland, rural growth centers
may prosper largely at the expense of surrounding areas. Remoteness, a defining characteristic of many rural places, will probably be a liability unless
matched by favorable scenery or climate. Finally, the small scale of most rural
economies—that is, their lack of agglomeration—will be another liability.

How then might rural policymakers enhance these rather grim economic
growth prospects? This section sketches four broad implications for policy:
taking advantage of emerging industries, bolstering lagging rural industries,
encouraging regional cooperation, and spurring change in rural institutions.

Taking Advantage of Emerging Industries

The evidence suggests that many successful rural counties will shift increasingly from a dependence on natural resource industries toward an industry
base—most likely focused on services—that exploits remoteness and scenic
amenities.

Rural places with scenic and recreational amenities often spawn growth in
service industries. A whole host of service industries—from hotels and motels
to restaurants and entertainment—have grown up in remote places that boast
mountains, lakes, or a warm winter climate. Branson, in southwestern Missouri, is a good example of tourism-based service-industry growth that capi-
talizes on both a relatively remote location and recreational amenities.

The outlook for rural growth in services, however, should not be over-stated. Apart from amenity-based growth, other types of service industries may require more agglomeration than many rural places can provide. These categories include business and financial services that spawned some of the most rapidly expanding businesses of the past decade. The lack of service synergy in many rural places appears largely to explain why rural areas lagged behind metropolitan areas in the 1980s. For instance, when county employment growth in services is arrayed by distance from metropolitan areas, service activity declines in step-fashion as the distance increases from a metropolitan area. Not only did rural America lose out on service jobs, the jobs it did gain were low-paying service jobs. Adjusted for inflation, the average wage for service jobs in metro areas grew 1.5 percent a year in the 1980s, whereas wages fell in completely rural counties.

Why has service growth bypassed many rural areas? There appear to be two contributing factors. First, there is no substitute for face-to-face interaction in marketing services; trust is hard to establish long-distance. Second, service companies seek locations where there is already a strong base of service companies, locations that are generally close to a major market. There are exceptions, of course. Overall, however, the gains in service jobs in suburban and urban areas swamp those in isolated places. There are real questions about how much of rural America can tap into the new service-based economy.

Transportation infrastructure will be important in helping rural communities exploit growth opportunities in the 1990s. The importance of access to markets is underscored by the greater incidence of interstate highways or metropolitan adjacency among winning rural counties. Those rural locations with good transportation infrastructure may develop industries that facilitate movement of goods to their final markets. For example, distribution centers and some manufacturing enterprises may spring up to facilitate or tap into new north-south trade flows. But unless transportation networks expand to link more remote rural places with markets, or at least position them as a stop along the journey from the origin of goods to their final destination, the distribution activities are unlikely to grow in remote rural places.

Bolstering Traditional Industries

If the past decade is an indicator, a majority of rural counties may well trail in economic performance in the 1990s. Many of these laggards will be tied to traditional rural industries, such as agriculture, manufacturing, forestry, and mining. These industries have suffered a diminished impact on rural economic growth because final markets for the goods of these industries are, in most cases, either mature markets characterized by slow growth or markets that are subject to intense competition, or both. Furthermore, these industries have all enjoyed enormous gains in productivity that have reduced the demand for labor inputs and in many cases have resulted in shuttered grain elevators, factories, or mines.

In the decade ahead, rural policymakers might do well to try boosting the value added by these industries in rural places. In agriculture, for instance, many rural places simply export bulk commodities instead of processed food products. Profit margins in bulk farm products are razor thin and likely to stay low. A comparison of where farm and food production takes place suggests that industrial states in the Northeast control a disproportionate share of the nation's food (Barkema, Drabenstott, and Stanley 1990). Most rural places face an uphill challenge attracting more food processing because they are distant from the nation's major retail markets. Moreover, firms that do relocate to rural areas may only reinforce economic growth in the trade centers that are already doing well in lagging regions.

The record of the 1980s also underscores the need for policymakers to encourage policies that open up new trade opportunities for rural businesses. Many of the goods produced in rural America have run into stagnant or declining markets in the past decade. Initiatives such as the North American Free Trade Agreement will bring new opportunities to many rural industries while encouraging even more gains in rural productivity. There nevertheless remains a need for a market infrastructure to support growth in rural exports. Given their generally small scale, many rural businesses may be slow in exploiting export opportunities. Programs that help rural businesses reduce the cost and increase the speed of contacting foreign buyers may be helpful.

Encouraging Regional Cooperation

Rural economic development is normally a local affair requiring the leadership and effort of many different segments of the community. The rural economy of the 1990s may require a broader frame of reference, however. The remoteness and small scale of many rural communities gives them two strikes against them from the outset. One way to overcome the lack of agglomeration is to pool resources with neighboring communities. Similarly, such cooperation may help redress transportation deficiencies. But regional cooperation is often anathema to local leaders.

The nation's Great Plains region illustrates the potential value of regional cooperation. Rural counties in this region are generally in the same economic boat: farm-dependent, a long way from markets, and far from metropolitan areas. Despite this commonality, the region has few institutions that strive to develop regional solutions. On the contrary, most states adopt beggar-thy-neighbor development strategies, and there are few examples of cooperation on a substate level.

By contrast, other regions have stronger institutions to help forge common regional economic policy approaches and have even actively promoted regional economic development groups (Fosler 1991). These entities establish priorities for joint actions by states and help identify narrower geographic areas with common economic interest. They also point out new institutions that are needed in the region or ways that old institutions can adapt.

The Great Lakes and the South have been especially active in promoting regional economic institutions. The Great Lakes region now boasts six groups: the Great Lakes Commission, the International Joint Commission (with Canada), the Council of Great Lakes Governors, the Center for the Great Lakes, Great Lakes United, and the Great Lakes Economic Policy Council. The South, which led the development of regional institutions, has the Southern Growth Policies Board, the Commission on the Future of the South, and the Southern Technology Council. Economic success will not result simply from the creation of regional commissions, but the evidence suggests that some good has come from the regional focus these groups have brought to common economic problems (Fosler 1991).

Regional thinking can usefully guide economic policy by widening the focus beyond local communities to a multicounty trade area. In the new rural economy, firms will move to rural locations only if they can find some of the same economic synergy (or agglomeration) benefits that metropolitan areas provide. The only way for a small rural community to begin to provide such benefits is by banding together with nearby communities. A good example of this pooled economic strategy is found in southeastern Iowa where "cluster towns" have developed. Generally a cluster includes a group of six or so communities that join forces to develop their area. With tourism as the unifying theme, the efforts have had positive results.

Spur Institutional Change

Many rural institutions were created when the land was settled more than a century ago and have changed little. The new rural economic landscape, however, requires many of these institutions to change. Two institutions are particularly noteworthy: public-service delivery systems and the Cooperative Extension Service. Changes in these institutions must be guided by the need to create more synergy, just as local communities must search for synergy with neighboring communities. Unfortunately, synergy is hard to spark within well-established institutions.

The rural public-service delivery system is already under pressure in many declining or stagnant communities, and the system will doubtless undergo a revolution in the coming years, born either of necessity or innovation. Administering public service delivery from county courthouses may no longer be cost effective. Reforming delivery to match economic development clusters, however, may offer distinct advantages both to taxpayers and to start-up businesses.

The Cooperative Extension Service remains tied principally to production agriculture, but the needs of the new rural economy are much broader. Much of rural America will rise or fall on the success of local entrepreneurs. Often these business startups require technical or managerial assistance to succeed. Though local bankers can often help entrepreneurs find additional assistance, business extension services are lacking in many parts of the country.

CONCLUSION

The overall economic decline of rural communities in the 1980s raises important questions about their viability in the 1990s. The foregoing comparison of rural places that flourished with those that declined suggests certain industries may emerge to lift some rural economies in the 1990s or sustain the growth that some rural places achieved in the 1980s. Rural communities with natural scenic amenities, such as mountains or lakes, may be able to capitalize on service industries related to retirement or tourism, while other rural communities may be able to tap into transportation networks and new flows of traded goods to bolster their economies. The new rural economic map suggests, however, that few rural places will have the locational attributes needed to take advantage of emerging industries. Far more rural places will be limited by their dependence on traditional natural resource industries. These places may need to rely on innovative policy actions such as promoting regional cooperation or changing rural institutions.

NOTES

Mark Drabenstott is a vice-president and economist and Tim R. Smith is a senior economist, both with the Federal Reserve Bank of Kansas City. The views expressed here are strictly those of the authors, and do not necessarily reflect those of the Federal Reserve Bank of Kansas City or the Federal Reserve System.

1. "Economic synergy" describes the beneficial interactions in a local economy that lead to the economic whole being bigger than the sum of the individual parts. Economists call this phenomenon "agglomeration economies."

2. The definition of nonmetropolitan counties as "rural" is consistent with the framework developed by Bender et al. (1985). In this chapter, "rural" and "nonmetropolitan" are used interchangeably. For a discussion of the 1983 Office of Management and Budgets (OMB) redesignation of metro/nonmetro status, see Hady and Ross (1990). See Drabenstott and Welch (1991) and Smith (1992) for more detailed comparisons of metro/nonmetro regional economic growth.

3. Definitions of nonmetropolitan areas were derived from those used by Bender and others at the Economic Research Service, U.S. Department of Agriculture. The definitions used in this paper include updates developed by Hady and Ross (1990) for four economic base types (farming, manufacturing, mining, and government). Manufacturing counties received at least 30 percent of total proprietor's income from manufacturing enterprises in 1986. Mining counties received at least 20 percent of this income from mining sectors in 1986. Farming counties realized at least 20 percent of their labor and proprietor's income from agriculture in 1981, 1982, 1984, 1985, and 1986. (The definition of farming-dependent counties adjusts for fluctuations in farm income over time by using a 5-year average. The year 1983 was dropped because it was an extremely aberrant year for farm income.) Government counties received at least 25 percent of their income from government payrolls in 1986. Retirement counties are identified by 1970–1980 immigration patterns. If the number of immigrants over the age of 60 comprised more than 15 percent of the 1980 over-60 population, the county was assumed to be a retirement county. Income in these counties is likely to depend highly on transfer payments, private pensions, dividends, and interest earnings. Mixed counties are those meeting more than one of the economic base criteria. Trade counties do not fall into any of the other categories mentioned and are assumed to be trade centers that derive income by providing goods and services to surrounding counties. "Other" counties were either poverty counties or federal land counties that did not qualify for any of the economic base categories. (The approach in cataloging the counties was to emphasize a single economic base for each county and allow the poverty and federal lands counties to sort to the economic base group where they belonged.)

4. Although many winners were retirement and trade centers, not all retirement and trade centers were winners. Within broad economic base categories, some counties fare better than others because they appear to have a favorable mix of such characteristics as local leadership, complementary industries, and high-quality work force. And whereas only a few winners were farm-dependent counties, the same favorable mix of local characteristics allowed these few counties to overcome the economic difficulties faced by other counties with a similar economic base.

5. Tim Smith (1989) discusses location factors most often identified in studies of business location. For examples of these studies, see Bartik (1985), Plaut and Pluta (1983), Wasylenko (1985), and Wasylenko and McGuire (1985).

6. Henry and Gibson (1988) make a similar comparison of rural winners and losers using a different time period, a different definition of winners and losers, and a different list of county characteristics. In Table 9.1, the values of the characteristics are measured as close as possible to the beginning of the period.

7. For example, Smith and Drabenstott (1992) survey recent evidence supporting a connection between higher education and economic development.

8. Maps of winners and losers in the nation's heartland show an apparent link between amenities and rural growth (Smith 1992). In that region winning counties were clustered in the Rocky Mountains and in the Ozarks of southern Missouri.

9. In this case we define proximity in terms of Beale Codes. Developed by Calvin Beale at the U.S. Department of Agriculture, these ten classification codes divide counties into a spectrum ranging from urban core counties to completely rural places with no significant city.

Code

Metropolitan Counties

0   Central counties of metropolitan areas of 1 million population or more
1   Fringe counties of metropolitan areas of 1 million population or more
2   Counties in metropolitan areas of 250,000–1,000,000 population
3   Counties in metropolitan areas of less than 250,000 population

Nonmetropolitan Counties

4   Urban population of 20,000 or more, adjacent to a metropolitan area
5   Urban population of 20,000 or more, not adjacent to a metropolitan area
6   Urban population of 2,500–19,999, adjacent to a metropolitan area
7   Urban population of 2,500–19,999, not adjacent to a metropolitan area
8   Completely rural (no places with a population of 2,500 or more), adjacent to a metropolitan area
9   Completely rural (no places with a population of 2,500 or more), not adjacent to a metropolitan area

10

UNDERSTANDING TRENDS IN RURAL LABOR MARKETS

GENE F. SUMMERS, FRANCINE HORTON,
AND CHRISTINA GRINGERI

In this chapter we discuss rural labor markets by describing the trends in the industrial structure of rural labor markets and the consequences of these changes in terms of employment and income.[1] We then provide an overview of the theories used by social scientists to understand the trends and their consequences.

Our discussion distinguishes labor markets from labor market areas. The term "labor market" refers to the social relations between buyers and sellers of labor, and "labor market areas" refers to localities in which market relationships occur. Within any geographic area or administrative unit, many labor markets may operate. Some markets may involve only local buyers and sellers (e.g., the farm labor market or the local retail sales labor markets), others may involve buyers and sellers who participate in regional or national markets (e.g., physicians, corporate managers, or university professors), and still others may involve mixtures of local, regional, and national markets. However, the labor markets operating within any locale combine to create characteristics of employment in the local labor market area (Tolbert and Killian 1987; Summers, Horton, and Gringeri 1990).

It is especially important to separate markets from market areas when determining the most appropriate public policy strategy to deal with employment issues. If locality is of no consequence, the employment issues may be reasonably addressed by macroeconomic policies. If, however, great diversity characterizes labor market areas, regional policies may be required to target industrial sectors, occupational groupings, social divisions, or population sectors (Deavers and Brown 1984; Brown and Deavers 1988; Deavers 1988; Osterman 1988).

TRENDS

Since the mid-1950s rural labor markets have shifted from a heavy dependence on agriculture and other natural resource-based industries to a greater diversity of economic activities (Brown and Deavers 1988; Castle 1988; Weber, Castle, and Shriver 1988; Duncan 1989; Drabenstott and Henry 1988; Falk and Lyson 1988; Summers, Horton, and Gringeri 1990; Barkley 1993; Singelmann and Deseran 1993). With the downturn in agriculture and natural resources as sources of employment, manufacturing and service industries have expanded as rural labor markets. In this section we will examine this sectoral shift and associated changes in the income and employment status of rural workers.

Employment by Sector

The service sector clearly has dominated growth in labor demand over the period from 1955 to 1990 for the entire United States. In 1990 there were 52.4 million more American workers than in 1955 and 51 million of them (97.5 percent) were employed in the service sector (Smith 1993). Manufacturing provided employment for only 2.2 million additional workers, and agriculture lost almost 3 million jobs. These trends have been replicated in rural labor markets, where from 1975 to 1989, 89 percent of the net employment growth was in the service sector (Smith 1993).

During a brief period in the 1970s both manufacturing and service sector labor markets were growing in rural areas: from 1969 to 1976 the rate of service sector employment growth in rural areas actually exceeded that of urban areas. According to Miller and Bluestone (1988) this growth was closely linked to rural manufacturing growth. After 1976 rural industrialization stagnated and the rate of service employment growth slowed with it, but the service sector continues to provide nearly all the net growth in rural employment. These statistics indicate broad trends in the restructuring of the U.S. economy, but one cannot conclude that they apply equally well to all rural labor markets. The rich diversity and complexity of market trends becomes more apparent by examining changes among regional and local labor market areas.

In a 1988 study of rural employment and commuting patterns, Killian and Hady (1988) found 182 labor market areas in rural America. They defined a sector as predominant if it accounted for more than 30 percent of employment in a labor market area. Agriculture remained the predominant labor market in 32 of the 182 rural labor market areas. Mining dominated twelve rural labor market areas while eight areas were heavily dependent upon wood products. By contrast, textile and apparel manufacturing was the dominant labor market in 12 market areas and durable manufacturing in 6. Public education and administration led the employment roster in 26 areas, and 86 were classified as "diversified." It is very evident that the nationally calculated 5.0 percent employment in agriculture and natural-resource industries is concentrated in relatively few rural labor market areas.

Many changes have occurred in the small towns and open countryside of rural America. Although the countryside is still largely covered by fields and forests, most rural people earn a living in manufacturing or service industries. Two-thirds of a farm family's earnings come from its income off the farm. National and world events affect life on Main Street, at the school, down at the courthouse, and on the farm. Changing rural labor markets also have altered employment and incomes.

Labor Market Outcomes

Trends in the structure of labor markets reveal nothing about the outcomes for participants. Therefore, we here examine trends in unemployment, underemployment, and the level of earnings provided by employment.

Unemployment rates in rural labor markets have increased significantly over the past twenty years. In 1973 the reported rural unemployment rate was 4.4 percent; in 1993 it was 6.5 percent (Fuguitt, Brown, and Beale 1989; USDA-ERS 1993). When adjusted to account for discouraged and involuntary part-time workers, the rates are 7.1 percent and 10.2 percent, respectively. During most of the intervening years, however, the adjusted rates were above 10.0 percent. Only in 1989 and 1990 did the rate fall below 10.0 percent, to 9.1 and 9.4 respectively.

From midcentury to the early 1980s, unemployment rates in rural areas generally were lower than in urban areas. In the early 1980s, however, this situation reversed, and for the next ten years rural unemployment remained higher than urban. Since 1991 the gap has closed, with both areas showing unemployment rates about 7.0 percent. When unemployment is adjusted to account for "discouraged workers" and those who are involuntarily employed only part-time, the 1993 rates rise to 10.2 percent unemployment for both areas.

Part-time employment has been increasing as a proportion of workers in rural and urban labor markets, although the change has been more noticeable in rural labor markets. Like unemployment, part-time employment has increased more rapidly in the rural labor markets during recessions, and the recovery has been less complete than in the urban labor markets. Thus, in 1990 the part-time employment rate in rural labor markets was 12.8 percent over-all, 21.7 percent for females and 6.8 percent for males (U.S. Bureau of the Census 1990a). The comparable 1990 urban rates were 11.4 percent overall, 18.3 percent for females and 6.4 percent for males. These figures show a substantial increase from 1988, when the annual average of part-time employment for economic reasons in rural labor markets stood at 5.9 percent, compared to 4.2 percent in urban markets. In 1973 the comparable percentages were 3.6 and 2.7, respectively, for rural and urban labor markets (U.S. Bureau of the Census, Current Population Surveys 1973–1988; Parker 1989).

Earnings of rural workers also fall below those of urban workers, and the gap is widening. Even when other income sources are added to earnings, rural families and households garner lower incomes than urban residents. In 1990 the median income of rural families was $27,591. Compared to the median $37,896 for urban families, the income of rural families was only 72.8 percent of their urban "cousins" (U.S. Bureau of the Census 1992a). The comparable ratio in 1980 was 78.5 percent (U.S. Bureau of the Census 1980). One may be tempted to discount these differences on the premise that costs of consumer items are substantially lower in rural areas, but the evidence suggests that housing is the only consumer item that is consistently lower in rural America. Most household consumption items actually cost more in rural areas than in urban areas. The common perception that overall cost-of-living is lower in rural than in urban areas is inaccurate, at least for residents of many rural communities.

LABOR MARKET THEORIES

Social scientists turn to general theories of work and society to interpret these trends in rural labor markets. We have arranged these theories into three groups according to their main focus: demand-oriented, supply-oriented, and institution-oriented frameworks. Demand-oriented explanations emphasize global, national, and regional changes in the structure and volume of product demand and other factors that affect the demand for labor. Supply-oriented explanations draw heavily on human capital theory with its stress on the importance of education and training of workers in competitive labor markets. And institution-oriented explanations emphasize organizational and institutional factors that shape the operation of labor markets.

Demand-oriented Theories

The demand for labor consists of employment opportunities that are structured according to occupations, industries, skill requirements, and location of work, all of which may vary over time and among places. Several factors may affect the level of labor demand at any time and place: the demand for the output (good or service) that labor produces; the productivity of labor (a combination of capital, technology, and worker skill); and the price of factors of production other than labor. Some demand-oriented theorists use national labor markets as their unit of analysis, whereas others address regional differentiation within the nation. In either case, these theorists attempt to explain the vicissitudes of labor market conditions by searching for exogenous factors to account for the labor demand changes that are occurring in labor markets and labor market areas. In the broadest perspective, one begins with the changing conditions in the global economy that affect the local demand for labor.

Global Economic Restructuring. Since the mid–twentieth century, the world has experienced economic, social, and political changes that several authors summarize as the global diffusion of capital, technology, and skills (Galston 1988; Harrison and Bluestone 1988). As these critical factors of production have diffused worldwide, they have helped generate a truly global economy with intensive global competition. This competition has intensified pressures on the economy of the United States. In particular, the traditional extractive and goods-producing sectors face greater international competition, forcing firms in these sectors to seek more efficient production tactics. Obviously, these sectors have been the predominant sources of demand for labor in rural markets; consequently, the global restructuring has hurt rural labor markets and market areas even more than labor markets in urban areas.

In all industrial nations, manufacturing output has steadily increased and maintained its share of the GNP while employing fewer workers, often by substituting capital and technology for labor (Bluestone and Harrison 1982; Summers 1984; Drucker 1986). Thus, rural labor market areas in the United States that are heavily dependent on low-skill, low-wage manufacturing for employment are experiencing declining labor demand. With promises of "high-technology" for even greater production efficiency, there is little reason to expect this structural change to reverse.

Export Base Theory. According to export base theory, the economy of any spatial system may be divided into two broad sectors: economic activities that produce goods and services for external markets and activities that produce goods and services for internal markets. These theorists assume that export activities drive the internal economic activities; they refer, for instance, to the export sector as "basic" and the domestic sector as "secondary." The crucial element is the generation of a money flow into the local economy that is then spent internally. In this manner, exports generate a demand for labor in the export activities and, by extension, in the secondary sector through the spending and respending of the money brought into the economy by the export activities (Andrews 1954; North 1955; Tiebout 1956; Thompson 1973).

Agricultural products, raw materials, and manufactured goods have composed the bulk of the export sector for many rural labor market areas, but global and national trends in these product markets threaten the labor demand in areas with a strong dependency on them. It is not necessary, however, to limit the export sector of rural labor market areas to the traditional of farming, forestry, mining, fishing, and manufacturing. Export activities can expand to include exportable business services, recreation, tourism, and residential development for people with passive incomes. Export base theory thus provides a possible guide for understanding the labor demand shift from agriculture, natural resource-based extraction and manufacturing to the service sector labor markets in rural labor market areas (Hirschl and Summers 1982; Killian and Hady 1988; Smith 1984; Smith, Hackbart, and van Veen 1981; Smith and Pulver 1981; Summers and Hirschl 1985).

The list of nontraditional rural economic activities with a potential for generating exportable goods and services is large and the range of possibilities not yet fully explored. The technological changes in communications favor a spatial dispersion of production activities and producer services; advances in telecommunications and transportation have overcome the cost of distance for at least some rural labor market areas (Noyelle 1983; Garnick 1984; Leven 1985). Advocates of the export base theory argue that as the export activities of rural labor market areas diversify and expand labor demand will continue to grow in a variety of service-producing labor markets. These markets include medical centers that serve a nonlocal clientele, universities and colleges attracting nonlocal students, recreation and tourism, research and laboratories of the federal and state governments, and business and consumer services.

Supply-oriented Theories

Supply-oriented explanations of rural labor markets and outcomes focus attention on the workers and their characteristics. The supply of labor consists of the number of people who are willing to sell their labor services for a specified wage to fulfill a stipulated set of required skills. A great many factors may operate to determine the labor supply in a market area, including the proportion of the population who have needed skills or are able to acquire them, the time required to acquire the skills, competing opportunities for work activities, and nonmonetary goals of the potential workers.

Human capital theory (Becker 1971; 1985) is the supply-oriented theory most commonly used to explain the operation of labor markets, including rural labor markets. According to this theory, employers hire and retain workers because of their productivity, which is a function of their skills and knowledge acquired through schooling, training or work experiences. Workers are paid a wage based upon their productivity compared to that of competing workers. Therefore, workers may increase their future earnings by investing in productivity-increasing activities such as schooling and training. Human capital theorists assume that all individuals follow this rational model of investment and that human capital differences among individuals therefore result from variations in their expectations of returns on their investments. Furthermore, workers differ in their assessments of the costs of acquiring human capital, in total returns on investments, and in calculations of discount rates and variations in their talent or ability.

Social scientists have used this theory in two ways to explain the observed trends in rural labor markets. First, the level of education and skills are lower in rural areas than in urban areas. Although it has diminished in recent years, this gap has prevailed throughout U.S. history and persists still. Therefore, some authors argue that the relative lack of human capital in rural labor market areas explains the higher rates of unemployment and lower incomes in contrast with urban areas.

Second, researchers have argued that the limited human capital of rural workers makes rural labor market areas more vulnerable to global competition for unskilled labor. A recent study by the National Academy of Sciences Panel on Technology and Employment concluded that although technology creates more jobs in the national economy than it eliminates, the negative impact of technology falls heavily on those persons without basic skills and with poor education (Cyert and Mowery 1987). The technological upgrading of jobs requires greater human capital for workers trying to enter these labor markets. Many rural workers do not have the requisite training and skills. Some workers lack even the basic literacy skills needed for higher-skill training, creating a pool of hard-to-employ workers (Ross and Rosenfeld 1988, 338). Many authors argue that dislocated workers who made their living in declining occupations or in declining industries in rural areas will require considerable retraining and re-education. Until rural workers have upgraded their skills, their high unemployment and low incomes will continue.

Institution-oriented Theories

Institution-oriented theories cover a broad spectrum of institutional arrangements, including social norms affecting individual behavior (those of employer and employee), rules of the firms that are buying labor services, union rules, and state and federal regulations governing labor markets and other societal institutions. These theories provide a conceptual framework for understanding the formal and informal rules that govern the operation of labor markets. They are distinguished by their challenge to the notion that supply- or demand-oriented theories are sufficient to comprehend the dynamics of labor markets and the outcomes of labor market participation.

Implicit Contracts. One group of institution-oriented theories focuses on decision making by employers and workers inside the firm. Efficiency wage theory and transaction cost analysis are two theories that offer explanations of decision-making behaviors when the assumptions of perfect rationality and profit-maximizing behavior are set aside. For example, efficiency wage theory argues that some employers pay more than the "going wage" in their market area in order to elicit greater effort from their employees or to solidify worker loyalty (Bulow and Summers 1986; Stiglitz 1987). The introduction of such an efficiency wage may be rare in rural labor markets because informal arrangements exist between employers and workers. In his analysis of two rural labor markets in Maine, Doeringer (1984) describes an informal "gift exchange" where workers accepted lower than market wages in exchange for "favors" to the workers and their families, such as promises of being rehired if layoffs ever occurred, time off from work for personal and family obligations, and giving first preference to family members when new workers were needed. Although one may interpret such employer-employee relations as paternalistic agreements, they nevertheless exist in many rural labor markets and explain in part the lower wages of rural workers.

The use of implicit (or informal) contracts is also a focus of transaction cost analysis. It is a common practice for firms to pay newly hired workers less than the market wage during periods of training, with the understanding that wages will rise after the initial period of on-the-job training. This transfer of information to the new employee is an informational transaction cost from the employer's point of view (Williamson et al. 1975). The use of this wage trajectory obviously benefits both the employer and the employee, who share the cost of training. Moreover, as the employee's productivity increases and wages rise, employer and employee benefit anew. When this arrangement decreases worker turnover, employers are able to reduce future transaction costs.

In labor markets where the informational transaction costs associated with training new employees are low, wage increases over time will not be expected. If the required job skills are simple, training will be of short duration and worker productivity will peak quickly. As a result, the cost to the employer of replacing workers would be relatively low. Therefore, transaction cost analysis would predict both relatively lower wage rates and higher unemployment rates in labor markets having these characteristics. Many of the jobs available in rural labor markets are of this type, especially in the service sector, which has been the major source of rural employment growth in recent years.

The sociotechnical theories emphasize technological developments, particularly the introduction of computers, in an ever-widening array of labor markets. Technological change requires new ways of organizing work that will increase production efficiencies through continuing on-the-job training, greater flexibility of labor use in the workplace, and improved product quality (Piore and Sabel 1984). The possibilities for institutional changes resulting from contemporary and future technological innovations are enormous and barely explored (Sorge and Streeck 1988). However, several developments already have had visible impacts on rural labor markets.

The sociotechnical perspective is a partial explanation for the rise of unemployment in rural areas during the 1980s. By then, computer technology allowed production activities to be decentralized. Manufacturers in New York City can now transport computer boards that control the machines on textile production lines to plants anywhere in the world, install them in the machines, and begin producing anew in less than twenty-four hours. Many manufacturing systems and information-processing industries share this capability. The availability of such computer technology and satellite communication systems allows firms to exploit the lower costs of production in sites around the world. As operations move to lower-cost sites outside the United States, rural areas suffer increased unemployment.

The effects of technological innovation do not always have such a negative effect on all workers. The paper industry, for example, is a rural U.S. industry that has put enormous effort into computerization and reorganization. Here the introduction of new technology has increased productivity through ongoing training of the workers who run the computerized production process (Zuboff 1984). This increase is being accomplished through the development of work teams and pay-for-knowledge schemes, the reduction of job classifications, and a wide variety of other labor-management cooperation schemes in both union and nonunion "shops." Although this transformation may result in a reduction in the number of workers needed, those employees who remain employed receive substantially higher compensation for their services.

Informalization of Work. A related institutional approach examines the "informalization" of labor markets. Informal sector employment is one type of low-wage, low-skill labor that employers may find increasingly profitable to locate in rural areas. By informal sector work, we mean the buying and selling of labor services in a manner that circumvents the laws, rules, and regulations that govern acceptable conditions of employment. Castells and Portes characterize informal sector work as "unregulated by the institutions of society, in a legal and social environment in which similar activities are regulated" (1988, 2). The product of this relationship is usually sold legitimately in the market, but the terms of informal work may not conform to legal requirements. The employment is unreported and thereby the "employer" and the "employee" avoid various payroll assessments: income taxes, unemployment tax, social security tax, workers' compensation, and so on. The "off-the-record" work may also involve unsafe working conditions, payment below minimum wage, dismissal without notice or recourse, and dependence for the worker.

Industrial homework in a variety of manufacturing sectors often relies on informal labor in which workers are paid by the piece or unit of production, off-the-record, and therefore lack fringe benefits or job security. Homework is income-generating activity done in the residence for an outside employer or an intermediary. The increase in informalization is most often explained as industry's reaction to the growing strength of the working class during the 1960s. Unions impede capital accumulation by organizing workers' demands for insurance, health and safety standards, and higher wage and benefit packages. Informalization is a way to decentralize and isolate the labor force in order to avoid the costs of unionization.

The fact that informal labor relations are "at home" in rural areas should come as little surprise, given the trends discussed earlier, particularly the supply of low-skilled workers. The greater prevalence of routine manufacturing jobs and the documented growth in low-wage and low-skill work in rural areas suggest that the line between formal and informal activities in this context may indeed be quite fine. Higher rates of poverty in spite of the presence of an earner in the household and greater disparity between rural and urban household income all point to the potential for informal activities to grow. The depressed rural economies mean greater numbers of people seeking work who may be willing to accept low piece-rates, job insecurity, and no benefits in exchange for a somewhat increased household cash flow (Gringeri 1993; 1994).

Dual and Segmented Labor Markets. Institution-oriented theories also focus on labor market inequalities, labor market discrimination, and the institutional environment that sustains them. Dual labor market theorists posit two types of labor markets. Primary labor markets consist of jobs with higher wages and employment stability than most jobs. They are concentrated in large firms located in sectors of the economy that are capital intensive. A small number of firms dominate primary labor markets and control nearly all of their product market. In a study of the steel industry, Stone (1974) points to a number of institutional structures that are characteristic of primary labor markets: "hierarchical job ladders, limited ports of entry, inducements to stay on the job, job-specificity and a sharp division between the physical and mental aspects of work" (75). Secondary labor markets generally contain unstable jobs, relatively low wages, little opportunity for advancement, and comparatively poor working conditions. Firms that make up secondary labor markets tend to be in highly competitive industrial sectors where large numbers of firms control relatively small segments of their product market. Segmented labor market theory expands this notion by further elaborating the primary and secondary labor markets.

This structural theory calls attention to the fact that women and racial and ethnic minority groups are concentrated in the secondary labor markets and that rural areas have a higher concentration of these markets than urban areas. It also examines the dynamic processes that sustain the labor market segmentation process over time and directly challenges assumptions by human capital theorists about worker preferences in job choice and just returns to worker productivity (Gordon 1972; Loveridge and Mok 1979). Thus, structural theorists partially explain rural and urban differences in income and employment, as well as gender and racial differences, by the institutional arrangements characteristic of industries and their associated labor markets (Falk and Lyson 1988, 1989; Lyson and Falk 1993; Singelmann and Deseran 1993).

SUMMARY

We have identified several major labor market trends in rural areas, noted the consequences of these shifting conditions for workers' employment and income, and surveyed briefly the theories used to explain the observed changes. One still might ask, are rural labor markets different in some fundamental way from those in urban areas? Do they require different theories or do the same theories apply to both? If the same theories apply to both, why then do we observe different trends when we compare urban and rural labor markets and market areas? One also might ask, are all these theories really necessary? Why isn't one theory sufficient? As a way of summarizing this chapter, let us address these questions.

Are rural and urban labor markets fundamentally different? Although rural and urban labor markets differ in important ways, the fundamental relationships between supply, demand, and institutions are the same in both rural and urban markets. The same theories apply to both; a unique theory (or set of theories) is not required to understand rural labor markets. Nonetheless, rural and urban labor markets differ substantially. If one studied only urban labor markets, one would not be able to transfer that knowledge directly to rural labor markets without the potential for making serious errors.

Urban and rural labor markets are different in part because the components (or elements) of labor supply and demand vary considerably across markets and market areas. On the supply side, rural workers on average have less education and training than their urban counterparts. Based on human capital theory, one would therefore expect lower wages in rural labor markets. Rural workers are also often more attached to their community of residence than urban workers and are therefore less geographically mobile. Knowing that employees have a strong attachment to the community or that other employment is not available nearby, an employer may offer a lower rate of pay than would otherwise be the case.

Important differences exist between rural and urban labor markets on the demand side as well. Service sector employment is increasingly important in both areas, but rural labor market areas are more likely to be dominated by a single industry. Furthermore, employment in rural areas is more likely to be in natural resource–based industries or in low-wage, low-skill manufacturing. In fact, rural labor markets, particularly those markets dominated by natural resource–based industries or by a single sector, are dissimilar from each other as well as from urban labor markets.

Thus, both the supply of labor, either in terms of the number of workers available or their skills, and the characteristics of labor demand vary across labor market areas. As a result of these compositional differences, urban and rural labor markets produce quite different outcomes, even though the principles governing the supply and demand relationships are the same.

The "rules of the game" may also differ between rural and urban labor markets. In rural areas the terms of agreement between the employer and employee are more likely to include nonmonetary considerations, as described by Doeringer (1984). For example, the worker may be allowed time off to care for a sick child without loss of pay, or be allowed to consume some of the product being made or sold without paying for it. Such arrangements are usually informal. Nothing is written down, and it may not even be discussed between the employer and employee; the arrangement is merely part of the local norms governing employment. Where such nonmonetary compensation arrangements occur, the wage rate is likely to be lower. This evidence suggests that institutional and social organizational factors also account for some of the differences found in rural and urban labor markets.

Are all the labor market theories necessary? Why isn't one theory sufficient? All of the theoretical orientations we have considered offer insight into rural labor market trends and outcomes. Alone, none appears to be complete or adequate. In some instances the theories pose alternative explanations for what is occurring in rural labor markets. More important, they illuminate different aspects of the social and economic environment in which labor markets operate. The variety of theories reflects the underlying complexity and diversity of rural labor markets.

To illustrate the role of theory, we conclude by reviewing the trends in rural labor markets noted in the first section of the chapter. The various theories help us to understand these trends and the differences between urban and rural areas.

1. Without a doubt, rural labor markets (as well as urban) have been greatly influenced by sectoral shifts of the economy and increased global competition. According to demand-side theories, the traditional extractive and manufacturing sectors have sought to increase productivity or move to lower wage locations in response to increased international competition. Rural labor markets are more likely than urban ones to depend on these sectors as the predominant source of demand for labor, and global restructuring may in fact have caused higher unemployment and lower income for rural households.

2. For rural labor markets dominated by one industry or sector, the fortunes of the area are likely to be more closely tied to the fortunes of that sector than in more diversified areas. For example, areas historically dependent on agriculture have been hard hit by the enormous shift of labor out of the agricultural sector.

3. The increase in unemployment has been, to some extent, an economy-wide phenomenon. Nonetheless, rural unemployment rates were considerably higher than urban rates in the 1980s. This gap may be attributed to factors that distinguish rural from urban labor markets, including the greater dependence on natural-resource industries and low-wage manufacturing, which have been subject to economic swings and global competition. In addition, rural workers may find it harder to find new employment because of relatively lower levels of education and training and because of fewer choices of employers.

4. Household and family income are lower in rural areas than urban, and the gap has been increasing. Lower earnings are consistent with lower average levels of education and training in rural areas. However, earnings of rural workers are lower than those of urban workers with the same education working in comparable jobs. If two workers have the same productivity, human capital theory predicts they will be paid the same wage. Here institutional theories offer further insight. Wages may be lower in rural areas as a balance to nonmonetary compensation and informal labor arrangements. A greater prevalence of industrial homework and a higher proportion of workers in secondary-sector-type jobs may also keep earnings lower in rural labor markets.

5. Part-time employment has risen faster in rural than urban markets. On the supply side, there has been an increase in the number and proportion of persons in the labor force who prefer part-time work. On the demand side, increased competition has produced greater instability in product markets, and employers may feel a need for greater flexibility in scheduling work. By maintaining a smaller permanent work force and using part-time (or temporary) workers during periods of increased demand, the desired flexibility can be achieved. From an institutional perspective, employers may find it economical to hire part-time workers, for they seldom receive health insurance, retirement benefits, vacation time, or sick leave.

These factors explain the general rise in part-time employment, but not the rural-urban difference. The rapid increase in rural part-time employment may be due to differences on the demand-side as well as institutional factors. Rural labor markets may be more dependent than urban markets on the particular sectors most likely to increase part-time employment, such as the low-skill manufacturing industries facing increased global competition. Moreover, depressed rural economies may result in more workers who are willing to accept part-time, temporary, and low-wage jobs.

By employing all the perspectives, the complexity and diversity of rural labor market areas can be better understood. Rural and urban labor markets are subject to the same fundamental principles of supply and demand, yet labor market outcomes and trends differ because of compositional and institutional differences between rural and urban areas. Understanding those differences makes for more informed policies.

NOTES

1. Throughout this chapter rural and urban will be used as synonyms for nonmetropolitan and metropolitan as defined by the U.S. Bureau of the Census (1991).

PART FIVE
DISTRESS AND POVERTY

In Part 4 economic performance was related to space and geography. Drabenstott and Smith, particularly, demonstrated further that economic performance has been quite uneven. Some areas that have done well historically have been in decline more recently. Whether such decline is permanent or temporary is of course enormously important, for poverty is difficult to escape once it has become established.

Persistent poverty is the subject of this part. How prevalent is it in rural places? Why does it exist? Why does it persist in one place and prove temporary somewhere else?

In the introductory chapter of this section, Gene Summers discusses the extent, severity, and location of rural poverty in the United States. He then discusses the various theoretical explanations for its existence.

In the following chapter Thomas Hirschl and David Brown test and evaluate some of these theoretical explanations by comparing and contrasting rural and urban poverty. Their article adds significantly to the literature on this subject as well as having implications for the design of public policy.

In the third and final chapter of this section, Janet Fitchen draws on personal research to explore the economic and social trends that affect rural poverty. Although she concludes that no single cause is responsible for rural poverty, she does identify the range of factors that contribute to what she believes is a worsening situation.

11

PERSISTENT RURAL POVERTY

GENE F. SUMMERS

Pastoral images of rural America as a "green and pleasant land" distort reality. For most rural residents life has been austere in the extreme. For Native Americans, life was simple and hard even before the European settlers came to North America. After the arrival of settlers in 1609, Native Americans were removed from their homelands east of the Mississippi and forced onto reservations where nearly half the Native American population continues to live in severe poverty.

Most of the voluntary migrants to North America came to escape poverty in their home countries. Many settled in the slums of the ports of entry, but many also became farmers and farm workers. Although some rural settlers prospered, most lived in poverty.

For the several million Africans brought to North America as slaves, poverty was a continuous and virtually inescapable condition. When slavery gave way to sharecropping and tenant farming, the former slaves and their children after them experienced continued unrelenting poverty. The Great Migration of rural African-Americans to northern cities in the early twentieth century and the second wave of migration in the 1950s brought tens of thousands of African-Americans from the rural South. For most of those left behind on farms and in small rural towns of the Black Belt and Lower Mississippi Delta, however, poverty remains a rural way of life.

For Mexican-Americans in the Southwest the story is somewhat different, but every chapter ends with relentless poverty. In 1848 the United States completed its capture of the northern one-third of the nation of Mexico. The class structure of a few wealthy landowners and thousands of peasants came with the land. Today, little has changed; over half of the rural Mexican-Americans in the Lower Rio Grande Valley still live in poverty. The transfer of

213

northern Mexico to the United States has benefited the wealthy class, but little of the increased largess has trickled down to the poor.

In the past century there have been several concerted attempts to reduce poverty, especially rural poverty, in the United States. At the end of the nineteenth century economic hardship was widespread and severe. A "rural uprising" was threatening the United States to such an extent that President Theodore Roosevelt appointed the Country Life Commission to address the problems of rural Americans. That report engendered a massive national effort to bring the rural component of society up to the standard of living of urban America. Great efforts were made and some progress toward that goal was realized, but the 1930s found rural Americans again in desperately poor conditions as the nation plunged into the Great Depression.

Many of the New Deal programs initiated by Congress during the 1930s were aimed at bringing relief to rural people, and, again, some progress was made toward that goal. In truth, however, the desired relief from rural poverty came only when the United States entered World War II. The war effort raised such an enormous demand for farm products that prices improved dramatically. Factories could hardly get enough workers to meet their war production demands, which meant many poor rural residents could move to cities where wages were better and the standard of living higher.

During the decade following the war, American industry expanded faster than at any time in history. By 1958 John Kenneth Galbraith would declare that the affluence of American society had made widespread poverty a thing of the past, only "pockets of poverty" remained in the 1950s (Galbraith 1958). These pockets of poverty were mainly in rural areas—the southern highlands (Appalachia), the Black Belt and the Lower Mississippi Delta regions of the former plantation South, the border counties of the Lower Rio Grande Valley, and the Native American Reservations, mostly in the Upper Great Plains and the Southwest. In 1963 President Lyndon Johnson launched his War on Poverty to wipe out these last vestiges of destitution and make the American Dream a reality.

A decade of progress followed, and the number of poor people dropped from approximately 40 million in 1960 to 24 million in 1973. During this period the population of the United States was growing, thus the actual percentage of people living in poverty was dropping even more dramatically than the numbers indicate; incidence of rural poverty fell from approximately 30 percent in 1960 to around 13 percent in 1970.

However, poverty rates increased sharply after 1979 in both rural and urban areas. By 1983 the poverty rate of central city residents had climbed to 19.8 percent, 9.6 percent in suburbs, and 18.3 percent in rural areas (Hoppe

1993). Since 1983 rural poverty rates have declined somewhat but have not fallen as far as the 1978 levels when rural poverty reached a low of 13.5 percent.

WHAT IS POVERTY?

"Poverty is ultimately," as Patricia Ruggles says, "a normative concept, not a statistical one" (Ruggles 1990, xv). One cannot define poverty without reference to social norms that vary over time, from place to place, and among groups. The point of reference in all instances is, however, a minimum standard of living to which all members of society should have access. Although the elements that constitute a "standard of living" include cultural, political, and social considerations, it is most common to express them in terms of economic well-being.

Currently, the U.S. government bases its determination of the "poverty line" on a method introduced in the early days of the War on Poverty. Mollie Orshansky, an employee of the Social Security Administration, recommended that poverty be defined as the amount of income needed to purchase a minimally adequate market basket of goods and services. In practice, the cost of the market basket was based on one commodity—food and specifically the "economy" or "thrifty" diet. The formula assumes that poor families spend one-third of their income on food, and therefore the cost of the thrifty diet (minimally adequate diet) was multiplied by three to arrive at the income poverty threshold. Adjustments are made according to family size and inflation as measured by the Consumer Price Index.

The U.S. Bureau of the Census uses this measure of poverty in order to assess the number of poor people. The federal Office of Management and Budget also uses it to set the eligibility standards for federally funded income maintenance programs, including the cash and in-kind transfers known collectively as welfare. There is much debate as to whether the count of poor people should be made before or after the value of welfare benefits are added to their earned money income.

WHO ARE THE RURAL POOR TODAY?

A recent report from the Rural Sociological Society describes the characteristics of the rural poor (Rural Sociological Society Task Force on Persistent Rural Poverty 1993). The portrait revealed in this report is enlightening, occasionally surprising, and disheartening throughout. The following sketch of America's rural poor is based on this recent publication.

There are two ways to describe the rural poor: to focus only on the population of poor people, seeking to describe the kinds of people who are poor; or to examine the prevalence of poverty among various segments of the United States population by calculating the probability of being poor for various groups of people, such as rural residents, women, African-Americans, the elderly, and so on. The answers yielded by these two approaches are seldom the same, but both are extremely important. Unfortunately, people often confuse the two sets of answers and therefore have misconceptions of the rural poor.

In 1990 there were slightly over 9 million rural residents of the United States who were poor. The overwhelming majority of these rural poor were white (72.9 percent). Fewer than one-fourth were African-Americans (23.6 percent) and Hispanics made up only 5.4 percent of the total. Nearly half (44.4 percent) of the rural poor lived in married-couple families (two or more related persons who live together). Only 17 percent of the rural poor were children living in families headed by a female householder with no husband present. Another 17.6 percent of the rural poor were children living in married-couple families. Thus, children made up 34.6 percent of the rural poor. The elderly made up 14 percent of the rural poor and 9.4 percent of the rural poor were disabled persons. Notice that one should not add these percentages, for individuals are counted in more than one way. Nearly two-thirds of rural poor families (64.6 percent) had at least one member working in formal employment and approximately one-fourth had two or more members working. These are the "working poor" of rural America.

Rural poverty is concentrated in the South; 55.3 percent of poor rural Americans lived in Delaware, Maryland, Virginia, West Virginia, North Carolina, South Carolina, Georgia, Florida, Kentucky, Tennessee, Alabama, Mississippi, Arkansas, Louisiana, Oklahoma, or Texas. There were 6.6 million rural white people living in poverty in 1990; 2.9 million of them lived in the South (43.6 percent). At the same time there were 2.1 million African-Americans living in rural poverty; 96.8 percent of them lived in the South. Thus, black rural poverty is almost exclusively a Southern phenomenon, but Southern rural poverty is not a black phenomenon; more than half of the rural poor living in the South are white.

The second approach to the question Who are the rural poor? is to examine rates of poverty for various segments of the population. If you are a white person living in a rural area of the United States, what is the probability of being poor? In 1990 the probability was .135; in other words, 13.5 percent

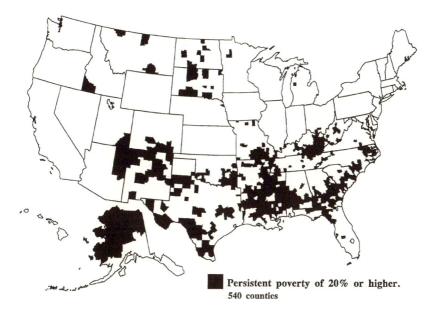

Figure 11.1. Nonmetro counties with persistent high poverty, 1960–1990. (Source: U.S. Bureau of the Census and Economic Research Service, USDA; courtesy Calvin Beale)

of white rural residents were poor; they had a poverty rate of 13.5. That same year the rural poverty rates were 40 percent for African-Americans, 35 percent for Mexican-Americans, and 30 percent for Native Americans. Rural racial and ethnic minorities are major victims of poverty with rates double and triple that of whites.

The only social characteristic that imposes a heavier burden than race or ethnicity is family status. Married-couple families living in rural America had a poverty rate of 9.9 percent in 1990. When children were present the rate increased to 14.0 percent. In sharp contrast, female-headed families (with no husband present) had a poverty rate of 43.2 percent. When children were present, that rate jumped to 56.8 percent. The importance of labor force participation in accounting for this enormous differential is discussed in Chapter 10. Suffice it here to note that married-couple families have two potential adult workers.

There are 540 rural counties that have had poverty levels of 20 percent or more in each of the last four censuses—1960 through 1990. In 1990 these counties were home to 30 percent of the rural poor. Their location is shown in Figure 11.1 (Beale 1993). It is immediately obvious that these same counties, for the most part, made up the "pockets of poverty" that were major targets of the War on Poverty. In 1960 the average poverty rate for these counties was 57.3 percent. In 1990 the average rate had declined to 28.7 percent, still double the rate for all other rural counties and more than double that of urban America, often exceeding that of the worst of the central cities. Moreover, for racial and ethnic minorities living in these counties, poverty rates often exceed 50 percent; female-headed families where children are present often have poverty rates exceeding 70 percent. Clearly, in many of these persistent poverty counties, racial and ethnic minorities are the predominant victims (Summers 1991).

WHY DOES RURAL POVERTY PERSIST?

Many answers to this question have been offered over the years, ranging from entrapment by a culture of poverty, to lack of education and job skills, to declining employment opportunities, to economic exploitation, to discrimination in education and labor markets, and to failed welfare programs. Space will not permit a thorough examination of each possibility. Instead, a broad framework for understanding the various explanations and a more detailed examination of the prominent theories of poverty will be provided. In most instances, theories of poverty describe structures and mechanisms of society that apply to both urban and rural poverty. Certain theories, however, appear to have particular relevance to an understanding of rural poverty.

Schiller (1989) suggests that the numerous attempts to explain poverty can be grouped meaningfully into three types: those explanations that place the blame for poverty on deficiencies of the poor themselves (their flawed character), those that blame poverty on the restricted opportunities of the poor, and those that blame government for destroying incentives for stable families and economic self-sufficiency (see Ropers 1991 for a similar treatment).

Deficiencies of the Poor

Several theories attempt to explain poverty by positing deficiencies of the poor as the cause of low incomes. According to this perspective, there are abundant opportunities for poor people to improve their economic condition. All indigents who want to better themselves and their families can do so. Therefore, people who remain poor do so because they have not made the necessary effort, they have refused to take advantage of the opportunities that are there, they have engaged in dysfunctional behaviors, or they have innately inferior abilities. This explanation of poverty assumes many forms.

The Culture of Poverty. Oscar Lewis is often credited with originating the notion that people are poor because of their cultural traits (Lewis 1966a). Lewis observed the lifestyles of the poor, mostly in Mexico and Puerto Rico, and concluded that their behavior patterns differed from the patterns of the nonpoor in ways that could be explained by their distinct values (Lewis 1959, 1966a, 1966b). Exclusion from participation in labor markets and the cash economy, he reasoned, can create individual apathy, alienation, and deviant behaviors. Once these cultural adaptation are made and passed from parents to their children, they become barriers to future adaptation when new economic opportunities arise. Thus a "culture of poverty" entraps those who share its values, beliefs, attitudes, and behavioral patterns. Lewis did, however, argue that the "culture of poverty" accounted for only a small proportion of impoverishment, perhaps 20 percent.

Other theorists have appropriated Lewis's theory to argue that all poor people develop a culture of poverty that they internalize as a preferred way of life. This distortion of Lewis's concept has been roundly criticized and generally lacks empirical support. Recent work by scholars such as Fitchen (1981, 1991), Cornell and Kalt (1990), Gringeri (1990), and others demonstrates that incorporating cultural elements into theory can enhance our understanding of poverty without blaming the victim.

Human Capital Theory. The basic argument of human capital theory says that the more education and work experience a person has, the better his or her job will be. Workers who are the most productive earn the most money, and those who are the most productive are those who are the most highly skilled. Moreover, for every individual who is willing to invest in his or her education, there is an employer who will reward him or her justly (Dudenhefer 1993).

Advocates of this theory argue that poverty in rural America persists because many rural workers lack the necessary skills to obtain jobs that pay wages above the poverty line. Poor people who live in rural areas must have insufficient education and irrelevant or limited work experience; otherwise, they would not be poor. The evidence shows clearly that rural adult residents have lower levels of educational attainment than urban adults. Within rural areas of high poverty, educational attainment of minority adults is less than white adults. Students in rural high schools have lower Scholastic Aptitude Test (SAT) scores than other students, at least lower than those of suburban students (Lichter et al. 1993).

The human capital theory appears to be robust and efficient as an explanation of earnings as a function of education and work experience under certain circumstances. It provides explanations of earnings for individuals who are active in formal labor markets that reward labor productivity and have low unemployment rates. "But human capital is only one-half of the equation. The other half involves employers and the rewards they give to workers in relation to the skills of those workers" (Dudenhefer 1993, 40).

Genetic Inferiority. One form of blaming the victim argues that impoverishment is due to the genetic inferiority of the poor. People with limited ability, particularly intelligence, are unsuited for many of the jobs in society that require average or better intellectual skills. No matter how much effort they expend, they will never be able to master the tasks required of jobs that pay wages more than the poverty line. When applied to individuals, *without reference to gender, race, or ethnicity,* there is considerable evidence to support the claim that some individuals are born with disabilities that limit their performance in formal labor markets. Persons with extreme disabilities are counted among the "deserving poor" and attempts are made by society to provide for their care. However, the number of such individuals in society cannot be more than a small percentage of the poor, for "work disability" accounts for less than 10 percent of the poor (Hoppe 1993). Racists often attempt to extend the genetic inferiority argument to explain the disproportionately higher poverty rates among racial and ethnic minorities. To date, research has produced no evidence to support such claims.

Restricted Opportunities

An alternative approach to explaining persistent poverty, especially in rural areas, is to examine the economic, social, and political environments of poor people. The basic thesis of those who take this approach is that individuals, groups of individuals, and even entire regions are persistently poor because of restricted opportunities (Schiller 1989). This approach is sometimes referred to as "blaming the system" (Ropers 1991).

The restricted opportunities approach has spawned numerous explanations. I group them here under three headings: labor demand deficiencies, racial discrimination (especially education and employment), and class exploitation. They all share the notion that impoverishment results from forces beyond the control of the poor themselves. Proponents of the restricted opportunities approach argue that only after equality of opportunity has been achieved can one cite personal deficiencies to explain impoverishment.

Labor Demand Deficiencies. This explanation of rural poverty focuses on the "demand side" of rural labor markets. For the vast majority of people, money income is earnings received from selling their labor services. How much work, or employment, a worker is able to get depends upon the demand for the labor services he or she is willing and able to provide. Simply stated, you can work only if there is a demand for the work you are able to do. In the previous discussion of the human capital theory, we learned that lack of education and skills might result in limited employment and low income. The labor demand deficiency theory says limited employment also results from a lack of employment opportunities.

Labor demand deficiencies may result from a variety of sources. Historically, the economic base and primary source of employment in rural areas has relied heavily on natural resource endowments—good soils and ample water for agriculture and forestry, mineral resources for mining, and bodies of unpolluted water for fisheries. Where these resources are of poor quality or are in limited supply one might expect to find restricted opportunities for employment and poor wages for workers in industries based on these natural resources. Thus, in some places rural poverty may be explained by the fact that some people live in areas where the natural resource base is too limited to provide incomes above the poverty line for more than a few people. An imbalance exists between the "population carrying capacity" of the resource base and the current number of people attempting to earn a living in the area.

In the late 1940s and throughout the 1950s there was an enormous thirst for the products of American farms. Two factors seem to account for much of this demand. First, there was a decade or more of pent-up demand by the American consumer due to the depression of the 1930s and the restrictions placed on would-be buyers during World War II. Second, at the end of the war only the United States had escaped the physical destruction of its infrastructure. The rebuilding of the war-torn countries generated an unprecedented market for products that almost no nation, except the United States, was in a position to supply.

Consequently, the high demand for labor in virtually all industries continued in the years following the war. Under these conditions, labor unions gained strength and were able to negotiate wage increases in many industries. Farms and firms of all kinds were seeking ways to reduce their "labor costs" by reducing their demand for labor while maintaining or increasing the output of the enterprise. The application of discoveries in science and engineering provided new technologies that resulted in the displacement of hundreds of thousands of rural workers. Although some displaced rural workers migrated to cities and larger towns where they were absorbed into the urban labor markets, many remained in rural areas where they faced limited employment opportunities and low wages. By the early 1960s this rural labor displacement and rural-to-urban migration had created an urban crisis of unemployment and poverty, without having solved the problem of rural poverty. In 1960 the aggregate unemployment in counties with persistent poverty was 57.3 percent and 29.7 percent in all other rural counties (Beale 1993).

By the 1970s it was abundantly clear that the United States no longer could maintain its postwar near monopoly of international commodity and products markets. The war-torn countries of Europe and Asia had rebuilt their production capabilities, in some instances incorporating state-of-the-art technologies that made U.S. firms relatively less efficient. At the same time, the value of the U.S. dollar became very strong against other currencies, which discouraged foreign exports but encouraged imports. The wages of U.S. workers were among the highest in the world, and U.S. firms had to compete with the lower-wage labor of newly industrializing countries.

Rural areas were seriously affected by the increased global competition. Plant closings in manufacturing industries left many small towns reeling as their major source of jobs disappeared. Loss of a major employer in a small local economy often has immediate and devastating effects on other firms and households in the community. Obviously, the families that depended upon the major employer for an income have lost a major or sole source of income. They must curtail their expenditures for consumer goods and services. Businesses that provide these consumer goods and services to local residents suffer losses and often cut back on the number or hours of workers they employ. According to proponents of the labor demand deficiency theory, this loss of employment opportunities has contributed significantly to the growth of rural poverty.

The industrial restructuring occurring in the United States also involves centralization of management functions, subcontracting for labor services, and an increased use of temporary and part-time employees. Many firms that have multiple locations for production or sales purposes are reducing the number of management functions performed at each site. Such changes in the organization of management also mean fewer jobs in the rural communities.

Cost savings and market flexibility considerations have encouraged many firms to turn to out-sourcing labor services and to an increased use of part-time and temporary workers. Out-sourcing is a form of contracting for labor services in which a firm enters into an agreement with another firm to provide services, often services that were previously provided by their own employees. An example would be when a Detroit auto manufacturer contracts with a firm in Chicago to provide a component for the auto it assembles in Indianapolis. The Chicago firm has no manufacturing plant at all. Instead, it contracts out the assembly of the component to "independent contractors" who do the work in their homes (see Gringeri 1993 for a documented description of this process).

Discrimination in Education. Education is undeniably a major determinant of earned income. The positive correlation between educational attainment (years of schooling) and income is very strong and consistent; an inadequate education is a major cause of poverty. Precisely because income earnings capacity is so strongly dependent upon educational attainment, equal access to educational opportunities is critical. When race, ethnicity, gender, social class of origin, or place of residence are entered into the analysis, substantial, consistent differences become apparent. Certain groups of Americans enjoy less access to educational opportunities than others. Those denied equal access face an increased probability of being poor. Therefore, discrimination in education is a major source of poverty, especially in rural areas with a high concentration of racial or ethnic minority populations.

Until 1954 racial discrimination in education was blatant and supported by the "separate but equal" doctrine established by the U.S. Supreme Court in 1896 (*Plessey v. Ferguson*). Although the court case dealt explicitly with the education of African Americans, the same doctrine was invoked to justify discriminatory practices affecting most residents of the United States whose ancestors were non-European. Despite the Supreme Court's 1954 decision in *Brown v. Board of Education* that "separate is inherently unequal," school segregation continues.

Studies have documented inequities in educational facilities and equipment, disparities in per pupil expenditure on education, and imbalances in the qualifications of classroom teachers when rural and urban schools are compared or when predominantly minority schools are compared with predominantly white schools. In many rural areas where housing segregation does not provide a convenient basis for school segregation, academies have been established for children of white families who can afford the additional expense of tuition, leading to both race and class discrimination.

Subtler forms of institutional discrimination occur within schools. Enrichment curricula and remedial educational opportunities often result in tracking systems that limit the educational opportunities of minority, lower class, and female students. This constriction occurs when culturally biased standardized tests are used to assign students to tracks. The racial, class, and gender biases of teachers also have been shown to result in differential treatment of students (AAUW 1992).

Not only do children who are discriminated against in school have a greater likelihood of being poor as adults, but these children's parents too were denied equality of educational opportunities. Thus, discrimination in education also contributes to the intergenerational persistence of poverty.

Discrimination in Labor Markets. There are disparities in earnings between rural and urban workers with the same educational attainment. Similar inequalities exist between minority and white workers, women and men, and workers whose parents are of different social classes. Such differences lead many social scientists to argue that discrimination in labor markets accounts for some of the observed inequalities in earnings returns to educational attainment.

Labor market discrimination comes in many forms. Employers and unions sometimes deliberately exclude minorities, women, and members of the lower class when hiring. Although this behavior is illegal, there is clear evidence that it continues (Fix and Struyk 1993). "Word of mouth" recruitment is a more subtle, but effective, means of denying access to unwanted applicants for job openings. Occupational segregation is yet another means of discriminating in labor markets. An employer may hire minorities, women, or people of lower class, but generally only for low-paying jobs with few opportunities for promotion.

The targeting of entire geographic areas for exclusion in order to avoid commerce with "undesirables" is known as "red-lining." It was first identified as a practice used by some bankers and insurance underwriters who declared selected geographic areas as ineligible for loans or insurance. Anyone applying for a loan or insurance who lived in such an area was automatically denied. Such areas were often rural towns or urban neighborhoods with high concentrations of low-income households or minority populations. Even though "red-lining" is now a violation of federal law, there is evidence that race, gender, and locational bias in credit and business loan practices still constrain the creation of minority and female-owned businesses, especially in rural areas. Thus, through quite subtle and indirect methods of discrimination, some rural poor are denied or have limited access to equal employment opportunities.

Business location decisions also may limit or deny rural workers, especially minority rural workers, from access to employment opportunities (Williams et al. 1992). A decision to avoid locating a plant or store in an area of high poverty or racial concentration may not be motivated by prejudice, but the effect is to limit the employment opportunities in the area, which results in de facto discrimination. Similar denial and limiting of opportunities occurs when firms close establishments in such areas.

Worker Exploitation. Another theory of poverty focuses on the structure and uses of economic and political power to explain why so many rural people and places remain impoverished. Proponents of this view argue that the root of poverty lies in the capitalist economic system. Society, so the theory goes, is divided into two classes of people, those who own the means of production (capitalists) and the wage laborers (workers). The boundaries between these two classes is very rigid, offering virtually no social mobility. The owners and managers of capital use their resources, economic power, and influence to maximize their profits and thereby increase their wealth and power. To do so they must minimize the costs of production, and since wages paid to labor are a major production cost, wages and all related labor costs are kept as low as possible. Furthermore, owners and managers of capital will seek to substitute technology and mechanization for labor whenever doing so increases efficiency (output per unit cost of inputs). They also may move production activities to locations where labor and other production costs are lower. Finally, they will wield their political power to restrain government actions that might increase their taxes, reduce their comparative advantages in trade, and strengthen the ability of labor to organize.

According to this view, when owners and managers of capital are unrestrained, worker exploitation results; profits are extracted from the workers by paying them less than the "real value of their labor." Thus, the economic and political elite are able to retain and perhaps increase their wealth by maintaining a large and impoverished class of workers who are sufficiently desperate that they are willing to accept work on the terms offered by the owners and managers of capital. From the point of view of impoverished workers, exploitation is better than starvation.

Some critics of the capitalist system argue that the exploitation of workers can be avoided only if the state owns the principal means of production. The recent collapse of communism in eastern Europe has undermined the credibility of this view. Other, more moderate, critics argue that the excesses of the system can be controlled through state regulation of the critical mechanisms of the economy and labor market practices. There are many varieties of intervention schemes, but they all aim to use state apparatus (legislative bodies, regulatory agencies, courts, police) to restrain abuses and guide the economy without taking ownership or management control of goods and services production in society.

In the United States, state intervention gained unprecedented momentum during the 1930s with the enactment of New Deal programs. Several programs to assist the poor were initiated during these years: Old Age and Survivors Insurance was initiated and later expanded to what we now call Social

Security, Aid to Dependent Children was started and later renamed Aid to Families with Dependent Children (AFDC), relocation assistance programs were provided to families in search of work, assistance to disabled persons was increased, unemployment insurance was introduced, workers compensation was launched, legislation to strengthen organizing efforts by unions was passed, and many other similar worker-oriented programs were established to limit the exploitation of workers. During World War II the role of the state in managing the economy was further expanded to coordinate the war effort, an expansion that continued during the Cold War years at a more restrained level. The War on Poverty during the 1960s and early 1970s further extended federal government programs to assist the impoverished and lower-income segments of society. This thirty-year period of increased government intervention is often referred to as "growth of the welfare state."

Failed Government Policies

The third major approach to explaining the persistence of rural poverty posits that the policies of the welfare state have undermined work incentives, destabilized the family, created a costly and unmanageable government bureaucracy, and handicapped the ability of owners and managers of capital to respond to market changes. Government intervention, perhaps motivated by the noblest of intentions, has produced a record of failed government policies.

According to this perspective poor people are not inherently flawed, and their impoverished condition does not result from their own deficiencies. Instead, the policies of the welfare state have produced high taxes, welfare benefits, racial quotas, and other distortions of the economy that pervert workers' perspectives and behaviors. Rather than helping the poor, government policies have actually destroyed work incentives and created "welfare dependency" for millions of poor people (Gilder 1981; Murray 1984; Kaus 1992; Mead 1992). Thus "restricted opportunities" also is a spurious explanation of rural poverty. Government interventions in the economy have distorted markets and undermined the ability of United States firms to compete in changing world markets. As government has attempted to respond to the plight of the poor by stipulating wage and benefit requirements, safety regulations, and hiring and promotion practices, the effect has been to raise the cost of labor to such a high level that firms cannot compete.

According to this view, firms are unable to grow and expand in ways that could create more jobs. Instead, employers are forced to find ways to substitute technology and mechanization for workers. They also may have to reorganize management to reduce costs. The practices of out-sourcing described earlier are said to be a result of government policies that have raised the costs of labor. Therefore, the deficiencies in labor demand in rural areas also are a result of failed government policies that are a brake on economic growth. Unregulated and unrestrained, the economy could create more jobs.

SUMMARY

This chapter has described the extent and persistence of rural poverty in the United States and provided an overview of the several explanatory theories employed by social scientists. Readers will naturally wonder which is the correct or best explanation. In fact, there is no single correct or best theory. Rural poverty has multiple causes, and each of these theories adds something to our understanding of this complex issue. Alone, no theory accounts sufficiently for the persistence of rural poverty in its diverse forms, but each approach is appropriate at a different level of analysis. The theories mutually complement one another, as the Rural Sociological Society Task Force on Persistent Rural Poverty concluded in 1993:

> Much theoretical work concerning poverty is organized around the framework of supply and demand for labor and is driven by moral assumptions such as the inherent value of work, legitimacy of access to consumption through work (except for children, disabled, and the elderly), and just pay for honest toil. . . . One body of theory emphasizes deficiencies of individuals as the source of poor earnings, and the other focuses on firm, sector, and market constraints on opportunities for earnings. These are inherently complementary rather than contradictory. Thus, the extended and rancorous debate of recent years is largely vacuous and counterproductive. Each theory provides useful, but limited, explanations of persistent rural poverty. (RSS Task Force on Persistent Rural Poverty 1993, 11)

Each of these three broad approaches to explaining persistent poverty attracts people who hold different ideologies, political values, and economic interests. Although social scientists are able to describe the various views and to conduct research that may reveal the empirical verity of claims for one or another of them, the political process will define the escape from rural poverty. Knowledge of our potential biases does not settle the controversy, but it may ease the sifting and winnowing of potential pathways from poverty for rural people and places.

We must continue to search for accurate and complete information about who are the rural poor; what distinguishes them from the rural nonpoor; how they differ from one another regionally, racially, culturally, and politically; and how they compare with the urban poor. The following two chapters summarize a great deal of the current state of knowledge about these issues. The clear message is that the rural poor are a very diverse segment of America's population whose quality of life is extremely debilitating. In many instances their life is as austere as that of the residents of the worst central city slums in America. Most Americans view such conditions as unacceptable in the world's richest nation, and leaders are being asked to create pathways from poverty, but the challenge is enormous.

12

THE DETERMINANTS OF RURAL AND URBAN POVERTY

THOMAS A. HIRSCHL AND DAVID L. BROWN

Scholarly and policy concerns about poverty and increasing social inequality were renewed by economic conditions in the 1980s. During this period, three significant trends appeared that concern the nation's poor. First and perhaps most significant, sustained economic prosperity failed to reduce poverty. Despite continuous economic growth between 1983 and 1989, reductions in the poverty population were modest, averaging 1.8 percent per year and only exceeding 2.5 percent in 1984 (U.S. Bureau of the Census 1990b; 1990c). Uncharacteristically, levels of inequality increased during this period of economic expansion, leading two observers to declare that the expansion failed to "lift all boats" (Danziger and Gottschalk 1993, 5). Second, the prevalence of poverty for mother-only families remained at the high level achieved by 1980 (Garfinkel and McLanahan 1986). Third, a combination of monetary inflation and administrative cutbacks reduced the effectiveness of government welfare programs, notably Aid to Families with Dependent Children, and of federal housing assistance (Levitan 1990).

Poverty is not evenly distributed across the American landscape, but scholarly efforts have largely focused upon the inner city poor in metropolitan areas (Anderson 1990; Jencks and Peterson 1991; Massey and Eggers 1990; Wilson 1987, 1991). In terms of sheer visibility, the poor population of the inner city commands the greatest attention from the nation's news media, policy analysts, and academic researchers, especially since the recent civil disturbances in Los Angeles and the Crown Heights area of New York City. The prevalence of rural poverty, however, resembles that in metropolitan central cities, and it, too, represents a major challenge for research and public policy. Recent analyses (Rural Sociological Society Task Force on Persistent Rural Poverty 1993; Duncan 1992a; McLaughlin and Sachs 1988; Morrissey 1991;

O'Hare 1988) demonstrate that, compared to metropolitan areas, nonmetropolitan areas exhibit higher poverty rates, experience more underemployment (Lichter and Constanzo 1987), and are more widely afflicted by long-term "persistent poverty" (Adams and Duncan 1992). Thus, although urban ghetto poverty is a major national problem, the problems of rural poverty are no less severe. The focus on the urban ghetto could prevent an accurate understanding of poverty if the circumstances of the ghetto are not representative of other places with similarly high poverty rates.

In this chapter we look across broad geographic areas to gain a comparative understanding of how poverty occurs in both urban and rural locales. Our specific purpose is to identify the factors associated with the higher prevalence of poverty among metropolitan central county and rural populations vis-à-vis the metropolitan fringe population. Do the same factors cause metropolitan central county and rural poverty, or is extreme poverty in these two diverse areas caused by different factors? To address these questions we model data from the Panel Study of Income Dynamics (PSID), a nationally representative sample of the United States population. The PSID is a unique data source, for it provides household-level information as well as information about the respondent's county of residence. Other national household samples, such as the Current Population Survey, suppress information about county of residence to protect respondent confidentiality. Use of the PSID, however, permits us to investigate both household level and contextual factors associated with poverty in rural and urban areas.

We address two specific propositions. First, the higher prevalence of poverty in rural areas and metropolitan central counties is explained by compositional differences in human capital (education and work experience), demographic characteristics (age and race), and household structure (single parent family versus married couple family). We interpret support for this proposition as indicating that poverty is higher in rural areas and metropolitan central counties because these areas have more people at risk of poverty. Our second proposition is that differences in local economic organization (unemployment, quality of jobs, and employment change in manufacturing industries) explain spatial differences in poverty. The second factor implies that the differences between rural and metropolitan central county on the one hand and suburban poverty on the other derive from dissimilar economic opportunity. A recent report by the Rural Sociological Task Force on Persistent Rural Poverty (1993) asserts that while these two sets of factors fail to offer a complete explanation of rural/urban poverty differences, they are clearly central aspects of any causal explanation. We put this assertion to an empirical test by modeling data from the PSID.[1]

RURAL/URBAN DIFFERENCES IN
THE CAUSES OF POVERTY

Poverty in the United States is geographically concentrated in central cities of large metropolises and in small towns and rural areas. In 1990 metropolitan central counties contained 29 percent of the nation's total population but 41 percent of persons below the poverty level, whereas nonmetropolitan areas contained 23 percent of all persons and 29 percent of the poor. In contrast, almost half the nation's total population resided in metropolitan ring areas (48 percent), but only 30 percent of the people falling below the poverty level resided there (U.S. Bureau of Census 1990b).

The purpose of this chapter is to identify the underlying causes of the residential concentration of poverty in rural areas and metropolitan central counties. Does poverty concentrate in metropolitan central counties and rural areas because the characteristics of people living in these locations are less favorable than the characteristics of people living elsewhere? Alternatively, does the explanation rest on a spatial unevenness in the opportunity structure that differentiates metropolitan central counties and rural areas from other residential and economic settings?

Individual and Household Attributes

An individual's stock of human capital is associated with his or her economic well-being or disadvantage. Although the intensity of labor demand, the geographic location of employers, and the wage structure and skill requirements of occupations constitute the organizational context within which human capital is applied, skills, knowledge, and experience qualify a worker for employment and subsequent advancement on the job. Human capital is associated with job security by facilitating adaptation to technological and other changes in the workplace. As Thurow (1975) has commented, workers' positions in the queue for locally available jobs are determined by their human capital and demographic characteristics. Moreover, an individual's stock of human capital is associated with the ability to migrate if appropriate jobs are not available locally.

Underinvestment in human capital is not strictly a metropolitan central county problem. Small towns and rural areas also contain a disproportionate share of the nation's underdeveloped and immobile human resources. In 1988, for example, a quarter of rural young adults had not completed high school, and only 13 percent had completed four or more years of college (corresponding percentages for metropolitan areas are 20 percent and 26 percent, respectively). Even though average educational attainment of rural youth has increased in recent years, it still falls behind urban educational levels (McGranahan and Ghelfi 1991). And, as O'Hare (1988) has pointed out, rural poverty rates exceed urban rates within each level of educational attainment. Hence, educational differences alone do not explain the relatively high level of rural poverty.

Employment by the household head and/or spouse is another individual level factor that has a strong negative effect on the chances that a household will have an income below poverty level. However, the antipoverty effects of employment are thought to be less in rural than in metropolitan areas because rural employment is more frequently in low wage industries or occupations, and rural jobs are more likely to be involuntarily part-time or seasonal (Lichter and Constanzo 1987).

Poverty has also been shown to be related to minority status and youth (Farley and Allen 1987; Preston 1984). Racial and ethnic minority status and young age are positively associated with the chance of household poverty regardless of residence; however, race and age composition differ markedly between metropolitan and nonmetropolitan areas. The high concentration of racial and ethnic minorities in metropolitan central cities, for example, contributes to high poverty rates in such areas. By contrast, few minorities live in rural areas outside of the South and Southwest (Fuguitt et al. 1989). The aggregate impact of race, then, on the chances of rural poverty is not great, at least at the national level.

Family structure, too, affects a person's probability of being poor. Families headed by single mothers, especially those with young children, have increased dramatically during the last two decades (Jaynes and Williams 1989; Garfinkel and McLanahan 1986). The rise of families headed by females has changed the dynamics of family income determination and exposed a large number of women and children to economic insecurity. The poverty rate of persons living in families headed by women far exceeds the rate for husband-wife families, 30.4 percent compared with 5.7 percent for married couple, and 12.0 percent for male-headed families (U.S. Bureau of the Census 1990c). The reciprocal relationship between economic conditions and family status is apparently a central aspect of the process through which poverty develops and is perpetuated in America.

Part of the relationship between family structure and poverty has to do with labor force participation for the obvious reason that ability to gain income from wage labor depends on the availability of family members to hold jobs (Duncan and Tickamyer 1988; McLaughlin and Sachs 1988). When adult family members are constrained from working by lack of human capital, parenting responsibilities, work-limiting disabilities, old age, or geographic isolation from sources of employment, earnings obviously diminish as a source of family income.

The rise of families headed by single mothers has occurred in both urban and rural areas, although more traditional husband-wife units continue to be somewhat more prevalent in the rural population (Fuguitt et al. 1989). By 1990 the share of younger rural families maintained by unmarried women had increased to 16 percent compared with 19 percent in urban areas. Almost half of young black rural families were headed by women (U.S. Department of Agriculture 1991). The association between the growth of these families and poverty appears to be strong regardless of rural-urban residence. Lower education and labor force participation of nonmetropolitan female household heads helps to explain their relatively high incidence of poverty (McLaughlin and Sachs 1988). The poverty rate of rural persons living in families headed by women, for example, far exceeds the rate for rural persons in husband-wife units (32.2 percent vs. 5.6 percent) (U.S. Department of Agriculture 1991). The situation for children living in mother-only families is particularly difficult regardless of residence. Sixty-one percent of rural children living with a single female householder fall below the poverty level compared with only 14 percent of rural children living in married-couple families (Rogers 1991).

In sum, we believe that the direction of relationships between individual and household characteristics and the chances of poverty are the same regardless of rural or metropolitan residence. Differences in these compositional factors help explain high rural and metropolitan central county poverty. However, residential differences in demographic and household composition may cause certain factors to play a larger (or smaller) role in determining poverty rates in rural areas versus metropolitan central counties. For example, even though rural blacks have very high poverty rates, we expect race to play a smaller role in causing national-level rural poverty because very few blacks live in rural areas outside of the South.

Labor Market Composition and Restructuring

The U.S. goods-producing sector has experienced significant job losses as part of the structural realignment of the nation's economy that has been occurring over the last three decades. The trend in employment away from the production of goods and towards service industries is being experienced by all developed nations and is likely to continue (Jones 1990). The U.S. Bureau of Labor Statistics projected that nine out of every ten new jobs from 1984 to

1995 would be in the service sectors. The decline of manufacturing employment and the rise of service employment has negative implications for the economic security of a large proportion of the nation's work force. The growth of manufacturing jobs allowed large numbers of workers to rise from poverty; many of these very same people are being displaced in the current structural transformation.

Even within the goods-producing sector, lower-skill production jobs have declined much more rapidly than average, further reducing the jobs available to workers with limited education or low levels of literacy and math ability. Between 1979 and 1985, for example, overall employment in the United States grew by 9 percent; white-collar manufacturing employment grew by 10 percent; and blue collar manufacturing jobs declined by 15 percent (Brown and Deavers 1989).

A large body of literature has focused on the negative impact of industrial transformations on women and on racial and ethnic minorities (Tienda et al. 1987; Fainstein 1986–1987). The literature also indicates that economic restructuring is especially problematic for persons who live in metropolitan central counties or in rural areas. Wacquant and Wilson (1989), for example, identify the loss of manufacturing jobs in the nation's urban economy as one of the most important contributing forces in the social and economic marginalization of many inner-city blacks. Kasarda (1985) has demonstrated a growing mismatch between the skills of the inner-city labor force and the types of employment opportunities expanding in the central city. Kasarda contends that many inner-city blacks are not qualified for the new white-collar jobs being created in central cities and that they are spatially isolated from lower-skilled jobs being created farther out in the suburban ring.

Similarly, the dramatic rise in rural poverty that occurred during the early to mid-1980s appears to be associated with economic stagnation and with the industrial and occupational restructuring of rural economies. Thirty years of structural change have left most rural workers dependent on economic opportunities outside of traditional agriculture and other natural resource-based industries. Although this structural transformation, especially the rise of rural manufacturing, has benefited many workers, the growing rural manufacturing base displays a disproportionate representation of labor-intensive establishments with a surfeit of relatively low-skill, low-wage jobs. These jobs tend to be vulnerable to broad cyclical swings in the nation's economy, and they have proven to be especially vulnerable to international competition. As a result, rural employment growth from 1982 to 1987 was only half as rapid as in urban areas (1.6 percent per year vs. 3.0 percent per year) and growth was practically nonexistent in industries that produce goods. Rural economies suffered from delayed recovery from the 1979–1982 recession and had significantly higher unemployment during the most recent recession as well (U.S. Department of Agriculture 1991).

The net effect on rural workers of recent economic trends and of longer-term structural changes has been to decrease the security and quality of their employment. Rural unemployment has been higher than urban unemployment since 1980; rural workers are more likely to be underemployed and underpaid (Shapiro 1989; Lichter and Constanzo 1987); and real earnings per rural job have declined, especially in the goods-producing sector that accounts for over one-third of rural employment (U.S. Department of Agriculture 1991). Hence, an increasing share of rural workers occupy marginal and frequently unstable jobs in peripheral industries that, because of declining product markets and technological change, are either stagnant or declining employers.

All regions and localities have not been affected equally by this broad trend. Many areas retain a significant share of employment in "core industries" that tend to have higher occupational status profiles, higher wages, more stable employment, and more desirable fringe benefits. Core industrial sectors include durable manufacturing, mining, construction, and transportation and communication services. As Bloomquist and Summers (1982) have demonstrated, local economies that specialize in core sector industries (or, to use their term, concentrated industries) tend to have greater income equality. Similarly, Tomaskovic-Devy (1987) has shown that differences in industrial structure are associated with intercounty variations in poverty rates.

DATA

We use here the 1985 wave of the PSID, the most recent wave available when the analysis was conducted. The PSID is a longitudinal file of persons in household units first interviewed in 1968 and every year since; the total number of households in 1985 was approximately 6,700. Part of the original impetus for drawing the sample was an effort to assess antipoverty programs; accordingly, households living below and near the poverty level were over-sampled. The PSID is therefore an appropriate data set to study the determinants of household poverty in varying residential locations.

The dependent variable in this study is income poverty at the household level. It is measured by the PSID income/needs variable, modified to conform to the U.S. Bureau of the Census definition of poverty (Institute for Social Research 1987, D3-D5). Income is defined as total family income that is the sum of taxable income of head and spouse, total transfers of head and spouse, taxable income of others, and total transfer income of others. Like most annual income surveys, the questions asked refer to the year preceding the interview year. Thus, our use of the 1985 wave yields information about income in 1984. Our analysis is therefore conducted for the year 1984, and we use 1984 variables when appropriate and available.

The significant independent variable is county of residence, which was classified in 1984 according to a scheme developed by the USDA Economic Research Service using 1980 census data (Institute for Social Research 1987). We have transformed the USDA categories into the following four county types: "metro core"—central counties of metropolitan areas with populations of 300,000 or more; "metro fringe"—fringe counties of metropolitan areas with populations of 300,000 or more; "other urban"—other metropolitan counties and nonmetropolitan counties that have an urban population of 20,000 or more; and "rural"—nonmetropolitan counties that have an urban population of less than 20,000. Our four-category classification system is based on 1980 metropolitan status and size of county urban population. The cutoff of 300,000 for metropolitan areas was chosen after examining several different cut points; we believe it differentiates the nation's larger cities from smaller cities and rural areas.

We included a number of other PSID variables in the study to control for the individual- and household-level determinants of poverty discussed earlier. We define human capital by including a dichotomous education variable consisting of no high school degree versus high school degree or higher, employment status of the household head and of the head's spouse, head's years of full-time work experience, and head's work-limiting disability status. Demographic characteristics include head's race (non-Hispanic white v. minority—largely African-American in the PSID), age, and family status, which is operationalized with a three-way measure consisting of unmarried and without children, single parent, and, the omitted category, married.

Contextual characteristics are operationally defined at the county level. Each PSID respondent record contains a federal information processing code (FIPS) that is used to link county indicators to the household records. The indicators are percent of the labor force unemployed in 1984, percent of county labor force employed in concentrated sector industries in 1984, and the percent change of county employment in manufacturing from 1975 to 1984.

We seek to identify whether residential status is a significant determinant of household poverty after controlling for the relevant causal factors. Our review of the literature suggests that observed differences between rural and

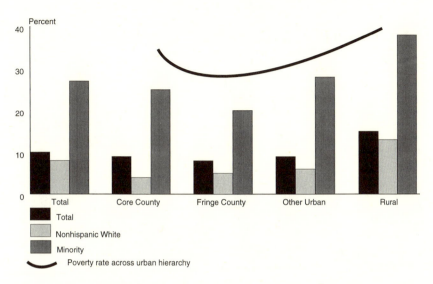

Figure 12.1. Household poverty rate by residence and race, 1984. (Source: Panel study of income dynamics, 1985 wave)

metropolitan central county poverty rates should be diminished by controlling for variables of household composition and contextual control. We first review aggregate poverty levels across the four different residential statuses. We then estimate a multivariate model to define the probability of being poor, contingent on various household and economic opportunity factors.[2]

ANALYSIS

Aggregate levels in household poverty rates by residence are presented in Figure 12.1, along with the overall rate.[3] Overall, 8.7 percent of the PSID households lived in poverty in 1984, and this varies greatly by residence and by race. Rural minority households have the highest poverty rate (36.4 percent), versus non-Hispanic white households residing in core metro counties, who have the lowest poverty rate (3.7 percent).

Figure 12.1 has three sets of vertical bars corresponding to the total poverty rate, the non-Hispanic white poverty rate, and the minority poverty rate. Within each of these three sets of bars, there is a "U" pattern moving from left to right (see the U drawn on the graph). Poverty is high in core counties, least in fringe counties, slightly higher in other urban counties, and highest of all in rural counties. Because rural poverty is highest, the right end of the U

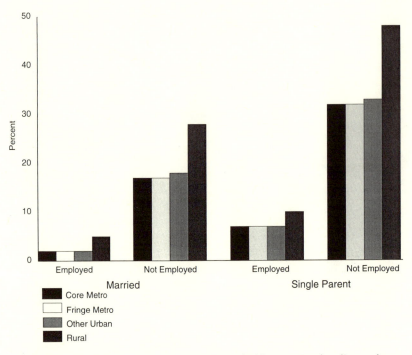

Figure 12.2. Probability of being poor: Household structure, head's employment status, and residence.

is higher than the left end. This aggregate pattern could be the result of compositional differences in people at risk of poverty, of differences in the structure of economic opportunity between different rural and urban areas, or of other factors not included in our analysis. In the statistical analysis that follows, we investigate the first two possibilities.

Multivariate Analyses

Figures 12.2 through 12.4 present results from a multivariate analysis testing for an association between residence and poverty, controlling for compositional factors. These factors include human capital variables (education, employment status of head and spouse, years of full-time work force experience, and work disability status), demographic factors (age and race), and household structure (single-parent family and married-couple family). If there is no statistically significant association between rural or urban residence and poverty controlling for these compositional factors, then the effect of residence in the model will be equal to zero, which would be graphically reflected by

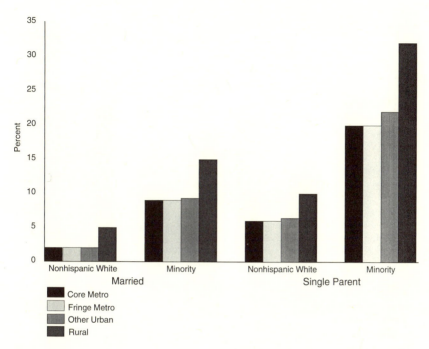

Figure 12.3. Probability of being poor: Household structure, head's racial status, and residence.

residence bars of equal height. Figure 12.2 simulates the effect of household structure and head's employment status on the probability of being poor; Figure 12.3 simulates the effect of household structure and race on the probability of being poor, and Figure 12.4 simulates head's work experience and education.

In all instances, single-parent families have higher poverty risk than married couple families, but this risk is greatly reduced by having a job, as illustrated by Figure 12.2. Likewise, Figure 12.3 illustrates the joint effects of household structure and head's racial status. This figure illustrates the plight of minority families (both married and single parents) who experience three times the poverty risk of non-Hispanic white families. This pattern indicates that the higher prevalence of single-parent families among minority households does not account for the higher risk of minority poverty and suggests that there are other factors, such as residential segregation, employment discrimination, and lack of capital resources, causing high minority poverty. Figure 12.4 shows that education has an antipoverty effect, even after controlling for work experience. Households in which the head has

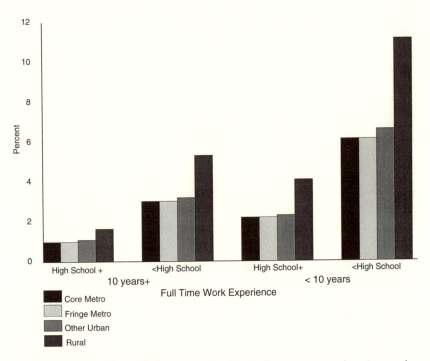

Figure 12.4. Probability of being poor: Head's work experience, education, and residence.

a high school degree experience less than half the risk of poverty of households in which the head does not have a high school degree, regardless of work experience.

An examination of the overall effect of residence in Figures 12.2 through 12.4 reveals that the rural bar is higher than the other three residence types for each group of bars. This means that the higher rate of rural poverty is not accounted for by differences in employment status, household structure, minority status, work experience, or education. Composition does, however, account for the differences among the other three residence types, for there is no reliable statistical difference between poverty rates once compositional factors are controlled. This rather dramatic finding indicates that the rural poverty rate is higher than the poverty rate in other areas even after controlling for the characteristics of at-risk households. One possible explanation for this difference? Economic conditions in rural areas are worse than in other areas, an explanation pursued in Figures 12.5 and 12.6.

Figures 12.5 and 12.6 simulate the effect of residence and local economic organization on the probability of being poor. Comparing the residence ef-

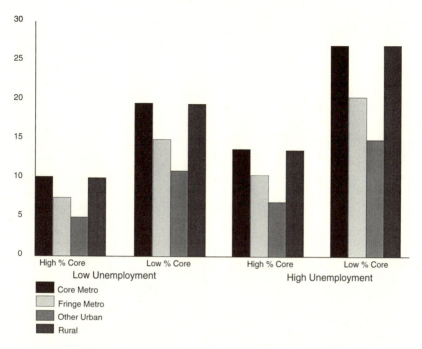

Figure 12.5. Probability of being poor: Unemployment level, percent of labor force in core industries, and residence.

fect in these two figures to the effect in the compositional models presented in Figures 12.2 through 12.4 reveals a very different pattern of results; that is, there is no difference between rural and metro core county poverty if one controls for these two aspects of local economic organization. In other words, these two residence types would have equal poverty rates under conditions of equal unemployment rates, equal percentages of employment in core industries, and equal changes in manufacturing employment. Fringe metro and other urban counties, however, would still have lower poverty rates under equal economic conditions. This fact indicates that these counties have characteristics that protect them from poverty, notwithstanding economic conditions, characteristics absent in rural areas and metro core counties. The evidence from Figures 12.2 through 12.4 suggests that these may be compositional factors, e.g., more households with higher education levels, fewer single-parent families, and so on.

Figure 12.5 shows that local employment composition, measured by percent of the labor force in core industries, has a powerful effect on the household risk of poverty even after controlling for unemployment level. House-

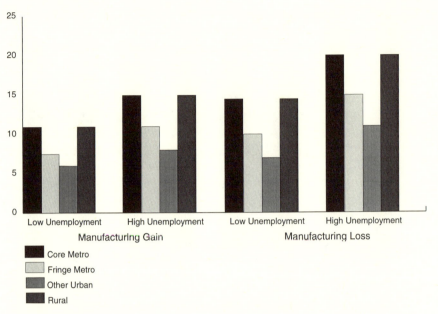

Figure 12.6. Probability of being poor: Manufacturing change, unemployment level, and residence.

holds in counties with a low percentage of employment in core industries face twice the risk of poverty as households living in counties with a high representation of these better jobs.

Figure 12.6 illustrates the symmetric effects of manufacturing employment loss and unemployment. Households in counties with high unemployment face a 40 percent higher risk of poverty than households in counties with low unemployment. Similarly, households in counties that have lost manufacturing jobs face a 40 percent higher risk of poverty compared to households in counties that gained manufacturing.

Our final analytical goal is to determine whether the combination of compositional factors and local economic organizational factors either eliminates or accounts for the effect of residence. The answer is no. When we estimate models that include both sets of variables, the pattern of results for the residence coefficients is identical to the model that includes only compositional variables (illustrated by Figures 12.2 through 12.4). Except for manufacturing change, all of the compositional and contextual variables show statistically significant effects on the odds of poverty. Thus, the effect of local economic organization on the probability of poverty is the same as illustrated in Figures

12.5 and 12.6, except that there would be no difference between counties that gained versus counties that lost manufacturing.

There are two possible interpretations of our finding that compositional and local economic organization factors, when considered together, fail to eliminate the effect of residence on the probability of poverty. First, our particular measures may not accurately represent the true effects of composition and context. We discount this explanation: the compositional measures we used are consistent with other poverty studies; furthermore, we investigated a wide variety of other measures of local economic organization (percent of county population below poverty, per capita income, occupation composition, and others) and obtained the same results. The second possible explanation is that another factor(s) not measured by our model accounts for rural/urban differences in the odds of poverty. We support this interpretation, and it is in fact consistent with the recent study authored by the Rural Sociological Task Force on Persistent Poverty (1993), which indicated that human capital and economic structure are only two of many possible explanations of residential differentiation in poverty. Nonetheless, our findings show that these two categories of variables contribute importantly to understanding the causes of poverty in rural and urban areas.

CONCLUSION

The purpose of this chapter is to test the proposition that rural/urban differences in poverty can be accounted for by compositional factors and factors related to local economic organization and opportunity. This analytical goal was pursued by modeling data from the PSID, and three patterns emerged. First, compositional factors (human capital, demographic characteristics, and household structure) are powerful poverty determinants, but rural-urban differences in human capital do not explain why rural poverty is higher than poverty in other residential settings. Indeed, when compositional factors are taken into account, the unique status of rural poverty comes sharply into focus.

Second, factors related to local economic organization may explain poverty differences between core metro counties and rural counties, but they fail to explain differences between these two county types, metro fringe counties, and other (smaller) urban counties. In general, the effect of local economic organization on poverty is less powerful than the effect of demographic, human capital, and family structure characteristics of rural and urban households. This result is not surprising since our model is intended to predict poverty at the household level.

When both household-level variables and local economic variables are included in the same model, the pattern of results for the residential coefficients resembles the model that only includes household composition variables. That is, there is still a substantively large and statistically significant greater risk of poverty for rural households versus households residing in any other area. We thus return to our initial question: Are population composition and local economic structure common causative factors associated with higher rates of central county and rural poverty? Our answer to this question is yes and no. Yes, these factors certainly are common causes of poverty in rural and urban areas. But no, there also appear to be other causes of rural and urban poverty not captured by these two sets of explanatory factors, at least not as characterized here. We believe that an explanation of factors differentiating rural and urban poverty must include the history of class and race relations in such areas (Brown and Warner 1991), as well as aspects of local social organization, including patronage in labor market relations and class- and race-based tracking in public schools (Duncan 1992b). Moreover, it must be remembered that the rural and urban categories are both exceedingly diverse, and explanations of high poverty in one area may be inadequate to explain high poverty in other areas with different histories, natural resource endowments, or race and class structures.

From a policy perspective, these findings about the different causes of rural versus urban poverty might be juxtaposed with research that demonstrates similar differences in welfare use. Compared to the urban poor, the rural poor are less likely to possess accurate eligibility information about the Food Stamp Program (Rank and Hirschl 1993), more likely to disapprove of welfare programs (Rank and Hirschl 1993, 1988), and generally less likely to use welfare (Hirschl and Rank 1991). Together, these findings indicate that where the need for welfare provision is greatest, the use of such programs is smallest. This conclusion suggests that social access to existing antipoverty policies may seriously constrain their effectiveness in rural communities.

This chapter highlights the need for more and better research on the causes of rural poverty put forth by the Rural Sociological Task Force on Persistent Rural Poverty (1993). Our analysis indicates that different causes of poverty in rural and urban areas are not explicable solely in terms of common social scientific approaches that emphasize human capital, labor market, family structure, and demographic factors. To better understand what is distinctive about the causes and amelioration of rural poverty, researchers should start from the premise that conventional approaches only provide a partial explanation and must be significantly enhanced by a historical and political context in order to generate a comprehensive explanation.

NOTES

1. The Rural Sociological Task Force on Persistent Poverty (1993) also listed a third theory of persistent rural poverty: the culture of poverty theory, which argues that a person's lifestyle precludes economic success. Our analysis does not directly test this theory.

2. We estimate three separate logit models, all with the same dependent variable, defined as 1 when household income is below the poverty cutoff and zero otherwise. The first model posits that income is a function of residential status (the trichotomous variable core metro, fringe metro, other urban, and rural as the omitted category), head's employment status (1 = employed, 0 = otherwise), spouse's employment status (1 = employed, 0 = otherwise), head's education attainment (1 = high school or higher, 0 = otherwise), head's work force experience (1 = head's full-time employment experience 10 years or more, 0 = otherwise), head's disability status (1 = head has work limitation, 0 = otherwise), head's racial status (1 = non-Hispanic white, 0 = minority), age (the trichotomous variable head less than age 25, head age 65 or more, and omitted category head's age 25–64), and family status (married, single parent, and the omitted category not married/no children). This model includes residential status with a series of household characteristics. The second model posits poverty as a function of residential status (same as first model), percent core employment (1 = percent core employment in the bottom quartile, i.e., less than 2.7 percent, 0 = otherwise), manufacturing job change (1 = manufacturing job loss, 0 = manufacturing job gain), and unemployment (1 = unemployment in the top 25 quartile, i.e., greater than 9 percent). This model includes residential status with these three measures of local economic organization. The third model includes all of the variables from models one and two. Coefficient estimates for each of these models are not presented, but are available from the authors upon request. Figures 12.2 and 12.5 are based upon the estimates of models one and two, respectively, and have been transformed to probabilities according to the formula provided by Peterson (1985):

$$P\ (\text{poverty} = 1; L = x) = \exp\ (x)\ /\ [1 + \exp(x)],$$
$$\text{where } L = \text{natural log } [P\ /\ 1 - P)]$$

In Figures 12.2 and 12.5, the values of the independent variables are set to their modal values unless otherwise specified by the table heading. Thus, in Figure 12.3, the values for residence status, family status, and employment status vary in combination with spouse's employment status (0 = not employed), head's education attainment (1 = high school or higher), head's work force experience (0 = head's full time employment experience less than 10 years), head's disability status (0 = head has no work limitation), head's racial status (1 = non-Hispanic white), and age (0 = head's age 25–64).

3. The household poverty rate shown in Figure 12.1 is generally lower than the person poverty rate reported by the Current Population Survey for the same year because of computational differences related to units of analysis (the person poverty rate in 1984 was 14.4 percent). For our purposes, the household rate is analytically superior, for household organization is strongly related to poverty dynamics.

13

WHY RURAL POVERTY IS GROWING WORSE: SIMILAR CAUSES IN DIVERSE SETTINGS

JANET M. FITCHEN

The existence of poverty in rural America contradicts popular beliefs about "the good life" in the countryside. Despite a benign and productive environment, the paradoxical reality is that the poverty rate is higher in rural America than in the nation as a whole, a rural disadvantage that has persisted over the decades. The rural poverty rate in 1992, for example, was 16.8 percent, compared to the national poverty rate of 14.5 percent. Politicians and the public focus almost exclusively on the inner cities but over 9 million rural residents live below the poverty line. Scholarly attention to rural poverty has grown considerably in recent years, as revealed by the work of the Rural Sociological Society's Task Force on Persistent Rural Poverty (1993) and in edited volumes on rural poverty (Duncan 1992a) and uneven development (Lyson and Falk 1993).

Poverty is not randomly distributed around rural America, however. In some areas it has not been a significant phenomenon at all or has recently diminished, but in other areas it is widespread, deep, and continuing—or it is increasing, which is the concern of this chapter. Given the uneven distribution of poverty in the countryside and the diversity of rural America itself, our understanding of rural poverty and its growth would be enhanced by supplementing national-level descriptive statistics with qualitative data from field research in specific rural places. This chapter is based on research conducted in dozens of rural communities around the nation, starting with in-depth field research in upstate New York (Fitchen 1981, 1991) and followed by scoping research in nine other states during 1992–1993. Research sites were selected to include different regions, economies, employment trends, and urban influences, as well as different historical, ethnic, and sociocultural characteristics.[1] Specific localities meeting those criteria were identified on the basis of high 1990 poverty rates (over 20 percent) or significant recent increases in poverty.

The geographically dispersed nature of this research provided firsthand observation of the diversity of rural poverty. Perhaps more striking than the differences, however, are certain macrolevel forces and national trends that span regions and cause worsening of poverty in widely separated rural locations. This chapter, therefore, will be neither a travelogue-type sampler of variations of rural poverty nor an explicit comparison of the several states but an analysis of why, as the twentieth century ends, numerous and diverse rural places still have high poverty rates or are experiencing an increase in poverty. The central sections of the chapter concentrate on causes that were identified in this research as contributing to rural poverty. They include certain economic transformations, migration patterns, and social and behavioral trends. Although these three types of causes are discussed separately, it is important to realize that in reality they interact. Indeed, a specific aim of this chapter is to emphasize that no single cause adequately explains why rural poverty is growing worse in many locations around the country: A holistic, integrated approach may better explain what is happening and why.

SOME ECONOMIC CAUSES OF INCREASING RURAL POVERTY

Although changes in the economy of any particular rural community are connected to and reflect transformations in the economies of nearby urban centers, the region, the nation, and the world, the effects are played out locally. Economic changes contributing to rural poverty in specific localities can be grouped under four headings: general stagnation and decline, restructuring of manufacturing, further transition to service-sector employment, and transformation of the food production industry. Some of these changes are regionally specific or localized, but most are widespread, and several may occur together. Each of the four will be illustrated with material from specific field research sites.

General Stagnation and Decline

Perhaps the most obvious and long-standing economic cause of high and persistent poverty in rural communities is a flat or sinking regional economy.

Stagnant economies, with perennially high unemployment and poverty rates, have continued to characterize entire regions as disparate as the Mississippi Delta, northern New Mexico, and northern Appalachia. In the Delta, where institutionalized structures of racism create and compound economic stagnation, even median income is at or below the official poverty line. The poverty rate in Delta counties where I conducted interviews averaged 44 percent; but 64 percent of residents are African-American, and for them the poverty rate is at least 60 percent. In Native-American and historically Hispanic parts of northern New Mexico, county poverty rates have exceeded 30 percent for decades. One county, for example, had a 1990 poverty rate above 36 percent and a median household income under $13,000, which is hardly more than half of the state median income. In this isolated county, where the official 1990 unemployment rate was nearly 17 percent, there simply are too few jobs. Economic stagnation is not confined to regions with a high proportion of minority residents, however. Appalachia, for example, has long had high rural poverty rates in the absence of significant minority populations, a pattern seen even in the region's northern edges in upstate New York.

In some places high poverty rates result from decline in extractive industries. Dependence on resource extraction, a situation that may not be recognized as a problem in good times, becomes a liability for communities if the core industry suffers a national or regional downturn and reduces or closes its local operations. Timber, fishing, mining, and oil, all inherently subject to cycles of good times and bad, were hit hard in recent decades, although differently and with regional and localized variation in length and depth of decline. In Michigan's Upper Peninsula slumping world markets of the 1970s coincided with depletion of the best copper and iron ores, throwing communities into serious, protracted decline because there was little else to keep residents employed after the mines shut down. In the Northwest during the 1980s, several communities formerly dependent on logging and milling suffered localized decline and significant increases in poverty (Cook 1993; Kusel 1991). Contrary to common perception the culprit is not the spotted owl or the Endangered Species Act but a long-term restructuring of the timber industry that has resulted in closure of many small lumber mills, more automation at remaining mills, and gradual shift of the industry to the Southeast.

Restructuring of Manufacturing Firms and Employment Practices

Popular images notwithstanding, manufacturing has been the backbone of many rural economies. According to official classification, nearly 40 percent of the nation's nonmetropolitan population lives in counties where manufacturing is the major source of local employment income. In the last few decades many rural communities have been dealt a double blow: decline in the number of manufacturing jobs as a result of factory closings and deterioration of remaining factory jobs as a result of restructuring. Many manufacturing firms have moved their operations from the Northeast and Midwest to rural communities in the less-unionized South and then to still cheaper labor markets in the Third World. When a local firm that had been the mainstay of employment is purchased by a national or multinational corporation headquartered far away, continued operation of the local plant is threatened even if it is turning a profit. Loss of a factory deals a major blow to small or mid-sized communities because they lack back-up employment for displaced workers. Few new factories have come in to replace the businesses that have been lost; at best there is substitution of smaller-scale assembly plants. This scenario prevailed in a central New York town, where workers lost well-paid jobs with good benefits when the distant corporation that had purchased the local plant decided to move operations to Mexico. Laid-off line workers who exhausted their unemployment benefits without finding adequate replacement jobs finally took entry-level or night-shift work in a small, new assembly plant and in several cases joined the ranks of the working poor.

The problem is not only that local factories are closing, but that employment conditions within remaining plants are also deteriorating. For many of the people still fortunate enough to be employed in the mills and factories of rural America, the rewards of work (including benefits as well as income) have diminished substantially (Shapiro 1989). Corporations attempting to remain profitable in highly competitive international markets have further reduced labor and benefit costs through additional automation or increased use of overtime, part-time employment, and temporary hiring. In one town in the Mississippi Delta, workers reported that their company, long known as a "good employer," now hires only temporaries and that existing full-time workers aren't retained long enough to move above the starting wage. With a large number of unemployed people available to take even these inadequate jobs, single mothers who had broken out of the welfare system reported that they were not able to get out of poverty even after a full year of working in this plant.

In the Southeast, the establishment of textile and garment manufacturing plants in the last few decades has resulted in relatively low unemployment rates, but poverty rates are still well above national averages. In one North Carolina county, for example, poverty remained high despite job growth: Unemployment was only 7.6 percent in 1990, but the poverty rate stood at 25 percent for the county and 30 percent or more in some of its towns. The problem lay less in the number of local jobs than in their meager rewards. Entry-level textile and apparel jobs were paying relatively low wages, and many workers were stuck at these levels because their jobs were part-time or temporary. Workers in a relatively new clothing manufacturing plant reported that they were unable to get enough hours to gain either adequate earnings or health benefits, partly because the labor-intensive operations in garment manufacturing are being transferred to "twin" plants in Mexico under the maquiladora system (see Tomaskovic-Devey 1990).

Along the Mexican border, the maquiladora system has spurred dramatic growth in manufacturing employment on both sides, bringing new factories not only to such metropolitan centers as El Paso and Ciudad Juarez but to adjacent rural areas as well. Ironically, this expansion of manufacturing employment has been followed by a significant increase in local poverty rates, due primarily to depressed wages caused by an excess labor supply, which in turn results from increasing immigration from Mexico (Saenz and Ballejos 1993).

Further Transition to Inadequate Service-sector Employment

In rural America as in urban, transition to a service economy has contributed significantly to the ranks of the "working poor" and "new poor" (Shapiro 1989). Where the shift entails transition from adequate manufacturing jobs to low-end retail jobs, even if there is a net gain in numbers of jobs, workers caught in the transition are apt to suffer income reduction. On the aggregate level, the community's income may be diminished and its poverty rate augmented.

The association between retail service employment and rural poverty is particularly evident in scenic places where tourism has become a major component of the local economy. As studies have demonstrated (Smith 1989), the addition of tourism jobs to a community is not likely to help marginal rural families avoid or climb out of poverty, for the majority of jobs it creates are inadequate for supporting families. In some places poverty rates even increase when people move to the area to take new tourist-related jobs but cannot stretch peak-season earnings to cover the slack season. From the mountains of upstate New York to resorts in central and coastal Oregon, communities with an increased number of tourism jobs find a greater proportion of their residents earning below-poverty incomes. In one rural Oregon county where tourism has fueled "a major economic boom," 3.5 million visitors in 1991 supported 3,275 jobs. But according to a local chamber of commerce, nearly half of these jobs were part-time or seasonal. The total payroll for these jobs, $33 million, amounted to only 44 percent of the payroll received by an equal number of local employees working in the traditional base industry, forestry and wood products. In such communities an increasing number of workers who tend lawns, clean condos, make motel beds, and serve restaurant meals, especially those who are single women with children, need and qualify for food stamps. Income inadequacy in tourist-boom communities is apt to be especially critical in terms of housing: In the county just discussed, while the wage ceiling in tourism jobs has edged up slightly from the entry-level wage of two years earlier, local rents have risen 25 percent and rental vacancy rates have fallen to less than 2 percent. The number of people eligible for public housing has soared, and working families with incomes just above the eligibility level are forced to double up or move out to peripheral communities.

Transformations in Food Production and Processing

Again contrary to public perception, agricultural decline now plays a small and diminishing role in creating more poverty (Deavers and Hoppe 1992). Even the farm crisis, despite its painful economic, social, and personal impacts, did not cause a significant rise in rural poverty, partly because most families who lost their farms changed fairly quickly to postfarm livelihoods and also because the rural farm-dwelling population has declined to less than 10 percent of the total rural population. Since the poverty count reflects people's residence, not their place of work, farm poverty is a very small component of rural poverty.

Paradoxically, growth in large-scale, intensive, irrigation-based agriculture is spatially and temporally associated with rising poverty rates, especially in the Southwest and California and in parts of the Northwest and Plains as well. This increase in poverty has been triggered by several recent production trends, as growers have shifted towards more profitable specialty fruit, vegetable, and nursery crops. These products are more labor-intensive, with work spread over a longer season, and contrary to earlier forecasts, growers have not moved towards mechanization but towards "Mexicanization" (Palerm 1991; Rochin et al. 1989). In such crops as strawberries, apples, pears, broccoli, and asparagus, and in specialty nursery plants, workers now are primarily Hispanics, including Mexican-Americans born in Texas or California, Mexican nationals who have traveled the migrant harvest stream for years, and very recent, direct arrivals from southern Mexico and Central America. Although a significant migrant labor force is still needed for peak seasonal work, increased demand for labor and the possibility of nearly year-round employment in the fields and in processing and packing plants that have sprung up nearby have enabled thousands of previously migrant workers to settle more permanently. Although most resident worker households have at least two adults engaged in agricultural labor and related activities, poverty prevails among them for several reasons: household size may be larger than average; underemployment and seasonal unemployment are still characteristic; work hours are further reduced by travel time and weather-related slack periods; a labor surplus depresses wages; and low wages for agricultural labor remain a dominant element in the nation's food production strategy.

The big difference now is that these low-income workers are not migrants but year-round residents of the crop-producing areas and that their individual and household poverty, in the aggregate, elevates community poverty rates. In southern New Mexico, where transition of more acreage from cotton to chilies has greatly increased labor demands, poverty rates in small towns have risen dramatically. In the most intensive fruit and vegetable production areas of California, community-level poverty rates in the 1990 census were running in the range of 25 to 35 percent and more. Local poverty may be considerably higher than indicated in official figures, however, in part because the sensitive issue of legal residency leads to a census undercount. Furthermore, the poverty of farm workers is not even classified as *rural* poverty, since most towns where workers have settled are situated within populous metropolitan counties. In Fresno County, for example, farm-worker poverty is officially counted as metropolitan rather than rural poverty. Poverty is also obscured by very healthy indicators of production, sales, and general economic activity (Bradshaw 1993).

While the ironic pattern of widespread and serious poverty spawned by the highly profitable vegetable and fruit industry is not new, it has accelerated in the last decade and expanded geographically. The pattern varies depending on climate and growing conditions, crop, and kinds and amount of labor required for growing, harvesting, processing, and packing. It is most intensely developed in the great agricultural valleys of southern and central California, but it is essentially similar in Texas and is rapidly spreading in New Mexico and Arizona. High poverty rates among settled farm workers have become common even in the Northwest, intensifying in and spreading from Washington's productive Yakima Valley and localized in association with specific crops in Oregon.

Upward mobility is not impossible for agricultural laborers, and many are better off than before they settled into year-round work. In some crops, such as strawberries, where small-scale farming can be profitable in certain locations, some Mexican farm workers have become farm operators (Wells 1990).

Upward mobility is also revealed in the life stories of Chicano students in the California university system who tell of childhood in farm laborer families. On the whole, however, the expanding labor needs of modern fruit and vegetable production create a situation in which large numbers of farm labor families are living in poverty, new laborers come in at the bottom to replace any who move upward or out of the agricultural system, and many communities experience residential turnover but no decrease in poverty. Communities with high rates of poverty among settled resident agricultural workers are reeling under the impact and bracing for more.

In much the same manner, major change in the production and processing of meat, poultry, and fish has brought increased poverty to other parts of rural America—even as it has brought more jobs. Since the early 1980s the meat-packing industry has decentralized away from large midwestern cities to areas of irrigated grain production and large feed lots in the High Plains (Stull et al. 1990). The world's largest and newest meat-packing plants have come to the countryside of Kansas and Nebraska and with them thousands of jobs and considerable commercial development. In the new mode of beef- and pork-packing, however, most jobs require less entry skill and pay lower wages than was the case in traditional meat packing, making the new jobs unattractive to local residents. To acquire a sufficient labor force, the companies recruit poor and unemployed people from distant states such as California. In southwestern Kansas, up to half of packing plant workers are minorities, including Southeast Asian refugees and, increasingly, Mexicans and other Latin Americans (Broadway 1994). Although entry wages are well above the prevailing hourly minimum, many workers have less than a forty-hour week, and the difficult and dangerous working conditions cause people to lose their jobs or quit, often before obtaining a raise or health benefits. Turnover in the work force is high, with a large local pool of people who have worked in packing but are not presently employed, circulation of unemployed workers from plant to plant within a tristate region (Kansas, Nebraska, and Texas), and a steady flow of recruits from places more distant. To be sure, the arrival of a new packing plant generates a spurt of local economic growth. In one city in rural Kansas, employment has increased by over 55 percent and population by 33 percent since two large packing plants were established in the early 1980s, and the official unemployment rate in 1990 was only 2 percent (Gouveia and Stull 1992). Nevertheless, most of the incoming workers, regardless of ethnic or regional provenance, are poor when they arrive and many remain poor or fall back into poverty periodically. The increased poverty connected to meat packing may not readily show up in census or other statistical data or even in a casual visit, because it is hidden within a generally healthy local economy and because low-income families attracted by packing jobs typically reside in bedraggled trailer parks located in a different municipality or county, forming a ring of impoverished settlements surrounding the bustling meat-packing town.

Similarly, localized expansion of poultry and fish production employment may maintain or intensify poverty in some communities. In the Southeast, the Plains, and the Midwest, new poultry processing plants bring more employment but fail to reduce local poverty because the new jobs are inadequate. Few workers earn sufficient hourly wages or are hired for enough hours to push their income above the poverty level. In Mississippi, catfish processing plants have brought some much-needed employment to small towns, but the industry's wage structure and hiring practices tend only to transform people from the category of nonworking poor to working poor.

In all these food-related industries, the new production and processing systems have brought overall economic growth and population increase to rural areas, but they may do little to reduce local poverty and may even bring increased poverty because they attract people who are poor and who may subsequently be unable to earn adequate incomes in the new jobs. This movement of poor people to places with food-production or food-processing jobs is yet another aspect of rural impoverishment and leads us to consider directly the role of migration in increasing rural poverty.

MIGRATION PATTERNS ADDING POVERTY TO SOME RURAL AREAS

Various migration patterns are having different impacts on local poverty rates. One form of migration, suburbanization, tends to reduce the poverty rate in rural areas where it occurs, especially in those adjacent to healthy metropolitan centers. A case in point is the fast-growing rural Mississippi County just south of Memphis, Tennessee. Here, the poverty rate is falling because people making the urban-to-rural move are apt to be better educated and able to earn more, through commuting or self-employment, than the preexisting population in the communities to which they move. As in any locality where affluent people are added to the population base, the percentage of local residents in poverty declines, even if the number of poor residents remains constant. Often, however, through mechanisms of rising housing costs and tighter land-use regulations, poorer people are displaced to lower-cost communities. In such cases, it should be noted, suburbanization is not a victory against rural poverty but a dispersion and peripheralization of rural poor people.

Four other migration patterns, however, are contributing to impoverishment of certain rural communities.

Immigration and Settlement of Immigrants in Rural Places

Although immigrants to the United States from Latin America and the Caribbean still mostly head to the cities, a major change contributing to rural poverty is that a greater share of new and recent immigrants now avoids or leaves the cities in favor of smaller towns. Numerous rural communities are becoming, in effect, "ports of entry" as newly created jobs in maquiladora manufacturing and in food production, processing, and packing are dispersed into the countryside. As indicated previously, although workers in such agricultural employment are poor and live in small towns, many are not counted in rural poverty statistics because they reside in the rural parts of counties classified as metropolitan and because the unit of analysis for most poverty studies is the county. This situation is true, for example, in southern New Mexico, where a rapid influx of Mexican-American and Mexican agricultural workers is impoverishing small towns in the rural portion of a metropolitan county.

Growth in rural poverty through immigration is remarkably similar all across the fruit- and vegetable-nursery industry. In each case, immigrant workers arrive poor and are apt to remain poor for some time, in part because language and educational handicaps restrict them to the lowest-level jobs. Many of the recently settled agricultural workers are among the 1.3 million immigrants who applied for legalized residence status under the Immigration Reform and Control Act of 1986 (IRCA), though an undetermined number (generally estimated as one-fourth to one-third of agricultural laborers in Western states) do not have legal residence documents. Despite their poverty in the new location, for many immigrants the move is part of a strategy to achieve a better standard of living, and many eventually pull up to and above the poverty line. Nonetheless, at the aggregate level of receiving communities, immigrant settlement substantially increases poverty. In some Oregon towns with newly concentrated vegetable and fruit production and processing, poverty rates are around 20 percent, compared to the state rate of 12.4 percent.

Increased poverty associated with rapid immigration has profound effects, including stress on schools and public health services, deterioration and crowding of local housing, fiscal problems for local governments, and strain on the private voluntary assistance network. In New Mexico's border area, one rural school district is growing so rapidly that an entire elementary school should be built each year, and special education and service needs are soaring, as are expenses for bilingual education. Neither state funding nor the local tax base can keep up with the burgeoning needs created by rapid immigration of people who are poor. These effects are not just temporary, however, for as some immigrants move up or out, new poor recruits take their places, filling the lowest-level jobs and the worst housing and creating ever more demand on overstressed local health and education programs. At least 150 towns in southern and central California have been identified as "enclave" settlements for Hispanic laborers (Palerm 1991), and two-fifths of these communities have Latino majority populations, in some cases close to 100 percent. Poverty rates in these towns range from the mid-20s to the upper-30s. In New Mexico and Texas, the rapidly growing *colonias* stand as stark testimony to increasing poverty tied to labor immigration and migration (Rochin and Castillo 1993). Much of the housing is seriously substandard, and the physical infrastructure is woefully inadequate. For example, in one of the newly created border-area *colonias* in west Texas, a settlement of about 1,000 residents, homes include very old trailers, converted buses, and the body of an ice-cream truck. In one *colonia* without public sewer and water, outhouses are common and residents fill household water containers from a public pump clearly marked with a skull and crossbones.

Internal Migration of Poor People to Towns with New Employment Opportunities

Closely related to the impoverishment resulting from immigration is an increase in local poverty resulting from internal migration of poor people from various parts of the United States, both urban and rural, to towns or small cities in rural areas that have recently expanded their employment base. The phenomenon is well illustrated by the meat-packing towns in the High Plains, although it also occurs in connection with manufacturing growth and tourism development if a large number of entry-level positions are created. This paradoxical form of community impoverishment also stems from expansion of local employment. The people who push up local poverty rates primarily are young adults who have moved from places with limited employment opportunities and who may arrive with limited employment experience.

In Kansas and Nebraska meat-packing towns, the most obvious and talked about of the internal migrants are relatively recent immigrants, particularly Southeast Asians from California, who come as part of "planned secondary resettlement," and Mexicans who perceive better economic opportunities for themselves in High Plains meat packing than in South Texas or in crop agriculture. The less-noticed inmigrants are the "nonethnic" whites, individuals and families unable to support themselves elsewhere, who are attracted by reports of good money to be made in meat packing. Some have undertaken this single long-distance move as part of redirecting their lives; others are "passing through" or "on the road," moving around the country in search of a better life. All of these inmigrants arrive poor, and although some have skills and educational preparation that enable them to get a good job, many others are unable to escape from poverty. Typical of the latter are the women interviewed at a skills training program who found that despite available jobs, making an adequate living can be elusive, either because of the nature of the jobs or because of their own educational and employment deficits, or both. Having come to the meat-packing town with a husband or boyfriend, they had experienced no improvement in household well-being, for their partners had been unable to succeed either, perhaps remaining unemployed for long periods, and the couple had then separated. On their own as single parents, the women remained in the new location, tried to support the family with a retail clerk job at the mall, and had eventually turned or returned to welfare. Thus, though jobs may be plentiful in such a community, more potential workers migrate in than industry can absorb or adequately support, and the "excess" become part of a floating low-income population.

Internal Migration of Poor People to Rural Towns with Limited Employment

A very different migration pattern that has increased poverty in certain rural locations is movement of poor people from larger and more prosperous towns and cities to smaller and economically weaker rural communities. Simply by their residence change, people who move from a metropolitan area transform their poverty from urban to rural and swell the ranks of the rural poor. Those people who move from one rural place to another are part of a spatial redistribution of rural poverty that augments poverty in communities where they settle.

This pattern of community impoverishment through residential relocation is generally part of an "exchange migration" or "succession" that proceeds through a fairly uniform sequence. It begins with loss of employment that accelerates outmigration from a rural community, creating a glut of unwanted housing and vacant commercial buildings. At the same time, low-income residents of cities and small towns, both nearby and distant, are being squeezed out by rising housing costs and meager employment incomes or welfare support. They report that they had been attracted to the depopulated rural town by its lower housing costs and by the better living conditions and schools that may prevail in spite of its decaying economy. "Pioneer" migrants are followed by relatives, friends, and others pushed out from cities and prospering towns where they can't make ends meet. The receiving community thus becomes a "resettlement destination," but as its population rebounds, the community also grows poorer.

This migration pattern is a relatively small phenomenon at the national level, though common enough to be captured in nationwide demographic analysis (Lichter, McLaughlin, and Cornwell 1994). Evidence of this "backfilling" phenomenon was found in some upstate New York communities (Fitchen 1991), in eastern Nebraska outside major metropolitan areas, and in the upper peninsula of Michigan on the periphery of the more economically healthy small cities. It also may be occurring in distressed timber-based communities in the mountains of California (Kusel 1991) and Oregon. The phenomenon also was apparent in the Washington wheat-growing area, where further consolidation and mechanization have left fewer farm jobs and diminished business opportunities for local residents. In a tiny Washington community of 600, the change was sudden and dramatic. Residents reported that twenty-eight houses had stood vacant and "run-down" two years before, but all had subsequently been rented, mostly to low-income families from dynamic towns and cities elsewhere in the state. Although the agricultural changes did not directly cause poverty, they contributed indirectly to an increase in local poverty by hastening outmigration and creating a housing glut.

In this exchange migration, the rural destination communities have few employment opportunities, especially for people with limited education or work history. Hence, people's choice of location might be perceived as economically irrational. But interviews with families who are part of this pattern show that such a move is apt to be beneficial for them because even a part-time low-wage job will cover a greater portion of the rent in a depressed community. Additionally, public assistance, food stamps, and Medicaid are all portable, and where rents are cheaper, a welfare allowance can more nearly cover family needs. Even though this internal migration pattern helps low-income families get by, it may not lift them out of poverty. On the aggregate level, the receiving community's poverty may be dramatically increased.

Differential Migration Away from Rural Places

Movement away from rural communities with sagging employment is another way in which migration impoverishes rural communities. As demographers have amply demonstrated (e.g. Lichter, McLaughlin, and Cornwell 1994), outmigration continues to be selective: Better-educated young adults with better job prospects and higher lifetime earning trajectories are more likely to leave, whereas those less prepared for employment are more apt to remain in their declining rural communities. If outmigration diminishes the total local population, but few low-income residents leave, then the local poverty rate is automatically increased. Even after some residents have departed, there may still be too few adequate jobs to absorb the remaining young adults, and poverty rates may therefore continue to climb as more youngsters enter adulthood and become parents but have only meager employment earnings.

Reasons for the so-called "failure" of some people to move away from depressed rural communities are less well documented but generally include a mix of social, cultural, and economic considerations (Hickey 1991) and appear quite similar around the country. When a factory in a Northeastern village or a lumber mill in the Pacific Northwest close down, many workers beyond middle-age lack formal education or skills to compete for adequate employment elsewhere. With their life savings tied up in houses unsalable in a depressed market and their social investments tied to local family and community, they settle for very long commutes to inferior jobs or else remain jobless. Younger adults who have grown up in a persistently poor rural locality may be held in place by a combination of fear of the unknown and a sense of inadequacy and low self-esteem. In upstate New York (Fitchen 1981) as in the Mississippi Delta (see Dill and Williams 1992), people who elect to stay in a depressed hometown use a mix of traditional informal economic self-provisioning strategies, kin-based support systems, and public assistance to patch together a living that allow them to remain in a depressed but familiar place but virtually guarantee that they will also remain poor.

Cultural factors, too, may keep people in place despite inadequate employment opportunities. In an isolated Indian community in the Northwest, for example, a bulging population of young adults is now entering a nonexpanding job market in a near-stagnant local economy, a situation quite certain to augment the persistently high poverty rate. But the central and centripetal force of culture, with its emphasis on ties to relatives, both living and ancestral, keeps young people in the area despite lack of jobs. A similar situation obtains in historically Hispanic and persistently poor communities in New

Mexico's mountainous north. Even in nonethnic rural populations, culture has a holding power. Thus displaced timber workers in the Cascade mountains of the Northwest expressed an ideological or value orientation that makes any other occupation or location virtually unimaginable (see also Hibbard 1993) and makes financial poverty an acceptable price for remaining in place.

SOCIAL AND BEHAVIORAL TRENDS THAT INCREASE PEOPLE'S VULNERABILITY TO POVERTY

Recent societywide social and behavioral trends are causing more rural residents to fall into poverty, making it less likely that people already poor will get out of poverty and fostering transmission of poverty to the next generation. Single parenting, teen pregnancy, inadequate education, and substance abuse have increased in rural America just as in cities and suburbs, though not only among the poor and not uniformly in all places. These behavioral patterns may be mutually reinforcing and tend to exacerbate other poverty-risk factors, such as ethnic discrimination and institutionalized racism. As these behaviors become more prevalent, especially if rural employment remains inadequate, they are likely to contribute to the perpetuation and growth of rural poverty.

Single Parenthood

In the past, the rural poor were much more likely than the urban poor to live in two-parent families, but the rural-urban marriage difference has recently diminished, mostly as a result of changing marriage patterns in rural areas (Lichter and Eggebeen 1992). Although "female-headed households" are still less prevalent than in central cities, at least 39 percent of rural poor households are now headed by women (Porter 1991, 30).

The relationship between single parenthood and increasing rural poverty is complex, however. High levels of poverty are not everywhere correlated with high levels of single parenthood, as became clear from comparisons among research sites. For example, two rural counties a few hundred miles apart in eastern Washington had poverty rates of around 20 percent in 1990, nearly double the state rate, but in one county the percentage of households headed by women was 50 percent higher than the state's 15 percent average, whereas in the other county it was just at the state level. In the Mississippi Delta, high single-parenthood rates are only a small part of the explanation of poverty. In some highly Hispanic communities in the Southwest and California, where poverty is endemic, single parenthood is not especially common.

Importantly, the changed rural economic context has made single parenthood more of an economic handicap than it was in the past or than it is in cities. Rural single-parent households are apt to be poorer (Lichter and Eggebeen 1992) and to remain poor longer (Ross and Morrissey 1989) than comparable urban households. The tighter link between single parenthood and poverty in rural America appears to lie in constricted employment opportunities for rural women, who receive lower wages and more involuntary part-time jobs. Where the thrust of recent economic development has been in tourism, for example, many low-earning service-sector workers are single women with dependent children. Single mothers are also prevalent in the work force in certain types of routine manufacturing and food processing plants, for example, in some of North Carolina's garment factories and knitting mills, in chicken processing, and in Mississippi Delta catfish packing. In these places, employment and marriage factors interact to push up poverty rates.

Teen Parenting

In virtually every research site, community service providers expressed concern over high rates of teen pregnancy. To the extent that teen parenting is a high-risk factor for poverty, as conventional wisdom, human service professionals, and national studies indicate (Schorr 1988, 11–15), there is reason to believe that poverty rates will increase in places with high levels of teen parenting. The situation is not uniform, however, as births to teens have risen more in some rural locations than others and not always in direct association with changing poverty rates.

In certain ethnic groups, parenting before age twenty is culturally normative, and social supports are in place for babies born to young married and single parents. As more Hispanics settle in rural communities, rural birth ages are bound to drop, both because of the Mexican cultural pattern of early childbearing and because of the increasing number of Hispanics of childbearing age now residing in these towns. In one Oregon research site, for example, Hispanics comprise only 9 percent of the county population but accounted for 18 percent of all births in 1990; and births to women under twenty had risen substantially. But ethnic change doesn't tell the whole story. Age of first birth has always been lower in the rural population than the urban, so births to rural eighteen- and nineteen-year-olds may represent little change from the past. In the changed economic context, however, teen parenting may now have relatively greater impact in raising rural poverty rates because young parents, even if married, cannot earn enough to support children. Especially critical now are increased births to younger single teen girls with no financial support from either partners or parents.

Inadequate Education

Elevated high-school dropout rates continue to characterize poorer rural populations, especially minorities. But the efficacy of completing high school as a route out of poverty—unless rural employment opportunities improve—is not entirely clear (Rural Sociological Society Task Force on Persistent Rural Poverty 1993, 39–67). From research observations conducted at job readiness classes in welfare-to-work programs in various states, two impressions (gleaned from interviews and observations but not documented quantitatively) are especially striking: the inadequacy of literacy skills among adults who had actually graduated from high school and the frequency of undiagnosed learning disabilities among those who had not. Even for the many women who do complete basic literacy education or obtain a GED (general equivalency diploma), the payoff may be discouragingly small: If the jobs they subsequently get pay only poverty wages, these women and their children will remain in poverty. Although good employment training programs appear to bring positive personal benefits for most participants, limited or inadequate rural employment opportunities remain critical barriers to reducing rural poverty.

Correlation of low educational attainment and low earnings in rural America is readily apparent in the case of Mexican-American workers in low-paid production work, both in vegetable and fruit growing and packing and in meat packing. Quite simply, adults with inadequate education are confined to the lowest-paid jobs. But they value education for their children and consider it essential for their upward mobility. In an Oregon community, for example, Mexican-American parents routinely reported that a primary reason for settling out of the migrant stream was so that their children could "go to school, stay in school all year, just one school." Parents acted on this commitment, not only by starting their children's education early, but also by participating in parental activities and responsibilities fostered by such programs as Head Start and by scheduling their visits back to Mexico to avoid interrupting children's schooling. Some children of Mexican-American farm workers not only graduate from high school but go on to college. In far more cases, however, the trajectory of education peaks early in high school. Teens leave school "temporarily" because they and their households need money.

Re-entry into school becomes more and more difficult as time passes, and the hope of gaining a slightly better job in the future does not warrant continuing to endure the negative aspects of school in the present. It is logical to expect that as the population of Mexican and Mexican-American agricultural workers expands spatially and numerically, rural high-school dropout rates will increase—unless some major changes occur both within the schools and in the economic and social conditions that perpetuate poverty in these rural places.

Self-destructive Behaviors

Rural America has not been immune to the sociobehavioral problems associated with poverty in the nation's cities. Drug abuse and drug-related gangs and violence have filtered in, though belatedly and slowly, and are of concern to social workers, health professionals, educators, religious leaders, and court officials. Drug abuse may be implicated in both the increase and the deterioration of rural poverty, particularly where it occurs in the context of and combined with other poverty risks, but alcohol abuse is still reported as more widespread. Also commonly associated with rural poverty is family violence. Sexual abuse of children was mentioned by teachers, social workers, and adult victims as a common but underestimated problem in their communities, and it is closely associated with subsequent early childbearing. Although these and other destructive behaviors may arise out of the stresses of poverty, they also can be active agents, making people more vulnerable to becoming or remaining poor.

Erosion of Extended Family Support Systems

Rural people who survive chronic poverty and multiple emergencies are quick to credit the assistance of family and relatives. However, both low-income interviewees and service providers in different regions and across diverse ethnic groups indicated that family networks might not be operating as effectively now as in the past to cushion the damaging effects of being poor. Primary reasons suggested for this failure include stress and ineffective family functioning, which in turn may have been brought on or exacerbated by poverty. Additionally, some young adults do not use family networks effectively, exhausting the resources and patience of one relative after another and "burning out" their potential sources of support. Even where extended family still serves as a safety net, it may not be effective as a source of contacts and resources that could help people escape the underlying situation that gives rise to so many emergencies, that is, the chronic poverty.

Kinship-based family support systems appear stronger in some ethnic groups and regions, as in cohesive Indian and Hispanic communities where extended family ties are perpetuated by cultural and social institutions. But even there, older residents and local human service professionals remarked with deep concern on what they perceive as a greater readiness of the younger generation to turn to formal agencies for assistance. This change was interpreted as a step away from traditional values and social systems toward the development of "a welfare element" dependent on "the system." In both ethnic and mainstream rural low-income populations, according to teachers in special programs for teen parents, the growing desire of young people to become "independent" coupled with availability of Aid to Families with Dependent Children (AFDC) for young single parents mean that fewer teen parents (single or coupled) are living with their parents and more are establishing separate households. This pattern would automatically push up a local poverty rate, since these newly established households are apt to be poor, whereas in the more traditional pattern, young parents remained in the home of their parents and therefore were not counted as an additional household in poverty.

To the extent that extended family support systems are less accessible or effective now than formerly, the other social and behavioral trends discussed here may have more serious negative consequences because they are not offset by social cushioning and informal support. In this weaker social context, teen parenting, single parenthood, school problems, and substance abuse may render the individual even more vulnerable to long-term poverty. Thus, although erosion of family support systems may not cause poverty to increase, it puts some individuals at greater risk of falling into or remaining in poverty.

CONCLUSION

Spanning the considerable diversity of poverty in rural America is an overarching commonality: the urgent need to reduce the poverty already present and to prevent its increase and entrenchment. This chapter has drawn on field research to convey the transcending similarity of processes that appear to be operating across the varied economic and social landscapes of rural America. A great deal of additional and more thorough research is needed. At the very least, we need to know the magnitude of the trends—in which and how many places they are occurring, and who and how many people are affected by them. In designing further studies and analysis of rural poverty, three points that have emerged in this field research might be considered.

First, increasing or worsening rural poverty is neither the result of a single cause operating everywhere in rural America nor of entirely different causes operating in different areas. In reality, several causes are operating; they are interconnected and interacting, and different combinations of causes operate to different extents in different places. Clarification of the relative role of economic, migrational, and sociobehavioral factors identified in this chapter and specification of the different combinations of causes operating in different places will require a multifaceted research approach.

Second, poverty afflicts not only people (the individuals, households, and population sub-groups that compose the official poverty count), but also places (the regions, counties, and communities) where poverty is created and where poor people reside. The importance of place as a dimension of rural poverty is recognized by rural scholars (see Lyson and Falk 1993) but generally given inadequate attention in both analysis and policy. Further research on rural poverty should pay more attention to place, and to the distinction between poverty of people and poverty of place.

Third, increases in poverty result from both system-level and individual factors, and the two are distinct, though interacting. Poverty has increased in certain rural places as a result of system-level factors, such as economic change, but sociobehavioral characteristics of individuals and households determine why, given these system-level changes, certain people have become poor or are poorer than other people. Where macrolevel causes of poverty coincide with factors that increase individuals' vulnerability, they reinforce each other, elevating people's chances of becoming or remaining poor and raising the local poverty rate. In further research, it might be helpful to distinguish between "poverty," the economic condition existing on the system level, and "the poor," the individuals or groups of people who fall into, are brought up in, transmit, remain in, or escape from poverty.

If we are serious about addressing the problem of poverty in rural America, these three analytical points, together with a better understanding of diversity and similarities, should inform public policy affecting both poverty and general rural conditions.

NOTES

The New York state research was supported from 1990 through 1992 by the Ford Foundation through the Aspen Institute's Rural Economic Policy Program. The national research was conducted during 1992–1993 while I was on sabbatical leave from Ithaca College as a Center Associate of the National Rural Studies Committee, affiliated with the Western Rural Development Center in Corvallis, Oregon, and funded by the W. K. Kellogg Foundation.

1. States included in this scoping research include North Carolina, Mississippi, New Mexico, California, Oregon, Washington, Kansas, Nebraska, and Michigan. Research methodology was adapted from earlier studies of poverty and community change in upstate New York. Background information on economic situations and poverty trends in each state was obtained from 1990 census data and secondary materials, extant studies of local poverty, and interviews with experts in state agencies and universities. On-site research, averaging about a week in each of several locations within a state, consisted of open-ended interviews with informants such as service providers, community leaders, educators, and other knowledgeable local residents; observations conducted in local agencies, schools, and programs serving low-income residents; collection of local documentation on poverty; and interviews with low-income residents. In each research site I promised to attempt to maintain anonymity of location, institutions, and individuals.

PART SIX
REGIONAL AND
ETHNIC DIVERSITY

Trite statement though it is, the diversity of rural America is one of its most significant and compelling characteristics. This diversity has been documented statistically in some of the preceding chapters, but no amount of statistics can drive home the significance of this diversity as strongly as firsthand observation. Not only does the physical topography vary greatly, ethnic backgrounds and local settlement history differ as well. Everyone, of course, cannot enjoy the privilege of observing America firsthand as the National Rural Studies Committee did in several regions of the country. Here in Part 5, however, a substitute has been provided. These six chapters provide a sampling of prevailing regional and ethnic diversity. Although comprehensive coverage is impossible, the reader will sense from reading these chapters the enormous range of conditions, problems, and human responses.

In Chapter 14 Paul Starrs describes the arid West. Although this vast region is generally sparsely settled, enormous concern exists over the way it is used. Therein has always lain, Starrs notes, the seeds of conflict. Successive waves of settlers have come to the West over the past four centuries, and each successive wave has made a different use of the landscape. Currently, urban interests and newcomers often want to prevent all change except, of course, for the change they themselves might make. Thus conflicts between cattlemen, miners, and timber workers who reside in the rural communities and environmental interests and newcomers have become increasingly common.

In Chapter 15, a change of focus from landscape to people, Refugio Rochin attacks the stereotype that all rural Latinos are migrant and seasonal workers, illegal aliens, and transients. They comprise almost 9 percent of the population, and about half of them are foreign born. These people, he argues convincingly, are assets, not liabilities. They have demonstrated a capacity to integrate themselves into society generally, and Rochin believes that we best serve ourselves by becoming sensitive to ways we can assist them.

C. Matthew Snipp, a sociologist and himself a Native American, contributes a chapter on American-Indian economic development. There are two superficially contradictory impressions generated by this chapter: The problems Native Americans face are immense and exceedingly difficult—but one senses that greater autonomy and self-rule are paying off, not just in economic development but also in self-esteem.

A historical view of the South is presented in a chapter by Charles Aiken, a historical geographer at the University of Tennessee. He illustrates how technological development and social change have restructured the southern countryside. The always contentious subject of race relations is brought to bear forthrightly and skillfully. In the following chapter on African-Americans, race, and poverty, Bruce Williams and Bonnie Dill make the case that economic development and poverty cannot be addressed meaningfully without considering race relations.

Finally, rural midwesterners are discussed by Sonya Salamon. In many respects the Midwest is the envy of the rest of rural America. Educational accomplishments are high and substantial self-determination exists. What are the ethnic and cultural forces that made these accomplishments possible? Though impossible for many other areas to emulate the accomplishments of the Midwest, an understanding of its history adds to our understanding and appreciation of the cultural diversity of sparsely populated places.

14

CONFLICT AND CHANGE ON THE LANDSCAPES OF THE ARID AMERICAN WEST

PAUL F. STARRS

From the air even a glancing look at the arid West of the United States reveals a land where the gaps between settlements are large and city lights are few. The quality of space in the West is different from the rest of the United States, and the unquiet relationship between places urban and rural is the product of a changing region colliding with the special relationship that veteran westerners claim to maintain with "their" land. A long-ago established pattern of land use with few competing alternatives, of wilderness and frontier living and sparse settlement, holds true today, though it daily becomes less definitive as the southwesterly migration to the Sunbelt pushes forward.

For more than a century—and in places like northern New Mexico for about four hundred years—the arid West has been set apart from the rest of North America as variously the "rugged" part of the continent, the "handsome" side of the United States, or as the Wild West, what Bernard DeVoto described as the "plundered province." Each epithet fits. The most important element of western life is change itself. The alterations do not come especially rapidly, but the clock of change ticks on, inescapable and not always welcome. Western landscapes are always works in progress, more so than in other parts of the United States.

Even defining the parameters of the West can be a mite ticklish. Geographically, mere subtleties distinguish the Southwest from California or the Great Basin from the Rocky Mountains or other parts of what is generally dubbed the "arid West." And, although the gorge of dyed-in-the-wool westerners rises, even California with its 31-plus million people, in almost all its significant components is pure "western." The arid West's landforms, drainages, and physique are as similar as the region's disparate cultures.

What then constitutes "the West"? Dryness: across much of the region no more than twenty inches of precipitation fall in an "average" year, except in the mountains. The federal government retains control (whether the proprietary role is "ownership" is always a touchy question) of significant portions of western land. Deeded private acreage is relatively scarce—a scattering of green fields or suburbs seen from the air, standing in marked contrast to public acreage or land reserved for other users. The military landscape is especially substantial and imperious. Far more than a token of the West is parks, or wildlife refuges, and other sections are custodial reservations for Native Americans. The economy of this frontier has long depended on the exploitation of natural resources, although this dependency is increasingly challenged.

Culturally, the West is also home to distinctive ecological modes. Donald Worster has noted that these include the cowboy and sheepherder as well as the irrigator and the water engineer. There is, indeed, a pastoral west and a hydraulic west (Worster 1987). Furthermore, as Peirce Lewis has explained, despite its awesome spaces the West really is not roomy—not, anyway, the usable parts—nor is it really "rich" in resources (Lewis 1992). Indeed, opportunities are sparse, and if some parts of the West seem enormously varied in terms of their people, residents tend to be concentrated in enclaves. Different languages and ethnicities are especially a part of the Southwest—until a decade or two ago, Spanish took precedence over English, in New Mexico, and Native American languages and other tongues sustained by nuclei of ethnic settlers held out against the pressures of homogenization (Starrs 1994). Part of the difference is purely of the emotions and senses. The West is growing fast, in a way that the most oblivious traveler cannot overlook: as airports and interstates turn eyes away from small-town life, they focus on the city's glitter gulch. Western space no longer seems to matter so much.

WATER

The word "rival," as a matter of fact, evolved from the Latin *rivalis,* meaning "one living on the opposite bank of a stream from another."
—*Maass and Anderson,* . . . And the Desert Shall Rejoice

The common obsessions of old-time westerners are land and water. Land is plentiful, although it is not always easily obtained or kept, but there is nowhere near enough water to satisfy demand. It goes almost without saying that there is certainly sufficient water for a West without interlopers—native plants and animals are well-adapted to precisely the water available from normal hydrologic processes, and before Euro-Americans arrived, the Native Americans had a rough peace with the natural water supply. The problem in the West, especially now, is that people settle where the water is not and engineer around natural limits.

Water has fulfilled many a use in the West, furnishing transportation for the likes of John Wesley Powell; inspiring an obsession in John C. Frémont, who sought a mythical Rio Buenaventura; meeting a desperate survival need for William Lewis Manley and the 49ers crossing Death Valley. For individuals, water enough could be found. But water for larger enterprises is more problematic. Mining requires access to water for removing, processing, and transporting ore. Irrigation is the massive consumer of western water, absorbing between 80 and 90 percent of all the developed water in the West. As it is increasingly practiced in the West, livestock ranching—the agronomic practice most perfectly suited to arid lands—is an enormous water user not because animals drink a great deal but because irrigated pastures and feeds like alfalfa are grown on watered fields. Tourism, however, is also a vast monopolizer of water (estimates are as high as 800 gallons per day for each guest), and in many western cities tourist trade is as real a threat as agriculture to a sustainable water supply. Attempts to control water and thereby dominate all subsequent uses of land are themes common to western literature, history, and even film (Starrs 1993).

Urban Water

Cities and their industry are another matter. Compared to the exotic activities of ranching or sluicing irrigation water across a dry field, defense manufacturing or computer assembly may seem tepid fare. They are nonetheless two of the big-money activities moving to the interior West, and they usually carry with them only a fraction of their work force. Firms are happy to move to places like Albuquerque, El Paso, Phoenix, Salt Lake City, Boise, Las Vegas, and Boulder where amenities are a consistent draw, crime and urban blight are relatively low (the cities are by and large newer), and educated local workers are available.

Not all movement is East to West; there is also a backwash from the Pacific. The flow of California migrants to other locales is fast becoming a flood; more than a quarter of a million residents abandoned California in 1992, and the state's small net population growth was due entirely to foreign immigration and a high birth rate. This eastward migratory sweep is in general welcomed by neighboring states. The West's febrile and only episodically strong natural resources economy (generally rural) is being replaced by tourism, industry, social service provision, and manufacturing (generally city-based and booming). In Arizona, manufacturing produces five times the income of agriculture, and tourism employs ten times as many people as mining. Water, meanwhile, remains a preoccupation. Among the first concerns expressed by the site assessment team of any enterprise is "what's the water like?" Cities trying to attract firms are learning to have an answer at hand, for with industry and manufacturing come new work forces, new home building, and fresh service sector jobs. In the West, the immigrant population growth of the last three decades is perceived by local government as the essence of economic health.

Cities control western water. The West's cities and their people have the wherewithal and the political influence (read: votes) to capture water, by eminent domain or purchase, from rural water users. Today, no luxury compares to a swimming pool or a golf course in the arid Southwest. Without water there is no golf course, no swimming pool, no street cleaning, no sewer hookups, no lawns, no spas, no fountains. And as the saying goes, when you have it, flaunt it: at the Treasure Island casino in Las Vegas, Nevada, a faux British frigate is "sunk" by pirate vessels six times a day on the hotel's private "lagoon."

Water is success. The state of Arizona testifies to the triumph of hydraulic engineering: Colorado River water from the nearly completed Central Arizona Project, an undertaking once advanced as a boon to rural Arizonans, now flows to Phoenix and the Valley of the Sun itself. Without water (and the evaporative or "swamp" cooler that preceded today's air conditioner), Phoenix (or equally Tucson, Tempe, and Truth or Consequences) would have a population but 10 or 20 percent its current size (Cunningham 1985). Water does not add to the quality of life in the arid West, water *is* the quality of life.

Historically, the control of water was necessary for even the smallest town with the sparest of water users. The original town plat for Santa Fe, Tucson, Albuquerque, or even Las Vegas, New Mexico, was gridded around ditch systems that brought a combination of potable and irrigation waters. Urban water users always retained first right to water, but only for sustenance needs.

The links between city and agriculture have slowly dissolved in the West as towns have grown larger and have begun developing their own separate and competing water systems, partly for health reasons. An adversarial pattern of developing water for urban use was set; Mormons embraced it as Indian pueblos had before, and so did cities throughout the arid West. Los Angeles set a riveting standard with grappling reaches east, northeast, and straight north for water, and other cities in the West were not far behind; Arizona, Colorado, Nevada, and New Mexico, especially, have taken the water customs, laws, and statutes that large California cities exploited in their search for water and turned them to still more sophisticated use. The water code now known as the "Law of Prior Appropriation" made long-distance water conveyance to cities and industry feasible. Increasingly, competition between cities and rural users for water is the rule.

Among the ironies of western water use is the tacit assumption in law that cultural differences really have no place in determining how water is allocated. The irony is powerful because the culture of water runs deep and has a physical expression everywhere in the West. The legal combat of Hispanic New Mexicans working to preserve access to traditional water rights is entrenched; the import of old Spanish and Mexican water laws are increasingly acknowledged, if not accepted. Books like John Nichols's *The Milagro Beanfield War*, Bill DeBuys and Alex Harris's *River of Traps*, and Stanley Crawford's lucid *Mayordomo* testify to the cultural roots of Hispanic water use. The rights of groups within Navajo, Apache, Hopi, various Pueblo Indian nations, and, in fact, all Native Americans to develop water as they see fit are contested not only by industry, government, and other claimants, but increasingly by environmental groups who find themselves at odds with Indian groups they long had assumed were "natural allies." Unsurprisingly, many Native Americans feel they deserve to develop their waters as they see fit— and they claim a primordial and preemptive right to water that state engineers and the federal government are loath to acknowledge.

Rural Rights to Water

The word "rights" is assuming an ever more important place in the western lexicon, especially as rural areas acknowledge that what they had assumed was theirs in perpetuity can be removed in an unconcerned sweep of a pen by urban legislators. Many ranchers assert that they have a usufructuary right to graze public lands—a right they claim is based, in places, on a hundred or more years of use and tradition. The same argument is advanced for water rights, with a few twists: there is also the public trust doctrine, which stipulates that government is required to sustain natural resources (including clean air, streams, forests, and rangelands) in excellent condition, since they are held in trust for the future public. Although offered supposedly as a benefit to the countryside, there is no mistaking that the brunt of any substantive change most affects rural residents. Advocates of public trust doctrine are most often city-based environmental attorneys opposed to the stains that resource use inevitably leaves on a rural landscape. The only way to keep a "resource" entirely clean, of course, is never to remove it from its figurative shrink wrap, like a proof coin in plastic. Of course, in such matters no single opinion is certifiably "correct."

The discussion of water in the Southwest is constantly evolving. The latest variant involves water marketing. The idea is simple: water already contracted for by rural farmers can be sold to cities, usually at an enormous markup, while the farmer leaves the fields untilled (or plants with less water-intensive crops) and pockets the cash. Cities benefit by getting water, otherwise unobtainable without an enormous investment in water purchasing, pipelines, and purification. Farmers benefit from a secure income for doing nothing, a time-honored tradition of subsidy that redounds especially to large growers (a certain size attained, farmers become "growers"). Environmental advantages accrue as unneeded crops are not grown, extra pesticides are not applied, and lands are not unduly cultivated.

The essential challenges to water marketing are also quite reasonable, and they symbolize the West's current state of mind: Why should a few growers, already benefiting from access to subsidized water, be allowed to take profits in the millions for doing nothing? Perhaps even more to the point, if the argument is that cities "need" the water and farmers can be pressured into giving it up, how is this remaking the West? How large should cities be allowed to grow—if water no longer limits urban expansion, what will? These questions are neither subtle nor remote. Responses are demanded now, and in most cases decisions favor cities over rural residents. Vote tonnage counts.

Lately, rural residents across the country display an uneasy attitude in their dealings with cities and their urban people. In the West especially, rules are changing fast. The struggle over water is emblematic. Rural folk have every reason to be afraid; their view of water, land, agriculture, and the whole of the rural western natural resources economy is something that contemporary migrants to the arid West, who hail from many parts of the country and the world, do not understand. A new vision of the West supplants the old. It is not like change in the Northeast or Midwest, the Southeast or the Pacific Northwest. This change is driven by a constant infusion of new blood, of outsiders who bring in new concerns, different ideas of what is "appropriate," who consider it entirely reasonable to make a green city paradise of a desert land. A barely veiled utopian impulse would remake the earth in a style to which people would like to become accustomed. No tradition or physical limitation seems sufficient to slow the pace. Cash and water are the means to an end, and rural westerners fear that their traditional livelihoods are literally circling the drain.

FEDERAL LANDLORDS AND LIVESTOCK RANCHING

After water, the second western obsession is land, much of which belongs to one government body or another. Many a western activity is rooted in exploitation by individuals of public properties. The statistics are simple, if only in terms of federal lands. Nevada is 87 percent federally controlled; Utah 64 percent; Idaho 63 percent; Oregon 52 percent; Wyoming 48 percent; California 45 percent; Arizona 43 percent; Colorado 36 percent; New Mexico 33 percent; Montana 30 percent. These numbers indicate that many of the lands not actively in crops or cities are controlled by the federal government. Anyone who wants to make use of these lands is required, by law, to obtain agreement from the appropriate government entity.

Since the older western economies were based on the exploitation of natural resources, ongoing negotiation was required between resource users and government. Governments were often co-opted into whole-hearted support of resource exploitation. Sometimes rather too much was given away, or the reins left too loose. By 1900, and certainly by the 1930s, federal and state governments had asserted a right to control the use of public lands, and the battle began. It continues, pitting government resource managers against both environmentalists and resource users. In the last decade the debate has grown notably louder. The supposed dominant doctrine, since the mid-1970s, advocates "multiple use," with no single group entitled to exclusive use of public resources. Most notable in this contest is the refusal to find a middle ground. Livestock ranchers, miners, loggers, and the companies they represent fear that to budge an inch is to lose a mile, and the most extreme environmentalist position is that of Earth First!: "No compromise in the defense of mother Earth." To outsiders, a militant unwillingness to compromise by all hands seems a singularly self-destructive attitude, but it has slackened little.

When livestock ranching was adopted by English-speaking settlers moving west, they borrowed a number of the Hispanic grazing techniques and moved onto public lands, using them freely as a form of commons. Some of the lands were titled up, but since the United States Congress took a dim (and palpably racist) attitude toward Hispanic land-holding practices, land claimants could not possibly obtain anywhere near the acreage they needed to graze their animals on private lands. They continued to use public lands and eventually began to pay the federal government a token fee for a nonexclusive use of the land.

The Cowboy Complex and Riposte

The economy of livestock grazing, especially of cattle, was distinctive and has achieved a worldwide cachet in the cowboy, or pastoral, economy. About 17 percent of the cattle in the United States spend some part of their life on public lands, almost all of which lie in the West (only 5 percent of the feed for American livestock comes from public lands, but public lands are the great breeding grounds for cattle, and those early months are critical). Like the western manipulation of water, this use of public lands is viewed increasingly as suspect. True, the historic damage wrought by livestock (and their owners) on public lands is considerable and slow to heal. Thus the use of public lands is said to be destructive and unwarranted. Since livestock ranchers have no titular right to graze, some opponents argue that their animals should be removed from public lands. Little surprise that "Cattle Free By '93" and "Out the Door by '94" are familiar slogans (HCN 1992; Starrs 1994a). A comparable argument can be made against mining, logging, irrigated farming, hydroelectrical production, or almost any other rural economy. Using land messes it up, and if only perfection is permissible, then the blackguards must be moved off and out and the environment protected by the extirpation of its enemies: cattle, miners, farmers, loggers, planners, sheep, Indians, ranchers.

The antigrazing movement, driven by literary figures like Edward Abbey and Page Stegner working in concert with urban westerners, produces a body of commentary that, if nothing else, earns points for clever titles: *Sacred Cows at the Public Trough, The Waste of the West: Public Lands Ranching,* Jeremy Rifkin's *Beyond Beef: The Rise and Fall of Cattle Culture;* articles such as Abbey's "Even the Bad Guys Wear White Hats," Philip Fradkin's "The Eating of the West," or Dyan Zaslowsky's "A Public Beef," get the message across. Sentiment against grazing is driven by a distaste for livestock, an adulation of wildlife, and a strong self-righteous sense that livestock ranchers are getting away with something on public lands. The Wildlife Society, Sierra Club, Earth First!, Earth Island Institute, Audubon Society, and the Natural Resources Defense Council form a goal-oriented collaboration against ranching that is having localized success. Meanwhile, a panicked and at times vitriolic response from livestock associations is not helping the prograzing cause in the least.

"Throw them off," goes one fairly rabid environmentalist argument, ignoring the 31,000 permittees, representing income for perhaps 130,000 rural westerners, and four or five times that many jobs (in feed stores, farm equipment sales, corner diners, vet clinics, stock yards, saddle shops, bars and bordellos). In so wealthy a country as the United States, perhaps there is no intrinsic reason to use public lands. Perhaps it does not matter that the country's rural residents have contributed a distinctive culture and an important (essential) boost to rural western economies, that many are better than fair stewards of the land, and that some have been good stewards for decades. Ranching simply may not compare to the number of residents massing in the dramatic cities of Colorado, Utah, Arizona, New Mexico, Texas, Nevada, and, of course, California. Precisely this point is made repeatedly by revisionist western historians bent on recasting the legends of the frontier West into something more realistic: the modern West is of cities and urban concerns (McMurtry 1990).

Urban Refugees and New Coalitions

New immigrants arrive in a steady stream, part of the pattern of western reverse migrants abandoning "city" life and its travails to move to exurban areas perceived as more healthy, safer (usually for children), and offering a quality of life not available in even the medium-sized western cities. This confidence in the bucolic advantages of western rural environments is touching to observers, if somewhat misguided. Crime, overcrowding, and rising costs move to the countryside, too. Yet a massive exodus of people (rich ones, lately) to Los Alamos, Flathead Lake, Boise, Moab, Santa Fe, and Boulder has spawned a fresh new generation of rural wannabes, while fomenting dismay in many longer-time inhabitants. They warily watch the usual suite of problems, including escalating land values and property taxes; impossible strains on rural schools, hospitals, and roads; and the rapid dilution of rural solidarity into a culturally mixed hodgepodge. The same story applies to the Red Rock Canyon country, or to Prescott, near Phoenix, or to the Carson and Washoe valleys near Reno, or to the Sierra Nevada foothills in California, or to once-small towns in the midelevation ranges of the Rocky Mountains near Denver that brim with new settlers.

The numerous urban people moving to rural areas are generally wealthier than the natives, and they bring with them a body of skills and a sense of empowerment that are alien to many long-standing rural residents. These new settlers are not bumpkins or rubes, they are educated people who have access to sophisticated techniques of organizing, politicking, and lobbying. Industry, government, and other special interest organizations that propose projects or changes in areas where these "reverse migrants" form a measurable part of the population are learning to beware, at some cost. Once settled in their chosen environment, they prefer to slam closed the barn door, something profoundly frustrating to other residents who have a more sanguine attitude toward innovation and rural development. In intriguing ways, "exurbanites" abandoning large cities (and suburbs) for a better life in the rural west are both a conspicuous boon and an enduring threat to rural tradition. Whether telecommuters or modern rustics, they are city people living in rural areas, not "rural westerners." Their land ethic is different or absent, they are tied to (and often living on) money from "outside," and will not and cannot adopt "rural values."

The old-time community of rural settlers whose lives and economies are based on the use of natural resources find their world in a swirl of change. Resource exploitation becomes ever less profitable as costs build. Many of the new expenses are simply a factoring-in of environmental costs that used to go uncalculated. But other costs accumulate as ranchers, miners, loggers, and even growers encounter competition for resources where a decade or two ago there was none. Especially troubling to these communities is that one of the uses most often proposed for public lands is no use at all—the removal or cessation of all the activities that made the communities in the first place, under pressure from environmental advocates or government managers who are taking a new look at the larger effects of resource exploitation. The human costs of this pollarding of rural culture are neatly compartmentalized but no less severe.

THE ARID WEST AS COLONY

When Bernard DeVoto described the western United States as a "plundered province," he addressed the peculiar relationship of West to East, of colony to colonizer, of resource supplier to the resource's extractor. The arid West, DeVoto argued, was both mendicant and tributary—aside from providing coal and oil and beef and lamb and scenery and recreational (a word worth deconstructing) opportunities, the region was also the taker of hundreds of pork barrel projects. DeVoto's analysis, published in 1934, is still partly true, but today the arid West leads the country more and more, instead of following behind.

The lack of control over their land has long troubled rural westerners. With the federal government—the custodian of 300 million acres of western land—based in regional offices or, even more remote, in Washington, D.C., the impression of outsiders dominating impotent communities has only grown. In the strongest western movement of the last two decades, communities have demanded additional voice in determining their destiny and have requested the return of some of the independence that was once so much a part of the western mystique.

The Sagebrush Rebellion of the 1970s and 1980s centered in Nevada but extended through much of the Southwest. It was an expression of disfavor with the colonial policies of the federal government and, simultaneously, an attempt to wrest control of land from centralized authority. The question of empowerment, of the right to control a region's destiny, is much in the news. The topic is complicated because it is in considerable part also born of familiar rural suspicions of urban interests.[1] Rural westerners view the principle of "one person one vote" as a viperous reality threatening their long-term survival. Luxuriating in numbers, packed cities call the shots. Fairness (democracy or not) is another issue. Who can forget the crude lessons of playground life, where the weighty bully slams one end of a teeter-totter into the dirt, leaving the person opposite dangling high and powerless to do anything but leap off. Thus do the West's rural residents view the ambiguity of urban interest in the region's resource lands.

Much of the arid West remains a frontier. If the old (and conservative) Census Bureau definition of the frontier as a region with fewer than two people per square mile holds true, then 150 counties—all in the West—are still frontier (Edmondson and Fost 1991, Popper 1984). The area involved is one-quarter of the United States (Alaska excluded), and it is home to less than one-quarter of 1 percent of the United States population. Chunks of Nevada, Utah, New Mexico, Montana, Idaho, and Wyoming qualify. But the vast majority of the population in the arid West is urban, following the census definition of a place with more than 2,500 residents. In California and Arizona, the proportion is over 90 percent. For Nevada, Colorado, Texas, and Utah, more than 80 percent is urban. Better than 70 percent of the residents of New Mexico, Oregon, and Washington are urban. But all the cities occupy only about 6 percent of the West's physical area.

The split between the urban and rural West is, then, only likely to become more pronounced. The cities draw. Rural places attract, as well, but not nearly so fast and in much smaller absolute numbers than the urban areas. Movement within the West is considerable, but there is also migration from outside. Signs like the preternaturally quick population growth of Nevada and Arizona over the last twenty years (in percent) and the unequaled growth of California (in raw numbers) indicate a changing relationship between the rest of the United States and the arid lands of the West (Starrs and Wright 1994).

The West is not just a colony any more. Much as Los Angeles was an enormous magnet to migrants through most of this century, the greater West is now drawing new residents. Jobs are not all of the attraction. Important to this movement is the search for a better way to live—"lifestyle migrants" are crucial. The parklands (national and state), the public lands (Forest Service and Bureau of Land Management, BLM), the wildlife refuges, and the greenbelts and conservation easements increasingly being accumulated by private conservation groups promise potential westerners that the land they are moving to will not too soon be spoiled.

Open space offers opportunity, deferred choices, and a bank of potential very different from the "geography of hope" that Wallace Stegner first praised more than thirty years ago (Stegner 1980). He was writing of wilderness, not of open space for its own sake. The pertinent question here is whether all the groups that make up the residents of the arid West will ever agree about the West's open spaces (Popper 1986). Much of that land is in a few private hands or is public, so choices about what will happen to it are not necessarily up to the democratic public.

CULTURAL DIVERSITIES

The Southwest echoes the larger arid West's great mix of people and cultures. Northern New Mexico offers an enclave of Castilian Spanish–speaking residents who place their cultural roots in southern and western Spain. In terms of population, Tucson and Phoenix reflect Latin America as much as the United States. The same can be said for New Mexico; Pueblos of upper Rio Grande New Mexico are urban settlements of Native Americans that have been dense with people for a thousand years, and the Southwest as a whole boasts a Native American population that is larger than in any other region of the United States. Among the Euro-American residents are Italians, Basques, Mormons, and dozens of other settler groups. Demographic discrepancies within the West's population come in bewildering variety—the numerous Hispanic and Mormon children; the retired sunbirds along the Colorado River; the established middle-age working communities across the region. The population characteristics show immense local variation, and learning to read them is to apprehend the diversity of the Southwest itself (Wilkinson 1992).

Yet there are only halting efforts across the arid West and Southwest to understand what these different groups—urban, rural, Indian, Hispanic, Asian, African-American, Anglo, young and old, wealthy and poor—have in common or might want to see done differently. The federal government is among the worst culprits: resource use, recreation, and management programs have been sculpted for a hundred years according to the doctrines of "progressive resource management," a euphemism for control by and for a small elite of educated, white, and Washington, D.C.–based career professionals, who typically manage for what is "best for the resource." Demands are beginning to build for a break in the monopoly—witness the insistence and self-righteousness of the rural protests against government management programs.

Another part of the problem is the vast assortment of factions, each of which has its own vision of what might be an appropriate future for the arid West and its public, private, and industry lands. The duel for influence is becoming increasingly serious, and, always ominous, lawyers are involved. Attempts to avoid conflict and litigiousness are the reasons why resource management decisions have so often been left up to government agencies and their interpretations of statute; the power of rural communities to solve their own problems internally is much reduced (Ellickson 1991). Attitudes towards resource use are changing. Some of these changes will please resource exploiters; others will offer more solace to the forces that favor preservation over use.

Finally, there is a brilliant variety of distinctly western landscapes, created by westerners stretching and testing and despoiling their surrounds. Although some of these landscapes imitate other parts of the United States, many are homegrown in the West. Geographers, landscape architects, sociologists, and environmental historians may puzzle over them, but their significance is inescapable. We owe a lasting debt to J. B. Jackson, who more than anyone else has assessed the West and the geographical significance of its landscapes. He has invited us to think about the now ubiquitous mobile homes that were initially an artifact of the rural West. The open, lazy western grid, with space so little prized, gets equal notice. The landscapes of mining, of land division, of Hispanic and Pueblo adobe are the stuff of Jackson's commentary. The water-supplying *acequias,* the ranch roads, and the distinctive forms of ranch buildings that are quintessentially "western" all have earned evaluation. This material landscape is the one perfect and unbiased expression of the people who live in the West.

Jackson is most useful because he offers additional lessons for considering the difficult question of a rural western environment that is in the throes of conversion into a pawn of the cities. Perhaps, he notes, letting go is enough . . . while learning to appreciate the new settlements and settlers of the arid West.

The story of the dying of small rural communities in every part of the world has become familiar to us all over the last century and a half. It is most impressive, most regrettable when it tells of the decay of a well-known and well-loved landscape, like that of New England or New Mexico, but the moral of the story is in almost every case the same: existence for people in the country became more and more difficult, more and more joyless and without reward. Low pay, monotonous work, a sense of being isolated and forgotten, a sense of diminishing hope for the future afflicted one village, one farmstead after another. For more than a century, here in America, we have seen it happening, so perhaps it is not too early for us to look elsewhere in the countryside to become aware of new communities, the new installations that are evolving in that rural landscape. . . . We can see the emergence, all over the state, of a new kind of community—new in that it represents a different kind of relationship with the environment, a deliberate confrontation with elements in the landscape that earlier generations sought to avoid. (1985, 7–8)

The geography of the arid West, and of New Mexico and the Southwest especially, is complex and at times fraught with violent disagreement. It is changing fast, and in ways so novel (Las Vegas, St. George, Santa Fe, Boulder) as to be almost unpredictable. What we can predict are the severe penalties that rural parts of the West will pay, as once rural enclaves are "discovered." Exciting new cities are born, built in a haze of freon coolant, mulberry and cottonwood pollen, humidity rising from golf courses, traffic, wall murals, and a flurry of languages. Not all communities will become a Taos or an Aspen or a Sedona—pinnacles of a "new age consciousness." But disturbance of these landscapes comes often enough: the communities will be challenged and some will fold or be unrecognizable in a matter of years. And the economies that once supported them—ranching, mining, small-holder farming, timber—are going to be tested to the point of disappearance, unless they can reach some accommodation with newcomers who neither understand, nor wish particularly to learn what these older western societies need to exist. They may perish. Others will take their place, but it will not be the same. Perhaps it shouldn't be.

NOTES

Revised and updated from "Dilemmas of a New Age—A Half-Millennium of Landscape Change in New Mexico and the Southwest," in: *National Rural Studies Com-*

mittee: A Proceedings, edited by Emery Castle and Barbara Baldwin (Corvallis: Western Rural Development Center at Oregon State University; 1992), 7–15. This chapter was prepared, in part, under funding from an S.V. Ciriacy-Wantrup Postdoctoral Fellowship in Natural Resource Economics, at the University of California at Berkeley. The hospitality of Professor Tim Duane and the Department of Landscape Architecture, College of Environmental Design, is gratefully acknowledged.

1. How familiar are these suspicions? Universal, it can be argued. Consider the remarkable Claude Berri/Marcel Gagnol film, *Jean de Florette* (1987) for a cinematic view of comparable French rural doubts about *arriviste* urbanites.

15

RURAL LATINOS: EVOLVING CONDITIONS AND ISSUES

REFUGIO I. ROCHIN

In my years as a professor at the University of California, I found that most non-Hispanic colleagues and students usually think of rural Latinos as poor farm workers only.[1] Few people asked me if Mexican-Americans or Chicanos were owner-operators of farms or rural entrepreneurs. Few wanted to know if Latinos have another legacy in rural America that could be incorporated into school curriculums. Few regard rural Latinos as legal residents with allegiance to the United States.

The intent of this chapter is to deliver a message: When we address conditions of rural Latinos, Hispanic-Americans, Chicanos, and so on, we should no longer stereotype them all as migrant and seasonal workers, illegal aliens, and transient groups. We should first view rural Latinos as part of America's society, players in a larger demographic trend that is changing the ethnic composition of rural communities as well as the balance of power and socioeconomic relations between different ethnic groups. Also, when we study rural Latinos, we should think in terms of their attributes and unique differences that contribute to the United States. The mention of rural Latinos should not connote social problems and foreign aliens: For decades, rural Latinos have been assets, not liabilities, serving in a number of roles to strengthen the nation's economy.

This message is presented in two parts. First, I focus on the history and the contemporary roles of Latinos in "rural" America: the often ignored contributions of Latinos to U.S. crop and livestock production; the origins of migrant and seasonal workers; the unionization of farm labor; and the emergence of rural *colonias,* Southwest communities with majority populations of Latinos. Second, I argue that U.S. agriculture is going through a phase of

"Mexicanization" rather than the "mechanization" predicted in the 1970s and 1980s.

Before we begin, however, an answer to an important question: What is a Hispanic-American or Latino?

The U.S. Census Bureau estimated the 1992 Hispanic population at 22.1 million, or about 8.8 percent of the total population (U.S. Bureau of the Census 1993). This population consisted of the following groups: 63.6 percent Mexican, 10.6 percent Puerto Rican, 4.7 percent Cuban, 14.0 percent Central and South American, 7.0 percent "other Hispanic" (i.e., persons with origins in Spain or persons who identify themselves as Hispanic, Spanish, Spanish American, Hispano, Chicano, and so on).

Latinos are of many racial, religious, ethnic, and cultural backgrounds and they experience widely varying levels of prosperity and success in the United States. The ancestors of some Latinos lived in parts of the United States long before these regions became part of the nation.

At last count, about half of all Latinos were foreign-born, with the majority born in Mexico (Cattan 1993). During the 1980s Latinos accounted for approximately one of every three legal immigrants to the United States. The largest immigrant group comes from Mexico, about 250,000 per year. In addition, as many as 1.3 million Mexicans entered the United States between 1980 and 1986 as undocumented aliens (Cattan 1993).

The 1986 Immigration Reform and Control Act (IRCA) instituted a legalization program by which long-time illegal residents were granted amnesty and were able to apply for legal residence between 1987 and 1989. Mexican immigrants were the largest beneficiaries of IRCA. Because of IRCA, and several thousands of fraudulent applications, the precise number of aliens residing illegally in the United States is not known and actual numbers depend on how much the enforcement of IRCA reduces the flow of undocumented immigrants and results in the compulsory departure of those who remain here illegally (Martin et al. 1994).

Since IRCA, approximately 95 percent of all aliens who have been apprehended without legal documents have come from Mexico, many as repeat offenders. Approximately 1 million aliens from over 140 countries have been apprehended each year since IRCA (Martin 1993).

Hispanic-Americans are found all over the United States, but 85 percent reside in just nine states and half in two states alone: California (7.7 million, a number larger than the populations of forty-two states) and Texas (4.3 million). Mexican-Americans (Chicanos) are highly concentrated in the southwestern states of California, Texas, Arizona, New Mexico, and Colorado; 83 percent of this region's Hispanics are of Mexican origin. Puerto Ricans, who are U.S. citizens by law, dominate the Hispanic population of New York. Cuban Americans form the majority of Hispanics in south Florida. Though not as geographically concentrated as the other groups, Central and South Americans tend to settle on the East and West coasts (Chapa and Valencia 1993).

Latinos have, on average, a relatively low level of educational attainment. About 51 percent of Latinos twenty-five and older have received a high school diploma or higher, compared to about 80 percent of the non-Latino population (Chapa and Valencia 1993). One reason for the lower rate is that adult Latino immigrants have tended to be poorly educated, arriving with less than an eighth-grade education. Few immigrants from Mexico and Central America speak English. Furthermore, many of the Latino youth fail to complete high school in the United States, although this pattern appears to be changing for the good (Meisenheimer 1992).

The Hispanic population's median age of 26.4 years, estimated in March 1992, is about nine years lower than the median age of non-Hispanics (i.e., 32). Mexicans are the youngest Latino subgroup, with a median age of just 24.4, and Cubans are the oldest, at 40.4 years (about five years older than that of non-Hispanic whites) (Garcia 1993).

About 10.1 million (7.8 percent) of the U.S. labor force is Hispanic-American (Garcia 1993). With a "labor force participation rate" (LFPR) of 80 percent, Latinos are more active in either working or looking for work than non-Latinos, who have an LFPR of 74 percent (Chapa and Valencia 1993, table 7). Still, the unemployment rates for both Latino males and females are generally one and a half times higher than those of non-Latino whites (Cattan 1993; DeAnda 1994).

Latinos have relatively higher rates of employment in farming, forestry, and fishing than non-Latinos. In 1992, 12 percent of Mexican men 16 years and older were employed in these occupations, compared to 4.2 percent of the non-Latino men. In general, less than 2 percent of all women work in farming, forestry, and fishing, but 2.7 percent of Mexican women (the highest rate) work in these occupations. It is projected that by the year 2010 Hispanics will have become the nation's largest minority group, surpassing African-Americans and changing work force demographics in many ways. We expect Latino persistence in rural America (Cardenas 1994).

In 1991 the aggregate before-tax money income of Hispanic households was $184 billion, about 5 percent of the United States total income figure of $3.6 trillion. Thus, the nation's population of Hispanics (8.8 percent of the total) barely received 5 percent of the nation's income in 1991. Although studies have shown that Latino affluence, that is, the number of "higher-income" Latino households, has increased dramatically over the past twenty years, the increase has not been sufficient to counteract the widespread poverty of large segments of the Latino community (Rochin and Soberanis 1992).

Based on 1991 income figures, 28.7 percent of Hispanic families fell below the poverty level, as compared to 9.4 percent of non-Hispanic families (Garcia 1993, 9). Hispanic families were larger in 1991 than non-Hispanic families (3.80 persons and 3.13 persons, respectively). Concomitantly, Hispanic families raised more children in poverty. In fact, about 40.4 percent of Hispanic children were living in poverty in 1991 as compared to only 13.1 percent of non-Hispanic children. Hispanic children represented 11.6 percent of all children in the United States but represented 21.5 percent of all children living in poverty in 1991 (Garcia 1993, 9).

High rates of seasonal unemployment explain some of the poverty of Latinos. Moreover, median weekly earnings are generally lower for Latinos than for non-Latinos. In farming, forestry, and fishing, the median earnings of Mexican men are about $325/week and for non-Latino men $516/week. For Mexican-origin women the median earnings are $285/week and for non-Latinas (white women) $393/week in these occupations.

Although a heterogeneous population of many nationalities, different political agendas, and various ethnicities, Latinos manifest a long-standing sentiment of community. Latino organizations have been able to draw support from across the groups to address important issues and needs. And despite negative attitudes toward Hispanics by non-Hispanics, such as those about "illegal aliens," the overwhelming majority of Latino citizens express a high degree of patriotism toward the United States and a strong positive optimism about their own financial outlook (Ford Foundation 1992). Few Hispanics define bilingual education in terms of maintaining Spanish language and culture. Instead, more than 80 percent of all Hispanics support bilingual education as a means to learn English (Ford Foundation 1992, 5). More than 76 percent of Mexican immigrants report an intention to stay permanently in the United States and roughly 75 percent desire U.S. citizenship, testifying to the continuing image of the United States as a land of opportunity (Ford Foundation 1992).

LATINOS OF RURAL AMERICA

Little has been written specifically about the makeup and status of Hispanics in rural America except for their work as migrant and seasonal farm workers.

Today there are approximately 2 million Hispanics who reside permanently in nonmetropolitan counties of America (Lyson 1991). Compared to nonmetropolitan whites (52 million) and African-Americans (5 million), Hispanics constitute a small proportion of the nonmetro population. In the 1980s, however, the number of Hispanics residing on rural farms increased by 59,000, from 78,000, while the rural farm population of whites declined by over a half million residents (Rochin and Castillo 1993). Moreover, since 1987 the number of "rural farm" Hispanics has been greater than the number of "rural farm" blacks, 137,000 and 88,000, respectively (Rochin 1993).

Both Hispanic men and women are disproportionately employed in agriculture: 12 percent of Latinos work in farming compared to only 4.2 percent of non-Latino men. Latinos can be found also in other industries of the rural economy. According to Lyson (1991), approximately 40 percent of rural Hispanic men work in construction and manufacturing and a majority of rural Hispanic women (53.6 percent) work in "services" (Lyson 1991, 10).

Rural Latinos have lower annual earnings than non-Latinos, in part because of the seasonal nature of employment. Lyson's study of income distribution in rural America indicated that relatively more Hispanic households in 1987 had incomes below $7,500 than white households (15.4 percent and 10.4 percent, respectively). Also, few rural Hispanic households had incomes above $40,000 compared to white households. Lyson (1991) also found that between 1979 and 1987 the income distribution for rural Hispanics worsened as fewer Hispanic households were in the top income quintile and more were in the lower quintiles.

In 1989 rural poverty rates were 40 percent for African-Americans, 35 percent for Mexican-Americans, and 30 percent for American Indians. Poverty rates for rural whites stood at nearly 13 percent in the same year (Snipp et al. 1992).

Legacy of Riches and Denial

It is no accident of nature that rural Hispanics are poor agricultural workers living in the Southwest. Let us recall, however, that the earliest Mexican-Americans were actually not immigrants in the Southwest: the territory was originally theirs. As noted by Carey McWilliams in his revealing book *North From Mexico* (1990): "It should never be forgotten that, with the exception of the Indians, Mexicans are the only minority in the United States who were annexed by conquest; the only minority, Indians again excepted, whose rights were specifically safeguarded by treaty provision" (102). That annexation by conquest, under the terms of the Treaty of Guadalupe Hidalgo executed on

February 2, 1848, took all the states of the Southwest away from Mexico and transferred rights of property and U.S. residence away from the earliest Hispanic-Americans. The lands that Mexico ceded to the United States were larger in area than Germany and France combined and represented one-half of the territory that Mexico possessed in 1821. When the treaty was signed, approximately 75,000 Spanish-speaking people (of mixed Spanish and Indian blood) were living in the Southwest.

In 1853 the United States took another bite of Mexican territory, the 45,532 square miles called the Gadsden Purchase. Soon thereafter, the rush of U.S. Easterners after gold, coupled with completion of the transcontinental railroad in 1869, opened more areas of the Southwest, with the railroad tycoons getting the lion's share of land. The Southern Pacific Railroad became the largest landowner in California with over 20 million acres in the central valley. In California, former Mexicans (called "Californios") were reduced to a relatively small fraction of the state's population between 1860 and 1900 as the eastern immigrants moved in. In Texas, former Mexicans (called "Tejanos") experienced the same fate as the "Hispanos" of New Mexico.

Self-serving legislation by eastern U.S. settlers and contrived judicial proceedings dispossessed nearly all Mexican titleholders of more than 800 Mexican land grants, even though the Treaty of Guadalupe Hidalgo contained provisions to honor the former titles (McWilliams 1990). Instead of land remaining in Mexican hands, extremely large tracts of land went to non-Latino settlers. Moreover, the Homestead Act of 1862 gave thousands of Anglo and European settlers 160-acre parcels, overlapping Mexican land grants. Today in New Mexico the federal government and *Hispanos,* Latinos who trace their heritage back to the eighteenth century, continue to dispute ownership of the land (Knowlton 1985). In several other niches of the Southwest, too, the traditional Hispanic legacy continues in farming and rural communities (Crawford 1988).

Thus disenfranchised, Hispanic-Americans were subjected to a harsh future of deprived riches and inheritances. U.S. history books dissociated the development of the Southwest from its Hispanic contributors, robbing Latinos of a history that would have brought them pride. Noteworthy, for example, is that colonial Spanish and Mexican-Indian settlers developed and diffused America's first grapes, raisins, apricots, peaches, plums, oranges, lemons, wheat, barley, olives, and figs. They also learned to assimilate and adapt the New World (Mexican) products of cotton and henequen, and the nutritional indigenous diet of corn, beans, squash (pumpkin), tomatoes, chili peppers, avocados, vanilla, chocolate, and a variety of other fruits and vegetables that are today a part of our agricultural wealth.

The Spaniards, and later the Mexicans who took over the Southwest territory from Spain in 1821, also established the system of large farm estates or *ranchos*. The colonial missions were the training grounds for the first agricultural work force in California, the mission (Pueblo) Indians. As Indians were forced or indentured to labor on vast *ranchos* of several thousand acres each, they and *mestizos* (people of mixed Spanish, Mexican, and Indian blood) developed western techniques of large-scale ranching and agriculture. In ranching, Mexicans introduced the rodeo, bronco-busting of the mustang, chaps, spurs, calaboose, stampede, barbecue, and many other traditions we think of as being typically American. In agriculture, our Hispanic forerunners introduced riparian rights and water-saving irrigation systems and technologies for the arid Southwest.

The Origins of Migrant Workers

Although the Southwest was transformed by the de-Hispanization of the region, Mexico was also changed by its peasant revolution and cries for agrarian reform from 1910 to 1917. The revolution coincided with a growing demand for labor in U.S. agriculture that resulted in a steady flow of Mexican migrants into the United States. By the mid-1920s, Mexican migrants replaced previous farm workers of Chinese, Japanese, Hindi, and other ethnic backgrounds who had been recruited near the turn of the century to meet the farmers' demands for agricultural labor (Fuller 1991).

The trip north was hardly a problem; the Border Patrol of the Immigration Service was not established until 1924. Readily available in growing numbers, Mexican refugees were actively recruited and encouraged to migrate north from Mexico by the organized efforts of U.S. growers and agricultural associations. By the 1930s, Mexicans were the largest single group in the fields of California. Their low wages and skilled hard work fueled much American agricultural prosperity (Fuller 1991).

In the 1940s World War II augmented the need for farm labor to harvest labor-intensive crops. In response the United States negotiated a deal with Mexico to enable Mexican farm workers to work legally in the United States under temporary contract arrangements (i.e., the Foreign Farm Worker Program). More than 1 million workers would come to the United States to work in the so-called Bracero (translated: hired hands) program until 1965. At the height of the program in the 1950s, about 10 percent of the U.S. farm labor force were Mexican-based migrant workers employed throughout the United

States, mostly in the southwestern states. They accounted for 40 to 70 percent of the peak work force in crops such as lettuce, cucumbers, melons, oranges, and tomatoes.

On December 31, 1964, the Bracero program ended. Nonetheless, U.S. agriculture continued to employ Mexican farm workers under Labor Code Section H2 "Temporary Foreign Worker Certification Program." Thereafter, Mexican workers entered the United States provisionally when farmers could prove that a domestic labor shortage was imminent and that employment of foreign workers would not adversely affect the wages or working conditions of similarly employed U.S. workers. In 1989 about 26,000 foreign worker jobs were certified under the amended H2A Program that exempts employers from paying Social Security or unemployment taxes (Whitener 1991, 14.).

The post-Bracero employment of Mexicans in the Southwest, together with the recruitment drive from midwestern labor markets, has long supported a migratory pattern among Mexican workers of annual summer migrations to other parts of the United States (Valdés 1991). From the Texas valley, a region of intense poverty (Maril 1989), streams of migrant workers have traveled as much as 4,000 miles annually to the upper midwest (the Great Lakes region), to the west coast into the state of Washington, and even to regions of the Eastern Seaboard.

Until recently, the U.S. Department of Agriculture (USDA) conceptualized three distinct streams for migrant and seasonal farm workers, made up largely of Latinos. For purposes of general reference USDA programs referred to the eastern, midwestern, and western paths, beginning and fanning out from south Texas. This depiction was made to design systems for tracking the children of migrant and seasonal workers for federal programs in health and education. However, various studies and observations now indicate that farm-worker migration of Latinos is a much more complex, unpatterned, and unpredictable phenomenon (Martin 1988). Most Mexican and Tejano migrants travel an average of less than 500 miles in pursuit of work. Many so-called "Tex-Mex" migrants have settled also in states like Michigan, Wisconsin, Indiana, and Illinois, adding to the competition faced by migrant and seasonal workers (Barger and Reza 1994).

Farm Labor Unions and Collective Bargaining

Farm-worker strife and conflict have usually accompanied periods of enlarged supply of migrant and seasonal workers in America's rural economy (Galarza 1976). The earliest farm labor strikes in California agriculture in the twentieth century were organized by Mexicans: in Oxnard in 1903, in Wheatland in 1913, in the Imperial Valley in 1928, in El Monte in 1933, in San Joaquin cotton fields throughout the 1930s, and, of course, within memory of most, the Delano grape strikes and boycotts beginning in 1965 and lasting ten years under the leadership of Cesar Chavez and the United Farm Workers union. In all cases, Mexican field-workers (joined by Filipinos) struck for higher wages, better working conditions, and the right to engage in collective bargaining (Sosnick 1978). However, the National Labor Relations Act purposely, and to this date, excludes farm labor from its provisions.

In 1975 California legislators passed the first mainland law (Hawaii was first in the nation) recognizing the rights of farm labor organizations to collective bargaining. Called the California Agricultural Labor Relations Act, most of its provisions were unprecedented in American history. It guaranteed union access to farms and democratic elections of officers (Rochin 1977). Between 1975 and 1985 hundreds of contracts were signed between unions representing farm workers and farm employers. Labor conflicts increased after 1985 over issues of further unfair labor practices (discrimination in wages and cheating workers), the use of pesticides, immigration, and exploitation by labor contractors, once the archenemy of the United Farm Workers.

The mounting problems coincided with the decline of the United Farm Worker union, a largely Chicano and Mexican body. In California, where it was estimated that the union represented more than 100,000 workers in 1982, there were probably fewer than 15,000 workers organized by the UFW a decade later. According to the UFW former Governor Deukmejian's (Republican) administration undermined the union by biasing the California Agricultural Labor Relations Board in favor of farmers and by underfunding its operations and slowing its responses to unfair labor practices (Ferris 1993).

Hispanic Farms and Farmers

Mexicans are not strictly field hands, rural Latinos include renters and owner-operators of farms as well. The 1980 Census of Population identified 11,520 Hispanic farmers, about 1 percent of all U.S. farmers. Why this low number? One reason may be that Mexican settlers re-entered the United States after much of the cheaper land had been handpicked by earlier immigrants. Also, U.S. farming became increasingly capital intensive and technical. The low income of Mexican workers lessened their chances to accumulate money to buy land and equipment. More important, many Mexican workers preferred returning to Mexico where they could acquire land at lower cost and obtain financial backing with less difficulty.

Despite their small number nationally, Hispanic-operated farms have increased in number: in 1982 there were 16,183, in 1987, 17,476 (U.S. Bureau of the Census 1988a). The overwhelming number of Hispanic farms (73 percent) are below 219 acres, about one-half of the national average. Most Hispanic farms are found within seven states: Arizona, California, Colorado, Florida, New Mexico, Texas, and Washington. Moreover, Hispanic farmers are primarily tenants, sharecroppers, and part-owners who rarely have marketed sales above $25,000. In only two states do more than 50 percent of the Hispanic farms have sales of $10,000 or more, namely, California (with 51 percent) and Florida (with 50.2 percent) (U.S. Bureau of the Census 1987b). We know very little about Latino farmers, but in Colorado and New Mexico, parallel Hispanic and Anglo farming has been found to differ somewhat in cropping patterns and livestock holdings. Hispanic farmers tend to specialize more in alfalfa and sheep whereas Anglo farmers have more potatoes and cattle (Eckert and Gutierrez 1990).

During the 1970s, a short-lived movement took place in California to convert Chicano farm workers into owner-operators of cooperative farms, mostly for horticulture production. The efforts were successful as long as the USDA and California's system of Cooperative Extension helped these farmers with technical assistance for production, finance, and marketing. By the mid-1980s most Chicano cooperatives were gone, for a variety of reasons. However, many former cooperative members continued farming as renters or sharecroppers, especially in the production of vegetables and strawberries (Rochin 1986).

Sharecropping appears to have been motivated in part by landowners' wish to bypass the state's labor laws, especially the Agricultural Labor Relations Act of 1975. As sharecroppers, Chicanos are treated by law as farmers and not as farm workers who can be protected by California's Agricultural Labor Relations Act and other laws covering work conditions and wage rates. Under sharecropping, landlords were protected for a while against federal immigration laws concerning aliens and could avoid paying fines, coverage for workers under OSHA, and labor contractor laws. According to Wells (1984): "Most basically, strawberry sharecropping is a response to a changed balance of power between agricultural labor and capital. . . . In the current context, sharecropping helps landowners cope with the rising cost and uncertainty of labor. Far from hindering rational production, modern sharecropping facilitates and is recreated by capitalist accumulation" (2–3).

Rural Colonia *Settlements*

In California, over 500,000 Hispanics live in numerous small rural communities varying in size and complexity from unstructured *ranchos* to towns and cities. Colorado, New Mexico, and Texas add nearly 1 million rural Hispanics to California's rural number. In California, for which there are data, nearly seventy rural communities have been found to have a majority of Hispanic people in each, ranging from 50 to 98 percent of the population. The average town size is 6,000 people. Most residents are of Mexican descent and are either farm workers or employees in agribusiness. Recent research (Rochin and Castillo 1993) indicates that during peak periods in agriculture, the population of Hispanic settlements is substantially enlarged by the presence of migrant farm workers. Since annual earnings in farm employment are typically well below the poverty level, the Hispanic residents in rural settlements constitute a large proportion of California's rural poor. The concern is that these communities show signs of becoming centers of a rural underclass of Hispanics laboring to support themselves in the agricultural economy. These places have relatively low tax bases and therefore lack many of the public amenities needed to provide adequate health care, schooling, and safety (Rochin and Castillo 1993).

The subordinate position of *colonia* residents has been sustained by agribusiness and immigration. The overwhelming dominance of large farms and their dependence upon low-skill labor predicates a political alliance of agribusiness firms supporting liberal immigration. Since IRCA there has been little enforcement of immigration laws in agricultural areas, which also means that farmers can take advantage of the massive population growth in Mexico, which provides an abundant supply of workers. Under these circumstances, farm and agribusiness interests are well-positioned to dictate wages and working conditions and hence the welfare of rural *colonias* and Chicanos.

TRENDS OF HISPANIC-AMERICANS IN AGRICULTURE

Both the supply of and demand for Hispanic (Mexican) workers for agriculture have influenced U.S. immigration policies (Martin et al. 1994). In particular, the Immigration Reform and Control Act (IRCA) that passed Congress in 1986 was strongly supported by U.S. agriculture, especially by the Farm Bureau Federation. It contained provisions for Seasonal Agricultural

Workers (SAWs) and Replenishment Agricultural Workers (RAWs), covering up to 1 million Mexican workers for farm employment (Martin et al. 1994).

One post-IRCA study found that about 75 percent of California's farm workers were born in Mexico and most of the rest were Mexican-American or Chicanos. In California's Central Valley, the state's salad bowl of farm products, 87 percent of the workers were born in Mexico, 6 percent were born in the United States, and 7 percent were born outside of the United States and Mexico (Alvarado, Riley, and Mason 1990). Moreover, based on 361 persons interviewed, Alvarado et al. found that 33 percent are U.S. citizens; 59 percent are legally in the United States on visas; and 7 percent are "undocumented" residents. One-half reported coming to work in the United States ten or more years ago; slightly under 8 percent reported coming less than four years ago. Almost all come from farm labor backgrounds (Alvarado et al. 1990).

According to the Final Report of the Commission on Agricultural Workers, the majority of undocumented workers who applied for legal resident status did so as SAWs. Commissioner Philip L. Martin added that the SAW program legalized mostly young Mexican men who continued to commute between the United States and Mexico. Consequently, the process of Mexican immigration was not stopped but abetted (Martin 1993).

Although the effects of liberal immigration policy are perhaps most pronounced in California, Mexican immigrants are also becoming an increasingly important part of agricultural work forces in Texas, Florida, and the other leading states with increasing fruit and vegetable production. There are indications from North Carolina, Washington, Wisconsin, and New York that the Mexican component of the farm worker population is increasing steadily. In fact, IRCA's National Agricultural Workers Survey (NAWS) has revealed that Latino immigrants and their descendants do most of the field work in the United States. Some workers continue to be undocumented and most are immigrants. In 1990 NAWS found that 71 percent of Seasonal Agricultural Service (SAS) farm workers were Latinos, twice as many as the percent employed two years earlier (Gabbard and Mines 1994).

According to accounts of the UFW, the Immigration Reform and Control Act of 1986 hurt their efforts to gain new members because of the large number of legalized Mexican immigrants who were in need of jobs. Many SAWs seemed to know very little about the UFW's past struggle, philosophy, and purpose. As more undocumented immigrants flowed into the rural economy, there was also more competition for jobs and only modest interest in joining politically oriented, attention-getting groups of workers. New workers were recruited increasingly by farm labor contractors, who, for a fee, would transport and supervise farm workers, a service of immense benefit to small and medium size farmers who did not speak Spanish and who wanted to avoid hassles with IRCA's policies to control employment of illegal aliens (Taylor and Thilmany 1992).

Post-IRCA Mexican immigrants include indigenous groups who journeyed north with serious economic needs and their own ideas about organizing through self-help. One group, for example, is composed of Oaxacan (Mixtec Indian) field hands who came to work fields and joined a campaign to organize Mexican Indians like themselves in California. Known collectively as the *Comite Civico Popular Mixteco,* founded in 1981 in one of Mexico's poorest states, the group began an organizing drive in San Diego County in 1988 among Indians who were literally living in the fields, in man-made caves and shrub covered areas near urban communities. Today this group is struggling for recognition and raising issues of racial and economic discrimination, both in Mexico and California (Zabin et al. 1993).

As we approach the twenty-first century, the Latino struggle for empowering farm workers is troubled. The movements' preeminent leader, Cesar Chavez, died in his sleep on April 23, 1993, in San Luis, Arizona, ironically near where he was born 66 years before. Cesar Chavez was an inspiration to Chicanos and Mexican workers from all walks of life. The year before his death he was accorded Mexico's highest honor by President Salinas de Gortari for humanitarian service to Mexicans. His famous adage, *si se puede* ("yes, you can do it"), endures among Chicanos. Added to the uncertainty of proceeding without Cesar Chavez, the UFW faces a much bigger predicament: Americans today are embroiled in metropolitan decay, community turmoil, and global issues, and they are more ignorant than ever before of Latino farm workers. For the television addict, the farm workers' struggle is not much more than an occasional "discovery" of migrant hardship, discounted as a Mexican problem of illegal immigration.

Other Patterns of Change

Rural Hispanics have changed in character and so have their conditions. Many rural Hispanics are finding nonfarm employment. The formation of *colonias* demonstrates an increasingly permanent and settled rural Hispanic or Chicano population. Because of IRCA, most Latinos are legal residents. Judging by previous historical patterns of immigration, Mexican immigrants are here to stay. The newcomers include Mexican Indians, urban Mexicans, and people of all ages who find housing in places with many more Latinos like themselves. More Mexican women have immigrated to the United States than ever before, a fact that abets U.S. settlement.

Mexican settlement is geographically concentrated in rural areas of the Southwest but is spreading to all states. Today several communities conduct daily business in Spanish, and many residents have few opportunities for learning English, even if they want to. Within *colonias* education is a perplexing problem. Although many recent Mexican immigrants enter the United States with more schooling than their predecessors, the education of most non–Hispanic Americans has advanced much more. To this day, we know very little about the educational and income mobility of *colonia* residents. Will they become locked into *colonia* life and dependence on farm jobs and agribusiness? How many will be self-employed or work in other rural occupations?

History and data show a distinct racial and ethnic bias in the employment pattern of hired labor in U.S. agriculture. Out West, Hispanic workers predominate in agriculture and are hired by large and medium-sized farms to perform a variety of specialized tasks. In the Southern states, Hispanic workers are replacing African-Americans, who used to be concentrated on larger farms as workers. Larger farms in the West and South tend to employ more Latinos for specialized tasks than do mid-or small-sized farms. In the Midwest, there appears to be a decline in midsized farms and a tendency towards more hired labor. In the Midwest there is no long history of a significant proportion of Mexican workers employed on farms. However, we do know that the Midwest is the place of consistent employment of migrant and seasonal workers during the summer, especially of Mexican-origin workers (Valdés 1991).

"Mexicanization" and Implications for U.S. Agriculture

Mechanization has been the traditional weapon of large farms seeking to reduce use of workers and to undercut the bargaining power of farm workers. Mechanization gives growers an alternative, albeit an expensive one, to paying higher farm labor wages. During the demise of the Bracero program in the 1960s, mechanization and its consequences were widely studied, but the predictions raised about declining employment opportunities and declining producer competitiveness never materialized.

Instead of mechanization, "Mexicanization" ensued. "Mexicanization," a term coined by Palerm (1991) in his study of Mexican and Chicano *colonias,* was certainly confirmed by IRCA's provisions. In describing how Mexicanization works, Palerm (1991) described the long-standing culture of migration between Mexico and the United States: the same workers go back and forth to the same employment areas and employers, then pass the tradition on to generation after generation of Mexican farm workers.

Rochin and Castillo (1993) have found that this process has created a stabilization of California's agricultural labor force that also has contributed to the growth of *colonias*. The process involves large numbers, upwards of 1 million persons entering annually from Mexico to find work, often in rural America. And the process is growing in several rural places all over the United States.

Five decades of Mexican workers in the U.S. agricultural economy (dating back to the Bracero era) have driven most other U.S. workers out of seasonal migratory farm work and has changed the composition of rural communities. Mexicans and Chicanos now shoulder the responsibility for the bulk of fruit and vegetable harvesting in the states where this production is concentrated. Recruitment for available jobs is done largely through Mexican families and friends and by labor contractors whose Mexican roots and residential connections allow them to muster hundreds of workers locally and from villages in Mexico and Central America on short notice. They literally guarantee the arrival of Latinos at harvest sites in California or other states within a four-day period.

Although Mexican immigrants want to learn English, Spanish is becoming the language of the fields, spoken by labor contractors and workers, though rarely used by farm operators or by most other black or white workers in search of farm employment. The implication is that if an individual cannot speak Spanish, their prospects for obtaining migratory or seasonal farmwork are almost nonexistent.

Conversely, Mexican/Chicano farm workers who speak Spanish only and who have little formal education or English training may face unsurmountable obstacles when and if they attempt to make the transition to the world of nonfarm employment. By settling into *colonias,* they bind themselves to rural communities of protection and culture, but they also become increasingly isolated from the rest of the United States that is non-Hispanic.

Relations between the United States and Mexico are improving, especially in reducing trade barriers. The North American Free Trade Agreement (NAFTA) is a case in point. Even so, NAFTA is unlikely to result in significantly reduced migration of Mexican workers to the United States in the short run because of inadequate employment opportunities in Mexico. Both the supply of Mexican farm workers and the demand for them remain strong. Some studies have predicted that the jobs in Mexico will be produced gradually over the 1990s and will depend upon Mexico's policies for "privatization" and its investment climate for U.S. dollars (Rochin 1992). At the same time, however, Mexico is abolishing its system of farm *ejidos* (which guaranteed usufruct to land without title) by allowing its farmers both to own and to sell their land. If Mexican peasants sell their land, where will they go? If landlessness occurs—as feared by Mexican academics—will social pressures mount in Mexico, resulting in a greater push of workers to the United States and into *colonias*? For now, we don't know.

CONCLUSION

Rural Latinos, Chicanos, and other Hispanic Americans constitute a diverse population within a larger demographic trend that is changing social and power relationships between people. By the year 2000, Hispanic-Americans will be called upon to carry a bigger role in sustaining the wealth of this country. Mexican-Americans in agriculture are still exploited and work under inhumane conditions that include unsuspected toxic chemicals, child labor, and high rates of sickness and accidents. Half of Hispanic-Americans are foreign-born and would benefit from policies that foster acculturation (not assimilation), English-language training, and community interethnic relations.

Although Chicanos form the majority in a significant number of border communities and in towns in such primary agricultural areas as California's Central Valley, higher education and colleges of agriculture have not responded to the potential for recruiting and educating rural Latinos from these neighboring towns to study agriculture and natural resources. The migrant farm-worker image is embedded too deeply in the minds of non-Latino educators. Very few of my U.C. Davis colleagues in agriculture, for instance, imagine Latinos as scientists and future leaders in agriculture. They are mesmerized by the farm-worker syndrome and not sensitized to the positive strengths of Chicanos as owner-operators of farms or rural entrepreneurs. But only consider: Mexico's agricultural economy, after all, is farmed by thousands of progressive Mexican farmers.

Public-policy analysts have sought for decades to improve the lot of migrant and seasonal farm workers. Now they must broaden their focus and work to improve the lot of rural Chicanos and Latinos. These analysts will have to learn more about the global economy, patterns of international migration, and the processes of "Mexicanization" of fields and *colonia* formation. They may even have to learn Spanish. Hispanic-Americans should be looked upon not as a disadvantaged population presenting endless social problems, but as a potential source of strength for the society and economy of the nation.

NOTE

1. I use the term "Latino" interchangeably with "Hispanic American" in general. Mexican-origin workers are part of this term. The term "Chicano" refers to Mexican-origin workers who reside in the United States.

16
AMERICAN INDIAN
ECONOMIC DEVELOPMENT

C. MATTHEW SNIPP

A century ago, American Indians were deemed a "vanishing race," for it was widely believed that American Indians were destined for extinction. This belief was not unjustified. By the end of the nineteenth century, American Indians were a shattered, dispirited people. Disease, warfare, famine, and outright genocide had reduced their numbers within a few generations from millions to less than a quarter of a million in 1890.[1] Once a self-governing, self-sufficient people, American Indians across the nation had been forced to give up their homes and land and subordinate themselves to federal authorities. Under Bureau of Indian Affairs (BIA) supervision, the forced resettlement to reservation lands or the Indian territory meant a demoralizing life of destitution, hunger, and often complete dependency on the federal government for material needs.

Today, American Indians are more numerous than they have been for several centuries, but they are still one of the most destitute groups in American society. An important change is that tribes now have more autonomy and are more self-sufficient than any time since the last century. In many rural areas, American Indians and especially tribal governments have become increasingly more important and more visible by virtue of their growing political and economic power. One reason for this change has been the concerted efforts of tribal leaders and federal officials to develop economic activity in and around the areas where reservations are located, especially as a means of combating poverty and providing economic opportunities. The balance of this chapter is devoted to the principal elements of economic development in Indian country.

Table 16.1. Educational characteristics of American Indians and Alaska natives, blacks, and whites, 1990 (in percent)

	American Indians and Alaska natives	Blacks	Whites
High school dropouts[a]	18.2	13.9	10.0
High school graduates[b]	65.5	63.1	77.9
College graduates[b]	9.3	11.4	21.5

Source: U.S. Bureau of the Census, Summary Tape File 3.

[a] Persons age 16 to 19 not enrolled in school without 12 years of schooling
[b] Adults age 25 and over

RESOURCES FOR ECONOMIC DEVELOPMENT

Economic statistics leave little doubt that American Indians are one of the poorest segments of American society. The numbers in Table 16.1 show the educational achievements of American Indians in relation to blacks and whites in 1990. These data plainly show that Indians lag far behind whites by any measure. American Indian youth drop out of high school at alarmingly high rates. In 1990 about 18 percent of American Indians ages 16 to 19 were not in school and had not completed the twelfth grade, compared with 14 percent of blacks and 10 percent of whites. Surprisingly, American Indians are more likely to have graduated from high school than blacks. This statistic suggests that American Indians eventually complete their schooling with a GED or diploma. Table 16.1 also shows that American Indians seldom complete four years or more of college. High drop-out rates and disrupted school experiences undoubtedly are major contributors to this problem.

The lack of schooling and collective disadvantages confronting American Indians translate into considerable economic hardship. The unemployment rate for American Indians in early 1990 was 14 percent, compared with 13 and 5 percent for blacks and whites, respectively (see Table 16.2). Although American Indians have slightly higher unemployment than blacks, they have virtually identical household incomes and poverty rates. These differences are slight but one possible explanation for them is that more black families than Indian families are headed by single women. Or alternatively, more Indian families than black families have the advantage of having a male (and hence better paid) worker in the home (Snipp 1989).

The current economic circumstances of American Indians in many ways reflect a long history of federal efforts to subordinate an otherwise self-governing, self-sufficient people. This process eventually culminated in wide-

Table 16.2. Unemployment, income, and poverty among American Indians and Alaska natives, blacks, and whites, 1990 (in percent)

	American Indians and Alaska natives	Blacks	Whites
Unemployment rate	14.4	12.9	5.2
People in poverty	30.9	29.5	9.8
Mean household income[a]	$26,206	25,872	40,308

Source: U.S. Bureau of the Census, Summary Tape File 3.

[a] 1989 dollars

spread welfare dependency that took root in the late nineteenth century. Welfare dependency has been a fact of life in Indian country since tribes were interned on reservations and forced to depend on military rations for survival. The dependency has become considerably more complex and manifest in federal programs such as the War on Poverty efforts or the projects sponsored by the Comprehensive Employment and Training Act of the 1960s and 1970s. The abrupt termination of many of these programs in the early 1980s reminded tribal leaders of the uncertainty of federal largesse and the need for financial independence.

Economic development has been viewed increasingly as an alternative strategy for raising tribal revenues to deal with reservation problems. Efforts to stimulate economic activity on reservations are not a new idea. Since the late 1970s, however, reservations have been pursuing a variety of alternatives, some of them closely tied to the unique legal and political status of reservations. Economic development in Indian country can be viewed in terms of the resources available for development—natural and human—along with the strategies that have been used to develop them.

Natural Resources

There are 278 federally recognized American Indian reservations ranging in size from less than 100 acres to the Navajo reservation—16 million acres covering parts of Arizona, Utah, and New Mexico, in all an area about the size of West Virginia. These reservations account for most of the 56.2 million acres of Indian lands supervised by the federal government. These reservations are extremely diverse in terms of the natural resources they possess, but the four major types of resources include agricultural land, timber, water, and mineral resources.

Agricultural Land. Since the late nineteenth century, the federal government has encouraged American Indians to adopt agriculture.[2] Yet the land allotment policies of this era actually caused declines in Indian agriculture (Carlson 1981). There is a long history of failed attempts to establish tribal farms and livestock herds. Some tribes suffered disastrous land losses during allotment. Other tribes, such as those in the Southwest, had practiced agriculture for centuries, but they refused to adopt non-Indian technologies and their collective farm systems were disrupted by allotment.

For most of this century, non-Indians have been responsible for the majority of agricultural production on tribal lands. For example, when members of the Ute tribe in Utah refused to become farmers, Indian agents leased their lands to nearby Mormon farmers. This response is typical of how agricultural land was and continues to be managed on most reservations (Lewis 1988): agricultural lands are leased and farmed primarily by non-Indians (Levitan and Miller 1993). One study in particular found that non-Indians cultivated the most productive farmland while Indians were more likely to control less productive grazing land (Levitan and Johnston 1975).

The productivity of tribal agricultural land is a serious problem. Not surprisingly, reservations were established in places unattractive for farming, and few reservations have highly productive lands. The BIA classifies less than 1 percent of all reservation lands as highly productive, and less than 5 percent of the giant Navajo reservation has highly productive farm land. For the average reservation, this proportion amounts to about one acre of productive agricultural land per resident (Summers n.d.).

There are notable exceptions to this rule of unproductive land. For example, the Passamaquoddy tribe in Maine used funds from land claims settlements to acquire and develop a high-quality blueberry farm that supplies gourmet markets, premium hotels, and Ben and Jerry's ice cream. The Ak Chin reservation south of Phoenix has what is undoubtedly the largest and most profitable agribusiness with over 10,000 acres of cotton and alfalfa in production (White 1990).

Timber. Although agricultural production is not widespread on many reservations, timber production is considerably more common. This timber is often cut and processed outside the reservation but a growing number of reservations have built mills to produce finished lumber. One of the oldest of these mills was established on the Menominee reservation in Wisconsin.

Historically, the BIA has had primary responsibility for overseeing tribal forests and for the harvesting and sale of tribal timber. In 1989, 237 federal reservations possessed nearly 16 million acres of forest land with potentially harvestable timber. Perhaps more significant is that in 1989, 149, or slightly over half of all federal reservations, had about 6 million acres in commercial forests. This acreage represents a significant resource: its total harvested value is estimated at $158 million.

In the 1970s and 1980s the BIA was the subject of numerous complaints as well as congressional investigations regarding its management of tribal forests. These complaints alleged fraud, mismanagement, and, in particular, "sweetheart" deals between BIA employees and lumber companies, improper accounting, and incompetent resource management (Richardson and Farrell 1983). These complaints, coupled with growing tribal self-determination have meant that tribes are considerably more involved in the management of this resource; indeed, a number of tribes have instituted specialized forestry programs. Another analysis (Krepps 1992) of reservation forest management did not directly indict BIA mismanagement, but it did conclude that tribes should have a greater involvement in timber management as a safeguard against bureaucratic incompetence.

Water. The *Winters* doctrine, a principle stemming from a Supreme Court decision over tribal water rights, guarantees that tribes have prior claims on water destined for their reservation. In the arid western United States, this right gives reservations a powerful claim on a scarce and vital resource. In 1988, for example, the Supreme Court ruled that American Indians were entitled to about half of the water in eastern Wyoming (Levitan and Miller 1993). This decision is perhaps most important for reservation development, especially in water-intensive projects such as agriculture.

However, developing water for lease or sale off the reservation is tangled in the complex legal web of water use and riparian rights and has not been extensively pursued. One reason for this hesitance is the expense of litigating water rights cases. In the 1980s the Wind River reservation spent $9 million protecting their water rights (Levitan and Miller 1993). It is nonetheless possible for tribes with extensive water rights, such as the Navajo, to lease their water to the arid cities of the Southwest, just as large growers have found it more profitable to lease their water than to use it for farming. Water also can be used to produce revenue in other ways; for instance, the Salish-Kootenai in Montana sell hydroelectric power from a dam on their reservation. The scarcity of water makes such projects controversial, however. The Navajo sell water to slurry coal from the Hopi reservation to power plants in Nevada, but although both tribes benefit from this use of water, they are also opposed to expanding it because of the potential adverse impact on underground water reserves (Levitan and Miller 1993).

Minerals. The minerals available on reservation lands run the gamut from gravel to zinc and copper to energy resources: uranium, coal, petroleum, and natural gas. Needless to say, the immense potential wealth associated with the latter has attracted the most attention. By some estimates, 40 percent of all uranium and 30 percent of the strippable coal west of the Mississippi is located on tribal lands (Jorgensen et al. 1978).

Despite the enormous real and potential value of these resources, the tribes possessing coal and petroleum are not significantly wealthier than other tribes (Snipp 1988), for two reasons. First, some tribes, such as the northern Cheyenne in Montana, view mining as a violation of their sacred relationship with the land. In fact, this belief is frequently a source of conflict among tribal members who adhere to traditional tribal beliefs and less traditional tribal members who wish to develop the resources. Second, and more important, for many years the BIA failed to exercise proper oversight in the process of making leases, and these oversights caused millions of tons of coal to be sold at prices far below market value (Richardson and Farrell 1983, Snipp 1988).

Congressional inquiries and complaints by tribal leaders resulted in revamping BIA leasing procedures. The tribes also became more proactive in the negotiations for lease agreements. One important way the tribes became more involved in leasing was in the creation of the Council of Energy Resource Tribes (CERT). The council was formed in 1975 to increase tribal involvement in lease negotiations and to provide technical assistance to aid tribes in negotiations. (Ambler 1990). Since the formation of CERT, many old leases have been renegotiated, and tribal involvement has considerably improved the prices received for energy resources. However, a sluggish world market for coal and petroleum has dampened the enthusiasm for exploiting these resources.

Human Resources

Besides sheer numbers of able-bodied workers, education, training, and work experience are the best indicators of the human capital reserves of reservations. The low levels of educational attainment and labor force participation already have been noted and need no further comment—they bespeak the limited human resources for reservation development. The shortage of job opportunities in reservation communities further exacerbates the shortage of human capital as the best-educated, most able-bodied workers leave the reservation for employment elsewhere.

Many tribes have decided to address the scarcity of human capital on their reservations by establishing tribal colleges. The first tribal college was established in 1968 by the Navajo tribe. During the next twenty years, another twenty-three tribal colleges were established on reservations across the western United States. Most of these institutions are small facilities with two-year community college programs. A few, such as Sinte Galeska College in South Dakota, have a limited number of four-year programs. Almost without exception, these institutions depend heavily on federal funding and struggle to maintain facilities and personnel adequate to meet accreditation standards. Because the students attending these schools have few economic resources, revenue from tuition or property taxes is minimal to nonexistent.

Although relatively new, tribal colleges have the potential to play a crucial role in the development of human resources on reservations. The students attending these colleges are typically older. They frequently have very poor academic preparation and are returning to upgrade their basic skills, obtain vocational training, or acquire a GED. These students are not being diverted from educational opportunities elsewhere; they are students who would not be attending college under most circumstances, except that the presence of a tribal college gives them an opportunity to do so (Carnegie Foundation 1989).

In 1989 an estimated 4,400 full-time equivalent students were enrolled at the twenty-four tribal colleges (Carnegie Foundation 1989). The actual number of students in tribal colleges is even higher, for most students are not attending full-time programs. Considering that low educational levels and a lack of human resources have been one of the main obstacles to economic development on most reservations, the advent of tribal colleges is a development of potentially profound importance. These institutions are training people who in the past would have been labeled "hard-core unemployed." Their proximity also means they are well-situated to coordinate the curriculum with the specific needs of economic development projects. Many of these opportunities are yet to be realized, but an infrastructure now stands where nothing existed only a few years ago.

STRATEGIES FOR ECONOMIC DEVELOPMENT

Since the late nineteenth century various tribes, mostly in Oklahoma, have tried to promote economic development. These early efforts were scuttled by officials in the Bureau of Indian Affairs because at the time, the federal government was committed to dissolving tribal allegiances. Thus any project that might help sustain the viability of tribal organization was strenuously resisted by government authorities (Miner 1976). This policy remained in place until the 1930s, when it was replaced by efforts to rejuvenate tribal organization. In subsequent decades a variety of strategies have been adopted for promoting economic development. These strategies have taken many different forms, but, very broadly either they have been guided by conventional development models or they have taken very unconventional routes to economic development.

Conventional Development Models

Beginning in the 1950s, and even earlier in some areas, federal officials and tribal leaders adopted more or less "textbook" models for economic development. Like other rural communities, tribes have tried to attract industry by emphasizing a low-wage work force and nonexistent taxes, or by building infrastructure such as roads or industrial parks. Unlike other rural communities, they also have tried to start up their own businesses in construction, light manufacturing, agriculture, and a hodge-podge of other activities. A variety of efforts have been undertaken to encourage entrepreneurship. Many of these efforts reached a peak under the Economic Development Administration (EDA) and the Small Business Administration (SBA). Despite severe federal cutbacks in the early 1980s, some of these programs continue to offer assistance. Currently, most conventional development strategies focus on tribal operations or individual entrepreneurs.

Tribal Operations. The activities of tribes in promoting economic development are divided between attracting industries from outside the reservation and starting their own businesses. Often the goal of attracting outside industries is job creation, making labor-intensive and often low-wage industries most appealing. Light manufacturing such as electronics assembly plants have been located on a number of reservations. A fishhook factory was briefly located in the Pine Ridge reservation in South Dakota. The strategy of attracting industries owned by non-Indians has been a mixed success, however. The jobs created by such firms are typically low-skill, low-wage jobs with few benefits. Management jobs are seldom filled by Indians. Although these firms have the virtue of providing employment, they do not often yield a significantly improved standard of living. Making the welfare poor into the working poor can be considered at best a small improvement. A second problem with such industries is that they pit reservation workers against workers in developing nations. Like other rural communities, reservations have watched local industries join the exodus overseas to obtain cheap labor. Some tribes have been able to resist this trend, however. According to Chief Philip Martin of the Mississippi Choctaw, his tribe has been successful with light manufacturing because they can offer superior workmanship to compensate for lower offshore labor costs.

Tribally owned businesses face other dilemmas. One crucial problem is deciding whether a tribal business will operate to maximize employment, or whether it will seek to become an efficient, highly competitive enterprise. In theory, there is no necessary conflict between these goals. In practice, such a conflict often exists when decisions about layoffs or dismissing incompetent employees must be made. The decision to choose between jobs or profits is often complicated further by the problem of tribal politics. Like other communities, American Indians often disagree about the best course of action for tribal government. In connection with economic development, disputes may arise over the types of development, who is involved, and the disposition of jobs and revenues. Decisions that are politically astute may be disastrous for tribal enterprises.

Some tribes have attempted to deal with conflict by establishing business committees separate from the tribal government. This move is intended to distance business decisions from tribal politics, but too often it merely shifts political disputes from the arena of tribal government to the business committee. Cornell and Kalt (1990) argue that political development is a necessary antecedent to economic development. For tribal governments to successfully undertake complex economic development projects, they must be able to exercise a great deal of administrative expertise as well as having the political stability to carry out long-range plans. Cornell and Kalt (1990) echo others (e.g., Vinje 1985) when they also note that economic development projects must be consistent with tribal culture and lifestyles, and especially with the political culture of the tribe. Tribes accustomed to diffuse, highly decentralized decision-making processes will not accommodate economic development projects organized with a highly centralized management plan.

Reservation Entrepreneurship. A 1984 Presidential Commission discouraged the involvement of tribal governments in business enterprises and recommended that entrepreneurship would most benefit reservation economics. However, the federal government has done very little to actually increase private enterprise by reservation Indians. American Indians desiring to start their own businesses face many of the same obstacles confronting non-Indians trying to start a small business.

American Indian entrepreneurs face particularly difficult problems raising investment capital. One reason should be obvious: most American Indians have extremely limited financial resources and thus have difficulty obtaining the personal equity expected by bank loan officers. A second reason is that reservation and other Indian lands are held in a trust by the federal government. American Indians, then, cannot sell their land, nor can they use it for collateral. In many ways, this arrangement is beneficial, for it preserves the remaining lands of American Indians. At the same time, however, it is an obstacle that non-Indian entrepreneurs need not face.

An experimental project for raising investment capital has been developed on the Pine Ridge reservation in South Dakota. With support from the First Nations Foundation, the Lakota Fund encourages the development of "micro-enterprises." This project, modelled after one developed in Bangladesh, begins by encouraging the formation of small borrower groups. Members of these groups take out small loans, usually less than $1,000, for the purpose of producing goods and services for sale; thread and fabric might be purchased to produce quilts, for example. Individuals are the loan recipients, but the group is responsible for loan repayments and the default rate is very low, less than 10 percent. The Lakota Fund also offers technical assistance in marketing and other business practices.

The Lakota Fund plays an important role in promoting reservation entrepreneurship by teaching basic skills needed for business. The projects it funds are, however, extremely small ("micro"), they generate small amounts of income, and it is not clear that the projects it sponsors will eventually become sizable businesses with paid employees. Nonetheless, it is an important experiment that deserves careful attention as a development model for other tribal communities.

Unconventional Development Strategies

Unconventional development strategies are based on the special legal and political status of American Indians—hence they are not options for economic development by non-Indians. This approach to economic development became more common in the late 1970s and 1980s, possibly because there was less federal support for conventional development projects. This approach also has been called the "legal road to economic development" (Olson 1988), and central to this strategy is the doctrine of tribal sovereignty.

The concept of tribal sovereignty is implicit in much of the preceding discussion, for it is a central organizing principle in relations between the federal government and American Indians. The legal theory behind tribal sovereignty dates back to the founding of the United States and early decisions of the Supreme Court (Barsh and Henderson 1980). Briefly, tribal sovereignty means that by treaty and other agreements tribes have reserved certain legal rights of self-government. These rights provide tribal governments with a measure of self-rule subject to the authority of the federal government and exempt from most state and all local authority. With only a few exceptions, tribal governments have most of the same powers as state governments.

The so-called "legal road to economic development" exploits the powers of tribal sovereignty, treaty rights, and other legal agreements for the sake of developing a market niche for tribal enterprises. The ability to use tribal sovereignty for creating a market niche is crucial to successful enterprise. And, indeed, a number of operations stem from treaty rights, land claim settlements, and the use of tribal sovereignty to create a market niche.

Two of the best-known developments stemming from treaty rights settlements are located in Maine and in the Puget Sound region of Washington State. In 1975 the Passamaquoddy and Penobscot tribes of Maine won a major court victory and a ruling that these tribes might be eligible to claim up to two-thirds of the state. After protracted negotiations, a federal task force concluded negotiations with these tribes with a settlement of $82 million. With this settlement, the tribes purchased lands, established investment portfolios, and initiated economic development projects. The Passamaquoddy invested a full third of their settlement in economic development projects such as a construction firm, a cement factory, and a blueberry farm. These projects were meant to produce income for tribal services and jobs for tribal members. Since the settlement, some of these projects have been more successful than others, but they have been sufficiently capitalized and well-managed that they are counted as successes by the tribe (White 1990).

The state of Washington in the 1950s and 1960s was the site of protracted struggles over Indian fishing rights. These struggles culminated in the court case of *U.S. v. Washington*, also known as the Boldt Decision. In 1974, federal judge George Boldt rendered a verdict that treaties signed with the Puget Sound tribes entitled them to 50 percent of the salmon harvested in this region each year in perpetuity. This major victory enabled these tribes shortly afterwards to initiate economic development projects based on fishing. The Lummi and the Quinault in particular have vertically integrated aquaculture programs with fish hatcheries and fish-processing plants. These tribes play central roles in Puget Sound conservation efforts and have a major stake in improving fisheries production. Furthermore, these activities are also a major source of tribal employment and revenue.

Because tribal sovereignty gives tribal governments the right to legislate for themselves, another direction in the legal road to economic development has been for tribes to make available goods and services restricted by local and state laws. Faced with shrinking federal subsidies in the mid-1970s, many reservations established retail tobacco stores ("smoke shops"). These shops sold tax-exempt tobacco products and they were relatively successful because they could undersell local non-Indian retailers.[3] The revenue from these establishments typically has been used to support tribal social service programs. Predictably, the success of smoke shops caused an outcry from local merchants about unfair competition and from state and local authorities about lost tax revenues. In 1978 these complaints erupted into a legal conflict involving the Seminole tribe of Florida. In *Vending Unlimited, Inc. v. State of Florida*, the courts ruled that the principle of tribal sovereignty meant that tobacco sales on reservation lands are exempt from state taxes (Kersey 1992, 109).

Compared to gambling, however, the controversy and revenues generated by tobacco shops are negligible. Shortly after the victory of *Vending Unlimited*, the Seminole developed a high-stakes bingo operation on their Florida reservation. This game offered jackpots of cars, vacations, and cash prizes exceeding $10,000. This extremely popular attraction produced tribal revenues that dwarfed the revenues from tobacco sales (Kersey 1992). Again predictably, Florida authorities attempted to halt this operation, which resulted in another landmark court case. In 1980 the federal district court ruled in *Seminole Tribe of Florida v. Butterworth* that the doctrine of tribal sovereignty meant that the Seminole retained rights of self-government that exempted them from state gambling regulations. This decision was appealed by Florida officials but was upheld by the federal appeals court in 1981.

As a result of the Florida decision, other tribes ventured cautiously into high-stakes bingo as a source of tribal revenue. Sharp reductions in federal aid to tribal social programs that occurred during the Reagan administration also encouraged tribal leaders to develop gaming operations. As bingo spread, tribes began testing the idea of having other types of gambling, a notion that was quickly challenged by state officials and was eventually settled by the United States Supreme Court. In 1987 the Court ruled against the state of California (*California v. Cabazon and Morongo Bands*) and established beyond question the tribes' right to develop gambling operations on their reservations.

The implications of the California decision were far-reaching. It meant that in principle, American Indian tribes could develop large-scale casinos that were entirely unregulated except by tribal authorities. This decision sparked a flurry of lobbying in Congress by state officials desiring control over gambling and by gaming industry groups concerned about growing competition.[4] Indian organizations, meanwhile, launched a counter-lobbying campaign to protect their gaming operations from what many viewed as an infringement on tribal sovereignty. The result of these efforts was the Indian Gaming Regulatory Act (IGRA) of 1988.

The IGRA legislation contained two mandates. First, it required tribes and state officials to negotiate formal agreements known as "compacts" about how reservation gambling would be operated, along with procedures for mediating stalemated negotiations. Second, it established different classes of gambling and stipulated that reservation gambling should be broadly consistent with the types of gaming allowed outside the reservation. That is, if a state allowed Class II gambling, which includes lotteries, tribes also would be allowed to offer Class I (bingo) and Class II games but not Class III (dice, roulette) gambling.

The IGRA legislation was a mixed victory for the parties involved. On the one hand, it set definite limits on tribal gambling, and it tied reservation gaming to state limits. On the other hand, it clearly permits tribes to develop gambling operations, and it does not allow state officials to directly regulate tribal gaming.

As of June 1993 there were 125 gambling establishments operated by American Indian tribes in twenty-four states (*Indian Gaming* 1993). Oklahoma, the former Indian Territory and the state with the largest American Indian population, had 21 Indian gaming operations followed by California with 16, Wisconsin with 14, and Minnesota with 13. About half of all Indian gaming operations are concentrated in these four states. The games offered, as well as their scale, vary enormously. Some are modest affairs that offer bingo games with moderate jackpots of a few thousand dollars. Others are large-scale full-service casinos that gross several hundreds of millions of dollars annually and promise players jackpots in the hundreds of thousands of dollars. Perhaps the largest of these casinos belongs to the Pequot tribe in western Massachusetts, which reportedly grosses about $400 million annually.

Indian gaming is a remarkable development. For several formerly impoverished tribes, Indian gaming has generated a stream of cash income that was once unimaginable. Although this income has helped tribes deal with some pressing social problems in their communities, it has generated other difficulties. For example, conflicts with state and local authorities have become more intense as a result of gaming disputes.

In 1993 considerable pressure was placed on Congress by state and local officials, as well as by the gaming industry, to curtail reservation operations. This pressure included a resolution passed at the National Governor's Association meeting that called for additional limits on Indian gaming, a document endorsed by all but one of the governors. The gambling industry also has vigorously lobbied against Indian gaming, including several bizarre episodes involving gambling magnate Donald Trump. These episodes included litigation filed by Trump against the BIA, public allegations by Trump that Indian gaming is controlled by organized crime, and a shouting match between Trump and Congressman George Miller during a committee hearing (Cruise 1993).

American Indian leaders, especially those with successful operations, are quick to point out the benefits of Indian gaming for their communities. Indeed these revenues have often meant better schools and improved public services for many reservations. Most reservations, however, do not have spectacularly successful gaming developments, and many American Indians do not live on reservations.

Nonetheless, tribal gaming has been an important if controversial development. In response to the governors and the gambling industry, Congress held hearings throughout 1993 about whether to further limit these establishments. Despite intensive lobbying on both sides of the issue, Congress has not yet acted to amend the legislation passed in 1988. Regardless of how Congress acts, Indian gaming is likely to remain a contentious matter for the foreseeable future.

CONCLUSION

Although few in number, American Indians have an enduring place in American society, and perhaps nowhere are they more visible than in rural areas. This visibility stems from the growing numbers of American Indians occupying reservation and other trust lands and, more important, from the revitalization of tribal governments since the 1950s. Tribal governments now have a larger role in reservation affairs than ever since their original resettlement on reservation lands.

The challenges facing tribal governments are daunting. American Indians are among the poorest groups in this nation. Reservation Indians have substantial needs for improved housing, adequate health care, educational opportunities, and employment, as well as the development and maintenance of reservation infrastructure. In the face of declining federal assistance, tribal governments are assuming an ever larger burden. On a handful of reservations, tribal governments have assumed completely the tasks once performed by the BIA.

As tribes have taken greater responsibility for their communities, they also have struggled with the problems of raising revenue and providing economic opportunities for their people. Although reservation land bases provide many reservations with resources for development, these resources are not always abundant, much less unlimited, and they have not always been well-managed.

It will be yet another challenge for tribes to explore ways of managing efficiently their existing resources. Legal challenges also face tribes seeking to exploit unconventional resources such as gambling revenues. Their success depends on many complicated legal and political contingencies. Despite the many obstacles confronting American Indian tribes, their history of resilience and persistence in the face of adversity gives good cause to be cautiously optimistic about their future.

NOTES

1. The American Indian population probably numbered around 5 to 7 million in 1500 (Thornton 1987, Snipp 1989). This number is possibly too conservative compared with higher estimates reaching 18 million (Dobyns 1983).

2. The General Allotment Act (1887) and related legislation was passed for the purpose of "civilizing" American Indians by forcing them to adopt Euro-American agricultural practices. This legislation privatized tribal lands, deeded parcels to American Indian families, and mandated that any remaining land be sold to non-Indians.

3. Tribes have made concessions with the states to collect some type of tax in exchange for being allowed to operate these establishments unmolested by local authorities.

4. Complaining that tribes have an unfair competitive advantage, Donald Trump has filed suit against the Bureau of Indian Affairs in an effort to stop Indian gaming and to protect his casino interests in Atlantic City, N.J.

17

THE RURAL SOUTH: A HISTORICAL VIEW

CHARLES S. AIKEN

The American South is a large section of the United States without precise borders, and those who study it have long debated the area's boundaries. Definitions range from the simplistic agrarian notion of the South as the Cotton Belt to the expansive concept of a realm of southern culture that extends northward beyond the Ohio River and westward across the Llano Estacado (Smith and Phillips 1942, 287–317; Zelinsky 1992, 117–134; Meinig 1969, 103–106). The least debated and most widely accepted definition is that employed by the Bureau of the Census. The census South extends from Delaware and Maryland through Texas and Oklahoma and encompasses sixteen states.

Because the southern realm is one of significant regional and historical diversity, the idea of multiple "Souths" has long persisted. In its most rudimentary spatial form, this concept posits two Souths. Well before the Civil War the Upland South with a white yeoman farmer tradition was recognized as distinct from the Lowland South with its plantation tradition. When the notion of a New South arose after the Civil War, the concept of an Old South was invented as the counterpart. Since the colonial period, an urban South has existed that is economically and culturally distinct from the rural South.

During the half century following the Great Depression of the 1930s, the rural South underwent sweeping changes. Many of the alterations that occurred after 1940 are not well documented, and some are unstudied. For an historical geographer, the sweeping transformation of the rural South is fascinating, for it affords the opportunity to study complete processes of landscape evolution and regional change. Among the significant changes are population redistribution and accompanying modifications in rural settlement patterns, spatial alterations in agriculture, impact of the civil rights movement, and emergence of yet another concept of two Souths. My discussion of the rural transformation is confined primarily to the Lowland South.

POPULATION REDISTRIBUTION AND CHANGES IN RURAL SETTLEMENT PATTERNS

In 1940 more than half of the South's 41,666,000 inhabitants were rural.[1] Although the 1920 census was the first to reveal that more than half of the nation's population was urban, twenty years later 63.3 percent of the census South's inhabitants were still rural compared with 43.5 percent nationwide (Table 17.1). In Alabama, Georgia, and Mississippi, the heart of the Lowland South, the rural population surpassed 70 percent. In 1990 only 31.4 percent of the South's population was rural. The South's actual rural population in 1990 was somewhat less, for the census invariably undercounts the population that is functionally urban, especially in sprawling Southern urban areas interspersed with farm and idle land. In 1940, 39.2 percent of the South's total population and 62.0 percent of the rural population resided on farms (Table 17.1). By 1990 the farm population had declined to only 1.4 percent of the total population and to 4.5 percent of the rural. Even in Georgia, Alabama, and Mississippi, the decline in importance of the rural farm and the growth of the rural nonfarm population were just as dramatic.

Blacks have comprised a significant part of the rural South's population since the colonial period. In 1900, 90 percent of the nation's black population lived in the South, and 83 percent of the South's blacks were rural. Despite the great urban migration of blacks during the first third of the twentieth century, 77 percent of United States blacks still resided in the South in 1940. Almost half of the blacks in the nation and 64.4 percent of those in the South were still rural. In 1990, 52.8 percent of the nation's blacks lived in the South, of whom 22 percent were rural (U.S. Bureau of the Census 1976; 1992a).

Although population statistics are important in themselves, they also allude to major geographical changes that they do not reveal. Underlying the figures are major redistributions of the rural population and significant changes in rural settlement patterns. Most studies of population redistribution in the United States treat interregional movements. Rarely do studies penetrate below the county level, but profound changes in population distribution have occurred within counties at the local scale. Historically, most of the South's rural population was dispersed across the countryside. The dominant spatial trend during recent years has been nucleation. Concentration of rural people

Table 17.1. Changes in population, 1940–1990.

	Total Population	Rural Population	% of Total	Farm Population	% of Total	Rural Nonfarm Population	% of Total
The South							
1940	41,666,000	26,375,000	63.3	16,344,000	39.2	10,032,000	24.1
1990	85,446,000	26,790,000	31.4	1,217,000	1.4	25,572,000	29.9
Difference 1940–1990	43,780,000	415,000		−15,127,000		15,540,000	
% Difference 1940–1990	105.1	1.6		−92.6		155.4	
Alabama, Georgia, Mississippi							
1940	8,141,000	5,778,000	71.0	4,103,000	50.4	1,675,000	20.6
1990	13,092,000	5,347,000	40.8	196,000	1.5	5,151,000	29.9
Difference 1940–1990	4,951,000	−431,000		−3,907,000		3,476,000	
% Difference 1940–1990	60.8	−7.5		−95.2		207.5	

Source: U.S. Bureau of the Census

in several new types of geographical situations occurred with the decline in the farm and growth in the rural nonfarm population. Unincorporated hamlets are important parts of the newly emerged settlement pattern (Hart 1981; Aiken 1985). The hamlets are of two basic types: unplanned assemblages of dwellings and planned subdivisions.

Unplanned assemblages of dwellings often begin as settlements of extended families. Parents give or sell to children small lots from a farm on which to build houses or place mobile homes. Splitting off lots for children may also occur on adjoining farms. Eventually lots may be sold to people who are not family members, and over a few years a group of a dozen or more dwellings evolves.

In 1960 official county plat books rarely contained maps of planned subdivisions that were not parts of incorporated places. Today, examination of plat books in almost any nonmetropolitan county in the South reveals pages of new subdivisions, many of which are located in the countryside (Aiken 1985). Developers have found ready markets for rural subdivision lots among urbanites, including retirees who want a home in the country, but the major market is the growing local rural nonfarm population.

Among the few studies that have assessed the rural subdivisions is an analysis of Loudon County, Tennessee (Williams 1982). Loudon is a nonmetropolitan county that adjoins the Knoxville Metropolitan Statistical Area. In 1954 Loudon County had only 6 planned rural subdivisions; in 1982 it had 112. Analysis of the inhabitants revealed that 47 percent had relocated from other parts of the county, primarily from dispersed rural dwellings. Five major types of rural subdivisions were identified, ranging from simple ones that were created by surveying lots along existing roads to large complex developments with numerous roads designed for aesthetic appeal (Williams 1982, 12–20).

In particular areas of the rural South, primarily in the Upland but in some places in the Lowland as well, large, densely populated rural settlement complexes, which often do not have even a municipality that meets the census population threshold of urban, have evolved. These complexes have some characteristics of metropolitan suburban fringes, but they are not parts of metropolitan areas. A federal or state highway usually provides the arterial focus. Along the highway and close to it on side roads are numerous dwellings, many of which might be in planned subdivisions. Interspersed among the dwellings are various businesses, including grocery stores, convenience markets, farm and garden supply stores, and barber and beauty shops. Small factories are located near major crossroads or on railroad sidings. Such a complex is essentially a rural city, for it functions spatially as a small dispersed urban area. The largest complexes may actually include one or more small municipalities. Although these new rural settlement complexes are largely unstudied, large portions of the rural population are concentrated in them, particularly in the Ridge and Valley in eastern Tennessee, Sand Mountain in northern Alabama, and the Upper Piedmont in the Carolinas and Georgia.

The changes in population distribution and in settlement patterns have varied from region to region. A description of the black population of the Yazoo Delta in Mississippi illustrates how sweeping the changes have been for one group of people in a nonmetropolitan region. Historically, blacks in the Delta were an essential part of the plantation system. In 1940, 89 percent of the 313,214 blacks in the eleven-county region of the Delta were rural farm residents. Most were members of tenant families, primarily sharecropper families. The settlement pattern was a dispersed one; houses of sharecroppers were scattered across the cotton fields (Prunty 1955, 467–474). Beginning in the 1930s with the reduction of cotton acreage under the Agricultural Adjustment Act and the commencement of large-scale agricultural mechanization with the introduction of tractors, plantations began to be reorganized spatially (Aiken 1978). After World War II mechanization proceeded rapidly, with the introduction of mechanical cotton pickers followed by the adoption of herbicides for weed control. As plantations were mechanized, the labor system changed from one that used sharecroppers to one in which agricultural workers were paid cash wages. On most plantations the reorganization occurred in stages as the new technology was adopted and the number of sharecroppers was reduced (Aiken 1978).

The demise of sharecropping was accompanied by major alterations in the settlement pattern of the Delta (Prunty 1955; 1962). The dispersed plantation settlement pattern of 1940 was superseded by a nucleated one (Figure 17.1), for tenant houses dispersed across fields impeded efficient use of new agricultural machinery. Although most dwellings were razed, some were relocated to main roads to house machinery operators and the diminishing number of sharecroppers. During the past twenty years, old houses on plantations increasingly have been replaced with small modern ones for the resident labor force.

Reorganization of plantations was accompanied by a great exodus of blacks from the Yazoo Delta. The black population declined from 313,241 to 178,296 between 1940 and 1980 (Aiken 1987, 565–566). Meanwhile, a significant modification occurred in the spatial distribution of the blacks who remained. In 1940, 80.8 percent of the blacks in the Yazoo Delta resided on farms; only 11.2 percent were urban. By 1980 the black farm population had declined to 3.1 percent of the total. The percent of the black population that

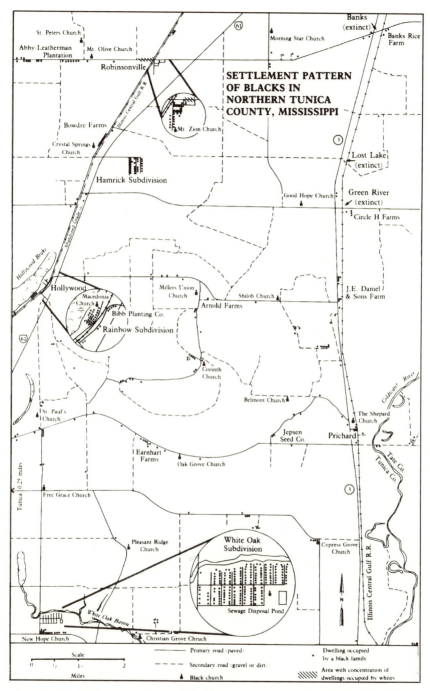

Figure 17.1. Settlement pattern of blacks in northern Tunica County, Mississippi. (Source: C. Aiken 1985; reproduced courtesy of the American Geographical Society of New York)

was urban had increased to 46. Rural nonfarm had become the dominant category, comprising 50.9 percent of the region's black population.

Mississippi was one of five states for which the Bureau of the Census prepared 1980 block data for all rural as well as urban areas. By using block data in combination with field analysis it is possible to study the microscale distribution of the black population in the Delta. The trend toward urbanization is much greater than indicated by summary census figures. In 1980, 12.1 percent of the blacks in the Delta resided in rural municipalities, incorporated places with populations less than 2,500. More important, almost 20 percent of the Delta's blacks lived within one mile of the corporate limits of municipalities and functionally were part of them. In 1980, 77.2 percent of the black population in the Delta was "municipal"; only 22.8 percent was "open-countryside rural" (Aiken 1987, 567–568). Much of the "open countryside" population was concentrated in planned subdivisions, some of which were sponsored by federal agencies, and in unplanned assemblages of dwellings. White Oak, located in Tunica County near the town of Tunica, is an example of a FmHA subdivision (Figure 17.1).

In 1960 almost 50 percent of the occupied dwellings in the Delta were dilapidated or deteriorated (Aiken 1987, 569). During the two decades following the initiation of the War on Poverty by the Johnson administration in 1965, the Farmers Home Administration and the Department of Housing and Urban Development spent more than $200 million to improve housing in the region. Single-family dwellings for home ownership, public housing, and multifamily rental projects were funded by the agencies. The improvement in the quality of housing has been profound. A full 42 percent of the housing units in the Delta occupied by blacks in 1980 were constructed after 1960 (Aiken 1987, 569).

Two factors are paramount in explaining the large concentrations of rural-nonfarm blacks on the margins of towns and cities: location decisions for federally funded housing and refusal of white-controlled municipal governments to annex black residential areas. With respect to location, federally funded housing in the Delta tends to follow lines of least resistance. One type of location is on the margins, but not within the political limits, of municipalities. Although the municipalities provide utilities and other services to the new residential areas, which with a few exceptions are predominantly black, white municipal officials refuse to annex them primarily because addition of large numbers of blacks will dilute white voting strength. In 1980 twelve of the fifty-seven municipalities in the Delta underbounded their actual populations at levels that were statistically significant. Among them were Indianola, Cleveland, and Belzoni (Aiken 1987, 567–574; Figure 17.2). On the edges

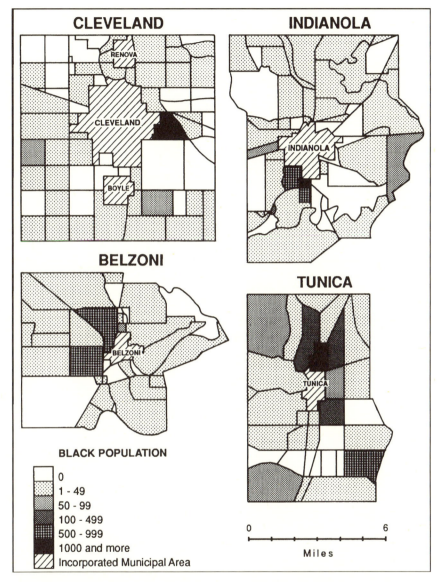

Figure 17.2. Black population of rural census blacks surrounding Cleveland, Indianola, Belzoni, and Tunica, Mississippi, 1980. (Source: C. Aiken 1987; reproduced courtesy of the Association of American Geographers)

Table 17.2. Changes in farms, land in farms, and cropland harvested, 1940–1987.

	Number of Farms	Acres Land in Farms	Acres Cropland Harvested
The South			
1940	3,007,100	370,169,000	103,290,000[a]
1987	823,900	281,243,000	59,248,000
Difference 1940–1987	−2,183,200	−88,926,000	−44,042,000
% Difference 1940–1987	−72.6	−24.0	−42.6
Alabama, Georgia, Mississippi			
1940	738,871	61,983,000	22,387,000[a]
1987	120,944	30,637,000	9,803,000
Difference 1940–1987	−617,927	−31,346,000	−12,584,000
% Difference 1940–1987	−83.6	−50.6	−56.2

Source: U.S. Bureau of the Census

[a] Harvested cropland figures are for 1939

of these municipalities, subdivisions of new, brick-veneer single-family houses, including FmHA 502 dwellings and HUD Section 23 leased public housing projects sprawl across the landscape interspersed with FmHA Section 515 apartment complexes (Aiken 1987, 572–574).

SPATIAL CHANGES IN AGRICULTURE

Analysis of a few elementary statistics also reveals major changes that occurred in southern agriculture after 1940 (Table 17.2). Between 1940 and 1987 the number of farms in the South declined from more than 2 million to 823,900, land in farms decreased from 370 to 281 million acres, and harvested cropland dropped from 103 to 59 million acres. In Georgia, Alabama, and Mississippi, declines were even more dramatic. Land in farms decreased 50.6 percent and harvested cropland decreased 56.2 percent between 1940 and 1987.

These statistics, like the ones for population, imply substantially more than they reveal. The decline in land on farms and in cropland has not been uniform across the South. Whereas some agricultural regions, including the Southern Piedmont, experienced declines so great that they are now essentially extinct as crop regions (Prunty and Aiken 1972), other areas, including portions of the alluvial Mississippi Valley, had increases in cropland. The major geographical trend during the past fifty years has been concentration of

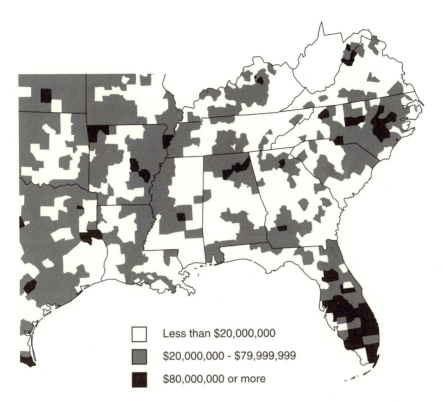

Figure 17.3. Average value per farm of agricultural products sold per county, 1987. (Source: U.S. Bureau of the Census)

agriculture in a few regions (Hart 1968; 1978). In 1987 most of the South's agriculture (exclusive of Texas and Oklahoma) was in three regions: the lower Mississippi Valley; the inner coastal plain of the Carolinas, Georgia, and Alabama; and central and southern Florida (Figure 17.3).

The regions that contain most of the South's agriculture are fully modern, and they rank among America's major agricultural areas in technology and productivity. Historically, however, these areas were perceived as inferior to others that are now virtually extinct as agricultural regions. The sandy-soil areas of the inner coastal plain became important for agriculture only after the introduction of commercial fertilizer following the Civil War. Most of the alluvial Mississippi Valley was still forested in 1900, and settlement was impeded by annual flooding, poor drainage, and malaria. Florida, which in 1986 ranked first among the southeastern states and ninth among the fifty

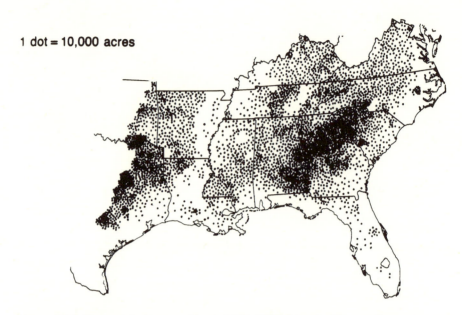

Figure 17.4. Decrease in harvested land, 1880–1982. Map by Thomas Frey. (Source: Healy 1985; reproduced courtesy of the Conservation Foundation)

states in value of agricultural products, is a twentieth-century place (U.S. Bureau of the Census 1986, 627). Parts of Florida that are now citrus orchards and vegetable and sugar cane fields were open-range ranch country and swamp in 1940 (Mealor and Prunty 1976).

During the decline and concentration of agriculture, cotton lost its lofty position. In 1940 cotton was still the fulcrum of southern agriculture, and the Cotton Belt was the agricultural heart of the South. In 1929, the last agricultural census year before the imposition of federal crop controls under Franklin Roosevelt's New Deal, the southern states (exclusive of Texas and Oklahoma) planted 23.5 million acres to cotton. By 1982 cotton had declined to 2.9 million acres, and the crop accounted for only 11 percent of farm income in the southeastern states, surpassed in value by vegetables, orchard fruits, and soybeans (Healy 1985, 24–25; Luke 1989).

Large areas of the South that once were important agriculturally, including the Southern Piedmont, the Alabama-Mississippi Black Belt, the Ridge and Valley in Alabama and eastern Tennessee, and the Nashville Basin in middle Tennessee, have almost gone out of crop production (Figure 17. 4). Across these areas much of the land has reverted to forest or lies idle, covered by broom sedge and tree saplings. The agriculture that survives occurs in islands, areas where the declines have not been as great (Prunty and Aiken 1972). Scattered among the forests and the old fields are the relics and fossils of a bygone agriculture. Large tracts in extinct agricultural regions are now owned and leased by timber products companies, and land that at midcentury grew cotton and corn now produces pulpwood.

Another important change implied but not revealed in agricultural statistics is spatial restructuring of southern farms. Between 1940 and 1987, while the number of farms in the South declined from 3,007,100 to 823,900, the size of the average farm increased from 123 to 341 acres (Table 17.2). In Georgia, Alabama, and Mississippi the number of farms decreased 84 percent while average farm size increased from 84 to 253 acres. Also between 1940 and 1987 major changes occurred in the types of farmers and the acreage of land in farms and cropland controlled by them (Table 17.3). Since 1940 the importance of tenants has declined in southern agriculture while the role of part owners has grown. In 1940 full owners comprised 44.2 percent of the South's farmers and controlled 41.4 percent of the land in farms. Tenants comprised 48.2 percent of the farmers and leased 33.2 percent of the land in farms. Only 7.2 percent of the farmers were part owners, and they controlled only 17.7 percent of the land in farms. By 1987 tenants had declined to 9.3 percent of the farmers and leased only 14.6 percent of the land in farms. Part owners, however, had increased to 25.8 percent of the farmers, and they controlled nearly half of the land in farms. Also, the southern tenant farmer at the close of the twentieth century was considerably different from the stereotypical, poverty-stricken renter of 1940. The average southern tenant farm contained 85 acres in 1940, but 535 in 1987.

The growth in farm size and in the importance of part owners points to another major spatial alteration in southern agriculture. In order to achieve economies of a scale to support larger machinery inventories and to increase profits, farmers began renting as well as purchasing additional land. Because a farmer often is unable to purchase or rent land next to what he already owns or leases, the increase in farm size has been accompanied by the growth in importance of "fragmented" or "dispersed" farm operations (Aiken 1971). After spatial concentration, the development of fragmented farms has been the most significant geographical trend in southern agriculture during the past fifty years. Some farmers with large machinery inventories choose to remain tenants and rent all of the land that they farm. Although such renters are classified by "share" and other traditional census tenant definitions, they actually are new types of tenants. Like most part owners, most of the new tenants are highly capitalized; they farm dispersed parcels but believe that there is more economic advantage in renting land than in purchasing it.

Table 17.3. Types of farmers and land in farms, 1940 and 1987.

	1940	1987	Difference 1940–1987	% Difference 1940–1987
The South				
Full owners				
Number	1,327,000	535,300	−791,700	−59.7
% of farmers	44.2	65.0		
Part owners				
Number	216,600	212,500	−4,100	−1.9
% of farmers	7.2	25.8		
Tenants				
Number	1,449,300	76,900	−1,372,400	−94.7
% of farmers	48.2	9.3		
Full owners				
Acres in farms	153,366,000	107,398,000	−45,968,000	−30.0
% Land in farms	41.4	38.2		
Part owners				
Acres in farms	65,515,000	132,716,000	67,201,000	102.6
% Land in farms	17.7	47.2		
Tenants				
Acres in farms	123,013,000	41,129,000	−81,884,000	66.6
% Land in farms	33.2	14.6		
Alabama, Georgia, Mississippi				
Full owners				
Number	245,100	81,100	−164,000	−66.9
% of farmers	33.2	62.0		
Part owners				
Number	32,500	30,800	−1,700	−5.2
% of farmers	4.4	23.5		
Tenants				
Number	458,900	7,500	−451,400	−98.4
% of farmers	62.1	5.7		
Full owners				
Acres in farms	28,363,000	13,888,000	−14,475,000	−51.0
% Land in farms	45.8	45.3		
Part owners				
Acres in farms	5,052,000	13,355,000	13,355,000	164.4
% Land in farms	8.2	43.6		
Tenants				
Acres in farms	26,243,000	3,395,000	−22,848,000	−87.1
% Land in farms	42.3	11.1		

Paul S. Taylor, who traveled widely across the American agricultural regions during the 1930s, was one of the earliest to note the emerging role of farms comprised of dispersed parcels (Taylor 1941). Geographers at the University of Georgia in the 1960s were among the first to identify and study fragmented farms in the South (Fisher 1967; 1970; Aiken 1971; Sublett 1975, 16–18). There are different types and sizes of fragmented farms, but relatively little is known of them. The dated format of the U.S. Census of Agriculture provides hardly any information. The best surrogate data in the Census of Agriculture are those for part owners and tenants. It can be assumed that most modern farmers who rent or own and rent usually cannot achieve economies of scale through purchase or lease of land that adjoins the land they already control.

One type of dispersed farm that emerged in the South is the "fragmented neoplantation" (Aiken 1971). This farm meets all of the traditional criteria for a plantation except for the ways in which ownership and spatial distribution of land are considered. Historically, in the South a plantation was defined as a continuous tract or separate tracts of land in close proximity under one ownership (U.S. Bureau of the Census 1915, 13). A fragmented neoplantation is composed of a headquarters farm, which is usually owned; dispersed farms, which are both rented and owned; and fields on landholdings where only crop bases are rented (Aiken 1971, 44). Most fragmented neoplantations are several thousand acres large and may be spread over areas of several hundred square miles. The 3,500-acre Presley fragmented neoplantation in Tate County, Mississippi, consisted of a headquarters farm, six rented farms, and rented cotton bases on six landholdings. The 5,000-acre Vandiver neoplantation in the Tennessee Valley of northern Alabama had only a 160-acre headquarters farm. The remainder of the acreage was rented from thirty-four landlords (Aiken 1971, 44–46). Fragmented neoplantations are common in the alluvial Mississippi Valley, where many landholdings that were traditional tenant plantations in 1940 have been integrated through purchase and lease into even larger operations.

IMPACT OF THE CIVIL RIGHTS MOVEMENT

A few great events of the twentieth century brought profound changes to the South. Among them was the civil rights movement. The changes initiated between 1954 and 1970 continue to make their impact. The two principal goals of the civil rights movement were the restoration of voting rights to blacks and the termination of legalized segregation. Three critical events were paramount in initiating the changes sought by blacks. The U.S. Supreme Court decision in *Brown v. the Board of Education of Topeka, Kansas* reversed the 1896 "separate but equal" decision of *Plessy v. Ferguson* and initiated the desegregation of public schools and other publicly owned facilities. The comprehensive Civil Rights Act passed by Congress in 1964 re-enforced and extended the *Brown* decision. Congressional passage of the 1965 Voting Rights Act insured blacks that devious means could not be used to keep them from voting or to spatially dilute their political power.

Most of the research on the civil rights movement and its impact in the South has focused on urban areas. Not only did a number of important events of the civil rights movement occur in the rural South, including the 1964 Mississippi "Freedom Summer" and the 1965 march from Selma to Montgomery across the heart of the Alabama Black Belt, but the impact on the rural South has been just as profound as on the urban. The initial reaction of many whites in the rural South to the 1954 U.S. Supreme Court decision was to deny the possibility that the school systems could ever actually be desegregated. Between 1955 and 1957 more than five hundred bills designed to circumvent or nullify the Supreme Court decision were passed by southern legislatures (Goldfield 1987, 68). To further insure that schools would not be desegregated, funding for black schools began to approach that for white ones, in the mid-1950s. Historically, more than four times the amount spent per black pupil was spent per white pupil in rural counties, and at the time of the *Brown* decision in 1954 many black children in the rural South did not have access to public high schools (Johnson et al. 1941, 25). New elementary and high schools began to be built for blacks, replacing legions of one- and two-room schools scattered across the rural countryside. When in the 1960s desegregation became inevitable, communities reacted in different ways (Aiken and Demerath 1968). A reaction by some whites was to abandon public schools for private ones. Numerous private academies sprang up across the South, sometimes occupying buildings of closed white public schools that were sold.

Today, across the rural South, most children attend integrated public schools. As in the nation's cities, however, in rural counties geographical patterns have emerged in which particular schools may be predominantly white or predominantly black (Aiken 1992). These patterns reflect both increased residential segregation in the restructuring of rural settlement patterns and the gerrymandering of school district boundaries. Private schools in the rural South are strongest in areas where the population is more than 50 percent black.

With restoration of voting rights, blacks have again come to play a major role in the politics of the South. At the section and state levels political realignments occurred, and the structures and strengths of the Democratic and Republican parties changed. Who in 1940 would have predicted that in the early 1990s Mississippi would have a Republican governor and two Republican United States senators? Or who in 1964 would have thought that by the 1990s the upstart Mississippi Freedom Democratic party would long have been merged with the state's Democratic party?

Although southern blacks have come to play vital roles in local, state, and national elections, they have not been as successful in seeking election to major political offices. In 1990 the southern states had no black U.S. senators and only five black representatives (Joint Center for Political Studies 1991, 13–14). All but one of the representatives were from metropolitan areas. The Second Mississippi Congressional District, which is essentially the Yazoo Delta, was the only nonmetropolitan one in 1990 represented by a black congressman. Several additional majority-black congressional districts that included counties were created in southern states following the 1990 census. At the local level blacks have pursued political office more successfully. In 1990 almost all of the 4,955 black elected officials in the South held local offices (Joint Center for Political Studies 1991, 12). Significant growth in the number of black elected officials occurred as the impact of the 1965 Voting Rights Act increased. In 1973 Mississippi had 152 black elected officials; in 1990 there were 669 (Joint Center for Political Studies 1973, xvi; 1991, 12).

Even with the 1965 Voting Rights Act, which was extended in 1982, much of the local political progress that blacks have made in the rural South has been achieved only through court suits and boycotts. Blacks have brought numerous court suits seeking changes in the ways in which officials are elected and in the geographical boundaries of voting districts. One type of suit seeks replacement of at-large elections with a system of districts or wards. Another type seeks the creation of majority black districts and wards. In December 1988, blacks were elected to the Dallas County, Alabama, Commission for the first time since Reconstruction and 23 years after passage of the 1965 Voting Rights Act. The legal struggle to have three majority-black districts created in this nonmetropolitan county, where 55 percent of the population is black, was in the federal courts for ten years (Nossiter 1989). As stated above, one of the reasons that some white-controlled municipal governments in the Yazoo Delta refuse to annex black residential areas is fear that white voting strength will be diluted. In 1980 the black residents of the southern fringe of Indianola initiated under the 1965 Voting Rights Act what was to become a lengthy court case that sought annexation of their neighborhoods. In settlement of the case, the U.S. District Court enjoined Indianola to annex an area that included all of the federally sponsored housing on the south side of the city prior to the 1990 census (Aiken 1987, 574–577).

Increasing election of blacks to county and municipal offices in the rural South means that biracial government is emerging. Although biracial government is the norm, there are counties and municipalities that have become politically controlled by blacks. Geographically, clusters of counties and small municipalities with majority black governments have begun to appear across the nonmetropolitan South. In Mississippi black elected officials now control part of the old Natchez plantation district and parts of the Yazoo Delta. More than twenty municipalities have black mayors and majority black governments (Joint Center for Political Studies 1991, 251–270).

The reaction of whites in small southern cities and towns to blacks assuming political control is similar to that of whites of inner cities of the nation's metropolises. Election of a black majority government usually means exodus of a significant part of the white population, especially if the election has been preceded by significant opposition by whites to blacks holding political offices (Aiken 1990). One of the most detailed analyses of blacks assuming political control of a southern county and city is Norrell's study of Macon County and Tuskegee, Alabama (1985). A long tragic history of whites attempting to impede political participation by blacks ended in 1972 with the transfer of political control of both the county and the city to blacks. This transfer was followed by a precipitous decline of the white population of Tuskegee between 1970 and 1990.

A NEW CONCEPT OF TWO SOUTHS

The impact of the civil rights movement on the South extends beyond benefits to blacks, for whites profit from no longer having to defend segregation. Economically, the passing of segregation by law and the restoration of voting rights to blacks helped pave the way for the emergence of the Sunbelt South of the late twentieth century. But all areas have not shared equally in recent economic progress. During the 1980s yet another concept of two Souths began to emerge. As the modern South of the late twentieth century began to materialize, the realization dawned that not all areas share equally in the economic progress. There is a South that is doing well economically, but there is another South that is left behind. Figuratively, there is the "Sunbelt South" and there are "shadows in the Sunbelt."

The recent concept of two Souths emerged in part from the Southern Governors Association and the Southern Research Policies Board (MDC 1986; Southern Governors Association 1986; Southern Growth Policies Board 1986). Not without controversy, the concept of two Souths has been aggressively promoted by a group of politicians, business leaders, and academicians, including William Clinton and Albert Gore, Jr. The new concept not only seeks economic and social improvements in the areas that have been left behind, it also outlines how economic growth is to be sustained in the Sunbelt areas. Great emphasis is placed on improvements in elementary and secondary education, on the role of local leadership, and on the importance of local initiative and innovation in the creation of new jobs. Geographically, the concept of two Souths recognizes that the southern states are part not only of a national but of a world economy.

The South that is doing well economically consists largely of the metropolitan areas, the first tier of nonmetropolitan counties surrounding the metropolitan ones, and a group of dispersed nonmetropolitan counties that are removed from metropolitan areas. The South that is left behind is essentially the remainder of the nonmetropolitan counties; that is, the South that is left behind is a large part of the rural South (Walker 1989). On the basis of socioeconomic factors the South can be divided into three principal types of areas, which are shown for the Southeast in Figure 17.5. The counties with the greatest problems are those in the "distressed" category. The Yazoo Delta, the Alabama Black Belt, and the Cumberland Plateau are among the regions with the large numbers of "distressed" counties. These areas have in common a high rate of poverty, high unemployment, low educational level, and nonmetropolitan situation.

Fundamental to addressing the problems of the rural South that is left behind is realization that it is not homogeneous, but a place of geographical, social, economic, and political diversity. Major differences exist among regions. Programs designed to improve conditions in one region may not work well in another region. Some regional differences are well-known, such as the racial contrasts between the Upland and the Lowland South. Lesser known are differences in age structure of the population, attitudes toward schools and formal education, and composition of local economies. Furthermore, it is important to distinguish the areas that have a strong, but specialized, local economy from areas in which the local economy has largely collapsed. Both the Yazoo Delta and the Alabama Black Belt are economically distressed (Figure 17.5). The Yazoo Delta, one of the nation's major agricultural regions, has a strong farm economy and a large poor, underemployed population that cannot be absorbed by the modern agricultural system. In parts of the Ala-

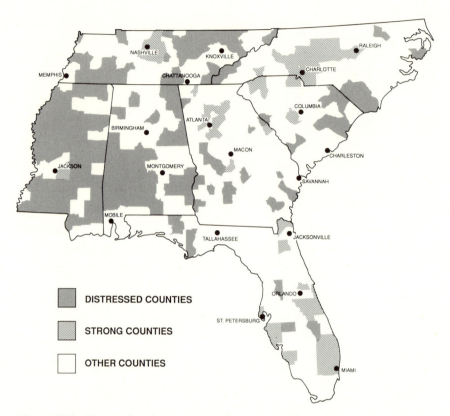

Figure 17.5. Distressed and strong counties in the Southeast (Source: Appalachian Regional Commission)

bama Black Belt the agricultural economy is largely gone, and a new local rural economy that can fully absorb and sustain the population has not developed.

CONCLUSION

Why did some agricultural regions decline and others remain viable? Why did certain communities handle integration and restoration of voting rights to blacks better than others? Why are there counties and municipalities across the nonmetropolitan South that have made significant economic progress and others that have been left behind? Does some overriding factor explain spatial variability in the rural South?

In 1951 William Faulkner was invited to Greenville, Mississippi, to address a meeting of the Delta Council, an organization of agricultural and business leaders. The five thousand people who heard Faulkner gave him a standing ovation, and the Delta Council later published the speech as a pamphlet. To most of the audience, the speech came off as an attack on the regimented programs and bureaucracy of the federal government and as a patriotic call for a return to the America that was envisioned by the founders (Blotner 1974, 1417). Analysis of the speech, however, reveals the major theme as neither patriotism nor an attack on the federal government, but the theme of responsibility (Aiken 1982, 201).[2] "That's what I am talking about: responsibility," stated Faulkner. "Not just the right, but the duty of man to be responsible, the necessity of man to be responsible if he wishes to remain free; not just responsible to and for his fellow man, but to himself" (Faulkner 1952, 42).

The theme of responsibility is tied directly to another powerful theme in Faulkner's works, that of the decline and failure of leadership (Aiken 1981; 1982, 193–202). Although Faulkner's stories of his imaginary Jefferson and Yoknapatawpha County, Mississippi, are universal in their meaning, the reality from which he drew his fiction was principally the rural and small-town Lowland South. Faulkner developed the theme of leadership decline and failure in his fiction and stressed responsibility in one of his few public addresses to fellow rural southerners, suggesting that he believed one of the major problems was a crisis in leadership. Other people, more recently and much more directly than Faulkner, have identified leadership as one of the critical problems of the rural South (Winter 1988).

Leadership operates within a historical dimension on different geographical scales. Across the rural South isolated counties and municipalities that have viable economies usually can be explained on the basis of the quality of local leaders. Frequently this leadership lies in only one or two individuals. To explain the demise of large agricultural regions such as the southern Piedmont one has to trace historically the loss of agricultural leaders at both the regional and local levels (Aiken 1993). In the small islands of the Piedmont where agriculture is still viable, endurance of local agricultural leadership is overt, taking precedence over any physical factor, including topography and soil, or any economic factor, including those of the infrastructure (Prunty and Aiken 1972).

At the sectional level, the significance of the new concept of two Souths is that it has the potential of making a major break from the economic and social philosophies that the South's leaders followed for more than a century. The era when fiscal conservatism in government took precedence over basic needs of people appears to be drawing to an end. In order to improve education and accomplish the economic and social reforms that the new concept of two Souths acknowledges, larger sums of public funds will have to be wisely spent, implying tax reform that should modify the regressive taxation policies of southern states.

Since the 1870s southern prophets have predicted the coming of a new and better South. Although the rural South is a vastly different and a much better place than it was at the end of the Great Depression, most rural southerners are too young to have known the South of the 1930s. For them, improvement is not measured from 1940 but from today. Unfortunately, many rural southerners still live in such destitute economic and social conditions that the last decade of the twentieth century may seem no different to them than did the 1930s to an earlier generation.

NOTES

Research for the sections on population redistribution and changes in settlement patterns in the Yazoo Delta was supported by the National Science Foundation under Grant No. SES-8420508.

1. My discussion of population in this historical overview of the South is primarily rural-urban. The distinctions between rural-urban and metropolitan-nonmetropolitan are discussed elsewhere.

2. In the context of the Delta and its plantation agricultural system, Faulkner's theme of responsibility is tied directly to his stories of Isaac McCaslin and the vanishing Mississippi wilderness (see Aiken 1981; 1982).

18

AFRICAN-AMERICANS IN THE RURAL SOUTH: THE PERSISTENCE OF RACISM AND POVERTY

BRUCE B. WILLIAMS AND BONNIE THORNTON DILL

In the 1990s several factors have contributed to a renewed interest in rural America: the realization that poverty persists in rural America, the continuing family farm crisis, and the attempt by some journalists and the popular press to explain the malaise of the urban underclass in terms of low-income rural lifestyles transported into our urban centers (see Lemann 1986, 1991; Dash 1989). This latter orientation specifically identifies African-Americans from the rural South as principal figures in the urban underclass problem.

The plight of rural African-Americans, who comprise one of the largest disadvantaged groups in the United States, is the central concern of this paper. Whereas much has been written about the lack of human capital resources—low education, limited skills and training, and so on—among this population, we contend that any discussion of this long-term impoverishment and lack of opportunity must be placed within the context of the sociopolitical and economic environment of rural society in general and of southern society in particular.

GENERAL OVERVIEW

The rural African-American population is distinct from its white and Hispanic counterparts in that it has a smaller farm population and is primarily concentrated in the southern region of the country. In 1988, only 111,000 African-Americans lived on farms U.S. Bureau of the Census 1989). This number represented only 2.2 percent of the total American farm population. It also

339

represented only 2.7 percent of the total African-American rural population. By 1990 only 69,000, or .2 percent, of rural African-Americans resided on farms (U.S. Bureau of the Census, 1992c).

According to the 1987 Census of Agriculture, in 1977, 34,150 African-Americans were full-owner farmers and another 15,026 were part owners of farms; by 1982 African-American farm ownership had fallen to 33,965 and 13,093, respectively; and by 1987 the totals had been reduced to 28,407 and 9,996, respectively (1987b, table 16). Hence, by 1987 African-American full-owner farmers represented only 2.3 percent of the total full-owner farmers in America and only 1.6 percent of America's part-owner farmers.

The Rural and Rural Farm Population: 1990 reports that the African-American rural population in 1990 was 4,091,000 persons. This represents 6.1 percent of the total rural population and 13.5 percent of the total African-American population (U.S. Bureau of the Census 1992c, 18). African-Americans are then the largest rural minority group in America, followed by persons of Hispanic origin numbering 1,846,000 individuals or 2.8 percent of the total rural population (U.S. Bureau of the Census 1992c, 19).

In 1992 the African-American population numbered 31.4 million, of which 17.1 million, or 54.4, percent lived in the South (U.S. Bureau of the Census 1992c, Table 3). Indeed, not only do the majority of African-Americans live in the South, but so do the vast majority of rural and farming African-Americans. Fully 94 percent of rural African-Americans reside in the South (Atkins 1989). Additionally, 87.8 percent of the African-American farm population resides in the South. The South, then, is truly the area of the country where the African-American rural experience is most readily articulated and defined.

THE SOUTH

The American South is a geographical region centered on the eleven states that seceded from the Union in 1861 and became known as the Confederate States of America: Alabama, Arkansas, Florida, Georgia, Louisiana, Mississippi, North Carolina, South Carolina, Tennessee, Texas, and Virginia. The U.S. Department of the Census defines the South as the Confederate states plus Delaware, the District of Columbia, Maryland, Oklahoma, and West Virginia. Whatever the debate over the specifics of the geographical boundaries of the South, there is little disagreement over the basic elements that distinguish southern culture and society.

The American South has a unique history. Slavery and racism have had a dominant influence in shaping the lives of most southerners: urban and rural, white, African-American, Indian, and Asian. Feagin states that "Southern culture has perhaps been the most distinctive regional culture, because of the racial oppression of black Americans and the subsequent rationalizations for that thoroughgoing racial discrimination" (1989, 79). Killian adds further that "for a Southerner, the salient fact was and is whether he was white or black; all else was secondary" (1970, 16).

This aspect of the South cannot be denied or ignored even today, when the real progress in race relations that has characterized the post–civil rights era is heralded in the mass media in cover page titles like "Race and the New South: How Blacks and Whites are Remaking the Old South" (*U.S. News and World Report* July 23, 1990). This article celebrates the fact that "in 1958, 72 percent of Southern whites opposed sending their children to school with blacks; just 13 percent of Northerners said the same. By 1980, only five percent of whites in both regions was opposed. And a Gallup Poll in June found Southerners slightly more optimistic than Northerners about race" (1990, 23).

In reality, many of the more blatant forms of discrimination, such as the Jim Crow practices and legal segregation that characterized the pre–civil rights South, have been replaced by more sophisticated, less apparent forms of racial discrimination that more closely parallel northern racism and race relations. Hence, racial discrimination remains extremely high and tensions remain low as long as African-Americans remain in their newly prescribed places. The recent white backlashes that occurred when African-Americans attempted to integrate Forsythe County, Georgia, and Shoal Creek Country Club in Birmingham, Alabama, serve as excellent examples of what lies just below the surface of the "New South" for those who dare to "cross the line."

This grim reality, however, is especially true for rural African-Americans who have remained most subject to the persistence of the racially based history and tradition that characterizes the rural South. This history has been well researched and documented in classic works by scholars such as Cash (1941); Davis et. al (1941); Dollard (1937); DuBois (1935); and a few of the more contemporary works of Genovese (1965; 1974); Jordan (1968); Woodward (1974); Harding (1981); and Cobb (1982; 1984; 1991).

THE SOUTHERN RURAL CLIMATE

For our purposes, the three most distinctive elements that define the rural South are the Bible Belt, the Black Belt, and the color/class line. Without reference to these elements it is nearly impossible to comprehend the magnitude of the social beliefs and community forces that restrict the opportunities of rural African-Americans to initiate significant change. Because religion is such a pervasive force in defining and maintaining southern mores and social stratification, there is a more intimate connection between Christianity, racism, and social control in the Bible Belt than exists elsewhere in the United States.

The Bible Belt

"Bible Belt" is a term used to define a region of the country where religion, particularly fundamentalism with its emphasis on the literal interpretation and authenticity of the Scriptures, is dominant. According to Wilson (1989), H. L. Mencken, who coined the term in the 1920s, identified the rural Midwest and South as the primary geographical locations of the Bible Belt and called Jackson, Mississippi, "the heart of the Bible and Lynch Belt." To say the least, conservative religion is paramount. A recent Gallup Poll study on religion in America concluded that "the Bible Belt is real, not just a political saying" (*Commercial Appeal* 1987).

It is commonplace that religion plays a very significant role in molding the attitudes of human beings in any given society. As Weber (1946, 1958, 1964) determined, religion gives meaning to the social world and provides a worldview. Durkheim (1951) established the sociological principle that religion also provides social cohesion and justifies or legitimizes the status quo. Finally, Karl Marx developed the idea that religion obscures the fact that people construct society and therefore can change it (Bottomore 1963). These three great principles inform our understanding of religion and society in the Bible Belt.

Southern religion differs from religion in other areas of the country. This difference is well summarized by Hill:

(1) The forms that are common in the region are relatively homogeneous. The range of popular options is narrow. (2) The South is the only society in Christendom where the evangelical family of Christians is dominant . . . (3) A set of four common convictions occupies a normative Southern religious position. Movements and denominations in the South are judged for authenticity in the popular mind by how well they support these beliefs: (a) the Bible is the sole reference point of belief and practice; (b) direct and dynamic access to the Lord is open to all; (c)

morality is defined in individualistic and personal terms; and (d) worship is informal. (1989, 1269)

Hill asserts also that the South is characterized by what he calls a "limited-options" culture, especially in the religious sphere. The conservative religion is reflected in conservative politics, economic development strategies, and orientations to race relations and social change. James Sessions adds, "The white Southern church has mainly been a conservative, reinforcing agent for traditional values of white Southern society" (1989, 1282).

Honor also characterizes southern values. Ayers (1989) believes it is a value that thrives in a rural environment characterized by low literacy—hence its survival in the South. Nonetheless, he also sees the notion of honor as conflicting with the ideals of Christian virtue. Although his analysis may apply to individual honor, race or ethnic group honor posits a whole new dynamic.

The sense of ethnic group honor functions with religion in the South to create an overpowering sense of white racial group identity, which helps to firmly maintain the color line between racial groups and the class line within the white community. Ethnic group honor admits the poorest white southerners into an exclusive club that sets them apart from all African-Americans (Light 1972). It also keeps these same poor souls from allying with their African-American counterparts to improve their mutual lot in life. Individual options remain few because of the social control inherent in this belief system.

Religion of African-Americans in the South has created a different dynamic. Although religion in southern African-American communities incorporates the same common convictions as that of the larger society, African-American ministers were able to introduce a spirit of communalism into their churches because of the total exclusion of African-Americans from the larger community. All classes of African-Americans were therefore thrown together in support of one another; the poor were not isolated from the nonpoor, as they were in white communities (Balswick 1989). This mutuality allowed a degree of freedom for African-Americans unavailable to poor white southerners, whose churches were generally controlled, directly or indirectly, by the upper-class white establishment (for an excellent case study discussion of this phenomenon, see Newman 1976).

The African-American church provided a base for the free expression of feelings and a focal point for group protest, mobilization, and self-support. Rural and urban African-Americans had the luxury of an institutional base for the articulation of their needs. These institutions, however, like their members, stood outside of the central political and economic structures of the larger white communities and therefore had and still have limited access to major community resources. It is truly ironic that poor whites, who are only symbolically included within the central power structure, have no comparable institution to speak specifically to their needs. One is led to ask: "Other than pandering to racial prejudice and bigotry, what institutions specifically speak on behalf of poor white southerners?" Inclusion within the central value system of the region reinforces class and racial divisions that in turn limit individual and group options.

The Black Belt

For our purposes, the Black Belt refers to that geographical part of the South historically associated with cotton production, large plantations, and a large number of African-Americans. This territory extends from Virginia into North Carolina, through mid- and lower Georgia, and into mid-Alabama, traversing the length of Mississippi along the Mississippi River basin, culminating in Arkansas and several Louisiana counties bordering the great river.

Today the counties comprising the Black Belt are essentially rural, poor, and still heavily populated by African-Americans. The 147 Black Belt counties are characterized by African-American residency of 40 percent or more (Falk and Lyson 1988). These 147 counties contain approximately 75 percent of the rural African-American population, and all of these counties are classified as "persistently low-income."

The concentration of the rural African-American population in the South and especially in the Black Belt counties has a tremendous impact on the past, present, and future economic status of everyone in the region. This impact cannot be fully examined without reference to the color line, or racism.

The Color Line

The South has a long and sordid history of racial oppression. A distinctive feature of that oppression has been the desire to maintain a color line to permanently separate whites and African-Americans at most levels of interaction. This tradition flows from the history of slavery and the fact that the African-American population was so large, especially in Alabama and Mississippi, where for a short time it exceeded the white population.

It is no accident, then, that these two states embodied racist dogma and demagoguery in the twentieth century. The result in the white South has been a sense of paranoia over African-American empowerment rivaling that of white South Africa. Although patterns of black political participation in the urban South have become more similar to patterns in northern cities, efforts to keep African-Americans at the bottom of the political and economic hierarchies are still quite prevalent in the rural South, where traditional plantation culture has its roots. As a result the rural South is one of the most disadvantaged sectors of the country, and rural African-Americans are one of the most destitute populations.

AFRICAN-AMERICAN POVERTY IN THE SOUTH

Rural poverty and the South are synonymous. Poverty has long been one of the major characteristics of the South (Woodward 1960). All but 18 of the 206 "persistently low-wage [income] counties" in America are located in the South, along with 53.6 percent of all of the nation's rural poor (Porter 1989). Recent studies of rural poverty suggest that its consequences are more acute in rural areas than in urban areas (Atkins 1989, Lee 1990). For example, rural children are more likely than their urban counterparts to experience severe health and nutritional deficiencies (Atkins 1989). Further, a rural family, of any race, with a working head of household is nearly twice as likely as its urban counterpart to be poor (Atkins 1989).

A report published by the Joint Center for Political Studies entitled "The Forgotten Poor: Blacks in Rural Areas" (1988) reveals that the situation is considerably worse for rural African-Americans. The report, "Poverty in Rural America" (Porter 1989), documents that 44.1 percent of nonmetropolitan African-Americans were poor in 1987, compared to 33.3 percent of central-city-dwelling African-Americans. A study by Cheong, Toney, and Stinner (1986) found that nonmetropolitan areas offer lower levels of economic opportunities for everyone, but especially for African-Americans.

As bad as conditions are for poor African-Americans, they are even more pronounced for poor African-American women. Traditional political, economic, and social forces (specifically religion and formal education) conspire to leave women in their traditional roles as helpmates in and out of the home. According to fundamentalist Christianity, God created woman as helpmate for man; as a helpmate, she has a secondary role of low status and power even if she does work (Flora and Johnson 1973). Outside of the home rural African-American women find themselves confined to the lowest-paying jobs, and they are isolated from collective action. Moreover, issues of race keep poor African-American and white women from working for their mutual benefit (Janieski 1985; Sacks 1988). Poor rural African-American women tend to have fewer options than other groups in this limited-options environment.

The absence of opportunities for work that provides a living wage exacerbates the problems of rural African-American women, particularly the numbers of single-mother households have grown significantly in recent years. In 1960, for example, 27 percent of poor black families were headed by single mothers with children. By 1980 that percentage had risen to 59 percent (Dill et al. 1989). According to a report by the Southeast Women's Employment Coalition (Women of the Rural South 1986), the feminization of poverty is becoming as extensive a problem in the rural South as it is in the urban North. The report concludes that the special needs of rural and poor women are not being addressed by state policymakers.

Explanations for the persistence of poverty among rural African-Americans have focused upon supply-side factors, as found in the human-capital and status-attainment perspectives, as well as on demand-side factors, which target social structures and labor market organization. Doubtless education, skills, culture, labor markets, and structural factors are all components of this problem. Again, however, none of these approaches treat discrimination as an essential component of the analysis. (For a full discussion of these perspectives and their limitations in explaining persistent rural poverty among racial and ethnic minorities, see *Rural Sociological Society* 1993.) In fact, we contend, racism and discrimination have important independent effects on the persistent impoverishment of the African-American community in the rural South.

Louis Swanson, in an intriguing article entitled "The Human Dimension of the Rural South in Crisis," attests that "an unsavory dimension of the rural South in crisis is the persistence of overt and subtle racism. . . . The historical patterns of Southern apartheid continue to occur for those areas with a high proportion of black residents . . . racism is still a formidable foe to the vitalization of the rural South and an important dimension of the current crisis" (1988, 96). Indeed, this theme is central in recent works on the history of the new South as we move away from the unwarranted assumption that "racism is no longer an issue in American society." Scholars such as Billings (1988); Brown and Warner (1989); James (1988); and Wright (1986), to name just a few, are forcing us to reevaluate the New South and its rural underpinnings.

JOBS: THE BOTTOM LINE

One of the primary reasons that rural African-Americans are in such dire straits is that they are concentrated in the worst-paying jobs or they have no jobs at all. Recent studies by Falk and Lyson (1988, 112) found that white males in the South hold 40 percent of the best jobs; African-American men hold no more than 10 percent of these but hold from 50 percent (in southern metropolitan areas) to 70 percent (in Black Belt counties) of operative and unskilled blue-collar jobs.

Falk and Lyson document that in rural areas of the South, African-American women experienced the worst employment opportunities. More than 90 percent of rural African-American women were employed in bad jobs (i.e., jobs characterized by low wages, few or no benefits, and/or hazardous working conditions). They conclude that "the figures become so pronounced that in Black Belt counties, it is nearly a truism to say that if a black woman is employed at all, it will be in a bad job" (Falk and Lyson 1988, 112).

A grim picture emerges as Falk and Lyson identify the modal job categories for white and African-American men and women in the South: white men are managers, supervisors, or farmers; African-American men are janitors (in southern metropolitan areas) or farm workers and laborers (in the Black Belt); white women are secretaries or clerks; African-American women are maids, cooks, or low-skill machine operatives (1988).

Again it is important to emphasize that the major reasons for this disparity are not lack of human capital or the geographic location of African-Americans (that is, rural or urban); racial discrimination is the cause (Cobb 1984; Lichter 1988; Wright 1986). It is no accident that employment opportunities for rural African-Americans have not changed significantly since 1970 and are not expected to change in the foreseeable future (Lichter 1988). The vast majority of rural African-Americans are still confined to "bad jobs" or no jobs at all. To understand the current situation in the rural South is to appreciate the impact of the plantation or rural South on the rest of the South. The predominance of agriculture as the primary southern industry combined with the traditional plantation system of production afford the rural plantation elite inordinate influence over state and local politics (Billings 1988). This influence extends to the all-important issues of defining the ideological foundations of southern race relations and the tangible opportunity structures for whites and African-Americans alike.

THE POLITICAL ECONOMY OF THE RURAL SOUTH

The basis of social organization in the South has been local control, exerted historically through the administrative unit of the plantation. Today local control tends to be exerted through county government. More than in any other part of the country, the political organization of the Old South states reflects a tradition of very strong, semi-autonomous county governmental structures.

The plight of rural African-Americans is intimately connected to county government. From the rural counties of the South came the impetus to organize the Citizens' Councils, the coalitions of political and business elites who spearheaded southern resistance to integration, during the early days of the civil rights movement (Cobb 1984). Through their local and state legislative positions, the rural elites used their political and economic power to direct the state wide anti-integrationist movements. Currently, it is at the county level that we find the most resistance to the progressive social changes that the southern states have reluctantly endorsed since the passage of national civil rights legislation in the 1960s. In other words, the routinely traditional taken-for-granted exclusion of African-Americans is most pronounced at the county level (Black and Black 1987). There also we find the greatest adherence to and propagation of the ideology of racism cum traditional southern religious beliefs.

Two notions must be emphasized here. First, the Delta and the Black Belt economies, as they exist today, are the conscious construction of the rural white elite (Lyson 1989); and, second, the class structure of the rural South is organized to maintain the "master-slave" past, relative to race (James 1988). Economic development will thus be controlled to the extent that human development needs are kept to a minimum. The elite class desires capital accumulation or capitalist growth without the social changes accompanying the modernization process.

Cobb (1984) calls the practitioners of this kind of economic development "Boondock Capitalists." They are willing to take lower profits than possible in order to preserve traditional relationships. The typical pattern is to recruit low-wage, low-skill industries into their counties. This pattern of economic development characterizes rural counties with large African-American populations.

Currently, this pattern differs from economic development in counties with small African-American populations in that high-wage industries are now actively sought along with low-wage industries. This scenario furnishes a classic example of Blumer's (1965) notion that industrialization is molded to fit within existing systems of discrimination rather than to destroy them. It is similar to the South African pattern of retarding economic development prior to the 1970s because continued expansion would have necessitated the training of black South Africans to supplement the shortage of skilled white labor.

Under this system of selected economic development, local elites accumulate large profits that are then invested not in their own communities but often in other states (e.g., in Mississippi we found that many rural elites have invested large portions of their wealth in North Carolina). The system is supported at the state level by state policies that discourage unions and maintain low property taxes and high regressive taxes (e.g., taxes on gas, food, and auto licenses).

State and local officials are also known to steer potential foreign and northern business and industrial investors away from heavily populated African-American rural counties (Cobb 1984; Lyson 1988). This informal practice is called the "30 percent solution" because it is applied to counties with 30 percent or higher African-American residency (Rosenfeld et al. 1985; Cobb 1984). Our own research confirms that this pattern of new capital investment is still pervasive in Mississippi (Williams et al. 1992).

Rural African-Americans existing within this environment find their options limited to a life of low-wage employment and welfare assistance. Although Brown and Warner (1989) present an excellent account of the totality of control that the rural white elite exert over African-Americans, it cannot be truly appreciated until one sees it firsthand. From banking, wholesale, and retail to the legal, educational, and political systems, elite group control is nearly airtight in the Delta and Black Belt counties.

To further complicate the problem, the transfer payments from the welfare system that hold many rural African-American families together have been integrated into the informal system of local control and exploitation. Local employers routinely lay off African-American workers as they become eligible for raises and/or promotions. These workers then are forced onto welfare for several months, at the least. If lucky, they are eventually recalled to work at their old salary and position levels. This cycle can be expected to repeat itself several times a year, every year.

This tactic is used specifically against African-American workers. Those people who acquire a reputation for questioning or challenging authority are refused transfer payments simply by an employer informing the welfare department that the employee was laid off. If the employee can produce no verification of termination, he or she can be denied unemployment benefits. Additionally, welfare assistance can be withheld temporarily at the discretion of the caseworker. This very informal ploy is quite effective in encouraging a docile, pliable labor force. It is fostered in many instances by collusion and nepotism on the part of employers and unemployment office and welfare department personnel. From the perspective of the worker, it is reinforced by a scarcity of legal assistance for African-Americans and a lack of unionization and legal, rational authority in the workplace.

Another informal tactic used by employers to maintain low wages in rural counties is to refuse to hire a worker who is currently employed by another local businessman. The business community has a "gentleman's agreement" not to tamper with one another's labor force. Additionally, African-American workers are hired as part-time workers more readily than white workers. This practice reduces the worker liability of the employer while it increases the need of the African-American worker for social welfare support. The added employment hardship of rural African-Americans (i.e., marginal employment and poverty-level earnings) leads Lichter (1989) to postulate that better education and skills training will not significantly improve the plight of rural African-Americans. This hardship may continue, then, unless we change the attitudes that perpetuate the "master-slave" tradition.

CONCLUSION

The plight of rural African-Americans is desperate but not quite hopeless, if we are willing to attack the problem at its root cause rather than concentrating on the effects. We have allowed the myth of the Old South to affect the opportunities of all who live there. The first step is to realize that what has been created through a process of education and propaganda can be undone only through reeducation. People are socialized to think of themselves as the guardians of an idealized past. Educational institutions, especially those of higher learning, must accept responsibility for setting the record straight. Universities should become the forums for the rational discussion of race relations in the South as the descendants of the rural elite come forth to be enlightened.

The issue of race cannot, therefore, be approached as an afterthought, as it is in the 1986 Southern Growth Policies Board Report, *Halfway Home and a Long Way to Go*. Combating racism is not listed among the ten major regional objectives advocated by the board. This omission is unconscionable in a region that is unique in America for the special roles that race and racism play within its borders. It is indeed encouraging that the 1990 Lower Mississippi Delta Development Commission Report, *The Delta Initiatives,* directly addresses this issue with major recommendations (1990, 61).

The opportunities of rural African-Americans will not be substantially altered until rural elites create a new vision for their communities. A recent study of small farming communities in Nebraska, *Clues to Rural Community Survival* (1987) suggests that vibrant rural communities are created from a combination of investment and economic development stemming from community pride and progressive leadership. Community leaders must have a vision for their respective communities, and for the rural South that vision must include the human development needs of the African-American population, but without a concentrated assault on the self-contained, self-perpetuating value system and worldview of the rural elite, this transformation is not likely.

Attacking the problems of rural African-Americans also represents a direct assault on the plight of poor white southerners, who are caught up in an economic and social system that inhibits their abilities to place class above racial interests. A direct blow to the racial foundations of southern rural culture would crucially undermine the economic, political, and social arrangements that have been built upon it. Granted, the problems of economic development that plague Southern rural communities would not disappear. The upheaval would nonetheless provide a level playing field for all residents—opening up the possibility of using limited resources to serve the needs of entire communities, rather than benefiting the few at the expense of the many.

19

THE RURAL PEOPLE OF THE MIDWEST

SONYA SALAMON

Why, as midwesterners coped with the disastrous 1993 flood, were usually cynical reporters motivated to write glowing reports about rural communities along the Mississippi? In their articles journalists from the *New Yorker* (Stewart 1993) and the *New York Times* (Rimer 1993) compared the generosity, selflessness, egalitarianism, and cooperation of Iowans, Missourians, and Illinoisans favorably to the gouging, exploitation, and class-biased reactions observed among Floridians after Hurricane Andrew in 1992. The distinctive social fabric of the Midwest that these reporters observed at its best derives from social patterns developed among agrarian peoples when the region was the frontier.

Customs such as cooperation, watchfulness, and volunteerism were forged on the prairie frontier to sustain families and communities. These customs and social processes endure despite the economic and political changes that have transformed midwestern rural society since the golden age of small towns at the turn of the century. Television, fast-food franchises, malls, vacations, nonagricultural jobs, and far-flung kin firmly integrate rural peoples into urbanized America. Midwesterners now struggle to preserve their peripheral small communities, believing that their way of life provides the best of both worlds: rurality in the context of urbanity. I describe here the special qualities of rural people of the Midwest and illustrate how these qualities are put to use when people mobilize as communities to collectively control their destiny.

As a researcher, I have visited Illinois small towns for almost twenty years. To the traveler, rural Illinois communities (and all of the Midwest) today are, in many respects, indistinguishable from the suburbs that ring Chicago. The visitor finds the same fast-food restaurants, the same gas stations, and the same motels and supermarkets. Disk-jockey patter on rural radio stations is the identical packaged routine I hear on the stations of the cities I drive through on the way to a rural community. But when I leave the car and interact with shop owners, supermarket checkers, and motel desk clerks contrasts become apparent. Local people are more open, friendly, and curious about me than people at home in Urbana, not a large town itself. Observing the joking among townsfolk in cafes, shopping at the local supermarket, and participating in ordinary street and store interactions offer me a window into the daily life of midwesterners: they greet strangers, strike up a conversation readily, include them in a joke, and in general are eager to make a good impression. They like their lives and feel confident others will too.

Nevertheless, negative stereotypes abound about people in the rural Midwest, perhaps stemming from high school memories of reading Edgar Lee Masters, Sherwood Anderson, or Sinclair Lewis, or from watching television sitcoms. Perhaps these stereotypes account for the reactions of hardened reporters to midwesterners they met during the flood. Puritanical, provincial, nosey, materialistic characters suffocate creative and individualistic heroes and heroines in early twentieth-century novels about the small towns that then characterized much of America. Classic social-science studies of midwestern communities similarly describe coercive conformity in which local gossip, criticism, and actions aggressively maintained an egalitarian and homogenous façade (Blumenthal 1932; Lynd and Lynd 1937; Atherton 1954; Vidich and Bensman 1958; Billington 1966; and Varenne 1977). Yet midwesterners' response to the great floods of 1993 were extolled as the epitome of unselfish cooperation, goodwill, and sacrifice for others. Each image contains truths; the struggle to survive has altered the social fabric of small communities. What once appeared to be an impermeable social structure has become fragile as the century draws to a close.

MIDWESTERN SMALL-TOWN PEOPLE

To appreciate the characteristic midwestern way of life requires an understanding of who the people are, what it means to have a small-town identity, and why particular taken-for-granted actions occur in response to ordinary events. The region is racially and ethnically homogeneous, has an infrastructure not very different from the region's urban areas (paved roads, highways, water systems, electricity, phones, good schools), and most areas of the region are within a one- or two-hour drive from population centers of 25,000 to 50,000. These latter factors are due largely to the character of local citizens and interweave with the region's homogeneity to shape peoples's prescriptions for social life.

A rapid peopling of the Midwest, much of it through railroad colonization, took place in the latter half of the nineteenth century (Hudson 1985). In just fifty years the Midwest was settled through one of the most extraordinary transfers of land and people the world has known (McNall and McNall 1983). Although the settlers were white and had Christianity, farming, and European peasant backgrounds in common, their cultural differences earned the Midwest the rubric "ethnic mosaic" (Salamon 1992). Germans, both Catholic and Protestant, Irish, Swedes, Norwegians, and Danes, along with a smattering of French, Poles, Belgians, Czechs, and Volga Germans, flocked to the area in search of precious land or religious freedom (Swierenga 1989). Balancing these immigrants from northern and western Europe were native-born settlers (northeasterners, Upland southerners, and midlanders) also having diverse dialects, beliefs, and religions (Fischer 1989). Towns became dominated by "Yankee" business and professional families, and the countryside sported immigrant-farmer enclaves (Salamon 1992).

The concentration of midwestern ethnic populations today reflects the intersection of European and U.S. historical events at the time of immigration. Significant concentrations of Germans, Swedes, Irish, and Norwegians remain where their ancestors originally settled after the opening of agricultural opportunities in the Midwest (Lieberson and Waters 1988). In the Corn and Wheat Belt states west of the Mississippi, 40 percent of all residents report some German ancestry, the largest ethnic group. The next largest white group in the region is the English (a combination of the census English and Scottish categories), which has less than half the German numbers (Salamon 1992). Those of Scandinavian heritage (Norwegians, Swedes, Danes, and Finns) differentially settled in the Upper Midwest and remain, with Germans, one of the most rural ethnic groups (Fuguitt et al. 1989).

The occupation of farming is particularly conducive to preserving early ethnic concentrations, and as a result, midwestern rural populations today are still overwhelmingly white (Table 19.1). A 1980 census study that matched present ethnic groups with immigrant groups found both groups highly involved in agriculture (Lieberson and Waters 1988). Occupational continuity is aided by an overall decline in farm numbers, although half the family farms in the nation are found in the Midwest (Beale and Kalbacher 1989). Farming is an occupation people are moving out of, not into, so that the original ethnic groups are not diluted by new ones.

Midwestern agriculture developed in such a way that the land-tenure system exemplified the Jeffersonian egalitarian ideal: dominated by self-suffi-

Table 19.1. Diversity among midwestern rural peoples

	Population	% of Total
Total Region	59,668,632	
Total Rural	16,894,436	100
White	16,507,122	97.70
Black	137,036	.81
Hispanic	146,824	.86
American Indian	150,306	.88

Source: 1990 U.S. Census

cient farmers, independent because they owned (or could hope to own) the land they worked (Bellah et al. 1985, 30–31). Jefferson advocated education and admonished agrarian citizenry to become politically involved: "Love your neighbor as yourself, and your country more than yourself" (quoted in Bellah et al. 1985, 31). After the initial settlement a land-tenure system emerged in which family farms, for which the family provided the majority of the management and labor, have dominated the Midwest (Bogue 1959; Bogue 1963). Such farmers, according to Jeffersonian tenets, have a vested interest in participating in the political system, and indeed active civic involvement has shaped the region socially and politically. For example, midwestern public school systems were initially locally controlled. This structure meant that communities, through their farmer-dominated school boards, selected teachers that matched their beliefs as well as their pocketbooks. Starting around the turn of the century, educational professionals sought to centralize education through school consolidations and eventually developed a more uniform curriculum throughout the Midwest. Illinois was slower than either Iowa or Indiana to centralize school governance, and students from its farmer-dominated systems consistently tested higher in core subjects (Fuller 1982). Their involvement in running community schools provided many ethnic settlers with a concrete democratic experience.

Traditionally, farmers have retired into town, and midwestern populations are older than rural populations elsewhere (see Fuguitt, Chapter 5). Almost 40 percent of elderly midwesterners live in rural counties, and the region (along with the rural South) has a concentration of three-quarters of the nation's nonmetropolitan elderly (Fuguitt et al. 1989). The concentration of elderly people is greatly influenced by the outmigration of younger people seeking employment, causing the region to have fewer births than deaths (Johnson 1993). In addition, most of the Midwest, with its harsh climate, does not attract retirement inmigrants, and its elderly tend to age in place.

These combined factors produce communities where the elderly constitute as great as 25 percent of the population. In smaller communities services such as medical facilities, group housing, or public transportation are less likely to be available locally or even in the county. Through agrarian customs of watching out for neighbors, aid in times of crisis, and social service, the elderly have maintained support for one another and the community as a whole. They are motivated to be neighborly because they consider everyone in town an acquaintance, and friendship requires actions that reinforce cohesive communities (Bellah et al 1985).

SOCIAL RELATIONS OF SMALL-TOWN MIDWESTERNERS

Midwestern small-town life revolves around a basic set of social institutions: family, neighbors and friends, school, and church. Midwesterners consistently have believed that their small towns provide a uniquely supportive, quiet, neighborly, friendly, family-oriented, slow-paced, relatively egalitarian, and safe space to dwell. In rural areas and small towns people feel they have control over their lives (Vidich and Bensman 1960; Hummon 1990). This small-town ideology shapes the way Midwestern rural people relate to one another and sets priorities for where and with whom people spend their time, energy, and financial resources. Midwesterners' commitment to a small-town ideology accounts for their actions.

The Relationship Between People and Their Communities

For rural midwesterners social life occurs among networks of kin, neighborhood, work, and church that overlap—by contrast, the social networks of city people are more segregated and specialized. In small towns everyone "knows everyone else." Kin, neighbors, and friends meet one another at work, at church, on main street, at school, or at leisure activities such as a high school basketball game. This situation is called a high "density of acquaintanceship," because a large proportion of residents are linked through primary social relationships (Freudenberg 1986). Daily life is carried out among a cast of familiars rather than among strangers in an anonymous city. People may not necessarily like one another, but because they know one another they expect to receive or give support if adversity strikes. A stable population fosters a high density of acquaintanceship in which people monitor one another's behaviors and property. Watchfulness functions in turn to control deviance, to make the socialization of children a community responsibility, and to assure care for those in need (Freudenberg 1986). Under these circumstances strangers are noticed: once while I was visiting a retired couple, for instance, their phone rang. A neighbor had called to report, "Your visitor left her lights on."

In midwestern small towns people are "in everything." The filling-station owner serves in the volunteer fire department, on the school board, as a church elder, and as coach of a soccer team. When people go out for lunch, shop, or attend the high school basketball game they can greet personally everyone seated around them. When a farmer eats the noon meal at the local cafe, the waitress can gossip with him about their high school reunion or whether his son was at the 4-H meeting the night before. Stories about an appointment forgotten, a mistaken perception, middle-aged spread, running out of gas, or a practical joke furnish material for daily teasing for years. Neighbors cheerfully acknowledge that "we don't like each other much, but we make do."

Children belong to everyone in the community. If a child misbehaves, someone will in all likelihood discipline him and the parents will hear about it before he reaches home. Furthermore, community authorities who are acquainted with a child and her family may expect some "acting up" as children test local limits and thus tolerate minor violations rather than enforcing the law harshly (Schwartz 1987). The elderly are similarly monitored. If an elderly person does not raise his or her window blinds by the usual time a watchful neighbor checks to see if anything has happened. A farmer in one Illinois community takes it on himself to plow out all the driveways and sidewalks of his elderly neighbors. The overlapping social networks that create a high density of acquaintanceship account for controlling deviance, caring for dependent residents (old and young), and monitoring youth. These networks support and regulate residents' behavior in ways crucial to creating a sense of community (Freudenberg 1986).

Egalitarian Relationships

An urban visitor plunked down in any small midwestern town is continually impressed by rituals that recognize, greet, and superficially include people in the ongoing social life. Driving in the countryside almost every truck or car driver will sketch a greeting: a hat tipped, a wave, a nod of the head. Walking down a street or in a local park a stranger is met with an acknowledgement of his or her presence. Eye contact is sought rather than avoided. Buying something in a store or purchasing a service is an interaction that bridges the gap between seller and the purchaser: even if we are strangers our shared experiences as human beings unite us. The weather, politics, sports, or parenthood are all potential topics in common. Frequent jokes show that people don't take themselves too seriously and don't hold themselves above their neighbor. Ideals of egalitarianism and pleasantness shape interactions despite economic and social differences.

In contrast to the present ideology of egalitarianism, differences were once emphasized between town and countryside, causing antagonistic relations in the nineteenth and early twentieth centuries. Historically, farmers resented villagers for taxing them without representation, ignoring their concerns about schools, assuming a socially superior position towards them, or taking their business for granted despite being economically dependent on them (Brunner et al. 1927). Today, farmers, who once outnumbered townsfolk, are less than 2 percent of the U.S. population and have become a minority throughout the rural Midwest (Beale 1989b). Surviving farm families run operations that probably generate a greater cash flow than many town businesses. When a farm couple drives in to eat their noon meal at the local cafe they are indistinguishable from the other patrons. The farmer or his wife are likely to be college graduates, school board presidents, church deacons, or members of the bank board. Distinctions between town- and countryfolk have diminished socially as well as economically. Thus the factors that previously divided countryside and village have relaxed, and the farmers have shed their inferiority complex. Furthermore, the economic and demographic realities of decline mean that midwestern people know they cannot afford to alienate anyone who shows commitment to the community (Aronoff 1993).

Life in small towns is not an idyll. There can be a down side of the density of acquaintanceship, as captured by the authors cited previously. When we surveyed households door-to-door, neighbors would explain who was a hermit or who was difficult, but a neighbor's assessments did not always accurately predict behavior. Perhaps an outsider could be more easily dealt with than someone with whom one has a long and complex relationship. People say that a person must have been born or at least educated in the community to be truly an insider. The trade-off for enduring community norms is that, once accepted, you receive support and your idiosyncrasies are tolerated. Historically, exclusive membership was reinforced by the group belonging to the same church, having a shared history, knowing everyone, intermarrying, and participating in community rituals such as festivals (McNall and McNall 1983). Tales abound of the difficulty of overcoming outsider status despite long residence in a community. For example, in a tightly knit German community a woman of Swedish ancestry married a local in the 1940s. She was an outsider marrying into a group where more than 80 percent of the marriages were Germans married to Germans from the community. Despite joining the major community church no one outside the immediate family spoke to her for over three years (Salamon 1992). Her children, however, born and raised in the community, found ready acceptance.

A middle-aged woman commented that her city workmates are surprised at the extent of her knowledge about everyone in town. She tells them, "That's how it is in a small town." To her, her community is paradise. "[Town] is the best community. . . . I have nothing bad to say about it . . . The people here are the greatest . . . you have a caring type of person." To demonstrate the supportiveness of the community, she and her husband described the agony of a son's serious accident. In a Springfield hospital (fifty miles away) the son had had successive operations over many weeks. Their community of 2,000 prayed for him and sent more than 300 cards. She overheard a nurse asking another "What kind of a kid is he—is he famous or something?" The reply was "No, he's from [town]; they're just like that." This woman is not alone in her satisfaction with and preference for living where she does. Midwesterners, like most rural residents, consider their communities superior and claim a high level of satisfaction with their lives (Hummon 1990).

Social Participation

Rural communities traditionally mobilized basic social support through various voluntary organizations such as church groups. Voluntary groups thrive in rural areas and range from the formal volunteer firemen, Women's Christian Temperance Union (WCTU), historical societies, and social-service clubs such as the Lion, Elks, Moose, and Masons to a myriad of informal neighborhood card groups. Such groups voluntarily supply the brains, muscle, and financial backing to accomplish such infrastructure initiatives as the purchase of a new fire engine, construction of a ball field, or replacement of the school roof. The bake sales, raffles, festivals, and parades we connect with small towns are all carried out by citizens who give of themselves to make their community a better place to live and work (Hatch 1979). An Illinois garage owner, proud of his son becoming the third generation in the family's fifty-year-old business, reflects the level of commitment found in small towns: "I'm on the town board and have been for twenty-five years . . . I've never run for mayor, but I've never needed to. I would run if no one else did. I wouldn't let the town down." Because town populations are so small, ad hoc groups supply services while simultaneously serving as the source of social life, social recognition, and gratification for good deeds. A farm woman whose husband serves on the school board, among other community activities, made much of how "you have to watch your reputation in a small town like this one." They both agreed that "it's important to be involved." Their activities maintain the family's reputation, and the community benefits from volunteerism.

Women supply much of the labor for the informal neighboring traditions that constitute "caring" in small communities. When a death occurs, for example, the church women's circle cooks and provides child care and other assistance while the family grieves. Older, frail people are driven to shops and to the doctor by female relatives or neighbors. While engaged in conversation, women monitor who drives down the street and what neighbors are doing. Neither women nor men, however, are as available as they once were to provide social support. Rural women currently appear in the work force at the same proportion (60 percent) as do urban women (Tickamyer and Bokemeier 1988). Nowadays, more woman formally govern small towns, own businesses, and run local newspapers. They have tried to find work, or make it, close to home, but many women must travel, just as their husbands must. As a consequence small-town people are stretched thin to cover the same volunteer duties that were relegated mainly to women in the past.

Community Institutions

The relative prosperity of the Midwest and the domination of the family farm (as opposed to the industrial or plantation farms of the South and West) were the foundation on which small, homogeneous communities were built (see Hobbs, Chapter 20). Local boosterism and community mobilization combined to assure decent roads, water and electricity, telephones, and other beneficial aspects of physical infrastructure. Churches, schools, town halls, libraries (often thanks to Andrew Carnegie) are a midwestern town's most substantial edifices, public monuments to the willingness of past residents to tax themselves substantially, and symbols of the commitment to the community ideal.

Midwesterners since frontier days have valued schools as a core institution worthy of social and capital investment. Along with educating children, schools serve local communities as centers for voting, club and service organization meetings, recreation, and adult education (Ilvento 1990). The centrality of the building in a community's social fabric accounts for the long, hard fights to retain local schools in the face of state pressure for regional consolidation of educational districts. Small-town residents are convinced that their locally controlled school districts make a difference educationally and socially. Evidence that nonmetro students in the Midwest tend to score higher than metro students on the National Assessment of Educational Progress (NAEP) (see Teixeira, Chapter 22) suggests that their position is justified. One western Illinois community taxes itself at almost twice the rate of a neighboring town to retain its small school. A couple with children in the school expressed a common view about taxes. Said the husband, "Local taxes are too high, but on the other hand we want to keep the school." His wife added, "If you're going to spend your money on something it might as well be the school. It's money well spent." The fight to keep their school is a fight to preserve the community's cohesion and identity. In particular, the school's small size is considered critical to producing community-minded students. "When you don't have many in the class everybody has to take leadership," explained a retired teacher.

Churches represent another pivotal social institution in small towns. Rarely does a midwesterner lack church affiliation. Social action in midwestern small towns tends to flow through churches and typically focuses on local causes. Flood efforts in the summer of 1993 took place in church facilities, and efforts throughout the state were mobilized through church groups. Ministers ensure that the elderly and youth are nurtured through church groups and provide a voice of morality. Women's Christian Temperance clubs remain a potent force in keeping communities "dry" throughout the rural Midwest.

Catholic, Lutheran, and other denominations connected historically with the original northern and western European ethnic settlers are often a town's most imposing structures—tall and built of brick. Not only is an organized church a source of religious support, but, like schools, churches provide a setting for youth groups, community meetings, elections, and government. If a single church dominates an ethnically homogeneous town, community and congregation overlap and cohesion is reinforced. A farm woman regards her community as supportive because "it's a Lutheran (Missouri Synod) community. When everyone belongs to the same church it creates pride and ties people together." She pointed out the similarity between the centrality of the church in her town and a neighboring town where "everyone there is Catholic." Thus, when the annual Lutheran Mission festival is held by this congregation, community is simultaneously celebrated. Such an arrangement is typical of communities where German Americans predominate (Salamon 1992). Historically, where Yankees (those who trace ancestry to the Protestant British Isles) predominate a diversity of churches serve the midwestern community. When multiple churches coexist, membership reflects a family's social standing in the community. Churches are ranked in a hierarchy that corresponds to a local hierarchy of income, education, occupation, family background, and landed wealth (Ploch 1990).

In most small towns a cafe serves as the arena for informal meetings during which the business of daily government takes place. On the surface nothing occurs but a voicing of opinions about the weather, the economy, and the latest gossip. The hidden agenda of such interactions, however, constitutes the working out of subtle consensus building about town issues. So important is the cafe as an arena that locals are depressed when it closes. A farmer described being desolate for almost year after the town cafe closed. He visited the surrounding towns for his breakfast coffee hour. "How would I know how to farm if I didn't find out during coffee hour," he joked. Finally, a couple took over the defunct cafe, allowing him to resume his beloved routine conversations about farm, community, and the markets each morning over breakfast. As a school board member, a church elder, and a 4-H leader, among other duties, the farmer's busy schedule was incomplete without the coffee-shop talk. In many communities women have their own coffee hour which serves a similar communal purpose. Townspeople are thus in such close contact that they are easily mobilized when illness, flood, fire, or other emergencies occur suddenly. Midwestern communities live up to their communitarian ideology when a crisis strikes.

SURVIVAL MENTALITY IN MIDWESTERN RURAL COMMUNITIES

Midwestern rural communities are engaged in a struggle for survival as their populations dwindle and, consequently, demand declines for local businesses and services. Although the actual disappearance of rural communities was relatively rare until the 1980s (Fuguitt et al. 1989), historical persistence does not preclude a community's demise in the 1990s. In the past, greater population density created competition among towns for residents and businesses. Rivalries engendered a fortress mentality. This competition was exemplified in the nineteenth century by violent "county-seat wars" unique to the Midwest over which town was to become the county center of government (Schellenberg 1981). Town business leaders historically joined organizations dedicated to "boosterism," a commitment to town "progress" through commercial and population expansion (Atherton 1954; Curti 1959) or to the maintenance of local pride and esteem (Hatch 1979). In its newest incarnation boosterism is recast as those characteristics leading communities toward "entrepreneurial" acts and initiatives to spur local economic development

(Flora and Flora 1988). Midwestern towns cannot afford complacency without agriculture to sustain the local economy (Fitchen 1991). Outsiders that only one or two generations ago might have been shunned are embraced if willing to make a commitment to community vitality. The only doctors willing to locate in small towns are often Indian, Filipino, or Pakistani. Similarly, the local motel is often run by Asians and the busiest restaurant is owned by a Chinese or Mexican family. Rural communities are thus becoming more heterogeneous (Fitchen 1991). These minority professionals are so desperately needed that they receive better treatment than they might have even in the very recent past.

Not all towns enjoy the cohesion needed to act as an entrepreneurial community. Illinois villages only a few miles apart differ visibly in the numbers of businesses still open on main street, the makeup of village residents, and the involvement of people in community affairs. In my twenty years of studying Illinois ethnic farming communities I found that knowing which ethnic group dominates the population provides a good predictor of community vitality (Salamon 1992). German-Americans, in particular, maintain vital villages. Germans are community oriented and are willing to work together because they believe that what benefits the community over the long term benefits them. Strong agreement about what a community should be and, often, a single dominant church facilitate group mobilization. Their initiatives typically emphasize preservation of what exists rather than economic development for its own sake.

Communities where Yankees dominate are fundamentally divided by distinct social strata and various churches, making community mobilization more difficult. Yankees tend to think of the village more as a commercial center than as a locus for ethnic solidarity. When the main street declines a Yankee village loses its purpose, but it is not a cause for concern as it would be among German-Americans. Yankee identity is not as dependent on the community as is German-American identity (Hatch 1979; Varenne 1977).

Let me illustrate how one community dominated by German-Americans worked together. About fifteen years ago a small western Illinois town found itself in danger of losing crucial businesses. Residents organized by the mayor invested in the restaurant and meat locker that were going under. "We all had the chance to buy shares. Nobody could buy more than $400 to $500," explained an elderly couple who invested in the venture. A recently received dividend surprised the husband. "I got a check from the restaurant the other day for $250. I never expected to see that money again. It was a contribution to the welfare of the community." To give families and teenagers something to do on weekends and in the summers, citizens of the same community started a highly successful bowling alley venture. A bowling alley provided a center that could be an alcohol-free gathering place for teens. Thus is a local population accountable for the type of community they live in. The patch-work of community types that exist across the Midwest reflects the ethnic mosaic of the original settlement (Salamon 1992).

The survival mode of small communities has altered the fabric of rural society. Whereas in the past town and country residents were competitive, they now realize they are "all in this together." Very small rural communities in particular capitalize on their authenticity as a resource to exploit for economic development. Attributes such as self-reliance, hard work, honesty, and a well-preserved ethnic identity are traits that midwesterners have discovered others value and will seek out. Although fifty years ago ethnic farmers were scorned as yokels, today ethnicity is a distinctive and marketable asset. Spillville, Iowa, thus celebrates the centennial of Antonin Dvorak's three-month stay among his Czech countrymen with a "Remembering Dvorak" festival. German-American communities along the Missouri River and in central Illinois, Norwegian and Swedish settlements in Wisconsin, and Irish hamlets in Iowa celebrate their uniqueness with homecomings, festivals, and parades. Ethnic identity and culture attract tourist dollars.

Lacking a distinctive ethnic identity, other communities have spruced up a charming central square or local park, covered bridges, or refurbished Victorian homes with the goal of luring travellers by evoking a simpler time. Community auctions, celebrations of old-time farming days, and small-town Fourth of July celebrations are the taken-for-granted material of the past that intrigues the jaded urbanite. If people can support themselves financially through such activities a community is more likely to maintain its youthful population and thus endure for another generation.

CONCLUSION: THE BEST OF BOTH WORLDS

Historically, it was thought that the best and brightest left rural communities for the city. As early as 1916 E. A. Ross reflected on the selective migration from Michigan, Iowa, Illinois, Wisconsin, and Missouri by commenting that communities were left as "fished-out ponds populated by bullheads and suckers." Yet the small-town way of life holds a sentimental appeal for urban and suburban residents who idealize its tranquility, people, and social relationships. Urbanites perhaps are aware that small-town residents are more satisfied with their communities as a whole and regard life there as safer, cleaner, a better place to raise children, and friendlier (Hummon 1990). In the 1970s Americans chose rural areas over urban places, creating a turn-about migration for the first time since the turn of the century (Beale 1989a). Rural life has become more attractive to rural people themselves now that satellite dishes, television, and videos bring urban experiences into the living room and good roads provide easy access to big-city attractions. An Illinois farm family deeply involved in church, the school board, the Chamber of Commerce, and other activities combines involvement in their small community with frequent trips to St. Louis to see professional baseball and hockey games, shopping at regional malls in Champaign and St. Louis, and eating meals in ethnic restaurants. Once a year they take a week's vacation in Canada, and the husband hunts in the Colorado mountains each fall. They can combine the rural ambience of farm and garden, quiet and security, with urban sophistication. They can be of the urban culture but not in it. Rural people, such as this farm couple, consider that their way of life combines the best of both worlds.

In a time when many Americans seek community and a community identity, rural midwesterners feel secure about these elusive qualities. Midwestern rural people have a robust and positive place identity. Their lives testify to the wisdom of Jefferson. The legacy of small family farms and democratic institutions since settlement is a concerned and well-educated citizenry, broadly involved in local government and committed to the common good (Bellah et al. 1985). People live among neighbors who know them and care about them in a environment shaped by a good physical infrastructure, strong social services, and active civic organizations. Rural dwellers in other parts of the nation aspire to what midwesterners take for granted. Midwesterners have endeavored to preserve their way of life by acting collectively, assuming that by working together the destiny of a community can be controlled. Midwestern rural people recognize that a community's future depends on dedicated citizens who value the small size, intimacy, slow pace, and simplicity that several generations ago their counterparts were anxious to exchange for bright city lights.

PART SEVEN
GROUP DECISION MAKING IN THE COUNTRYSIDE: THE SOCIAL AND INSTITUTIONAL CONTEXT

The individualism of rural people may be more idealized perception than description of reality. Cooperation, both formal and informal, has always characterized group behavior in the countryside. The distances involved and the common problems that must be faced have contributed to the uniqueness of rural institutions.

Daryl Hobbs begins the section by examining the social organization of rural America. He poses two questions: Are rural institutions truly effective instruments? And is anything to be gained by considering rural institutions separately from urban institutions?

Ronald Oakerson, a political scientist, contributes the following chapter, in which he first identifies the source of authority for each unit of government that operates in rural places and then appraises the conduct and performance of rural government. He concludes his chapter with a discussion of group problems and the capacity of rural institutions to deal with them.

The subsequent three chapter address various aspects of rural education and training. In Chapter 22 Ruy Teixeira rigorously and thoroughly compares the quality of rural and urban education and training. His findings challenge many prevailing perceptions about the quality of rural schools. Joan Fitzgerald then compares rural and inner city technical education as a tool for community development, calling attention to the importance of entrepreneurship and discussing ways of fostering it. Next, David Reynolds analyzes the history of rural school consolidation in Iowa.

In the final chapter of this section William Browne and Louis Swanson advance an iconoclastic view of rural public policy. They identify reasons for the federal government's minimalist policy in rural areas while supporting a larger presence in terms of agricultural programs. They argue further that this minimalist involvement is likely to continue in the future and identify measures to make the policy more effective.

20

SOCIAL ORGANIZATION
IN THE COUNTRYSIDE

DARYL HOBBS

> Our rural institutions are remarkably faithful to the problems they were created to address, but society has changed and so have the problems.
>
> *(Castle 1986, 528)*

The social, economic, and political life of country residents is as organized, and as enriched and affected by organizations, as the lives of their urban and suburban neighbors. The complexity, comprehensiveness, and diversity of social organization in the countryside differs little from that found in urban America. Indeed, because of the persistent intrusion of the institutions of a mass society into the countryside, both rural and urban America are served and affected by many of the same national institutions: health, education, social services, trade unions, and so on. Some scholars contend that the notion of a separate rural society has in fact been rendered obsolete (e.g., Gallaher 1980; Padfield 1980a; Friedland 1982; Vidich 1980).

Other observers, meanwhile, present empirical evidence to show that the eclipse of the rural community and its associated organizational forms has not been complete and that distinctive and effective forms of rural organization remain (e.g., Summers 1986; Luloff 1990; Center for New West 1992). They contend that institutions of the larger society have joined, but not supplanted, structures of local rural origin. In this chapter I attempt to identify what is distinctive about the social organization of rural America, while also describing some of the effects of vertical organizational integration on rural life. I also examine rural social organization to determine whether it is more or less effective in empowering and representing rural interests than urban social organization. Insofar as social organization is linked with effectiveness, the

369

continued, widening gap between rural and urban well-being invites consideration of the role played by organization. I take Castle's observation of the need for institutional and organizational innovation as a guiding premise. To the extent, however, that rural America is subject to the services and constraints of national institutions, it becomes pertinent to ask whether so-called urban institutions have been any less faithful to the purposes they were created to address? In those cases the need for institutional innovation may transcend a rural-urban dichotimization.

WHAT IS SOCIAL ORGANIZATION?

Social organization, that is, institutions, formal organizations, and other routinized ways of dealing with problems of life, are the constraints adopted by a society, locality, or any other social collectivity that shapes human interaction and reflects a capacity to achieve well-being for its members (North 1990). Pertinent to this analysis, North draws a distinction between institutions and organizations. Institutions are the rules of the game in a society, "analogous to the rules of the game in a competitive team sport" (North 1990, 4). Extending that analogy, organizations are the teams, players, and strategies they adopt to compete (North 1990, 5). Although institutions establish the framework and purposes for organizations that come into existence, the action of organizations themselves, as their strategies test the limits of existing institutional rules, contributes to institutional change.

Organization, especially in the social history of the United States, has usually been linked with purpose, problem solving, and representation of interests (Tocqueville 1969; Benson 1982). It was Tocqueville who identified voluntary associations as the problem-solving strategy of choice among American communities. In the context of a modern, complex society, organization reflects more than distinctive customs and ways of life; it is a measure of the power and effectiveness of different populations and groups, their capacity to set and achieve goals. In North's analysis it is institutional and organizational capacity that most differentiates the haves from the have-nots.

The circumstances of rural settlement contributed to distinctive rural institutions that, at least for a time, established the framework for what rural organizations emerged and for what purpose. Although the institutions of the larger society have slowly gained hegemony, they have not totally supplanted those of local origin, and the coexistence of local and national institutions creates an inherent conflict between the old and the new, or as Padfield (1980b) describes it, between rural fundamentalism and an ideology of growth.

THE NEED FOR ORGANIZATIONAL EFFECTIVENESS: THE RURAL DEFICIT

Rural America has long lagged behind urban America in income, highly skilled and well-paid employment, services, and other "objective" measures of quality of life. And those deficits have grown as rural capital continues to be drawn into urban centers of commerce and industry. A perception persists, however, that whatever deficits rural residents and localities suffer in "objective" measures of well-being are compensated by higher levels of "subjective" well-being, such as a presumed spirit of cooperation, sharing, and friendliness in family and community relationships (National Rural Electric Cooperative Association [NRECA] 1992). Such perceptions are at least partly responsible for continued metropolitan sprawl into the countryside, migration of retirees into rural areas, and the emergence of rural "playgrounds for the affluent." Despite the persistence of such impressions, growing evidence attests to deterioration even of the subjective quality of rural life. Rural Americans now consider an increase in crime, loss of family farms, alcohol abuse, and increased use of illegal drugs to be the four greatest threats to the future of rural America (NRECA 1992).

Concurrently, on the "objective" side, rural poverty rates have recently grown to levels exceeding those of inner cities, and lack of higher-skill and higher-paying employment is contributing to continued population loss. Thus there is room to question how well the needs and interests of rural Americans are being represented by their contemporary social infrastructure. In exploring the foundations of the rural institutions that Castle observes have been "remarkably faithful" to the purposes they were created to serve, I show how those foundations have changed along with society and its problems. Concern about present and future well-being of rural residents informs the assertion that innovation and restructuring of rural institutions are required to enhance the organizational capacity of rural localities.

THE UNDERREPRESENTATION OF RURAL INTERESTS

Organizational capacity is not simply a reflection of the number of institutions and organizations serving a population; it is their effectiveness in representing interests that matters. Indeed, in terms of numbers of organizations, much of rural America could be described as overorganized but underrepresented; still, many rural poor or minority communities are both underrepresented and underorganized.

By "overorganization," we mean the greater actual number of organizations (e.g. churches, interest groups, local governments, etc.) per capita in rural localities than in urban. In a study of 400 New York villages, Harp (1973) found a mean of twenty-six voluntary associations per village. And, as Oakerson reports in the following chapter, nonmetropolitan areas include only 22 percent of the nation's population but nearly 62 percent of total U.S. local governments—and the number is growing: from 1932 to 1987 the number of nonmetropolitan municipalities grew by 17 percent and the number of special purpose districts more than doubled (Oakerson 1992). The number of rural organizations has grown in response to increases in the number and specialization of rural interests.

As one indication of underrepresentation, we cite the absence of rural development as a policy priority at either state or national levels, despite continued deterioration of rural conditions relative to the rest of the nation. The result of small scale rural organizations and growing specialization of rural residents' interests is fragmented representation (Fisher and Knutson 1989; Honadle 1993). If ever there was a coherent rural interest, it is gone today. Instead there are many rural interests, some better organized and represented than others.

LOCAL VARIATION IN ORGANIZATION

Although we refer in general terms to the social organization of rural America, the mix of organizations and institutions varies greatly by locality and region and is, in sum, as diverse as its people, its economy, and its geography. The diversity is long-standing and persists in part because forms of social organization dedicated to preserving local traditions, distinctiveness, and identity have been joined by institutions and organizations dedicated to drawing rural producers and consumers into a mass society and a global economy. Diversity exists not only between localities, as it always has, but within them as well.

Despite the pervasive effects of mass society, some rural localities remain socially and economically viable and retain a capacity to act (Luloff 1990). Recent research reports great variation in the organizational capacity of rural communities to achieve local change and development (e.g., Green et al.

1990; Flora and Flora 1988). Summers (1986) concludes that the vitality of a small town depends on the organizational structure and value of community decision making.

THE FOUNDATIONS OF RURAL SOCIAL ORGANIZATION

Two features of rural America have historically contributed most to its distinctive forms of organization: the dominance of the family farm as the initial rural industry (and the dominant national industry until early in the twentieth century) and the prevalence of geographically separated small settlements. Before improved mobility and greater market penetration the two characteristics were interdependent—most of the small settlements existed to serve the needs of the surrounding farm population. The settlements became farm towns. Social organization and other social attributes reflected those conditions. The interdependence of farm and town also fostered, and reinforced, agrarianism as a dominant, pervasive, and persistent rural value.

The dispersed settlements and their social and economic roles became identified as community, which was equated in the minds of many with a territory and a coterminous pattern of common identity and cooperative relationships. Although the idea of community connotes many different meanings (Fowler 1991), community was, in the early rural context, simultaneously a description of locality, purpose, and a statement of value. They generally coincided in a town.

Thus each of the two most pertinent features of the organizational foundation of rural America—an agricultural industry composed largely of small family farmers dispersed geographically among small settlements—was also linked with an important value. Agriculture as an industry became identified with agrarianism, and the dispersed settlements were the foundation for communitarian values. The combination contributed to institutionalizing of family farms and rural communities themselves, which then inspired many associated forms of organization.

Agriculture, dispersed settlements, and the values associated with them are important not only for understanding how rural America initially organized itself, but also because changes in agriculture and in the meaning and significance of space have significantly affected rural social organization and have exacerbated the need for institutional innovation.

Although agriculture and agricultural towns have changed dramatically, the values they spawned persist and support the public perception of a "rural mystique" (Willits et al. 1990). A recent national poll (NRECA 1992) reflects the persistence of that mystique, showing that the public overwhelmingly attributes to small towns and rural areas the virtues of strong sense of family, friendliness, a commitment to community, responsible citizenry, resourcefulness, and so on, even while acknowledging that urban areas boast superior quantity and quality of services.

Despite the rural deficit in objective conditions, the strength of subjective perceptions emphasizes the power the rural mystique retains in shaping public responses to rural needs and circumstances. Although Browne (1989) finds that organizations predicated on a rural mystique are less likely to be politically effective, congresspeople continue to invoke "saving the family farm" as a rationale for recent agricultural legislation, even as the family farm has become more difficult to define. Reform and restructuring of rural institutions is limited in part by the persistence of perceptions shaped by the past.

DISPERSED SETTLEMENTS AND THE RISE OF COMMUNITY

Churches, schools, and local governments were among the first organizations to appear in the countryside. Although trade centers became the nucleus of agricultural communities, churches and schools were frequently established in the open country and formed the basis for rural neighborhoods. Early rural sociologists generally differentiated communities from neighborhoods along functional lines (e.g., Brunner and Kolb 1933). Communities were identified by the presence of a wide range of institutions and necessary services, whereas neighborhoods were usually organized around a single organization, usually a church or school. Neighborhoods were often the basis for work exchange among farmers as well.

In much of rural America the spatial isolation of settlements—and who settled them for what reason—turned those settlements into communities with a comprehensive way of life. Spatial isolation resulted in social isolation and buffer against significant intrusion from the dominant society and culture. Local circumstances and certain dominant characteristics of the local population such as religion, ethnicity, race, occupation, or social class contributed to the development of locally distinctive cultural, organizational, ceremonial, and ritual forms. Thus different localities created their own institutionalized solutions to recurring problems: their own "little traditions" (Gallaher 1980).

Religion and ethnicity usually went hand in hand, particularly in settlements established by the European immigrants who flooded the Midwest and West following the Homestead Act of 1862. Although more than a hundred years have passed since original settlement, Salamon (1984) finds that ethnicity remains an important influence on social, economic, and farm life in those places even today.

ECONOMIC SPECIALIZATION

Rural communities generally were and are highly specialized economically. Although agriculture was the most typical specialization, the existence of other settlements was predicated on logging, fishing, mining or, more recently, oil, recreation, or manufacturing. Under conditions of spatial isolation, a dominant occupation, just as religion or ethnicity, provided a foundation for a distinctive pattern of local social organization.

The economic foundation of a locality had great implications for social class as well. Although social class played a secondary role in rural localities initially dominated by family farms, it was a more decisive organizational factor in areas with a clear division between management and labor. Even in agriculture there are class-based differences that affect social organization, as in the rural South where first plantations and later sharecropping prevailed. More recently Goldschmidt (1978) has documented major social organizational differences between two California agricultural communities, one dominated by family farmers and the other by concentrated ownership and dependence on hired labor.

FROM RURAL SETTLEMENTS TO COMMUNITY

Although shared characteristics and shared space are important to the concept of community they are not sufficient; a shared life, self-consciously accepted, is required (Fowler 1991, 4). It is the shared life materializing in a collection of institutions that Park (1952) claims distinguishes community from other social constellations. Residents directly experience within the community the institutions and institutional constraints of the locality and the larger society.

Spatial isolation reinforced local traditions, which in turn framed and limited the behavior of community members (Vidich 1980). Locality was at once the source that met residents' needs, however they defined them, and the basis for institutions that constrained choices. Life was less complicated because few alternatives were socially acceptable (Vidich 1980). Although different institutions—political, economic, religious, family—served different purposes and were the basis for different organizations, they tended to be governed by common values and thus wove a single fabric. Institutional specialization and differentiation in the degree we know it today existed only in fledgling form.

What evolved was a community that formed a basis for obtaining goods and services, served as a source of identity for residents, and structured social relationships, stratification, and cooperation. The conditions of settlement favored the cooperative behavior that, as observed by North, is more likely to occur "when individuals repeatedly interact, when they have a great deal of information about each other, and when small numbers characterize the group" (1990, 12).

THE MEANING OF SPACE

Rural space became more than a geographic constraint, it was invested with social value and became a defining attribute of the little traditions. With the open country pattern of farmer settlement, community boundaries extended into the countryside to mark a settlement and its surrounding trade area as a community. The boundaries signified more than convenience, however; they were dividing lines between little traditions. People belonged to, and were thus constrained by, one little tradition or another. Crossing the lines meant being subject to a different set of rules and customs. The association of the American rural community with territory was so indelible that it became the dominant theoretical perspective on community until quite recently (Martindale and Hanson 1969).

Although increased mobility and the persistent penetration of the institutions of the larger society have mitigated the limiting effect of space on rural life, the territorial rural community remains a source of identity for many rural people. Most of the rural localities born in the last century remain today, and their residents continue to invest them with social value, despite their altered economic and social relationships. Space does however continue to impose a cost, especially on rural residents who lack mobility. Dillman and Hobbs (1982) have observed that today's rural disadvantaged are most likely those who are restricted to the offerings of their locality.

THE SOCIAL ORGANIZATION OF AGRICULTURE

The special role of agriculture in the overall development of U.S. rural and community life is not simply attributable to production from the land. The actual form of production (large numbers of small farmers owning and operating their own land) in much of rural America contributed most to the institutions and organizations established to support agriculture and rural life. Despite local differences in organization, most rural people shared dependence on agriculture, the methods by which it was practiced, and the ideologies that surrounded it. This homogeneity of farmers' interests and practices helped reinforce the social foundations of the settlements.

Furthermore, U.S. agriculture from Jefferson forward was imbued with a set of values thought to be essential to an effective democratic society. Because it supported these values, agriculture early on became more than a business; it was widely perceived by its practitioners and supporters as comprising a way of life. Agrarian values elevated small owner-operated farms to an embodied virtue as well as a business and inspired the formation of a number of different kinds of rural institutions and organizations.

The Jeffersonian ideal of a democratic society of small farms and businesses bolstered by education was well suited to settlement and expansion of the frontier. The ideal was later reinforced by 1862 passage of the Homestead Act, which was instrumental in attracting both U.S. urban dwellers and large numbers of European immigrants to settle the land, and the Morrill Act, which created what was to become the land grant university system. The Morrill Act augmented the Jeffersonian ideal of education and later, through the Cooperative Extension Service, added to the rural institutional framework by assisting in the creation of numerous rural and agriculturally related associations. The Morrill and Homestead acts also established the federal government as an institution destined to join, affect, and in some cases, supplant local community and agricultural institutions. Those acts reflected a national interest in an economically and socially productive agriculture. Significantly, leadership for the Morrill Act came not from farmers but from educated middle-class professionals (Bonnen 1987).

After the Civil War, growing industrialization generated new markets for agricultural production, and the completion of railroads provided the means to link agricultural producers with the external markets. An early consequence of increased market dependency was the emergence of farmer's movements that provided the foundation for what would become general farm organizations. Agriculture led the way in breaking from local institutional constraints and connecting with the institutions of the larger society.

During the late 1800s the Grange and Farmer's Alliances were two of the more prominent movements, with the Grange, originally established as a farmer's social and educational organization, rising to prominence on the issue of widespread farmer discontent with railroad prices and monopoly. The philosophical foundation of these movements was generally populist; farmers were attracted in large numbers to the Populist Party, which made a major bid for national power in 1896. These movements reflected a growing farmer distrust of business of all kinds, including many found at the local level. McGranahan (1983) emphasizes that as the interests of farmers began to extend beyond the locality, the interests of local merchants, whose customers and business were bound to the locality, began turning to ways of expanding and diversifying local economies. Thus began the separation of the interests of farmers and local merchants endemic to today's rural communities. Merchants' interests inspired new forms of organization. In a 1927 study of 140 rural villages, Brunner and Kolb (1933) found 83 that reported having Chambers of Commerce or industrial development organizations.

Two still-active general farm organizations originated in the period from 1900 to 1920: the Farmer's Union, begun in Texas, gained greatest prominence in wheat growing areas of the Great Plains, and the Farm Bureau, begun in Iowa, attracted greater membership in the Corn Belt and the South. These organizations, along with the Grange, are called general farm organizations because their focus shifted from protest to a broad-based program of education, improving farm production, and lobbying for legislation favorable to farmers and rural residents. All three emphasize an organizational structure built up from the local level through state and national organizations. The Farm Bureau, largest in membership and, for a time, in political influence, was most attentive to developing a local organization base. Initially, the Farm Bureau was greatly assisted in this effort by the Cooperative Extension Service, with which it maintained a close relationship in many states until after World War II.

These organizations are historically important because their programs, generally devoted to improving the well-being of farmers, were initially also mechanisms for representing rural interests nationally. They were instrumental in lobbying for rural mail delivery, rural electrification, and improvement in rural roads and highways, innovations that benefited farmers and town residents alike. They also expedited a rural transition from the jurisdiction of local institutions to national and reflected the view that farm interests and rural interests coincided—a belief that still affects national rural policies.

FARMER COOPERATIVES

The farmers' growing dependence on external markets gave rise to local organizations, such as cooperatives, that specialized in creating links with larger markets. Cooperatives were an organizational form that "fit" the rural environment of the period. They were importantly based on communitarian and agrarian values and served the practical need of connecting with external markets and suppliers. The original impetus for agricultural cooperatives was both local and an outgrowth of social movements. Like the more general farmer social movements, they were inspired by the populist agenda of countering perceived adverse effects of big business on agriculture. The social movement phase of cooperatives was most active from 1890 to 1930.

Though they grew out of localized social movements, cooperatives moved rather quickly to adopt rational business forms, and their purposes soon subjected them to national institutional constraints. General farm organizations (especially the Grange, the Farm Bureau, and the Farmer's Union) were also active in helping to establish local and regional agricultural cooperatives. Even today many local farm supply and marketing cooperatives retain the name of one those organizations.

The Clayton Act (1914) strengthened the legal basis of cooperative business, and passage of the Capper-Volstead Act (1922) cleared the way for cooperative businesses to combine commodity marketing efforts by exempting them from certain provisions of the Sherman Anti-Trust Act. Accordingly, local cooperatives began organizing federated regional cooperatives in order to gain greater market power. Regional cooperatives were generally conceived as a cooperative of cooperatives. The 1920s and 1930s were the most active years for formation of regional cooperatives. Through many consolidations, mergers, and name changes, most of today's regional cooperatives, which include such nationally prominent names as Agway, Farmland Industries, Land O'Lakes, and Harvest States, trace their origins to that period.

There were 7,374 agricultural cooperative associations in 1921; the number peaked at about 12,000 in 1930. Membership in marketing and farm supply cooperatives reached a peak in 1954–1955 with 7.6 million farmers belonging to nearly 10,000 associations. Since then the number of associations has gradually declined, to 4,663 in 1990. The merger and consolidation of local associations to gain larger-scale economies has been most responsible for the declining numbers of cooperatives.

The long-term trend among farm cooperatives has followed the course of other rural institutional trends. What began as locally controlled organizations serving principally local needs have gradually given way to larger, more complex regional organizations. Local cooperatives now operate virtually as franchises or branches of large regional cooperatives. This change coincides with the shift in the orientation of agricultural producers from local to national and even global markets. Cooperatives, like other forms of rural and agricultural association, are concerned about their future, and they make the organizational changes necessary to compete in larger and more highly specialized markets.

THE EXPANDING ROLE OF NATIONAL GOVERNMENT

Throughout the twentieth century the federal government has expanded its role in direct provision of agricultural services, finance, credit, and markets. Greater federal involvement not only added directly to the stock of rural and farm organizations but also contributed a cause for further organization: influencing government policy. Three major kinds of rural organizations resulted: groups such as the general farm organizations that came into existence to affect federal legislation; entities that were direct federal creations, such as the Soil Conservation Service; and organizations whose existence was made possible by federal legislation, such as rural electric cooperatives. All three types continue to occupy a prominent place among rural organizations. Their intended purpose was to increase agricultural productivity and contribute to the well-being of farm families. Most were either statutorily or practically limited to agricultural or rural purposes, thus making them uniquely rural organizations even though national in origin. Most of these groups were established before 1950 and persist today. The few recent creations of federal initiatives are neither distinctively rural nor limited in application to agriculture. Examples include rural Hill-Burton hospitals, area vocational schools, and many regional planning commissions.

Locus of control distinguishes the role played by federal line agencies from other organizations created by the federal government. The line agencies are under direct federal control with only limited advisory input from localities. The Soil Conservation Service is something of an exception, for it has created local organizations to promote and facilitate soil conservation practices and structures. Although the Cooperative Extension Service was a direct result of federal legislation (Smith-Lever Act 1914), the locus of control has been predominantly state and local. The "cooperative" feature of the extension service directs that the origin of its educational programs and their support will be shared by federal, state, and local sources. Although there are extension offices in all counties (rural and urban), most local and state programs of the

Cooperative Extension Service have traditionally been oriented first toward agriculture producers, rural families, and youth.

An important feature of the Cooperative Extension Service is that it was a way of adding to the stock of rural organizations. The extension service organized many affiliated local associations such as Homemaker and 4-H clubs and a significant number of county farm bureaus as a means of carrying out their educational programs. But extension also played a major role in organizing autonomous production and marketing cooperatives, rural electric cooperatives, dairy herd improvement associations, farm business associations, county fair boards, and so on. Although most of the extension service's organizational efforts occurred prior to 1950, many of the associations it helped to create remain today, and extension continues to provide educational and technical assistance.

Cooperatives have a special relationship with the federal government. Although the federal government did not participate in organizing cooperatives (except indirectly through extension), favorable federal legislation did much to establish the legal basis of cooperatives and to facilitate the formation of regional cooperatives. Federal support for cooperatives was also evidenced by the establishment in 1926 of the Cooperative Marketing Agency (now the Agricultural Cooperative Service) within the U.S. Department of Agriculture to promote the idea of cooperatives and to provide them with educational and technical assistance.

The federal government played an explicit role in the formation of rural electric and farm credit cooperatives. Both grew out of New Deal legislation: Farm Credit Administration, for example, was formed in 1933 to extend credit to farmers' marketing and purchasing associations. Throughout various name changes the farm credit system has remained a source of loan funds for local and regional Production Credit Associations and the Federal Land Bank (cooperatives). The Rural Electrification Administration (REA) was created by executive order in 1935 (passed into law in 1936) to provide loan funds to cooperatives organized to provide electricity to people on farms and in the open country. The act that created the REA specifically required loans to be made to cooperative forms of organization. Consistent with their broad rural agenda, general farm organizations lobbied aggressively on behalf of REA.

THE AGRICULTURE RULES CHANGE

The New Deal era marked the last direct involvement of the national government in creating local forms of rural and agricultural organization. The federal role in agriculture has continued to expand but has taken the form of financing and administering the agricultural commodity price support and supply management programs. The changed federal role has directly influenced agriculture and the organizations that represent it.

In addition to creating new agricultural and rural agencies and associations, the New Deal era produced legislation that redefined agricultural production and, thereby, the organizations that represented farm and rural interests. New Deal programs established a legal basis for commodity production and initiated what was to become a fixture of U.S. agricultural production, the guaranteed loan and price support programs linked to specific commodities (Bonnen 1987; Friedland 1984). The social contract between government and a relatively undifferentiated agricultural (and rural) sector was thus recast.

The accelerating rate of agricultural mechanization following World War II, along with price supports and other new production technologies, expedited the substitution of capital for labor and increased the rate of farm consolidation. Concurrently, land-grant university research and extension reinforced a transition from multicrop general farming to specialized commodity production, a trend that continues today.

The transition was accompanied by new and different producer interests and therefore a change in the types of organizations representing them. Farmers no longer automatically held interests in common but began to specialize along commodity lines. Accordingly, general farm organizations became less effective in representing producer interests, for interests of different commodity producers were often competitive. New organizations, specialized by commodity, began to appear such as the American Soybean Association, the National Corn Growers Association, the National Pork Producers Association, and the National Cattlemen's Association. Most agricultural commodities are now represented by a specific association, which is financially supported by a "check off," whereby some fraction of commodity sales is withheld at the point of sale and sent directly to the association.

Commodity organizations differ notably from general farm organizations. Commodity organizations are principally devoted to promoting domestic and international sales of their commodity, affecting legislation favorable to commodity producers, and supporting research to develop new products and uses of the commodity. Their primary focus is national and international, although most of the major commodity organizations have state and local associations in regions that produce the commodity. Commodity organizations are unlikely to have a local agenda unless a local issue of direct relevance to commodity producers arises.

A recent analysis of the relative influence of different farm-related organizations on the 1985 farm bill reinforces the different roles of commodity groups, general farm organizations, and other farm interest groups (Browne 1989). In his survey of congressional staff, Browne found that staff reported that specialized commodity groups had more influence on farm legislation than general farm organizations and other agricultural interest groups because of their ability to address narrow policy questions in a highly specific fashion. Browne also reports that "legislative staff people find little use for information about sector-wide concerns, generalized farm or business problems, social conditions of underclasses and public interest problems about the environment or nutrition" (1989, 378).

The emergence of politically powerful commodity organizations and the relative decline in influence of general farm organizations has redefined the relevance of agriculture for rural community development and helps explain the inattention to rural development policy nationally. Fisher and Knutson, for example, emphasize that "commodity groups have little or no interest in policy outside of price and income policy, international trade policy and environmental policy. Since commodity groups have become the strongest politically of the farm organizations, little attention is given by farm leaders to rural development policy" (1989, 63).

This transition from a few broad interest organizations to a much greater number of specialized commodity groups has compounded the fragmentation of rural interests. Ironically, the land-grant university system, once a contributor to rural integration, has, through its own specialization, reinforced that fragmentation. These transitions effectively severed agricultural interests from rural interests, and rural interests have further subdivided as other sectors of the rural economy, such as manufacturing, have overtaken agriculture in their contributions to rural income and employment (Henry, Drabenstott, and Gibson 1986). Not surprisingly, Honadle (1993) notes that the groups claiming to represent rural America are perceived as competing with one another—each has its own solutions to rural problems.

CHANGE PRODUCES TWO KINDS OF FARMS

As specialized commodity producers have grown in size and proportion of total agricultural production and rural economies have diversified, another kind of "farmer" has become numerically important, particularly in the eastern half of the nation where rural industrialization and metropolitan sprawl have been extensive. These are "part-time" farmers, so defined because they are typically employed full-time off the farm or have other sources of income larger than farm income. Generally defined as those farms having gross farm commodity sales of less than $50,000 per year, they comprised 75 percent of the total number of farmers in 1987, yet produced only 12 percent of total output (Census of Agriculture 1987). Most of the part-time farmers do not identify farming as their principal occupation. Their occupations and interests are diverse and they do not necessarily share commercial agricultural interests. Commodity producers are more likely to view farming as "a business," whereas the choice to farm part-time in conjunction with some other occupation is more often based on a desire to practice agrarian values. The growth in the number of part-time farms has come at the expense of a shrinking middle group of "family farms": the group that has long been regarded as epitomizing agrarian values. Although the number of middle-sized family farms is dwindling, the impression of those farms as typical continues to prevail, especially in political debate over farm programs.

The bifurcation of agriculture has had implications as well for the viability of rural localities. Large-scale commodity producers tend to obtain production inputs from suppliers specializing in higher volume and to market their products through larger regional markets. Concomitantly the smaller, part-time producers purchase relatively few inputs and market small quantities. Consequently, the marketing outlets and agribusinesses that were once a foundation of the local business community have disappeared from many small, formerly farm towns. Agribusinesses supporting agriculture, including cooperatives, have tended to follow the same trend of concentration and expansion in scale as their larger customers and retail trade in general. Ironically, it is now difficult to find many farm businesses in what were once farm towns. In many rural localities the foundation of local business and commercial organization is lost.

Thus the small family farm, an essential foundation stone of distinctively rural forms of social organization, is not what it used to be, and nor, therefore, is rural America. The transition of commercial agriculture from local to national institutional control is largely complete. Virtually all present organizations designed to serve agricultural and rural needs are derived from national rather than local institutions. Despite the transition, agriculture as a sector has not fully shed its roots nor its traditional values. Agricultural policies, formed far from where the production occurs, tend still to equate agriculture with small family farms and agricultural policies with broader rural well-being, neither of which is consistent with current data. Sorting out the effect of these changes remains on the rural agenda.

INCORPORATION OF RURAL INTO MASS SOCIETY

Agriculture aside, it is no longer possible to analyze rural social organization without reference to the larger society and global economy within which it is embedded. There has been a transition from community to society with a concomitant "shift in the center of wealth and civilization from agricultural to industrial and urban" (Vidich 1980, 112). Accordingly, many of the conditions of urban life are being reproduced in small communities. Local institutions, established to serve distinctive local needs, either continue to exist in residual form or are incorporated into those of the mass society. The transition has also necessitated new forms of organization to mediate the inside-outside interface in the local community. Such organizations typically have allegiance to both the community and the institutions beyond, resulting in a rural ambivalence and contradiction (Benson 1982). Differences in social organization between the rural then and the rural now are greater than present differences between urban and rural.

The incorporation of local institutions into those of the mass society has produced a dendritic (treelike) pattern of social organization in contemporary rural America. Rural localities tend to remain separate with little relationship and mutual cooperation, except insofar as obtaining services requires, but they are firmly connected with, and dependent on, the institutions and organizations of the larger society. With economic viability at stake, they tend to compete with each other for location of those organizations: everything from schools and Wal-Mart stores to branch plants of national industries. The competition tends to preserve the dendritic pattern and constrain cooperation among localities; it also reflects a desire and a capacity to act independently.

The strong, multiple connections with the dominant society and the absence of much, if any, collaboration between localities helps account for much change in rural social organization having originated outside the locality. The definition and solution of local problems has been largely surrendered to external institutions and organizations. Correspondingly, community effectiveness is now frequently measured by success in attracting outside sources (Flora and Flora 1988).

In some institutional sectors, such as health, education, and retail trade, the changes have had a standardizing effect. The hospitals, schools, and franchise businesses tend to look and operate very much the same regardless of location. Conversely, in the economic production sector, changes such as rural industrialization, tourism, and the like have contributed to greater local economic specialization and therefore to perpetuation of rural diversity. On the consumption side rural localities have become more alike; on the production side they have become more specialized and dissimilar. The net effect of both changes has been that all rural localities become less autonomous and more dependent. Thus the institutional structure of the larger society, greater dependence on external economic investment, and greatly enhanced physical and communication mobility have largely, but not completely, replaced family farm agriculture and isolated settlements as the foundations of rural social organization.

THE EFFECT OF NATIONAL INSTITUTIONS ON RURAL LOCALITIES: THE CASE OF PUBLIC SCHOOLS

The standard institutional environments of modern society excite standard patterns of response, despite persisting local traditions. No institution better exemplifies this truth than public education, in which the national institution provides the framework for public schools in all matters from finance to organizational rules, regulations, and procedures. Local variation among rural schools, at the instigation of public policy, has been reduced in favor of greater uniformity. Rural schools have generally become smaller versions of urban schools.

One of the early distinctive rural organizational forms was the "one-room country school," an organizational adaptation to farming and a dispersed rural population. Generally the eight-grade one-room schools were established in rural neighborhoods; high schools, where they existed, were usually located in the trade centers. It was, in fact, the need for farm children to provide labor on the farm that established what was to become the nation's school calendar and length of the school day. The school day began after farm children had helped with morning farm chores and ended early enough for children to repeat the ritual in the evening. The summer "vacation" allowed children to be available full-time during the busiest agricultural season.

Until about 1920 schools were mostly locally financed and therefore locally controlled, although states had established departments of education and were supporting "normal" schools to provide professional teacher training. But the state and federal role in financing (and regulating) education was minimal. In 1920 local sources accounted for 83.2 percent of total spending for public education, states contributed 16.5 percent, and federal spending was negligible (Jansen 1991). Succeeding decades, however, have witnessed an inexorable process of rural schools incorporated into a national education institution. The rationale for incorporation has been rural school improvement. Indicative is the change in sources of funding. By 1987 funding from local sources had diminished to 43.9 percent of total school revenues, the contribution of states had grown to 49.8 percent, and the remaining 6.4 percent came from federal sources. Along with the shift in funding has come a greatly expanded role of the state in regulation and professionalization of public schools.

As state regulation and professionalization expanded, a standardized model of the "good" school evolved, leading to what Tyack (1974) referred to as the "one best system." The one best system was a model based on a standard comprehensive curriculum, taught by specialized teachers, and a hierarchical organization with professionally trained administrators to direct the enterprise. The institutionally designed and ratified comprehensive school, in order to be affordable, required a relatively large enrollment and a substantial revenue base. Accordingly, enrollment size also became a measure of a "good" school; a standard to which many rural schools failed to measure up. Not only one-room schools but many rural high schools were judged to be too small to support faculties of specialists.

What followed had a great effect not only on rural schools but on rural neighborhoods and communities as well. At the behest of state departments of education and with legislative assent, rural schools were strongly encouraged to consolidate. Facilitating the consolidation movement were improvements in transportation that made travel to more distant schools feasible. The number of U.S. school districts declined from 128,000 in 1930 to 84,000 in 1950 and down to 15,000 in 1987. Consolidation basically eliminated the one-room country school as a feature of rural culture and many small-town high schools were consolidated out of existence as well. Most rural neighborhoods and many towns thus lost a significant focal point of identity and social relationships: their school. Because of the social and economic importance attached to schools, consolidation was a threat to many rural communities and was strongly resisted. Peshkin (1982) recounts the inter- and intracommunity conflict generated from a twenty-year-long school consolidation battle involving several small Illinois towns. The threat of state-mandated school consolidation continues to be widely resisted by rural communities (Sher 1986).

School consolidation was one of the early and most influential factors in expanding the geographic size of the rural "community" (service area) beyond the nearest small town. Since then everything from regional shopping malls to health care and marketing of farm products have reinforced rural regionalization with a corresponding reduction in the social and economic role of the community. But the effect of incorporating rural schools into the "one best system" has been more far-reaching than consolidation alone. The national presumption notwithstanding, local control of education is now more perceived than real. Moreover, the extent of state control and regulation has increased as a consequence of recent school reform efforts. Greater external regulation has contributed to rural schools becoming more socially and intellectually isolated from the communities in that they serve. The standardized curriculum, which is oriented toward inculcation of national values and symbolic understandings, excludes local traditions and beliefs (Gamradt and Avery 1992). Thus the school, as an agency of socialization, is focused more on national than on local integration.

Conflicting standards and values also emerge in the administration and control of schools. According to at least one study, the combination of increased professionalization of teachers and administrators coupled with declining income in many rural localities is producing conflict between school boards and the teaching and administrative staff regarding compensation and benefits (Schmuck and Schmuck 1992).

Although recent school-reform initiatives have generally strengthened the role of the state in defining educational problems and prescribing their solutions, there is growing recognition that local social capital (community and family) exerts a powerful independent effect on educational outcomes (Coleman 1987). Some reform efforts are beginning to turn toward decentralization and encouraging greater interaction between school and community.

EFFECTS ON RURAL COMMUNITIES

Although most of the nineteenth-century settlements remain in place, many of them have lost the attributes associated with community. Community has not altogether disappeared from rural America, but rather both the relational and territorial bases of rural community have changed. The relational aspect of community has fallen victim to the specialization of interests linked to nonlocal institutions. Cooperation among residents does not serve the breadth of interests it formerly did. Concomitantly, the institutional constraints of locality have lost much of their force. As technologies have facilitated the expansion of social and economic space, criteria other than physical proximity have become the basis for relationships of rural people. Common interests no longer arise solely from common geographic location. Community, where it exists, is more likely to be based on social nearness than common residence (Kramer 1970). Accordingly, new bases for community are emerging from geographically extended relationships (Korsching, Borich, and Stewart 1992).

Economic change has also contributed to the changing function and demographic composition of rural localities. The agricultural transition eroded the economic viability of many rural localities. Since the turn of the century, agriculture has released labor as it has increased productivity. A result has been a long-term irreversible migration of youth and young adults from most rural localities to larger urban labor markets. The declining population eroded the economic base of support of many rural community businesses, necessitated increased regionalization, and modified the age distribution and therefore the interests of the population. In an effort to remain economically viable, many rural localities turned to organizing themselves to attract outside investment, inviting factories to relocate from urban to rural areas to take advantage of lower wage rates. The effectiveness of the strategy, particularly in the southeastern states, is demonstrated by that fact that manufacturing employment had become the largest source of rural income by the late 1970s (Bender et al. 1985). Significantly, national policies and investments in infrastructure and job training reinforced local initiatives. Although these efforts were undertaken to "save" rural localities, they also redefined the basis of social organization and integration. Success in attracting outside investments further reduced local autonomy, and more rural organizations were left with diminished purpose.

In place of a community interest, one is now more likely to find many interests in the same locality divided along age, occupational, gender, and social-class lines. The path to acting on those interests has increasingly been found through specialized organizations outside the locality rather than cooperation at the local level, a phenomenon that has had a centrifugal effect on localities. Local interests tend to diverge both spatially and organizationally rather than to converge in the locality, and the structure of power and influence becomes polarized between local and nonlocal interests (Martindale and Hanson 1969). Diminished local social integration is accompanied by a decline in local autonomy and self-sufficiency, a condition Gartrell (1983) refers to as an "underdevelopment" of rural communities. The common purpose and cooperation that enable a locality to act effectively on its own behalf is frequently absent, although some communities have achieved or retained such a capacity (Luloff 1990; Summers 1986).

REDEFINITION OF SPACE

With increased mobility and institutional consolidation the geographic basis of rural social organization expanded beyond the bounds of the traditional community, making space an increasingly irrelevant factor in the definition of community. Communities are, in effect, being pulled in different directions—away from hometowns, downtowns, and other geographically demarcated places and toward an array of different service networks located elsewhere (Center for New West 1992).

Academic thinking about community has changed as community has divorced itself from territory. Martindale and Hanson (1969) note that analysts who think of territory as an essential attribute of community are likely to conclude that community is disappearing. By contrast, those who think of community in interactional or relational terms (e.g., Wilkinson 1986) view community as persisting and important. The Center for the New West, in their recent assessment of the rural Great Plains, quote Fishman's (1990) observation that the "community of place" is being superseded by "communities of networks." Fishman identifies three networks—household, consumption, and workplace—that provide new bases for community relationships.

PERSISTENCE OF DIFFERENCES

Localities do retain certain social and organizational differences despite the standardizing influences of the mass society. Recent research confirms variation in sense of community and local capacities. Goudy, in a study of twenty-seven rural Iowa localities, found substantial differences between them in the degree of attachment residents felt toward their community. Not surprisingly, length of residence in the community, higher social standing, and a later stage in the life cycle lead to a greater sense of community, more sorrow when forced to think about leaving, and greater interest in local affairs (Goudy 1990, 189). Similarly, Flora and Flora (1988), in a study of midwestern rural communities following the farm crisis of the mid-1980s, found that the localities that had flourished during that period manifested the ability to tolerate controversy, to take advantage of outside resources, and to define their community broadly, including collaboration with adjoining places. Other recent studies such as Green et al. (1990) and John, Batie, and Norris (1988) find that the capacity of rural localities for social organization is more important than location, natural resources, and other endowments in differentiating rural localities that are thriving from those that are not.

No less socially and economically dependent than other rural communities, the communities analyzed by these studies suggest the possibility of new and effective forms of cooperation and collaboration emerging from today's rural conditions. These and other recent research studies support the feasibility and efficacy of rural institutional innovation.

THE PEOPLE LEFT BEHIND: MINORITY AND PERSISTENT-POVERTY COMMUNITIES

Many rural localities are disadvantaged not only by increased dependence and loss of autonomy but also by persistent poverty. Many have not changed their relative income position since a 1960s presidential commission on rural poverty labeled them "the people left behind." The proportion of the population falling below federal poverty guidelines has, in recent years, been greater in rural America than in urban America and has been growing. As in urban America, the rural poor tend to be highly concentrated. Regions such as the Black Belt of the rural South have high concentrations of low-income population. The U.S. Department of Agriculture reports more than 240 nonmetropolitan counties as persistently poor because they have fallen in the lowest quintile in per capita income for the past forty years (Bender et al. 1985). Although nationally a majority of the rural poor are white, most of the persistent-poverty counties include high concentrations of minority population. In rural areas as well as urban, African-Americans, Native Americans, and Hispanics are more likely to be poor and to be concentrated in poor communities.

It is one of the paradoxes of social organization that those who stand to benefit most from organization tend to participate least. More associations representing a greater range of interests are found in wealthier than in poorer communities regardless of race or ethnicity. Even where organizations exist, participation is highly related to income (Goudy 1990). Social class is a powerful determinant of the extent of organization and its effectiveness.

Lacking a viable economic basis for a local economy and with little to sell in the marketplace other than labor, poor rural localities tend to have few indigenous organizations beyond family and church (Kramer 1970). Those voluntary associations that do exist are usually social rather than economic or political in orientation (Kramer 1970). Research shows that while there are racial and ethnic differences in patterns and styles of social organization, it is economic marginality, more than race or ethnicity, that is associated with a lack of organization. Besides churches and local governments, institutions found in poor localities have usually originated in the larger society and are predominantly controlled by external interests. Notable among these, as we have seen, are public schools. Chronic unemployment, underemployment, and general economic marginality inhibit effective participation in the institutions of the larger society as well.

CONCLUSION

As the capacity of traditional rural communities to provide social integration has diminished, national interest in community and localism has increased (e.g., Bellah et al. 1986; Schweke and Toft 1991; Center for New West 1992). Parallel explanations exist for these seemingly contradictory trends. Noting a growing national interest in community, Bellah et al. (1986) attribute the renewed interest in localism to frustration with the increasing impersonality and fragmentation of interests of a mass society: the same factors associated with declining community integration in rural areas. Perceived deficiencies in national institutions could be expected to evoke similar complaints among both rural and urban populations, since it is now national, more than local, institutions that provide the framework for both rural and urban relationships. The desire for new forms of social integration and the need for institutional innovation encompass both rural and urban America. We thus restate the problem with which we began this chapter—rural America is not alone in needing institutional innovation.

Despite the renewed national desire for community, no consensus has emerged about what community is and where it is to be found (Fowler 1991; Bellah et al. 1986). That context may help account for why polls continue to show most Americans attributing those qualities of social relationships they associate with community to rural areas and small towns. As this chapter has emphasized, those perceptions do not accord with contemporary rural community and social life. The critical question is not, then, whether the rural town represents a viable national model of community, because it no longer does, but whether another basis for community will evolve to replace it.

Recent research does not provide an answer to that question, but it does suggest some principles and considerations for new bases of rural (and urban) organization and integration.

A Need for New Measures of Well-being and of Institutional Performance

To an important degree, contemporary institutions are a product of the measures devised to reflect their performance, for example, jobs, per capita income, students' standardized test scores, physicians per 10,000 population, and so on. Measures like these generally chronicle a rural deficit. Recent research finds, however, that the economic success of rural communites is unrelated to such traditional measures as median family income, total population, presence of an interstate highway, or adjacency to a metropolitan area. (John, Batie, and Norris 1988). Instead, the research finds that local leadership, ability to mobilize resources, attitudes of the population, and cooperation among local and outside organizations are the distinguishing characteristics of "successful" rural communities.

Marshall (1986) observes that organizations tend to produce those things they measure and reward. If schools measure and reward standardized test score performance that is what they will likely achieve. Missing are measures of education, health, well-being. Institutional innovation will likely require new measures of performance and the expectations those measures reflect. There is a need for a perspective on what constitutes the good life—a perspective that can be translated into organization.

The Irrelevance of the Rural-urban Dichotomy in Policymaking

There is a widely perceived conflict between rural and urban interests (e.g., Honadle 1993), an artificial separation that reduces certain policy choices to a zero sum. The impression of conflict rules out an appreciation of the importance of a viable rural America for a stronger urban America. Examples abound. The quality of the urban work forces have, for much of this century, been dependent on the quality of education and training rural-to-urban migrants received. Similarly, for issues such as poverty, rural and urban are not important bases for policy initiative. At stake also are conflicting interests concerning food policy and agricultural policy, environmental policies, and land use. Having lost population and political power, rural interests tend to lose in a policy context that frames choices in terms of a rural-urban dichotomy. Rural localities will more likely benefit from policies addressed to both rural and urban needs.

The Need for New Organizations to Represent Rural Interests

Although analysts such as Schweke and Toft (1991) have noted the emergence of a "new localism," it is pertinent in the rural context of multicommunity regionalism to ask what is "local" and what should be the "local" basis for organization. In the early rural settlements residents depended on what their locality had to offer; they are now more often dependent on what their region has to offer. The locality, as we have emphasized, became a principal basis for rural social organization. Regions, however, have not generally become a basis for organization. Behavior has changed but there has been little concurrent change in the scope of organizations. Therefore, although many rural people have a vital interest in developments in their region, there are few organizations through which to express those interests. Regional development tends to be an aggregate of whatever actions are taken in or by individual communities.

Although the behavior of rural people generally reflects regionalization, identities and emotions often remain attached to individual towns, complicating the prospects for cooperation between towns in a region. Nevertheless a viable approach to improving the connection between interests and organization has been to emphasize the need for greater collaboration among existing organizations to achieve common interests (Center for New West 1992). A specific strategy has been a recent emphasis on multicommunity collaboration (Korsching, Borich, and Stewart 1992), which seeks to expand the resource base of localities in order to achieve goals. Communities, however spatially defined, will still need to act on their own behalf.

Even within localities there are benefits to be gained from greater collaboration among organizations. Achieving cooperation among local organizations to achieve broader community purposes is a characteristic of entrepreneurial communities (Flora and Flora 1988).

The Importance of Locality for Some Kinds of Organizations

To be sure, rural community has lost some of its identification with place, but place is not therefore irrelevant as a basis for social organization. Place continues to be an important source of resident identity and, though it may impede some forms of collaborative activity, attachment to place can motivate other forms of cooperation as Goudy's (1990) research shows. Perceived quality of life tends to retain an association with place, and some places are perceived to have more of it than others.

The relevance of place to social organization depends on the problem. Recent research shows benefits to be gained from regional, or multicommunity, collaboration in economic development, health care, and local government services (Korsching, Borich, and Stewart 1992). Conversely, the importance of locality for public education continues to be a focus of debate, both rural and urban. At stake in the debate over school choice and desegregation is the importance attached to where education occurs. Many observers argue that proximity and local support are more important to students' educational performance than differences in quantitative measures of school quality (Coleman 1987).

The Potential Advantages of Rural Organizations for Achieving Institutional Innovation

From a dominant institutional perspective the small size of rural organizations and the diversity (fragmentation) of rural interests seem to be liabilities. Those characteristics, however, in conjunction with a problem-solving orientation, are associated with a higher probability of innovation. Whether those characteristics are a liability or an asset depends on how they are perceived and acted on. Although small, informal organizations have been shown to have an advantage in creativity, those very characteristics contributed to the single fabric that constrained choices in the early rural communities (Vidich 1980). A difference is toleration of diversity. Diversity is a threat to the single fabric, but a resource to innovation (Flora and Flora 1988).

A problem-solving focus is also important to organizational innovation. In the case of rural localities, of course, an important consideration is whose definition of the problem provides the focus. If the problem is "given" by a dominant institution (the typical case), it is less likely to inspire creativity than if the problem is defined by community interaction. It is essential to identify a problem that is likely to stimulate creativity and is potentially amenable to solution.

A growing body of literature documents the creativity of rural communities in devising new approaches to education, health care, and economic development. Most studies report that local leadership has been a crucial factor.

The dominant principles of the mass society have been specialization, centralization, and standardization. Accordingly, as rural America was drawn into the mass society, conventional wisdom regarded the application of those principles as the "fix" for reducing the rural deficit. The strategy was applied, but, although rural America was significantly transformed in the process, its deficit was not "fixed." Instead the principles are being reevaluated nationally as a perceived need has emerged to "reinvent" government, health care, education, and other institutions. It is no longer self-evident that the key to rural improvement lies in extending urban institutions into the countryside.

Attention focuses increasingly on a need to accommodate diversity, to adapt to local circumstances, and to shift locus of control closer to where services are needed and provided. In this environment it is possible that some of the distinctive aspects of rural social organization, rather than being perceived as a problem to be solved, may prove instead to be aids to developing new forms of social integration. Although rural localities cannot, on their own, fix significant structural problems, recent research has shown the importance of "less visible" aspects of social organization for local innovation, change, and development. The return on public investments may well be increased if policies and programs encourage and support the creative efforts of rural localities.

21
STRUCTURES AND PATTERNS OF RURAL GOVERNANCE

RONALD J. OAKERSON

Rural areas across America present extremely varied problems. This diversity derives from variations in geography and resources, from history and its enduring institutions, and from cultural differences that stem originally from the settlement patterns of different immigrant streams. Diversity, in short, forms the basic challenge of rural governance.

Rural areas also exhibit common characteristics, however, that distinguish them from urban areas. Low population densities combined with a strong focus on the use of the natural resource base distinguish rural governance problems. Rural communities evince a preoccupation with the natural environment and its transformation parallel to the preoccupation of cities with the built environment and its development. Thus it is hardly a surprise that much of rural governance is concerned with the relationships between people and natural resources—especially land and water. Of course, rural dwellers face the same issues faced by most people anywhere—housing, education, transportation—problems that are sometimes complicated and sometimes simplified by the relatively low densities at which rural people live. Responding to its characteristic problems amid the diverse circumstances of time and place, rural America has developed a distinctive yet varied structure of governance.

In this chapter, I introduce the basic institutions of rural governance. My purpose is to describe the dimensions of the institutional endowment of rural America, as well as to analyze its overall governance structure by explaining how its parts fit together. I also examine the conduct and performance of this institutional complex in order to offer a provisional assessment of institutional performance, especially as it relates to the challenges of rural diversity.

THE INSTITUTIONS OF RURAL GOVERNANCE

The institutional arrangements for governing rural America can be represented as a kind of edifice, an elaborate institutional structure that rests on a foundation of property rights, is framed by the legal and political structure established by federalism, and operates through an infrastructure made up of local governments and civic associations, as well as state and federal administrative agencies. This set of institutions is best understood structurally, as a configuration, not as a set of independent elements. The study and the practice of rural governance require that we learn to use an "institutional architecture," a design science that fits differently constituted institutional components to one another intricately and coherently.

The Institutional Foundation: Property Rights

Private property rights establish a foundation, not only for market organization (as is widely accepted), but also for public organization. By defining and limiting the prerogatives of private action within certain bounds, property rights establish both the institutional threshold at which public action is required to accomplish a common purpose and the permissible boundaries of public action vis-à-vis private actors. Private property and public organization are complementary institutional arrangements; one should be studied in terms of the other.

In the American system of governance, property rights form the "more permanent" substructure of a somewhat "less permanent" institutional infrastructure. The more secure and immutable nature of property rights derives mainly from constitutional protection, accorded both by the Fifth Amendment, which limits the national government, and by the Fourteenth Amendment, which limits the states. Changes in property rights, though not impossible, occur very slowly and usually through a process of adjudication rather than legislation.

Differences in property rights, together with differences in the physical nature of assets or resources, account for many of the differences observed in public organization. Property rights can be divided variously, leading to different forms of public organization. The variation between land rights and water rights, discussed below, illustrate these relationships.

Land Rights. The importance of the private ownership of land in the organization of rural America can scarcely be exaggerated. Beginning in 1875, the U.S. Congress, chose to survey, divide, and sell the vast public domain that eventually stretched across the continent and today accounts for nearly 80 percent of the territory of the United States (Carstensen 1988). In an act that predated the U.S. Constitution, Congress established the legal framework for the subsequent disposal and settlement of public lands, creating the township grid used for dividing land into separate parcels in the various federal territories that were eventually organized and admitted to the union as states. The creation of private rights in land was a deliberate product of the public policy of the U.S. government, a choice that was reiterated in a series of congressional enactments over the course of the nineteenth century.

There remains, however, a large public domain within the United States (Wunderlich 1993). Rural land is presently divided roughly fifty/fifty between public and private holdings. The nation's single largest landowner by far is the U.S. government, which owns roughly 690 million acres—30 percent of the total land area of the United States. This fact alone gives the federal government a prominent local role in much of rural America: what the U.S. government owns, it governs. State and local government holdings plus Indian reservations add another 165 million acres to the total public domain, raising it to 37 percent of the entire land area. Privately held farmland amounts to some 878 million acres, 38 percent of the total land area. Nearly all agricultural land, except for grazing lands, is privately held.

In the system of private property, grazing rights are, in fact, an anomaly, one that combines public ownership with private, for-profit use. Much of the western range remains in the public domain simply because no one opted to buy it. Ranchers enjoy renewable grazing rights in accordance with public policy, but the rights can be terminated without payment of compensation. Controversy over grazing fees, often deemed too low, and charges of overgrazing have been a regular feature of the arrangement.

Private ownership of land entails a basic allocation of authority characterized by individual authority over land use and the governance of land tenure primarily through the marketplace. As freeholders, rural landowners historically have exercised wide latitude in deciding how to use their land, whether to convert it from one use to another, and when and to whom to sell it. Private discretion over use and conversion has been limited mainly by police-power regulations, in particular zoning, as determined by local authorities accountable to local communities of interest. Market control over land tenure is limited primarily by the power of eminent domain subject to the Fifth and Fourteenth amendments, which permit a governmental authority to compel sale for a public purpose but require the payment of just compensation. The nature of these constraints, judicially rather than administratively applied, leaves most of the initiative in the use and transfer of private land to landowners.

Water Rights. Considerably more complex than land rights, water rights also reflect greater diversity from state to state. The basic water right is a right to appropriate water—to withdraw it—from a water source. Unlike land rights, water rights typically do not guarantee the owner any particular amount of water (Advisory Commission on Intergovernmental Relations [ACIR] 1991). In many states water rights are tied to overlying or adjacent (riparian) lands. Thus, landowners often have an unlimited right to pump groundwater or divert water from a stream that passes through or by their land as long as the water is put to a beneficial use on site. A number of western states, however, also have established water rights based on prior appropriation and use. If, through prior use, several appropriators have established their rights to withdraw water from the same source, and if the water becomes scarce, the most senior appropriator has the superior right and may exclude others, the most junior appropriator being excluded first. In neither arrangement, however, is the water right separately transferable. If tied to land, the water right can be transferred only with the land, not separately. If tied to prior appropriation, the right held by a senior appropriator cannot be sold; instead, by failing to use it, the senior appropriator yields the right to the next most senior appropriator.

Whereas rights to land establish the basis for a land market, water rights do not similarly lay the foundation for a water market without further public organization or adjudication (Blomquist 1992). Given the common-pool nature of water resources, competing rights to appropriate or withdraw water from the same source create a situation in which no one has secure access to a fixed quantity of water. Without such a guarantee, it is difficult to assign economic value to a water right. Therefore, in order to create fully tradeable rights to water, a public organization able to define and limit withdrawals is usually needed together with an adjudication that redefines water rights as rights to specific shares of a common water source, available for any use.

Property rights in land and water establish the foundation—the institutional base—to which the elements of rural public organization are added as institutional increments. The framework for this institutional creativity, however, is supplied by federalism.

The Institutional Framework: Federalism

Federalism has had a profound effect on the character and direction of rural public organization. Although the institutional parameters of federalism have changed in basic ways over the course of American history, one feature—arguably its most important—has remained constant: State law does not depend on prior national authorization. This statement contains the central meaning of the Tenth Amendment's reference to "reserved powers," and it gives state legislatures the law-making independence they have used to generate the institutional infrastructure of rural America in all its variety. States are not in general required to seek authority to act from Congress, a legal fact that has greatly reduced the costs in time and effort of responding to diverse state and local problems. State lawmakers have freedom both to respond to local problems and to tailor their response to local circumstances.

Virtually all state policy, however, can be preempted by congressional action. Under the supremacy clause of the U.S. Constitution, the states are broadly exposed to federal preemption, which is limited only by the reach of the enumerated powers granted to Congress—powers that have been expanded virtually without limit in this century by means of judicial construction. In fact, since the decision of the U.S. Supreme Court in *Garcia v. Metropolitan Transit Authority of San Antonio* (1985), the states appear to enjoy little constitutional protection against a federal invasion of their customary powers, although in the more recent decision of *New York v. United States* (1990), a decision relevant for rural America, the Court was willing to strike down an act of Congress that obligated states to dispose of nuclear waste within state boundaries.

Nevertheless, the states retain substantial political protection against unwanted preemption, in particular when important localized concerns are shared among a minimum of forty-one senators—the number required to defeat a motion of cloture in the U.S. Senate. If carried, a motion of cloture limits debate and thus requires a vote. Among the significant consequences of federalism is equal representation of the states in the Senate, an institutional fact that gives rural states a weight in voting greatly disproportionate to the size of their populations. Although the number of rural states depends on how one defines rural, one might reasonably include all of the western states plus Alaska, part of the Midwest, most of the South, and the northern part of New England. Even a state such as California has significant rural interests to protect, though in some cases rural interests will be more than offset by strong urban interests if the issue includes a sharp urban-rural conflict. Arguably, more than half the states have important rural interests.

In sum, federalism establishes freedom to legislate at the state level but exposes states to the possibility of federal preemption, attenuated politically, however, by equal representation of the states in the Senate. Acting within this context, state legislatures have played a pivotal role in establishing the general legal framework of rural public organization. Unlike the independent position of the states in the federal system, local governments are legally dependent on the laws and constitution of each state for prior authorization to act. Moreover, local governments can only be created and vested with legal authority pursuant to appropriate legislation by the state. A very large portion of the rural institutional infrastructure was created by local communities that used the enabling authority given them by state law (ACIR 1987).

To a great extent, therefore, state policy operates indirectly, establishing the legal conditions for collective action, rather than undertaking collective action directly. Federal policy has often operated even more indirectly by seeking to encourage state provision of enabling legislation to facilitate the local participation required for the success of federal programs. Nevertheless, federal policy has affected rural areas in nearly every major facet of rural life: land, agriculture, water resources, public works, energy, parks and recreation, education, and public assistance. In a few important policy domains (public lands and agricultural commodity programs) the federal influence has been predominant. More frequently, however, state law has provided the primary organizing framework for collective action with respect to rural problems, and federal policy augments, modifies, or extends state policies.

One more point on federalism: The states are subject to constitutional constraints applied via the Fourteenth Amendment, which extends due-process rights to include protection against state action and requires that citizens of each state be accorded the "equal protection of the laws." In 1962 the Supreme Court held in *Baker v. Carr* that the demands of equal protection required that both houses of bicameral state legislatures be apportioned according to population. This ruling effectively weakened the representation of rural areas. In only about four or five states can a majority of the state population be considered rural. Outside those few states, rural power was significantly diminished, creating the opportunity for much greater influence on rural governance by nonrural populations, even as it diminished the oft-criticized influence of rural areas on urban governance.

The Institutional Infrastructure I: Local Governments

The infrastructure of rural governance is composed of a variety of local institutions, mostly units of local government. The local governments found in rural areas typically include counties, school districts, towns and townships, municipalities, and various special purpose districts, although the mix varies from one state to another. Each type of local government has a different history and serves distinct, though often overlapping, functions. Institutions of local government can be distinguished in terms of the four broad purposes for which they are created: first, to provide uniform services to local communities on a statewide basis; second, to enable local communities to provide diverse services based on local demand; third, to enable property owners to act collectively in order to increase the efficiency of economic production, usually agriculture, or conserve natural resources; and, fourth, to organize local clientele to receive and use services from state or federal agencies.

Local Governments as Instruments of State Service Provision. Counties, local subdivisions of state governments, are present in all but two states (Connecticut and Hawaii). Seventy-five percent of counties lie outside metropolitan areas. Nearly everywhere, they perform a similar set of functions, best understood as state functions carried out in local communities (e.g., registration of deeds, births, and marriages; conduct of elections; and the performance of judicial functions). Yet the organization of county government relies on locally elected officials and to a large extent on taxes levied locally to carry out functions that are not only required by state law but usually specified and regulated in detail. From one perspective, the county is an anomalous institution—an administrative arm of state government that nevertheless operates outside the state bureaucracy and is directly accountable to a local electorate.

Local Governments as Instruments of Local Settlements. Whereas counties were established to serve statewide purposes, other local governments were designed to serve local interests in local ways. Towns or townships, like counties, are a state subdivision, but less common and more variable. Originating in New England, townships gained fame from Alexis de Tocqueville's *Democracy in America,* which treats them as the paradigm case of American local self-governance. In New England, townships were planned and laid out just before being settled. Thus the establishment of a township government was simply part of the broader founding of a community; its boundaries would closely match those of a distinct settlement. In 1785 Congress decided that the public domain comprising the Northwest Territory would be divided into six-mile-square units, called townships, in order to conduct a land survey as a prelude to being sold and settled. The township grid was eventually extended to cover nearly 80 percent of the territory of the United States. Subsequently, states used the same township boundaries to organize township governments, which were then aggregated to form counties. West of the Appalachians, therefore, the township tended to acquire a less communitarian, more conventional character than the New England town, a character derived from an arbitrary set of boundaries unrelated to physical geography or intentional patterns of settlement.

Over the last century, the importance of rural townships in most states outside the Northeast has declined relative to counties; this process accelerated after the Great Depression. Townships were created expressly to serve the needs of local communities, but the local accountability and local revenue-raising capability of county governments also suited them to this purpose. Nonexistent in the South, rural townships remain basic units broadly available to serve discretionary local purposes only in the New England states plus New York, Pennsylvania, New Jersey, and Wisconsin. Elsewhere, townships have either been abandoned or their scope of authority reduced to only a few functions. Nevertheless, there remain approximately 17,500 townships nationwide, two-thirds of which are located in nonmetropolitan areas.

Townships and counties can both be viewed as "default units" of local government (Oakerson and Parks 1989). Unless a local community chooses to create another unit of government, either the township or county serves by default as the basic unit for accomplishing local purposes. Default units form the institutional base of local governance, a base to which other types of units—such as municipalities and special purpose districts—are added as increments. The nature of the institutional base varies substantially, however, among states, affecting the shape of the eventual structure.

Municipalities, variously called "villages," "boroughs," "towns" (not to be confused with those towns equivalent to townships), or cities, are added to the institutional base to serve specific communities. Surprisingly, the majority (roughly 60 percent) of the 19,200 municipalities that exist nationwide are found outside metropolitan areas. Unlike most townships and counties, municipalities tend to be created by local initiative, subject to the procedures and requirements of state law, with locally determined boundaries designed more or less to match a more densely populated area of settlement. Sometimes, a municipality overlies more than one township or county. Municipalities can be found in rural areas except in New England, where, outside of large cities, the township functions effectively as the local municipality. In Pennsylvania, townships are also considered to be municipal corporations, with the result that there is no "unincorporated" territory anywhere in the state.

Most public schools are provided by independent school districts organized separately from other local governments, though sometimes with coterminous boundaries. In many states townships initially provided for public schools; a portion of each township was originally reserved by Congress for the purpose of supporting public education. State efforts to consolidate school districts have greatly reduced their numbers, leaving less than 15,000 districts at present, nearly 60 percent of which are rural. Average school district size varies considerably, however, from state to state. Throughout most of the South, county boundaries have historically served as a basis for school district boundaries as well, creating relatively large districts. A few predominantly rural states retain large numbers of small districts, for example, Nebraska and North Dakota, as well as the rural areas of New York.

In addition to townships, counties, and school districts, which subdivide states, and municipalities, which dot the landscape, various special purpose governments have been created to undertake a single function (or a limited number of closely related functions). Special districts may or may not be fully independent of other local governments, have boundaries coterminous with those of other local governments, exercise independent taxing authority, or elect their own governing officials. The purposes that they serve include virtually any purpose associated with local government. Among the most numerous types are fire-protection districts, park districts, and water and sewer districts. Smaller than a township or bigger than a county, they are flexible and diverse. Nearly 30,000 special districts have been formed nationwide, more than half of which are found in rural areas.

Special districts generally are created in two types of circumstances. In one scenario, a community located within a large "default unit" (usually a county) seeks to organize collectively for a limited purpose as opposed to the broader set of purposes served by a municipality. For this reason, "independent" districts, which exercise their own taxing authority, tend to be found in greater numbers in states without strong townships; townships frequently organize "dependent" special districts for this purpose, which in some cases are no more than taxing districts. The other circumstance occurs when a group of municipalities or townships (or a municipality plus surrounding unincorporated territory) seek to create an overlying special district in order to obtain economies of scale on the supply side (e.g., a sanitary wastewater treatment plant) or a sufficient number of consumers to justify provision on the demand side (e.g., enough library patrons to justify the provision of a library). Two states lead the nation in their reliance on independent special districts: Illinois (where local parks and recreation are provided largely by means of special districts) and California (with its diverse natural resource base).

There is a single great exception to the pattern of local government sketched above: the Indian reservation. Unlike the other settlement units, reservations were created by authority of the U.S. government and, therefore, enjoy greater legal independence from overlying state (and local) governments. The American Indian Self-Determination and Education Act of 1975, the current enabling legislation, confers significant political autonomy on tribal reservations, allowing them to create their own institutions of self-governance (Snipp and Summers 1991). The extent to which activities conducted on reservations are subject to state law is a matter of dispute. Although the full implications of tribal autonomy are still somewhat ambiguous and subject to considerable controversy in state and local politics, many tribal governments have vigorously seized upon their legal status to pursue activities contrary to state law. Of perhaps greater long-term significance is the potential created by institutional autonomy for tribes to craft a relationship between private and collective action more consistent with the communitarian traditions of tribal cultures. In this sense tribal governments are more than local governments in the conventional American mold, for they often undertake private economic activities collectively, in the common interest of their members.

Local Governments as Instruments of Collective Action Among Agricultural Producers. Special purpose districts also are created to serve the economic interests of producers, as well as the consumer interests of community residents. Unlike organizations composed of local residents, special districts of this type are often composed of landowners and serve the interest of economic production, in most cases agriculture. The most numerous special districts in rural areas are organized around natural resources, in particular, water. Water districts vary greatly in size and are organized for purposes that include irrigation, groundwater management, drainage, local water supply, and various combinations thereof. Like other special districts, they are created primarily at local discretion.

The most numerous water-related districts are drainage districts, usually created in order to organize a group of farmers who seek to drain "excess" water from farmland but who may have difficulty agreeing on the apportionment of costs and possibly on securing the necessary level of participation (Bollens 1957). If one or two farmers whose participation is necessary act as holdouts, they can effectively negate a voluntary effort. A district is formed by drawing on state legislation that usually allows farmers to petition a local governing body or court to create the district. The petition requirement is ordinarily quite stiff, varying from one-third to two-thirds of the affected landowners or, perhaps, of the affected land area. As an organization of landowners, the district represents an institutional accommodation to and extension of private property rights. The method of finance authorized by law is usually limited to assessments against improvements to property (in addition to bonds). Once created, districts tend to be largely self-governing. They elect their own officers, raise their own revenue, and administer their own affairs with little interference from state and local governments.

Irrigation districts are created to attend to the reverse problem—moving water onto fields where rainfall patterns provide insufficient moisture to grow crops. Institutionally, they closely resemble drainage districts (Bollens 1957).

Groundwater management districts are somewhat different. In this case the problem is to manage the use of a common-pool resource where private property rights create unlimited rights to appropriate water for on-site use. Like drainage districts, groundwater districts are a form of public organization created as a complement to private property rights. The collective problem is to curtail individual use in order to maintain the water table and preserve the groundwater basin as a replenishable resource. The underground basin is also useful simply as a water storage facility. To be effective, district boundaries should conform rather closely to the natural boundaries of the underground basin. When organized as a district, overlying proprietors are able to act collectively, foreclosing holdouts and apportioning water quotas and costs among users. Districts that manage groundwater supplies also frequently engage in related activities, such as importing water to replenish a basin, maintaining barriers to saltwater intrusion (along the West Coast), supplying water to consumers, and irrigation. As noted in the foregoing discussion of property rights, an adjudication to create quantifiable rights may enable districts to establish a water market based on tradeable water rights that are no longer tied to the ownership of overlying land (Blomquist 1992).

Local Governments as Instruments of Clientele Organization for State or Federal Services. Local public organizations also have been created in rural areas with the main purpose of receiving and organizing the use of services from state or federal agencies. Soil and water conservation districts and local farmers' organizations tied to county extension offices are the two principal instances.

Soil conservation districts, in fact, present an interesting contrast to water districts. The soil conservation problem is intrinsically different from the water problems typically addressed by districts. Drainage, irrigation, and groundwater all present problems of spatial externality within a local community—they involve groups of adjacent landowners or land users who need to act collectively in order to advance their individual self-interest. The district is a device for facilitating such group action among a community of freeholders. Soil conservation presents a problem of temporal externality—it is concerned with actions that maximize net income at one particular time but diminish the value of the resource and thus reduce the stream of income from the resource over time. Farmers who are pressed by market conditions (and commodity price supports) toward the adoption of short-term survival strategies may be unwilling or unable to adopt strategies directed at long-term investment in soil conservation (Napier 1991). Such investments require forgoing present income for future income. Local farmers who act collectively are no better able to overcome this circumstance than farmers who act individually.

Not surprisingly, soil conservation districts originated from a broader federal initiative, not from the initiative of local farmers (Bollens 1957). Soil conservation was considered a national problem but one whose solution depended on local circumstances and information. The result was an intergovernmental arrangement that connected the federal Soil Conservation Service (SCS) with state conservation committees and local conservation districts. The commonality around which districts were to be organized was a common set of conservation practices, appropriately fitted to local circumstances. The state legislation for creating soil conservation districts was based on model legislation prepared by the SCS and recommended to all state governors in 1937 by President Franklin D. Roosevelt. The formation of a district typically requires only a small number of local petitioners, who present their petition to the state soil conservation committee for action.

About half of the existing soil conservation districts have boundaries that are coterminous with local government boundaries, usually counties, thus they fail in many cases to realize the objective of creating districts that conform to variable topographical conditions. District activities are financed mainly by federal and state appropriations. The district's board of governors is rarely involved in district activities, which are instead dominated by SCS technicians. Farmers have looked upon the district not as an instrument of local collective action but as an "activity of the national government through which people are told how to farm" (Bollens 1957, 167). Although usually given the authority to adopt mandatory land-use regulations, few districts have actually used the authority. Instead the districts have become a conduit for federal and state support of voluntary conservation projects, whereby participants agree to certain practices as a condition of financial subsidy. Politically, the districts are an important source of clientele support for the SCS in Congress.

County extension agents originated with the Smith-Lever Act of 1914, which provided for a program to disseminate information on improved methods of farming being developed by federally supported agricultural colleges and experiment stations. Because county agents were to be financed jointly by federal and state governments, complementary state action was required to implement the program. Many states decided, much as in the later case of soil conservation, that farmers should be collectively organized to facilitate the dissemination of information (Olson 1965). This recognition—sometimes a requirement of state funding—led to the formation of "farm bureaus." Functionally, farm bureaus resembled soil conservation districts, created to organize the local dissemination of information, although institutionally they were private, voluntary organizations, which do not require an enabling act. Simultaneously, they served the purpose of organizing a local clientele to support the provision of services supplied by federal agencies, including the Cooperative Extension Service associated with the U.S. Department of Agriculture. Local farm bureaus soon affiliated to create the American Farm Bureau Federation, which continues to organize clientele support for the Cooperative Extension Service.

There are still other local clientele organizations. Locally elected committees of farmers advise the implementation of agricultural stabilization policies in local areas, which are administered by an agent of the federal Agricultural Stabilization and Conservation Service. Established in this case by federal law, the committees serve the familiar purpose of organizing the local delivery of a federal service. Other clientele groups are often organized as cooperatives (e.g., farm cooperatives or rural electric cooperatives) that receive services or other benefits from state or federal agencies. Although not created or expressly authorized by government, they are important elements of the local institutional infrastructure relevant to rural governance.

The Institutional Infrastructure II: State and Federal Agencies

Both state and federal governments have created multiple agencies that produce services or (less frequently) administer regulations related to rural America. The service-producing agencies divide mainly into three categories: direct service agencies that supply services directly to individuals in specific localities, auxiliary service agencies that supply auxiliary or intermediate services to local agencies, and informational agencies that disseminate information for use by individuals through a local governmental institution.

The direct service agencies can be viewed as nonlocal agencies (i.e., agents of nonlocal governments) carrying out local functions. The services convey benefits directly to individuals, rather than to other service producers, many of whom are users of public lands. Included are state forest and parks agencies, plus the U.S. Forest Service, National Park Service, Bureau of Land Management, and Fish and Wildlife Service, all of which represent state and federal governments in their roles as local property owners. Yet they pay no local property tax, and in many ways they displace local governments, providing, for example, their own roads, police, and fire protection. One of their major functions is to regulate the relationships among the heterogeneous uses of public lands, in particular, the relationships between extractive and nonextractive activities (e.g., timber production versus recreation).

The political relationships that sustain these agencies differ substantially (Clarke and McCool 1985). The U.S. Forest Service is a highly professional agency historically dominated by professional foresters, who place considerable emphasis on research and scientific forest management based on a sustained yield philosophy (J. Wilson 1989). The National Park Service, which manages similar lands, is more concerned with managing people than natural resources and, consequently, is more sensitive to a variety of political constituencies and to public opinion (J. Wilson 1989). The Bureau of Land Management is more nearly a clientele agency, closely tied to its principal beneficiaries, ranchers who graze their herds on public lands. The Fish and Wildlife Service, an agency with a checkered history, administers wildlife refuges (now concentrated in Alaska) and fish hatcheries. Fishers and hunters may owe the availability of fish and game in part to the service, but they don't usually fish and hunt on land the service administers. Because Fish and Wildlife, compared to the other direct service agencies, has a weak public image and lacks a strong, well-defined clientele relationship, it is often overcommitted and underfunded compared to the others (Clarke and McCool 1985).

The auxiliary service agencies are focused almost entirely on water resources. Four federal agencies are authorized to build and maintain water resource facilities: the U.S. Army Corps of Engineers, Bureau of Reclamation (BOR), Soil Conservation Service (SCS), and Tennessee Valley Authority (TVA). Of these, the corps and the SCS are the only agencies that operate nationwide. The SCS specializes in small watersheds and upstream protection, while the corps concentrates on larger scale projects. The BOR operates only in seventeen western states, reflecting its original mission to develop irrigation works in order to assist in the "reclamation" of arid and semiarid lands. Large-scale water resource projects, however, are designed to serve multiple purposes, effectively bringing the BOR into competition with the Corps of Engineers. The TVA is the only regionally focused federal water resource agency. Although at one time considered a model for integrated water resource development, the TVA has not been closely emulated in other parts of the country. The political viability of all four agencies is tied to clientele support, much of which is organized through the local institutional infrastructure. Although producing similar services, each agency serves a somewhat different clientele (Clarke and McCool 1985).

With the partial exception of the TVA, the federal water resource agencies are mainly suppliers of large-scale intermediate services, on which state and local public agencies draw to deliver services directly to individuals. Large water resource projects (e.g., constructing and maintaining dams and reservoirs) fall largely into this category. Although flood control can be viewed as a direct service, it is also a pure public good, lacking separable individual users. Otherwise, water resource projects supplied by the corps or the BOR serve indirect purposes, such as water supply and recreation, that are ultimately provided and managed by other public agencies, either state or local. They function, therefore, as large-scale producers of selected intermediate goods and facilities, operating in the context of a multiorganizational structure of service producers.

The Cooperative Extension Service and (in the main) the Soil Conservation Service deliver quintessential local services, usually to individual farmers; in this sense they parallel direct service producers. Yet, like auxiliary service producers, they operate through an infrastructure of local organization that, to earlier observers, began to resemble a federally created and managed system of rural local government or "agricultural democracy" (Grodzins 1966). Both agencies principally collect, assemble, and disseminate information, usually take it directly to individuals, adapting it to their circumstances. Both entities have acquired a dependency on local political constituencies that make autonomous "federal direction" of the system problematic and render their delivery of services to specific communities highly dependent on locally prevailing political relationships. In some cases this dependency can mean service that is focused on local elites. Efforts to broaden the mission of cooperative extension to include information relevant to local communities on a wider range of topics, especially community governance and economic development, have been underfunded and therefore have met with only mixed success (Brown and Glasgow 1991). Broadening the range of information disseminated means broadening the clientele being served. Although there are potential payoffs to the agency, the broader clientele may be less easily defined and mobilized and therefore more difficult to use as a source of political support.

INSTITUTIONAL CONDUCT AND PERFORMANCE

A typical rural area contains a host of local governments of various types: townships, school districts, villages, various water-related districts, fire districts, cemetery districts, a soil conservation district—each often with its own governing body. Such systems of public organization have often been subjected to a standard critique: divided authority fragments responsibility; overlapping jurisdictions confuse accountability and frustrate coherent policy formation; lack of central direction dilutes policy and inhibits effective implementation. American local government is regularly criticized for its fragmentation of authority among more than 83,000 local governments. More than 54,000 local governments (roughly 65 percent of the total) are located in nonmetropolitan areas, making population per government more than five times as great in metropolitan than in nonmetropolitan America. If the standard recommendations of many administrative reformers were followed, the result would be the dissolution of most of the institutional infrastructure now used in rural governance (Ostrom 1989).

Yet the fragmentation decried by critics is closely linked to the local capacity for collective action prized by rural communities throughout the country. The nature of local decision making in this system goes well beyond operational and policymaking autonomy on the part of established local governments. It extends as well to the constitutional autonomy of local people, whether as settlements seeking to provide themselves with services and amenities or as groups of economic producers seeking greater productivity. The ability of local groups to form new public instrumentalities, including municipalities and special purpose districts, is a constitutional capability that allows local communities not simply to act collectively, but to create the required institutional infrastructure to act collectively, infrastructure that is often closely matched to local circumstances.

The formation of new special purpose districts, for example, is frequently preferred to relying on existing local governments because of the districts' flexible boundaries and lower decision-making costs. Local government boundaries, especially those laid out on a township grid, are unlikely to correspond closely to the domain of a specific problem (e.g., a drainage area). Moreover, a group that wants to proceed with a project such as drainage or irrigation is able to do so by means of a district, without having to involve others in their collective decision making, except to a limited extent at the initial point of district formation. Local consent is the main political constraint on the decision to constitute a district. Although the decision-making (transaction) costs of constituting a district can be quite high within the affected community, they are lower than the often prohibitive costs of decision making in a purely voluntary arrangement, and they may often be lower than trying to accomplish the same purpose through an existing large-scale bureaucracy or by securing action from a large, general-purpose jurisdiction, such as a state. At the same time, unintended costs to others (the social costs of public action) can be minimized by the local character of the district and the need for a relatively high level of local consensus. The system allows local solutions to local problems to be implemented without waiting on overlying authorities to act, provided that those affected can forge a substantial consensus.

Local collective action reduces the dependency of rural communities on state and federal bureaucracies. Instead of relying on administrative coordination, local governments and special districts coordinate their own activities on the basis of mutual consent, subject to the rule-making capabilities of state legislatures and the judicially enforceable obligations they may create among themselves. Collective action can occur at multiple scales of organization—smaller units nested within larger units—on the basis of a qualified independence among overlapping jurisdictions. Instead of an overarching bureaucracy, multiorganizational arrangements emerge to take care of mutual interests, capture limited economies of scale, coordinate operations as needed, and resolve conflicts (Ostrom 1989). When such arrangements are formed among independent local units, jointly organized intermediate bodies, and overlying state or federal agencies, the resulting configuration takes on the shape of industrial organization typical of market economies (Ostrom and Ostrom 1965). Just as in a highly differentiated private industry (e.g., the computer industry or motion picture industry), the various components of a good or service are produced by different organizations, each operating at a different scale of production, and linked by contractual arrangements. The chief difference between the public and private sectors is that most of the producers in a public service industry are government agencies, each one accountable to its own political constituency.

For example, rural areas are often served by a public water industry—not a water bureaucracy—that consists of a large number of small local water agencies that supply water to consumers and, perhaps, regulate a local water source; a smaller number of regional agencies that manage larger scale sources of supply, such as surface reservoirs and aqueducts; and a still smaller number of state and federal overhead agencies that supply information and expertise and undertake the development of new sources of supply (Ostrom 1971). The local water agencies may include private water companies, municipal water agencies, and water districts of various types, whereas regional agencies may be organized by overlying special districts, county governments, or state or federal governments. The large overhead agencies include both state water departments and federal agencies, each specializing in particular types of water resource development. Larger-scale public agencies offer economies of scale as well as the opportunity to obtain financial support through the political bargains struck among a large number of political constituencies. The latter results in the federal subsidy of development programs that often benefit rural areas. At the same time, smaller-scale public organizations are left relatively free to respond to local problems in local ways.

Similar industrylike arrangements can be found in nearly every arena of local public organization, especially in metropolitan areas outside central cities (ACIR 1987). The exact shape of the industry depends, however, on the nature of the good being supplied, as well as on the previous institutional endowment. Small school districts, for example, often operate in the context of regional agencies that supply auxiliary services to districts and undertake the production of specialized kinds of education, such as vocational-technical education, education for severely handicapped children, or "alternative" education (see ACIR 1988, 1992). Sometimes regional agencies are organized by local districts acting jointly; other times, they are organized by state education agencies to serve local districts (e.g., BOCES in New York, Intermediate Units in Pennsylvania). Either way, the functions performed regionally are fairly standard and derive from educational technologies and the scale economies inherent in the production of certain auxiliary services and service components.

This system of public organization does not conform to a single hierarchy. It is a system composed, rather, of multiple, overlapping hierarchies, loosely held together through multiorganizational and intergovernmental arrangements within the overall constitutional and legal framework of American government (Ostrom 1989). The system has developed in great part from local initiative, supplemented by state and federal initiatives in particular instances. The overall pattern of institutional development in the United States enabled rural communities to attain an extraordinary diversity of public organization. Local autonomy and influence, though never absolute, is almost always considerable.

The aggregate performance of the system is subject to considerable variation, however, both from one part of rural America to another and from one type of rural problem to another. The performance of local governments in general varies widely, whether rural or urban. The institutional variety characteristic of the system as a whole is unevenly distributed among the fifty states. Some states have built a rich infrastructure of rural institutions; others have not. As a result, collective problem-solving capabilities vary substantially across the American countryside.

Morton Grodzins (1966), a path-breaking student of American federalism, argued that citizen participation in rural communities tended to exceed that found in urban communities. He observed a relatively high degree of participation across various types of rural governments, including those created in response to federal initiative. He was careful, however, to distinguish participation from control. There is considerable anecdotal evidence for the persistence of rural political machines in some areas, especially areas with a high incidence of poverty or dominance by a single industry, such as the Appalachian coalfield of eastern Kentucky and southern West Virginia (Caudill 1963, Perry 1972). Under conditions of severe underemployment of human resources, public goods often have local value primarily for the private benefits they engender: jobs provided, contracts awarded, and favors done. These circumstances nurture machine politics in urban or rural communities alike. The local machine dominates the distribution of selective private benefits inherent in the provision of a range of local public goods and services—schools, roads, even welfare. Some rural areas exhibit a more distinct class structure, which is reflected in elite dominance of local governance. Distinct class structure is also more prevalent in states where local government has been dominated by county-level institutions, which afford fewer opportunities than a strong township system for the expression of political diversity through local governments.

Empirical evidence solidly supports the proposition that, other things equal, small local government agencies outperform large local government agencies on a number of indicators related to the provision of local services that involve face-to-face relationships, such as police and education (Ostrom 1976, Niskanen and Levy 1974, Kiesling 1967). Rural areas that are endowed with relatively small default units (e.g., strong townships) and with small school districts may, therefore, be better equipped to address some types of local problems. These studies suggest that the major problem across rural America is not the lack of uniformity in local institutions but insufficient diversity in some states of the institutional repertoire available to local communities.

The principal limitation on the technical efficiency of local governments as producers of services in rural areas is not the number of small governments (so-called fragmentation) but low population density. Consolidation of governments cannot alter a demographic fact. Given low densities, consolidation creates "scale" only by sacrificing proximity (increasing service-delivery distances and thus diminishing the sought-after economies) and frequently community as well. In the case of schools, consolidation can hinder effectiveness by aggregating the school population to the point that students do not share a common community background and the "social capital" that community provides (Salamon and Davis-Brown 1990). If particular services or service components can benefit from consolidation, various institutional arrangements are available for organizing such services separately, including intergovernmental agreements and special purpose districts that create organizational overlays.

The successful use of special purpose districts to solve collective problems is well documented in the few cases that have been carefully studied (Blomquist 1992, Hawkins 1976). Given a relatively open-ended enabling environment created by state law, local communities are frequently able to develop complex and elaborate arrangements of self-governance in relation to important local resources, often linking themselves as well to external sources of support. Such efforts are not successful in every instance, however (Blomquist 1992). A heavy reliance on local initiative and local consent can never ensure success. Therefore, a degree of tolerance for local failure is necessary in order to maintain local autonomy and the opportunity to learn from local failures. From this perspective, the best prospect for continued improvement of institutional performance is continued attention to institutional design and creativity, reshaping and extending the institutional capabilities of various communities of interest to respond to problems. The alternative is state and federal preemption of local problem solving.

Consider, for example, recent developments in the organization of soil conservation efforts. The apparent inability of soil and water conservation districts to control soil erosion adequately through the collective action of farmers in specific communities is predictable from the nature of the problem. The federal government opted in 1985 for a more aggressive effort to regulate farming practices, using participation in farm price-support programs to leverage the adoption of soil conservation measures (Napier 1991). The designation of the SCS to administer these regulations has cast an agency with a strong tradition of delivering helpful advice and information, backed by subsidies, in the politically difficult role of regulating and, if need be, penalizing members of their clientele.

The nature of the soil erosion problem, although not responsive to local district control, may also not be well suited to federally imposed controls. The need for local information and adaptation to local circumstances remains, just as when the federal soil conservation program was initiated during the New Deal. Moreover, one of the principal economic factors now contributing to the cost-effectiveness of soil conservation is the social cost of the water-borne, off-site side effects of soil erosion (Napier 1991). These effects vary substantially from one area to another. Conservation measures that are economically justified in one area may not be justified in another. Watershed-based jurisdictions may, therefore, provide the more appropriate domain in which to undertake the regulation of soil conservation practices, encompassing agricultural producers and those affected by erosion-based water pollution in the same public jurisdiction (Lovejoy and Fletcher 1991). Greater, more carefully crafted institutional diversity, not uniform national policies, provides these problem-solving capabilities.

The federal agencies involved in rural America are no more subject to an effective hierarchy of authority than their local counterparts. Scattered through at least three major cabinet departments—agriculture, interior, and defense—similar agencies such as the Corps of Engineers and the Bureau of Reclamation, or the Forest Service and the National Park Service have no common superior except the President and Congress. This freedom has led to a durable pattern of independence and rivalry among related agencies. Often the object of strenuous criticism and determined reform efforts, this system nonetheless has survived and continues to thrive. One factor in the success of the federal infrastructure is how closely it is adapted to the state and local infrastructure within the framework of federalism. Moreover, interagency rivalry often spurs federal agencies to higher levels of achievement (Clarke and McCool 1985). Instead of establishing monopoly suppliers (often thought to be inherent in public organization), Congress has created alternative vendors from which to choose. Moreover, the differing values and interests that are at stake in the governance of rural America often find forceful advocates in the political forum among the various agencies that share rural responsibilities.

CONCLUSION: FACING THE FUTURE

Perhaps the fundamental challenge facing institutions of rural governance is to accommodate increasing levels of demand on rural areas from nonrural constituencies. Environmentalism, tourism, waste disposal, access to land and water—all these issues increasingly concern nonrural residents whose aggregate demand for rural resources far exceeds the demands of rural people. The decline in the percentage of the U.S. population living in rural areas (not, it should be noted, an absolute decline in rural population, which has held steady) exposes rural residents increasingly to policies imposed by nonrural residents. Such constituencies almost certainly will be represented in many decisions affecting the future of rural America and the resources it holds, a conclusion that can be supported by pointing to the large percentage of rural land area owned by the U.S. government—land in which metropolitan residents are, so to speak, the majority shareholders.

As nonrural demands on rural America multiply, urban-rural conflict can be expected to increase as well. For example, Allegany County, New York, the state's poorest and one of its most rural counties, recently resorted to 1960s-style civil disobedience and threats of violence to turn back a state-led effort to locate a nuclear waste dump in the county (Fitchen 1991). In the past the relatively low salience of most rural issues for nonrural people ordinarily worked in favor of rural interests. Numerous interests have emerged, however, often without strong roots in the life of rural America, for whom rural issues have high salience. In this new setting, the low salience of rural issues among the general population no longer serves the interests of rural communities. In short, rural America needs friends—political allies—from outside the rural community itself. Rural communities must convince others that rural values are important to nonrural communities and that rural communities remain the most reliable trustees of those values. In order to make this argument convincingly, rural America may have to give up some of its former claim on the federal treasury and concede some of its political autonomy, especially concerning the use of natural resources.

The basic case for sustaining the institutional infrastructure of rural governance as it has developed over the last two centuries is found in the stunning diversity of the American countryside. From the stone-walled farmland of New England, to the lake regions of the upper Midwest, to the irrigation communities of southern California, each locale presents unique problems and opportunities, addressed largely by a homegrown collection of local governments, civic groups, and professional associations. Rural diversity is clearly a source of material and cultural values prized by rural and nonrural residents alike (Castle 1993). This basic fact remains relevant even in the face of increasing rural-urban interdependence and interpenetration.

If there is an immediate threat to the effective governance of rural diversity, it comes from potential monopolies of power and influence: from reformers who seek to create neat hierarchies (Ostrom 1989), from agencies that grow too large relative to their rivals (see Clarke and McCool 1985), and from congressional intolerance of local accommodations and the political temptation to preempt state and local creativity by imposing national solutions on what are perceived to be national problems. In the long run, such strategies threaten the institutional foundation and framework of rural governance, and carry consequences that extend far beyond the residents of the countryside.

NOTES

I would like to thank Barbara Baldwin, Bob Black, Bill Blomquist, Emery Castle, and Elizabeth Davis for their very helpful comments on an earlier draft.

22

RURAL EDUCATION AND TRAINING: MYTHS AND MISCONCEPTIONS DISPELLED

RUY A. TEIXEIRA

This chapter provides an overview of human capital issues facing rural America, where human capital is defined as the productivity-enhancing skills acquired by individuals through education, training, and other means. My purpose is not to be comprehensive, but rather to stimulate discussion on how rural human capital development can best serve the overall goal of rural economic development.

BASIC FACTS ON HUMAN CAPITAL LEVELS IN RURAL AMERICA

Human capital levels are generally assumed—correctly—to be lower in rural (nonmetro)[1] America than in urban (metro) America. Close scrutiny of the data reveals, however, that the magnitude of these differences is less than usually supposed.

Educational Attainment

The most obvious way to compare levels of educational attainment of rural and urban workers is to look at summary measures of educational attainment across the two geographical designations and assess the magnitude of the differences between them. This information provides an important baseline for comparison, and I provide such information in considerable detail.

Another way to compare educational attainment across rural and urban ar-

Table 22.1. Educational attainment of people aged 25 and older, 1990 (in percent)

Schooling Completed	Metro	Nonmetro
Graduate or professional degree	8.0	4.5
Bachelor's degree	14.5	8.5
Associate degree	6.4	5.4
Some college, no degree	19.5	16.1
High school graduate	28.6	34.7
High school dropout	23.0	30.8

Source: Greenberg, Swaim, and Teixeira 1993.

eas is to consider the usefulness of a given level of education to individuals in those areas. It may be the case that a level of education relatively low by urban standards suits many rural individuals well. Therefore, I accompany the following presentation of the basic data on educational attainment (and other aspects of human capital) with a consideration of variations in demand for skill across rural and urban areas.

1990 census data indicate that nonmetropolitan (nonmetro) adults have somewhat lower educational attainment levels than their metropolitan (metro) counterparts (Table 22.1). In contrast to earlier periods, however, the metro and nonmetro distributions have some important similarities. In both areas, a typical worker has a high school diploma but not a bachelor's degree. This broad middle of the education distribution comprises 55 percent of the metro work force and a nearly identical 56 percent of the nonmetro labor force. By contrast, in 1960 the median rural educational attainment was only 9.3 years, compared to 11.1 in urban areas.

Still, a rural gap in educational attainment remains, both at the top and at the bottom of the distribution. In 1990, 31 percent of the nonmetro population aged 25 and older had not finished high school, compared to 23 percent of the metro population. A rural gap in educational attainment is also evident at the top end of the distribution. Forty-eight percent of metro adults attended at least some college, 23 percent earned a bachelor's degree, and 8 percent a professional or graduate degree. The corresponding nonmetro shares were significantly lower at 35, 13, and 5 percent.

It is important to emphasize, however, that the long-term trend has been for the educational attainment gap between rural and urban areas to close, a convergence illustrated by calculating high school completion rates for younger cohorts. As shown in Table 22.2, the nonmetro gap in high school graduation rates among these cohorts was halved between 1971 and 1991.

Table 22.2. Educational attainment of 25- to 44-year-olds, selected years

Item	1971	1975	1979	1983	1987[a]	1991
Completed high school			Percent			
Metro	73.7	79.6	83.2	85.7	87.1	87.7
Nonmetro	65.6	70.7	77.8	80.8	82.7	83.7
			Percentage points			
Nonmetro gap	8.1	8.9	5.4	4.9	4.4	4.0
Completed four or more						
years of college			Percent			
Metro	17.0	21.4	24.0	26.8	27.5	27.8
Nonmetro	10.8	13.8	17.5	18.0	16.2	16.2
			Percentage points			
Nonmetro gap	6.2	6.6	6.5	8.8	11.3	11.6

Source: Greenberg, Swaim, and Teixeira 1993.

[a] The metro/nonmetro classification of counties was revised between 1983 and 1987 using 1980 census data.

On the upper end of the distribution, though, the rural-urban gap in completing a bachelor's or more advanced degree actually increased after 1971. Specifically, the share of the metro population ages 25–44 with at least four years of college increased by 10.8 percentage points between 1971 and 1991, while the nonmetro increase was a smaller 5.4 points. Note, however, that this divergence exaggerates actual rural-urban differences in school continuation, because it reflects, at least in part, an intensified rural brain-drain (rural youth attending college increasingly migrated to urban areas where the economic returns on their education were higher). Note also that, given the existence of this differential in returns to education, some of the rural-urban gap in college completion rates—whatever its true magnitude—may simply reflect a rational approach to investment in education by rural individuals.

On balance, then, these rural-urban comparisons of educational attainment indicate some grounds for concern (particularly in terms of college completion rates) but do not suggest a massive human capital deficit in rural America. Instead, the bulk of the rural work force appears to match up fairly well with their counterparts in urban areas.

Educational Achievement

The data in the previous section suggest that the educational attainment levels of average rural workers pose less of a problem than generally supposed. It could, however, be objected that the attainment levels of these rural workers are not the issue, achievement levels are. In other words, the typical rural student may now be staying in school and getting a diploma, but, due to the poor quality of rural schools, he or she may be learning much less than his or her urban counterpart.

By this logic, the current abundance (by historical standards) of rural high school graduates could be deceptive: these graduates may not know enough to be good workers. A related concern is that rural high schools may not adequately prepare their best students for the most challenging colleges and universities. Thus the skills acquired by rural students could still be a severe problem despite the historical upgrading in terms of years of schooling.

To measure levels of student achievement, it is necessary to turn to the National Assessment of Educational Progress (NAEP), a nationwide, representative survey of the cognitive achievement levels of students across the United States. The NAEP was started in 1969 as an annual survey of 9-, 13-, and 17-year-olds. (Since 1980 it has been done biennially.) The NAEP is the only existing data set which allows statistically valid comparisons of achievement levels of students in the United States. Up to 100,000 students are tested during each survey year, distributed so that 4,000–6,500 students are tested in a given subject at each of the three age/grade levels. Because the main interest here is in the quality of the rural work force, I will focus my analysis on the twelfth-graders in the data set—the next cohort to be entering the work force.

The NAEP usually tests each subject area only every other test year. Therefore, to look at a full range of subjects, it was necessary to look at two recent assessments, 1988 and 1990. The 1988 NAEP tested students in reading, history, civics, geography, and writing. The 1990 NAEP tested student knowledge of math and science, and also tested reading, the only subject repeated from 1988.

The mean achievement scores of twelfth-graders broken down into metro-nonmetro categories are remarkably similar (Table 22.3). The only overall subject in which there is a statistically significant difference at the 95 percent level of confidence is reading in 1988. Note, however, that even this modest difference disappears in the 1990 data because metro twelfth-graders improved only slightly in reading from 1988 to 1990, while nonmetro twelfth-graders had a much larger increase in achievement levels. Statistically significant, though small, differences also exist in two subfields of mathematics, algebra/functions and measurement. The mathematics composite, however, which measures overall achievement across all fields of mathematics, shows no significant difference between metro and nonmetro students.

Table 22.3. Mean achievement scores of twelfth-graders

Subject	Metro	Nonmetro
Reading (1988)	288.0 (1.0)	284.1 (1.7)[a]
Reading (1990)	288.7 (1.2)	288.3 (1.8)
History (1988)	295.7 (1.2)	292.8 (2.1)
Civics (1988)	296.6 (1.4)	296.0 (1.7)
Geography (1988)	293.5 (1.2)	291.2 (2.2)
Writing (1988)	223.9 (1.6)	224.8 (2.1)
Science Composite (1990)	293.7 (1.5)	292.4 (2.4)
Life sciences	295.8 (1.3)	295.4 (2.2)
Physical science	291.2 (1.8)	289.0 (2.8)
Earth and space science	291.8 (1.6)	290.6 (2.9)
Nature of science	298.6 (1.6)	296.9 (2.6)
Mathematics Composite (1990)	296.3 (1.3)	293.1 (2.1)
Algebra and functions	298.0 (1.3)	293.6 (2.2)[a]
Geometry	297.5 (1.5)	293.0 (2.5)
Measurement	295.3 (1.4)	291.6 (2.2)[a]
Numbers and operations	295.0 (1.2)	292.4 (1.9)
Data analysis and statistics	295.3 (1.3)	295.0 (2.3)
Estimation (1990)	293.1 (1.2)	293.7 (1.6)

Source: Teixeira and Greenberg, forthcoming.

Note: Standard errors in parentheses.
[a] Metro-nonmetro difference is significant at the 95 percent level of confidence.

Although the general pattern of results in Table 22.3 does indicate a very slight metro advantage, the data clearly do not suggest that the average rural student is being shortchanged by inferior schools.[2] All the differences in the table are less than 5 points on a scale that theoretically ranges from 0 to 500. (Over 90 percent of twelfth-graders actually score between 225 and 375, still a large range.) In one subject (writing) nonmetro students even score a little higher than their urban counterparts.

It could still be argued that a comparison of metro and nonmetro twelfth-graders is misleading because of higher nonmetro dropout rates. These high nonmetro dropout rates mean, the argument runs, that the worst students are filtered out of nonmetro school systems before the twelfth-grade test is even administered. Hence the deceptive equivalence between metro and nonmetro students: nonmetro schools are worse, but the skimming phenomenon gives them better kids to work with, propping up the average nonmetro score.

This hypothesis can be tested by looking at the scores of eighth-graders in the three subjects of math, science, and reading. Very few students have

Table 22.4. Mean achievement scores of eighth-graders

Subject	Metro	Nonmetro
Reading (1990)	261.5 (1.3)	259.6 (2.0)
Science Composite (1990)	262.9 (1.7)	263.7 (1.6)
Mathematics Composite (1990)	266.2 (1.4)	261.5 (1.5)[a]

Source: Teixeira and Greenberg, forthcoming.

Note: Standard errors in parentheses.
[a] Metro-nonmetro difference is significant at the 95 percent level of confidence.

dropped out of school before eighth grade, so if the similarities between metro and nonmetro scores are caused by the greater number of nonmetro dropouts, we would expect greater metro/nonmetro differences among eighth-graders than among twelfth-graders.

As the data in Table 22.4 show, there is nothing in the eighth-grade data to support the hypothesis that metro/nonmetro score equivalence is driven by the relatively high nonmetro drop-out rate. In science, for example, eighth-grade nonmetro students actually do marginally better than metro students (although the difference is not statistically significant). And, while metro eighth-graders do score slightly higher than nonmetro eighth-graders in math and reading, only the math difference—less than 5 points on a 500-point scale—is statistically significant.

Because differences in the United States are often regional in character, it is useful to further disaggregate the data into four geographic regions (Table 22.5). Across most regions, these data confirm the previously observed pattern of only small differences between metro and nonmetro average achievement levels. Note, however, that in the South substantially larger nonmetro/metro differences can be observed. But even here the differences are not large—no more than 9 points in any one subject. The most surprising finding from this table is that in the northeastern and midwestern states nonmetro students generally score higher than metro students. This phenomenon is particularly noticeable for nonmetro science students in the Midwest, whose average science score is a statistically significant 12 points higher than metro science students. Thus, with the possible exception of the South, it does not appear that nonmetro students are learning less in school than metro students. Indeed, in some areas of the country they appear to be learning more.

Table 22.6 presents a further disaggregation of the data by the commonly used Beale system of detailed urban/rural categories. In reading, the population size of the county does not seem to have any obvious direct effect on

Table 22.5. Mean achievement scores of twelfth-graders, by region

	Metro		Nonmetro	
Northeast				
Reading (1988)	286.9	(2.4)	289.8	(5.5)
Reading (1990)	289.7	(2.8)	293.9	(1.3)
History (1988)	297.0	(2.6)	298.6	(16.3)
Civics (1988)	293.9	(2.6)	297.2	(10.2)
Geography (1988)	293.4	(3.2)	306.1	(5.6)[a]
Writing (1988)	231.8	(4.0)	222.8	(7.9)
Science Composite (1990)	298.5	(4.1)	303.7	(1.4)
Mathematics Composite (1990)	301.0	(2.7)	303.9	(1.0)
Midwest				
Reading (1988)	289.5	(1.3)	286.7	(4.3)
Reading (1990)	289.2	(1.0)	294.6	(2.3)[a]
History (1988)	298.0	(2.0)	297.6	(4.3)
Civics (1988)	298.5	(2.1)	304.8	(3.1)[a]
Geography (1988)	298.1	(1.3)	298.8	(3.6)
Writing (1988)	221.0	(2.3)	230.4	(2.9)[a]
Science Composite (1990)	291.6	(2.4)	303.5	(4.1)[a]
Mathematics Composite (1990)	296.9	(3.0)	299.4	(0.7)
South				
Reading (1988)	287.8	(1.5)	279.7	(1.4)[a]
Reading (1990)	287.2	(2.8)	279.2	(3.7)[a]
History (1988)	290.6	(2.0)	287.7	(2.3)
Civics (1988)	294.0	(2.5)	286.8	(3.0)[a]
Geography (1988)	284.5	(2.5)	280.9	(3.7)
Writing (1988)	215.9	(3.8)	218.9	(3.1)
Science Composite (1990)	281.7	(3.6)	275.8	(4.4)
Mathematics Composite (1990)	287.8	(1.7)	279.3	(4.5)[a]
West				
Reading (1988)	288.2	(1.7)	286.7	(4.3)
Reading (1990)	288.2	(3.0)	289.1	(4.9)
History (1988)	295.7	(2.0)	292.6	(2.7)
Civics (1988)	299.4	(3.0)	299.5	(4.1)
Geography (1988)	295.7	(2.2)	292.2	(3.8)
Writing (1988)	223.2	(2.2)	228.1	(6.4)
Science Composite (1990)	297.3	(2.8)	293.9	(9.3)
Mathematics Composite (1990)	296.3	(2.3)	296.3	(7.5)

Source: Teixeira and Greenberg, forthcoming.

Note: Standard errors in parentheses.
[a] Metro-nonmetro difference is significant at the 95 percent level of confidence.

Table 22.6. Mean math and science scores by detailed urban/rural categories (1990 data)

	Math		Science		Reading	
Metro areas						
Central counties with population of 1 million or more (Beale code 0)	292.2	(2.7)	289.7	(3.4)	285.1	(2.4)
Fringe counties with population of 1 million or more (Beale code 1)	302.0	(2.4)	299.1	(3.9)	291.3	(2.4)
Counties with populations of 250,000 to 1 million (Beale code 2)	297.3	(2.9)	295.4	(3.9)	288.4	(3.2)
Counties with populations of less than 250,000 (Beale code 3)	291.9	(2.0)	289.8	(5.4)	292.0	(2.8)
Nonmetro areas						
Counties with urban populations of 20,000 or more (Beale codes 4, 5)	299.9	(1.9)	303.3	(4.0)	292.1	(2.5)
Counties with urban populations of less than 20,000 (Beale codes 6, 7)	289.5	(2.9)	286.1	(3.8)	285.3	(3.4)
Completely rural counties (Beale codes 8, 9)	287.3	(12.9)	286.3	(13.6)	288.8	(7.2)

Source: Teixeira and Greenberg, forthcoming.

Note: Standard errors in parentheses.

students' test scores. That is, scores fluctuate with county size but not in any easily definable pattern and only over a range of 7 points.

Mathematics and science scores look somewhat different. Here it is interesting that larger nonmetro counties do quite well, better than almost all the metro categories, whereas there is a drop in scores of over 10 points when county urban population goes below 20,000. This drop is still not very large in a 500-point scale, but it does suggest that the very smallest nonmetro counties may not be able to offer their students the same educational opportunities in subjects that involve advanced facilities or teacher education as the

Table 22.7. Percentage of students enrolled in schools that offer advanced curricula

Advanced placement course	Metro	Nonmetro
American government (1988)	21.8 (3.5)	6.6 (3.8)[a]
American history (1988)	57.3 (4.2)	23.1 (6.8)[a]
English language (1988)	54.1 (4.4)	29.5 (4.1)[a]
English literature (1988)	59.9 (4.1)	24.6 (6.2)[a]
Calculus (1990)	90.4 (2.4)	48.6 (7.7)[a]
Second-year biology (1990)	75.1 (3.7)	68.3 (5.8)
Second-year chemistry (1990)	62.2 (4.4)	44.6 (7.6)[a]
Second-year physics (1990)	32.9 (4.5)	7.5 (5.7)[a]

Source: Teixeira and Greenberg, forthcoming.

Note: Standard errors in parentheses.
[a] Metro-nonmetro difference is significant at the 95 percent level of confidence.

larger counties. (Because reading scores are probably more dependent on the general quality of the student's school, rather than on particular subject offerings, they would be less likely to reflect a school district's inability to provide advanced courses.)

Although most rural twelfth-graders, even those in the smallest counties and the smallest schools, are achieving at levels equal to or only slightly worse than their urban counterparts, the fact remains that fewer rural than urban twelfth-graders go on to college, as described in the previous section. Part of the explanation for this may be that rural schools on average offer fewer advanced courses than urban schools (Table 22.7). The differences here are quite substantial. For example, only 48.6 percent of nonmetro students attend schools that offer calculus, compared to 90.4 percent of metro students. And only 7.5 percent of nonmetro students have the opportunity to take second-year physics, compared to 32.9 percent of metro students.

These data can be further broken down by Beale categories (data not shown). These data reveal that the smallest nonmetro counties offer their students fewer advanced courses than the larger ones, suggesting that students in rural areas, particularly in remote areas, may not be well prepared to go on to do college-level work or even to meet the minimum entrance requirements for some colleges.

The fact that nonmetro schools offer fewer advanced classes than metro schools (Table 22.7) may also explain why metro students are slightly more likely than nonmetro students to reach advanced levels of achievement. Table 22.8 presents calculations of the percentage of students, metro and nonmetro, who score 20 percent or more above the mean in each subject area.

Table 22.8. Percentage of twelfth-graders scoring 20 percent above the mean

	Metro	Nonmetro
Reading (1988)	4.0 (0.7)	2.8 (0.9)
Reading (1990)	4.5 (0.6)	4.0 (0.8)
History (1988)	3.9 (0.6)	2.5 (0.7)
Civics (1988)	4.4 (0.6)	4.4 (0.7)
Geography (1988)	4.7 (0.8)	3.0 (0.9)
Writing (1988)	17.8 (1.0)	17.6 (1.5)
Science Composite (1990)	9.0 (0.9)	6.4 (1.5)
Mathematics Composite (1990)	3.9 (0.6)	3.1 (0.8)

Source: Teixeira and Greenberg, forthcoming.

Note: Standard errors in parentheses.

Although the differences are not statistically significant in any of the subjects, the data do display a uniform pattern: more metro than nonmetro students score at advanced levels.

To summarize, the message conveyed by these data on educational achievement could not be clearer. Rural students are not receiving inferior quality education, and the general public presumption that they are receiving an inferior education is simply wrong. Indeed, when rural students stay in school—and there is still some room for improvement here—the general education they receive is roughly on a par with that in other areas of the country. There is obviously a need to improve the access of rural students to advanced courses that facilitate access to higher education. A genuine gap exists between metro and nonmetro areas in this regard. But this gap in no way supports the standard assumption that the average rural worker suffers severely from poor educational preparation.

Vocational Training

Of course, a discussion of educational attainment and achievement does not exhaust the issue of human capital development. Indeed for much of work force outside of professional and managerial occupations, postschool vocational training—formal company training programs, informal on-the-job instruction, and so on—is as important (or more important) for skill development as attending school. In addition, a large (though declining) portion of the rural work force was educated when average educational attainment levels in rural areas were quite low, making skill development through training par-

Table 22.9. Skill-improvement training on current job, 1983 and 1991 (in percent)

Group of workers	Metro		Nonmetro	
	1983	1991	1983	1991
All workers	36.8	43.4	36.8	39.9
Gender				
Men	37.6	43.1	37.2	39.3
Women	35.9	43.7	36.3	40.6
Race/Ethnicity				
Hispanic	23.2	29.5	24.1	27.3
Black (non-Hispanic)	30.7	37.4	27.8	27.1
White (non-Hispanic)	38.7	45.9	37.8	41.4
Education				
Dropout	17.1	19.3	19.0	18.2
High school graduate	31.0	35.8	33.3	34.7
1–3 years college	42.2	47.8	44.5	49.0
4 years college	51.1	57.9	55.3	65.3
5+ years college	60.5	67.8	68.4	72.8
Region				
Northeast	31.9	40.0	38.6	42.6
Midwest	37.6	44.8	36.7	42.1
South	37.6	44.8	34.0	36.3
West	40.6	43.2	41.7	44.0

Source: Greenberg, Swaim, and Teixeira 1993.

ticularly important for these workers. A basic assessment of human capital development in rural areas must therefore encompass the area of postschool vocational training.

Do rural workers have adequate training opportunities after joining the labor force? Data for 1991 suggest that rural workers do not have as many opportunities to improve their job skills as urban workers (Table 22.9), though the magnitude of this deficit is fairly small (40 percent of nonmetro workers as compared to 43 percent of metro workers had received training on their current job). That said, it is worrisome that this gap in training rates opened up between 1983 and 1991. Although some U.S. employers appear to have concluded that their long-run competitiveness requires increased investment in work-force training, this trend was markedly weaker in rural areas.

A related concern is that enterprise-based training may be least available to those rural workers in greatest need of improved vocational skills. The data in

Table 22.10. Types and sources of skill-improvement training for workers receiving training on their current job, 1991 (in percent)

Training Type/Provider	Metro	Nonmetro
Type of training		
Managerial	27.9	23.7
Computer	34.7	29.3
Academic (three Rs)	14.5	14.6
Other technical	62.9	66.4
Training provider		
School	32.0	33.3
Company program (formal)	42.5	37.1
On-the-job (informal)	39.7	39.4
If school		
High school vocational education	4.4	4.0
Private vocational school	9.7	13.3
Two-year college	41.0	41.5
Four-year college	50.5	46.8

Source: Greenberg, Swaim, and Teixeira 1993.

Table 22.9 shows workers with low levels of formal education receiving much less postschool training. Obviously, the coincidence of low educational attainment and a paucity of job training provides undesirable reinforcement for those stuck in low-skill, dead-end jobs. Training rates are also low for racial and ethnic minorities. Only about one in four rural blacks and Hispanics report any training on their job as compared to over 41 percent of other (predominantly white) rural workers. In addition, training rates are quite low in the rural South, where educational attainment is lowest and where most nonmetro blacks and Hispanics live.

The training provided to rural workers also differs in several respects from that provided to urban workers (Table 22.10). One difference is that nonmetro workers receive less training in managerial and computer skills than metro workers. A second is that nonmetro workers are less likely to participate in formal company training programs. The latter tendency is probably due, at least in part, to the smaller size of rural firms. Most small firms cannot afford to establish formal training programs and must instead rely on either informal instruction from co-workers or external training providers.

Finally, among external providers, nonmetro firms differ from metropolitan employers by relying more on private vocational schools and less on four-year colleges. This difference reflects the fact that many rural firms are not located near public or private schools that can provide specialized vocational training for their work force.

In sum, these data suggest that there are grounds for concern about the training opportunities accorded rural workers. But the data do not indicate a massive shortfall in rural human capital development, any more than the education data do. We must conclude that the common perception of rural workers as suffering mightily from human capital deficits is incorrect. In many ways, in fact, rural workers match up surprisingly well with their urban counterparts. If rural workers are faring poorly—and they are—the primary causes may lie elsewhere, outside of the realm of human capital development.

HOW IMPORTANT ARE HUMAN CAPITAL LEVELS TO RURAL AREAS?

Obviously, human capital levels are of some importance to rural America but the real issue here is how much? The answer is not clear, despite the claims of many who see higher rural educational levels as a panacea for rural problems.

In fact, there are a number of grounds for questioning the efficacy of more education as a strategy for rural development. Rural areas, as mentioned at the beginning of this chapter, have upgraded human capital levels dramatically from their very low levels of thirty years ago (when the median rural resident had only a ninth-grade education). The years since 1980, however, have seen a troubling divergence of economic outcomes between metro and nonmetro areas despite this enriched stock of rural human capital. This divergence includes slower employment growth, higher unemployment, relative and absolute earnings deterioration, higher levels of underemployment, relative decline in nonmetro per capita income and higher poverty rates (Lichter 1993).

Can all this decline really be due to the fact that, despite dramatic upgrading in rural educational levels, a rural-urban human capital gap—albeit smaller than generally believed—still exists? This possibility seems implausible given such other indicators as the relative decline in nonmetro returns to education and the outmigration of a substantial percentage of the better educated nonmetro population to metro areas.[3] The indicators actually indicate a relative lack of demand for high-skill workers in rural areas in the 1980s.

In fact, skill demand was quite weak in rural areas in the 1980s, both relative to urban areas and relative to nonmetro trends in the 1970s. This relationship holds no matter what measure of job skill requirements is used (i.e., the educational levels of job incumbents or direct ratings of job skill levels taken from the Dictionary of Occupational Titles [DOT]).[4] In the 1970s, the decade of the "rural turnaround," job mix analyses show that rural growth rates in skill requirements of jobs were close to those in urban areas. In fact, in some cases the skill growth rates in rural areas were even a little bit higher. For example, general educational development (GED) required—a DOT measure—grew at a ten-year rate of 2.9 percent in rural areas, compared to 2.2 percent in urban areas.[5] Similarly, average years of education required grew at a ten-year rate of 1.9 percent in rural areas in the 1970s, compared to 1.3 percent growth in urban areas. In the 1980s both rural and urban areas experienced slowdowns in the rate of growth of job skill levels.[6] But rural areas experienced a much more dramatic slowdown in skill-level growth— rates only about one-third to one-tenth of those in the previous decade, For example, growth in handling data skill requirements (DOT measure) in rural areas fell from a ten-year rate of 4.8 percent in the 1970s to .7 percent in the 1980s, growth in verbal aptitude requirements from 2.9 percent to .4 percent, and growth in GED requirements from 2.9 percent to just .3 percent.

Nor do the optimistic scenarios of a skills explosion in the economy, due to rapid movement into a high skill economy in the 1990s, presage high skill demand in rural areas (Johnston and Packer 1987). Even under an optimistic assumption of equal occupational growth rates across rural and urban areas, rural areas are projected to emulate their poor performance of the 1980s. For example, from 1990 to 2005, verbal aptitude skill requirements are projected to rise at a ten-year rate of .8 percent in rural areas and GED skill requirements at a rate of .9 percent. Other skill measures show a similar pattern.

Further food for thought is provided by estimates of the relationship between educational levels and local economic growth in rural areas. The relationship is not a strong one, to say the least, as shown by two recent analyses based on county data, aggregated into "commuting zones."[7] The first study, conducted by Killian and Parker (1991), was unable to find a significant effect of local educational levels on employment growth in rural areas in either the 1970s or 1980s. The second, by McGranahan (1993), shows that average years of education have had no significant effect on the growth of relatively high-skill or "complex" manufacturing jobs in rural areas in the last two decades.[8] Together, these studies provide strong support for the contention that growth in skill demand has been weak in rural areas and that, therefore, inadequate human capital cannot be the main obstacle to rural development.

IMPORTANT RESEARCH AND POLICY ISSUES FOR THE 1990s

This discussion of rural human capital suggests several areas of concern for the future. First, given the exceptional labor market disadvantages suffered by high school dropouts, continued progress is needed in reducing the proportion of dropouts in the rural work force.[9] This recommendation seems particularly sensible in light of the perfectly decent education provided by the average[10] rural school to those who do stay in school.

A second area of concern is the relatively low proportion of the rural work force with a degree from a four-year college. The gap here is significant and has even increased in recent years (though some of this is clearly due to out-migration of the well-educated students to urban areas). One way to help remedy this situation is to increase the proportion of rural schools that offer advanced courses in college preparatory subjects. As shown by the NAEP data, rural students are currently dramatically underserved in this regard, despite the reasonably good job that rural schools do in imparting general academic skills.

A third area of concern is a gap that appears to be developing in the amount of postschool vocational training available to rural and urban workers. Although this gap is not presently large, the trend is highly undesirable given the importance of such training to the bulk of the rural work force. The overwhelming proportion of rural work force of the year 2000, after all, are already on the job today. It follows that training, not schooling, will be the vehicle for improving their human capital, if it is to be improved at all.

All of these rural human capital deficits, however—relatively many high school dropouts, relatively few college graduates, relatively little postschool vocational training—must be considered in the context of relatively weak skill demand in rural areas. Indeed, given relatively weak demand, a rural deficit in skill supply is, at least to some extent, a natural outcome of economic dynamics, rather than a "problem," in the true sense of the term.

The roots of weak skill demand in rural areas must be addressed, then, if upgrading rural human capital is to have the desired positive effects. Of course, it is probably impossible to completely eliminate the differential in human capital demand between rural and urban areas—due to agglomeration economies and other spatial factors that impinge on such demand—but narrowing that differential should be feasible.

If, as the data suggests, rural areas are not primarily hobbled by their relative lack of human capital, what are they hobbled by? Where do the deficits truly lie? What really keeps the high-growth sectors of the economy away from rural areas? Lack of infrastructure? Lack of critical mass? "Rurality"? Answering these questions—and then addressing them in a policy sense—will help ensure that improving human capital levels in rural areas improves not only the welfare of rural individuals, but of rural places.

NOTES

1. The terms "rural" and "nonmetro," as well as "urban" and "metro," will be used interchangeably.

2. Based on time trend data from the NAEP (Greenberg and Teixeira 1993), there may have been slightly more basis for such a viewpoint in the past. These data show that the metro-nonmetro achievement gap was slightly larger in the mid-1970s but has diminished in the intervening years. It is interesting to note that this convergence of achievement scores parallels the convergence of attainment levels documented in the previous section.

3. See McGranahan and Ghelfi (1991) for data and discussion.

4. The Dictionary of Occupational Titles (DOT) is a compendium of occupational titles in common use in civilian U.S. labor markets. The compendium is based on survey information collected at irregular intervals by job analysts for the U.S. Employment Service. A variety of information about each occupational title is contained in the DOT, including ratings of the educational development, training time, physical capabilities, temperaments, and aptitudes necessary for the job. There have been four editions of the DOT: 1939, 1949, 1965, and 1977, plus a substantial revision of the fourth (1977) edition, issued in 1991. The fourth edition contains information on well over 12,000 different occupations.

5. For technical details on how this analysis was performed, see appendix to Teixeira and Mishel (1992).

6. Note that these findings contradict the conventional wisdom that the 1980s were marked by an explosive growth in the skill levels of jobs. Of course, it could be argued that these findings, since they are based on analyses of job mix (changes in the distribution of jobs in the economy), fail to capture the tremendous changes taking place within jobs. In other words, the distribution of jobs may not have changed much, but the content of the work that individuals do within particular jobs has radically shifted. Data on the changing content of work within occupations does not support this proposition, however. Indeed, these data show the same sluggish growth in job-skill requirements revealed by analysis of job mix changes. See Teixeira and Mishel (1993) and Teixeira and Mishel (forthcoming) for specific figures and discussion.

7. There are 763 commuting zones in the United States (excluding Alaska), of which about 508 may be considered nonmetro. See Killian and Parker (1991), Appendix A, for technical details.

8. Interestingly, years of education (ages 25–44) has had a significant negative effect on the growth of low-skill or "routine" manufacturing jobs in rural areas. That is, the lower the educational levels, the higher the growth in routine manufacturing em-

ployment. For technical details on the distinction between complex and routine manufacturing, see appendix to McGranahan and Ghelfi (1991).

9. Note, however, that 1990 census data already show the dropout rates of metro and nonmetro 16- to 19-year-olds to be virtually identical.

10. Of course, just because the average rural school is providing a reasonably good education doesn't mean all rural schools are. Indeed, the figures on average educational achievement undoubtedly cloak substantial variation among individual schools in rural and urban areas. Students and schools that are faring particularly poorly may need special remedial assistance simply to reach the average levels of educational achievement referred to here.

23

LINKING EDUCATION AND COMMUNITY DEVELOPMENT: RURAL AND INNER CITY STRATEGIES

JOAN FITZGERALD

A recent report suggests that our education system has neglected the school-to-work transition for the "forgotten half" of students who do not go to college (William T. Grant Foundation 1987). Consensus has emerged on many fronts that our education crisis can be partly solved by better linking education to economic development at the local level, particularly in many rural and inner-city areas where economic restructuring has created high unemployment. Technical preparation (tech prep), a program that links education with work-based learning in businesses, has been adopted as one way to facilitate school-to-work transitions in many states. This chapter presents data from a study of the implementation of tech-prep programs in rural, urban, and suburban sites in the state of Illinois. I focus on how well the links between schools and local businesses have been forged and conclude the chapter with a reflection on the promise and problem of establishing effective links between education and economic development, with particular emphasis on rural areas.

THE LINK BETWEEN EDUCATION AND
ECONOMIC DEVELOPMENT

The discussion of education reform, as it relates to the changing needs of employers in the 1990s, is often framed in terms of increasing the supply of educated workers. Both supply- and demand-side policies, if implemented in isolation, are inadequate for reversing patterns of uneven development that have

436

left rural and inner-city areas underdeveloped. If it is not linked to education reform and skills enhancement, economic development can at best attract the same kind of low-end employment that has come to dominate many rural economies. Thus, on the demand side, policy needs to encourage firms to make the high-skill, high-wage choice. Likewise, if education is not linked to a broader development strategy, it represents what Swanson (1990) refers to as a rural transitional development strategy—one that focuses on shifting rural capital and human resources to areas of higher demand in response to market forces.

There is considerable diversity in rural economies (Killian and Hady 1988). Many rural areas, however, are characterized by declining industries and less-educated people. Although it might seem logical to conclude that if rural areas had a more highly educated work force they would attract growing industries, McGranahan and Ghelfi (1991) reveal the fallacy of this argument. Rural economic growth in the 1970s and early 1980s was the result of low-end production jobs moving from urban areas in search of low-skill, low-cost labor. The lower education levels of rural workers did in fact serve to lure these firms (Johnson and Beale 1993). Indeed, Bloomquist (1988) used the product cycle model to classify rural manufacturing and found that it was dominated by mature "bottom of the cycle" firms. The predominance of mature, low-skill industries is significant to future rural development. Firms in mature industries are not likely to provide on-the-job training or other opportunities for upgrading the skills of rural workers. Thus, there are few opportunities for the rural adult labor force to acquire the skills that might make it more attractive to employers requiring a more highly skilled labor force.

Evidence does not, however, suggest that increasing the education levels of rural people alone will attract high-wage, high-skill employers. In fact, the relationship between education and economic development appears to be negative (Falk and Lyson 1988; Schaffer and Sander 1988). Killian and Parker (1991) found the independent effect of schooling levels on local growth to be insignificant in both metropolitan and nonmetropolitan areas. Educational investment paid off for rural residents only to the extent that they were willing to migrate to areas offering higher paying jobs (O'Hare 1988; Pollard and O'Hare 1990; Killian and Parker 1991). Indeed, the out-migration of young, educated rural residents leads Swanson (1990) to conclude that human resource policy has operated to facilitate rural depopulation: the biggest export of rural areas may be their high school and college graduates.

On the supply side, it seems clear that our education system has to increase the number of students who are ready for college or work. We now recognize that the requirements for both groups of students are converging. All students need to leave high school with strong mathematical skills, written and verbal communication skills, critical thinking skills, and the ability to work cooperatively. If we are going to place all the students graduating from the school-to-work programs being developed, demand-side public policy must encourage employers to adopt high-skill, high-wage forms of production organization (see Fitzgerald 1993a). Tech prep offers an opportunity to link these two approaches.

TECH PREP AND THE SCHOOL-TO-WORK TRANSITION

The overriding objective of the Carl D. Perkins Vocational and Applied Technology Education Act of 1990 is to increase the competitiveness of the United States in the world economy by upgrading the skills of the labor force. Improving the quality of vocational education is the primary means through which the legislation seeks to achieve this end. The legislation has the potential to transform vocational education from a second-class curriculum to one that equips students with knowledge and skills that can be applied to the workplace and to higher education. It provides funding for innovations in vocational education and guidelines requiring several changes from existing approaches. Perkins funds are to be used specifically to develop innovative approaches to vocational education.

The definition of tech prep used in the Illinois State Plan is typical of that used by many states: "A combined secondary and postsecondary program which: leads to an associate degree or two-year certificate; provides technical preparation in at least one field of engineering technology, applied science, mechanical, industrial, practical art or trade, agriculture, health, or business and builds student competence in mathematics, science and communications (including through applied academics) through a sequential course of study and leads to placement in employment." Many states and local school districts are using funds from the 1990 Carl D. Perkins Vocational Education Act to develop tech-prep programs. A defining characteristic of tech prep is the integration of academic and vocational curriculum. Tech prep is guided by the belief that vocational education does not have to exclude college as an option.

Several specific curriculum innovations are mandated by the legislation. First, rather than focusing on narrowly defined job skills, the vocational curriculum will teach students about all aspects of an industry. The rationale for this requirement is that students are likely to change jobs many times in their lifetimes and will need more than one narrow job skill. Learning all aspects of an industry will allow students to attain high rungs of the career ladder in a given occupational area. Thus they learn planning, management, financing, technical and production skills, underlying principles and technology, labor and community issues and health, and safety and environmental issues. In order to gain competency in these areas, students must be proficient in the basic components of the academic curriculum, including mathematics, reading, writing, science, and social studies.

Second, the Perkins legislation requires a merging of academic and vocational education. This integration provides students with a broad base of knowledge crucial to success in future work environments and also offers vocational students the necessary background to pursue a college degree, if they so choose, after graduation.

Third, the Perkins Act requires that business, labor, parents, and the broader community be involved in the development and implementation of programs. The rationale for requiring business participation is itself threefold. Businesses can help schools determine what types of jobs are likely to be in demand in the near future and can help identify the types of skills students will need in the identified occupations. Moreover, tech-prep programs in many states are required to have a work-based learning component. Local businesses are needed to provide on-the-job training and internships for the students. Finally, businesses can provide a more general service to the schools by bringing teachers and students into the workplace so they can see firsthand how work is structured. These programs can range from simple tours to hiring teachers over the summer on actual jobs in the occupations in which they teach (see Fitzgerald 1993b).

Through these links with the demand side of industry, tech prep holds the promise of linking education with economic development. The link to employers is thus an integral part of the success of tech prep in preparing students for employment. Yet my study of implementation in Illinois suggests that it is precisely this crucial link that is missing in many rural and inner-city programs.

TECH PREP IN ILLINOIS

The study examined implementation of tech prep in fifteen sites throughout the state that are in their second or third year of program planning. Five of the sites are rural, four serve medium-size cities and their surrounding areas, five are suburban sites within the Chicago metropolitan area, and one site is in the city of Chicago. The case studies of the fifteen sites are based on interviews, funding proposals, and other documents on tech prep produced by each site, as well as on secondary data. Interviews were conducted with program directors and coordinators, teachers, and business, community, labor, and parent representatives involved in program planning and implementation. The analysis presented here focuses on the level of business involvement in the programs (see Fitzgerald 1993b for discussion of other issues related to implementation).

The following list presents sixteen ways in which businesses are involved in tech prep. The intent was to use the list to create a hierarchy of participation, with increasing levels of involvement moving down the list, but it quickly became evident that reality was more complicated. It is difficult to assign levels of commitment to activities. There is great variation, for example, in the amount of commitment evident in the most prevalent form of business participation, that is, serving on tech prep advisory committees. Some advisory committees meet infrequently and only comment on activities or curriculum after they have been undertaken. Others meet monthly or even more often and are assigned specific responsibilities, such as developing the course requirements or an entire curriculum.

Business Activity	Description
Serve on advisory committee	Attend meetings (monthly to semi-annually) and provide advice on curriculum changes and tech prep activities
Provide advice on curriculum development	Respond to a survey on what schools need to teach, or more involved assistance beyond advisory board meetings
Participate in curriculum development	Writing of curriculum with teachers for specific courses
Provide guest speakers	Provide guest speakers in classrooms or for broader school audiences
Provide tours for students	Develop a tour of the business operation for students that explains occupations and their activities and educational requirements

Provide tours for teachers	Develop a tour of the business operation for teachers that explains occupations and their activities and educational requirements
Participate in career day programs	Provide a speaker and information to discuss occupations and future jobs prospects in the industry in which the business is classified
Participate in job shadowing programs	Provide opportunities for students and teachers to shadow employees to better understand the requirements of particular types of jobs
Offer internships for students	Provide paid internships for students in place of employment
Offer internships for teachers	Provide paid (or subsidized) experience for teachers to learn first-hand how occupations have changed and to better understand their skill requirements
Donate supplies, equipment, or money	Provide equipment on which students train or materials that can be used in the classroom
Operate a mentoring program	Establish one-on-one or small group relationships with students to help them develop a better understanding of different careers, and to offer advice on educational choices
Offer topical workshops for teachers	Provide workshops for teachers that address current changes and issues in the industry
Assist in program marketing	Provide financial or other support for marketing efforts. Promoting the program publicly to improve parental response

Offer scholarships or awards	Motivate students to participate by offering public recognition of their efforts
Commit to preferential hiring agreements	Agree to hire students who graduate meeting specified criteria

Another problem in establishing the level of business involvement is that the number of activities covered is not necessarily a good indicator of the quality of participation. It is difficult to evaluate, for example, whether it is better to have twenty business representatives who simply show up at meetings twice a year, or a few representatives who make substantial contributions to curriculum development or other activities. In a community dominated by one dominant employer, the contributions of that one firm may be as valuable as those of twenty businesses in another community.

Despite the problems of quantifying levels of business involvement, it became evident through the interviews with tech-prep directors that certain types of support are essential to developing high-quality programs. In terms of their direct support to tech prep, curriculum development assistance, providing internships for students, and preferential hiring agreements are the most important contributions businesses can make. Internships or other programs to upgrade the skills of teachers also are of critical importance. Many teachers are unaware of changes in technology that have altered drastically the types of skills required in their occupational areas. At a minimum, businesses can offer tours or lectures on changes in the workplace. Ideally, teachers should receive hands-on experience with the latest technology in their fields.

Significant differences in the level and quality of business participation seem closely related to conditions of the local economy. It is clear from the business involvement in the fifteen sites that those businesses with the greatest hiring needs are the most motivated to involve themselves heavily in tech-prep programs. This phenomenon suggests that the characteristics of the local economy and local businesses affect the level of business participation. Clearly, schools in areas characterized by mature industries and employment decline will not be able to obtain work-based learning experiences in growing industries for their students. This problem is especially evident in rural and inner-city programs.

The tech-prep programs being developed at Illinois Eastern Community College typify the problems rural districts face in soliciting business support. Illinois Eastern is located in the southeastern part of the state. Unemployment in the eight counties served by the community college averaged between 9 and 10 percent during the 1990–1992 period. The tech-prep planning team has confronted many barriers in soliciting business involvement. Part of the problem stems from the large, predominantly rural region that Illinois Eastern Community College covers. The director has few contacts with businesses in the small communities in his district. An invitation from the director at Illinois Eastern resulted in only nine out of the twenty-eight area businesses agreeing to serve on the Tech Prep Advisory Council.

Such personal contacts are essential to soliciting support from the business community. For example, in the tech-prep program with one of the highest levels of business support, the co-directors hold leadership positions in several business associations, community service groups, and city and county development committees. They both have long-standing relationships with local business. These relationships were essential to building business support. In another suburban Chicago program, a retired businessman volunteered to solicit business support for the program. Although the Illinois Eastern program would benefit from more localized efforts at business recruitment, the director has neither the resources nor the staff to assign to the task. In addition to there being relatively few viable businesses in the Illinois Eastern region, spatial constraints seem to be a barrier to developing strong relationships with a dispersed business community.

Efforts to educate local companies about the tech-prep program and its benefits to employers also have proved unsuccessful. Local businesses have not seen the value of participating in tech prep, for most of them are not hiring new employees. Evidence from the fifteen sites suggests that businesses most motivated to become actively involved are those who anticipate hiring within the next few years and those large companies concerned with public relations. Given the high rate of plant closures and layoffs in many rural communities, it is not surprising that business representatives are not active in program development.

Another weakness of business involvement in rural areas is that many of the businesses involved in tech-prep planning activities do not represent the same industrial sectors as the programs. Occupational programs are selected based on predicted future job demand, and since many local industries are in decline, the programs are chosen in industries growing in other parts of the state. Thus, while the Illinois Eastern tech-prep programs are in manufacturing technology, business, and child care, the local businesses serving on the Tech Prep Advisory Committee include an auto dealership, a flower shop, a bank, an insurance company, a fast-food chain, a hospital, and a grocery store. There may be jobs available in these industries, but there are not enough for schools to develop programs for the occupations within them. The advisory committee has made several recommendations, such as dropping shorthand from the curriculum, and businesses have commented on general employability skills, but because they are not in the same industries as the programs being developed, critical needs are simply not being met. Although business representatives may be able to provide information on what sorts of skills employers are seeking they cannot offer a work-based learning component. Furthermore, because most of them are not hiring at all, business participants have not committed to preferential hiring.

The rural Southeastern Illinois Community College program has also experienced difficulty in garnering business involvement in tech prep for reasons similar to those of Illinois Eastern Community College. There is little diversity in the local economy. The largest industries in the region are coal-mining and agriculture, and both are in decline. The unemployment rate has reached as high as 15 percent in the last two years. Representatives from the coal-mining industry have spoken to students at school regarding the industry and provided tours of the mines, but internships cannot be offered due to insurance and liability issues. Since most jobs in mining are unskilled, there is little motivation for the companies to advance tech prep.

Another reason for the lack of involvement is that many of the businesses in rural areas are branch-plants. As a long literature in branch-plant economies has demonstrated, branch-plant managers are less likely to get involved in local politics or to support local initiatives such as tech prep in the schools.

In contrast, the Kishwaukee Education Consortium (KEC) serves a district that is predominantly rural but includes parts of DuPage County, one of the fastest growing parts of the Chicago metropolitan area. There are no large cities within its service area. The local economy is strong, with low unemployment and a diverse economic base. The main businesses in De Kalb, the largest city in the service area, are General Electric, Amoco, Barber-Green (a subsidiary of Caterpillar), IDEAL, Harvester, and Johnson Controls. A Nestlé Midwest distribution center is currently under construction.

The program receives support from many businesses. Business support was built from long-standing relationships between community college administrators and business organizations. The co-directors of the program are involved and hold leadership positions in a large number of business associations, community service groups, and city and county economic development committees. One of the co-directors, the vice president of Kishwaukee Community College, is also chair of the De Kalb Chamber of Commerce. They emphasize that these relationships have been essential to building business partnerships. They also note that the relationship-building process took a long time—almost ten years.

The De Kalb County Economic Development Corporation views vocational education as a vehicle for economic development and has been involved in several projects to improve tech-prep programs. The corporation consists of CEOs of the area's major companies, mayors from the region, and other business leaders. The city of De Kalb also has gotten involved by using tax increment financing to finance equipment for KEC projects. The funding applies to the entire KEC district, which is larger than the city's boundaries. Thus economic development and education reform are linked through informal and formal mechanisms.

Part of the motivation for the county's and the city's involvement is that many local businesses have aging labor forces. To develop a trained work force, KEC is working with De Kalb County Economic Development Corporation to develop an academy program in manufacturing technology. The academy is similar to an apprenticeship program in many ways. A key component of the program is business sponsorship of students. Sponsorship will be industry specific, with a single business sponsoring two to three students. The participating businesses will employ students during the summer as interns and will commit to hiring them after graduation. The technical curricula of the academy will be developed by industry representatives, and there will be strong focus on core academic classes, especially mathematics. The occupational areas to be included in the future are being identified by participating employees. For example, business has noted a need for skilled office employees, and an academy for office systems is being discussed.

ALTERNATIVE VISIONS FOR RURAL-BASED TECH PREP

The study identified two major problems rural schools have encountered in developing tech-prep programs. First, community colleges serve large geographic areas with many distant small towns. This spatial constraint makes it difficult for the tech-prep director who does not have strong contacts with business representatives throughout the college's service delivery area. Strong ties between school and business are essential to building relevant programs. Second, if tech-prep programs are developed in occupations with high growth potential, the jobs are likely to be located outside the rural area. This reality has two implications for the programs: there will be few local employers with the capacity to provide a work-based learning component for the program, and even if a work-based component could be simulated, the students' employment opportunities after graduation will require them to move or to commute, possibly long distances, to work.

These problems in linking the business sector with tech prep suggest that a different approach must be taken in rural areas. Two strategies hold out limited hope. The first possibility is to link tech prep with new employment activity in growing sectors. This strategy probably would work better in places adjacent to metropolitan areas (Deavers 1992; Fuguitt 1991). Glasmeier (1992) suggests that there is some limited potential for high tech industry development in some rural areas. A recent issue of *Economic Development Digest* cites several states, including Iowa, North Dakota, South Carolina, and Mississippi, that have developed programs using telecommunications to link education and economic development initiatives.

A second possibility is to link tech prep with entrepreneurship strategies. This approach would provide students with business skills in areas underserved in the local economy and could also prepare them for a wide variety of occupations.

LINKING GROWTH INDUSTRIES TO TECH PREP

Moraine Valley Community College, which serves a suburban and rural county, demonstrates how economic development and education strategies can be linked. The college is active in local economic development through several programs. The college's efforts to link education and economic development resulted in the creation of an economic development corporation, the Economic Development Corporation of the South Suburbs (EDCSS). The EDCSS provides information and assistance to new, expanding, and relocating businesses. Businesses are assisted with site selection, export and financial information, training, and other services.

Rather than waiting for businesses to ask for assistance, EDCSS staff visit companies, analyze their production organization, and offer suggestions of how to incorporate production-enhancing technology or reorganize the physical layout of the plant. If new equipment requires upgrading workers' skills , EDCSS will work with the company to design the training program. The EDCSS works closely with new businesses opening in the area. For example, EDCSS is working with Reading Energy, which is opening a trash incinerator in a small town served by the college. The facility will employ between eighty-five and ninety-five people, and Moraine Valley has offered to provide the necessary training for employees hired by the facility.

Moraine Valley's Business and Career Institute offers customized training, workshops, consultation, and strategic planning services to local and nonlocal businesses on a not-for-profit basis. Courses offered to employees include basic skills, ESL, computer skills, and many other specific courses. Programs include computer-aided design, electronics, automotive technology, medical records, and criminal justice. The institute is housed in the Center for Contemporary Technology. The center offers programs in computer numerical control, information management systems, electronics, environmental control, metallurgical technology, CAD/CAM, computer-integrated manufacturing, nondestructive testing, welding technology, and other related areas.

ENTREPRENEURSHIP AS THE LINK BETWEEN EDUCATION AND LOCAL ECONOMIC DEVELOPMENT

Entrepreneurship is thriving in many rural economies. Lin, Buss, and Popovich (1990) examined the rate of new successful business starts in rural areas and concluded that rural areas can provide good entrepreneurial climates. Particularly encouraging is that their results held even in states not commonly viewed as having good business climates. In the four states examined, rural economies produced new firms at the same rate as metropolitan and metropolitan-adjacent counties. These firms represented the same diversity of industries as their metropolitan and metropolitan-adjacent counterparts and created substantial employment in rural counties.

Revolving loan funds for microenterprises are springing up in communities of all sizes throughout the United States. Many of these programs are modeled after the Grameen Bank program in Bangladesh. The U.S. Small Business Administration funds several of these initiatives. The Center for Rural Affairs operates a Rural Enterprise Assistance Program that administers a revolving loan fund and provides technical assistance in business plan development and business management for entrepreneurs. The autumn 1993 issue of *Strategy Alert,* the newsletter of the Community Information Exchange, details several microenterprise and entrepreneurship programs operating in rural areas throughout the country.

The Center for Law and Education, a national nonprofit policy and advocacy organization in vocational curriculum reform, has directed much of its work in connecting Carl D. Perkins legislation to community development. Specifically, the center has established the Vocational Education Project to help redirect vocational education to better meet the needs of education, employment, and community development. The project has developed a "Model for Vocational Education and Community Revitalization" to address these needs. The model suggests that community development can include: involving students in assessment of the community's needs and production of goods or services contributing to the community's welfare, and linking to other community development planning, institutions, and enterprises.

One strategy promoted by the Vocational Education Project, especially in poor communities, is creating enterprises in schools that serve the broader community. The center is working with the Youth Enterprise Network (YEN) in Chicago to develop enterprise programs in three high schools. The network is a vocational program in business ownership operating in three Chicago high schools. It is a collaborative school reform effort undertaken by Bethel New Life, Chicago Cities and Schools, and the Chicago Workshop on Economic Development (CWED) with the three high schools, with the assistance of the Center for Law and Education. The YEN demonstrates how vocational education can incorporate entrepreneurship into a broader community development strategy.

The YEN program began by preparing teachers to develop and teach the new curriculum. Teachers took seminars in entrepreneurship at Chicago State University and attended workshops on curriculum development and teaching all aspects of the industry. The new curriculum provides YEN students with the academic and applied skills needed to own and operate a business. The programs follow the Carl Perkins "all aspects of an industry" guidelines, preparing students for multiple careers within an industry. Each year the necessary writing and mathematics skills are incorporated into the students' academic courses. For example, the specific skills needed to conduct market research, do feasibility analyses, develop business plans, and manage business operations are integrated into the academic and vocational curriculum. Students apply these skills by doing a local market analysis, developing a business plan, and setting up a business within the school. The focus of these activities is to identify business opportunities within the neighborhood. In the three schools involved, businesses started include a school supply store, a credit union, a second-hand infant clothing store, an apparel boutique, a cafe, and a greeting-card shop featuring the designs of art students.

The cafe operated at Orr Community Academy demonstrates the skills students have acquired while operating their business. During the first year, students participated in a desktop catering business. During the second year, planning for the school cafe began. Students were responsible for pricing and selecting all equipment and furniture needed to start the cafe, they learned to select and cost out the menu and locate suppliers, and they also handled the scheduling and addressed management-employee relations issues. This approach takes students far beyond learning how to cook.

The Rural School Based Enterprise Program in North Carolina provides another example of how entrepreneurship can be integrated into the school curriculum (Nachtigal 1990). The program assists the creation of school-based enterprises at rural high schools and community colleges, effectively turning rural schools into small-business incubators. Students learn entrepreneurial skills and how to identify development opportunities in the local economy. Like YEN, the program focuses on establishing enterprises and increasing employment in the community. Rural students research, plan, set up, operate, and own small businesses in cooperation with local educational institutions. There is an academic component for credit in which students take courses in applied economics, entrepreneurship, and small business ownership/management. The academic component is linked to an experiential component in which students operate their own business. These businesses are not merely school projects that end with the school year but are intended to become an ongoing part of the community's economic and employment base. After the businesses are initiated through the educational institution, the students that founded them continue to operate them.

Businesses that have developed from this program include a T-shirt silk-screening company, a company producing athletic uniforms and related items, a boat rental operation, a "leisure time" activities store, a New York–style delicatessen, and a child-care center. Students research the need for certain businesses in the community and the economic viability of such businesses in order to increase the potential for their success. The program attempts to address the lack of opportunities for students in rural areas while stimulating the local economy through business development. Thus, programs addressing community development and incorporating community in their curricula can be fitted for specific urban and rural development needs.

The critical difference between the YEN and rural school-based enterprise programs and similar programs led by business is that entrepreneurship is touted not as a ticket out of inner-city neighborhoods or rural communities but as a means of community development. The organizations developed the program because they had identified schools as one of the few neighborhood institutions with the facilities and human resources needed for community development. Other institutions are being drawn in as well. The Center for Urban Economic Development at the University of Illinois at Chicago has been conducting workshops with the students to familiarize them with the broader community economic development process. Eventually, even broader reforms, such as restructuring the school day to make the school more available to youth, families, and community members, are being planned.

Entrepreneurship programs have their place, but self-employment cannot serve as a substitute for other types of employment. Overall, the small businesses created are extremely vulnerable (Bates and Nucci 1989). Nevertheless, linking tech prep with entrepreneurship programs can link the demand and supply sides of rural and inner-city development efforts. As one component of a broader tech-prep program, this approach can furnish students with skills that can be used in a number of employment contexts.

CONCLUSION

Rural development strategies based solely on increasing the education levels of rural people will not increase the economic prospects of rural places. Rather, federally funded school reforms, such as the tech-prep programs being implemented under the Carl D. Perkins legislation, need to be integrated with local economic development activities to increase the demand for skilled workers. The two approaches to developing this integration discussed here— community college-based economic development corporations and entrepreneurship—provide examples of how such integration can be established. Although neither remedy can revitalize the most isolated and declining rural economies, each can contribute growth opportunity.

The discussion of obstacles to implementing vocational education programs under the Carl D. Perkins legislation also can prove useful to state program planners under the new federal school-to-work legislation. This study of implementation reveals that programs in rural, suburban, and inner-city schools face very different opportunities and problems.

NOTES

This research was primarily funded by the Joyce Foundation. Additional funding was provided by the Western Rural Development Center at Oregon State University.

24

RURAL EDUCATION: DECENTERING THE CONSOLIDATION DEBATE

DAVID R. REYNOLDS

School consolidation has been advocated by school administrators for more than a century, yet it remains one of the most difficult and contentious social policy issues in rural America (DeYoung 1992, 232). Banovetz and Dolan (1990, 99) suggest that consolidation constitutes the "grand debate" in rural education. As presently constituted, it pits what is good for society—usually defined in terms of the equal availability of educational opportunities—against what is good for community—the preservation of distinctive rural community norms and values (cf. Bender 1978). Were these always choices? Was consolidation a necessary response to the changing nature of rural community wrought by changes in communications technology and by farm consolidation and rural depopulation? Can a historical analysis of how consolidation came to dominate reform ideology provide insight into the fundamental policy issues surrounding rural education and, perhaps, also suggest how the grand debate can be transcended? I seek to illuminate these issues in this chapter, an examination of rural educational reform in Iowa from 1895 to the mid-1960s.

Iowa had more one-room schools than any other state in the United States—almost 14,000 in 1895. For more than a generation these numbers had been the source of great pride in the dispersed rural communities that blanketed the state. On the eve of World War I, Iowa became the center of national and even international attention as educational elites attempted to persuade the state's farmers to abandon these schools in favor of the modern consolidated school. Despite some early "successes," the movement failed to live up to expectations. Instead of being one of the first, Iowa was one of the last states to complete the task of consolidating its rural schools. What went wrong?

THE POLITICAL ECONOMY OF RURAL
EDUCATIONAL REFORM

Worried by the social and economic changes wrought by the rapid industrialization of the Midwest in the last three decades of the nineteenth century,
a small but influential cadre of urban-agrarian elites coalesced into what
was to become one of the more important rural reform movements of
the Progressive Era, the Country Life movement (Bowers 1974). Country
Life reformers saw the family farmer as the foundation upon which U.S. industrialization was based but saw the continued hegemony of prototypical
agrarian values—independence, self-reliance, thrift, diligence, conservatism—
threatened if something was not done to preserve and protect them (Danbom 1979). Farming still involved spatial and temporal rhythms of production and community life quite different from those of the cities, and the social
relations characterizing rural life still possessed strong elements of reciprocity.
Face-to-face communication in both market and cultural transactions was still
dominant, but Country Lifers thought the nature of this communication was
being transformed as selective rural to urban migration continued (Neth
1987). Could the productivity of midwestern agriculture be sustained if rural
areas lost the more productive family farmers and their children to more re-
munerative economic pursuits in the cities (U.S. Senate 1909, 21–22, 30–36,
37–51)? With higher food prices, urban-industrial growth in the country as a
whole would be undermined.

If the social and economic disadvantages of rural life seemed clear enough,
ways of overcoming them without also destroying its supposed advantages
were not. The Country Life Commission appointed by President Roosevelt
in 1907 recommended a few specific reforms such as federal road building,
parcel post, and federal public health initiatives, but more fundamental
changes seemed necessary (Danbom 1979: 44). In particular, new rural institutions were needed to stem the flow of people, especially of farm youth, to
the cities (Boorstin 1974, 134–135). To this end, the reform of educational
institutions in rural areas figured prominently in the thinking of the Country
Life reformers (see Bailey 1908, 1920; Cubberley 1914; Carney 1912; Saloutos and Hicks 1951; Lapping 1992), and national educational leaders were
more than pleased to lend their support.

In the cities a new system of education that had been installed in the last
quarter of the nineteenth century appeared to be achieving success in reproducing the ideology and class structure of industrial capitalism (Spring 1972;
Bowles and Gintis 1976; Reynolds and Shelley 1990). Country Lifers argued
that a redirected rural education was needed if agriculture was to hold its own

in an increasingly commercial, industrialized society (see, e.g., Anderson 1906). The farmer needed to become "confident of his mastery over the forces of nature" by practicing scientific agriculture without losing his belief in the moral superiority of rural over urban life (Keppel 1960, 142). This confidence, it was thought, could be nurtured by making the study of modern agricultural life the centerpiece of a new curriculum for the rural public schools.

The first national study of rural schools in the United States was undertaken in 1896–1897 by a commission appointed by the National Education Association (NEA). In comparison with the apparent efficiency and standardization of the urban schools, the rural schools were criticized for remaining "as individualistic, inefficient, and chaotic as ever" (Fuller 1982, 106). Needed curricular changes could not be made without first putting in place a better system of rural school supervision. The prevailing pattern of an elected superintendent overseeing the country schools of a county was seen as little better than no supervision at all. As the necessary first step in reform, the report urged that small one-room schools be closed and that pupils be transported at local public expense to larger, centrally located, graded schools (NEA 1897). The commission maintained that population decline required rural school consolidation in some areas, and this particular form of consolidation was argued for on the grounds that it would improve the quality of rural education. This tactic was the first salvo in the efforts of leading educators to implement what Tyack (1974) has aptly called the "one best system" for the organization of the public schools in the U.S. (see also Hobbs, Chapter 20).

The leaders in the new field of educational administration were even more convinced than those in the Country Life movement that the enthusiasm earlier settlers had shown for educating their children had degenerated into complacency. Consolidation was viewed as a means to stimulate a renewed interest in education among rural students and their parents, leading to increased enrollments in both elementary schools and high schools. Unlike the Country Lifers, these reformers wanted parents to take a greater interest in the rural schools but essentially to relinquish their control over the education of their children to the professional educator. Consolidation would enable professionals to bring the educational advantages of the city to the country. It would increase the funds available for the provision of greatly expanded rural public school facilities, for a higher quality but standardized curriculum, and for the transportation of rural students to schools. According to this view, the only educationally significant differences between rural and urban schools would be that the former would be located in "rural" areas and would place greater emphasis on instruction in scientific agriculture. It was understood that rural schools would still be smaller, have fewer teachers, fewer students, and possess smaller tax bases.

In placing emphasis on achieving equality rather than on fostering new forms of rurality, reformers in the emerging field of educational administration differed quite significantly from the Country Life reformers. In the early years of the new century, then, there were two sets of rural school reformers and two logics of consolidation: one emphasized the role of school consolidation in rural community revitalization and the other emphasized the equalization of educational opportunity between urban and rural children. The two sets of reformers agreed that rural school consolidation was a necessary first step. Rural education needed to be systematized and brought more firmly under the control of the state. This alliance over means rather than ends was no doubt given political momentum by the apparent success of the consolidation of industrial and commercial firms in the rise of American industry to world prominence during this period (Davenport 1909; King 1913).

For Country Life reformers and national educational leaders to agree on the efficacy of consolidation was one thing, selling it to rural people was another. The latter required that reform be channeled into concrete political action. The creation of the consolidation movement entailed school reformers building alliances with other more narrowly focused "progressive" movements in their states.

SCHOOL CONSOLIDATION IN IOWA: A RESPONSE TO POPULATION DECLINE?

The period 1900–1914 is usually referred to as the Golden Age of Agriculture. For the first time in a generation, farm prices were high at the beginning of the period and continued to move upward. In Iowa, generally recognized as possessing the richest, most productive tillable soils in North America, prosperity wrought a number of demographic and economic changes in the countryside.

The state's rural population had peaked in 1880 and remained relatively constant until the end of the century (Brindley 1912). In the first decade of the new century, however, the rural population declined by 114,750, or 6.9 percent (Andriot 1983). Population changes in rural areas, however, were highly uneven geographically (see Figure 24.1). Nonetheless, in 1910 almost 70 percent of the population remained rural (and small town) and was over-

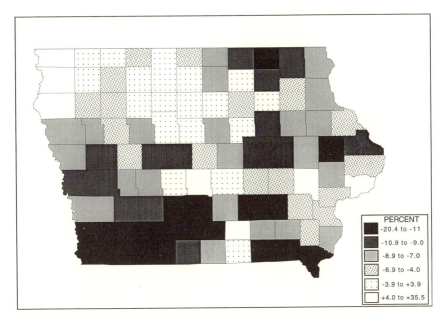

PERCENT
- -20.4 to -11
- -10.9 to -9.0
- -8.9 to -7.0
- -6.9 to -4.0
- -3.9 to +3.9
- +4.0 to +35.5

Figure 24.1. Percent change in rural population in Iowa counties from 1900 to 1910.

whelmingly accounted for by farm families. The populations of all cities in the state increased over the decade (U.S. Bureau of the Census 1913a) but not as rapidly as in other midwestern states. Although Iowa remained "rural," it was losing rural population more rapidly than the industrial bases of its cities were expanding to absorb the rural surplus (Brindley 1912).

There was a 5.1 percent reduction in the number of farms and an increase in average farm size from 151 acres in 1900 to 164 in 1910 (U.S. Bureau of the Census 1932). The distribution of farm sizes was very strongly regionalized by 1910 (Figure 24.2). These changes were accompanied by even more dramatic decreases in the number of school-age children in various parts of the state.[1]

As the rural population decreased and agricultural prices increased, agricultural land values rose sharply, increasing by 123 percent between 1900 and 1910 (U.S. Bureau of the Census 1913b), and continued to soar for another decade. The value of real property subject to taxation for the support of the rural schools increased much more rapidly than the number of pupils decreased. Hence, rural population loss was not accompanied by any fiscal incentive for farmers to abandon their one-room schools in favor of alternative means of providing public schooling.

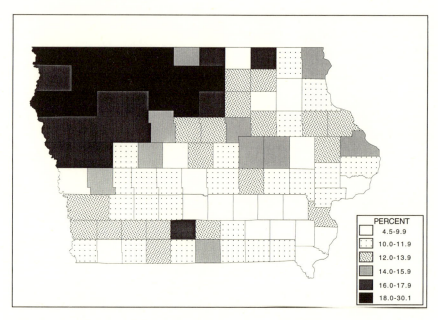

Figure 24.2. Percent of farms with more than 260 acres, 1910.

Before 1900 almost all suggestions for the reform of Iowa's schools began within the leadership of the Iowa State Teachers Association (ISTA), an organization tightly controlled by the leaders of the state's major colleges and universities, and by a few superintendents from the state's larger cities (Hart 1954, 13–28). From the late 1860s onward ISTA had pushed successfully for the creation of graded schools and high schools in all villages, towns, and cities and for the implementation of "modern" systems of supervision and management. With the active complicity of the state superintendent and ISTA, boosters in progressively smaller and smaller urban places pressed the legislature to reduce the number of inhabitants required of a place for it to organize as an "urban" independent district, until by 1894 it was a mere 100 (Aurner 1914–1915, I: 264–278; III: 210–255).[2] Iowa possessed two school systems—a modern one for the almost 800 cities, towns, and villages, and a traditional one for rural children.

Country school teachers were not viewed as members of the teaching profession.[3] The state teachers' college trained teachers for urban schools. If country school teachers received any special training at all they received it in the normal training class of one of the larger high schools.[4] Reformers within Iowa's educational establishment argued that only the rural public schools needed "legislative help to insure the proper delegation of power" (Riggs 1909, 28). "Social efficiency" demanded the closure of country schools and their replacement with modern schools. As the prominent Country Life activist and ISTA leader, George H. Betts, put it, education "must relate itself immediately and concretely to the business of living" (Betts 1913, 1).

From the reformers' perspective, the quality of education in the country school was necessarily below that of the larger, efficiently managed urban school. Here reformers argued that Iowa had a "rural school problem" as severe as that found anywhere.[5] Except for soliciting evaluations of the physical conditions of rural school buildings and grounds from county superintendents, the only attempt to document the severity of the rural school problem was a compilation in 1903–1905 of the numbers of rural schools with enrollments and attendances below certain levels. Ironically, these data provided little support for the view that rural education in Iowa was in crisis.[6]

Undaunted, reformers continued to view the country school as a carryover from Iowa's pioneer days and ill-suited to meet the demands of twentieth-century farm practice and rural life (Campbell 1919). They refused to engage in debate the many farm families who thought that the country schools remained well-suited to their needs or who placed a higher priority on improving the quality of teaching in their schools.[7] Borrowing one of the tenets of the Country Life movement, reformers argued that if farmers did not invest more in their children's education, then rural areas would continue to lose their young people to the cities at an increasing rate, thereby undermining the reproduction of rural life even further and, by extension, undermining core American values (see Figure 24.3).

In fact, the real problem with the country school lay deep in the reformers' profound distrust of rural people and their culture. The reason the country school was "inefficient" was that it was controlled by the wrong people, and as Betts (1913: 26) put it, "a stream cannot rise higher than its source." Reformers were surprisingly candid about what they thought to be the appropriate class composition of school boards and the proper delegation of authority between local elites and professionals within a school district. Rather than being "communities" in a meaningful sociocultural sense, school districts should simply be territories of convenience, a spatial means of achieving the agglomeration economies and the proper delegation of authority thought necessary to provide a high-quality education at a reasonable cost. This view had merit, but so too did its converse. This truth was denied in the emerging discourse of consolidation. The perpetuation of any social and cultural differences based on or reinforced by locality was considered antithetical to equality.

Figure 24.3. "Give the Iowa boy and girl the best"; cartoon from Mapleton, Iowa, newspaper, June 24, 1915.

In many respects, reformers misinterpreted the nature of the changes that were occurring in the Iowa countryside. Most serious was their failure to realize that rural to urban migration in Iowa during this period was not a simple case of rural depopulation wherein farmers and their children left the farm in search of a better life in the city. Migration generally conformed to one of three patterns: the movement of retired farmers to nearby villages and small towns; the migration of young and middle-aged men, who either had not obtained or did not expect to obtain their own farms, into low-status occupations in nearby cities and towns; and the temporary movement of young people to the city for higher education and then into high-status occupations in urban places near home (Jensen and Friedberger 1976: 6.34–6.35). Contrary to appearance, the movement of these people was into occupations vital to the integration of a distinctive regional economy benefiting both rural and urban components alike.

Iowans valued their rural communities even when they were no longer their permanent places of residence. Reformers seriously underestimated how important the rural school was in institutionalizing the sense of collective identity rural people felt for their local communities. When a school is institutionalized in this way, "its perpetuation is seen as an end in itself. . . . [P]arents do not regard the school merely as a place to send their children to learn how to read, but as "our" school" (Alford 1960, 352). Reformers did not perceive resistance to rural school consolidation in communitarian terms but viewed it either as an unthinking, shortsighted clinging of farmers to an aberrant educational philosophy or as a form of social degeneration engendered by social and cultural isolation. These misunderstandings and misinterpretations were to have unfortunate consequences on both the rhetoric of rural school consolidation and the way in which its implementation was attempted.

After a decade of agricultural prosperity in the period 1896–1905, there was no rush in the rural districts to abandon the country schools and establish graded elementary and high schools serving rural students. To expedite reform, a top-down approach to the territorial restructuring of the control of the rural school appeared necessary. In three consecutive sessions beginning in 1906, reformers tried in vain to persuade the General Assembly to abolish country school districts and reconstitute them on a larger territorial scale, first at the township and then at the county levels. After these legislative failures, it was obvious that any changes in the organization of rural school districts would need to be formally initiated in localities and subjected to local voter approval. This necessity fundamentally altered the strategy reformers could pursue; henceforth they would have to proceed under existing laws or attempt to change them while working within the constraints of local democracy.

THE CREATION OF A DOMINANT CLASS ALLIANCE AND ITS DISCOURSE

In 1906 the General Assembly passed a law permitting the formation of new, territorially larger school districts without the explicit approval of the boards of directors of the preexisting districts affected. Such "consolidated" districts could be proposed by a petition signed by as few as one-third of the voters in the proposed district and voted into existence by the dual majority vote of those in the urban and rural portions of it. The intent of the law had simply been to provide a less politically cumbersome means for the school district of a town or city to expand into an urbanizing countryside. With other options now foreclosed, the task of reformers was to revise this law so that it would not only permit consolidation but actively encourage it.

In 1911 educational reformers took the first major step along this path by urging that the 1906 law be modified to require that whenever an urban place containing a school population of twenty-five or more was to be included within a consolidated district the school had to be located in that place. This stipulation appeared to remove the location of the school from "politics." By insuring that consolidated districts would include at most only one "urban" place, it also guaranteed the almost unanimous support of the residents of small towns for any and all consolidation proposals including them, thereby rendering them "natural" centers around which local consolidation movements could be organized.

Another important reform bill securing passage in 1911 was the so-called "free-tuition" law. It required every school district not having its own high school to pay the tuition for its students to attend any public high school in the state, provided that the tuition paid not exceed that charged at the nearest high school. The bill had been heavily lobbied for by the state superintendent and other educational leaders because they thought that it would not only provide the additional stimulus necessary for rural people to see finally the advantages of rural school district consolidation but would also create a powerful justification for state regulation of the high schools.

In 1912 the consummate political maneuverings of the new Superintendent of Public Instruction, Albert M. Deyoe, succeeded in building a powerful alliance between educational reformers and economic and political elites, united in the belief that a redirected rural education under the supervision of professional educators was necessary for future economic and social progress in the state. Organizationally, the Better Iowa Schools Commission (BISC) was the political centerpiece of this new effort.[8] All but one of the major reform bills proposed by BISC were passed and signed into law in 1913. Of these, by far the more significant were a bill granting the state superintendent's office full departmental status in state government, thereby providing a clear break with the tradition of direct popular control of the schools, and a bill granting state aid to consolidated school districts if they included courses on agriculture, domestic science, and other vocational subjects taught by state-approved teachers. The amount of state aid allocated was based on the number of classrooms contained in the school building. The maximum amount of aid provided was just sufficient to offset the anticipated cost of adding the teaching of these subjects to a school district's curriculum. To receive any state aid, however, transportation had to be provided for rural students and all twelve grades had to be housed in a single facility. Small-town newspaper editors across the state now found it easier to argue that the demise of their country schools was inevitable. As the editor of the *Pocahontas County Sun* opined: "It is evident to all that consolidation is sure to come. The legislature is holding out inducements now for the schools to consolidate in the way of bonuses, but in the near future it is evident that the matter will be dealt with in a different manner. The laws will compel consolidation and the people will have nothing to say" (*Pocahontas County Sun,* April 10, 1913).

Implementation and the Containment of Resistance

From mid-1913 until the U.S. entry into World War I, the principal locus of struggle over educational reform in Iowa shifted from the legislature to the small towns and rural areas across the state. The state's newly created Department of Public Instruction (DPI) under the indefatigable leadership of Deyoe, now assisted by a corps of state inspectors and a network of experts from the state's educational establishment, worked closely with the business elites of the small towns and some of the more successful commercial farmers across the state in a massive effort to convince farmers to abandon their rural schools in favor of the state-aided consolidated school. Efforts were initially targeted to stimulate interest in consolidation in the rich, cash-grain area in the north central and northwest parts of the state where there were larger farms, fewer people, and fewer towns. Arguably, the movement met with its greatest success in areas where it was least needed. Deyoe and his assistants urged local boosters to include enough taxable property in a proposed district to build and operate a school of a size qualifying for the maximum amount of state aid and gerrymandered to ensure that the district did not include enough opponents to defeat the measure. In 1912 there were but 12 consolidated school districts in the state. This number had swollen to 80 by the end of 1914, 187 by 1916, and 235 by 1917 (Brown 1922, 101; May 1956, 39) (see Figure 24.4).

Almost from the outset the campaign borrowed some of the rhetoric of the Country Life movement to build grassroots support for "modernizing" rural life. It was argued that open-country communities based on reciprocity and neighborliness were either already defunct or fast disappearing and that a resuscitated rural community life was needed. Improvements in transporta-

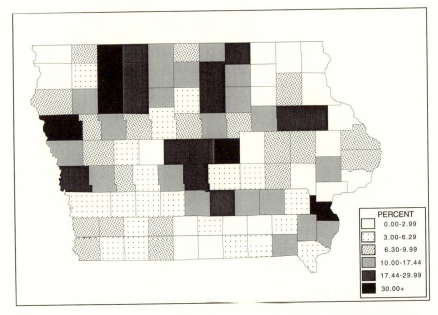

PERCENT
0.00-2.99
3.00-6.29
6.30-9.99
10.00-17.44
17.44-29.99
30.00+

Figure 24.4. Percent of country area included in a consolidated district, 1917–1918.

tion and agricultural technology and increases in farm prices suggested that rural social relations were becoming more town-centered, commodified, and modern anyway; rural society was inexorably being incorporated into mass society (see also Hobbs, Chapter 20). With fully up-to-date schools it was claimed that small urban places would become new "community centers" in a resuscitated country life (Deyoe 1915).

The more than 1,000 villages with populations below 800 were identified as the "natural centers" for consolidated schools (Campbell 1921; Welch 1921). Unlike larger towns that served as major marketing centers, villages were closely linked in their social relations with the surrounding areas because they were the principal places of retirement for farmers. Towns above this size, it was argued, were not "rural-minded" and were the very places to which rural teenagers migrated prematurely in search of jobs.

Rural Opposition to Consolidation

Although the leaders of educational reform shared a common ideology, they realized that many rural people did not share it. No issue dealing with rural public schooling, before or since, produced greater animosity and conflict between rural people and state leaders than school consolidation did when it was being contested in the hustings from 1906 to 1921.[9] Even in the areas where consolidation succeeded electorally, several elections were usually necessary before a consolidation would pass.

The list of specific objections rural Iowans had to consolidation was a long and varied one, but they tended to share five general concerns. First and most basic, rural people objected to consolidation on the grounds that it would result in a significant loss in rural parents' input to and control over the education their children received. Most farmers were content with *their* country schools, a complacency buoyed in part by agricultural prosperity. Continuing prosperity throughout the period severely undercut some reformers' contention that success in farming was causally connected to the amount of education a farmer had or to the nature of his educational facilities.[10] It also was well known that Iowa had the lowest level of illiteracy nationally and that the proportion of Iowans completing the eighth grade was consistently among the highest in the nation (Jensen and Friedberger 1976, 8.2). Many farmers thought it audacious that the public schools abrogate the family and community responsibility of teaching children about agriculture. Others opined that the "book farming" would "educate the farm child away from the farm" altogether or transmit aspirations to children that would damage their conception of farming as a way of life (Jensen and Friedberger 1976). A related cultural fear was that the mixing of rural and town children on the turf of the latter would continue the tradition of social discrimination by townspeople against farm children.

A second but related concern was that consolidation was being thrust upon rural neighborhoods whether they wanted it or not. Almost invariably one or more country schools deemed of high quality by most persons in a locality had to be included in a consolidation proposal for the district to meet the minimum areal extent specified by law (sixteen sections). When voters discovered that, even though a majority of them and their neighbors opposed consolidation, their children could be forced into a consolidated district, they were incredulous. This phenomenon gave credence to the contention of opponents that consolidation, billed as a means of improving rural education, typically killed many of the best country schools.

Third was the omnipresent issue of increased taxation. In the early phases of the movement, consolidation was erroneously billed as a means of actually lowering taxes. By 1913 the issue was not whether consolidated schools cost more than one-room schools but whether the benefits of the consolidated school were worth the much greater additional cost.[11] Typically, in areas with high land values the additional cost was judged worthwhile. Here it was also possible to raise more additional revenue per acre for school purposes than in less well endowed districts. This variation had several generally undesirable effects. By introducing considerably greater variation in per-pupil expenditures in rural areas, the apparent equality between rural districts that had previously so clearly distinguished them from urban areas was undercut. The resultant incentive for gerrymandering also exacerbated a place-based form of class divisiveness between farmers. Exclusive reliance upon property taxation, coupled with the rapidly escalating agricultural land values of the period, meant that the tax burdens for building and operating a consolidated school fell disproportionately on farmers rather than on townspeople. It led to the justifiable contention that consolidation resulted in farmers paying for the building of "town" schools. In 1905 one farmer in the Buffalo Center consolidated district remarked sarcastically that consolidation "has given us the great privilege of furnishing 45 percent of the pupils and of paying 65 percent of the cost" (May 1956, 40).

Fourth, the difficulty, inconvenience, and potential hardships of transporting rural students, particularly the younger ones, on Iowa's unimproved roads were almost invariably singled out for criticism by consolidation opponents. Even the reformers themselves conceded that the poor condition of roads placed limits on the territorial size of a district, but they viewed this issue as only a temporary impediment.

Fifth, farm families often opposed consolidation because it was presented as the only viable alternative to the country school. If a primary objective of consolidation was to improve the accessibility of rural students to "rural-minded" high schools (see, e.g., Deyoe 1912), many wondered why no effort was made to direct state aid to the country schools and encourage the formation of high schools serving the students from the surrounding four to nine country school districts.[12]

Silencing Dissent

From the outset the rhetoric of consolidation found a receptive audience primarily in villages and small towns that either did not have a four-year high school but wanted one or that already had one but could not afford to bring it up to the new state standards. The reformers targeted their efforts to these places, a strategy that was contradictory both educationally and territorially. It meant that those country school districts nearer to larger urban places would retain their country schools while paying the tuition to send their students to high schools in the very towns where, many reformers argued, the social environment would undermine important rural values. Apparently, those living in wealthier farm areas where the farms were larger, the population less dense, and the towns more widely dispersed were to be the principal beneficiaries of school consolidation.

The new political geography of school districts was fraught with spatial and economic inequalities and was politically contentious locally. Far too many villages existed throughout much of the state for all of them to be viable sites for consolidated schools. Elsewhere, so few villages existed that consolidated districts needed to be excessively large territorially. The school consolidation movement produced sharply different controversies from one part of the state to another. Where local communities were more strongly ethnic and where farm sizes were smaller and incomes low, consolidation was a political dead letter right from the start.[13] The hegemony of the consolidation discourse in reform circles, if not in the countryside, limited the organizational capacity of rural people to respond except in a fragmented, place-based manner.

Reformers realized that as long as the consolidation laws remained general laws that focused exclusively on the procedures through which people in a locality might initiate proceedings to form a consolidated district, persistent local proponents would win the day politically. Eventually they would hit upon a set of boundaries that would gain majority support in the rural portions of a proposed district. With at least 1,000 locations from which to launch local consolidation efforts, far more potential consolidated districts existed than were required or desirable. This situation created a powerful incentive for various forms of "defensive consolidation." Many rural localities sought inclusion in a consolidated district focused on a village of their choosing before they could be forced into that of another. Alternatively, if they wanted to unite with other rural neighborhoods without locating the school in a town or village or if they wished to maintain the country schools for the elementary grades but build a centrally located high school for the higher grades, they had to try to form an open-country consolidated district. Rural places that did not consolidate retained the traditional country school, but, ironically, in some parts of the state, the only sure way for a rural district to avoid losing territory to a consolidated district was to form one for the express purpose of not establishing a consolidated school.[14] Local "debates" over consolidation, where they emerged at all, almost invariably concerned the location of district boundaries rather than educational issues.

School consolidation was never an "experiment." Once a consolidated district had voted the bonds to build a new school, consolidation was essentially irreversible. By the end of World War I, reformers billed consolidation as the inevitable next step in social progress. School consolidation had been set within a discourse in which experts, townspeople, and only some farmers could see no other solution to the "rural school problem"—the consolidation discourse was hegemonic.

The question attracting the most attention in areas where consolidation efforts were mobilized and in each session of the legislature between 1913 and 1921 was what to do with those omnipresent territories that, in terms of spatial accessibility alone, would belong in a proposed district but that were controlled by opponents. Ironically, escalating conflict in the hustings over this issue eventually brought the consolidation movement in Iowa to a complete halt in 1921. In that year, the law was changed to include a proviso prohibiting consolidated districts from expanding their boundaries outward to include additional territory without the approval of voters in the additional territory. The proviso also deleted the requirement that school sites be in villages or towns. The intent of these changes was simply to remove the incentive for defensive consolidation, but with its geopolitical incentives to consolidate now removed, consolidation became a political dead letter. The onset of agricultural depression in 1921 sealed the fate of the consolidation movement in Iowa. Only a handful of consolidations would occur between 1922 and 1945. By the end of this period, 385 consolidated districts were still operating (see Figure 24.5). In 1928–1929 these schools enrolled approximately 20 percent of the rural students in the state. Consolidation had resulted in the closure of 2,663 country schools since 1913; ironically, the average enrollment of the closed schools was 27.1 while those remaining averaged only 16.1. Had consolidation been implemented as a rational response to enrollment decline in rural areas? In a word, no.

THE INTERWAR YEARS: WHAT HAD THE CONSOLIDATION MOVEMENT WROUGHT?

Although the consolidation movement helped create a lively interest in the rural public schools, resulted in a significant expansion in the numbers of four-year high schools across the state, and improved the access of many rural students to a more "modern" school apparatus, it never lived up to its billing as a way to equalize the elementary education opportunities of urban and rural children.

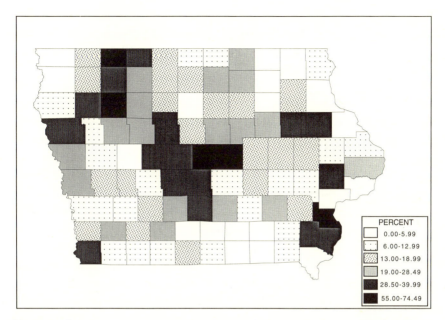

Figure 24.5. Percent of county area included in a consolidated district, 1927–1928.

What began as an attempt to improve the quality of rural education in all parts of the state was transformed quickly and unwittingly into an effort to improve education in only the most rural of rural areas in the wealthier portions of the state. With the onset of economic depression, the allocation of even fewer resources over more and larger schools ensured on average that the quality of elementary education afforded students was not a great improvement over that provided in the remaining country schools. A study conducted by the Iowa Child Welfare Research Station of performance on the Stanford Achievement Test in the 1920s, for example, showed that country school students in grades 1 to 3 did better than those in consolidated schools, whereas consolidated school students in grades 4 to 8 performed better than their country school counterparts (reported in Jensen and Friedberger 1976, 7.5). If the country schools had a weakness, it was in how their students performed in reading and language use, but this relative underchievement could have resulted from the generally shorter school terms in the country schools rather than from a poorer quality of instruction. Both types of schools produced students who scored higher than the national norm in arithmetic, spelling, and nature study and lower in history and literature.[15]

Consolidation and the Access of Rural Students to a
High School Education

It is also doubtful whether consolidation resulted in significantly greater access of rural students to high schools of a quality comparable to those of the state's larger cities and towns. In 1912–1913, the year before the consolidation movement began and before the state had developed a system for approving high schools, there were 804 public high schools offering one or more years of instruction. Practically every city, town, or village in the state had some form of high school even before the consolidation movement got into full swing. Consolidation was not primarily a means of establishing new high schools in places where none had existed previously; it was a movement to increase the size and to standardize the curriculum of those already in existence.

Between 1913 and 1930, there was a remarkable increase in the relative and absolute numbers of students attending high school in Iowa.[16] During this period the popularity of the high school increased everywhere throughout the state, not just in the rural areas.[17] The consolidation movement undoubtedly was a contributing factor, but the "free-tuition" law enjoyed even greater success in increasing the numbers of rural children attending the nonconsolidated high schools in the state.[18]

Beginning in 1911–1912, students residing in rural districts that did not consolidate could attend any high school in the state at their home district's expense, a privilege not granted to other students in the state. In 1912–1913, almost twelve thousand students took advantage of this law. The number of students availing themselves of this opportunity increased each year until 1930–1931, when almost 40,000 exercised the option. As early as 1913–1914 tuition students accounted for slightly more than 25 percent of the total high school enrollment in the state; by 1930–1931 their numbers accounted for fully one-third of high school enrollment, the vast majority of which comprised graduates of the country schools. Not surprisingly, the residents of rural districts within a reasonable weekend commuting distance from a town or city with a good high school had little interest in consolidation. As the financial resources of school districts dwindled with the deepening of the Depression and town districts sought to increase their numbers of rural tuition students by providing free transportation, this option came to be preferred over consolidation in most localities. It became so popular that as late as 1954 less than 30 percent of the total area of the state was included in a school district with its own high school (Smith 1969b, 109).

The consolidation movement did indeed help to make small high schools more accessible spatially to larger numbers of rural students, but, as a state-commissioned study by the Brookings Institution (1933) first pointed out, far too many of these small schools existed for them ever to possess local revenues approaching those available to high schools in the larger towns and cities. A movement initiated to equalize the educational opportunities between rural and urban children served primarily to re-institutionalize urban-rural inequalities in a different form. This, however, was not acknowledged within DPI until late in the 1940s (Smith 1969b, 109).

Consolidated schools differed from the nonconsolidated schools primarily in that they tended to be smaller and combined the elementary and high school grades in a single facility. Recent historical work has shown that most of the long-standing criticisms of the country school applied with equal force to educational conditions in the smaller consolidated and town schools of the state in the 1920s and 1930s (Jensen and Friedberger 1976, 7.15–7.16).

Economic Hardship and the Rise of a New Sense of Community

As early as 1920 Iowa was second only to California in the percentage of its school-age children attending high school (Troxel 1928, 191). As Country Lifers had hoped a decade or more earlier, the formation of consolidated districts did help contribute to new forms of "community," resulting in many instances from the sheer necessity of having to pull together to make a success of a situation from which there was no turning back. The formation of de facto high school districts through the exercise of the "free tuition" law had a similar effect. There was, however, another stimulus leading to the creation of a new sense of community. The gap between the social status and prestige of teachers (and educational administrators) and the longer-term residents of the small-town and consolidated school districts frequently created a serious cultural tension which threatened to undermine local support for the public schools. Educators resolved the dilemma by turning the high school into the social and recreational center for the surrounding area, "with basketball teams, marching bands and plenty of hoopla to whip up enthusiasm of residents for a local institution" (Jensen and Friedberger 1976, 7.17). Grudgingly, educators had come to realize the pivotal role of the school in institutionalizing community identity and thereby engendering broad-based support for the public schools. Perhaps because they were not permanent members of the rural community themselves, they overwhelmingly valued "community" merely as a means to an end and not as an end in itself. In this way a new form of "community" fostering new local identities based on small-town rivalries, institutionalized and legitimated through high school athletic competitions, rose to prominence (cf. Callahan 1962).

Population and Enrollment Changes: 1930–1950

During the Depression and throughout World War II, the consolidation discourse lost none of its hegemony in reform circles either in Iowa or nationally. Reformers assumed that worsening economic conditions had simply forced it off the political agenda. Literally nothing else, however, stood still. New Deal farm policies and the outbreak of war would eventually bring renewed prosperity to midwestern agriculture, but it was slow in coming and was accompanied by increasingly rapid changes in the organization of agricultural production. Particularly evident was the decrease in the relative proportion of farm land in the middling family farm sizes (50 to 179 acres) and an increase in the proportion of large farms (more than 259 acres) (Hart 1972, 273–274). The population living in rural areas decreased at an increasing rate each decade between 1930 and 1970.[19] In 1930, 60.4 percent of Iowa's population lived in rural areas; by 1970 this figure had dropped to 42.8. For the state as a whole the population aged 5 to 14 years decreased by 12.9 percent in the 1930s, but increased by 2.2 percent in the 1940s, by 29.3 in the 1950s, and by 4.2 percent in the 1960s. By the early 1950s these population changes translated into significant enrollment decreases in both the remaining rural independent school districts and in the consolidated school districts. A few new consolidated districts were formed in the late 1940s, but overwhelmingly the tuition student option was exercised. In areas where enrollment decline was most severe two or three country school districts often merged to form a new district with a sufficient number of pupils to justify the continuance of one of their country schools. Between 1930 and 1950 the number of country schools was reduced almost by half through such "voluntary" action—most of it coming in the 1940s (Table 24.1). This trend continued into the 1950s.[20] Thus as enrollment in the country schools dwindled, the enrollments in remaining schools were maintained. Although the high school retained its importance in the social life of rural Iowans during the Depression, attending high school did not lead to appreciably greater success in the job market—a fact that contributed to a marked decrease in high school enrollments. These losses were even more precipitous than the decline in the number of school-age children in rural areas. Statewide, elementary school enrollment decreased by 5.5 percent between 1930 and 1950, but high school enrollment dropped by more than 23 percent in that

Table 24.1. Enrollment in Iowa's country schools, 1912–1913 to 1959–1960

Year	Number of Country Schools	Enrollment in Country Schools	Average Number of Students
1912–1913	12,258	226,880	18.5
1917–1918	11,252	204,515	18.2
1921–1922	10,828	173,259	16.0
1929–1930	9,595	154,594	16.1
1934–1935	9,179	135,929	14.8
1939–1940	8,533	119,417	14.0
1944–1945	7,243	103,673	14.3
1949–1950	4,960	86,703	17.5
1954–1955	3,232	68,106	21.1
1957–1958	2,067	50,942	24.6
1959–1960	863	30,861	35.8

Source: Calculated by author from Department of Public Instruction, State of Iowa, *Biennial Reports*, 1913–1960.

same period (Table 24.2). In districts with their own high schools (the urban independent and the consolidated districts), elementary school enrollments actually increased during this period at the expense of the country schools. In 1930 country schools accounted for 40 percent of elementary school enrollments in the state; by 1950 this figure was only 23.5 (Table 24.2).

POST–WORLD WAR II REORGANIZATION: SOMETHING DIFFERENT OR MORE OF THE SAME?

By the 1950s Iowa had a "new" rural school problem, only now the small, seemingly inefficient high school replaced the country school of yore as the principal focus of concern. "Our major concern is not with the rural school . . . Our most serious problem is in the large number of small, inefficient high schools which we are operating. Three years ago we had the dubious distinction of having 5 percent of all the high school districts in the entire United States" (DPI 1960, 6). The parameters of the problem were remarkably similar to those first articulated a half century earlier. Following a decade of plummeting enrollments, the 1950s, like the 1910s, experienced an economic boom accompanied by an upswing in the number of school-age children. In the both the 1900s and the 1940s, "rural" children were not perceived as having access to the same quality of education afforded "urban" children.

Table 24.2. Enrollments in school districts by type: 1929–1930 to 1959–1960

Year	Country	Elementary[a]	High School[b]	Total	Percentage Elementary[c]
1929–1930	154,594	231,647	146,629	532,870	40.0
1939–1940	119,417	244,654	139,410	503,483	32.8
1946–1947	94,894	249,985	114,252	459,113	27.5
1949–1950	86,703	278,239	112,778	477,720	23.5
1959–1960	30,861	426,125	141,117	598,103	6.8

Source: Calculated by author from Department of Public Instrauction, State of Iowa, *Biennial Reports,* 1930–1960.

[a] Elementary school enrollment in districts with high schools.
[b] High school enrollment in districts with high schools.
[c] Percentage of elementary school enrollment in country schools.

Quality in both decades was defined by the size of schools and the number of grades and classes into which they were organized. Formerly, "rural" had been viewed by reformers quite literally as open farm country; by the 1950s "rural" had come to conform more closely to the U.S. Census definition of "rural" (i.e., people not living in urbanized places with populations in excess of 2,500). In the 1910s reformers were concerned with ensuring greater access to both graded and high schools; in the 1950s access to a high-quality high school education was the preoccupation. A new generation of educational reformers argued that most of Iowa's high schools were simply too small to offer the breadth and depth of curricula needed to provide rural students with skills that would enable them to compete for the best jobs in the burgeoning postwar economy.

Local proponents of earlier consolidation efforts now often found themselves prisoners of the "old" consolidation discourse: if the country school had to give way to educational progress then so too had the small-town high school. Even these people surely had some regrets, however, for the country school and the small high school had both been significant integrating institutions in their respective place-based communities and had imparted an important sense of collective identity. The community identities fostered by consolidation were based largely on pride of place resulting from the simple fact that the high school was the one "place" where the shared activities of students, parents, townspeople, and other residents had been institutionalized, providing an identity to the local community for almost everyone in the school district. The fact that extracurricular activities, particularly in the form of athletic events, were a major part of the institutionalization of the school and often engendered intense rivalries between neighboring school districts made community identities all the more real.

At long last, the principal issues at stake in the consolidation debate—in both its original form and in its reincarnation—were clear: the choice was between what was good for society, equality of educational opportunity for all individuals in the larger society, and what was good for community, a sense of collective identity and a set of shared values and a means of reproducing them. In the earlier consolidation debate, most reformers had asserted that the goals of equality and community were compatible, provided that new forward-looking communities could be created. Curiously, few if any saw the two goals as essential to one another and none of them articulated a role for the public schools in achieving both simultaneously. Despite the centrality of the school in fostering community identity, educational reformers left the pursuit of community to the institutions of civil society; school facilities merely provided the infrastructure. They repeatedly stressed that education was a societywide function and that the pursuit of equality of education, a primary goal of the state, should be achieved through its system of public schools over which it exercised ultimate authority (see, e.g., Alford 1960, 370). The territorially extensive rural community identities that had been fostered through the extracurricular activities of high schools in the interwar years were caricatured and lampooned as distractions from achieving equality of opportunity in education. Ironically, the choice between society and community became apparent only when it was clear that community had already lost resoundingly. The consolidation of Iowa's remaining country schools with the newly reorganized "community" districts was largely complete by the mid-1960s, but the pressure to form still larger districts continued.

Resistance to the reorganization of school districts was based on community defense sentiments similar to those expressed earlier in the century. Formerly, the community defended was the open-county rural community typically focused on either or both the country school and church, while latterly it focused on the small-town high school. Until the mid-1970s, when U.S. education as a whole came under attack for its tenuous connection with parents and the local communities it served, professional educators simply ignored community-based arguments or otherwise denied their legitimacy. From the 1970s onward, an increasing number of studies has documented that the educational advantages of the large over the small high school in Iowa and elsewhere are much less than had been presumed (Baker 1970; Dunne 1977; Goodlad 1984; Monk and Haller 1986; Turner 1985). There is also a growing consensus of what characteristics constitute an effective school educationally—e.g., relationships between students, teachers, and administrators based on mutual respect; individualized instruction; an emphasis on basic skills; parental and community involvement and support; a tolerance of individual initiative and innovation—and a realization that none of these have any necessary relationship to school size (Nachtigal 1990, 97). If anything, recent work suggests that urban schools have at least as much to learn from rural schools as rural counterparts have to learn from urban ones.

In 1991–1992 Iowa students led the nation in terms of average ACT and SAT scores—a position Iowa has held every year save one since these test scores have been published (U.S. Department of Education 1993a). In an international comparison of high-school students' proficiency in mathematics in 1991–1992, Iowa students topped those of all other states; in 1992 Iowa eighth-graders tied those in North Dakota in having the highest average mathematics proficiency scores in the country (U.S. Department of Education 1993b). In 1990 Iowa had the highest high-school completion rate in the nation (93 percent) and was closely bunched with four other upper midwestern states in having the lowest high-school dropout rates in the nation (U.S. Department of Education 1993b). In that same year Iowa ranked eleventh in the nation in terms of the percentage of persons 25 years old and over with a high-school diploma or higher. Additional statistics could be cited, but they would simply confirm what is already clear: in terms of typical measures of the quality of the educational outputs, Iowa schools are at or near the top in the nation. The only "standard" measure of educational success on which Iowa has never ranked near the top is in the percentage of its population 25 years and older with some college education (cf. Teixeira, Chapter 22). In 1990 Iowa ranked thirty-seventh among the states on this indicator of "quality." Education in Iowa has been high-school focused ever since the early 1920s; in 1990 Iowa was second (to Pennsylvania) in the percentage of its population 25 years and older whose highest level of education attained was high school graduation (U.S. Department of Education 1993a),[21] yet further evidence that both the support for and enrollment in public schools has a pervasive communitarian basis in Iowa. For most Iowans, attending the small country schools in high numbers prior to World War I was, in significant measure, an affirmation of community membership. After the war, the free-tuition law and the consolidation movement jointly stimulated a greater interest in the high school among rural Iowans, and they gradually expanded their community allegiances and identities to include small towns across the state. As Jensen and Friedberger (1976) suggest, however, most Iowans did not accept the reformers' view that the public school was primarily a vehicle of social and economic advancement.

High quality is not a recently acquired characteristic of Iowa's public schools. Throughout the entire twentieth century they have consistently ranked among the best schools in the nation. Iowa has had the lowest percentage of illiteracy in every U.S. census year this century, except for 1960, when it dropped to second. From 1870 through 1950, Iowa invariably was one of the leading states in terms of the percentage of its school-age population enrolled in school, never being lower than thirteenth and more typically figuring among the top five states. Relative to other states, Iowa ranked higher in this percentage before rather than after the consolidation movement began in the 1910s. If only input indicators of educational quality are considered (e.g., per pupil expenditures, state aid per pupil, teacher salaries, teachers' years of experience, and percentage of teachers with advanced degrees), Iowa appears quite average on many points but quite exceptional on others. Iowa has always had low pupil-to-teacher ratios and small class sizes, it has invested a relatively high proportion of its average personal income in the public schools, and, as has been stressed throughout this chapter, it has always been a leader in the number of schools per capita. Has the quality of education in Iowa remained high because of, or despite, rural school consolidation? Could both be correct? The evidence presented above suggests the latter.

CONCLUSION

While the overall system of public schooling in the United States is now widely perceived to be in crisis, rural education remains preoccupied with consolidation. Most writers on rural education fail to realize that the present discourse of consolidation, like its early-twentieth-century progenitor, has not involved critical debate over the quality of rural public schools at all but is the continuation of a much longer hegemonic discourse over consolidation as an end in itself. Failure to recognize this distinction means that we are likely doomed to repeat past mistakes rather than to learn from them.

The logic of rural school consolidation and reorganization has always entailed a simple spatial logic. It assumes that the primary determinants of educational quality are school size, the extent to which the curriculum is designed and implemented by professionals, the amount of revenue available for expenditure, and finally, that all three of these in turn are directly related to the size and territorial extent of school districts. The issue of quality is otherwise treated as unproblematic. Any links between school quality and community quality are either assumed or ignored, as are any differences between rural and urban communities. The spatial problem is one of assigning and transporting pupils to places where professionals will provide "education" and assigning taxpayers to those jurisdictions used to generate revenue to pay for that education. Following this logic, if the costs of transportation were to vanish or at least become relatively insensitive to distance, then the logic of consolidation is transformed fundamentally. Historically, the school has been a place where students, teachers, and administrators come into direct physical contact to engage in educational activities; for reasons of spatial efficiency the numbers of such places have been small relative to the numbers of students involved. If education does not require the simultaneous presence of students, teachers, and administrators on the scale required in the past, then the school as a place specializing in the provision of education must be reconsidered. What kind of place should it be? If it is a place where lifelong education occurs, how can specialization be justified at all? The traditional concept of school district is also in need of a fundamental rethinking.

These kinds of questions would be nonsensical were it not for the revolution in telecommunications technology in contemporary society. Advances in such technology have the capability of robbing the grand debate over consolidation of much of its traditional spatial logic. Schools could indeed be almost everywhere there is a port on the fiber-optic "information highway" that can be linked directly to wherever "students" might need or want to be. "Distance learning" could become the dominant form of schooling for most people. Remaining problems—ones that cannot be dispelled by further technological revolutions—include the issues of who will control the system, who will have access to it, how much will it cost, and who will pay for it. These are obviously crucial sociopolitical issues. How they are resolved will largely determine whether or not the consolidation debate is transcended. It would be a mistake, however, to assume that the advent of "distance learning" will necessarily obviate any "need" for further school consolidation in rural areas. If meeting the costs of connecting to a state or national telecommunication system are left to already existing school districts, the advantages affluent suburban school districts supposedly already have over central city and rural districts will likely be further increased. This discrepancy could force rural districts to unite in order to provide the resources necessary to achieve access to the system—much as small districts are currently urged to merge so as to meet stricter state standards at a reasonable cost. There is nothing necessarily egalitarian about distance learning. For low-income people, it could well occur only in places strongly resembling traditional schools, whereas for the more affluent students, educational choices could indeed abound.

Essentially, important policy issues in rural education devolve into two general classes—those concerning the locus of societal/community discretion and those concerning cost sharing. First and most important is what relationship should exist between local communities and the larger society and how this relationship should find expression in the school. Local communities consist of dense networks of social and economic relations within which people's daily lives unfold. How then can society have meaning if divorced from community? Should the public school seek to instill an appreciation of how local communities are embedded in society and give it texture and meaning? Even in the age of telecommunications, the concept of school as an important place where people learn about themselves in relation to their community, to others, and to society retains its relevance. What, moreover, are appropriate roles for parents, community members, teachers, and school administrators in maintaining a high-quality school? In rural areas and small towns there is a strong presumption that local communities will be less spatially extensive and that parental and community roles can and will be greater than in urban and suburban areas where the levels of population turnover are higher.

Next is the vexing issue of paying for public education and its infrastructure. Should the state provide all or most of the revenue needed to ensure wide access to communication technology vitiating the need for large schools? Should it also pay the salaries of the teachers and administrators still needed but leave the task of providing support for teachers to parents and community volunteers? Can some more appropriate means of sharing the costs of education between the state and community be found? Answers to these questions may well force a fundamental redefinition of the concept of the school as a place where all or most formal education is obtained. Whether rural and urban communities require different kinds (not sizes) of schools in order to achieve outputs of comparable quality also demands serious reconsideration. The hegemony of the consolidation discourse meant that these questions were finessed for three-quarters of a century. Only in the 1970s did debate over these matters begin—but the discussion all too quickly elided into a contest over the educational advantages of big schools over small schools.

New technology cannot, indeed should not, determine the answers to these questions, but it has helped reveal the critical policy issues. Rural school consolidation has not yet been replaced as a dominant discourse in educational reform, but it has lost its hegemony. Perhaps more socially constructive reforms in rural education can now be seriously discussed in an appropriate political forum. Let the real debates finally begin.

NOTES

1. Although the total population of the state decreased by 115,000 between 1890 and 1910, almost 40 percent of this increase was accounted for by the decrease in the number of persons aged 5 to 14 alone—the equivalent of the enrollment of approximately 1,800 country schools. In 1903–1904, the average number of persons between the ages of 5 and 21 years residing in a country school district was 30.5 (Biennial Report 1905, II: 117). The comparable figure for 1912–1913 was 25.4, a loss of 16.7 percent. In 1912–1913 the average enrollment in country school districts was 18.5.

2. "Urban" independent districts consisted of what Iowa law designated as city, town, or village independent districts. Since there was some presumption that these districts would possess graded-elementary schools and possibly some "high-school" level instruction, they were permitted to assess higher millage levies on the assessed value of property within them for public school purposes than was permitted in country school districts.

3. Country schoolteachers were neither recognized in ISTA's organizational structure nor on the programs of its annual meetings and were even denied participation in selecting members to its all-important Education Council (Smith 1969a, 414; Hart 1954, 51–58).

4. The state teacher's college offered no course of study designed for country schoolteachers until 1913, after it had come under intense pressure to assume more responsibility for training rural schoolteachers from key members of the state legislature and the state's Board of Education (Lang 1991, 323–325). The state had no formal system for training country schoolteachers until 1911, when a program providing state aid to high schools offering a state-approved program of normal training was first initiated.

5. The "rural school problem" entailed a veritable litany of educational sins of omission and commission. Teachers in the country schools were said to be inexperienced, poorly trained and underpaid, unsupervised, their tenure too short, and their teaching methods dated. Particularly singled out for ridicule was what an increasing number of the new educational experts thought to be an over-reliance on the recitation method and the use of older pupils to help instruct younger ones. The school year was too short and regular attendance levels too low and irregular. There were too few students to permit the "grading" necessary for converting education from a cooperative to a competitive endeavor. School facilities were too small, unkempt, unsanitary, outdated, and ill-equipped. Most of all, the rural school was criticized for having remained essentially unchanged while the institutions of the larger society around it were changing rapidly (Sabin 1898; Beard 1909; Deyoe 1912).

6. At no time between 1895 and 1920 did the county superintendents indicate that more than 13 percent of the rural schools were in "poor" condition. Typically, almost 60 percent were evaluated as in "good" condition. The special survey of student enumerations, enrollments, and attendance levels in 1903–1904 also failed to turn up anything very startling. Almost three-fourths of all rural school districts contained more than twenty school-age children and during the winter term (when more chil-

dren could attend), more than three-fourths of the rural districts had an average daily attendance of ten or more.

7. In this regard it is important to note that legislation to make school attendance compulsory and to grant the state more authority in the licensing of teachers won quite widespread approval in rural areas during the period 1901–1906 and passed much more easily than it did in other states (cf. Fuller 1982). A reasonable interpretation is that rural Iowans generally embraced efforts to improve their single-teacher schools and to increase their enrollments.

8. This commission consisted of educational experts, including several self-styled country life experts and high-profile Progressive politicians, handpicked by Deyoe and ISTA leaders for their influence not only in the Progressive wing of the Republican party but also with important business leaders in the state. Consistent with Progressive ideology, the educational experts took the lead in identifying the desired legislation while the political experts attempted to mobilize the requisite grassroots and legislative support for it. Only one farmer was on the commission (BISC 1912, 57–58).

9. The extent and depth of this conflict is indicated by the fact that conflicts over consolidation produced more litigation than any educational issue before or since. Between 1906 and 1925, seventy such cases were appealed to and heard by the Iowa Supreme Court. Countless others were heard by the district courts but went unappealed.

10. Jensen and Friedberger (1976) document that during this period success in farming was in fact largely unrelated to educational achievement beyond that received in the rural schools.

11. The best estimates available suggest that the shift from the rural independent to consolidated district was accompanied on average by about a threefold increase in school tax levies per acre of farm land in 1915 and a fourfold increase by 1921 (Phillips 1923, 38). The actual increase in tax levies was determined by the size and form of the school apparatus itself and by the geography of assessed valuations.

12. Evidence dating from the 1890s onward was available suggesting that this alternative to consolidation was both successful and popular (see, e.g., Biennial Report 1902; Aurner 1912, 1915, vol. 3).

13. Reformers did not push for the consolidation of rural school districts in parts of northeast and much of southern Iowa on the grounds that the uneven topography there made the transportation of pupils at public expense impractical. Not insignificantly, however, uneven topography also went hand-in-hand with small farms and relatively low farm incomes.

14. At least thirty and perhaps as many as sixty such "consolidated" districts were formed between 1913 and 1922.

15. Similar results were obtained in a massive nineteen-state study examining the achievement scores of 15,000 students in both consolidated and country schools under the auspices of the National Education Association in 1920–1922 (see Fuller 1982: 241–243).

16. In 1913–1914, total enrollment in the state's high schools was 48,770; by 1930 high-school enrollment burgeoned to 120,526. In 1930, 777 state-approved four-year public high schools accounted for 27.5 percent of the state's total public school enrollment (Brookings Institution 1933, 142). 1913–1914 is the first year for

which reasonably accurate high-school enrollment data is available. Prior to the creation of DPI in 1913, no means existed for the state to compel districts or county superintendents to supply these.

17. In the twenty-year period from 1913–1914 to 1933–1934, the total high-school enrollments in Iowa increased from 48,770 to 129, 845, an increase of 166 percent. During this same period the number of rural students attending high school under the provisions of the state's free-tuition law increased from 12,587 to 34,720, an increase of 175 percent.

18. In 1919–1920, "tuition" students comprised 26.7 percent of the state's total public high school enrollment (Biennial Report 1920)—a figure considerably higher than the number of rural high school students attending consolidated schools in 1927–1928 (the first year in which all of the consolidated schools had finally been built). Most of these tuition students were graduates of the one-room country schools. In 1921–1922, when roughly half of the new consolidated schools had been built, the high-school departments of consolidated schools accounted for 24.5 percent of the total high-school enrollment in the state as opposed to 29.1 percent accounted for by tuition students. In 1927–1928, when all of the consolidated schools had been built, the comparable figures were 22.6 and 27.3 percent, respectively.

19. The decreases in the percentages of persons not living in places with 2,500 or more residents for the 1930s, 1940s, 1950s, and 1960s were 2.5, 4.3, 5.5, and 6.7, respectively.

20. In 1957–1958 there were 2,545 school districts in Iowa with an average daily attendance of less than 25; 1,240 of these districts did not operate any school at all (U.S. Office of Education 1958).

21. In 1976 Iowa led the nation is the percentage of persons 18 years and older whose highest level of educational attainment was four years of high school (U.S. Office of Education 1981).

25

LIVING WITH THE MINIMUM: RURAL PUBLIC POLICY

WILLIAM P. BROWNE AND LOUIS E. SWANSON

Rural America, with its myriad problems and opportunities, is too diverse for a comprehensive, "one size fits all" policy. The needs of rural people are most appropriately met at the local level; therefore, the relevant policy question is: Can the federal government facilitate local development initiatives? Such a qualitative shift in emphasis would require a great deal of local and national effort to overcome the inertia of decades of minimalist rural policy. Although such states as Wisconsin, Pennsylvania, and Missouri, and their land-grant universities (LGUs), have a historical commitment to working with local people, the national effort has been uneven and sometimes nonexistent. In this chapter we propose that federal rural policy should involve less federal control and allow for greater flexibility among rural communities. Our focus is on federal rural development programs.[1]

The current fractured constellation of categorical grants and other programs that have some rural focus has no clear statement of goals, no consistent delivery system, and no guiding federal agency. Congress, particularly through the agricultural committees, is unlikely to sponsor a comprehensive rural policy or allocate additional resources. But congressional inaction need not mean policy failure. Many rural communities and areas mobilize and organize their scarce resources without a comprehensive federal policy. A new policy that would mobilize federal assistance to support local initiatives may minimize the federal role but foster locally identified and implemented development efforts. A rural policy that would emphasize local and regional autonomy but that would not require large federal outlays or a major congressional commitment may in fact be feasible.

The United States has never mounted a comprehensive attack on declining jobs, weak economic growth, population loss, and the consequences of national economic restructuring in rural places. (Osbourn 1988; Browne 1991; Effland 1993). In 1967 the National Advisory Commission on Rural Poverty submitted recommendations to address a wide range of rural social problems. Most of these recommendations were ignored by federal policymakers. Congress has continued to disappoint rural advocates by its inaction since the 1972 Rural Development Act, particularly in its failure to address rural development needs prior to and in the 1990 Farm Bill.

As a result, it has become fashionable once again to speak of grass-roots initiatives as the proper place for rural public policy. Grass-roots development efforts, facilitated by federal support, have the advantage of targeting scarce dollars to communities willing to invest their own time, effort, and money. It is not, however, clear that policies employing the rhetoric of greater local control would actually be welcomed by Congress, rural policy professionals, or assorted rural development interest groups. The same interests that have shaped the current fractured and institutionally administered federal programs may well oppose greater input from broad segments of rural residents. This potential opposition, combined with the lack of truly national advocacy, bodes poorly for the future of a national rural policy.

Ironically, a reluctance to share federal power locally does not characterize the more complex and expensive farm programs. United States Department of Agriculture (USDA) agencies such as the Agricultural Stabilization and Conservation Service (ASCS), the Soil Conservation Service (SCS), and the Cooperative Extension Service (CES) have structured their operations and built political legitimacy around local boards of those who use their programs. Program support spreads through clusters of neighbors. Hamilton (1992) has explained the empowerment of federal farm programs as a result of federal agency and local farmer cooperation.

The federal government is not alone in discouraging broad-based local control. Local elites and elected officials often shun programs that require long-term, broad-based citizen participation. Their lack of interest raises three questions. Why do rural development programs not incorporate the same level of citizen input and oversight as major farm programs? Why, instead, does significant local participation in rural development programs suffer the same problems that plagued the neighborhood-based, maximum-participation urban initiatives of the 1970s (Kotler 1969; Altshuler 1970)? And, if there were greater local input, is it reasonable to assume rural programs would lead to improved local communities?

These questions are prompted by our reading of the past and our evaluation of the present. The absence of locally based programs reflects historic conditions that limit or prevent greater local control of nonfarm rural social and economic development. These conditions include the location of rural development in congressional committees focused on farming, the diversity of rural social and economic issues, turf protection by existing agencies and development organizations, and a lack of enthusiasm by some rural officials about directing their own local rural development.

Farm institutions are not well equipped to become effective rural institutions, at least not in any direct sense (Browne 1991). Professional policy analysts may assume that the concept of rural development connotes a similar meaning and provokes a shared sense of urgency among rural residents and their leaders. This heroic, convenient assumption is incorrect. Therefore, a shift toward federal assistance in facilitating greater local control should be sought only with proper preparation and care.[2]

FARM AND RURAL INSTITUTIONS: TOP DOWN OR BOTTOM UP?

A dual transformation in rural America has occurred during the last half century (Browne et al. 1992). During this period many rural areas shifted their economic base from natural-resource extraction to manufacturing and service enterprises. Simultaneously, many rural class structures and economies changed from a high proportion of owner-operators, though often with low incomes, to hourly wage and salary positions. This transformation did not improve the relative economic and social well-being of most rural people. Furthermore, many nonfarm social and economic programs, such as the War on Poverty, job retraining programs, or the improvement of transportation infrastructures, did not reduce the gaps in relative income and well-being between metro and nonmetro areas. Most rural areas continue to be left behind (Whiting 1974; Rural Sociological Task Force on Persistent Rural Poverty 1993; Summers, Chapter 11).

The Great Depression of the 1930s created a crisis for federal public policy. Indeed, the Depression posed a crisis in the performance of the modern centralized state bureaucracy as a development institution (Hamilton 1992). Nowhere was this crisis more apparent than in the rural areas where almost half of the U.S. population resided. The immediate congressional response was the creation of temporary relief programs. Among farm programs, partnerships were formed between the federal government and local users. This partnership was a remarkably innovative and uniquely American option, given local distrust of centralized state bureaucracies. Local participants on the active joint local boards had an important effect on their performance.

The benefit for the federal bureaucracy was a legitimacy that stemmed from grass-roots support. This associative state became a pillar for proactive policy cooperation.

The relationship between administrators and farmers was tied to the problems of effective intervention in sharply fragmented and diverse farm commodity markets. How could the radically new public-policy concepts of the Agricultural Adjustment Administration (AAA) and SCS, which required large bureaucracies and imposed production constraints, gain popular support or necessary legitimacy? How could a comprehensive federal farm policy address the great diversity of agricultural farming systems and commodities? The simple solution to both problems was to give a degree of program control, particularly local oversight, to local farmers and landowners. Local participants were likely to be at least from the middle class and more likely still to be larger landowners. Although these new programs were granting a greater degree of control in the management of farm programs to local participants, those participants were usually local elites. Surviving today are ASCS (once AAA) and Conservation District Boards (CDB). The CDBs also use local advisory committees, the models for New Deal farm programs.

Cooperation with local users became the foundation for establishing large federal bureaucracies to facilitate the recovery of U.S. agriculture. A similar path was followed in the effort to bring electric power to isolated rural areas. Although the Rural Electricification Administration was built on regional rural cooperatives rather than on county-based boards, the objective was the same: to gain political legitimacy for bureaucracies that would otherwise face serious political opposition by making local users, usually local elites, partners in the assessment of program priorities and in the distribution of program benefits.

These temporary programs and their associated institutions have now survived for sixty years. Serious questions have been raised, however, regarding the equity with which the programs are delivered and with which the local boards are composed. Perhaps the most publicized challenge was to the AAA in the South, especially in cotton and sugar regions. Because program benefits were directed primarily toward landowners rather than producers, sharecroppers and tenants benefited very little. The formation of the Southern Tenant Farmers Movement was a direct reaction to this program inequity.

Similar charges that boards favor local elites have been leveled at the conservation districts. These very inequities, particularly in the South, gave the programs political credibility in the Congress of the 1930s, where committees were chaired by senior southern legislators. Elites were not, however, so very elitist as to be out of touch with many local needs. Such broad-based legitimacy, despite the diversity of farming circumstances, made it possible for an omnibus set of federal farm programs to emerge and survive for decades in Congress. The development and operation of these programs were associated with a highly productive farm sector.

PAST FEDERAL EFFORTS TO EMPOWER LOCAL PEOPLE

Nonfarm federal rural development programs have flirted with local control on a few occasions, such as the venture to create Rural Area Development Committees (RADCs) in the 1950s and early 1960s. Similarly, the Office of Economic Opportunity (OEO) and the War on Poverty of the late 1960s and 1970s sought to establish competing elites in local areas in order to promote broad citizen participation based on the motto of "maximum feasible participation" (Moynihan 1969). Each of these efforts was eventually eliminated either for lack of effectiveness or political liability. More recently, the New Federalism provided a very different emphasis.

The RADCs depended upon the voluntary establishment of local committees to oversee rural development. They were not granted any funding for programs and were dependent upon the good will of USDA agencies such as the Farmers Home Administration. There was no vested responsibility for these committees to develop and administer development programs and there was no incentive for local governments to support financially their work. Unsurprisingly, most committees were short lived. Nevertheless, their experience did demonstrate the need for multicounty development organizations to assist county and town governments in gaining federal grants and avoiding the duplication of expensive services. Several area development districts emerged from the RADC ashes and are now represented by the National Association of Development Organizations (NADO). However, these development organizations are financially supported by state and local governments and have limited regional planning authority.

Although OEO's efforts to empower groups that were otherwise disenfranchised at the local level achieved some success, the groups were eliminated eventually. Their greatest opposition came from existing local elites who believed these federally supported groups represented a direct political challenge to existing community power. The efforts of the OEO to foster local involvement and empowerment were the exception to the vast majority of nonfarm federal programs available to rural areas. Most programs were top-down administrative structures with little provision for local diversity and broad-based participation.

The 1980s witnessed a shift of responsibility for rural development from the federal government to state and local government. This shift is generally referred to as New Federalism and is associated primarily with the Reagan administration. The political attractiveness of New Federalism was not a belief in the efficacy of local governments to create and sustain their own development efforts. New Federalism attracted support because it addressed the federal government's fiscal crisis by conveniently transferring responsibility for administering and funding unwieldy and expensive entitlement programs, notably health care, to the states. The virtual elimination of community block grants to nonmetropolitan counties and rural places further reflected this reduced emphasis on federal spending. Significant development responsibility was thus passed to rural areas without the corresponding funding to the state and local governments for the administration of such programs.

None of these efforts, the RADCs, the OEO, or the latest New Federalism, have been successful in stimulating broad-based local development. The RADCs failed because of a lack of federal financial and political support and the absence of clearly defined goals for development. There was little incentive for local citizens to invest their scarce time and resources simply to create an appearance of a local partnership. The OEO programs were selectively successful, particularly from the viewpoint of disenfranchised segments of local populations, but they also were seen by entrenched local elites as threatening federal impositions. The New Federalism, finally, is not a development policy but a political means of addressing the federal government's fiscal problems. Proponents were not much concerned about the capacity of state and local governments to cultivate and administer development efforts.

Thus, the rural areas have experienced limited funding, unyielding federal policy mandates, and, most importantly, few opportunities for community leaders who want to make strategic choices about local development. With the exception of the various agricultural programs, federal programs have been less than impressive.

THE CHALLENGES OF DEVELOPING LOCAL CONTROL

The failure of federal development efforts to significantly improve the quality of life in rural America, with some notable exceptions such as rural electrification, has only exacerbated the rural development policy dilemma (Swanson 1989). Available policy options have been whittled away. The federal government's role has become particularly limited, for the politics of the federal government's fiscal problems of the past fifteen years severely restricts the allocation of new monies to rural nonfarm programs. Moreover, congressional agricultural committees are absorbed with commodity and environmental programs and their attendant interest groups and farm constituents. Food safety and nutrition also crowd their agendas. This situation is aggravated by opposition from agricultural and environmental interest groups to rural programs that they view as competitors for scarce funds and policy attention. Finally, even if the necessary effort and thoughtfulness were available for rural development, many agricultural committee members are unfamiliar with rural development concerns (Browne 1991).

The USDA has been unable to organize a comprehensive rural development policy—and we emphasize "comprehensive." Part of the blame must rest with the Congress, which has given little guidance and even less funding to nonfarm rural development. We do not mean to suggest, however, that we see no recent interest in things rural or that all rural people and rural groups are neglecting local problems. New programs such as the Alternative Agriculture Research and Commercialization (AARC) center at USDA have encouraged federally funded programs to work with rural communities to create jobs. The recent establishment of an under-secretary for small communities and rural development is especially noteworthy and may reflect a change in priorities at USDA. Even so, new efforts are still shackled to the past. Programs are primarily limited to FmHA loans and categorical grants for specific federal goals, such as the improvement of physical infrastructure. The SCS's rural development programs, CES (primarily through state extension), and Rural Development Agency efforts to develop voluntary local rural development councils do encourage greater citizen participation. But funding for all these efforts probably amounts to less than 1 percent of USDA's annual operating budget.

The land-grant universities have been equally unconcerned about rural development. Some colleges of agriculture have shifted scarce resources to rural development, but most have not, leaving most LGUs inadequately prepared to pursue rural development agendas even if opportunities emerged.

The situation reviewed in the preceding paragraphs suggests strongly that group rural development efforts will depend heavily on local initiative. Furthermore, if such efforts are to succeed they must be based on careful planning. This call for greater local participation does not reflect resignation; indeed it recognizes a point of view previously articulated in a highly idealized form. Greater local participation in the past hailed from such sources as agrarian populists, represented in the poetic license of Wendell Berry (1977) and the advocacy of community activist Harry Boyte (1989). To an extent even mainstream sources are currently joining in. Established organizations such as NADO, the National Association of Towns and Townships (NATT), and the National Association of Counties (NACO) have argued that rural communities can effectively identify and implement development programs. A recent advocate is the Democratic congressman from Kentucky, Scotty Baesler, who has proposed to establish federally funded, but not federally directed, Rural Development Boards (RDBs) in a manner similar to farm programs. All these initiatives show a need for more careful and continuous planning (see Pulver 1990). These affirmations of local capacity differ considerably in terms of their faith in local activism, the form they propose for local participation, and the range of activities they believe local communities can reasonably tackle. Much work remains before any of the proposals can serve to coordinate and integrate federal public policies.

Meanwhile, of course, the devil is in the details when public policy evolves. It is popular to uncritically extol grass-roots democracy. The idealistic work of Berry and Boyte is designed as a rhetorical championing of pluralist local decision making, but their ideas can hardly be taken at face value. Local politics is almost always found wanting against the ideal of the rural community (Sokolow 1990).

The experience and the lessons of the past need to be applied rather than relived and relearned. Local elites often use their influence to reduce broad-based citizen participation. Gaventa's (1980) case study of Middlesboro, Kentucky, offers a poignant exploration of how local elites can disenfranchise community members. Sokolow (1990) and Luloff (1990) argue that local entrepreneurs often avoid active participation in community development efforts. Luloff and Swanson (1994) contend that community disaffection greatly restricts the capacity of a community to tap all of its resources. The conclusion is that local politics and social control efforts can effectively hamstring the potential benefits of broad-based development efforts.

Past efforts to enhance local participation reveal two significant conflicts: institutional versus grassroots interests and local people versus local activists. Both conflicts are inherent in any public-policy approach and may impose significant constraints on what can be expected to work. Furthermore, the congressional agenda is so full and its resources so overextended that rural policy matters often command little attention. The prevailing paradigm holds that farm development is the route to rural economic health, a belief espoused by policy analysts whose interests are dominated by farm, food, and environmental issues of agriculture (Browne 1991). Rural policy needs what it is unlikely to get, a definitive shift in how Congress views the problem. Rural public policy should therefore utilize its greatest source of identity—its minimalist tradition—while shifting toward greater local control.

What does this analysis portend? At best, rural advocates may be able to establish a framework for assistance from the federal government. The framework should provide for technical assistance, transfer of expertise from federal agencies to local communities, modest sums of money for development, community-based planning, and a freedom from the constraints of myriad restrictions and mandates placed on local efforts.

Minimum support and maximum freedom can be obtained without additional federal funding, but existing federal programs for rural assistance would have to be redirected. Federal regulations need to be more flexible to accommodate the enormous rural diversity that exists across the nation and that is documented throughout this book. Current programs that provide transportation, housing, and other infrastructure support to rural places can and should be made far more user friendly and available on request.

Local governments are often hostile to rural development efforts. Sokolow (1990) argues that local officials often view rural development as getting in the way of traditional work. Local government agenda are crowded, and municipal, county, and township personnel often compete for federal and state dollars. Nevertheless, long-term value will result from broad-based, pluralistic decision-making processes. Successes and failures alike will add to the knowledge of local leaders.

Thus, the trick to making minimal rural policy work is freedom from institutional restraints, or old policy history, both in Washington and in local government offices. Of course, the real need is to discover incentives that will interest both Congress and local leaders in rural issues. Unfortunately, existing institutions are slow to adjust to policy needs when intense, sustained grass-roots demand does not exist.

There is a great need for more flexibility between the federal agencies administering rural programs and the people and organizations at the local level. Most federal agencies do not have a continuous or direct association with the communities that bid for their categorical grants. This lack of contact poses two problems. First, agencies are guided by program goals rather than by the actual needs of rural communities. Second, rural communities must bend their development priorities to the goals and requirements of specific categorical grants, an accommodation that diverts their scarce development efforts away from more pressing needs. Even when rural communities are successful in capturing a competitive grant they have little discretionary power to adapt their programs to changing local circumstances. We believe this problem to be relatively more serious in rural places. Big-city mayors, with greater political clout, have much more discretionary administrative authority than their rural counterparts.

Nonlocal development organizations, such as Area Development Districts (ADDs), are needed to keep track of federal programs and assist local governments and private sector institutions in locating, writing, and submitting grant proposals. It is no accident that the most successful rural development efforts are associated with a community's capacity to write and submit grant proposals (Martin and Wilkinson 1984). This arrangement intensifies the polarization among have and have-not rural communities, with the haves once again gaining an advantage. Consequently, this implicit triage policy (Swanson 1989) for allocating scarce federal funds perpetuates the marginalization of persistently poor rural communities.

Broad-based participation in local decision making is not universally feasible. In many communities, where local class structures are polarized between the haves and have-nots, there is no tradition or will among the elite to participate in broad-based public policy initiatives. In other places, local entrepreneurs and community volunteers are too busy to participate or are uninterested in local development and surrender the playing field to groups with vested interests, such as real estate speculators or representatives of activist groups. This lack of broad participation translates to the absence of clearly defined grass-roots support for new and uncertain rural policy efforts.

Most groups claim to be grass-roots because, if the claim sticks, it will improve their policy legitimacy, for a grass-roots issue has by definition a broad base of community support. The community in all of its diversity is not necessarily represented, however, in local decisions.

Bonnen (1992) has noted that no organized grass-roots constituency exists for a rural development policy. Farm policy, in contrast, has clearly defined beneficiaries. Environmental programs, as another example, reflect an entirely different level of public awareness about societywide problems than do the plight of rural communities. If no one believes that widespread benefits can be obtained from a comprehensive rural policy, any attempt to mandate broad-based participation in community development efforts will be self-defeating.

RE-CREATING LOCAL INSTITUTIONS

We began this chapter with a question: Is it reasonable to assume that rural programs would lead to improved rural places if they accommodated greater citizen input? Our answer: It depends. Many of the factors contributing to the persistence of a minimalist approach to rural policy are likely to persist. Given these traditional conditions and the need for development efforts, greater local participation is obvious. Communities need the opportunity to learn from their own experience. A broad base of involvement, as opposed to control by local elites and special interest groups, is welcome whether or not it brings immediate beneficial results. Continuing with past programs that empower those who benefit from the status quo or mandating the participation of special interests even though they claim to represent the grass roots will simply reproduce the existing situation. The capacity for development and the types and difficulty of their development problems vary greatly by rural community. The land-grant universities have a responsibility to assist rural communities in improving their development capacity, including continuous assistance in identifying goals and strategic plans.

A minimal federally directed community-based rural policy will require new institutions to encourage participation and provide incentives for greater diversity among those who do participate. Such institutions should avoid the problems of RADCs and the OEO, problems that stemmed from mandated structures that were more important than involvement and cooperation. Congress is unlikely to advance development by changing community class structures or enforcing the participation of specific people or interest groups. But Congress may, in a limited way, encourage processes that will widen representation by social classes and groups presently uninvolved. This expansion does not mean, nor should it require, that those who cooperate must like each other or share one another's values. What they must share is a common local interest in developing programs that meet local needs. No one should force or mandate a consensual process; forums for involvement are needed where grass-roots demands will reflect immediate goals and strategies for particular communities. If successful, such efforts will create a constituency even if one had not existed presently.

Initiatives that re-create local institutions are not new to rural America, but they are uncommon. Floyd County, Iowa, for example, developed a Vision for Agriculture development plan. In an aging population, county residents were worried about who would farm the land in the future, and they worked with state university officials to determine twenty objectives for county growth. In northern Minnesota, Democratic congressman Collin Peterson reassigned two of his Washington staff to his district. Their job was to work with community groups to foster local rural development. Both examples demonstrate that institutional responses can follow grass-roots needs if community citizens can be encouraged to cooperate. Such efforts will be necessary if more federal programs, such as AARC, are to provide opportunities for rural communities. For both Floyd County and northern Minnesota, the emphasis was on development results, not on mandating particular participation.

Congressman Baesler, as noted earlier, has proposed a modest rural development program that builds upon the successful components of farm programs. A federal-local partnership will be forged between the USDA and rural development boards. These boards will be authorized to develop programs within specified fiscal limits to identify and pursue local development needs. Baesler proposes that RDBs be composed both of appointed members and elected members. Here, then, an attempt is made to learn from the experience of the OEO. The responsibility for making the RDBs work will rest with local communities and supporting public institutions such as the LGUs and ADDs.

With only modest policy change, more local community opportunities can be created for addressing declining jobs, fostering economic growth, retaining populations, and otherwise improving the local capacity for development. This change entails, more than anything else, recreating local institutions on at least a small scale. Existing institutions of government need to break from their old policy histories. New forums that stimulate local citizen participation, especially among community leaders, need to be identified and encouraged. In communities that meet these challenges, rural development needs may be addressed with some success.

NOTES

The authors thank Emery Castle, Elizabeth Davis, Barbara Baldwin, Glen Pulver, and Ron Hustedde for helpful critical comments.

1. Local people have always worked toward their own development needs. Glen Pulver (1990) notes that rural communities often address development on a hit and miss basis. They attempt to do something they read or hear about, or they follow the allure of federal and state monies tied to categorical grants. The result is usually less than satisfactory and leads to local frustration. Without resources to support broad-based local goal setting and strategic planning such programs will not achieve their goals. We agree with Pulver's concern and his call for continuous education and technical assistance for rural citizens committed to improving community well-being. We focus here on what might be a feasible federal supporting role.

2. For a comprehensive statement on the reasons why a coherent rural policy does not exist, see Bonnen 1992.

PART EIGHT
IN CONCLUSION

26
AN OVERVIEW

EMERY N. CASTLE

The economic activity and social life of the countryside have been transformed in this century. Part of this transformation has been triggered by improvements in transportation and communication that have also affected the rest of our society. The automobile, for example, has had an enormous impact, as Peirce Lewis so eloquently states in Chapter 3. Transformation has stemmed also from technical change specific to the traditional extractive industries, as noted by Mills, Crosson, and Weber in Chapters 6, 7, and 8. In places where the extractive industries have been major players in the local economy, their increased efficiency often results in a loss of population, unless other economic activities can compensate—and Drabenstott and Smith make it clear that in vast areas of the nation such compensation has not occurred. One need only drive through parts of the Plains states and the intermountain West to see evidence of economic and social distress firsthand.

Economic distress does not characterize all of nonmetropolitan America, but social adjustment does (Drabenstott and Smith, Chapter 9). Many areas close to burgeoning metropolises have grown both in population and economic activity. Other places have developed as a result of outstanding natural, cultural, or social amenities. Such growth, of course, requires major social adjustments and often places local institutions under enormous pressure.

The social costs arising from these sorts of adjustments are not necessarily reflected only in monetary terms. Some places have been unable to compensate for lost economic activity. Communities have declined, even disappeared, and the social infrastructure has suffered. The landscape has suffered as well. Forests have been harvested and soils have been eroded. Even though the extractive industries have become more efficient as measured by our economic system, there have been social impacts not reflected in efficiency indicators.

495

Economic distress has lasted a long time in some places. At the extreme, rural poverty is more severe in the hinterlands than in the inner cities and is becoming even worse, as documented by Summers in Chapter 11. Hirschl and Brown (Chapter 12) discover significant differences between rural and inner-city poverty. Their findings indicate that rural poverty is often incurred by the fact that some rural people are excluded from mainstream decision making in both the private and public sectors. In Chapter 18 Williams and Dill take on this issue squarely, asserting that in a place where race is an important social issue, policies, plans, and programs designed to alleviate poverty but which ignore race relations are "unconscionable." We might add "ineffective" as well.

The communication revolution is often hailed as a means to diminish or eliminate the liability of distance or remoteness. Clearly this revolution has not had such effects, nor does it seem likely to have such effects any time soon. There is apparently no substitute for the advantage that comes from numerous economic activities located near one another. "Agglomeration economies" is the term used by economists and regional scientists to describe this phenomena.

What should an enterprising community do to increase economic activity? If it is located near other major economic activity, or if it can offer outstanding natural, cultural, or social amenities, it has a good chance of being successful. If it does not have these advantages it will find itself competing with other places that boast similar or better endowments. The supply of rural places that would like to have economic expansion far exceeds the demand for such places. Herein lies a major danger. Competition for increased economic activity may result in mistakes that damage the long-term prospects of an area, such as destructive competition among communities that engage in smokestack chasing. In Chapter 13 Janet Fitchen identifies some of the hazards of expanded economic activity that is based on low wages or temporary advantage. The community may have difficulty coping with low income, unemployed, and possibly, poorly educated workers.

There are optimistic signs in the midst of the generally bleak picture painted above. In Chapter 5 Glenn Fuguitt uses demographic evidence to suggest that a minor rural turnaround may now be occurring. If the trends identified by Fuguitt continue, they will probably be most marked in areas that have the desirable characteristics identified by Drabenstott and Smith.

What about the crime, congestion, and environmental degradation of urban and metropolitan places? Will these factors tend to drive more people to the countryside? It would be hazardous to generalize broadly. In the first place, some of these problems exist in less densely populated places, although perhaps not to the same extent or in the same way. Further, as noted by Mills in Chapter 6, locational preferences are only a part of the picture and can be misleading if they are not considered in the context of economic opportunities. The countryside is not likely to attract disgruntled city dwellers unless they have economic opportunities in the countryside or can commute to or otherwise take advantage of such opportunities in more populous places.

The picture that emerges is one of change and adjustment in the countryside. Some communities will decline, and regional expectations must become more realistic as well. Some areas will grow; fingers of development will extend from the more populous places. Suburbanization, often in the form of the galactic city, as described in Chapter 3 by Lewis, will continue to render obsolete our traditional notions of urban and rural.

Why devote special attention to rural America? After all, the United States is predominately urban, according to all but geographic measures. Moreover, change characterizes our entire society, and economic distress is not unique to the countryside. Even if the hinterlands have been forgotten, does it matter? If it does matter, what can be done about it? The answers to such questions are important but far from obvious.

I conclude that special attention for rural people and places is justified and supported by the chapters of this book. I base my conclusion on the interdependence of the city and the countryside and on the enormous diversity of rural people and places. Weber (Chapter 8) treats the economic interdependence of metropolitan and nonmetropolitan places in an explicit way, and several other chapters deal with the subject as well. There are two dead ends and one viable way of thinking about this reality. To ignore the interdependency and consider rural places in isolation from the urban is a dead end because the rural cannot be understood if it is considered in isolation, and public and private decisions, based on such an assumption, will not have anticipated outcomes. To consider the rural as simply an extension of the urban is also a dead end. Although aggregate comparisons may show little difference between, let us say, metropolitan and nonmetropolitan places, the enormous diversity within rural America insures that one will go far afield by assuming rural situations to be similar to the average or representative urban condition.

We therefore reject considering the rural either as something apart from or as a simple extension of the urban. One viable alternative remains—to consider the rural as an essential component of a predominantly urban society. Twenty-five percent of the nation's population and 97 percent of the nation's space is to be found there. Our conclusion, therefore, is that the rural is an important and diverse component of urban life. It is in the interest of the city for the countryside to enjoy comparable social and economic health. Three dimensions are of particular relevance:

- The people of rural America.
- The goods and services rural places provide for their urban counterparts.
- The natural amenities in the countryside and the management of rural space.

Granted that we should not treat rural people and places as a forgotten, neglected appendage of a predominately urban nation, what, then, should our attitude be? If neglect is not in the best interest of the traditional city, the galactic city, or the countryside, can a superior positive attitude be formulated? As used here, the term "attitude" is broader than "public policy"; the latter is implicit in the former. In general, a desirable attitude is one that recognizes the special needs and unique dimensions of the rural without awarding special privileges to rural people and places. Such an attitude is easier to describe than it is to practice.

THE PEOPLE OF RURAL AMERICA

A quarter of the population resides in rural America, and the nation's economic and social health is therefore affected significantly by the productivity and welfare of rural people. The special circumstances that exist in the countryside need to be considered when attitudes and actions toward these people are formulated. One circumstance is diversity. Even though rural diversity makes it difficult to design and administer policies from a central place, it is an asset as well. There is much to be learned from the experience of different people as they cope with particular circumstances and problems. Three examples illustrate the point.

In Chapter 19 anthropologist Sonya Salamon identifies important social characteristics of the rural people of the Midwest. Their educational attainments are the envy of the entire nation. They have numerous formal and informal means of cooperation to address group problems. Unsolved problems exist, to be sure, and there are conditions in their favor over which they have little or no control. Surely there is much to be learned from both the successes and failures of such people.

In Chapter 16 Snipp describes the enormous economic problems of the Native Americans who wish to preserve some semblance of their culture. Significant progress has been made toward the solution of some of their problems since they have been able to escape the paternalism of the Bureau of Indian Affairs. A related lesson may be suggested at the end of Chapter 17 by Charles Aiken who provides a historical view of the rural South. Aiken cites Faulkner's admonition that man must be responsible if he is to be free. Perhaps rural America could benefit by reflecting on the experience of the Native Americans, many of whom have learned that they must accept the responsibility for their fate, including possible hardship, if they are to escape the paternalism of the federal government.

Diversity in social organization has arisen as rural people have faced different conditions (Hobbs, Chapter 20). Density of population often becomes an important variable in determining the size of governmental units used to address particular problems, as noted by Oakerson in Chapter 21. Rural schools provide a vivid example. Rural schools have long been viewed with concern by professional educators who have used urban schools as a standard of measurement. Much of the argument advanced for school consolidation (without accompanying empirical evidence) has been that larger schools are necessary for a high-quality education (Reynolds, Chapter 24). In some states, in fact, competency testing was required of rural school children but not of their urban counterparts. However, as Teixeira (Chapter 22) has shown, the empirical evidence fails to show that rural education currently is markedly inferior to urban education, albeit local variation exists.

The social diversity of rural America must be reflected in the formulation and administration of programs directed toward rural people and places. The various entitlement programs are the single most important public-policy activity of the federal government in the countryside. Social security and welfare issues affect all rural people directly or indirectly. Many people are now rural because benefits are not "place specific" and it was possible for them to choose their place of residence without sacrificing benefits. This flexibility has been of value both to rural America and to the individuals affected. In other instances, policies have been less enlightened. Health benefits often are related to cost of living, and cost of living may be perceived as being less in rural than in urban places. Thus a climate may be created that will make rural health services even more inadequate in the future than they have been in the past. We need to devise ways to escape such vicious circles.

The particular educational and training needs of people in rural places also need to be understood. Education is often oversold as a way for communities or people to overcome rural stagnation. As Fitchen (Chapter 13) and others have noted, education is not a panacea. Yet, enormous cost is associated with error in the opposite direction. If education is neglected, those who must migrate to escape rural stagnation are terribly handicapped. In Chapter 23 Joan Fitzgerald contrasts technical training needs and opportunities in the inner cities with those of rural places, and Teixeira (Chapter 22) challenges many prevailing stereotypes about the nature of education and training in rural areas as it has existed to this time.

Historically, educational programs have been directed specifically toward rural people and places. Perhaps the most notable has been the Land-Grant University program, a unique partnership of local, state, and federal participation that provides both resident and nonresident education enhanced by major research opportunities for youth and adults. There is a remarkable consensus among the scholars who have studied this operation that it has had a major beneficial impact on agriculture, home economics, and forestry, areas in which it has concentrated greatest attention. But major concern has also been expressed about the relevance of much of the current effort. In Chapter 15 Refugio Rochin notes that higher education and colleges of agriculture have not responded to the potential for recruiting and educating rural Latinos to study agriculture and natural resources. One would also hope such institutions would be deeply concerned about the total educational needs of these people, not just agriculture and natural resources. One is reminded of Hart's demonstration in Chapter 4 that "rural" and "farm" no longer mean the same.

THE GOODS AND SERVICES PROVIDED BY RURAL PLACES

The national welfare depends significantly on the goods and services coming from the countryside. An accurate general understanding of the conditions required for a productive rural economy is of great importance. Obviously the nation as a whole will benefit if these goods and services are available in abundance, with high quality, and at a low cost.

The extractive industries have been, and remain, a major economic activity in the rural areas. Although they are no longer important as an employer of rural people as they once were, furnishing jobs is not the only measure of their value. If their productivity should decline, they would require more natural resources to carry on their production, or the nation would have to import more. Are special programs for extractive industries justified? Numerous programs have had the extractive industries as a principal concern. As noted, the land-grant universities and the United States Department of Agriculture have devoted substantial resources to education and research for

American agriculture. Research suggests that there has been a very high rate of return on this social investment. Conditions have changed, however, and it is unclear that the existing programs will continue to yield similarly high returns in the future.

Considerable debate now rages over whether special programs such as the LGUs should be continued. If they are continued, how should they be changed, if at all? The lessons of this volume would suggest that such debate is appropriate. It is not the productivity of the industries in rural places alone that is of concern here. The educational and informational needs of rural people are also important. As Summers (Chapter 10) has noted, rural labor markets have their own particular attributes. If people were educated differently would these attributes change? Many rural people do not remain rural all of their life. Even though rural-to-urban migration is less than it once was, many people, often youthful people, go from rural to urban places each year. Are they prepared to contribute to the urban society? This question is an important component of the debate concerning the future of programs following the land-grant university model.

THE NATURAL AMENITIES AND THE MANAGEMENT OF RURAL SPACE

The protection of the natural environment is of growing concern in the United States. There are numerous environmental organizations, many of which came into existence in recent years. Most of these environmental organizations are based in urban areas and draw membership and support from those places, although rural space amounts to approximately 97 percent of the total U.S. land area.

The extractive industries use a vast amount of space. Industries such as mining may not require a great deal of land in the aggregate, but others such as farming and forestry do. The way these industries are conducted has a great deal to do with the natural environment. Realistically, it cannot be otherwise.

The rise of environmentalism probably stems from several considerations. One surely is that certain limits of the natural environment can be observed. There are fewer virgin forests, some plant and animal species are disappearing, and air and water is not as clean as it once was. In tandem with these developments, per capita income has risen. As incomes rise, a smaller percentage of per capita income is spent on the necessities—basic food, clothing, and shelter requirements—and more income is available for the enjoyment of the natural amenities. Thus it is not surprising that environmentalism is, in significant part, an urban phenomenon, for it is in urban areas that wealth and people are to be found. The bulk of the natural environment is rural, however, and therein lies the seed of serious conflict.

There is a pressing need for the nation to change its attitude toward the management of rural space and the role of technical change in the management of that space. Paul Starrs communicates a sense of this issue in his sweeping treatment of the landscape of the arid American West (Chapter 14). Again, 97 percent of the nation's space is to be found in the countryside and it is in the countryside that much environmental policy will be put into practice. Urban interests of an environmental persuasion often look askance at the technology employed by the extractive industries. And there is little doubt that much contemporary practice leaves a great deal to be desired. However, as Crosson has noted (Chapter 7), technologies that make it possible to produce more per unit of land will ease the competition for land between agricultural and environmental uses.

This call for understanding and for a change in attitude toward rural people and places may be misinterpreted as a bid for a special national policy or expanded federal activity designed specifically for such people and places. I hope not. Obviously, attitude will influence policy, and I am calling for a special attitude toward rural people and places. But even if such a shift in attitude were to occur, there would still be room for considerable difference of opinion about how active government should be in addressing rural issues. The authors of this book themselves would vary significantly in this respect. Some analysts would recommend new programs and additional government expenditures; others believe the diversity and complexity of rural America mitigates against effective centralized action. Many would surely agree with the logic of Browne and Swanson (Chapter 25) that even with a minimalist federal policy stance, great flexibility is needed if variations in local circumstances are to be reflected adequately in decision making. The field investigations of the National Rural Studies Committee have, at the very least, convinced me that the people of rural America have a good grasp of their own problems and that they are resourceful and resilient people. People who would intervene on their behalf should do so only with a deep understanding of their aspirations, their capacities, their opportunities, and the ways they are connected to the rest of the nation.

REFERENCES CITED

Adams, Terry K., and Greg Duncan. 1992. "Long-Term Poverty in Rural Areas." In *Rural Poverty in America,* ed. Cynthia M. Duncan. New York: Auburn House.

Advisory Commission on Intergovernmental Relations (ACIR). 1987. *The Organization of Local Public Economies.* Washington, D.C.

———. 1988. *Metropolitan Organization: The St. Louis Case.* Washington, D.C.

———. 1991. *Coordinating Water Resources in the Federal System: The Groundwater–Surface Water Connection.* Washington, D.C.

———. 1992. *Metropolitan Organization: The Allegheny County Case.* Washington, D.C.

Ahearn, Mary C., Janet E. Perry, and Hisham S. El-Osta. 1993. "The Economic Well-being of Farm Operator Households 1988–90." Agricultural Economic Report 666. Economic Research Service, U.S. Department of Agriculture, January.

Aiken, Charles S. 1971. "The Fragmented Neoplantation: A New Type of Farm Operation in the Southeast." *Southeastern Geographer* 11(1): 43–51.

———. 1978. "The Decline of Sharecropping in the Lower Mississippi Valley." In *Man and Environment in the Lower Mississippi Valley,* Vol. 7 of *Geoscience and Man,* ed. Sam B. Hilliard, pp. 151–165. Baton Rouge: School of Geoscience, Louisiana State University.

———. 1981. "A Geographical Approach to William Faulkner's 'The Bear.' " *Geographical Review* 71(4): 446–459.

———. 1982. "The Image of the Plantation in Southern Fiction: The Case of William Faulkner." In *Proceedings of the Tall Timbers Management Conference,* pp. 189–206. Tallahassee, Fla.: Tall Timbers Research Station.

———. 1985. "New Settlement Patterns of Rural Blacks in the American South." *Geographical Review* 75:(4): 283–404.

———. 1987. "Race as a Factor in Municipal Underbounding." *Annals of the Association of American Geographers* 77(4): 564–579.

———. 1990. " A New Type of Black Ghetto in the Plantation South." *Annals of the Association of American Geographers* 80(2): 223–246.

———. 1992. "School Desegregation in the Plantation Regions of the American South." Paper presented at the National Meeting, Association of American Geographers, San Diego, California, April 18–22.

———. 1993. "Gone with the Wind: Planters and the Demise of the Piedmont Cotton Region." Paper presented at the National Meeting, Association of American Geographers, Atlanta, Georgia.

Aiken, Michael, and N. J. Demerath III. 1968. "Tokenism in the Delta: Two Mississippi Cases." In *Our Children's Burden: Studies of Desegregation in Nine American Communities*, ed. Raymond W. Mack, pp. 40–107. New York: Random House.

Albrecht, Don E. 1993. "The Renewal of Population Loss in the Nonmetropolitan Great Plains." *Rural Sociology* 58: 233–246.

Alford, R. R. 1960. "School District Reorganization and Community Integration." *Harvard Education Review* 30(4): 350–371.

Altshuler, Alan A. 1970. *Community Control.* New York: Pegasus Press.

Alvarado, A. J., G. L. Riley, and H. O. Mason. 1990. "Agricultural Workers in Central California in 1989." *California Agricultural Studies* 90(8). Sacramento, Employment Development Department, September.

Amato, Paul R., and Jiping Zuo. 1992. "Rural Poverty, Urban Poverty, and Psychological Well-Being." *Sociological Quarterly* 33: 229–240.

Ambler, Marjane. 1990. *Breaking the Iron Bonds.* Lawrence: University Press of Kansas.

American Association of University Women (AAUW). 1992. *How Schools Shortchange Girls.* Annapolis Junction, Md.

Anderson, Elijah. 1990. *Streetwise.* Chicago: University of Chicago Press.

Anderson, W. L. 1906. *The Country Town: A Study of Rural Evolution.* New York: Baker and Taylor.

Andrews, Richard B. 1954. "Mechanics of the Urban Economic Base: General Problems of Base Identification." *Land Economics* 20: 164–172.

Andriot, J. L., ed. 1983. *Population Abstract of the U.S. 1983,* Vol. 1. McLean, Va.: Andriot Associates.

Aronoff, Marilyn. 1993. "Collective Celebration as a Vehicle for Local Economic Development: A Michigan Case." *Human Organization* 52: 368–379.

Arthur, W. Brian. 1990. "Positive Feedbacks in the Economy." *Scientific American* (February): 92–99.

Atherton, Lewis. 1954. *Main Street on the Middle Border.* Bloomington: Indiana University Press.

Atkins, Joe. 1989. "Study Says Rural Poverty 'Most Severe' in South." *Clarion Ledger,* April 12, 3A.

"Attitudes of Regions Studied." 1987. *Commercial Appeal,* November 12, A11.

Aurner, C. R. 1914–1915. *History of Education in Iowa.* 3 vols. Iowa City: State Historical Society of Iowa.

Ayers, Edward L. 1989. "Honor." In *Encyclopedia of Southern Culture*, ed. Charles R. Wilson and William Ferris. Chapel Hill: University of North Carolina Press.

Baerwald, Thomas. 1978. "The Emergence of a New Downtown." *Geographical Review* 68: 308–318.

Bailey, L. H. 1908. *The State and the Farmer.* New York: Macmillan.

———. 1920. *The Country-Life Movement.* New York: Macmillan.

Baker, J. F. 1970. "A Study of the Relationships and Educational Effectiveness of the Upper Levels of School Size and Selected Student Characteristics and Behavior." Ph.D. dissertation, University of Iowa.

Balswick, Jack. 1989. "Religion and Social Class." In *Encyclopedia of Southern Culture*, ed. Charles R. Wilson and William Ferris. Chapel Hill: University of North Carolina Press.

Banovetz, J. B., and D. A. Dolan. 1990. "Rural Education." In *Research in Rural Issues: An Annotated Bibliography*, ed. W. Jones, pp. 99–152. DeKalb: Western Illinois University.

Barger, W. K., and Ernesto M. Reza. 1994. *The Farm Labor Movement in the Midwest: Social Change and Adaptation Among Migrant Farmworkers*. Austin: University of Texas Press.

Barkema, Alan, Mark Drabenstott, and Julie Stanley. 1990. "Processing Food in Farm States: An Economic Development Strategy for the 1990s." *Economic Review* (Federal Reserve Bank of Kansas City), July/August.

Barkley, David L., ed. 1993. *Economic Adaptation: Alternatives for Nonmetropolitan Areas*. Boulder, Colo.: Westview.

Barkley, David L., and Sylvain Hinschberger. 1992. "Industrial Restructuring: Implications for the Decentralization of Manufacturing to Nonmetropolitan Areas." *Economic Development Quarterly* 6: 64–79.

Barsh, Russell Lawrence, and James Youngblood Henderson. 1980. *The Road: Indian Tribes and Political Liberty*. Berkeley: University of California Press.

Bartik, Timothy. 1985. "Business Location Decisions in the U.S.: Estimates of the Effects of Unionization, Taxes, and Other Characteristics of States." *Journal of Business and Economic Statistics* 3 (January).

———. 1991. *Who Benefits from State and Local Economic Development Policies?* Kalamazoo, Mich.: W. E. Upjohn Institute for Employment Research.

Bates, T., and A. Nucci. 1989. "Small Business Size and Rate of Discontinuance." *Journal of Small Business Management* 27: 1–8.

Beale, Calvin L. 1989a. "The Revival of Population Growth in Nonmetropolitan America." In *A Taste of the Country: A Collection of Calvin Beale's Writings*, ed. Peter Morrison, pp. 137–152. University Park: Pennsylvania State University Press.

———. 1989b. "Significant Trends in the Demography of Farm People." *Proceedings of the Philadelphia Society for Promoting Agriculture 1987–88* (February): 36–39.

———. 1993. "Poverty Is Persistent in Some Rural Areas." *Agricultural Outlook* (September): 22–27.

Beale, Calvin L., and Glenn V. Fuguitt. 1990. "Decade of Pessimistic Nonmetropolitan Population Trends Ends on Optimistic Note." *Rural Development Perspectives* 6 (June–September): 14–18.

Beale, Calvin L., and Judith Kalbacher. 1989. "Farm Population Trends: Shrinkage, Shifts, and Fewer Heirs." *Farmline* 9: 19.

Beard, E. J. H. 1909. "The Rural Schools." *Proceedings of the Fifty-Fifth Annual Session of the Iowa State Teachers Association* 26: 38–45.

Beauford, E. Yvonne, and Mack C. Nelson. 1988. "Social and Economic Conditions of Black Farm Households: Status and Prospects." In *The Rural South in Crisis*, ed. Lionel J. Beaulieu. Boulder, Colo.: Westview.

Beck, E. M., Patrick M. Horan, and Charles M. Tolbert. 1978. "Stratification in a Dual Economy: A Sector Model of Earnings Determinants." *American Sociological Review* 43: 704–720.

Becker, Gary S. 1971. *Human Capital: A Theoretical and Empirical Analysis with Special Reference to Education.* 2d ed. New York: Columbia University Press.

———. 1985. *Human Capital.* New York: National Bureau of Economic Research.

Bell, Michael M. 1992. "The Fruit of the Difference: The Rural–Urban Continuum as a System of Identity." *Rural Sociology* 57: 65–82.

Bellah, Robert N., Richard Madsen, William M. Sullivan, Ann Swidler, and Steven M. Tipton. 1985. *Habits of the Heart.* Berkeley: University of California Press.

Bellamy, Donald. 1988. "Economic and Sociodemographic Change in Persistent Low Income Counties: An Update." Paper presented to the Southern Rural Sociological Association, New Orleans.

Bender, Lloyd D., et al. 1985. *The Diverse Social and Economic Structure of Nonmetropolitan America.* Rural Development Research Report 49. Washington, D.C.: U.S. Department of Agriculture, Economic Research Service.

Bender, T. 1978. *Community and Social Change in America.* New Brunswick, N.J.: Rutgers University Press.

Benson, J. Kenneth. 1982. "A Framework for Policy Analysis." In *Interorganizational Coordination,* ed. David Rogers, David Whettan, et al., pp. 137–201. Ames: Iowa State University Press.

Berry, Wendell. 1977. *The Unsettling of America.* San Francisco: Sierra Club Books.

———. 1981. *Recollected Essays: Nineteen Sixty-Five to Nineteen Eighty.* San Francisco: North Point Press.

Better Iowa Schools Commission (BISC). 1912. "Report of the Better Iowa Schools Commission." *Proceedings of the Fifty-Eighth Annual Session of the Iowa State Teachers Association* 58: 55–118.

Betts, G. H. 1913. *New Ideals in Rural Schools.* Boston: Houghton Mifflin.

Bibb, Robert, and William H. Form. 1977. "The Effects of Industrial, Occupational, and Sex Stratification on Wages in Blue-Collar Markets." *Social Forces* 55: 974–996.

Biennial Reports of the Superintendent of Public Instruction. 1898–1927. *Iowa Documents.* Nos. 28–43.

Billings, Dwight B. 1988. "The Rural South in Crisis: A Historical Perspective." In *The Rural South in Crisis,* ed. Lionel J. Beaulieu. Boulder, Colo.: Westview.

Billington, Ray. 1966. *America's Frontier Heritage.* New York: Holt, Rinehart, and Winston.

Black, Earl, and Merle Black. 1987. *Politics and Society in the South.* Cambridge: Harvard University Press.

Bloomquist, Leonard E. 1988. "Performance of the Rural Manufacturing Sector." In *Rural Economic Development in the 1980s,* ed. David L. Brown et al., pp. 49–75. Rural Development Research Report Number 69. Washington, D.C.: USDA, Economic Research Service.

Bloomquist, Leonard, and Gene F. Summers. 1982. "Organization of Production and Community Income Distribution." *American Sociological Review* 47: 325–338.

Blomquist, William. 1992. *Dividing the Waters: Governing Groundwater in Southern California.* San Francisco: ICS Press.

Blotner, Joseph. 1974. *Faulkner: A Biography.* 2 vols. New York: Random House.

Bluestone, Barry, and Bennett Harrison. 1982. *The Deindustrialization of America: Plant Closings, Community Abandonment, and the Dismantling of Basic Industry.* New York: Basic Books.

Blumenthal, A. 1932. *Small-Town Stuff.* Chicago: University of Chicago Press.

Blumer, Herbert. 1965. "Industrialization and Race Relations." In *Industrialization and Race Relations,* ed. Guy Hunter. London: Oxford University Press.

Bogue, Allan G. 1963. *From Prairie to Cornbelt.* Chicago: University of Chicago Press.

Bogue, Margaret Beattie. 1959. *Patterns from the Sod: Land Use and Tenure in the Grand Prairie, 1850–1900.* Illinois Historical Collections Series, vol. 34. Springfield: Illinois State Historical Library.

Bollens, John C. 1957. *Special District Governments in the United States.* Berkeley: University of California Press.

Bonnen, James T. 1987. "U.S. Agricultural Development: Transforming Human Capital, Technology, and Institutions." In *U.S.-Mexico Relations: Agricultural and Rural Development,* ed. Bruce F. Johnston, Cassio Luisellit, Celso Cartass Conteras, and Roger D. Norton, pp. 267–300. Stanford, Calif.: Stanford University Press.

———. 1992. "Why Is There No Coherent U.S. Rural Policy?" *Policy Studies Journal* 20(2): 190–201.

Boorstin, D. J. 1974. *The Americans: The Democratic Experience.* New York: Vintage Books.

Bottomore, T. B. 1963. *Karl Marx.* New York: McGraw-Hill.

Bowers, W. L. 1974. *The Country Life Movement in America, 1900–1920.* Port Washington, N.Y.: Kennikat.

Bowles, S., and H. Gintis. 1976. *Schooling in Capitalist America.* New York: Basic Books.

Boyte, Harry. 1989. *Commonwealth: A Return to Citizen Politics.* New York: Free Press.

Bradshaw, Ted K. 1993. "In the Shadow of Urban Growth: Bifurcation in Rural California Communities." In *Forgotten Places: Uneven Development in Rural America,* ed. T. A. Lyson and W. W. Falk, pp. 218–256. Lawrence: University Press of Kansas.

Brindley, J. E. 1912. "A Study of Iowa Population as Related to Industrial Conditions." *Agricultural Extension Bulletin No. 27.* Ames: Iowa State College.

Broadway, Michael. 1994. "Beef Stew: Cattle, Immigrants, and Established Residents in a Kansas Beefpacking Town." In *Newcomers in the Workplace: Immigrants and the Restructuring of the U.S. Economy,* ed. L. Lamphere, A. Stepick, and G. Grenier, pp. 25–43. Philadelphia: Temple University Press.

Bromley, Daniel W. 1985. "Resources and Economic Development: An Institutionalist Perspective." *Journal of Economic Issues* 19(3): 779–796.

Brookings Institution. 1933. *Survey of Administration in Iowa.* Institute of Government Research. State of Iowa.

Brown, David L. 1989. "Demographic Trends Relevant to Education in Nonmetropolitan America." In *Rural Education: The Changing Landscape,* ed. J. D. Stern. Washington, D.C.: U.S. Department of Education.

Brown, David L., and Kenneth L. Deavers. 1988. "Rural Change and the Rural Economic Policy Agenda for the 1980s." In *Rural Economic Development in the 1980s,* ed. David L. Brown and Kenneth L. Deavers, pp. 1–28. Rural Development Research Report No. 69. Washington D.C.: USDA, Economic Research Service.

——. 1989. "The Changing Context of Rural Economic Development Policy in the United States." In *Rural Labor Markets,* ed. William Falk and Thomas Lyson, pp. 253–277. Greenwich, Conn.: JAI Press.

Brown, David L., and Nina L. Glasgow. 1991. "Capacity Building and Rural Government Adaptation to Population Change." In *Rural Policies for the 1990s,* ed. Cornelia B. Flora and James A. Christenson, pp. 235–246. Boulder, Colo.: Westview.

Brown, David, and Mildred Warner. 1989. "Persistent Low Income Areas in the United States: Some Conceptual Challenges." In *National Rural Studies Committee: A Proceedings,* ed. Emery Castle and Barbara Baldwin. Eugene: Western Rural Development Center, Oregon State University.

Brown, David L., and Mildred E. Warner. 1991. "Persistent Low Income Nonmetropolitan Areas in the United States: Some Conceptual Challenges for Development Policy." *Policy Studies Journal* 19: 22–42.

Brown, G. A. 1922. *Iowa's Consolidated Schools.* Des Moines: Department of Public Instruction, State of Iowa.

Browne, William P. 1989. "Access and Influence in Agriculture and Rural Affairs: Congressional Staff and Lobbyist Perceptions of Organized Interests." *Rural Sociology* 54: 365–381.

——. 1991. *The Institutional Failure of National Rural Policy.* Prepared for the Rural Economic Policy Program. Washington, D.C.: Aspen Institute.

Browne, William P., Jerry R. Skees, Louis E. Swanson, Paul B. Thompson, and Laurian J. Unnevehr. 1992. *Sacred Cows and Hot Potatoes: Agrarian Myths in Agricultural Policy.* Boulder, Colo.: Westview.

Brunner, Edmund De S., Gwendolyn S. Hughes, and Marjorie Patten. 1927. *American Agricultural Villages.* New York: George H. Doran.

Brunner, Edmund De S., and John H. Kolb. 1933. *Rural Social Trends.* New York: McGraw Hill.

Bryson, Bill. 1988. "Fat Girls in Des Moines." In *Granta: Home,* pp. 23–44. New York: Viking Penguin.

Bulow, Jeremy I., and Lawrence H. Summers. 1986. "A Theory of Dual Labor Markets with Application to Industrial Policy, Discrimination, and Keynesian Unemployment." *Journal of Labor Economics* 4: 367–414.

Butler, Margaret A. 1993. *The Farm Entrepreneurial Population 1988–90.* Rural Development Research Report No. 84. Washington, D.C.: U.S. Department of Agriculture, Economic Research Service.

Callahan, R. 1962. *Education and the Cult of Efficiency.* Chicago: University of Chicago Press.

Campbell, M. 1919. "A Dying School System for Children Who Are Just Beginning to Live." *Midland Schools* 33(10): 339–342.

——. 1921. "A Brief History of Consolidation in Iowa." *Bulletin of the Iowa State Teachers College* (Department of Rural Education) 22(3): 3–16.

Cardenas, Francisco. 1994. "It's Full Speed Ahead: In a Scant 12 Years Hispanics Will Be the Largest Minority." *Hispanic Business* 16(4): 26.

Carlino, Gerald. 1985. "Declining City Productivity and the Growth of Rural Regions: A Test of Alternative Explanations." *Journal of Urban Economics* 18.

Carlino, Gerald, and Edwin S. Mills. 1987. "The Determinants of County Growth." *Journal of Regional Science* 27(1): 39–54.

Carlson, Leonard A. 1981. *Indians, Bureaucrats, and Land.* Westport, Conn.: Greenwood Press.

Carnegie Foundation for the Advancement of Teaching. 1989. *Tribal Colleges: Shaping the Future of Native America.* Princeton: Princeton University Press.

Carney, M. 1912. *Country Life and the Country School.* Chicago: Row, Peterson and Company.

Carstensen, Vernon, ed. 1968. *The Public Lands: Studies in the History of the Public Domain.* Madison: University of Wisconsin Press.

———. "Patterns on the American Land." 1988. *Publius: The Journal of Federalism* 18(4): 31–40.

Cash, W. J. 1941. *Mind of the South.* New York: Knopf.

Castells, Manuel, and Alejandro Portes. 1986. "World Underneath: The Origins, Dynamics, and Effects of the Informal Economy." Paper presented at the Conference on Comparative Study of the Informal Sector, Harper's Ferry, West Virginia.

Castle, Emery N. 1986. "Rural Institutions for the Future." In *New Dimension in Rural Policy: Building Upon Our Heritage,* ed. Ronald C. Wimberly, Dale Jahr, and Jerry W. Johnson, pp. 523–528. Joint Economic Committee Congress of the United States. Washington, D.C.: U.S. Government Printing Office.

———. 1988. "Policy Options for Rural Development in a Restructured Rural Economy: An International Perspective." In *Agriculture and Beyond: Rural Development Policy,* ed. Gene F. Summers et al., pp. 11–27. Madison: University of Wisconsin, College of Agricultural and Life Sciences.

———. 1993. "Rural Diversity: An American Asset." *Annals of the American Academy of Social Science* 529: 12–21.

Cather, Willa. 1918. *My Antonia.* New York: Knopf.

Cattan, Peter. 1993. "The Diversity of Hispanics in the U.S. Workforce." *Monthly Labor Review* 116(8): 3–15.

Caudill, Harry M. 1963. *Night Comes to the Cumberlands: A Biography of a Depressed Area.* Boston: Little, Brown, and Company.

Center for the New West. 1992. *Overview of Change in America's New Economy.* Denver, Colo.

Chapa, Jorge, and Richard R. Valencia. 1993. "Latino Population Growth, Demographic Characteristics, and Educational Stagnation: An Examination of Recent Trends." *Hispanic Journal of Behavioral Sciences* 15(2): 165–187.

Cheong, Kenwon, Michael B. Toney, and William F. Stinner. 1986. "Racial Differences Among Young Men in the Selection of Metropolitan and Nonmetropolitan Destinations." *Rural Sociology* 51(2): 222–228.

Christenson, James A., and Cornelia B. Flora. 1991. "A Rural Policy Agenda for the 1990s." In Cornelia B. Flora and James A. Christenson, *Rural Policies for the 1990s,* pp. 333–337. Boulder, Colo.: Westview.

Clarke, Jeanne Nienaber, and Daniel McCool. 1985. *Staking Out the Terrain: Power Differentials Among Natural Resource Management Agencies.* Albany: State University of New York Press.

Clues to Rural Community Survival. 1987. Lincoln: Heartland Center for Leadership Development, University of Nebraska.

Cobb, James. 1982. *The Selling of the South: The Southern Crusade for Industrial Development, 1936–1980.* Baton Rouge: Louisiana State University Press.

———. 1984. *Industrialization and Southern Society: 1877–1984.* Lexington: University of Kentucky Press.

———. 1991. *The Most Southern Place on Earth: The Roots of Southern Regional Identity.* New York: Oxford University Press.

Coleman, James. 1987. "Families and Schools." *Educational Researcher* 16(6): 32–38.

Coleman, James B. 1988. "Social Capital in the Creation of Human Capital." *American Journal of Sociology* 94 Supplement: 95–120.

Columbus, Christopher. 1989. *The Diario of Christopher Columbus's First Voyage to America, 1492–1493.* Abstracted by Fray Bartolomé de las Casas. Transcribed and translated into English by Oliver Dunn and James E. Kelley, Jr. Norman: University of Oklahoma Press.

Congressional Quarterly. 1984. *Farm Policy: The Politics of Soil, Surpluses, and Subsidies.* Washington, D.C.: Congressional Quarterly.

Conzen, Michael P., ed. 1990. *The Making of the American Landscape.* Winchester, Mass.: Unwin Hyman.

Cook, Annabel Kirschner. 1992. "The Increasing Prevalence of Children in Single-Parent Families in Washington: 1970–1990." In *Washington Counts,* no. 4. Pullman: Cooperative Extension, Washington State University.

———. 1993. " Changes in Employment and Poverty: Differences Between Timber-dependent and Metro Areas in Western Washington." Paper presented at Pacific Sociological Association, Portland, Oregon.

Cornell, Stephen, and Joseph P. Kalt. 1990. "Pathways from Poverty: Economic Development and Institution-building on American Indian Reservations." *American Indian Culture and Research Journal* 14: 89–125.

Crawford, Stanley. 1988. *Mayordomo: Chronicle of an Acequia in Northern New Mexico.* Albuquerque: University of New Mexico Press.

Crévecoeur, J. Hector St. John de. 1963. *Letters from an American Farmer.* New York: Signet.

Crosson, P. 1986. "Soil Erosion and Policy Issues." In *Agriculture and the Environment,* ed. T. Phipps, P. Crosson, and K. Price. Washington, D.C.: National Center for Food and Agricultural Policy, Resources for the Future.

———. 1991a. "Cropland and Soils: Past Performance and Policy Challenges." In *America's Renewable Resources,* ed. K. Frederick and R. Sedjo. Washington, D.C.: Resources for the Future.

———. 1991b. "Rural Land Management and the Welfare of Rural People." In *Proceedings of a Meeting of the National Rural Studies Committee,* Reading, Pa., May 16–17, ed. E. Castle and B. Baldwin. Corvallis: Western Rural Development Center, Oregon State University.

Cruise, Cathy. 1993. "Federal Officials Refute Trump Allegations; Committee Members Offended by Remarks." *Indian Gaming* 3(3): 18.

Cubberley, E. P. 1914. *Rural Life and Education.* Boston: Houghton Mifflin.

Cunningham, Bob. 1985. "The Box That Broke the Barrier: The Swamp Cooler Comes to Southern Arizona." *Journal of Arizona History* 26(2): 163–174.

Current, Richard N., et al., eds. 1978. *Words That Made American History: Since the Civil War.* Vol. 2, 3d ed. Glenview, Ill.: Scott, Foresman.

Curti, Merle. 1959. *The Making of an American Community.* Stanford, Calif.: Stanford University Press.

Cyert, R. M., and D. C. Mowery. 1987. *Technology and Employment: Innovation and Growth in the U.S. Economy.* Washington, D.C.: National Academy of Science Press.

Dahmann, D., and L. Dacquel. 1992. *Residents of Farms and Rural Areas 1990.* Current Population Reports, Population Characteristics, Series P-20, no. 457. Washington, D.C.: USDA and U.S. Department of Commerce.

Danbom, D. B. 1979. *The Resisted Revolution.* Ames: Iowa State University Press.

Danziger, Sheldon, and Peter Gottschalk, eds. 1993. *Uneven Tides: Rising Inequality in America.* New York: Russell Sage Foundation.

Dash, Leon. 1989. *When Children Want Children.* New York: William Morrow.

Davenport, E. 1909. *Education for Efficiency.* Boston: Heath.

Davis, Allison, et al. 1941. *Deep South: A Social Anthropological Study of Caste and Class.* Chicago: University of Chicago Press.

DeAnda, Roberto M. 1994. "Unemployment and Underemployment Among Mexican-Origin Workers." *Hispanic Journal of Behavioral Sciences* 16(2): 163–175.

Deavers, Kenneth L. 1988. "Rural Economic Conditions and Rural Development Policy for the 1980s and 1990s." In *Agriculture and Beyond: Rural Development Policy,* ed. Gene F. Summers et al., pp. 113–123. Madison: University of Wisconsin, College of Agricultural and Life Sciences.

———. 1992. "What Is Rural?" *Policy Studies Journal* 20(2): 184–189.

Deavers, Kenneth L., and David L. Brown. 1984. "A New Agenda for Rural Policy in the 1980s. *Rural Development Perspectives* 1(1): 38–41.

Deavers, Kenneth L., and Robert A. Hoppe. 1992. "Overview of the Rural Poor in the 1980s." In *Rural Poverty in America,* ed. Cynthia M. Duncan, pp. 3–20. New York: Auburn House.

deBuys, William. 1985. *Enchantment and Exploitation: The Life and Hard Times of a New Mexico Mountain Range.* Albuquerque: University of New Mexico.

DeVoto, Bernard. 1934. "The West: A Plundered Province." *Harper's Monthly Magazine* 169: 355–364.

Deyoe, A. M. 1912. "The School as an Efficient Factor in the Educational, Social, and Recreational Activities of the Community." *Midland Schools* 26(1): 46–48.

———. 1915. "Public School Activities in Iowa." *Midland Schools* 29: 147–153.

DeYoung, A. J. 1992. *Struggling with Their Histories: Economic Decline and Educational Improvement in Four Rural Southeastern School Districts.* Norwood, N.J.: Ablex.

Dill, Bonnie Thornton, Michael Timberlake, and Bruce B. Williams. 1989. "Race and Poverty in the Rural South: Racial Composition and Economic Development." Paper presented at the annual meeting of the ASA, San Francisco.

Dill, Bonnie Thornton, and Bruce B. Williams. 1992. "Race, Gender, and Poverty in the Rural South: African American Single Mothers." In *Rural Poverty in America,* ed. Cynthia M. Duncan, pp. 97–109. New York: Auburn House.

Dillman, Don A., and Daryl Hobbs, eds. 1982. *Rural Society in the U.S.A.: Issues for the 1980s.* Boulder, Colo.: Westview.

Dixon, R., and A. P. Thirwall. 1975. "A Model of Regional Growth Rate Differences on Kaldorian Lines." *Oxford Economic Papers* 27(2): 201–213.

Dobyns, Henry. 1983. *Their Number Become Thinned.* Knoxville: University of Tennessee Press.

Doeringer, Paul B. 1984. "Internal Labor Markets and Paternalism in Rural Areas." In *Internal Labor Markets,* ed. Paul Osterman, pp. 271–289. Cambridge: MIT Press.

Dollard, John. 1937. *Caste and Class in a Southern Town.* New Haven: Yale University Press.

Drabenstott, Mark, and Mark Henry. 1988. "Rural American in the 1990s." In *Rural America in Transition,* ed. Mark Drabenstott and Lynn Gibson, pp. 39–58. Kansas City, Mo.: Federal Reserve Bank of Kansas City.

Drabenstott, Mark, Mark Henry, and Lynn Gibson. 1988. "The Rural Economic Policy Choice." In *Rural America in Transition,* ed. Mark Drabenstott and Lynn Gibson, pp. 59–84. Kansas City, Mo.: Federal Reserve Bank of Kansas City.

Drabenstott, Mark, and Kelly Welch. 1991. "Rural America's Competitive Challenge: Strategies for the Future." In *Increasing Understanding of Public Problems and Policies—1991.* Oak Brook, Ill.: Farm Foundation.

Drucker, Peter. 1986. "The Changing World Economy." *Foreign Affairs* 64 (Spring): 768–791.

DuBois, W. E. B. 1935. *Black Reconstruction.* New York: Harcourt, Brace and Company.

Dudenhefer, Paul. 1993. "Poverty in the Rural United States." *Focus* 15 (Spring): 37–46.

Duncan, Cynthia M., ed. 1992a. *Rural Poverty in America.* New York: Auburn House.
_____. 1992b. "Individual Opportunity and Community Development in Chronically Poor Communities." Paper presented to the annual meeting of the Rural Sociological Society, University Park, Pa.

Duncan, Cynthia M., and Ann R. Tickamyer. 1988. "Poverty Research and Policy for Rural America." *American Sociologist* 19: 243–259.

Duncan, Marvin R. 1989. "U.S. Agriculture: Hard Realities and New Opportunities." Federal Reserve Bank of Kansas City *Economic Review* 3–20.

Duncombe, Herbert Sydney. 1966. *County Government in America.* Washington, D.C.: National Association of Counties.

Dunne, F. 1977. "Choosing Smallness: An Examination of the Small School Experience in Rural America." In *Education in Rural America: A Reassessment of Conventional Wisdom,* ed. J. P. Sher, pp. 81–124. Boulder, Colo.: Westview.

Durkheim, Emile. 1965. *The Elementary Forms of the Religious Life.* New York: Free Press.

Eckert, Jerry, and Paul Gutierrez. 1990. "Contrasts and Communalities: Hispanic and Anglo Farming in Conejos County, Colorado." Paper presented at the annual meeting of the Rural Sociology Society, Norfolk, Virginia, August 8–11.

Edmondson, Brad, and Dan Fost. 1991. "The Frontier Is Still Here." *American De-mographics* 13(7): 50–52.

Effland, Anne B. W. 1993. "Federal Rural Development Policy Since 1972." *Rural Development Perspectives* 9(October): 8–14.

Elazar, Daniel J. 1988. "Land and Liberty in American Civil Society." *Publius: The Journal of Federalism* 18(4): 1–30.

Ellickson, Robert C. 1991. *Order Without Law: How Neighbors Settle Disputes.* Cambridge: Harvard University Press.

Elo, Irma T., and Calvin L. Beale. 1983. *Natural Resource and Rural Poverty: An Overview.* Washington, D.C.: National Center for Food and Agricultural Policy, Resources for the Future.

Emerson, Ralph Waldo. 1957. "Nature." In *Selections from Ralph Waldo Emerson,* ed. Stephen E. Whicher. Boston: Houghton Mifflin.

Erickson, Rodney A., and Marylynn Gentry. 1985. "Suburban Nucleations." *Geographical Review* 75(1): 19–31.

Fainstein, Norman. 1986–1987. "The Underclass/Mismatch Hypothesis as an Explanation for Black Economic Deprivation." *Politics and Society* 4: 403–452.

Falk, William W., and Thomas A. Lyson. 1988. *High Tech, Low Tech, No Tech: Recent Industrial and Occupational Change in the South.* Albany: State University of New York Press.

———. 1989. *Rural Labor Markets.* Research in Rural Sociology and Development: A Research Annual, vol. 4. Greenwich, Conn.: JAI Press.

Farley, Reynolds. 1988. "After the Starting Line: Blacks and Women in an Uphill Race." *Demography* 25: 477–495.

Farley, Reynolds, and Walter R. Allen. 1987. *The Color Line and the Quality of Life in America.* New York: Russell Sage Foundation.

Faulkner, William. 1952. "The Rights of Man: An Address to the Delta Council." Reprinted in *Delta Review* 2:3 (1965): 40–42.

Feagin, Joe. 1989. *Race and Ethnic Relations.* 3d ed. Englewood Cliffs, N.J.: Prentice-Hall.

Ferris, Susan. 1993. "Fields of Broken Dreams." *Image* (Sunday Magazine of the San Francisco *Examiner*), July 18, 4–12.

"Financing Rural Community-Based Development." 1993. *Strategy Alert.* 39 (Autumn). Washington, D.C.: Community Information Exchange.

Fischel, W. 1991. "Land Use Conflicts at the Rural-Urban Border." In *Proceedings of a Meeting of the National Rural Studies Committee,* Reading, Pa., May 16–17, ed. E. Castle and B. Baldwin. Corvallis: Western Rural Development Center, Oregon State University.

Fischer, David Hackett. 1989. *Albion's Seed: Four British Folkways in America.* New York: Oxford University Press.

Fisher, Dennis, and Ronald D. Knutson. 1989. "Politics of Rural Development." In *Farm Foundation: Increasing Understanding of Public Problems and Policies—1989,* pp. 62–72. Oak Brook, Ill: Farm Foundation.

Fisher, James S. 1967. "The Modification of Rural Occupance Systems: The Central Georgia Piedmont." Ph.D. dissertation, Department of Geography, University of Georgia.

_____. 1970. "Federal Crop Allotment Programs and Responses by Individual Farm Operators." *Southeastern Geographer* 10: 47–58.

Fishman, Robert. 1987. *Bourgeois Utopias: The Rise and Fall of Suburbia*. New York: Basic Books.

_____. 1990. "America's New City: Megalopolis Unbound." *Wilson Quarterly* 14(1).

Fitchen, Janet M. 1981. *Poverty in Rural America: A Case Study*. Boulder, Colo.: Westview.

_____. 1991. *Endangered Spaces, Enduring Places: Change, Identity, and Survival in Rural America*. Boulder, Colo.: Westview.

Fitzgerald, J. 1993a. "Labor Force, Education, and Work." In *Theories of Economic Development,* ed. R. Bingham and R. Mier, pp. 125–146. Newbury Park, Calif.: Sage.

_____. 1993b. *Program and Policy Issues in Implementing Tech Prep in Illinois*. Chicago: University of Illinois Center for Urban Economic Development.

Fitzsimmons, James D., and Richard L. Forstall. 1993. "Metropolitan Areas: Definitions for the 1990s and Evaluation of Concepts." Paper presented at the annual meeting of the Association of American Geographers, Atlanta, Georgia, April 9.

Fix, Michael, and Raymond J. Struyk, eds. 1993. *Clear and Convincing Evidence: Measurement of Discrimination in America*. Washington, D.C.: Urban Institute Press.

Flora, Cornelia B., and Jan L. Flora. 1988. "Characteristics of Entrepreneurial Communities in a Time of Crisis." *Rural Development News* 12: 1–4.

Flora, Cornelia B., and Sue Johnson. 1973. "Discarding the Distaff: New Roles for Rural Women." In *Rural U.S.A.: Persistence and Change,* ed. Thomas Ford. Ames: Iowa State University Press.

Ford Foundation. 1992. "Latinos: Speaking in Their Own Voices." News release of forthcoming book by Rodolfo O. de la Garza, Angelo Falcon, F. Chris Garcia, John A. Garcia, and Louis DeSipio, New York, December 15.

"The Forgotten Poor: Blacks in Rural Areas." 1988. *Focus*. July.

Fosler, Scott. 1991. "Economic Development: A Regional Challenge for the Heartland." In *Regional Economic Development and Public Policy*. Kansas City, Mo.: Federal Reserve Bank of Kansas City.

Fowler, Robert Booth. 1991. *Dance with Community: The Contemporary Debate in American Political Thought*. Lawrence: University Press of Kansas.

Freshwater, D. 1989. "A Synopsis of the Proceeding of the Rural Development Symposium." In *Towards Rural Development Policy for the 1990s: Enhancing Income and Employment Opportunities,* Joint Economic Committee, Congress of the United States, Washington, D.C.: Government Printing Office.

Freudenberg, William R. 1986. "The Density of Acquaintanceship: An Overlooked Variable in Community Research?" *American Journal of Sociology* 92: 27–63.

Frey, William H. 1993. "The New Urban Revival in the United States." *Urban Studies* 30: 741–774.

Friedland, William H. 1982. "The End of Rural Society and the Future of Rural Sociology." *Rural Sociology* 47: 589–608.

_____. 1984. "Commodity Systems Analysis: An Approach to the Sociology of Agriculture." In *Research in Rural Sociology and Development,* ed. Harry Schwarzweller, 1: 221–235. Greenwich, Conn.: JAI Press.

Frost, Robert. 1979. *The Poetry of Robert Frost,* ed. Edward C. Lathem. New York: Henry Holt.

Fuguitt, Glenn V. 1991. "Commuting and the Rural-Urban Hierarchy." *Journal of Rural Studies* 7: 459–466.

———. 1992. "Population Trends in Rural America, 1960–1990." Madison: University of Wisconsin–Madison Center for Demography and Ecology Working Paper 92–19.

Fuguitt, Glenn V., and Calvin L. Beale. 1993. "The Changing Concentration of the Older Nonmetropolitan Population 1960–1990." *Journal of Gerontology: Social Sciences* 48: S278-S288.

Fuguitt, Glenn V., Calvin L. Beale, and Michael Reibel. 1991. "Recent Trends in Metropolitan-Nonmetropolitan Fertility." *Rural Sociology* 56: 475–486.

Fuguitt, Glenn V., David L. Brown, and Calvin L. Beale. 1989. *Rural and Small Town America.* New York: Russell Sage Foundation.

Fuguitt, Glenn V., Tim B. Heaton, and Daniel T. Lichter. 1988. "Monitoring the Metropolitanization Process." *Demography* 25: 115–128.

Fuller, Varden. 1991. *Hired Hands in California's Farm Fields.* Giannini Foundation Special Report. Berkeley: University of California, Division of Agricultural and Natural Resources.

Fuller, Wayne E. 1982. *The Old Country School: The Story of Rural Education in the Middle West.* Chicago: University of Chicago Press.

Gabbard, Susan M., and Richard Mines. 1994. "A New Understanding of Farm Worker Demographics." In *Immigration and U.S. Agriculture,* ed. Martin, Huffman, Emerson, Taylor, and Rochin. Berkeley: University of California, DANR Press.

Galarza, Ernesto. 1976. *Farmworkers and Agribusiness in California 1947–1960,* Notre Dame, Ind.: University of Notre Dame Press.

Galbraith, John Kenneth. 1958. *The Affluent Society.* Boston: Houghton Mifflin.

Gallaher, Art, Jr. 1980. "Dependence on External Authority and the Decline of Community." In *The Dying Community,* ed. Art Gallaher, Jr., and Harland Padfield, pp. 85–108. Albuquerque: University of New Mexico Press.

Galston, William. 1988. "Rural Economic Development in a Competitive Global Economy." In *Agriculture and Beyond: Rural Economic Development,* ed. Gene F. Summers et al., pp. 1–9. Madison: University of Wisconsin, College of Agricultural and Life Sciences.

———. 1993. "Rural America in the 1990s: Trends and Choices." In *Population Change and the Future of Rural American: A Conference Proceedings,* ed. Linda L. Swanson and David L. Brown. Economic Research Service, U.S. Department of Agriculture, Staff Report AGES 9324.

Gamradt, Jan Armstrong, and Patricia G. Avery. 1992. "Country Kids, City Kids: Community Context and Geopolitical Identity." *Journal of Research in Rural Education* 8(1): 61–74.

Garfinkel, Irwin, and Sara S. McLanahan. 1986. *Single Mothers and Their Children.* Washington, D.C.: Urban Institute.

Garnick, Daniel H. 1984. "Shifting Balances in U.S. Metropolitan and Non-metropolitan Area Growth." *International Regional Science Review* 9: 257–273.

Garreau, Joël. 1981. *The Nine Nations of North America.* Boston: Houghton Mifflin.

_____. 1988. "Edge Cities." *Landscape Architecture* 78(8): 51–55.

_____. 1991. *Edge City: Life on the New Frontier.* New York: Doubleday.

Gartrell, John W. 1983. "Agricultural Technology and Agrarian Community Organization." In *Technology and Social Change in Rural Areas,* ed. Gene F. Summers, pp. 149–162. Boulder, Colo.: Westview.

Gaventa, John. 1980. *Power and Powerlessness: Quiescence and Rebellion in an Appalachian Valley.* Oxford: Clarendon Press.

Genovese, Eugene D. 1965. *The Political Economy of Slavery.* New York: Vintage.

_____. 1974. *Roll Jordan Roll: The World the Slaves Made.* New York: Pantheon.

Gilder, George. 1981. *Wealth and Poverty.* New York: Basic Books.

Glasgow, Nina, Karen Holden, Diane McLaughlin, and Graham Rowles. 1993. "The Rural Elderly and Poverty." In *Persistent Poverty in Rural America,* chap. 8. Boulder, Colo.: Westview.

Glasmeier, Amy. 1992. *The High-Tech Potential: Economic Development in Rural America.* Washington, D.C.: Center for Urban Policy Research.

Goldfield, David R. 1987. *Promised Land: The South Since 1945.* Arlington Heights, Ill.: Harlan Davidson.

Goldschmidt, Walter. 1978. *As You Sow: Three Studies in the Social Consequences of Agribusiness.* Montclair, N.J.: Allenheld Osmun.

Goodlad, J. 1984. *A Place Called School.* New York: McGraw Hill.

Gordon, David M. 1972. *Theories of Poverty and Underemployment.* Lexington, Mass.: D.C. Heath.

Gottman, Jean. 1961. *Megalopolis: The Urbanized Northeastern Seaboard of the United States.* New York: Twentieth-Century Fund.

Goudy, Willis J. 1990. "Community Attachment in a Rural Region." *Rural Sociology* 55: 178–198.

Gould, David, and Roy J. Ruffin. 1993. "What Determines Economic Growth?" *Economic Review* (Second Quarter).

Gouveia, Lourdes, and Donald D. Stull. 1992. "Dances with Cows: Beef Packing's Impact on Garden City, Kansas, and Lexington, Nebraska." Paper presented at Conference on New Factory Workers in Old Farming Communities, Queenstown, Md., Wye Conference Center.

Green, Gary P., Jan L. Flora, Cornelia Flora, and Frederick E. Schmidt. 1990. "Local Self-Development Strategies: National Survey Results." *Journal of Community Development Society* 21(2): 55–73.

Greenberg, E. J., P. L. Swaim, and R. A. Teixeira. 1993. "Can Rural Workers Compete for the Jobs of the Future?" In *Agriculture's Changing Horizon: Outlook '93 Proceedings,* pp. 919–930. Washington, D.C.: U.S. Department of Agriculture.

Greenberg, E. J., and R. A. Teixeira. 1993. "Educational Achievement in Rural Schools." Unpublished manuscript. Washington, D.C.: Economic Research Service, U.S. Department of Agriculture.

Gringeri, Christina E. 1990. "The Nuts and Bolts of Subsidized Development: Industrial Homework in Two Rural Midwestern Communities." Ph.D. dissertation, University of Wisconsin, Madison.

_____. 1993. "Inscribing Gender in Rural Development: Industrial Homework in Two Midwestern Communities." *Rural Sociology* 58: 30–52.

_____. 1994. *Getting By: Women Homeworkers and Rural Economic Development.* Lawrence: University Press of Kansas.

Grodzins, Morton. 1966. *The American System.* Chicago: Rand McNally.

Grossman, Gene M., and Elhanan Helpman. 1991. *Innovation and Growth in the Global Economy.* Cambridge: MIT Press.

Hady, Thomas, and Peggy Ross. 1990. "An Update: The Diverse Social and Economic Structure of Nonmetropolitan America." Agriculture and Rural Economy Division, Economic Research Service, U.S. Department of Agriculture, Staff Report No. AGES 9036.

Hamilton, David. 1992. *From New Day to New Deal.* Chapel Hill: University of North Carolina Press.

Harding, Vincent. 1981. *There Is a River.* New York: Harcourt, Brace Jovanovich.

Harp, John. 1973. "Formal Voluntary Organizations: Agents of Stability and Change." *Search* (Cornell University College of Agriculture) 3(7): 1–27.

Harrison, Bennett, and Barry Bluestone. 1988. *The Great U-Turn: Corporate Restructuring and the Polarizing of America.* New York: Basic Books.

Hart, I. H. 1954. *Milestones.* Des Moines: Iowa State Education Association.

Hart, John Fraser. 1968. "Loss and Abandonment of Cleared Farm Land in the Eastern United States." *Annals of the Association of American Geographers* 58(3): 417–440.

_____. 1972. "The Middle West." *Annals of the Association of American Geographers* 62(2): 258–282.

_____. 1978. "Cropland Concentrations in the South." *Annals of the Association of American Geographers* 68(4): 505–517.

_____. 1981. "Migration to the Blacktop: Population Redistribution in the South." *Landscape* 25(3): 15–19.

_____. 1984a. "Population Change in the Upper Lake States." *Annals of the Association of American Geographers* 74(2): 221–243.

_____. 1984b. "Resort Areas in Wisconsin." *Geographical Review* 74(2): 192–217.

_____. 1986. "Change in the Corn Belt." *Geographical Review* 76(1): 51–72.

_____. 1988. "Small Towns and Manufacturing." *Geographical Review* 78(3): 272–287.

_____. 1991a. "Part-Ownership and Farm Enlargement in the Midwest." *Annals of the Association of American Geographers* 81(1): 66–79.

_____. 1991b. "The Perimetropolitan Bow Wave." *Geographical Review* 81(1): 35–51.

_____. 1992. "Nonfarm Farms." *Geographical Review* 82(2): 166–179.

Harvey, David L. 1993. *Potter Addition: Poverty, Family, and Kinship in a Heartland Community.* New York: Aldine DeGruyter.

Hatch, Elvin. 1979. *Biography of a Small Town.* New York: Columbia University Press.

Hawkins, Robert B., Jr. 1976. *Self-Government by District: Myth and Reality.* Stanford: Hoover Institution Press.

Hayami, Y., and V. Ruttan. 1985. *Agricultural Development: An International Perspective.* Baltimore: Johns Hopkins University Press.

HCN *(High Country News).* 1992. "An Alternative to the Bumper-Sticker Approach to Grazing." March 23, 24(5).

Healy, Robert G. 1985. *Competition for Land in the American South*. Washington, D.C.: Conservation Foundation.

Heimlich, Ralph E., and C. Tim Osborne. 1993. "The Conservation Reserve Program: What Happens When Contracts Expire?" *Choices* (Third Quarter): 9–14.

Henry, Mark, Mark Drabenstott, and Lynn Gibson. 1986. "A Changing Rural America." *Economic Review* (July/August): 23–41.

———. 1988. "A Changing Rural Economy." In *Rural America in Transition*, ed. Mark Drabenstott and Lynn Gibson, pp. 15–37. Kansas City, Mo.: Federal Reserve Bank of Kansas City.

Henry, Mark, and Lynn Gibson. 1988. "Searching for Rural Success." In *Rural America In Transition*, ed. Mark Drabenstott and Lynn Gibson. Kansas City, Mo.: Federal Reserve Bank of Kansas City.

Herbers, John. 1986. *The New Heartland: America's Flight beyond the Suburbs and How It Is Changing our Future*. New York: Times Books.

Hibbard, Michael. 1993. "The Failure of Sustained-Yield Forestry and the Decline of the Flannel-Shirt Frontier." In *Forgotten Places: Uneven Development in Rural America*, ed. T. A. Lyson and W. W. Falk, pp. 195–217. Lawrence: University Press of Kansas.

Hickey, Jo Ann. 1991. "Why Do People Stay Behind in Lagging Rural Regions Rather than Move to Nearby Growth Centers?" Paper presented at Rural Sociological Society meeting, Columbus, Ohio.

High Country News. See HCN

Hill, Samuel S. 1989. "Civil Rights and Religion." In *Encyclopedia of Southern Culture*, ed. Charles R. Wilson and William Ferris. Chapel Hill: University of North Carolina Press.

Hirschl, Thomas A., and Mark R. Rank. 1991. "The Effect of Population Density on Welfare Participation." *Social Forces* 70: 225–235.

Hirschl, Thomas A., and Gene F. Summers. 1982. "Cash Transfers and the Export Base of Small Communities." *Rural Sociology* 47: 295–316.

Hirschman, A. O. 1958. "Interregional and International Transmission of Economic Growth." In *The Strategy of Economic Development*, chap. 10. New Haven: Yale University Press.

Hodson, Randy D. 1978. "Labor in the Monopoly, Competitive, and State Sectors of Production." *Politics and Society* 8: 429–480.

Holland, David, Bruce Weber, and Edward Waters. 1992. "Modeling the Economic Linkage Between Core and Periphery Regions: The Portland, Oregon, Trade Area." Graduate Faculty of Economics Working Papers in Economics No. 92-103.

Honadle, Beth. 1993. "Rural Development Policy: Breaking the Cargo Cult Mentality." *Economic Development Quarterly* 7(3): 227–236.

Hoppe, Robert. 1993. "Poverty in Rural America: Trends and Demographic Characteristics." In *Persistent Poverty in Rural America*, pp. 20–38. Boulder, Colo.: Westview.

Horan, Patrick, and Charles M. Tolbert. 1984. *The Organization of Work in Rural and Labor Markets*. Boulder, Colo.: Westview.

Howes, Candace, and Ann R. Markusen. 1981. "Poverty: A Regional Political Economy Perspective." In *Nonmetropolitan America in Transition*, ed. Amos H.

Hawley and Sara M. Mazie, chap. 11. Chapel Hill: University of North Carolina Press.

Hudson, John C. 1985. *Plains Country Towns.* Minneapolis: University of Minnesota Press.

Hummon, David M. 1990. *Commonplaces: Community Ideology and Identity in American Culture.* Albany: State University of New York Press.

Ilvento, Thomas W. 1990. "Education and Community." In *American Rural Communities,* ed. A. E. Luloff and Louis E. Swanson, pp. 106–123. Boulder, Colo.: Westview.

Indian Gaming. 1993. "List of Indian Gaming Operations." 3: 14–15.

Institute for Social Research. 1987. *Panel Study of Income Dynamics: User Guide.* Ann Arbor, Mich.: Inter-University Consortium for Political and Social Science.

Iowa, Department of Public Instruction. 1928. *Iowa Educational Directory, 1927–1928.* Des Moines: State of Iowa.

_____. 1960. *Reorganization of Iowa School Districts: 1954–1955 to 1959–1960.* Des Moines: State of Iowa.

Jackson, J. B. [John Brinckerhoff]. 1960. "The Four Corners Country." *Landscape* 10(1): 20–26.

_____. 1970. *Landscapes: Selected Writings of J. B. Jackson,* ed. E. H. Zube. Amherst: University of Massachusetts Press.

_____. 1980. *The Necessity for Ruins and Other Topics.* Amherst: University of Massachusetts Press.

_____. 1984. *Discovering the Vernacular Landscape.* New Haven: Yale University Press.

_____. 1985. "Looking at New Mexico." In *The Essential Landscape: The New Mexico Survey Project,* ed. Jackson et al., pp. 1–9. Albuquerque: University of New Mexico Press.

_____. 1990. "The House in the Vernacular Landscape." In *The Making of the American Landscape,* ed. Michael Conzen, chap. 18. Winchester, Mass.: Unwin Hyman.

Jackson, Kenneth. 1985. *Crabgrass Frontier: The Suburbanization of the United States.* New York: Oxford University Press.

Jackson, W. 1991. "Nature as the Measure of a Sustainable Agriculture." In *The Broken Circle: Ecology, Economics, and Ethics,* ed. F. Bormann and S. Kellert. New Haven: Yale University Press.

James, David R. 1988. "The Transformation of the Southern Racial State: Class and Race Determinants of Local State Structure." *American Sociological Review* 53(2): 191–208.

Janieski, Dolores. 1985. *Sisterhood Denied: Race, Gender, and Class in the Southern Tobacco Industry, 1600–1970.* Philadelphia: Temple University Press.

Jansen, Annica. 1991. "Rural Counties Lead Urban in Education Spending, but Is That Enough?" *Rural Development Perspectives* (October–January): 8–15.

Jaynes, Gerald David, and Robin W. Williams, Jr. 1989. *A Common Destiny: Blacks and American Society.* Washington, D.C.: National Academy Press.

Jencks, Christopher, and Paul Peterson. 1991. *The Urban Underclass.* Washington, D.C.: Brookings Institution.

Jensen, Leif. 1988. "Rural-Urban Differences in the Utilization and Ameliorative Effects of Welfare Programs." Paper presented to the meeting of the Southern Rural Sociological Society, New Orleans.

Jensen, R. J., and M. Friedberger. 1976. *Education and Social Structure: An Historical Study of Iowa.* Mimeograph. Final Report to National Institute of Education, Newberry Library, Chicago.

John, DeWitt, Sandra S. Batie, and Kim Norris. 1988. *A Brighter Future for Rural America?* Washington, D.C.: National Governor's Association.

Johnson, Charles S., et al. 1941. *Statistical Atlas of Southern Counties: Listing and Analysis of Socio-Economic Indices of 1104 Southern Counties.* Chapel Hill: University of North Carolina Press.

Johnson, D. N.d. "The Performance of Past Policies: A Critique." In *Alternative Agricultural and Food Policies in the 1985 Farm Bill,* ed. K. Farrell and G. Rausser. Berkeley: Giannini Foundation, University of California.

Johnson, Kenneth M. 1993. "When Deaths Exceed Births: Natural Decrease in the United States." *International Regional Science Review* 15: 179–198.

Johnson, Kenneth N., and Calvin L. Beale. 1993. "Nonmetropolitan Demographic Trends Since 1990." Paper presented at the annual meeting of the Southern Demographic Association, New Orleans, October 22.

Johnson, Kevin R. 1993. *"Los Olvidados:* Images of the Immigrant, Political Power of Noncitizens, and Immigration Law and Enforcement." *Brigham Young University Law Review* (4): 1139–1256.

Johnston, W. B., and A. E. Packer. 1987. *Work Force 2000: Work and Workers for the 21st Century.* Indianapolis: Hudson Institute.

Joint Center for Political Studies. 1973. *National Roster of Black Elected Officials.* Washington, D.C.

———. 1991. *Black Elected Officials: A National Roster.* Washington, D.C.

Jones, Barry. 1990. *Sleepers Wake! Technology and the Future of Work.* New York: Oxford University Press.

Jordan, Winthrop D. 1968. *White Over Black.* Chapel Hill: University of North Carolina Press.

Jorgensen, Joseph G. 1984. "Land Is Cultural, So Is a Commodity: The Locus of Differences Among Indians, Cowboys, Sod-Busters, and Environmentalists." *Journal of Ethnic Studies* 12(3): 1–21.

Jorgensen, Joseph G., Richard O. Clemmer, Ronald L. Little, Nancy J. Owens, and Lynn A. Robbins. 1978. *Native Americans and Energy Development.* Cambridge, Mass.: Anthropology Resource Center.

Kaldor, Nicholas. 1970. "The Case of Regional Policies." *Scottish Journal of Political Economy* 17(2): 337–348.

Kasarda, John D. 1985. "Urban Change and Minority Opportunities." In *The New Urban Reality,* ed. P. Peterson, pp. 33–67. Washington, D.C.: Brookings Institution.

———. 1989. "Urban Industrial Transformation and the Underclass." *Annals of American Political and Social Science* 501: 26–47.

Kaus, Mickey. 1992. *The End of Equality.* New York: Basic Books.

Keats, John. 1957. *The Crack in the Picture Window.* Boston: Houghton Mifflin.

Keppel, A. 1960. "Country Schools for Country Children: Backgrounds of the Reform Movement in Rural Elementary Education, 1890–1914." Ph.D. dissertation, University of Wisconsin, Madison.

Kerner, O. H. 1968. *The Report of the National Advisory Commission on Civil Disorders*. New York: Bantam Books.

Kersey, Henry A., Jr. 1992. "Seminoles and Miccosukees: A Century in Retrospective." In *Indians of the Southeastern United States in the Late 20th Century*, ed. J. Anthony Paredes, pp. 102–119. Tuscaloosa: University of Alabama Press.

Kiesling, Herbert. 1967. "Measuring a Local Government Service: A Study of School Districts in New York State." *Review of Economics and Statistics* 49: 356–367.

Killian, Joyce E., and David M. Byrd. 1988. "A Cooperative Staff Development Model That Taps the Strength of Rural Schools." *Journal of Staff Development* 9: 34–39.

Killian, Lewis M. 1970. *White Southerners*. New York: Random House.

Killian, Molly Sizer, and Thomas F. Hady. 1988. "The Economic Performance of Rural Labor Markets." In *Rural Economic Development in the 1980s*, ed. David L. Brown et al., pp. 181–200. Rural Development Research Report No. 69. Washington, D.C.: USDA, Economic Research Service.

Killian, Molly Sizer, and T. S. Parker. 1991. "Education and Employment Growth in a Changing Economy." In *Education and Rural Development: Rural Strategies for the 1990s*, ed. R. W. Long. Washington, D.C.: USDA, Economic Research Service.

King, I. 1913. *Education for Social Efficiency*. New York: Appleton.

Knowlton, Clark S. 1985. "Land Loss as a Cause of Unrest Among the Rural Spanish-American Village Population of Northern New Mexico." *Agriculture and Human Values* 2: 25–39.

Knox, Paul L. 1994. *Urbanization: An Introduction to Urban Geography*. Englewood Cliffs, N.J.: Prentice-Hall.

Korsching, Peter F., Timothy O. Borich, and Julie Stewart, eds. 1992. "Multicommunity Collaboration: An Evolving Rural Revitalization Strategy." Conference Proceedings, RRD 161. Ames, Iowa: North Central Regional Center for Rural Development.

Kotler, Milton. 1969. *Neighborhood Government: The Local Foundations of Political Life*. Indianapolis: Bobbs-Merrill.

Kramer, Judith. 1970. *The American Minority Community*. New York: Thomas Y. Crowell Company.

Krepps, Matthew B. 1992. "Can Tribes Manage Their Own Resources? The 638 Program and American Indian Forestry." In *What Can Tribes Do? Strategies and Institutions in American Indian Economic Development*, ed. Stephen Cornell and Joseph P. Kalt, pp. 179–204. Los Angeles: American Indian Studies Center, University of California.

Kunstler, James Howard. 1993. *The Geography of Nowhere: The Rise and Decline of America's Man-Made Landscape*. New York: Simon and Schuster.

Kusel, Jonathan. 1991. "Well-Being in Forest-Dependent Communities." Vol 2. Berkeley, Calif.: Department of Forestry and Resource Management.

Lang, W. C. 1991. *A Century of Leadership and Service: A Centennial History of the University of Northern Iowa*. Vol. 1, *1876–1928*. Cedar Falls: University of Northern Iowa.

Lapping, M. B. 1992. "American Rural Planning, Development Policy, and the Centrality of the Federal State: An Interpretive History." *Rural History* 3(2): 219–242.

LeClere, F., and D. Dahmann. 1990. *Residents of Farms and Rural Areas 1989.* Current Population Reports, Population Characteristics, Series P-20, no. 446, Washington, D.C.: USDA and U.S. Department of Commerce.

Lee, Mitgang. 1990. "Rural Children at Top Risk for Failure, Says New Study." *Commercial Appeal,* May 23, A2.

Lemann, Nicholas. 1986. "Origins of the Underclass." *Atlantic* (June/July).

———. 1991. *The Promised Land.* New York: Knopf.

Leven, Charles L. 1985. "Regional Development Analysis and Policy." *Journal of Regional Analysis* 25: 569–592.

Levitan, Sar A. 1990. *Programs in Aid of the Poor.* 5th ed. Baltimore: Johns Hopkins University Press.

Levitan, Sar A., and William B. Johnston. 1975. *Indian Giving: Federal Programs for Native Americans.* Baltimore: Johns Hopkins University Press.

Levitan, Sar A., and Elizabeth I. Miller. 1993. *The Equivocal Prospects for Indian Reservations.* Washington, D.C.: Center for Policy Studies, George Washington University.

Lewis, David Rich. 1988. "Farming and the Northern Ute Experience, 1850–1940." In *Overcoming Economic Dependency: Papers and Comments from the First Newberry Library Conference on Themes in American History,* ed. Frederick E. Hoxie, pp. 142–164. Occasional papers in Curriculum Series no. 9. Chicago: Newberry Library.

Lewis, Oscar. 1959. *Five Families: The Children of Sanchez.* New York: Random House.

———. 1966a. "The Culture of Poverty." *Scientific American* 215: 19–25.

———. 1966b. *La Vida: A Puerto Rican Family in the Culture of Poverty—San Juan and New York.* New York: Random House.

Lewis, P. 1991. "The Urban Invasion of the Rural Northeast." In *Proceedings of a Meeting of the National Rural Studies Committee,* Reading, Pa., May 16–17, ed. E. Castle and B. Baldwin. Corvallis: Western Rural Development Center, Oregon State University.

Lewis, Peirce. 1983a. "The Galactic Metropolis." In *Beyond the Urban Fringe: Land-Use Issues of Nonmetropolitan America,* ed. R. H. Platt and G. Macinko, pp. 23–49. Minneapolis: University of Minnesota Press.

———. 1983b. "The Geographic Roots of America's Urban Troubles." *Earth and Mineral Sciences* 52(3): 25–29.

———. 1987. "America Between the Wars: The Engineering of a New Geography." In *North America: The Historical Geography of a Changing Continent,* ed. R. D. Mitchell and P. A. Groves, chap. 17. Totowa, N.J.: Rowman and Littlefield.

———. 1990. "The Northeastern United States and the Making of American Geographical Habits." In *The Making of the American Landscape,* ed. Michael P. Conzen, pp. 80–103. Boston: Unwin-Hyman.

———. 1992. "Misunderstanding the West in General and New Mexico in Particular." In *National Rural Studies Committee: A Proceeding,* ed. Emery Castle and Barbara Baldwin, pp. 36–39. Corvallis: Western Rural Development Center, Oregon State University.

Lichter, Daniel T. 1988. "Race and Underemployment: Black Employment Hardship in the Rural South." In *The Rural South in Crisis,* ed. Lionel J. Beaulieu. Boulder, Colo.: Westview.

———. 1989. "Race, Employment Hardship, and Inequality in the American Nonmetropolitan South." *American Sociological Review* 54: 436–446.

———. 1993. "Demographic Aspects of the Changing Rural Labor Force." In *Population Change and the Future of Rural America: A Conference Proceeding,* Staff Report no. AGES 9324, ed. Linda L. Swanson and David L. Brown. Washington D.C.: Economic Research Service, U.S. Department of Agriculture.

Lichter, Daniel T., Lionel J. Beaulieu, Jill L. Findeis, and Ruy A. Teixeira. 1993. "Human Capital, Labor Supply, and Poverty in Rural America." In *Persistent Poverty in Rural America,* pp. 39–67. Boulder, Colo.: Westview.

Lichter, Daniel T., and Janice A. Constanzo. 1987. "Nonmetropolitan Underemployment and Labor Force Composition." *Rural Sociology* 52: 329–344.

Lichter, Daniel T., and David J. Eggebeen. 1992. "Child Poverty and the Changing Rural Family." *Rural Sociology* 57: 152–172.

Lichter, Daniel T., and Glenn V. Fuguitt. 1982. "The Transition to Nonmetropolitan Population Deconcentration." *Demography* 19: 211–221.

Lichter, Daniel T., and Tim B. Heaton. 1986. "Black Composition and Change in the Nonmetropolitan South." *Rural Sociology* 51(3): 343–353.

Lichter, Daniel T., Diane K. McLaughlin, and Gretchen T. Cornwell. 1992. "Migration and the Loss of Human Resources in Rural America." In *Investing in People: The Human Capital Needs of Rural America,* ed. Lionel J. Beaulieu and David Mulkey, pp. 224–226. Boulder, Colo.: Westview.

Lieberson, Stanley. 1993. "Contemporary Immigration Policy: Lessons from the Past." Presented at Middlebury College Fifteenth Annual Conference on Economic Issues, Immigrants and United States Immigration Policy, April 3.

Lieberson, Stanley, and Mary C. Waters. 1988. *From Many Strands: Ethnic and Racial Groups in Contemporary America.* New York: Russell Sage Foundation.

Light, Ivan H. 1972. *Ethnic Enterprise in America.* Berkeley: University of California Press.

Lin, Xiannuan, Terry F. Buss, and Mark Popovich. 1990. "Entrepreneurship Is Alive and Well in Rural America: A Four State Study." *Economic Development Quarterly* 4: 254–259.

Long, John F. 1981. *Population Deconcentration in the United States.* Special Demographic Analysis 81–1. Washington, D.C.: U.S. Government Printing Office.

Long, Larry. 1988. *Migration and Residential Mobility in the United States.* New York: Russell Sage Foundation.

Lovejoy, Stephen B., and Jerald J. Fletcher. 1991. "Water Quality and Agriculture." In *Rural Policies for the 1990s,* ed. Cornelia B. Flora and James A. Christenson, pp. 235–246. Boulder, Colo.: Westview.

Loveridge, Ray, and L. Mok. 1979. *Theories of Labor Market Segmentation.* London: Martinus Nijhoff.

Lower Mississippi Delta Development Commission. 1990. *Delta Initiatives: Final Report.* Memphis: Mercury Press.

Lucas, Robert E., Jr. 1988. "On the Mechanics of Economic Development." *Journal of Monetary Economics* 22: 3–42.

Luke, Robert. 1989. "Agriculture Retains a Prominent Role Despite Pressures." *Atlanta Journal and Constitution,* March 12, 5S.

Luloff, A. E. 1990. "Community and Social Change: How Do Small Communities Act?" In *American Rural Communities,* ed. A. E. Luloff and Louis E. Swanson, pp. 214–227. Boulder, Colo.: Westview.

Luloff, A. E., and Louis E. Swanson. 1994. "Community Agency and Disaffection." In *Human Capital in Rural Development,* ed. Lionel Beaulieu and David Mulkey, chap. 14. Boulder, Colo.: Westview.

Luloff, A. E., and Louis E. Swanson, eds. 1990. *American Rural Communities.* Boulder, Colo.: Westview.

Lynd, Robert, and Helen Lynd. 1929. *Middletown.* New York: Harcourt, Brace and World.

———. 1937. *Middletown in Transition.* New York: Harcourt, Brace and World.

Lyson, Thomas A. 1988. "Economic Development in the Rural South: An Uneven Past—An Uncertain Future." In *The Rural South in Crisis,* ed. Lionel J. Beaulieu. Boulder, Colo.: Westview.

———. 1989. *Two Sides to the Sunbelt.* New York: Praeger.

———. 1991. "Real Incomes of Rural Black and Hispanic Workers Fell Further Behind in the 1980's." *Rural Development Perspectives* 7(2): 7–11.

Lyson, Thomas A., and William W. Falk. 1993. *Forgotten Places: Uneven Development in Rural America.* Lawrence: University Press of Kansas.

McGranahan, David A. 1983. "Changes in the Social and Spatial Structure of the Rural Community." In *Technology and Social Change in Rural Areas,* ed. Gene F. Summers, pp. 163–178. Boulder, Colo.: Westview.

———. 1993. "Education and Employment Growth in Complex and Routine Manufacturing." Manuscript. Washington, D.C.: USDA, Economic Research Service.

McGranahan, David A., and Linda M. Ghelfi. 1991. "The Education Crisis and Rural Stagnation in the 1980's." In *Education and Rural Economic Development,* ed. Richard W. Long, chap. 3. ERS Staff Report AGES 9153. Washington, D.C.: USDA, Economic Research Service.

McGranahan, David A., J. C. Hession, F. K. Hines, and M. F. Jordan. 1986. *Social and Economic Characteristics of the Population in Metro and Nonmetro Counties, 1970–1980.* Washington, D.C.: USDA, Economic Research Service.

McKibben, Bill. 1993. *The Age of Missing Information.* New York: Penguin Books.

McLaughlin, Diane K., and Leif Jensen. 1991. "Poverty Among the Elderly: Metropolitan-Nonmetropolitan Comparisons." Paper presented to annual meeting of the Rural Sociological Society, Columbus, Ohio.

McLaughlin, Diane K., and Carolyn Sachs. 1988. "Poverty in Female-Headed Households: Residential Differences." *Rural Sociology* 53: 286–306.

McMurtry, Larry. 1990. "How the West Was Won or Lost: The Revisionists' Failure of Imagination." *New Republic,* October 22, pp. 32–38.

McNall, Scott G., and Sally Allen McNall. 1983. *Plains Families.* New York: St. Martin's Press.

McWilliams, Carey. 1990. *North from Mexico: The Spanish-Speaking People of the United States.* New ed. updated by Matt S. Meier. New York: Praeger.

Maril, Robert Lee. 1989. *Poorest of Americans: The Mexican Americans of the Lower Rio Grande Valley of Texas.* Notre Dame, Ind.: University of Notre Dame Press.

Marshall, Ray. 1986. "New Skills for the Changing Economy." In *Technology, the Economy and Vocational Education,* ed. Stuart Rosenfeld. Research Triangle, N.C.: Southern Growth Policies Board.

Marston, Ed, ed. 1989. *Reopening the Western Frontier.* Washington, D.C.: Island Press.

Martin, Kenneth E., and Kenneth P. Wilkinson. 1984. "Local Participation in the Federal Grant System: Effects of Community Action." *Rural Sociology* 49(Fall): 374–388.

Martin, Philip L. 1988. *Harvest of Confusion: Migrant Workers in U.S. Agriculture.* Boulder, Colo.: Westview.

———. 1993. "Good Intentions Gone Awry." In *Western Wire,* pp. 14–20. Corvallis: Western Rural Development Center, Oregon State University.

Martin, Philip L., Wallace Huffman, Robert Emerson, J. Edward Taylor, and Refugio I. Rochin, eds. 1994. *Immigration Reform and U.S. Agriculture.* Berkeley: University of California, Division of Agriculture and Natural Resources.

Martindale, Don, and R. Galen Hanson. 1969. *Small Town and the Nation.* Westport, Conn.: Greenwood Publishing Company.

Massey, Douglas, and Mitchell Eggers. 1990. "The Ecology of Inequality: Minorities and the Concentration of Poverty, 1970–1980." *American Journal of Sociology* 95: 1153–1188.

Massey, Douglas, and Andrew Gross. 1991. "Segregation, the Concentration of Poverty, and the Life Chances of Individuals." Manuscript. University of Chicago.

May, G. S. 1956. "Iowa's Consolidated Schools." *Palimpsest* 37(1): 1–64.

MDC. 1986. *Shadows in the Sunbelt.* Chapel Hill: University of North Carolina.

Mead, Lawrence M. 1992. *The New Politics of Poverty: The Nonworking Poor in America.* New York: Basic Books.

Mealor, W. Theodore, Jr., and Merle C. Prunty. 1976. "Open-Range Ranching in Southern Florida." *Annals of the Association of American Geographers* 66(3): 360–376.

Meinig, D. W. 1969. *Imperial Texas: An Interpretive Essay in Cultural Geography.* Austin: University of Texas Press.

Meisenheimer II, Joseph R. 1992. "How Do Immigrants Fare in the U.S. Labor Market?" *Monthly Labor Review* 115(12): 3–19.

Mieszkowski, Peter, and Edwin Mills. 1993. "The Causes of Metropolitan Suburbanization." *Journal of Economic Literature* 7(3): 135–147.

Miller, James P., and Herman Bluestone. 1988. "Prospects for Service Sector Employment Growth in Non-metro America." In *Rural Economic Development in the 1980s,* ed. David L. Brown et al., pp. 135–157. Rural Development Research Report no. 69. Washington, D.C.: USDA, Economic Research Service.

Mills, Edwin. 1990. "Do Metropolitan Areas Mean Anything? A Research Note." *Journal of Regional Science* 30(3): 415–419.

———. 1992. "Large Metropolitan Areas: Their Functions and Prospects." In *National Rural Studies Committee: A Proceeding,* ed. Emery Castle and Barbara Baldwin. Corvallis: Western Rural Development Center, University of Oregon.

Mills, Edwin, and Bruce Hamilton. 1993. *Urban Economics.* 5th ed. New York: Harper and Collins.

Miner, H. Craig. 1976. *The Corporation and the Indian.* Columbia: University of Missouri Press.

Mishel, L. R., and R. A. Teixeira. 1991. *The Myth of the Coming Labor Shortage: Jobs, Skills, and Incomes of America's Workforce 2000.* Washington, D.C.: Economic Policy Institute.

Monk, D., and E. Haller. 1986. *Organizational Alternatives for Small Rural Schools.* Ithaca, N.Y.: Cornell University Press.

Mooney, Patrick H., and Jess Gilbert. 1991. "Farmland Tenure Policy." In *Rural Policies for the 1990s,* ed. Cornelia B. Flora and James A. Christenson, pp. 259–269. Boulder, Colo.: Westview.

Mormont, Marc. 1987. "Rural Nature and Urban Nature." *Sociologia Ruralis* 27: 3–20.

Morrison, Peter A., ed. 1990. *A Taste of the Country: A Collection of Calvin Beale's Writings.* University Park: Pennsylvania State University Press.

Morrissey, Elizabeth. 1991. *Work and Poverty in Metro and Nonmetro Areas.* Rural Development Research Report, no. 81. Washington, D.C.: U.S. Department of Agriculture.

Moynihan, Daniel P. 1965. "The Negro Family: The Case for National Action." Reprinted in *The Moynihan Report and the Politics of Poverty,* ed. Lee Rainwater and William L. Yancey. Cambridge: MIT Press.

———. 1969. *Maximum Feasible Misunderstanding: Community Action in the War on Poverty.* New York: Free Press.

Murray, Charles. 1984. *Losing Ground: American Social Policy 1950–1980.* New York: Basic Books.

Myrdal, G. 1957. *Economic Theory and Underdeveloped Regions.* London: Duckworth.

Nachtigal, Paul. 1990. "Rural Education in a Period of Transition." In *Proceedings of the National Rural Studies Committee,* ed. Emery Castle and Barbara Baldwin, pp. 95–104. Corvallis: Western Rural Development Center, Oregon State University.

Napier, Ted L. 1991. "Soil Conservation." In *Rural Policies for the 1990s,* ed. Cornelia B. Flora and James A. Christenson, pp. 247–258. Boulder, Colo.: Westview.

National Center on Education and the Economy. 1990. *America's Choice: High Skills or Low Wages.* Rochester, N.Y.: National Center on Education and the Economy.

National Education Association. 1897. *Report of the Committee of Twelve on Rural Schools.* Chicago: University of Chicago Press.

National Rural Electric Cooperative Association. 1992. *Public Attitudes Toward Rural America and Rural Electric Cooperatives.* Washington, D.C., June.

Nelson, Lowry. 1961. "Farm Retirement in the United States." *Geriatrics* 16: 465–470.

Neth, M. 1987. "Preserving the Family Farm: Farm Families and Communities in the Midwest, 1900–1940." Ph.D. dissertation, University of Wisconsin, Madison.

Newman, Dale. 1976. "Work and Community Life in a Southern Textile Town." *Labor History* 19(2): 204–225.

Niskanen, William A., and Mickey Levy. 1974. *Cities and Schools: A Case for Community Government in California.* Berkeley: University of California, Graduate School of Public Policy.

Norrell, Robert J. 1985. *Reaping the Whirlwind: The Civil Rights Movement in Tuskegee.* New York: Random House.

North, Douglas C. 1990. *Institutions, Institutional Change, and Economic Performance.* New York: Cambridge University Press.

North, Douglass C. 1955. "Location Theory and Regional Economic Growth." *Journal of Political Economy* 63: 243–258.

Nossiter, Adam. 1989. "Blacks Finally March into Power in Selma, Alabama's County." *Atlanta Journal and Constitution,* January 8, 12A.

Noyelle, Thierry J. 1983. "The Rise of Advance Services: Some Implications for Economic Development." *Journal of the American Planning Association* 49: 281–290.

Oakerson, Ronald J. 1992. "Size, Function, and Structure: Jurisdictional Size Effects on Public Sector Performance." *Proceedings of the National Rural Studies Committee, Fifth Annual Meeting,* pp. 84–93. Corvallis: Western Rural Development Center, Oregon State University.

Oakerson, Ronald J., and Roger B. Parks. 1989. "Local Government Constitutions: A Different View of Metropolitan Governance." *American Review of Public Administration* 19(4): 279–294.

O'Hare, William P. 1988. "The Rise of Poverty in Rural America," *Recent Population Trends and Public Policy Reports,* no. 15. Washington, D.C.: Population Reference Bureau.

———. 1992. "America's Minorities—the Demographics of Diversity." *Population Bulletin* (Washington, D.C: Population Reference Bureau) 47(4).

Olson, Mancur. 1965. *The Logic of Collective Action.* Cambridge: Harvard University Press.

Olson, Mary. 1988. "The Legal Road to Economic Development: Fishing Rights in Western Washington." In *Public Policy Impacts on American Indian Economic Development,* ed. C. Matthew Snipp, pp. 77–112. Albuquerque: Institute for Native American Development, University of New Mexico.

Osbourn, Sandra S. 1988. *Rural Policy in the United States: A History.* Washington, D.C.: Congressional Research Service, Library of Congress.

Osterman, Paul. 1988. *Employment Futures: Reorganization, Dislocation, and Public Policy.* New York: Oxford University Press.

Ostrom, Elinor. 1976. "Size and Performance in a Federal System." *Publius: The Journal of Federalism* 6(2): 33–73.

Ostrom, Vincent. 1971. *Institutional Arrangements for Water Resource Development.* Springfield, Va.: National Technical Information Service.

———. 1989. *The Intellectual Crisis in American Public Administration.* 2d ed. Tuscaloosa and London: University of Alabama Press.

Ostrom, Vincent, and Elinor Ostrom. 1965. "A Behavioral Approach to the Study of Intergovernmental Relations." *Annals of the Academy of Political and Social Science* 359(May): 137–146.

Padfield, Harland. 1980a. "Theory of the Dying Community." In *Dying Community,* ed. Art Gallaher, Jr., and Harland Padfield, pp. 1–22. Albuquerque: University of New Mexico Press.

———. 1980b. "The Expendable Rural Community and the Denial of Powerlessness." In *The Dying Community,* ed. Art Gallaher, Jr., and Harland Padfield, pp. 159–185. Albuquerque: University of New Mexico Press.

Palerm, Juan Vicente. 1991. "Farm Labor Needs and Farm Workers in California, 1970 to 1989." California Agricultural Studies, 91-2, Employment Development Department, Sacramento.

Park, Robert E. 1952. *Human Communities.* New York: Free Press.

Parker, Tim. 1989. "Non-metro Employment: Annual Averages, 1988." Press Release, February 27, 1989. Washington, D.C.: USDA, Economic Research Service.

Perry, Huey. 1972. *"They'll Cut Off Your Project": A Mingo County Chronicle.* New York: Praeger Publishers.

Peshkin, Alan. 1982. *The Imperfect Union: School Consolidation and Community Conflict.* Chicago: University of Chicago Press.

Peterson, Trond. 1985. "A Comment on Presenting Results from Logit and Probit Models." *American Sociological Review* 50: 130–131.

Phillips, D. P. 1923. "What Does the Farmer Pay for a Consolidated School?" M.A. thesis, State University of Iowa.

Piore, Michael J., and Charles F. Sabel. 1984. *The Second Industrial Divide.* New York: Basic Books.

Plaut, T. R., and J. E. Pluta. 1983. "Business Climate, Taxes and Expenditures, and State Industrial Growth in the U.S." *Southern Economic Journal* 50: 99–119.

Ploch, Louis A. 1990. "Religion and Community." In *American Rural Communities,* ed. A. E. Luloff and Louis E. Swanson, pp. 125–150. Boulder, Colo.: Westview.

Pollard, Kelvin. 1993. "Faster Growth, More Diversity in U.S. Projections." *Population Today* 21(February): 3, 10.

Pollard, Kelvin, and William P. O'Hare. 1990. *Beyond High School: The Experience of Rural and Urban Youth in the 1980s.* Washington, D.C.: Population Reference Bureau.

Popper, Frank J. 1984. "Survival of the American Frontier." *Resources [Resources for the Future]* 77(Summer): 1–4.

———. 1986. "Commentary: Zen Public-Land Policy." *American Land Forum Magazine* 7(4): 11–13.

Porter, Kathryn H. 1989 and 1991. "Poverty in Rural America: A National Overview." Washington, D.C.: Center on Budget and Policy Priorities.

President's National Advisory Commission on Rural Poverty. 1967. "The People Left Behind." Washington, D.C.

———. 1968. *Rural Poverty in the United States.* Washington, D.C.: Government Printing Office.

Preston, Samuel H. 1984. "Children and the Elderly: Divergent Paths for America's Dependents." *Demography* 24: 435–457.

Prunty, Merle C. 1955. "The Renaissance of the Southern Plantation." *Geographical Review* 45(4): 459–491.

———. 1962. "Deltapine: Field Laboratory for the Neoplantation Occupance Type." In *Northwestern University Studies in Geography,* no. 2. Evanston, Ill.: Department of Geography, Northwestern University.

Prunty, Merle C., and Charles S. Aiken. 1972. "The Demise of the Piedmont Cotton Region." *Annals of the Association of American Geographers* 62(2): 283–306.

Pulver, Glen C. 1990. "The Response of Public Institutions to the Changing Educational Needs of Rural Areas." In *Proceedings of the National Rural Studies Committee,* ed. E. Castle and B. Baldwin. Corvallis: Western Rural Development Center, Oregon State University.

"Race and the New South." 1990. *U.S. News and World Report,* July 23, 22–27.

Rank, Mark R., and Thomas A. Hirschl. 1988. "A Rural-Urban Comparison of Welfare Exits." *Rural Sociology* 53: 190–206.

———. 1993. "The Link Between Welfare Participation and Population Density." *Demography* 30: 607–622.

Report of the 1986 Commission on the Future of the South. 1986. *Halfway Home and a Long Way to Go.* Research Triangle Park, N.C.: Southern Growth Policies Board.

Reynolds, D. R., and F. M. Shelley. 1990. "Local Control in American Public Education: Myth and Reality." In *Geographic Dimensions of United States Social Policy,* ed. J. F. Kodras and J. P. Jones, pp. 107–133. London: Edward Arnold.

Richards, Robert O. 1978. "Urbanization of Rural Areas." In *Handbook of Urban Contemporary Life,* ed. D. Street and Associates. pp. 551–591. San Francisco: Jossey-Bass.

Richardson, Jim, and John A. Farrell. 1983. "The New Indian Wars." *Denver Post,* Special reprint, November 20–27.

Riggs, J. F. 1909. "The Next Step in School Legislation." *Proceedings of the Fifty-Fourth Annual Session of the Iowa State Teachers Association* 54: 26–29, 199–205.

Riley, Robert. 1985. "Square to the Road, Hogs to the East." *Illinois Issues* 11(7): 22–26. Republished (1985) in *Places* 2(4).

———. Circa 1990. "The New Rural Landscape: Some Thoughts in Progress." Typescript.

Rimer, Sara. 1993. "Washing, Baking, and Lugging, Too: Frontier Women of the Flooded Plain." *New York Times,* August 5.

Rochin, Refugio I. 1977. "New Perspectives on Agricultural Labor Relations in California." *Labor Law Journal* 28(7): 395–402.

———. 1986. "The Conversion of Chicano Farm Workers into Owner-Operators of Cooperative Farms, 1970–1985." *Rural Sociology* 51(1): 97–115.

———. 1992. "Hispanic Americans in the Rural Economy: Conditions, Issues, and Probable Future Adjustments." In *Proceedings, National Rural Studies Committee.* Las Vegas, N.M.

Rochin, Refugio I., and Monica D. Castillo. 1993. "Immigration, *Colonia* Formation, and Latino Poor in Rural California: Evolving Immiseration." Monograph no. 93–1. Claremont, Calif.: Tomas Rivera Center.

Rochin, Refugio I., and Pat Soberanis. 1992. "Middle-Class Squeeze." *Policy Brief.* Claremont, Calif.: Tomas Rivera Center.

Rochin, Refugio I., Yoshio Kawamura, Douglas B. Gwynn, and Edward Dolber-Smith. 1989. "California's Rural Poor: Correlations with 'Rurality,' Economic Structure, and Social Dimensions." In *Rural Development Issues of the Nineties: Perspectives from the Social Sciences,* ed. Thomas T. Williams, Walter A. Hill, and

Ralph D. Christy. Tuskegee, Ala.: Proceedings of the Forty-sixth Annual Professional Agricultural Workers Conference.

Rogers, Carolyn C. 1991. "The Economic Well-Being of Nonmetro Children." Rural Development Research Report, no. 82. Washington, D.C.: USDA, Economic Research Service.

Romer, Paul M. 1990. "Are Nonconvexities Important for Understanding Growth?" *American Economic Review* 80: 97–108.

Ropers, Richard H. 1991. *Persistent Poverty: The American Dream Turned Nightmare.* New York: Plenum Press.

Roseman, Curtis C. 1993. "Ethnic Diversity in Nonmetropolitan America." Paper presented at the annual meeting of the Population Association of America, Cincinnati, April.

Rosenfeld, Stuart, Edward Bergman, and Sarah Rueben. 1985. *After the Factories.* Research Triangle Park, N.C.: Southern Growth Policies Board.

Ross, Peggy J., and Elizabeth S. Morrissey. 1989. "Rural People in Poverty: Persistent Versus Temporary Poverty." In *National Rural Studies Committee: A Proceedings,* ed. Emery Castle and Barbara Baldwin. Corvallis: Western Rural Development Center, Oregon State University.

Ross, Peggy J., and Stuart A. Rosenfeld. 1988. "Human Resource Policies and Economic Development." In *Rural Economic Development in the 1980s,* ed. David L. Brown et al., pp. 333–357. Rural Development Research Report, no. 69. Washington, D.C.: USDA, Economic Research Service.

Ruggles, Patricia. 1990. *Drawing the Line: Alternative Poverty Measures and Their Implications for Public Policy.* Washington, D.C.: Urban Institute Press.

Rural Sociological Society Task Force on Persistent Rural Poverty. 1993. *Persistent Poverty in Rural America.* Boulder, Colo.: Westview.

Ruttan, Vernon. 1979. "Induced Institutional Innovation." *Journal of Agricultural Economic Research* 33(3): 32–35.

Sabin, H. 1898. *Twenty-Eighth Biennial Report of the Superintendent of Public Instruction.* Des Moines: State of Iowa.

Sacks, Karen Brodkin. 1988. *Caring by the Hour.* Urbana: University of Illinois Press.

Saenz, Rogelio, and Marie Ballejos. 1993. "Industrial Development and Persistent Poverty in the Lower Rio Grande Valley." In *Forgotten Places: Uneven Development in Rural America,* ed. T. A. Lyson and W. W. Falk, pp. 102–124. Lawrence: University Press of Kansas.

Salamon, Sonya. 1984. "Ethnic Origin as Explanation for Local Land Ownership Patterns." In *Research in Rural Sociology and Development,* vol. 1, ed. Harry Schwarzweller, pp. 161–186. Greenwich, Conn.: JAI Press.

————. 1992. *Prairie Patrimony: Family, Farm, and Community in the Midwest.* Chapel Hill: University of North Carolina Press.

Salamon, Sonya, and Karen Davis-Brown. 1990. "Rural Communities in Transition." In *Proceedings of the National Rural Studies Committee,* Third Annual Meeting. Corvallis: Western Rural Development Center, Oregon State University.

Saloutos, T., and Hicks, J. D. 1951. *Agricultural Discontent in the Middle West, 1900–1939.* Madison: University of Wisconsin Press.

Schaffer, Peter V., and William H. Sanders III. 1988. *Investing in Education: Payoff and Employment Growth.* Urbana: Policy Forum Institute of Government and Public Affairs, University of Illinois.

Schellenberg, James A. 1981. "County Seat Wars: Historical Observations." *American Studies* 22: 81–95.

Schiller, Bradley R. 1989. *The Economics of Poverty and Discrimination.* 5th ed. Englewood Cliffs, N.J.: Prentice-Hall.

Schmuck, Richard A., and Patricia A. Schmuck. 1992. *Small Districts Big Problems.* Newbury Park, Calif.: Corwin Press.

Schorr, Lisbeth B. 1988. *Within Our Reach: Breaking the Cycle of Disadvantage.* New York: Doubleday.

Schwartz, Gary. 1987. *Beyond Conformity or Rebellion.* Chicago: University of Chicago Press.

Schweke, William, and Graham S. Toft. 1991. "The New Localism." *Entrepreneurial Economy Review* (Winter): 3.

Sessions, James. 1989. "Civil Rights and Religion." In *Encyclopedia of Southern Culture,* ed. Charles R. Wilson and William Ferris. Chapel Hill: University of North Carolina Press.

Shaffer, Ron. 1989. *Community Economics: Economic Structure and Change in Smaller Communities.* Ames: Iowa State University Press.

Shapiro, Isaac. 1989. "Laboring for Less: Working but Poor in Rural America." Washington, D.C.: Center for Budget Priorities.

Sher, Jonathan. 1986. *Heavy Meddle.* Raleigh: North Carolina School Boards Association.

Sher, J. P., and R. P. Tompkins. 1977. "Economy, Efficiency, and Equality: The Myths of Rural School Consolidation." In *Education in Rural America: A Reassessment of Conventional Wisdom,* ed. J. P. Sher, pp. 43–77. Boulder, Colo.: Westview.

Shryock, Henry S., Jacob S. Siegel, et al. 1971. *The Methods and Materials of Demography.* Washington, D.C.: U.S. Bureau of the Census.

Singelmann, Joachim, and Forrest A. Deseran, eds. 1993. *Inequalities in Labor Market Areas.* Boulder, Colo.: Westview.

Smith, Eldon D., Merlin M. Hackbart, and Johannes van Veen. 1981. "A Modified Regression Base Multiplier Model." *Growth and Change* 12: 17–22.

Smith, J. Russell. 1930. *Home Folks.* Philadelphia: John C. Winston.

Smith, J. Russell, and M. Ogden Phillips. 1942. *North America: Its People and the Resources, Development, and Prospects of the Continent as the Home of Man.* New York: Harcourt, Brace.

Smith, Michal. 1989. "Behind the Glitter: The Impact of Tourism on Rural Women in the Southeast." Lexington, Ky.: Southeast Women's Employment Coalition.

Smith, R. N. 1969a. "Department of Public Instruction in Iowa." In *Education in the States: Historical Development and Outlook,* pp. 401–432. Washington, D.C.: National Education Association.

———. 1969b. *Development of the Iowa Department of Public Instruction, 1900–1965.* Des Moines: State of Iowa, Department of Public Instruction.

Smith, Stephen M. 1984. "Export Orientation of Non-manufacturing Businesses in Non-metropolitan Communities." *American Journal of Agricultural Economics* 66: 145–155.

———. 1993. "Service Industries in the Rural Economy: The Role and Potential Contributions." In *Economic Adaptation: Alternatives for Non-metropolitan Areas,* ed. David L. Barkley, pp. 89–104. Boulder, Colo.: Westview.

Smith, Stephen M., and Glen C. Pulver. 1981. "Non-manufacturing Business as a Growth Alternative in Non-metropolitan Areas." *Journal of the Community Development Society* 12: 33–47.

Smith, Tim R. 1989. "Foreign Direct Investment: A Source of Jobs for Tenth District States?" *Economic Review.* Kansas City, Mo.: Federal Reserve Bank of Kansas City.

———. 1992. "Determinants of Rural Growth: Winners and Losers in the 1980s." Working Paper. Kansas City, Mo.: Federal Reserve Bank of Kansas City.

Smith, Tim R., and Mark Drabenstott. 1992. "The Role of Universities in Regional Economic Development." In *The Economics of American Higher Education,* ed. William E. Becker and Darrell R. Lewis. Boston: Kluwer Academic Publishers.

Snipp, C. Matthew. 1988. "Public Policy Impacts on American Indian Economic Development." In *Public Policy Impacts on American Indian Economic Development,* ed. C. Matthew Snipp, pp. 1–22. Albuquerque: Institute for Native American Development, University of New Mexico Press.

———. 1989. *American Indians: The First of this Land.* New York: Russell Sage Foundation.

Snipp, C. Matthew, H. D. Horton, L. Jensen, J. Nagel, and R. Rochin. 1992. "Persistent Rural Poverty and Racial and Ethnic Minorities." Final Report for the Rural Sociological Society Working Group on Persistent Rural Poverty. Madison: Department of Rural Sociology, University of Wisconsin.

Snipp, C. Matthew, and Gene Summers. 1991. "American Indian Development Policies." In *Rural Policies for the 1990s,* ed. Cornelia B. Flora and James A. Christenson, pp. 166–180. Boulder, Colo.: Westview.

Snyder, T. D. 1987. *Digest of Educational Statistics.* Washington, D.C.: U.S. Department of Education.

Sokolow, Alvin D. 1990. "Leadership and Implementation in Rural Economic Development." In *American Rural Communities,* ed. A. E. Luloff and L. E. Swanson, chap. 12. Boulder, Colo.: Westview.

Sorge, A., and Wolfgang Streeck. 1988. "Industrial Relations and Technical Change: The Case for an Extended Perspective." In *New Technology and Industrial Relations,* ed. Richard Hyman and Wolfgang Streeck. Oxford: Blackwell.

Sosnick, Steve H. 1978. *Hired Hands: Seasonal Workers in the United States.* Santa Barbara: McNally and Loftin.

Southeast Women's Employment Coalition. 1986. *Women of the Rural South: Economic Status and Prospects.* Lexington, Ky.: Southeast Women's Employment Coalition.

Southern Governors' Association. 1986. *Cornerstone of Competition.* Washington, D.C.

Southern Growth Policies Board. 1986. *Halfway Home and a Long Way to Go.* Research Triangle Park, N.C.

Spring, J. 1972. *Education and the Rise of the Corporate State.* Boston: Beacon Press.

Starrs, Paul F. 1993. "The Ways of Western Death: Mor(t)ality and Landscape in Cormac McCarthy's Novels and Sergio Leone's Films." *Wide Angle: A Quarterly Journal of Film History, Theory, Criticism, & Practice* 15(4): 4–17.

———. 1994a. "Cattle Free By '93 and the Imperatives of Environmental Radicalism." *Ubique* (American Geographical Society) 14(1): 1–4.

———. 1994b. *Ranching's Realm: Landscape and Livestock in Western North America.* Baltimore: Johns Hopkins University Press.

———. 1994c. "A Sense of Where You Are, or, the Relevance of Regions." *Spectrum: The Journal of State Government* 67(3).

Starrs, Paul F., and John B. Wright, Jr. 1994. "California, Out—Great Basin Growth & the Withering of the Pacific Idyll." *Geographical Review* 84(4).

Stegner, Wallace E. 1980. "Coda: Wilderness Letter." In *The Sound of Mountain Water,* Stegner, pp. 145–153. New York: E. P. Dutton.

Stewart. James B. 1993. "Annals of Disaster: Battle on the Sny." *New Yorker* 69(25): 30–40.

Stiglitz, Joseph. 1987. "The Causes and Consequences of the Dependence of Quality in Price." *Journal of Economic Literature* 25: 1–48.

Stilgoe, John R. 1982. *Common Landscape of America, 1580 to 1845.* New Haven: Yale University Press.

Stone, Katherine. 1974. "The Origins of Job Structures in the Steel Industry." *Review of Radical Political Economics* 6: 61–97.

Stull, Donald D., Janet Benson, Michael J. Broadway, Arthur L. Campa, Ken C. Erickson, and Mark A. Grey. 1990. "Changing Relations: Newcomers and Established Residents in Garden City, Kansas." Institute for Public Policy and Business Research, University of Kansas. Report no. 172.

Sublett, Michael D. 1975. *Farmers on the Road: Interfarm Migration and Farming of Noncontiguous Lands in Three Midwestern Townships, 1939–1969.* Chicago: Department of Geography, University of Chicago.

Summers, Gene F. N.d. "Social Characteristics of Reservations." Mimeograph. Madison: Department of Rural Sociology, University of Wisconsin.

———. 1986. "Rural Community Development." *Annual Review of Sociology* 12: 347–371.

———. 1991. "Minorities in Rural Society." *Rural Sociology* 56: 177–188.

Summers, Gene F., ed. 1984. "Deindustrialization: Restructuring the Economy." *Annals of the American Academy of Political and Social Science,* vol. 475. Berkeley Hills, Calif.: Sage Publications.

Summers, Gene F., Sharon Evans, Frank Clemente, E. M. Beck, and Jon Minkoff. 1976. *Industrial Invasion of Non-metropolitan America: A Quarter Century of Experience.* New York: Praeger.

Summers, Gene F., and Thomas A. Hirschl. 1985. "Retirees as a Growth Industry." *Rural Development Perspectives* 1: 13–16.

Summers, Gene F., Francine Horton, and Christina Gringeri. 1990. "Rural Labor Market Changes in the United States." In *Rural Restructuring: Global Processes and Their Responses,* ed. Terry Marsden, Philip Lowe, and Sarah Whatmore, pp. 129–164. London: David Fulton Publishers. Also in *Proceedings of the National Rural Studies Committee,* ed. Emery Castle and Barbara Baldwin, pp. 61–80. Corvallis: Western Rural Development Center, Oregon State University.

Swanson, Louis E. 1988. "The Human Dimension of the Rural South in Crisis." In *The Rural South in Crisis,* ed. Lionel J. Beaulieu. Boulder, Colo.: Westview.

———. 1989. "The Rural Development Dilemma." *Resources* 96: 14–17.

———. 1990. "Dilemmas Confronting Rural Policies in the U.S." In *Proceedings of the National Rural Studies Committee,* ed. Emery Castle and Barbara Baldwin, pp. 21–30. Corvallis: Western Rural Development Center, Oregon State University.

Swanson, L. L., and M. A. Butler. 1988. "Human Resource Base of Rural Economies." In *Rural Economic Development in the 1980s: Prospects for the Future,* ed. D. L. Brown, J. N. Reid, H. Bluestone, D. A. McGranahan, and S. M. Mazie. Washington, D.C.: USDA, Economic Research Service.

Swierenga, Robert P. 1989. "The Settlement of the Old Northwest: Ethnic Pluralism in a Featureless Plain." *Journal of the Early Republic* 9: 73–105.

Taylor, J. Edward, and Dawn Thilmany. 1992. "California Farmers Still Rely on New Immigrants for Field Labor." *California Agriculture* (University of California) 46(5): 4–6.

Taylor, Paul S. 1941. "Good-by to the Homestead Farm." *Harpers Magazine* 182(May): 589–597.

———. 1988. "Feds, State Take Opposite Sides in Meriwether School Merger Fracas." *Atlanta Journal and Constitution,* July 17, 1E and 10E.

Teixeira, R. A., and E. J. Greenberg. Forthcoming. "The Myth of Inferior Rural Education." *Rural Development Perspectives.*

Teixeira, R. A., and L. Mishel. 1992. "The Myth of the Coming Labor Shortage in Rural Areas." Washington, D.C.: Economic Policy Institute.

———. 1993. "Whose Skills Shortage—Workers or Management?" *Issues in Science and Technology* 9(4): 69–74.

Teixeira, R. A., and L. Mishel. Forthcoming. "Skills Shortage or Management Shortage?" In *The New Modern Times: Factors Reshaping the World of Work,* ed. D. Bills. Albany: SUNY Press.

Testa, Mark, Nan Marie Astone, Marilyn Krugh, and Kathryn N. Neckerman. 1989. "Employment and Marriage Among Inner-City Fathers." *Annals of American Political and Social Science* 501: 79–91.

Thompson, Wilbur R. 1973. "A Preface to Urban Economics." In *Contemporary Economic Issues,* ed. N. W. Chamberlain, pp. 1–48. Homewood, Ill.: Richard D. Irwin.

Thoreau, Henry David. 1960. *Walden.* New York: Doubleday.

———. 1981. "The Bean Field." In *Walden and Other Writings,* ed. William Howarth. New York: Modern Library College Editions.

Thornton, Russell. 1987. *American Indian Holocaust and Survival.* Norman: University of Oklahoma Press.

Thurow, Lester. 1975. *Generating Inequality.* New York: Basic Books.

Tickamyer, Ann R., and Janet Bokemeier. 1988. "Sex Differences in Labor Market Experiences." *Rural Sociology* 53: 166–189.

———. 1989. "Individual and Structural Explanations of Nonmetropolitan Women and Men's Labor Force Experiences." In *Rural Labor Markets,* ed. William W. Falk and Thomas A. Lyson, pp. 153–171. Greenwich, Conn.: JAI Press.

Tickamyer, Ann R., and Cynthia M. Duncan. 1990. "Poverty and Opportunity Structure in Rural America." *Annual Review of Sociology* 16: 67–86.

Tiebout, Charles M. 1956. "Exports and Regional Economic Growth." *Journal of Political Economy* 64: 160–169.

Tienda, Marta, Wilma Ortiz, and Shelley Smith. 1987. "Industrial Restructuring, Gender Segregation, and Sex Differences in Earnings." *American Sociological Review* 52: 195–210.

Tolbert, Charles M., and Molly Sizer Killian. 1987. *Labor Market Areas for the United States*. Staff Report no. AGES870721. Washington, D.C.: USDA, Economic Research Service.

Tocqueville, Alexis de. 1965. *Democracy in America,* ed. Phillips Bradley. New York: Vintage Books.

————. 1969. *Democracy in America.* Trans. George Lawrence, ed. J. P. Mayer. New York: Doubleday.

Tomaskovic-Devy, Donald. 1987. "Labor Markets, Industrial Structure, and Poverty: A Theoretical Discussion and Empirical Example." *Rural Sociology* 52: 56–74.

————. 1990. "Back to the Future: Human Resources and Economic Development Policy for North Carolina." Raleigh: Department of Sociology, Anthropology, and Social Work, North Carolina State University.

Troxel, O. L. 1928. *State Control of Secondary Education*. Baltimore: Warwick and York.

Truesdell, Leon E. 1949. *The Development of the Urban-Rural Classification in the United States: 1874 to 1949*. Current Population Reports, Population Characteristics, Series P-23, no. 1. Washington, D.C.: U.S. Bureau of the Census.

Turner, R. 1985. "Dimensions of Quality in School Education." *School and University Review* 15: 1–5.

Tyack, David. 1974. *The One Best System: A History of American Urban Education.* Cambridge: Harvard University Press.

U.S. Bureau of the Census. 1913a. *Thirteenth Census of the United States, 1910.* Vol. 2, *Population*. Washington, D.C.: Government Printing Office.

————. 1913b. *Thirteenth Census of the United States, 1909 and 1910.* Vol. 6, *Agriculture*. Washington, D.C.: Government Printing Office.

————. 1915. *Plantation Farming in the United States*. Washington, D.C.: Government Printing Office.

————. 1932. *Fifteenth Census of the United States, 1930.* Vol. 2, Part 1, *Agriculture: The Northern States*. Washington, D.C.: Government Printing Office.

————. 1953. *Statistical Abstract of the United States, 1953*. Washington, D.C.: Government Printing Office.

————. 1973–1988. *Current Population Survey*. Washington, D.C.: Government Printing Office.

————. 1976. *Historical Statistics of the United States, Colonial Times to 1970*. Washington, D.C.: Government Printing Office.

————. 1980. *1980 Census of the Population and Housing*. Washington, D.C.: Government Printing Office.

————. 1985a. *Census Geography: Concepts and Products*. Washington, D.C.: Government Printing Office.

————. 1985b. *County Business Patterns*. Electronic file. Washington, D.C.

————. 1987a. *Census of Agriculture*. Washington, D.C.: Government Printing Office.

_____. 1987b. *Census of Agriculture, 1987.* Vol. 1, Part 41, *Summary and State Date,* Table 35. Washington, D.C.: Government Printing Office.

_____. 1988a. *Rural and Farm Population, 1987.* Current Population Reports, Series P-27, no. 61. Washington, D.C.: Government Printing Office.

_____. 1988b. *Census of Agriculture: Geographic Area. United States Summary and State Data.* Washington, D.C.: Government Printing Office.

_____. 1988c. *Statistical Abstract of the United States.* Washington, D.C.: Government Printing Office.

_____. 1989. *Rural and Rural Farm Population: 1988.* Current Population Reports. Series P-20, no. 439. Washington D.C.: Government Printing Office.

_____. 1990a. *1990 Census of the Population and Housing.* Washington, D.C.: Government Printing Office.

_____. 1990b. *Poverty in the United States: 1990.* Current Population Reports, Series P-60, no. 175. Washington, D.C.: Government Printing Office.

_____. 1990c. *Statistical Abstract of the United States.* 110th ed. Washington, D.C.: Government Printing Office.

_____. 1992a. *1990 Census of Population, General Population Characteristics, United States.* Washington, D.C.: Government Printing Office.

_____. 1992b. *Population Projections of the United States by Age, Sex, Race, and Hispanic Origin.* Current Population Reports, Series P-25, no. 1092. Washington, D.C.: Government Printing Office.

_____. 1992c. *Residents of Farms and Rural Areas: 1990.* Current Population Survey, Series P-20, no. 457. Washington D.C.: Government Printing Office.

_____. 1992d. *Statistical Abstract of the United States, 1992.* Washington, D.C.: Government Printing Office.

_____. 1993a. *The Black Population in the United States: March 1988.* Current Population Reports, Series P-20, no. 471. Washington, D.C.: Government Printing Office.

_____. 1993b. *Hispanic Population of the United States: March 1992.* Current Population Reports, Series P-20, no. 465. Washington, D.C.: Government Printing Office.

U.S. Bureau of Economic Analysis. 1985. *Regional Income and Employment.* Electronic file. Washington, D.C.

U.S. Bureau of Education. 1930. *Biennial Surveys of Education, 1918/20–1926/28.* Washington, D.C.: Department of Interior.

U.S. Department of Agriculture. 1960. *Agricultural Statistics.* Washington, D.C.: Government Printing Office,

_____. 1974 and 1992. *Agricultural Statistics.* Washington, D.C.: Government Printing Office.

_____. 1990. *Major Land Uses (1945–1987).* Diskette Contents and Documentation, unpublished. Washington, D.C.: Economic Research Service.

_____. 1992. *Economic Indicators of the Farm Sector: Production and Efficiency Statistics 1990.* ECIFS 10–3. Washington, D.C.: Economic Research Service.

U.S. Department of Agriculture, Economic Research Service. 1991. *Rural Trends and Conditions.* Washington, D.C.

_____. 1993. *Rural Conditions and Trends* 4(Summer): 16–17.

U.S. Department of Education. 1993a. *National Center for Educational Statistics, Digest of Education Statistics.* Washington, D.C.: Government Printing Office.

———. 1993b. *National Education Goals Report, Vol. 2: State Report.* Washington, D.C.: Government Printing Office.

U.S. Office of Education. 1958. *Biennial Survey of Education: 1956–58.* Washington, D.C.: Government Printing Office.

———. 1981. *National Center for Educational Statistics, Digest of Education Statistics.* Washington, D.C.: Government Printing Office.

U.S. Senate. 1909. "Special Message from President Roosevelt." *Report of the United States Country Life Commission.* Senate Doc. 705, 60th Congress, 2d Sess.

Valdés, Dennis Nodín. 1991. *Al Norte: Agricultural Workers in the Great Lakes Region, 1917–1970.* Austin: University of Texas Press.

Varenne, Herve. 1977. *Americans Together: Structured Diversity in a Midwestern American Town.* New York: Teachers College Press.

Vidich, Arthur J. 1980. "Revolutions in Community Structure." In *The Dying Community,* ed. Art Gallaher, Jr., and Harland Padfield, pp. 109–132. Albuquerque: University of New Mexico Press.

Vidich, Arthur, and J. Bensman. 1958. *Small Town in Mass Society.* Princeton: Princeton University Press.

Vinje, David L. 1985. "Cultural Values and Economic Development on Reservations." In *American Indian Policy in the Twentieth Century,* ed. Vine Deloria, Jr., pp. 155–175. Norman: University of Oklahoma Press.

Wacquant, Lois J. D., and William J. Wilson. 1989. "The Cost of Racial Exclusion in the Inner City." *Annals of American Political and Social Science* 501: 8–25.

Walker, S. Lynne. 1990. "A New UFW? A Statewide Campaign Is Under Way to Organize Another Segment of California's Field Workers." *California Farmer,* April 21, 34–54.

Walker, Tom. 1989. "Storied Sun Belt Prosperity Has Bypassed Much of the Rural South." *Atlanta Journal and Constitution,* March 12, 4S.

Wardwell, John M. 1989. "Nonmetropolitan Migration: Facts of the 1980s—Theories of the 1970s." Unpublished paper, Washington State University, Pullman.

Wasylenko, Michael. 1985. "Business Climate, Industry, and Employment Growth: A Review of the Evidence." Occasional Paper no. 98, Metropolitan Studies Program, Syracuse University.

Wasylenko, Michael, and Therese McGuire. 1985. "Jobs and Taxes: The Effects of Business Climate on States' Employment Growth Rates." *National Tax Journal* 38 (December).

Waters, Edward C., David W. Holland, and Bruce A. Weber. 1994. "Inter-regional Effects of Reduced Timber Harvests: The Impact of the Northern Spotted Owl Listing in Rural and Urban Oregon." *Journal of Agricultural and Resource Economics* 19(1): 141–160.

Weber, Bruce A., Emery N. Castle, and Ann L. Shriver. 1988. "Performance of Natural Resource Industries." In *Rural Economic Development in the 1980s,* ed. David L. Brown et al., pp. 103–133. Rural Development Research Report no. 69. Washington, D.C.: USDA, Economic Research Service.

Weber, Max. 1946. *From Max Weber,* ed. H. H. Garth and C. Wright Mills. New York: Oxford University Press.

———. 1958. *The Protestant Ethic and the Spirit of Capitalism.* New York: Scribner's.

———. 1964. *The Sociology of Religion.* Boston: Beacon Press.

Weinberg, Daniel. 1987. "Rural Pockets of Poverty." *Rural Sociology* 52: 398–409.

Welch, F. A. 1921. "Some Problems of the Village School." *Midland Schools* 35(5): 147–148.

Wells, Miriam J. 1984. "The Resurgence of Sharecropping: Historical Anomaly or Political Strategy?" *American Journal of Sociology* 90: 1–29.

———. 1990. "Mexican Farm Workers Become Strawberry Farmers." *Human Organization* 49: 149–156.

White, Robert H. 1990. *Tribal Assets: The Rebirth of Native America.* New York: Henry Holt.

Whitener, Leslie A. 1991. "The Agricultural Work Force: Patterns and Trends." Leader, Agricultural Labor Section, ARED/ERS/USDA. Remarks presented at Surgeon General's Conference on Agricultural Safety and Health, April 30–May 30, 1990. Paper revised July 1, 1991.

Whiting, Larry R. 1974. *Communities Left Behind: Alternatives for Development.* Ames, Iowa: North Central Center for Rural Development.

Wilkinson, Charles F. 1992. *The Eagle Bird: Mapping a New West.* New York: Pantheon.

Wilkinson, Kenneth P. 1986. "In Search of the Community in the Changing Countryside." *Rural Sociology* 51: 1–17.

Williams, Bruce, Michael Timberlake, Bonnie Thornton Dill, and Darryl Tukufu. 1992. *Race and Economic Development in the Lower Mississippi Delta.* Research Paper 15. Memphis: Memphis State University, Center for Research on Women.

Williams, David K. 1982. "Rural Residential Subdivisions in Loudon County, Tennessee." M.S. thesis, Department of Geography, University of Tennessee, Knoxville.

Williams, Raymond. 1973. *The Country and the City.* New York: Oxford University Press.

Williamson, Oliver, Michael Wachter, and Jeffrey Harris. 1975. "Understanding the Employment Relationship: The Analysis of Idiosyncratic Exchange." *Bell Journal of Economics* 56: 250–278.

William T. Grant Foundation Commission on Work, Family, and Citizenship. 1988. *The Forgotten Half: Pathways to Success for America's Youth and Young Families.* Washington, D.C.

Willits, Fern K., Robert C. Bealer, and Vincent L. Timbers. 1990. "Popular Images of 'Rurality': Data from a Pennsylvania Survey." *Rural Sociology* 55(Winter): 559–578.

Wilson, Charles R. 1989. "Bible Belt." In *Encyclopedia of Southern Culture,* ed. Charles R. Wilson and William Ferris. Chapel Hill: University of North Carolina Press.

Wilson, Edward O. 1984. *Biophilia.* Cambridge: Harvard University Press.

Wilson, James Q. 1989. *Bureaucracy: What Government Agencies Do and Why They Do It.* New York: Basic Books.

Wilson, William J. 1987. *The Truly Disadvantaged*. Chicago: University of Chicago Press.

————. 1991. "Studying Inner-City Social Dislocations: The Challenges of Public Agenda Research." *American Sociological Review* 56: 1–14.

Wilson, William Julius, and Kathryn M. Neckerman. 1986. "Poverty and Family Structure: The Widening Gap Between Evidence and Public Policy Issues." In *Fighting Poverty: What Works and What Doesn't*, ed. Sheldon Danziger and Daniel H. Weinberg, chap. 10. Cambridge: Harvard University Press.

Winter, William F. 1988. "Charting a Course for the Rural South." In *The Rural South in Crisis: Challenges for the Future*, ed. Lionel J. Beaulieu. Boulder, Colo.: Westview.

Woods and Poole Economics. 1992. *The Complete Economic and Demographic Data Source 1992*. 3 vols. Washington, D.C.

Woodward, C. Vann. 1960. *The Burden of Southern History*. Baton Rouge: Louisiana State University Press.

————. 1974. *The Strange Career of Jim Crow*. New York: Oxford University Press.

Wordsworth, William. 1993. "Preface" to *Lyrical Ballads, with Pastoral and Other Poems (1802)*. In *The Norton Anthology of English Literature*, ed. M. H. Abrams, 6th ed., vol. 2. New York: W. W. Norton.

Worster, Donald W. 1987. "New West, True West: Interpreting the Region's History." *Western Historical Quarterly* 18(2): 141–156.

Wright, Gavin. 1986. *Old South, New South: Revolutions in the Southern Economy Since the Civil War*. New York: Basic Books.

Wunderlich, Gene. 1993. "Agricultural Landownership and the Real Property Tax." In *Land Ownership and Taxation in American Agriculture*, ed. Gene Wunderlich, pp. 3–16. Boulder, Colo.: Westview.

Zabin, Carol, M. Kearney, A. Garcia, D. Runsten, and C. Nagengast. 1993. *MIXTEC Migrants in California Agriculture*. Davis: California Institute for Rural Studies.

Zelinsky, Wilbur. 1992. *The Cultural Geography of the United States*. Rev. ed. Englewood Cliffs, N.J.: Prentice-Hall.

Zuboff, S. 1984. *In the Age of the Smart Machine*. New York: Basic Books.

ABOUT THE CONTRIBUTORS

CHARLES S. AIKEN, professor of geography at the University of Tennessee, Knoxville, specializes in rural geography and geography of the American South. He has written on the decline of agricultural regions, the spatial restructuring of farms, the microscale redistribution of nonmetropolitan population, and the geography of fictional literature.

DAVID L. BROWN is professor and chair of rural sociology at Cornell University. His research and teaching focus on migration and population redistribution, spatial inequality, and rural policy in the United States and other developed nations.

WILLIAM P. BROWNE is professor of political science, Central Michigan University. He has published twelve books and nearly seventy articles on public policy problems. His research has been supported by the Economic Research Service, USDA, and the National Center for Food and Agricultural Policy.

EMERY N. CASTLE is a professor in the University Graduate Faculty of Economics, Oregon State University, specializing in resource and environmental economics. He is a past president of Resources for the Future, a Washington, D.C.–based public policy institute.

PIERRE CROSSON is a senior fellow and resident consultant at Resources for the Future. He has published widely on the relationships among agricultural production, land use, and the environment.

BONNIE THORNTON DILL is professor of women's studies and affiliate professor of sociology at the University of Maryland, College Park. Her research focuses on African-American women and families, and she is currently studying single mothers in rural southern communities. Her published works include *Women of Color in U.S. Society,* coedited with Maxine Baca Zinn (1994) and *Across the Boundaries of Race and Class: Work and Family Among Black Female Domestic Servants* (1994).

MARK DRABENSTOTT is vice-president and economist at the Federal Reserve Bank of Kansas City and oversees the bank's research on the seven-state Tenth Federal Reserve District. Long interested in farm and rural economies, he serves as chairman of National Planning Association's food and agriculture committee.

JANET M. FITCHEN was a cultural anthropologist whose research and writing centered on rural issues in the United States, especially poverty. Formerly chair of the Anthropology Department at Ithaca College, she had accepted a position as associate professor in rural sociology at Cornell University before her untimely death from a brain tumor in April 1995.

JOAN FITZGERALD is on the faculty of the University of Illinois at Chicago College of Urban and Public Affairs and the Center for Urban Economic Development. Her research focuses on issues related to school-to-work transition.

GLENN V. FUGUITT is professor emeritus of rural sociology and sociology at the University of Wisconsin–Madison. His research has concentrated on migration and population redistribution, particularly as they relate to nonmetropolitan areas in the United States, and he is a co-author of *Rural and Small Town America* (1980).

CHRISTINA GRINGERI is assistant professor in the Graduate School of Social Work at the University of Utah. She is author of *Getting By: Women Homeworkers and Rural Economic Development* (1994) and continues to be involved in issues of rural poverty, women and work, and social policies and programs.

JOHN FRASER HART has been professor of geography at the University of Minnesota since 1967. He is the author of *The Look of the Land* (1975) and *The Land That Feeds Us* (1991) and is working on a forthcoming book, *Reading the Land.*

THOMAS A. HIRSCHL is associate professor of rural sociology at Cornell University. His teaching and research interests concern poverty and social stratification, and he is the author of recent articles in *Demography, Social Forces,* and *Rural Sociology.*

DARYL HOBBS is professor of rural sociology and director of the University of Missouri Office of Social and Economic Data Analysis. His specialties are social change, rural development, and public policy.

WILLIAM HOWARTH, professor of English at Princeton University, is the author or editor of *The Book of Concord* (1982), *Thoreau in the Mountains* (1982), and many other works in the field of American literature and environmental history.

FRANCINE HORTON is a doctoral candidate in sociology and a research assistant in the Department of Rural Sociology at the University of Wisconsin–Madison.

PEIRCE LEWIS is professor of geography at Pennsylvania State University, University Park. He teaches and writes about ordinary human landscapes of the United States: how those landscapes got to be the way they are and what they reveal about the American condition.

EDWIN S. MILLS, professor of real estate and finance, Kellogg Graduate School of Management, Northwestern University, has written and taught about urban and real estate issues for over twenty-five years. His work has included studies in the United States and several South and Southeastern Asian countries.

RONALD J. OAKERSON is professor of political science at Houghton College and a member of the National Rural Studies Committee. He is a former senior analyst with the U.S. Advisory Commission on Intergovernmental Relations.

DAVID R. REYNOLDS is professor of geography at the University of Iowa. His research focuses primarily on the political geography of social and economic change in North America, and he gives special attention to exploring the linkages between regional economic development and the politics of place. Recent articles have appeared in *Progress in Human Geography, Political Geography,* and *Economic Geography,* and he is currently completing a book on the geography of political struggles over the reform of rural education in the Midwest during the Progressive era and how those struggles influenced the development of systems of public education in the region.

REFUGIO I. ROCHIN is professor of agricultural economics and sociology and director of the Julian Samora Research Institute, Michigan State University. A specialist in rural poverty and labor markets, Rochin was professor of agricultural economics and Chicano studies at the University of California–Davis from 1971 through June 1994.

SONYA SALAMON is professor of family studies in the School of Human Resources and Family Studies, University of Illinois at Urbana Champaign. Two decades of anthropological research on Illinois farm families and small rural communities have resulted in a book, *Prairie Patrimony: Family, Farming, and Community in the Midwest* (1992), and in more than thirty published articles.

TIM R. SMITH is a senior economist at the Federal Reserve Bank of Kansas City. As a member of the bank's regional economics group, he specializes in industry studies and research on regional economic development issues.

C. MATTHEW SNIPP is professor of rural sociology and sociology and director of the American Indian Studies Program, University of Wisconsin–Madison.

PAUL F. STARRS is professor of geography at the University of Nevada and works on cultural geography and resource issues in the United States, Europe, and Latin America. He is especially interested in the always evolving and often tumultuous relationship between the American West's urban and rural places.

GENE F. SUMMERS, a professor in the Department of Rural Sociology, University of Wisconsin–Madison, is a past president of the Rural Sociological Society and chair of that group's Task Force on Persistent Rural Poverty. His research and writing have focused on ways of reducing rural poverty, including community economic development, rural labor markets, and rural industrialization.

LOUIS E. SWANSON is professor of sociology in the College of Agriculture at the University of Kentucky. His research has focused on agriculture and rural community change with an emphasis on public policy. In addition to over fifty articles and book chapters, he has co-authored *Sacred Cows and Hot Potatoes: Agrarian Myths in Agricultural Policy* (1992) and *Rural Communities: Legacy and Change* (1992); co-edited *American Rural Communities* (1990) and *Agricultural Policy and the Environment: Closed Fist or Open Hand* (1994); and edited *Agriculture and Community Change in the U.S.* (1988). He has also been a visiting scholar at the National Center for Food and Agricultural Policy at Resources for the Future.

RUY A. TEIXEIRA has written extensively on rural labor market issues and is currently codirector of the National Rural Enterprise Survey at the Economic Research Service, USDA. He is also the author of numerous books and articles about American politics and director of the policy and public opinion program at the Economic Policy Institute.

BRUCE A. WEBER is professor of agricultural and resource economics at Oregon State University and a member of the National Rural Studies Committee. His teaching, research, and extension-education programs focus on rural economies and government finance.

CLIFTON WHARTON, JR., is former vice president of the Agricultural Development Council and edited *Subsistence Agriculture and Economic Development*. He is the former president of Michigan State University and former chancellor of the State University of New York System. In 1993 he was U.S. Deputy Secretary of State.

BRUCE B. WILLIAMS is associate professor of sociology at the University of Mississippi. He received his Ph.D. from the University of Chicago and has used his ethnographic research orientation to study race, poverty, and economic development in the Mississippi Delta. He is the author of *Black Workers in an Industrial Suburb: The Struggle Against Discrimination* (1987).

INDEX